Understanding Early Civilizat

This book offers the first detailed con documented early civilizations: ancient China, the Aztecs and adjacent peoples i …, the Classic Maya, the Inka, and the Yoruba. Unlike previous studies, equal attention is paid to similarities and differences in their sociopolitical organization, economic systems, religion, and culture. Many of this study's findings are surprising and provocative. Agricultural systems, technologies, and economic behaviour turn out to have been far more diverse than was expected. Yet only two basic types of political organization are found – city-states and territorial states – and they influenced economic behaviour at least as much as did environmental differences. Underlying various religious beliefs was a single, distinctive pattern that is unique to early civilization and must have developed independently in different regions of the world. Many other shared religious beliefs appear to have been transformations of a shared heritage from earlier times. Esteemed lifestyles that differed idiosyncratically from one early civilization to another influenced human behaviour in ways that often persisted despite changing material and political circumstances. These findings and many others challenge not only current understandings of early civilizations but also the theoretical foundations of modern archaeology and anthropology. The key to understanding early civilizations lies not in their historical connections but in what they can tell us about similarities and differences in human behaviour.

Bruce G. Trigger was James McGill Professor in the Department of Anthropology at McGill University. He received his PhD from Yale University and has carried out archaeological research in Egypt and the Sudan. His interests included the comparative study of early civilizations, the history of archaeology, and archaeological and anthropological theory. He received various scholarly awards, including the presitigious Prix Léon-Gérin from the Quebec government, for his sustained contributions to the social sciences. He was an honorary Fellow of the Society of Antiquaries of Scotland and an honorary member of the Prehistoric Society (U.K.). His numerous books include *The Children of Aataentsic: A History of the Huron People to 1660* (1976), *A History of Archaeological Thought* (Cambridge 1989), *Early Civilizations: Ancient Egypt in Context* (1993), *Sociocultural Evolution* (1998), and *The Cambridge History of the Native Peoples of the Americas, Volume 1* (Cambridge 1996), co-edited with Wilcomb E. Washburn.

Understanding Early Civilizations

A Comparative Study

BRUCE G. TRIGGER
McGill University

CAMBRIDGE
UNIVERSITY PRESS

University Printing House, Cambridge CB2 8BS, United Kingdom

One Liberty Plaza, 20th Floor, New York, NY 10006, USA

477 Williamstown Road, Port Melbourne, VIC 3207, Australia

4843/24, 2nd Floor, Ansari Road, Daryaganj, Delhi - 110002, India

79 Anson Road, #06-04/06, Singapore 079906

Cambridge University Press is part of the University of Cambridge.

It furthers the University's mission by disseminating knowledge in the pursuit of education, learning and research at the highest international levels of excellence.

www.cambridge.org
Information on this title: www.cambridge.org/9780521705455

First published 2003
First paperback edition 2007

A catalogue record for this publication is available from the British Library

Library of Congress Cataloging in Publication data
Trigger, Bruce G.
Understanding early civilizations : a comparative study / Bruce G. Trigger.
p. cm.
Includes bibliographical references and index.
ISBN 0-521-82245-9
1. Civilization, Ancient. 2. Social archaeology. 3. Prehistoric peoples. I. Title.
CB311 T77 2003
930–dc21 2002074052

ISBN 978-0-521-82245-9 Hardback
ISBN 978-0-521-70545-5 Paperback

Contents

Illustrations

Preface

In 1959, my final year as an undergraduate at the University of Toronto, I produced a paper entitled 'A Definition of Urbanism' for a course in which Ronald Cohen, then a young assistant professor, sought to introduce his students to the most recent trends in ecological and neoevolutionary analysis. I compared the ecological, demographic, economic, social, political, and cultural characteristics of five urban centres: Tenochtitlan, Akhetaton, Rome, and an ancient Mesopotamian and a medieval Western European city. I concluded that the eclectic range of features exhibited by these urban centres did not support Gideon Sjoberg's (1955, 1960) general construct of the 'preindustrial city' and that the early development of cities must have been multilinear rather than unilinear. My recent rediscovery of this early work in a dusty filing cabinet reminded me of how long I have been interested in comparative studies of early civilizations.

In the autumn of 1959, as a graduate student at Yale University, I had the opportunity to study the theory and methods of cross-cultural comparison under the expert guidance of George Peter Murdock and Clellan Ford. In 1963–64, I learned still more about this subject from Raoul Naroll, a senior colleague at Northwestern University. To these anthropologists, none still living, the present work owes a great debt.

After that time, my interest in comparative studies was in abeyance while I worked on settlement archaeology, historical archaeology, and the history of archaeology. Since 1970, however, I have taught approximately every second year a course at McGill University entitled 'The Social Institutions of Early Civilizations' and more recently 'Comparative Studies of Early Civilizations'. This course encouraged my interest in how early civilizations functioned and resulted in the publication of a few papers based on the comparative study of such societies (Trigger 1972, 1976b, 1979, 1985a, 1985b, 1990a, 1990b).

When I finished writing *A History of Archaeological Thought* (1989), I began to search for a way to evaluate the rival claims of cultural ecologists, who viewed societies as shaped by adaptive factors, and postmodernist cultural relativists, who regarded all human behaviour as culturally determined. It seemed to me that research was being guided to an unhealthy extent by theoretical dogmatism. I sought therefore to determine empirically what aspects of human behaviour and beliefs were shaped by factors that were common to all human beings and what aspects were shaped by idiosyncratic features of cultural systems by examining seven early civilizations distributed around the world, all but two of which had displayed predominantly independent trajectories of development. In this way, I hoped to provide an ontological basis for a more informed understanding of human behaviour. The results of my research are presented in this book.

The cross-cultural comparison of decontextualized traits concerning large numbers of societies around the world is, as Murdock often pointed out to his students, merely a quick way to discover robust patterning in sociocultural behaviour that requires closer study. When dealing with a small sample such as is available for early civilizations, data must be considered within a more contextualized framework if researchers are to understand their significance. The need to present data in their functional context (a kind of comparative equivalent of 'thick description') explains the great length of this book. As a result, it has also become a summary of my understanding of what is currently known about the seven best-documented early civilizations. It therefore fulfils my earlier promise to publish a synoptic description of these civilizations as well as a detailed analysis of how and why they resembled and differed from each other (1993: viii).

Since 1989, I have spent most of my otherwise unallocated time working on this book. I began writing it in November 1997, and the final draft was completed in June 2001. The most recent references are to works published early that year. The structure of the book was greatly influenced by various summaries of my research that I was invited to present when this research was still in its early stages. The first of these presentations was in the Department of Archaeology at the University of Bergen, Norway, when I was visiting that university as a guest of the Centre for the Study of the Sciences and the Humanities in February 1991. A second lecture, 'Constraint and Freedom in the Shaping of Early Civilizations', was delivered a year later to the Department of Anthropology at the University of Toronto during a visit sponsored by the Snider Lectureship Fund. The following December, similar talks were presented at University College London, at Cambridge University, and as a Munro lecture at the University of Edinburgh. The stimulating discussions that followed each of these presentations greatly assisted my work. Of still greater value for guiding my research were four lectures that I gave on ancient Egypt as an early civilization while I was visiting the Department of Sociology, Anthropology, and Psychology at the American University in Cairo. A year later these lectures were published as *Early Civilizations: Ancient Egypt in Context* (1993). The reactions to that volume were of great help to my later work.

Much of Chapter 2 is based on an unpublished lecture entitled 'Cross-Cultural Comparison and Postmodernism' that I gave at the University of Bradford while I was a guest speaker at the Theoretical Archaeology Group Conference held there in December 1994. The comparative discussion of writing systems in Chapter 25 is largely based on a more comprehensive study of the development of writing systems published in the *Norwegian Archaeological Review* (1998b).

Among colleagues and graduate students who have augmented or altered my perception of early civilizations in crucial ways or drawn my attention to vital literature I especially wish to thank John Baines, Mario Bunge, Stephen Chrisomalis, Jerimy Cunningham, Csilla Dallos, Bernardo Dubrovsky, Harvey Feit, Katja Goebs, Hilary Gopnik, Peter Gose, John Hall, Alice B. Kehoe, Andrea McDowell, Joyce Marcus, Lynn Meskell, Steven Mithen, Laura Nader, Joan Oates, Thomas C. Patterson, Anne Pyburn, Jérôme Rousseau, Philip Salzman, Frank Smith, Michael E. Smith, W. J. Stemp, Elisabeth Stone, Darko Suvin, Alexander von Gernet, Barbara Welch, Robin Yates, and Norman Yoffee. I also thank the many undergraduates who have taken my early-civilizations course over the years for the contributions that their discussions, questions, and essays have made to my understanding of these societies. The students of the classes of 1999 and 2001, which were taught while I was writing this book, were especially helpful. I have almost certainly inadvertently failed to acknowledge others who substantially assisted me over the past twelve years. To them I apologize.

Throughout the book I have referred to early civilizations in the past tense. This includes the Yoruba, despite the many continuities in their civilization through the colonial era to the present. I also have sought as far as possible to free descriptions of early civilizations from the use of terms, such as demesne, feudal, peasant, prebend, and *oikos*, that relate primarily to medieval European or Classical Greek and Roman civilizations. The resulting circumlocutions may seem strange at first, but I believe that this procedure helps to reduce bias in the understanding of early civilizations.

The only language of an early civilization that I have studied is Egyptian. Standardizing the spellings of words in the various other languages spoken in the early civilizations has proved vexatious, since each language has been transliterated in different ways into the Roman alphabet. While trying, whenever possible, to follow current conventions, I was forced to accept as given the spellings of some words that occur only in single secondary sources. I have presented ancient Egyptian words without suppositious vowels and generally have preferred transliterations that use as few diacritics as possible.

While I have read much of the primary documentation that is available in English by authors such as Sahagún (1950–82) on the Valley of Mexico, Cobo (1979, 1990) on the Inka, and Samuel Johnson (1921) on the Yoruba, I have more often cited secondary sources on the ancient civilizations on the grounds that their authors' evaluations of the primary documentation are more informed than my own. My referencing of factual material aims mainly to identify variant or contested interpretations of data, guide interested readers to further sources of information, and provide an idea of the interpretive literature on which my descriptions of early civilizations are based. I have listed at the end of the book only those works that have actually been cited.

I cannot claim to possess the expert knowledge about each early civilization that specialists on those civilizations do and am sure that such readers will find factual errors and egregious deficiencies in my understanding of particular early civilizations. Yet attempts to create multiauthored studies of early civilizations have their own pitfalls. I hope that a single interpretive viewpoint more than compensates for my heavy reliance on secondary sources.

My research for this book was greatly assisted by the award of two successive Killam Fellowships administered by the Canada Council. These relieved me of most teaching and all administrative duties at McGill University during calendar years 1990 and 1991. During calendar years 1992 and 1997 I benefited from McGill University's enlightened policy of sabbatical leave. Without such generous support it would have taken much longer to complete this book.

The final editing of the manuscript and seeing it through press have been substantially assisted by the annual stipend attached to the James McGill Professorship that I received in January 2001. I thank Zarin Machanda for her word processing of the manuscript that was submitted to the Press, Barbara Metzger for her expert copyediting, which produced a more readable book, and Kittisac Chanthaboune for preparing the illustrations. I also thank Jessica Kuper for her most helpful editorial advice, Frank Smith, Camilla T. Knapp, and Catherine Felgar for seeing the work through press, Barbara Chin for securing permissions, Robert Swanson for preparing the index, and Elizabeth Lewis for her important contributions to correcting proofs.

Readers who are interested in theoretical discussions and conclusions rather than the evidence on which they are based can read Chapters 1 to 4, the summaries and analysis of my findings in Chapters 13, 18, and 27, and the concluding discussion in Chapters 28 and 29. It is, however, impossible to evaluate the discussion independently of the evidence.

This book is lovingly dedicated to my wife, Barbara Welch. Her enthusiastic encouragement and critical input into its creation have vastly exceeded the call of duty. The two of us share, along with much else, a predilection for comparative studies, which in her case is directed towards Caribbean islands and banana production.

Understanding Early Civilizations

Introduction

1 Rationalism and Relativism

The most important issue confronting the social sciences is the extent to which human behaviour is shaped by factors that operate cross-culturally as opposed to factors that are unique to particular cultures. In part this debate addresses to what degree and in what ways human behaviour is influenced by calculations of self-interest that all human beings make in a similar manner as opposed to particularistic, culturally conditioned, and largely autonomous modes of conceiving reality. Marshall Sahlins (1976: ix) has labelled this confrontation the 'contest between the practical and the meaningful'. The debate goes beyond this, however, to consider to what extent humans may be biologically predisposed to understand reality and behave in similar ways. This debate has pitted materialists against idealists, behaviourists against advocates of cultural studies, processual archaeologists against postprocessual ones, and traditional cultural ecologists, as well as Darwinian archaeologists and sociobiologists, against neo-Boasian postmodernists. It has also split what remains of academic Marxism into two warring camps.

At the centre of this debate is a fundamental question: given the biological similarities and the cultural diversity of human beings, how much the same or how differently are they likely to behave under analogous circumstances? The answer to this question is crucial for understanding human behaviour and cultural change and for shaping the future course of human development (Trigger 1998a). In recent years theoretical positions have been elaborated with great subtlety and refinement, but there is no sign of consensus. As a contribution to this debate, this book seeks to establish empirically what features seven early civilizations, located on four continents, had in common and in what ways they differed from one another. I am assuming that, in the demonstrated absence of historical connections, shared features were either produced by patterns of thought and behaviour common to all human groups or shaped by similar environmental or functional constraints and therefore constitute examples of parallel development or coevolution. Cross-cultural variation reflects the influence of cultural patterns that are free of such constraints. I hope that these case studies will reveal to what extent different sorts of explanations of human behaviour are useful for explicating particular data.

Anthropology, as a product of Western civilization, has simultaneously pursued two antithetical but complementary goals: to demonstrate that people everywhere are biologically much the same and to celebrate the extent of cultural variation found throughout the world. Both of these concerns can be traced back to the eighteenth century, the first being linked to the rationalism of the Enlightenment and the second to Johann Herder and the romantic reaction against the Enlightenment. These two positions have continued to dominate Western politics and intellectual life and have influenced the development of Western civilization in many ways.

RATIONALISM

Rationalists stress the features that all human beings share as members of a single species. They maintain that, despite cultural differences, human needs, drives, motivations, desires, feelings, and sentiments are everywhere much the same. They define culture as humanity's learned modes of thought and behaviour, and they understand such learned behaviour as a far more efficient and therefore evolutionarily superior way for humans to adapt to changing conditions than natural selection (Boyd and Richerson 1985). Travellers often remark that it is possible for people from radically different cultures to understand most aspects of each other's behaviour even when they cannot speak one another's language (D. Brown 1991: 3). Dan Sperber (1985) argues that ethnographic research is possible only because behavioural differences are not very great. The primary role of reason is thought to be to enable human beings to satisfy biological and psychological needs that are fundamentally the same everywhere. Sahlins's (1976) distinction between this sort of 'practical reason' and 'cultural reason', by which he means decision making constrained by the idiosyncratic values of specific cultural traditions, is somewhat problematical. All human thought is symbolically mediated, and therefore practical reason is culturally encoded and generally transmitted from one generation to another in the form of unquestioned norms of behaviour. In this respect it is no different from cultural reason. The crucial distinction between practical and cultural reason is the capacity of practical reason to transcend individual cultures by serving interests that are grounded in panhuman traits.

Rationalists also view culture as adapted to the practical needs of everyday life rather than shaped by beliefs that are independent of such constraints. They treat the past not as a source of enduring identities, ideals, and models for action but as something to be transcended by creating ways of doing things that are better suited to changing circumstances and represent a fuller realization of human potential (Peel 1983: 7). Religious beliefs, values, and cultural traditions they tend to view as epiphenomenal. Thus they consider consciousness and ideas to be shaped by material calculations and to serve principally as a way of encoding and reinforcing practical behaviour.

From the rationalist perspective, the behaviour of any individual largely resembles that of all humans, and social processes are the collective outcome of innumerable individual decisions relating to personal status and well-being that are based on available knowledge and experience. In general, rationalism values the study of behaviour, especially adaptive behaviour, more highly than the study of beliefs and consciousness. This is often justified by advocating a positivist epistemology. It also privileges the study of cross-cultural similarities and sometimes dismisses 'unique, exotic, and non-recurrent particulars' as the result of historical accidents and therefore of no scientific interest (Steward 1955: 209). This emphasis on cross-cultural recurrences and rational explanations of human behaviour does not encourage an interest in cultural traditions. It does encourage an interest in sociocultural evolution.

Rationalist explanations of the uniformities in human behaviour assume a variety of forms. One of the most popular is that ecological or economic factors determine or at least severely constrain the development of sociopolitical organization and belief systems. Factors such as least effort, relative scarcity, and individual or collective security are invoked to explain why people behave the way they do. This approach generally minimizes the importance of human agency and accounts for change in terms of the rational calculation of the relative selective advantages of different strategies – in Sahlins's (1976: 89–90) words, displacing mind from human beings to the ecosystem. It also minimizes the consideration of what is specifically human about human behaviour. A second type of explanation, most closely associated with classical Marxism, sees intrasocietal competition for power and control of material resources as the principal factor bringing about change in human societies. In its original form this explanation was restricted to class societies, but in recent years neo-Marxists have attempted to extend it to preclass societies by postulating analogous forms of competition among lineages, genders, and age-groups (Bloch 1985).

Many rationalists accept that, while reason facilitates and helps to control human behaviour, it does not motivate it. Reason has evolved to serve drives that are rooted in human nature. Human nature, in turn, is grounded in a common biology that expresses itself in similar organic needs, forms of intelligence, and psychology that generate similar impulses and drives. (Debates continue as to whether biological factors produce significant behavioural differences between males and females, but racist attempts to establish biologically grounded differences among various ethnic groups have foundered.) The assumption is that, because of their biological similarities, human beings living under analogous conditions will respond in much the same way to similar problems. Bronislaw Malinowski (1939), for example, attempted to ground social institutions in biological and psychological needs, and George P. Murdock (1945) and Donald E. Brown (1991) identified universals in human action, thought, feelings, statuses, social roles, the division of labour, the underlying structure of language, reasoning, classification, psychological predispositions, and symboling. Brown (1991: 55–60) points out that even historical particularists such as Franz Boas and Clark Wissler acknowledged the existence of behavioural universals rooted in a common human nature. Boas (1963 [1911]: 154) observed detailed, far-reaching, and numerous similarities in thought and action among the most diverse peoples.

According to many rationalists, the existence of these universals refutes the behaviourist view of the human mind as a *tabula rasa* on which experience is objectively recorded and rationally analysed. Early social philosophers such as Thomas Hobbes, Jean-Jacques Rousseau, and John Locke attributed specific (though differing) natures to human beings. Karl Marx also assumed that an underlying sociability and generosity were reflected in hunter-gatherer societies and would be reflected once again in the socialist societies of the future. At the same time, in his desire to avoid supporting conservative ideas that human behaviour was biologically determined and immutable, he contrarily asserted that human nature was not innate but determined by the types of societies in which human beings lived (Fuller 1980: 230–64; Geras 1983).

Rationalists now tend to assume that basic human behaviour has been shaped by millions of years of hominid evolution, during which natural selection has 'wired' the human brain to cope with various specific as well as general problems (D. Brown 1991: 85; Mithen 1996). Much of this selection is thought to have been related to the problems of living in small social groups, which involved intragroup status competition as well as the need for cooperation to cope with both internal and external problems. It is argued that their living under these conditions until just a few thousand years ago accounts for the behavioural similarities shared by all human groups (Carrithers 1992).

Individual interests are complex and cannot be reduced to rational calculations relating only to personal benefits or the ecological adaptation of groups.

Individuals rank the objectives they wish to pursue differently, and their differing understandings may lead to different strategies for achieving the same goals. They may sometimes decide that their personal goals are best served in ways that accord with social objectives (Hardin 1968). Under these circumstances, even in small-scale societies, behaviour can be highly diverse, and varied individual decisions may play a significant role in the formulation of social strategies. Individual goal-driven behaviour may combine with ecological and other external constraints in complex ways. In an attempt to deal with this diversity, those who believe that sociocultural phenomena are shaped most powerfully and directly by ecological or economic factors frequently assert that the greatest degree of cross-cultural regularity among societies at the same level of development is associated with their economic institutions. They also assume that more cross-cultural diversity will be found in social and political institutions, because these institutions are less directly constrained by environment and technology, and still more diversity in art, philosophy, and religious beliefs, which are the aspects of behaviour most likely to be influenced by historical idiosyncrasies (Friedman and Rowlands 1978*b*: 203–5; Gellner 1982).

ROMANTICISM

Romanticism began as a protest against the rationalism of the Enlightenment, which many intellectuals believed ignored the importance of emotions and sensibilities and of attachments to friends, families, religions, communities, regions, ethnic groups, and nations. More generally, romanticism celebrated the cultural diversity that characterizes human societies. In the late eighteenth and early nineteenth centuries, it became identified with the conservative reaction against the French Revolution, which, in accordance with the rationalism of the Enlightenment, had demanded that all human beings should stand equal before the law, enjoy the same freedoms and opportunities for self-development, and share responsibility for promoting the common good.

The most recent expression of romanticism in the social sciences is the postmodernist view of cultural traditions as historically constructed 'sense-making systems' that shape people's perceptions and values and their reactions to new experiences. Postmodernists view cultures as highly diverse and idiosyncratic, and through the advocacy of anthropologists such as Victor Turner (1967, 1975), Marshall Sahlins (1976; 1985), Clifford Geertz (1979; 1984), and James Clifford (1988) their ideas have acquired enormous influence. Embracing cultural relativism and historical particularism, modern cultural anthropology once again has much in common with that of Boas.

Cultural relativists assert that human beings live within meaningful schemes of their own devising, which are contingently constructed and therefore never the only ones possible. While many of them recognize that material factors exert real influences on the cultural order, they reject the suggestion that any particular cultural form can be read from a given set of material forces (Sahlins 1976: 206). Which animals are considered appropriate to eat in a particular culture is determined historically rather than rationally (171). Economic necessity can never account for the forms assumed by cultural change, which are invariably constrained and shaped by established but purely conventional ways of doing things. Such conventions are subject only to the endless modifications brought about by individual decodings and re-encodings of knowledge. The resulting idiosyncratic diversity of understandings within each culture makes cultural change complex and unpredictable. Because relativists ascribe such great importance to ideas, they accord only minimal influence to biological constraints; both human behaviour and human nature tend to be viewed as culturally determined.

Extreme forms of relativism minimize the adaptive role of cultures and embrace an idealist cultural determination. Clifford Geertz (1965: 101) maintains that the human essence is manifested in variation rather than in universal characteristics. The only governance of human behaviour is provided by 'systems of significant symbols'. This cultural variability makes interethnic understanding very difficult. In one culture avoiding eye contact is a sign of respect; in another it may indicate insecurity or unreliability. White signifies mourning in one culture and black does so in another. While classical economists, as rationalists, consider the profit motive a human universal, cultural relativists maintain that the production and distribution of goods are determined by concepts that are highly variable from one culture to another.

Carried to its extreme, cultural relativism encourages the development of a radical subjectivism in which every decoding of a message becomes another encoding and it is impossible to comprehend fully what goes on in the mind of a close relative, let alone that of someone from a different culture. Ideas and beliefs, rather than the material conditions of life, are of overwhelming importance in determining behaviour.

Many cultural relativists attribute the determining or constraining power of culturally transmitted behaviour to a generally uncritical acceptance of what is learned, whether conscious beliefs or unconscious habits. Practical considerations or universal self-interest are generally considered insufficient to alter the beliefs and habits that control what people perceive, believe, and hold to be appropriate. In short, people adapt to the world not as it is but as they perceive it to be. Beliefs guide behaviour along culturally specific trajectories, as a result of which peoples with different cultures behave differently even in essentially similar circumstances. This is the essence of Sahlins's (1976) cultural reason. Such views are of considerable antiquity. The seventeenth-century philosopher Francis Bacon maintained that 'custom is the principal magistrate of man's life' (quoted in Boyd and Richerson 1985: 81), while the American sociologist William Sumner (1906) argued that humans for the most part inherited rather than chose their beliefs.

Others attribute the determining power of culture to deep structures that unconsciously shape the development of beliefs in much the same fashion as grammar implicitly patterns speech. The anthropologist Claude Lévi-Strauss (1962) has emphasized universal structuring principles of the mind that realize themselves in a series of binary oppositions by means of which culture is created and can be understood. He views cultures as unconsciously utilizing different sets of oppositions that encourage their elaboration along distinctive lines.

Still others have argued that the deep structures of languages, particularly as these are expressed in grammars, encode and thus emphasize different aspects of reality. Indo-European languages, for example, stress concepts of time by incorporating elaborate tense indicators into their verbs, while in Semitic languages verbs are used to distinguish whether actions are completed or still in progress. Linguists such as Edward Sapir (1921) and Benjamin Whorf (1956) have proposed that such differences among languages make their speakers think and behave differently, even though such speakers are not consciously aware of them. Others deny that such differences are of major significance, arguing that anything that can be said in one natural language can be said in all others, even if it may be much harder to do so in one language than in another. A similar objection may apply to the relation between cultural structuralism and what people think.

Christopher Hallpike (1986: 288–371), although not a cultural relativist, argues that historically related cultures are guided by inflexible core principles or key ideas that are not functionally related to particular subsistence patterns. These core principles – general beliefs about the nature of the cosmos and social organization – supply patterns that shape the development of cultures and social behaviour. Hallpike maintains that, because peoples tend to accept particular core principles as givens, such propositions can influence the development of historically related cultures for millennia.

Karl Marx and other materialists have objected that a theory that treats culture as an independent variable and assigns ideas a primary role in influencing behaviour is incapable of accounting for change (Bloch 1985: 31). Change requires either external pressures on individuals or goal-directed individual action upon society or the natural environment that alters social relations. For such purposive action to occur, material interests that are external to culture must be brought into play. The alternative approach, championed by extreme relativists, is to treat culture as an indeterminate script that slowly changes as a result of largely unintended transformations that occur in the course of individual decodings and encodings of information. This implies that cultural change has no inherent direction, except perhaps that brought about by the greater survivability of some forms of behaviour in direct competition with other forms. The latter sort of cultural selection is, however, of little direct interest to extreme relativists, since it suggests unwelcome limitations on cultural variability.

Postmodernism has encouraged a revival of the Boasian position that, while each culture can be studied and understood on its own terms, individual cultures cannot legitimately be evaluated against any absolute criteria. Ian Hodder (1986; 1987) maintains that, because each culture is a system of meaning that is the product of its own history and is based on unique assumptions, different cultures can be understood and evaluated only on their own terms. Moreover, he argues, because of the intervention of frameworks of culturally specific meaning there is 'no direct, universal cross-cultural relationship between behaviour and material culture' (Hodder 1986: 12). Rather than seeking to understand one aspect of a culture in isolation from the rest, he maintains, anthropologists must try to discover how the different parts of a culture are cognitively linked to form a meaningful whole. To understand the principles that guide agricultural production, for example, it is necessary to study the specific cultural context in which such production occurs. Comparing agricultural production in different societies in isolation from other features of these societies is bound to be misleading and imposes an erroneous materialistic interpretation on human behaviour. Agricultural production may be guided primarily by religious beliefs in one culture and by calculations of monetary profit in another – or, as Maurice Godelier (1978) put it, any aspect of culture can potentially serve as infrastructure. To address this argument it would have to be determined to what extent agricultural production primarily guided by religious concepts would differ from production based on calculations of monetary profit. Some materialists argue that such differing approaches to food production would simply be alternative devices for culturally encoding the same rational principles of ecological adaptation (Rappaport 1968).

Extreme cultural relativists deny that any effective form of cross-cultural comparison is possible – a position that essentially eliminates the basis for anthropology as a comparative study of human behaviour. Others, Geertz among them, argue that comparison is possible provided that it is an exhaustive, hermeneutically driven translation of the ideas of one culture into the thought patterns of another. This is such a difficult, time-consuming enterprise that no more than two cultures can be effectively compared. In general, because they view cultures as systems of knowledge transmitted from earlier periods, relativists prefer to understand them historically.

CONFRONTATION AND ACCOMMODATION

The dichotomy between rationalism and relativism poses many problems for anthropologists. Relativism encourages an interest in culturally specific habits, religious beliefs, art, values, and conceptions of the self that rationalist approaches tend to view as of minor importance. At the same time, it devalues an interest in the search for cross-cultural regularities in human behaviour which is central to a rationalist approach. If a rationalist approach by itself were capable of explaining all aspects of human behaviour, all cultures at the same level of development would closely resemble one another, any differences being attributable to environmental variation. If the range of variation in learned behaviour were limited only by cultural factors, every culture would be different except insofar as they were historically related.

The actual range of cross-cultural similarities and differences does not correspond with an extreme version of either of these scenarios. There is far more cross-cultural uniformity than extreme relativism would allow but less than a purely rationalist explanation would indicate. Even the most extreme relativists admit that universal prerequisites relating to biological necessities such as food, shelter, and biological reproduction impose limitations on cultural variation. Likewise, most rationalists allow that idiosyncratic cultural variation occurs but distinguish between the cross-culturally recurrent, adaptive features of culture, which are believed to be most evident in subsistence patterns and other forms of economic behaviour, and more variable cultural features such as art styles and religious beliefs. Behaviour in the former sphere is seen as restricted by the inflexibility of natural laws and the scarcity of natural resources, while cultural variation reflects the relative freedom of the human imagination. Marvin Harris (1974; 1977; 1979) has gone the farthest in trying to demonstrate that what appear to be cultural idiosyncrasies are adaptively determined, but his case studies remain more polemical than convincing. The challenge is to stop simply supporting one or the other of these alternative positions in a partisan manner and examine in greater detail the nature of cultural similarities and differences as the basis for constructing a more realistic theory of the factors shaping human behaviour and cultural change.

Rationalists and relativists agree that all human behaviour is culturally mediated and that such mediation defines a uniquely human form of adaptation.

Robert Boyd and Peter Richerson (1985) have demonstrated that most beliefs and behavioural patterns that have been culturally transmitted for long periods are superior to recent innovations, both because they have been tested longer and because during that time they have been selected to serve the interests of societies as well as of individuals. Rationalists and relativists do not agree, however, whether culture is phenomenal or epiphenomenal. This debate centres on the extent to which the factors that influence human behaviour are determined primarily by culturally transmitted beliefs or by panhuman drives and aspirations and on the extent to which personal experience can reveal the limitations or inappropriateness of traditional beliefs. As Childe (1956b: 59–60) once asked, how, and under what conditions, does a society decide that burning garbage is a more effective way to stop cholera than burning witches?

Today it is fashionable to argue that all so-called scientific interpretations are subjective and inevitably underdetermined by the available evidence (B. Barnes 1974). In the social sciences most interpretations are provisional and usually vigorously contested, while high-level theories are generally understood to lie beyond the realm of direct proof. There is no conclusive evidence that a materialist, behaviourally oriented approach is any more or less objective than an idealist, culturally oriented one. Yet some evidence is better than no evidence, and imperfect theories are stepping stones towards a better understanding. Cultural and ecological determinism are equally pernicious. Cultural determinism excludes in advance the consideration of cross-cultural regularities, while ecological determinism rules out the consideration of cross-cultural idiosyncrasies.

To circumvent this dilemma, I propose to undertake a comparative examination of similarities and differences in seven early civilizations. My aim is to determine to what extent and in what ways these cultures were shaped, on the one hand, by cross-culturally operative factors such as calculations of self-interest that are grounded in human nature and, on the other, by highly variable, culturally constituted, and hence historically specific and irreplicable modes of thinking. I am assuming that, if behaviour is determined by culturally inherited beliefs that are not subject to evaluation on the basis of panhuman criteria, it will tend to vary idiosyncratically from one early civilization to another. If behaviour is shaped by tendencies that are rooted in human nature, it will tend to display cross-cultural uniformities.

It is also necessary to investigate the constraints imposed by functional limitations. There appear to be only a limited number of ways in which societies at a particular level of complexity can function well, or even function at all.

Hallpike (1986: 141–42) has argued that such functional limitations become more restrictive as societies grow more complex and competition among societies at both the same and different levels of complexity increases. The convergence that comes about as a result of functional limitations suggests that processes of social and cultural change may be more variable than their outcomes. Childe (1958) argued that underlying the vast array of prehistoric European Neolithic cultures was a strictly limited number of forms of social and political organization. More recently Kent Flannery (1972) maintained that the factors leading to the development of complex societies are far more varied and idiosyncratic than the structures they produce. George P. Murdock (1949; 1959b) demonstrated that only a limited number of systems of kin terms possess sufficient logical coherence to survive as stable structures. He also documented that there were many more ways to shift from one kinship system to another than stable outcomes. The main difference among functional limitations appears to be that in the social and behavioural realm they relate mainly to making efficient use of limited resources, while in the cognitive sphere they have to do with limiting the production of a debilitating degree of symbolic variation (Gellner 1982).

If social organization and cultural coherence exhibit more order than processes of sociocultural change, functional studies may be more important for understanding regularities in human behaviour and for addressing what are often viewed as evolutionary as opposed to historical processes than many neoevolutionists have believed. This constitutes a strong argument that the synchronic-comparative approach adopted in this book may in some respects be even more useful for understanding sociocultural evolution than the study of actual sequences of change. It can also be argued that anthropological archaeologists have erred in trying to explain changes without first seeking to understand how what is changing functioned.

Constraint can be viewed as imposed on human behaviour by ecological and biological factors (as the latter constitute human nature), functional limitations, and cultural patterns. Ecological uniformities and functional limitations promote various kinds of cross-cultural convergences and uniformities, while ecological variations and divergent cultural patterns promote and sustain cross-cultural variation. Ecological factors and functional limitations encourage rational, conscious and individual responses to situations, while cultural patterns invite passive acceptance or active elaboration of established trajectories. It is evident that to some extent individuals and groups are able to reinterpret and alter cultural patterns for their social and material advantages and so that they can interact more effectively with the natural environment.

THE PROPOSED STUDY

Unlike most anthropological analyses, this study focuses not on how seven early civilizations evolved but on what their similarities and differences can tell us about factors that influence human behaviour. This requires determining what kinds of similarities were shared by all seven early civilizations, whether these similarities were general or specific, and whether some early civilizations shared certain features but not others. To what extent were specific sets of features shared by the same civilizations, making it possible to define subvarieties of early civilizations? What features varied idiosyncratically from one early civilization to another? How were these various types of features functionally correlated? My goal is to subject theories of sociocultural change to empirical testing.

The study I am undertaking is the sort of comparison that extreme relativists maintain is impossible. No one, they claim, can understand one or more other cultures sufficiently well to make comparisons that are more than projections of ethnocentric fantasies. To abandon an effort to understand patterning in human behaviour on the grounds of such dogmatic and unsubstantiated assertions would be a shameful act of intellectual cowardice.

In the next three chapters, I will assess comparative research, define early civilizations, and discuss some of the problems I have encountered in my research and how I have dealt with them. This will be followed by the examination in turn of the sociopolitical organization, the economy, and the beliefs, knowledge, and values of the seven early civilizations in order to ascertain the extent of their similarities and differences. This survey will differ from many previous ones, which have generally privileged the investigation of similarities or differences according to the theoretical preconceptions of the researchers. In three sectional summaries and an integrative chapter, I will assess the theoretical implications of my findings.

2 Comparative Studies

Comparative studies are potentially of great value for understanding human behaviour and cultural change, but all too often a lack of rigour renders them uninformative or even highly misleading. There is never enough information to explain all aspects of any early civilization, and this lack of information has stimulated many anthropologists to extrapolate what is known about one society to other, presumably similar ones. The societies being compared often represent different levels of development, and even societies on the same level cannot be assumed to be sufficiently alike to justify such extrapolation.

It is proposed, for example, that Maya political organization may have had significant 'feudal' characteristics, and attempts have been made to understand it better by comparisons with the feudal societies of medieval Europe and premodern Japan (Adams and Smith 1981). Yet, how can such comparisons be justified, let alone prove useful, when so little is known for certain about Maya political organization? While 'feudalism' signifies that land is granted by an overlord in return for political support and military service, nothing is known about relations between landholding and political authority among the Classic Maya. In Maya studies 'feudalism' tends to be used loosely to refer to any form of delegated authority. Beyond this, the civilizations being compared in this example were not at the same level of development. The feudal orders of medieval Europe and premodern Japan both evolved out of the collapse of more centralized forms of government and coexisted symbiotically with international religions of foreign origin that strongly assisted their political functioning. This type of religion was not associated with early civilizations. Other scholars have compared Maya political organization with that of West African peoples, such as the Yoruba, and with the so-called galactic polities and theatre states of Southeast Asia (Fox et al. 1996; Demarest 1992).

In the cultural sphere, Susan Gillespie (1989) has noted parallels between Aztec and Central African beliefs that kings originated as strangers to the people they ruled. Yet limited comparisons of this sort leave unresolved the question of whether such parallels are isolated historical coincidences or examples of a more general phenomenon. A more comprehensive study of the concept of the king as a stranger by Gillian Feeley-Harnik (1985) suggests that this theme recurs in many cultures that lack obvious historical connections. The idea of the king as a stranger may be related to a broader set of beliefs that kings and ruling classes differ, either supernaturally or ethnically, from their subjects. Familiar examples include the distinctions that were drawn during the eighteenth century in Britain between an aristocracy that traced its descent from Norman conquerors and indigenous Anglo-Saxon commoners and in France between the upper classes, which claimed to be of Frankish (German) origin, and the rest of the population, which was assumed to be descended from subjugated Romano-Celtic peoples. These distinctions ceased to be important with the emergence of a modern sense of national identity (Olivier 1999: 177).

A detailed and independent understanding of each early civilization is a prerequisite for comparative study. Using information about one early civilization to fill gaps in our knowledge of another inevitably creates the appearance of greater cross-cultural uniformity than was actually the case.

HISTORY OF COMPARATIVE STUDIES

Cross-cultural comparative studies must be distinguished from more detailed and intensive comparisons of a smaller number of societies. Cross-cultural comparisons examine data concerning selected features in a large number of societies in order to determine whether regularities are present that seem worthy of more detailed study and explanation. For example, a comparison of subsistence patterns and political organization would suggest that no hunter-gatherer society has ever developed a hereditary monarchy. Various explanations can be offered for this, including the lack of need for formal governance in small, mobile societies and the inability of such societies to produce a surplus capable of supporting such an institution. It would be very surprising if more intensive investigations produced evidence of even one example of that combination.

The first effort to collect information that would allow research to be carried out in this fashion was the British philosopher Herbert Spencer's *Descriptive Sociology*, which he began planning in 1859 as background for his *Principles of Sociology* (1876–96). *Descriptive Sociology* was compiled by Spencer and three assistants and published (partly posthumously) in fifteen volumes between 1873 and 1932. These volumes, organized by region, consisted of tables of statements summarizing the institutions and, if known, the histories of particular societies and reproducing extracts from the works cited. An additional section in which the extracts would be grouped under thematic headings, such as political, ecclesiastical, or ceremonial institutions, was never completed (M. Harris 1968: 159–61).

The first study to use a statistical cross-cultural approach to discover patterning in ethnographic data was that of Edward B. Tylor, who in 1889 read a paper to the Royal Anthropological Institute using data relating to marriage practices and subsistence patterns in several hundred societies around the world to provide evidence that matrilocal residence had preceded patrilocal residence. In keeping with the times, Tylor's findings were organized in a unilinear evolutionary format, with the developmental sequence being inferred from different subsistence patterns.

Tylor's approach was pursued by the Dutch sociologist S. R. Steinmetz (1930 [1900]) who set out to code ethnographic data concerning 1,000 to 1,500 'peoples and phases'. Although he did not achieve this goal, his student H. J. Nieboer (1900) examined relations between slavery and economic factors in 65 hunting and fishing societies, 22 pastoral groups, and 219 agricultural societies. Steinmetz's approach also inspired T. S. van der Bij's (1929) cross-cultural study of warfare, J. H. Ronhaar's (1931) examination of matrilineal societies, and Jan Tijm's (1933) comparative study of the role of women in North American Indian societies (M. Harris 1968: 612–13).

In their book *The Material Culture and Social Institutions of the Simpler Peoples*, the British sociologists L. T. Hobhouse, G. C. Wheeler, and Morris Ginsberg (1915) sought to determine the extent to which modes of food production were correlated with other aspects of culture, such as political and juridical organization, family structure, warfare, social stratification, and property, in an initial sample of 640 societies. Amplifying Nieboer's classification, they distinguished three grades of hunting societies, three of agriculturalists, and two of pastoralists.

The most sustained application of the statistical cross-cultural comparative method resulted from the creation at Yale University, in 1937, of the Human Relations Area Files (until 1949, the Cross-Cultural Survey), a systematic compilation of ethnographic sources relating to more than 240 cultures. Over the years, hundreds of thousands of pages of ethnographic material have been filed under uniform subject headings. The creation of these files opened the way for a vast number of cross-cultural studies addressing many different topics and, in the words of Marvin Harris (1968: 614), ushered in 'a whole new era of the comparative method'. Beginning in the 1950s, George P. Murdock, who had played a leading role in the development of the Human Relations Area Files, organized the compilation of a 'World Ethnographic Sample' and an *Atlas of World Cultures* (Murdock 1981), in which 563 cultures were described with respect to several dozen sets of coded features. This *Atlas* has made possible the investigation of correlations between numerous predetermined aspects of culture.

The principal feature of general cross-cultural research as it has developed since the nineteenth century has been the use of large samples and the search for correlations between specific features of cultures. This sort of research has sought almost exclusively to establish cross-cultural uniformities rather than differences. It therefore accords best with the rationalist approach, which postulates a high degree of uniformity among cultures. While the capacity of this approach to falsify assumptions by failing to find empirical evidence of correlations renders it capable of refuting or weakening as well as confirming rationalist theories (Weber 1976 [1896]: 285–86), it is generally associated with the search for positive correlations that accord with a rationalist outlook.

This sort of cross-cultural approach was especially attractive to the American archaeologists who adopted a more behaviourist and neoevolutionary approach in the 1960s. The development of radiocarbon dating in the 1950s had permitted the correlation of prehistoric sequences around the world and the determination of rates of change, making it possible for the first time for archaeologists to generalize about the nature of cultural change. In an effort to improve the behavioural interpretation of archaeological data, Lewis Binford rejected the haphazard analogies that hitherto had been employed and argued that interpretations had to be based on lawlike generalizations. This required establishing strong correlations between physical artifacts and specific forms of behaviour in living cultures that could be used to infer behaviour from material culture in the archaeological record (Binford 1962; 1972; 1978).

An example of this approach is Binford's (1971) systematic correlation of mortuary practices with dimensions of social behaviour such as age, sex, and social position in forty societies around the world. In this paper, which followed standard Human Relations Area Files procedures, Binford demonstrated that more behavioural dimensions were distinguished in burials in sedentary societies than in non-sedentary ones. In 'Willow Smoke and Dogs' Tails' (1980), however, no data or scores for individual hunter-gatherer societies were presented, and on the correlation chart only seven outlying societies were identified by name. Binford's explanation of centrally based hunting as an ecological adaptation to high latitudes was therefore very difficult to assess. In more recent work, Binford (1983) based generalizations about hunter-gatherer camp layouts and other forms of spatial behaviour on ethnographic observations he made among the Nunamiut Eskimo of Alaska, provided that these observations were not contradicted by the sometimes casual observations that he and other anthropologists have made among the San hunter-gatherers of southern Africa and the Australian Aborigines. This trend has been reversed only in Binford's (2001) detailed ethnographic study of ecological adaptation among hunter-gatherer societies.

Apart from Binford's work, little use has been made of statistical cross-cultural studies by neoevolutionary archaeologists or, with rare exceptions such as Robert Carneiro (1970a), by neoevolutionary social anthropologists. While George P. Murdock (1949), R. B. Textor (1967), and other social anthropologists made considerable use of general cross-cultural research to investigate regularities in human behaviour, only a small number of social and cultural anthropologists have consistently used cross-cultural data for delineating cultural similarities and differences (Ember and Ember 1983; Otterbein 1989). Declining interest in systematic cross-cultural comparison in both archaeology and anthropology has discouraged the comparative study of early civilizations.

CHALLENGES TO CROSS-CULTURAL GENERALIZATION

From the beginning, the validity of statistical cross-cultural studies as a method for delineating regularities in human behaviour was seriously challenged on a number of grounds. In the discussion that followed Tylor's presentation of his paper, the geneticist Francis Galton questioned its conclusions by enquiring rhetorically in how many cases the traits Tylor was examining had spread by diffusion or migration from one society to another rather than occurring independently. Tylor regarded this objection to his method as so serious that he ceased to use it. Subsequent research has made it clear that diffusion plays an important role in shaping the distribution of cultural traits. In a study using data concerning all documented North American aboriginal groups, Harold Driver (1966) demonstrated that historical-diffusional factors explained kin-avoidance practices much better than existing functional and evolutionary theories.

Beginning in the 1960s, comparative anthropologists sought to devise various answers to what became known as Galton's problem (Naroll 1961). Their proposed solutions were based on the assumption that, since diffusion was most likely to influence contiguous areas, studying the results of coevolution or parallel development required worldwide samples that were either maximally dispersed or stratified according to linguistic families which it could be assumed indicated populations that had separate histories. Researchers asking a general question such as whether matrilineal descent was functionally correlated with one type of subsistence more than any other tended to use a standard worldwide sample of over 250 societies, while a more specific question such as Binford asked about logistics in hunter-gatherer societies might be addressed using a sample of only 40 or so relevant societies (Ford 1967; F. Moore 1961).

Still other comparativists advocated employing very large or even exhaustive samples numbering thousands of societies (Driver 1966: 147; Jorgensen 1966: 168–69). This procedure made it possible to render informed and specific judgements about the extent to which distributions of traits resulted from diffusion or independent development. While studies of this sort have been carried out for North America (Jorgensen 1974), the information and resources are generally lacking to do this on a worldwide scale. Ruth Mace and Mark Pagel (1994) have suggested that studies of parallel development require the identification of independent events of cultural change rather than independent cultures. This is done historically, by constructing phylogenies of cultures and relating independent instances of culture change to them.

While there is no clear and effective way to distinguish cross-cultural regularities resulting from historical connections (homologies) from similarities resulting from independent development (analogies) in the cultural sphere, as can be done in biology, the samples that have been developed by the Human Relations Area Files and the statistical methods employed in analysing the data they contain seem capable of identifying at least some analogies. Powerful functional constraints reveal themselves in the form of strong worldwide correlations. Weaker 'tilts' and 'trends' indicate both the random countervailing influences of diffusion and the relatively weak and slow-acting nature of less powerful functional constraints (Coult and Habenstein 1965). Weak correlations may also indicate the involvement of multiple factors, the operation of which can be understood only as a result of the detailed study of a number of cases (Roberts 1996). A worldwide sample thus appears to be able to identify only those parallel developments that result from strong functional constraints. Unfortunately, robust correlations that go beyond what is self-evident tend to be infrequent.

Some critics of coevolutionary interpretations have proposed that various cultural similarities can be traced back twelve thousand years or more to a common culture that gave rise to the later ones of Northeast Asia and the Americas. They argue that the shared shamanistic beliefs of Siberian and New World hunter-gatherer cultures formed a substratum for the development of similar religious beliefs associated with the much later Chinese, Korean, Mexican, and Peruvian civilizations (K. Chang 1983; 1984; P. Furst 1977; Seaman and Day 1994). Still more radical diffusionists seek a single original culture from which all other cultures are derived, just as some linguists attempt to trace the origin of all modern languages back to a single mother tongue (Ruhlen 1994). This sort of approach proposes a historical explanation for the common features shared by hunter-gatherer cultures throughout the world. Other anthropologists maintain that specific ancient beliefs which spread with the earliest human populations around the world have persisted throughout later human history. Weston La Barre (1984) has labelled beliefs that are so ancient and widespread that they seem inextricable from all human thought 'archoses'. While such historical explanations cannot be ruled out, many similarities in cultures at all levels of complexity are accounted for far more convincingly from an evolutionary perspective. These include social institutions, forms of behaviour, and beliefs that are characteristic of complex societies but not of nomadic, hunter-gatherer ones and that recur throughout the world in situations for which the archaeological record does not provide any evidence of significant historical contact.

Beginning in the 1950s, British and Dutch social anthropologists objected to the statistical comparison of individual traits wrenched from their sociopolitical context (M. Harris 1968: 616–33; Köbben 1952; 1973). They argued that, because all aspects of social relations are parts of socially integrated wholes and individual cultural traits acquire their functional significance from the roles they play in such social systems, anthropologists must first seek to understand every trait in relation to the rest of the social system. Even if cross-cultural samples were chosen with greater care than in the past, the comparativists' decontextualization of traits was viewed as the continuation of practices associated with long discredited nineteenth-century evolutionism.

Social anthropologists were not in principle opposed to the comparative study of human societies. A. R. Radcliffe-Brown (1952) believed that the ultimate goal of social anthropology was to become the equivalent of comparative anatomy, with societies being treated as if they were equivalent to organisms. On the basis of this analogy, it was argued that, before societies could be compared, anthropologists needed to determine in detail how each society was constructed and how it functioned. This could be done only through the detailed analysis of ethnographic data collected during the course of lengthy fieldwork. The use of both historical and archaeological data was rejected because these data were not sufficiently contextualized or verifiable. As a result of the high standards set for collecting data, social anthropologists became so concerned with studying individual societies that most of them lost interest in carrying out comparative studies. Some of the best comparative work, by the American social anthropologist Fred Eggan (1966), examined cultures that were historically related to each other in an effort to understand why variations had arisen within single traditions.

Comparative studies were strongly repudiated by the new cultural anthropology that developed in the 1970s (Clifford 1988; Geertz 1973; V. Turner 1967; 1975). Like Boasian anthropologists, the new cultural anthropologists supported a humanistic, historical orientation in opposition to a generalizing, behaviouristic, and scientific one. Inspired by postmodernist relativism, they argued that every culture was a unique combination of traits that could be understood only in terms of their relation to the culture of which they were a part. Like social anthropologists, they associated comparative studies with cultural evolutionism and what was now viewed as its untenable assumption of cross-cultural uniformity. As a result of their cognitive rather than behavioural emphasis, cultural anthropologists proclaimed that each culture was a unique, self-contained system of meanings that could be understood only on its own terms. This position was reinforced by demonstrations that material culture, beliefs, and behaviour can distort, invert, and naturalize, as well as reflect and reinforce social reality (Hodder 1982a). On these grounds, cultural anthropologists went even farther than social anthropologists and rejected in principle the possibility of making meaningful cross-cultural comparisons. Yet, in practice there has been considerable ambivalence about comparisons. Ian Hodder, who in some of his writings asserted the incomparability of cultures, elsewhere proposed that regularities in the way garbage is used to mark social boundaries by various African societies and by European gypsies permitted archaeologists to discern social boundaries in Neolithic Western Europe (Hodder 1982b: 67; 1986; 1987).

The decline in comparative studies thus has a curious aetiology. Social anthropologists identified the general comparative approach's decontextualization of data and its search for cross-cultural regularities with the research methods of long-discredited nineteenth-century evolutionists, and new cultural anthropologists identified the search for these regularities with the neoevolutionism they were seeking to discredit. Yet neoevolutionists showed little interest in large-scale cross-cultural studies, apparently because they did not regard cross-cultural uniformity as something that had to be demonstrated (Fried 1967; Sahlins 1958; 1968; Service 1971). Much neoevolutionary theorizing relied on ethnographic data concerning the specific part of the world with which these anthropologists were most familiar, generally Oceania. As a result, data from Africa and North America were not checked to determine how similar societies exhibiting the same general level of complexity in various parts of the world were to one another. The failure of social anthropologists to challenge such assumptions of uniformity reflected their growing belief that anthropological data were too contaminated, as a result of acculturation to dominant colonial societies, to be useful for revealing key patterns at earlier stages of development (Schrire 1984).

There are indications of a renewed interest in comparative studies. These include Mace and Pagel's (1994) paper, referred to above, and C. L. Costin's (1996) advocacy of cross-cultural studies for understanding the relations between gender and craft specialization. Such research is inspired by a desire to distinguish between cultural universals, which may be biologically grounded, and idiosyncratic variations that clearly are not. Sociologists such as Ernest Gellner (1988), John Hall (1986), and Michael Mann (1986) have also shown great interest in the comparative study of complex societies, although their interest is oriented towards establishing the uniqueness of Western civilization.

Comparative studies and in particular statistical studies are a way to discover patterning in human behaviour, which in turn needs to be explained. For the most part, such studies have concentrated on documenting similarities rather than differences and therefore have been linked primarily to evolutionary and rationalist approaches. The search for similarities is not, however, inherent in the method, which can be used to document cross-cultural variation as well as uniformity.

COMPARATIVE STUDIES OF EARLY CIVILIZATIONS

The comparative study of early civilizations has followed a somewhat different course from that of general cross-cultural research. This is partly because the number of historically independent early civilizations is limited but more importantly because many non-anthropologists study early civilizations and the humanist approach to them tends to be non-comparative. Based on Johann Herder's belief that each civilization should be studied and appreciated for its own sake, this approach tends to treat each early civilization as unique. Similarities among them have generally been explained from the perspective of *Weltgeschichte* (world history), which maintains that all cultures have interacted with and to some extent influenced one another. Instead of considering the possibility of coevolution, humanists have traditionally offered diffusionary explanations of similarities. Only a few have studied early civilizations from a comparative perspective.

The archaeologist Gordon Childe (1934) and the Orientalist Henri Frankfort (1956) conducted detailed comparisons of the civilizations of ancient Egypt and southern Mesopotamia and concluded that they had evolved in distinctive ways and remained fundamentally different from one another. Southern Mesopotamia had developed as a series of city-states sharing a common culture, while ancient Egypt was united very early in its history as a divine monarchy, and its high culture had developed at the royal court. Childe, a materialist and a possibilist, attributed this difference to a contingent divergence in the ways the ruling classes in these two civilizations had devised to extract food surpluses from farmers. Frankfort, an idealist, attributed these differences to what Hallpike (1986) would later call distinctive 'core principles'. Frankfort believed that these core principles were elaborated out of distinctive ideas that had existed prior to the rise of civilization in these two regions.

The most influential comparative study of early civilizations was that of the ecological anthropologist Julian Steward (1949), who compared civilizations in ancient Egypt, Mesopotamia, northern China, highland Mexico, and Peru. Steward viewed cultures as adaptive systems and believed that they developed along similar lines in similar environments. Yet, unlike many nineteenth-century unilinear evolutionists, he thought that it was necessary to take account of the impact of different environments on cultures, an approach that he called multilinear evolution. Under the influence of Karl Wittfogel (1938; 1957), he proposed that all the earliest civilizations had developed in a single type of arid environment, where irrigation was necessary to sustain dense populations. All other civilizations, he argued, were secondary ones, having come into existence only as the result of influences emanating from the first.

According to Steward, the earliest civilizations had evolved in arid environments as population growth and the need to coordinate labour to build and maintain irrigation systems led to the development of centralized controls, which radically transformed the political organization of these societies. Steward believed that the earliest civilizations had been governed theocratically by priests but with increase in population and in interstate conflict, had fallen more and more into the hands of military leaders. Early civilizations became locked into cycles of increasing violence, which eventually undermined their economies and led to population declines. This made possible a new cycle of economic development, followed in turn by more violence and another decline. Steward regarded the civilizations that had evolved in arid regions as essential for the development of complex societies in all other environmental settings, but at the same time he thought of them as evolutionary dead ends. The development of more complex civilizations required environments that had more potential for economic and demographic expansion.

As an evolutionist and an ecological determinist, Steward believed that, because ecological factors played a crucial role in shaping cultures, the cross-cultural variation of early civilizations was limited. He also argued that anthropology could develop as a science only if anthropologists abandoned the preoccupation with the 'unique, exotic, and non-recurrent particulars' that had fascinated the Boasians and focused instead on explaining the cross-cultural similarities in structure and developmental trajectories of societies found in similar natural settings (Steward 1955: 209). He held that the 'cultural core', which he defined as the cross-culturally similar economic, political, and religious patterns that resulted from different societies' coping with similar environmental challenges, had to be delineated empirically. Yet in retrospect it is clear that he imposed a pattern of structural similarities and shared developmental trends on the five early civilizations he was studying that was far more uniform than was warranted by the facts.

Much less was known about early civilizations in the 1940s than is known today, and this encouraged Steward to extrapolate what was known about particular early civilizations to others. He also ignored available evidence and chose not to employ sound comparative methods in his efforts to impose upon early civilizations the uniformity that he wished them to exhibit. He did not take note of the significant differences that Childe and Frankfort had already delineated between ancient Egyptian and Mesopotamian civilizations. He misrepresented northern Chinese subsistence patterns, which had been based on rainfall agriculture, and did not examine the Classic Maya, Yoruba, or Cambodians, who had created civilizations in tropical-forest environments. For a long time he and his followers argued that all civilizations occurring in tropical forests had to be secondary ones and that because of environmental limitations they could flourish only briefly in such locations. Since then it has been demonstrated that the most spectacular early complex culture in Mesoamerica, that of the Olmec, developed in the tropical forest bordering the Gulf of Mexico beginning around 1200 B.C. It also appears that the development of both highland and lowland Maya cultures was influenced more by the Olmec culture than by parallel developments in Central Mexico (Coe 1977; Flannery 2000). Finally, there is evidence of the spectacular growth of Maya culture in the tropical lowlands during the late first millennium B.C., at the same time that complex societies were developing in highland Mesoamerica. While the Classic Maya culture flourished during the first millennium A.D., Maya urban centres had developed considerably earlier in the lowlands and continued to flourish on the Yucatán Peninsula until the Spanish conquest in the sixteenth century. Archaeological evidence indicates that Yoruba civilization developed in the tropical forest of West Africa during the first millennium A.D. and only later spread north onto the savanna (Shaw 1978). Thus there is no reason to deny that early civilizations were able to develop and flourish outside those arid regions where irrigation agriculture was required to support dense populations.

Nevertheless, because Steward's findings were compatible with the unilinear preconceptions of the neoevolutionary anthropology that developed in the 1960s, they exerted great influence on how anthropologists perceived the organization and development of early civilizations (see, e.g., Service 1975; Sanders and Price 1968). Field research, much of it carried out by neoevolutionary archaeologists, eventually revealed the severe problems that resulted from Steward's preoccupation with cross-cultural uniformities. In historical perspective, it must be concluded that his 'Cultural Causality and Law' was not only the most influential cross-cultural study of early civilizations ever published but also the most pernicious.

Another comparative study that belongs to the neoevolutionary tradition is *The Early State*, edited by Henri Claessen and Peter Skalník (1978). It was based on specially prepared (but not standardized) summaries of the sociopolitical features of twenty-one early states, a category that included not only early civilizations but also secondary civilizations and certain less complex centralized polities that are often called chiefdoms. More specific features were used to divide these early states into three types (inchoate, typical, and transitional), which were arranged to form an evolutionary sequence. Early civilizations were assigned to the typical (Egypt, Inka) and transitional (Aztec, Shang China) varieties, although on the basis of rather arbitrary criteria. Structural differences were interpreted as indicating successive stages of unilinear development, and, while different factors were acknowledged as promoting the development of states, it was assumed that, as a result of functional constraints, the result was always very much the same.

A very different sort of comparative study, Robert McC. Adams's *The Evolution of Urban Society* (1966), was a detailed comparison of early Mesopotamian civilization with that of the Aztec of Central Mexico. Adams found these two civilizations, which had developed totally independently of one another, to be structurally very similar and attributed these similarities to functional limitations on what is possible in social and political organization. In contrast to Steward, Adams paid attention to the differences between these two cultures as well and regarded both differences and similarities as worthy of scientific explanation. My present research demonstrates that, apparently by chance, Adams opted to compare two early civilizations that closely resembled one another, just as Childe and Frankfort had compared two that were very different. Thus the very different conclusions that these eminent scholars reached resulted largely from differences in the units they were comparing.

An important recent contribution to the comparative study of early civilizations is *The Archaeology of City-States*, edited by Deborah Nichols and Thomas Charlton (1997). While this volume also considers city-states in later preindustrial societies, most of the case studies concern early civilizations. Although the editors note that most contributors recognize the city-state as being only 'one of two or three major forms of early states', they view city-states as a cross-cultural regularity. They also espouse Steward's goal of 'trying to differentiate the patterns of cultural order from the background noise of cultural diversity' (Charlton and Nichols 1997a: 5), and this perspective has encouraged them to apply the label 'city-state' to early civilizations that might more appropriately have been classified as territorial states and ones for which too little information was available to permit any certain classification. The general conclusion that while 'city-states are normal products of worldwide social evolutionary trajectories . . . early territorial states, like Egypt, are quite exceptional' (Yoffee 1997: 262) appears to flow at least as much from the premises of the volume as from the evidence. Norman Yoffee seems uncertain how many territorial states are examined in this volume, referring to Egypt at one point as 'our single example of a territorial state' (260) but elsewhere including the Inka and Tiwanaku states in that category (262).

In spite of these limitations, the case studies document significant variation among city-states, whether within the same or different early civilizations, and draw attention to significant factors that may have shaped their development. Nevertheless, the volume as a whole documents a continuing commitment to a unilinear evolutionary perspective. The influence of unilinear evolutionary thinking is particularly evident in David Wilson's (1997) opposition not only to 'multistage state typologists' such as Claessen and Skalník but also 'modified stage typologists' such as myself, who postulate that different types of early civilizations may have existed at the same level of development. Wilson argues that 'the systematic features common to all states, or any other kind of society . . . should be of more interest in the cross-cultural perspective advocated by Steward [than] the unique local features of societies' (231).

Archaic States, edited by Gary Feinman and Joyce Marcus (1998), includes several theoretical papers arguing that early civilizations were characterized by resistance to state power and therefore by instability and periodic breakdown and exploring the possibility that early civilizations changed in nature over time. Marcus (1998) rejects the suggestion that most early civilizations consisted of city-state systems and argues that early civilizations first developed as large states, which in many cases later broke apart to form city-state systems. Feinman (1998) suggests that larger polities may have been required to produce pristine states than were needed to sustain later cycles of state development. This approach argues in a unilinear evolutionary fashion that much of the variation among early civilizations reflects the particular stage of development each civilization had reached and that, because all the oldest states were non-literate, their earliest phases can be studied only archaeologically. This theory does not, however, correspond with what is known about Egypt and Mesopotamia, which suggests that early civilizations initially developed in more varied ways than Marcus's proposal envisions.

These behaviourally oriented papers are complemented by John Baines and Norman Yoffee's (1998) magisterial comparison of the cultural development of early civilizations in Egypt and Mesopotamia. This study shows how, early in the histories of these two civilizations, the upper classes developed highly distinctive conceptions of what a civilization should be like that they never lost sight of, despite repeated cycles of political unity and disunity. Egyptian leaders did not abandon the ideal of political unity, which was deeply embedded in their religious and cultural beliefs, while in Mesopotamia the early assumption that unity was cultural rather than political never wholly disappeared. Baines and Yoffee suggest that idiosyncratic cultural features are likely to have played a far greater role in the political processes of early civilizations than the other contributors to this volume recognize.

THE PRESENT STUDY

This study compares seven early civilizations that developed in different parts of the world: Old and Middle Kingdom Egypt (2700–1780 B.C.), southern Mesopotamia from Early Dynastic III to Old Babylonian times (2500–1600 B.C.), northern China in the late Shang and early Western Zhou periods (1200–950 B.C.), the Valley of Mexico in the late fifteenth and early sixteenth centuries A.D., the Classic Maya (A.D. 250–800), the Inka kingdom during the early sixteenth century A.D., and the Yoruba and Benin peoples of West Africa from the mid-eighteenth century to the beginning of the colonial era in the late nineteenth century (Figs. 2.1, 2.2). The Yoruba states and Benin, selected to represent sub-Saharan Africa, constituted the best-documented and one of the culturally most advanced early civilizations of that region (Frobenius 1913, 1: 153). The same is true of the Late Aztec period in the Valley of Mexico in the broader context of highland Mesoamerica, of the Inka kingdom in the context of Peru, of the Shang state in relation to all of China, and of southern Mesopotamia in relation to the Middle East. Ancient Egypt and the Classic Maya were the sole early civilizations that developed in their particular areas.

It will be argued below that each of these civilizations developed substantially independently of the other six. With one exception, none of the languages spoken in these early civilizations is historically related to those associated with any other. The Akkadian language spoken in Mesopotamia belonged, as did other Semitic languages, to the same Afroasiatic language family as ancient Egyptian, but Sumerian, the other main language of southern Mesopotamia, was not related to ancient Egyptian.

Each early civilization was 'primary' or 'pristine' in the sense that its institutions do not appear to have been shaped by substantial dependence upon or control by other, more complex societies. Henry Wright (1998: 172) defines primary states as ones that arose from interaction among prestate societies only; 'secondary civilizations' frequently display combinations of features that would not have been present at the same time had these civilizations not developed under the influence or tutelage of more advanced neighbours. The administrative skills of international religions such as Christianity and Buddhism played a major role in the development of nascent states in northern Europe, Nubia, Korea, and Japan, but international religions did not develop until early civilizations had evolved into more complex preindustrial ones (Trigger 1978).

To qualify for this study, early civilizations did not have to have been 'pristine' in the more specific sense of being first to develop in a particular region of the world. That would be necessary only if Marcus (1998) were correct that first-generation early civilizations differed in some striking fashion from all later ones. Late Aztec–period civilization in the Valley of Mexico has been described as a third wave of urban development in that region, which drew upon the cumulative experiences of over fifteen hundred years of complex societies in Central Mexico (Charlton and Nichols 1997b). The city-state configuration that existed in Late Aztec times differed considerably from those which had evolved earlier, not least as the result of a much higher overall population density. Yoruba civilization likewise had flourished for many centuries prior to European contact and appears to have experienced one or more phases of widespread disruption during the prehistoric period. The Maya civilization drew upon previous Olmec achievements, the Inka upon earlier state building in the southern highlands and along the north coast of Peru, and the Egyptian perhaps upon contemporary developments in Southwestern Asia. Yet, at the periods we study them, these civilizations do not appear ever to have been directly subordinated to neighbouring early civilizations. Inka civilization developed in a region of the Andean highlands where political institutions had not previously advanced beyond the chiefdom level. The material culture that was distinctive of the Inka state also developed from local antecedents and was stylistically different from that associated with older civilizations in the southern highlands (J. Moore 1996: 798). Thus, even if the civilizations being examined were not 'primary' in the narrow sense, neither were they 'secondary'. They were instead manifestations of indigenous traditions of early civilizations that arose from local prestate societies. The decision not to study secondary civilizations ruled out the employment of a large sample to reveal significant cross-cultural patterning.

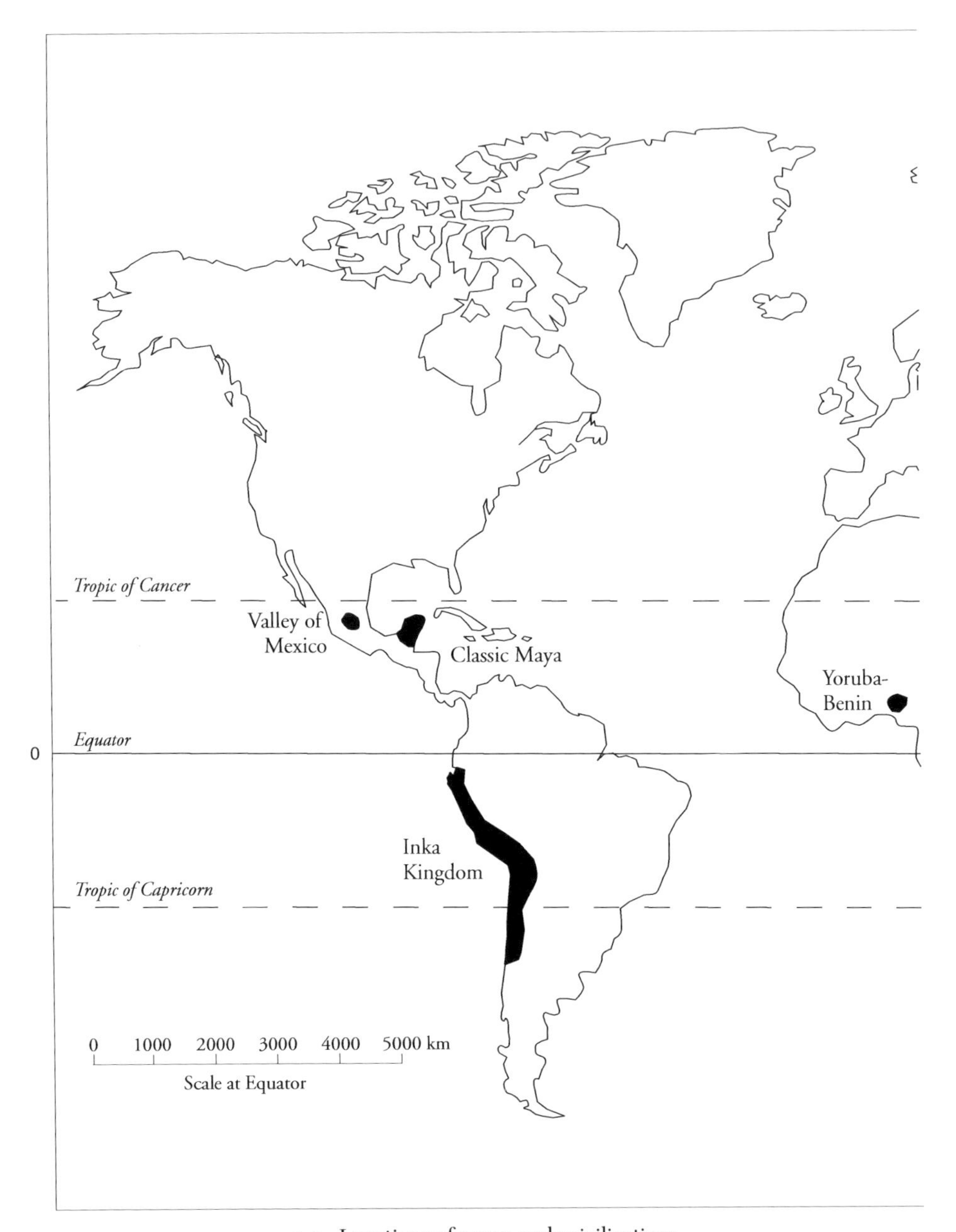

2.1. Locations of seven early civilizations.

My early training in social anthropology inclined me to believe that comparative studies cannot produce optimal results without analysts' first seeking to understand the functional relations that endow individual traits or institutions with behavioural and cognitive significance. To avoid treating social and cultural traits out of context, I sought to understand each of the seven early

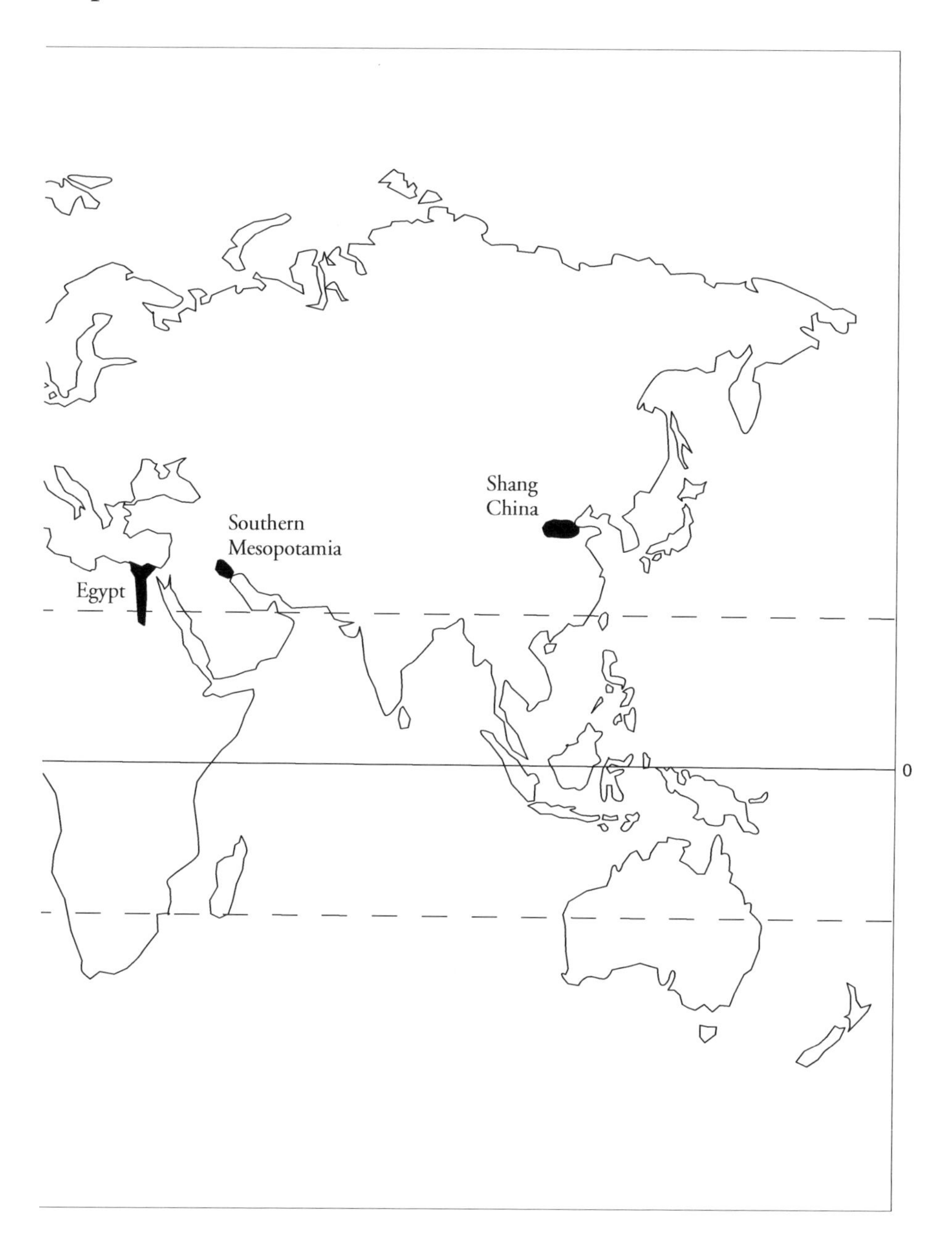

civilizations as a functioning system before I compared them. This meant intense study of the available archaeological data and written sources. Archaeological findings supply valuable information about technology, subsistence, circulation of goods, settlement patterns, and the distribution of wealth, and data of this sort are becoming increasingly abundant and comparable for early

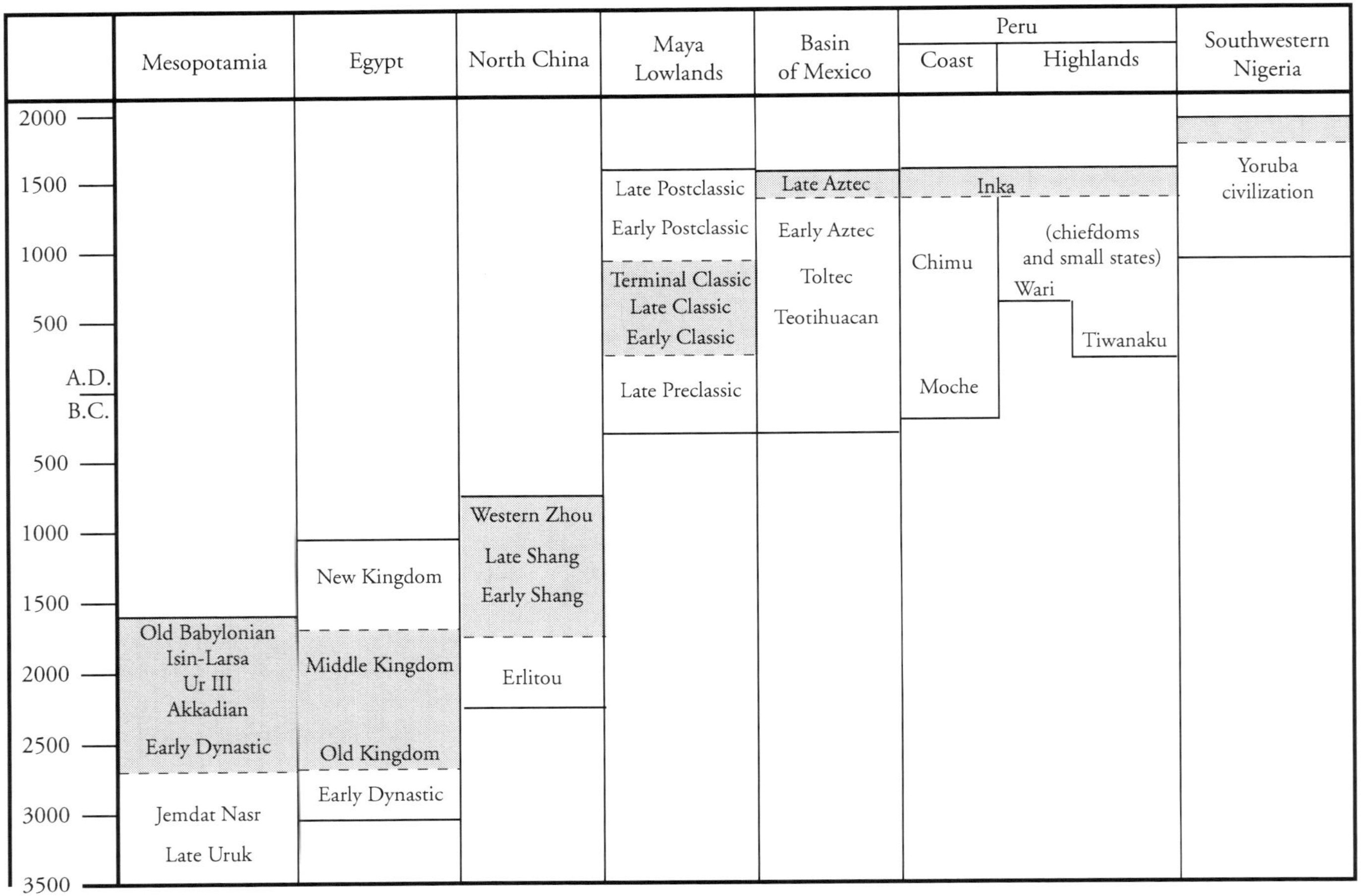

	Mesopotamia	Egypt	North China	Maya Lowlands	Basin of Mexico	Peru: Coast	Peru: Highlands	Southwestern Nigeria
2000								
1500				Late Postclassic	Late Aztec	Inka		Yoruba civilization
1000				Early Postclassic Terminal Classic	Early Aztec Toltec	Chimu	(chiefdoms and small states) Wari	
500				Late Classic Early Classic	Teotihuacan		Tiwanaku	
A.D. / B.C.				Late Preclassic		Moche		
500								
1000		New Kingdom	Western Zhou Late Shang					
1500	Old Babylonian		Early Shang					
2000	Isin-Larsa Ur III Akkadian	Middle Kingdom	Erlitou					
2500	Early Dynastic	Old Kingdom						
3000	Jemdat Nasr	Early Dynastic						
3500	Late Uruk							

2.2. Comparative chronology of early civilizations (periods examined in this book shaded).

civilizations. It is, however, very difficult to infer social and political organization from archaeological evidence alone. Many sites have been excavated that belong to the Indus Valley civilization, but it remains unresolved whether it was a state, a number of kingdoms, or a stateless commonwealth. So few written documents on this early civilization have been preserved that it seems unlikely that this and other questions will ever be answered (Kenoyer 1997; Maisels 1999: 186–259; Possehl 1998). Before the decipherment of Maya writing, similar problems beset the understanding of Classic Maya civilization. Scholars tended to assume that the Maya had theocratic rulers and debated whether these rulers presided over a series of city-states or a large territorial state (J. Thompson 1970). Once the Classic Maya inscriptions could be read, Maya society looked more like other early civilizations than most Mayanists had believed. What many scholars had thought might be sculptures of gods or theocratic priests turned out to be representations of kings, and it became certain that the Classic Maya were organized as a series of independent city-states.

A holistic understanding of early civilizations such as is necessary for this study also requires information about religious beliefs, cosmologies, and secular and spiritual values. While religious structures and tombs loom large in the archaeological record, the beliefs that inspired these monuments can be recovered only from written or verbal records. I have therefore sought to examine the oldest phase of civilization in each region for which we have not only good archaeological evidence but also substantial written records produced either by a literate minority within the societies being examined or by European visitors and colonists. The three civilizations mainly recorded in written form by European visitors were ones that either lacked visual recording systems completely (Yoruba) or did not possess varieties that could record the spoken word (Inka, Valley of Mexico). This requirement of substantial written sources meant that I could never study the earliest stage in the development of civilization in any particular area. Societies that evolved their own writing systems did not become fully literate until after they became early civilizations. Effective documentation of speech began several hundred years after the initial development of civilization in Egypt and after even longer intervals in Iraq and northern China and among the Maya. In the Valley of Mexico, Peru, and West Africa the states being studied had existed for varying lengths of time before Europeans first recorded information about them and were not necessarily the earliest civilizations in their regions. The vast majority of the surviving Maya texts relate to the Late Classic period, which, because of the Maya custom of constructing new temples and palaces on top of older ones, is also far better documented archaeologically than any earlier period. What makes cultures suitable for comparison is not how early they occur in a developmental sequence but whether, structurally and culturally, they conform to the definition of an early civilization.

Archaeologists are usually concerned with how civilizations evolved but generally have much less information on earlier phases than on later ones. This is because there were often fewer early sites to begin with, these sites were generally smaller, and the more important sites, which continued into more recent times, were covered over by later buildings and hence have less chance of being excavated. Thus requiring written evidence to be part of the sample meant that I would usually be studying periods that are archaeologically better documented as well.

I would have liked to include at least one early civilization from the Indian subcontinent, especially since Jonathan Kenoyer's (1997) archaeological analysis leads him to suggest that principles of social segregation resembling the later *jati* (caste) system were already present in the Indus Valley civilization. Yet not enough archaeological and contemporary historical evidence was available to include either the Indus Valley or the early phases of the later Gangetic civilization in my sample. Much of what passes for knowledge of pre-Mauryan Gangetic civilization is based on highly speculative and often ideologically driven conflations of limited archaeological data and later texts (Allchin 1995; Chakrabarti 1997; Erdosy 1988). This omission deprived my sample of significant variations in social organization and beliefs that may have been associated with the earliest civilizations of South Asia.

The civilizations in my sample are examined over periods that last from less than a century in the case of Inka Peru to almost a millennium each for ancient Egypt and Mesopotamia. The length of time over which each early civilization is studied has been determined by pragmatic considerations. Civilizations for which written documentation was provided by European visitors (Valley of Mexico, Inka, Yoruba) can be studied only for the brief period between earliest European contact and the establishment of direct colonial control. In the case of civilizations that produced their own literary documentation (Mesopotamia, Egypt, China, Maya), the earliest surviving written records are generally more limited in volume and content, and much longer periods are required to provide necessary information. These periods must, however, be spans of time during which no major irreversible changes occurred in the organization of the civilization. While the Old and Middle Kingdoms can be combined to provide information about the earliest phase of Egyptian civilization that is documented by written records, Egyptian social organization was sufficiently altered by the beginning of the New Kingdom that including most forms of information from that period in the present study seemed inappropriate. I therefore refer to the more abundant New Kingdom data principally to clarify how Egypt was different in earlier times. I do not deny that Egyptian society and culture changed significantly between the start of the Old Kingdom and the end of the Middle Kingdom, but these changes, in contrast to those that followed, do not appear to have markedly altered the existing pattern of Egyptian civilization. Where possible, the primary focus will be on the Old Kingdom, especially the Fifth Dynasty.

The study of Mesopotamian civilization is limited to southern Iraq, which contemporary documents such as the temple hymns of Enheduana suggest regarded itself as a culturally distinct group of city-states that did not include kingdoms located farther north, such as Assur and Mari (Postgate 1992: 26). While urban centres emerged in this region in the fourth millennium B.C., substantial written documentation first becomes available in the Early Dynastic III period. The lasting incorporation of southern Mesopotamian cities into larger regional states, which became normal only after the Old Babylonian period, places that period at the very end of the time span being considered. J. N. Postgate (1992: xxi) observes that Old Babylonian culture had deep roots in the third millennium and that, while later periods are largely irrelevant for understanding earlier times, what is known about it usually ends up having been true earlier as well. Thus, he argues, scholars can profitably generalize about southern Mesopotamia from 3000 to 1500 B.C. In contrast, Jean-Louis Huot (1989: 10) sees the reign of the Akkadian monarch Naram-Sin as a major watershed in Mesopotamian history, while Norman Yoffee (1995: 282–83) objects that Postgate's approach unduly homogenizes successive historical periods. Taking account of these differing opinions, the main focus of my study will be on the Early Dynastic III period, although fuller epigraphic documentation invites considering specific data from as late as the Old Babylonian. I reject, however, the notion that Mesopotamian culture did not change in any way during this time span.

Although there is a powerful temptation to project what is known about later phases of early civilizations back to earlier, less well-documented periods, it is dangerous to attempt this. Injudicious extrapolations to poorly documented periods of early civilizations are likely to be as misleading as what was achieved a century ago when Egyptologists employed what Greek and Roman authors had written about Egyptian customs to infer Egyptian behaviour in the New Kingdom. The result was like trying to reconstruct life in Elizabethan England from what is reported about England in modern newspapers. Formal Christian religious beliefs may have remained generally similar, but not social organization, scientific knowledge, values, or daily life. Just as scholars cannot justify using what they know about one early civilization to fill gaps in their knowledge of another, so they cannot use information about later phases in the development of a civilization to remedy deficiencies in what is known about earlier periods (Houston 1993: 7).

I therefore avoid using what the Spanish recorded about Maya culture in the sixteenth century A.D. to augment what is known about Classic Maya culture more than seven hundred years earlier. Likewise, there is no general warrant for projecting specific Western Zhou or still later Chinese customs back into Shang times. While I focus primarily on Shang civilization after the appearance of written texts about 1200 B.C., I will, where it seems appropriate, discuss early Western Zhou customs when little specific is recorded about analogous aspects of Shang culture. It does seem justified, however, to use information about Yoruba culture in the twentieth century to supplement what is known about poorly documented aspects of Yoruba life in the late precolonial period. In this case the time gap is relatively short, and sparse but significant older data permit examination of the appropriateness of these extrapolations.

I do not attempt to present data as if they referred to the way of life that existed in each civilization only at a single point in time in the style of the anthropologists' traditional 'ethnographic present'. On the contrary, I agree with the social anthropologist E. E. Evans-Pritchard (1962) that the best way to determine how the various parts of a culture are functionally interrelated is to observe how they change in relation to one another over time. Seeing how bureaucratic structures changed as different factions among the upper class competed with one another and sought to alter existing arrangements to their own advantage is particularly useful for understanding political organization. My aim in doing this is not to study change for its own sake but to understand each early civilization better.

An important question is whether the sample of seven early civilizations used in this study is large enough to reveal the full range of variation in early civilizations. It is clear from the very different conclusions that Childe and Frankfort drew from their comparisons of Egypt and Mesopotamia and Adams from his comparison of Mesopotamia and the Valley of Mexico that a sample consisting of only two civilizations can be highly misleading about the general nature of early civilizations. It has been argued that civilizations such as those of the Indus Valley (Possehl 1998) and Teotihuacan (Cowgill 1997) may have been constructed on radically different principles from those associated with any historically documented early civilization. These arguments have been revived in the context of recent discussions of heterarchical political organization and corporate power (Blanton et al. 1996; Crumley 1987; Ehrenreich, Crumley, and Levy 1995). Yet none of the suggested examples has provided certain evidence of early civilizations that lie beyond the general range of variation documented in the present sample.

As early as the 1920s it was recognized that not all early civilizations were of the same type. One of the aims of the present study is to determine whether the seven civilizations being examined can be assigned to two or three different categories or vary idiosyncratically. If the first option can be sustained, the sample is probably reasonably representative of the full range of variation in early civilizations. If no two civilizations turn out to be similar in any significant way, the sample is almost certainly inadequate.

Finally, this study must evaluate the persistent claim that the similarities shared by these seven early civilizations are or might be the result of historical connections rather than of parallel evolution. From the hyperdiffusionist point of view, there is only one pristine civilization: the first, whether real or hypothesized, to develop anywhere in the world (Hancock and Faiia 1998). For the most part, this claim is an attempt to call into question the likelihood that cultural coevolution ever occurred. With the nineteenth-century German ethnologist Friedrich Ratzel, its advocates dogmatically assert that one must rule out any possibility of diffusion before one can argue in favour of parallel evolution. Yet the claim that early civilizations developed independently of one another does not require proof that there was absolutely no contact between them.

The Classic Maya and the Aztec were closely related historically and culturally, having evolved as part of a widespread Mesoamerican way of life based on the cultivation of maize, beans, and squash (Blanton et al. 1981). Yet their very different environmental settings and dissimilar economic, social, and political organizations are reasons for studying both. Despite many shared religious beliefs, in the Valley of Mexico the concept of divine kingship was less extreme and less central to the functioning of the state than that held by the Classic Maya (Cowgill 1997). Art and architectural styles, agricultural practices, and the organization of cities were also dissimilar in the two regions. Because of such differences, I decided that adding the Classic Maya did not compromise the integrity of my sample, especially since it remained too small to be manipulated statistically.

Likewise, the ancient Mesopotamian and Egyptian civilizations were located only a few hundred kilometres apart, and both had developed from the Neolithic *oecumene* that had extended over much of the Middle East and North Africa and was based on the cultivation of wheat, barley, and flax and the herding of cattle, sheep, and goats. They participated in common trading networks, and a few artifacts of Mesopotamian origin turn up in the formative stage of Egyptian civilization along with artistic motifs and architectural elements that appear to copy Middle Eastern prototypes (Frankfort 1956; Joffe 2000; Mark 1998). Yet, despite such clear historical connections, no two civilizations in our sample were more different from one another in almost every respect.

More limited and indirect historical connections appear to link the remaining civilizations in our sample with each other and with those already discussed. North Chinese civilization developed from local Neolithic cultures that had evolved their own agricultural economy based on millet, sorghum, pig, dog, and silkworm production. While it is evident that early claims of massive Western influence on the development of Chinese civilization were grossly exaggerated, some traits – most notably the horse-drawn chariot, which appeared during the Shang Dynasty – may be of Western Asian origin. There is, however, no evidence of influences of Western origin prior to 1300 B.C. or of any direct link between Mesopotamian and early Chinese civilization (K. Chang 1962; Ho 1975).

There is also evidence of cultural contacts between Mesoamerica and Peru. At an early period corn, beans, and other tropical crops spread south from Mesoamerica and were incorporated into an indigenous Andean agricultural complex based on highland grains and tubers and the herding of cameloids. Various shared iconographic motifs, including eagles, serpents, and jaguars, also date from an early period (Willey 1955). In late prehistoric times trade between coastal Peru and Mesoamerica introduced knowledge of bronze-working into the Michoacán area of western Mexico (Hosler 1988).

Archaeological evidence refutes the persistent efforts of colonial apologists, pan-Africanists, and Yoruba exposed to Islamic influences to derive Yoruba culture from ancient Egypt or the Middle East (Diop 1974; Lucas 1948). It is clear that West Africa was a creative region in its own right and that Yoruba culture developed from a local Neolithic complex that was based on indigenous root and seed crops, particularly yams (Shaw 1978). Common traits such as headrests suggest, however, that various indirect contacts linked Egypt and West African cultures with each other and with other parts of Africa (Celenko 1996).

Finally, as noted above, it has been argued that certain cosmological and religious concepts that recur in the Chinese, Mesoamerican, and sometimes Peruvian civilizations may be derived from a common set of shamanistic beliefs that date from the Palaeolithic period in Northeast Asia and were carried into the Americas by the first Amerindians (P. Furst 1977; Seaman and Day 1994; Willey 1985). Arguments in favour of the trans-Pacific diffusion in later pre-Columbian times of ideas concerning the zodiac, geomancy, and techniques for making bark cloth have been advanced by professional archaeologists but not widely accepted (Kelley 1971; Tolstoy 1963; 1966).

Thus there are indications that limited cultural contact may have occurred during the development of these seven early civilizations. Nevertheless, archaeological evidence makes it clear that each of these civilizations evolved separately and largely independently in its own region. General patterns of civilization did not diffuse from one region to another. If diffusion accounted for major similarities in economic, social, and political organization, those civilizations that were geographically closest and therefore most easily accessible to one another ought to have displayed the greatest similarity. Despite their propinquity, ancient Egypt and Mesopotamia were structurally far more different from one another than Egyptian civilization was from that of the Inka or Mesopotamian civilization was from that of highland Mesoamerica or the Yoruba. Structural similarity does not correlate with geographical or temporal propinquity or with similarities in environmental settings. While the Classic Maya and Aztec civilizations were historically related and shared many cultural traits, their structural differences make their inclusion in this sample of vital interest. It is therefore possible, without stridently rejecting claims that there were varying degrees of historical contact among these civilizations, to treat them as examples of independent development and hence as equivalent units for comparative study.

3 Defining 'Early Civilization'

Identifying early civilizations for comparative study requires ascertaining the general features that distinguish them from both simpler and more complex societies. Such criteria do not constitute an 'ideal type', which, according to Max Weber (1949), seeks to order reality by selecting and accentuating certain elements of it. Instead, they identify a natural but not necessarily exclusive category within which it is possible to conduct a more detailed study of differences and similarities. Nevertheless, even postulating such a category as 'early civilizations' attracts charges of subjectivity and ethnocentric bias. Do early civilizations constitute a natural class that is susceptible to the kind of comparative study I am proposing? Does degree of complexity have any real meaning? Is it possible to measure complexity objectively? Do not fundamental historical differences render all societies inappropriate for comparative analysis? Extreme relativists would answer the last question with a resounding yes.

'Early civilization' is undeniably an evolutionary concept. It assumes the existence of less complex societies, some of which evolved into early civilizations, and more complex ones, which either developed out of early civilizations or grew up alongside of and ultimately replaced them. The aim of my research is not to evaluate the concept of sociocultural evolution (but see Trigger 1998a) or to try to account for how and why early civilizations developed. Yet, in order to demonstrate that the societies I am examining are at the same level or stage of development, it is necessary to argue that sociocultural evolution is a valid scientific concept.

SOCIOCULTURAL EVOLUTION

The idea of social evolution has been violently attacked in recent decades as a myth created by Western European scholars, beginning in the eighteenth century, to justify colonial exploitation in many parts of the world (Diamond 1974;

Patterson 1997; Rowlands 1989). Although there is much truth to this charge, I reject the suggestion that the idea of evolution as an approach to the study of human history is inherently and inescapably colonialist and racist. Archaeological research inspired by an evolutionary perspective has demonstrated the creativity of indigenous peoples around the world and the progress they achieved in prehistoric times, and growing knowledge of these achievements has played a significant role in undermining the justifications offered for colonialism and assisted independence movements.

Extreme relativists also object that the concept of cultural evolution attributes a spurious linearity and regularity to cultural change. It is only, they argue, by rejecting evidence that does not conform to expectations – that is, by imposing a false pattern on human history – that evolutionists have been able to suggest such regularity (Giddens 1984: 236; 1985). Cultural evolutionary explanations are denounced for their reliance on ecologically deterministic explanations of culture change. This, it is maintained, denies the importance of ideas in guiding human behaviour and the role of individual preferences and contingent events in shaping human history. Very little attention is paid by these critics to the role that relativists assign to cultural traditions as factors restricting or inhibiting individual choice. Evolutionary approaches are viewed as materialist attempts to deny the diversity of human behaviour and the capacity of culturally mediated ideas to create still more diversity.

It has been demonstrated archaeologically that all modern societies are descended from Upper Palaeolithic hunter-gatherer bands and these in turn from still earlier scavenging societies. Along the way, societies that abandoned hunter-gatherer economies experienced major changes in social organization and understandings of the universe and the place of humans in it. As knowledge of the past has increased, many concepts formerly associated with evolutionary theory have been recognized as erroneous and abandoned. A teleological view of sociocultural evolution has been slowly but remorselessly discarded. Evolutionary specialists no longer claim that a specific trajectory is inherent in sociocultural evolution and shapes human behaviour independently of human will. Such views are now summarily dismissed as 'God-surrogates' (Gellner 1988: 144) intended to preserve a belief that human history was the unfolding of some predetermined plan at a time when faith in divine providence was yielding to a more secular outlook. Today it is recognized that change is neither more nor less normal than stasis, that most innovation tends to promote random or multilinear rather than orthogenetic cultural change, that cultural change occurs for many different reasons and in highly contingent ways, and that, because of this, it is not predictable in specific instances. It is also recognized that greater social complexity is not necessarily accompanied by an increase in human happiness and that the concept of progress is a purely subjective one that has no place in scientific discourse.

In spite of this, a strong tendency has been noted for sociocultural change to move in the general direction of greater complexity. This results from the greater capacity of more complex societies to compete successfully with less complex ones for control of territory and other resources. As a result of such competition, in all but the poorest and most marginal environments (and increasingly even in these) smaller-scale societies must either acquire the key attributes of more complex societies or be displaced or absorbed by them. Convergence of this sort occurs far more readily in human societies than among other animal species because of the unique degree to which human behaviour is learned. As small-scale societies are deprived of resources and become less able to maintain a satisfactory lifestyle, many individuals in such societies adopt new forms of behaviour either to survive or because they are positively attracted by more successful ways of doing things. It is the short-term competitive advantages of societies that determine their relative viability. Small-scale hunter-gatherer societies may as a type possess greater long-term viability than industrial societies, but in direct competition it is the industrial societies that prevail (Trigger 1998a: 170–77). Increasing complexity also appears to foster a more scientific understanding of the material world and of human behaviour, as well as the development of higher levels of both social and self-control (Elias 1978; 1982). These attributes also appear to have a selective advantage.

Thus cultural selection provides a general direction to cultural change that justifies attempts to identify various stages in the development of greater cultural complexity, including early civilizations. This does not mean that all societies evolve along a single trajectory to a common future or that cross-cultural differences are less important than similarities. Unlike nineteenth-century evolutionists, who posited the successive development of specific types of society, cultural selectionists allow for the development and survival of many different sorts of societies in particular social and natural settings (Yoffee 1993). Any form of cultural evolutionism that seeks to account only for sociocultural regularities is bound to be scientifically inadequate. In order not to mask variability and bias their conclusions, anthropologists who employ an evolutionary perspective must pay as much attention to cultural differences as they do to cultural similarities. They must accept the possibility that features common to a particular stage or level of social complexity may be few by comparison with dissimilar ones. They also must determine empirically to what extent early civilizations or any other types of society were or were not clearly distinguished from other types.

DEFINING 'EARLY CIVILIZATION'

Unilinear evolutionists in the nineteenth century and more recently neoevolutionists believed that all societies at the same stage of development were very similar. Societies could therefore be assigned to a particular stage on the basis of a small number of distinctive criteria or even a single trait. In the past, civilization was often equated with the presence of writing, on the ground that the ability to record speech made possible new forms of innovation, commerce, and understanding (Morgan 1907 [1877]: 12). Yet this association cannot be sustained any more than any other attempt to define early civilizations in terms of specific items of material culture. In Egypt, Mesopotamia, China, and among the Maya, scripts that could be used to record speech were invented at a relatively early period. In highland Mexico, Peru, and West Africa recording devices of this sort did not develop. Yet there is no perceptible difference in the overall degree of social, economic, and political complexity reached by early civilizations that utilized writing and those that did not.

The situation is not improved by employing longer trait lists. Childe (1950) attempted to distinguish the earliest cities, and by implication early civilizations, from Neolithic villages in terms of ten criteria: (1) large urban centres, (2) craft workers, merchants, officials, and priests supported by the surpluses produced by farmers, (3) primary producers paying surpluses to a deity or divine ruler, (4) monumental architecture, (5) a ruling class exempt from manual labour, (6) systems for recording information, (7) the development of exact practical sciences, (8) monumental art, (9) the regular importation of raw materials both as luxuries and as industrial materials, and (10) resident specialist craft workers politically as well as economically under the control of secular or religious officials. Charles Maisels (1999: 25–27) has pointed out that Childe's final point is composed of three separate criteria: (10) peasants, craftsmen, and rulers form a community, (11) the social solidarity of the community is represented (or misrepresented) by the preeminence of temples and funerary cults, and (12) a state organization is dominant and permanent. Childe clearly believed that these features had evolved in a coevolutionary fashion and were all present in any social system that had reached a certain level of complexity. His definition of early civilization resembled the trait lists that were still used in the 1950s to define archaeological cultures. Such listings of features were later used by evolutionary anthropologists to delineate stages of cultural development.

One problem with such enumerative definitions is that even small disagreements about how specific criteria are defined or interpreted affect what societies are assigned to a particular category. In his effort to produce a general characterization of early civilizations, Childe defined terms such as 'city', 'monumental architecture', 'systems of recording', and 'exact sciences' in a loose or abstract rather than an operational manner. Cities in fact differed considerably in size, layout, and function in early civilizations, and scholars who used highly specific definitions of urbanism maintained that some civilizations, such as those of ancient Egypt and the Maya, lacked them (J. Thompson 1970; J. Wilson 1960); yet no anthropologist was prepared on that account to deny these two particular literate societies the status of civilizations. At the same time, the highly urbanized Yoruba have often been denied the status of a civilization or of having 'cities' rather than 'towns' because they were non-literate (Sjoberg 1960). The Shang Chinese occasionally have been described as a 'chiefdom' or 'prestate society', but those who did so never denied that they constituted a 'civilization' (Treistman 1972: 130). Each early civilization was the result of individual historical processes that produced distinctive material and institutional expressions. Such complex entities cannot usefully be defined by establishing a monothetic set of specific attributes that each of them must possess.

A useful characterization of early civilizations must instead be framed in terms of the general sorts of social, economic, and political institutions and the associated types of knowledge and beliefs that were required for societies of that degree of complexity to function. Behaviour is accorded priority not because material culture, especially technology, was unimportant but because it was embedded in society. Technology, settlement patterns, art, and architecture can be understood only in terms of the roles they played in materially supporting such institutions, facilitating social interaction, and promoting the ideological objectives of various segments of society. Cross-cultural regularities in beliefs and values must be interpreted in relation to the social conditions that produced them. A useful definition must therefore be constructed within a social anthropological framework. In the following sections, I will survey the common features that anthropologists have attributed to early civilizations in recent decades and determine how these general features differ from those associated with more and less complex societies.

Anthropologists apply the term 'early civilization' to the earliest and simplest forms of societies in which the basic principle governing social relations was not kinship but a hierarchy of social divisions that cut horizontally across societies and were unequal in power, wealth, and social prestige. In these societies a tiny ruling group that used coercive powers to augment its authority was sustained by agricultural surpluses and labour systematically appropriated from a much larger number of agricultural producers. Full-time specialists (artisans, bureaucrats, soldiers, retainers) also supported and served the ruling group and the goverment apparatus it controlled. Rulers cultivated a luxurious style of life that distinguished them from the ruled.

The horizontal divisions found in these societies are usually termed 'classes'. Classes are distinguished by their generality from more specific interest groups, based on common cultural, ethnic, religious, regional, or occupational affinities, that unite to pursue their members' specialized objectives. They are fewer, usually last longer, cut across entire societies, and influence virtually every aspect of their members' lives. Patricia Crone (1989: 101–2) maintains, however, that no preindustrial society had classes because, in contrast to the working classes in industrial societies, farmers, who constituted the majority of people in preindustrial societies, could not easily develop common goals beyond the local level and were therefore unable to unite as a group to pursue their economic interests in opposition to the ruling stratum. Crone argues that, because of this, preindustrial societies may have been horizontally divided into strata, ranks, or orders but not into classes. She thus equates the term 'class' with what some Marxists call 'classes for themselves', by which they mean social orders that are not only aware of themselves but also united in the pursuit of common political goals (Terray 1975). She also maintains that in preindustrial societies wealth was mainly determined by status, whereas in more rapidly changing and vertically mobile industrial societies class membership tends to be determined principally by wealth. The close association between wealth and class in industrial societies reflects the high degree of vertical mobility that results from the economic expansion and rapid social change that are inherent in capitalist societies.

Crone is not alone in recognizing that social scientists must choose between a broad definition of 'class' that can be applied to all varieties of complex societies, taking account of the different forms that it assumes in different types, and a definition that would restrict 'class' to modern industrial societies. The latter sort of definition treats preindustrial societies as having different kinds of stratification that arise from factors other than owning capital or the means of production (Bottomore 1974: 953). Historical usage both supports and undermines Crone's usage. While the term 'class' (*classis*) was an ancient Roman one, it came to be widely used only in modern Europe in the early nineteenth century, replacing earlier terms such as 'rank' and 'order', to denote hierarchical divisions that were increasingly being defined in economic terms. Nevertheless, the Romans used the term 'class' to designate the division of their society into formal orders based on personal wealth, which in turn defined individual and family rights and responsibilities in relation to the Roman state. This indicates that classes, even as narrowly defined by Crone, existed in some preindustrial societies.

Yet I agree that the terminological issue she has raised is not trivial – that farmers had difficulty in organizing for broadly based social action in preindustrial societies and that in these societies wealth tended to be derived from political power far more frequently than political power was derived from wealth. There is also evidence that in early civilizations major social divisions were perceived very differently from the way we regard them; the members of different social strata were sometimes assigned separate supernatural origins and different roles that were considered in accord with a divine plan. Every complex society had its own particular view of the nature, origin, and roles of its social strata. Crone's argument raises the possibility that different terms might profitably be employed to designate social hierarchies in industrial and preindustrial societies.

At the same time, while the roles played by wealth, power, prestige, education, and manners in acquiring membership in particular societal levels can vary greatly from one society to another, it appears that in all complex societies there is a strong correlation between wealth, power, and prestige. This suggests that similar concerns drive the development of and sustain horizontal divisions in all complex societies, even if the basic ways in which these divisions develop and maintain themselves change as societies increase in scale and complexity. Material concerns are not absent at any level, and economic and political motives appear inextricable regardless of how they are pursued. Even if farmers were unable to unite as a single group to achieve their political goals in early civilizations, they were as aware of the social hierarchy and of their place in it as members of the ruling group. Such knowledge played a major role in ordering individual behaviour in early civilizations and sometimes resulted in political action in the form of farmers' revolts or workers' demonstrations. Thus farmers constituted *de facto* 'classes in themselves' even if they did not constitute 'classes for themselves', and I am prepared to use the term 'class' as a cross-cultural label for the major hierarchical divisions found in early civilizations. 'Early civilization' can thus be summarily defined as the earliest and simplest form of *class-based* society.

EARLY STATES AND EARLY CIVILIZATIONS

Early civilizations were not the first societies to be divided into classes. Small-scale societies such as the sedentary, food-collecting Tlingit and Kwakiutl peoples of coastal British Columbia or the agricultural Kayan of Borneo were held together by kinship relations, and their leaders depended on public opinion for such support as was at their disposal, but they were divided into at least three hereditary strata or classes: chiefs or nobles, commoners, and slaves

(Donald 1997; Rousseau 1990; 2001). Early states such as Buganda, the Zulu kingdom in southern Africa, early historical Hawaii, and the seventeenth-century Powhatan polity in Virginia consisted of several thousand to several hundred thousand people, living in kinship-based communities or small chiefdoms held together by rulers who regularly used force to maintain their authority. The core of such an early state (or complex chiefdom) was an ethnic group, tribe, or ruler's kindred to which other groups willingly or unwillingly paid tribute. This tribute supported a higher standard of living for the core group, which was entirely or partly freed from agricultural labour, giving its members more time to carry out administrative tasks and suppress rebellions. Political control was based on patron-client relations, and the success of a polity depended largely on the personal qualities of its paramount leader (Earle 1991; Price and Feinman 1995; Upham 1990). Borders fluctuated and cores fragmented when political leadership failed. While the ruling group's lifestyle was more luxurious than commoners', the gap between these two groups was less marked than it was in early civilizations. These rudimentary classes were superimposed on hierarchically structured kinship networks or ethnic groups, with kinship remaining the basis of sociopolitical organization.

In early civilizations, in contrast, class displaced kinship and ethnicity as the main organizing principle of society. While kinship remained important at the local level and in reinforcing relations among the upper classes, endogamous classes allocated rights and responsibilities and protected the interests of a privileged minority. Power was based primarily on the control of agricultural surpluses, which the upper classes extracted in various ways from the rest of the population. While the technology remained simple, the organization and management of human labour sometimes became quite complex. Authoritative power in the form of institutionalized administrative positions replaced the more informal patron-client relations found in early states. Each state was administered by multiple levels of officials who were able to mobilize the entire population for defence and public works and provided the political security that allowed farmers to prosper and increase in numbers. Governments were sufficiently stable to endure over many generations. There was more strategic and symbolic emphasis than in early states on controlling territory; borders tended to be more clearly defined and guarded. This and the increased importance of class resulted in more restricted roles for kinship and ethnicity than at earlier stages of political development.

Central governments possessed ultimate control over justice and the use of force. The ruling class was able to exert various forms of coercion, but demands for the production of surpluses, corvée labour, and mandatory military service were kept at a relatively low level, and officials often reciprocated for such work with food and entertainment. Although most early civilizations had slavery, it was less extensive and oppressive than in many later preindustrial societies. The scale and productivity of early civilizations nevertheless permitted the upper classes to extract sufficient surpluses to support a markedly more elaborate lifestyle than that enjoyed by the lower classes or by anyone in less complex societies and to create monumental art and architecture that required a wide range of raw materials, highly skilled craftspeople, and professional planners and administrators. These creations became symbols of their power and leadership ability.

The upper classes claimed privileged relations with the supernatural, and rulers frequently were ascribed divine or semidivine status. Just as class had replaced both real and metaphorical kinship as a basis for organizing societies, so religious concepts replaced kinship as a medium for social and political discourse (Sahlins 1976: 211–12). There is little evidence that such issues were formulated in terms of explicitly political or economic concepts; this would have been especially difficult where paramount rulers claimed absolute and divinely sanctioned authority. As had been the case in less complex societies, religious concepts did not differentiate clearly between what we regard as the social, natural, and supernatural realms. Yet, despite a general tendency to view nature as animated by supernatural power and able to understand and respond to human entreaty, there is abundant evidence that the people who lived in early civilizations, like all other human beings, clearly understood the relation between cause and effect in their everyday dealings with the natural world. They were also keenly aware of self-interest and how it could be most effectively pursued in the social realm.

LATER PREINDUSTRIAL CIVILIZATIONS

Later preindustrial civilizations, what Talcott Parsons called 'Advanced Intermediate' societies as opposed to 'Archaic' ones (Sanderson 1990: 110), developed either directly from early civilizations or as secondary civilizations on the borders of early ones that they eventually dominated and transformed. Among them were the Assyrian and Persian Empires, Classical Greece, Republican and Imperial Rome, Mauryan India, Han Dynasty China, and the feudal and mercantile states found in Europe, Japan, and elsewhere in medieval and early modern times. These societies were organized either as city-states or regional states, with the latter tending to predominate. One of the key features that distinguished these societies from early civilizations was the widespread use of money, usually in the form of metal coins, to facilitate exchange and store wealth. The mass production of coins of small value, often made of copper, incorporated low-wage earners more deeply into market and wage economies. This was associated with the growing diversification of economies and the increasing importance of production, exchange, and financial services as sources of income (Heichelheim 1958: 251–54). Even in feudal societies, where a non-commercial form of landholding was associated with political power, money played an increasingly important role in facilitating the accumulation of wealth. In Western Europe this process led to the rise of capitalism (Braudel 1982; Wallerstein 1974). Money also served as a common denominator for calculating an individual's total assets, and this made it possible for the abstract concept of wealth to replace control of land or crop surpluses as a measure of position and status. A common measure of wealth also made it easier for an increasing number of individuals to invest in a variety of economic activities.

In many later preindustrial civilizations, military forces were more numerous, specialized, and institutionally distinguished from the state and from society in general. In early civilizations full-time soldiers tended to be few and to be led by kings, government officials, and local authorities. As military technology and tactics grew more complex, professional armies were created that were commanded by career officers. When the civil administration of the Roman Empire declined, generals used the disciplined and still well-financed military power at their disposal to override civil authorities and compete with one another for imperial office. In all societies where armed forces became institutionally distinct from the government, controlling the military became a growing source of concern for government officials (Mann 1986: 163–67).

Whereas in early civilizations supernatural powers were regarded as inherent in nature, in the course of the first millennium B.C. in Greece and parts of the Middle East, India, and China, the natural world became increasingly desacralized. Instead of being regarded as animated by supernatural energy, which endowed trees, rocks, and stars with reason, emotions, and will, as well as power, the physical universe came to be viewed as inanimate and plants and animals as lacking the reason and insight possessed by human beings. The world and the things in it became entities that human beings might try to understand through observation and thereby control more effectively.

This new understanding meant that the natural, social, and supernatural realms were for the first time explicitly distinguished from one another. The realization that the natural and social realms needed to be understood in different ways encouraged the development of new and more aggressive forms of enquiry into the nature of things. Some philosophers denied the existence of the supernatural altogether; others regarded the supernatural realm as remote and largely irrelevant for everyday human affairs. Most people, however, viewed deities as increasingly transcendent: human beings and the world depended on the gods for their creation and survival, but the gods were not believed to depend upon any aspect of their creation. New international religions, such as Zoroastrianism, Buddhism, Christianity, and Islam, stressed individualism and the difference between the real and the ideal. Instead of being identified with a particular state or civilization, these new religions claimed to be relevant for all human beings, and they promised personal salvation to all who believed their teachings and were prepared to live as they prescribed. Even those forms of Judaism which rejected proselytization regarded their god as the ruler of all peoples and places (Eisenstadt 1986; Gellner 1988). Religious loyalties thus extended over much broader areas than political and ethnic ties or than religious systems had done in early civilizations. Communities of believers in international religions played a major role in facilitating international trade and communication in a world in which production and exchange networks were becoming increasingly important and extensive (Mann 1986: 363–71).

These views affected political life. Old rituals in which monarchs mediated between the human and the supernatural realms persisted in some later preindustrial civilizations, but the conceptual separation of the natural, social, and supernatural realms promoted a view of kings as humans who at most received divine protection. The sacral kingship associated with early civilizations was replaced by diverse forms of government. Democracies, oligarchies, tyrannies, and military dictatorships flourished alongside both limited and absolute monarchies. Power increasingly depended on the ability of rulers to use military force to maintain high levels of agricultural productivity and sustain the bureaucracies that collected the revenues required to meet the state's expenses. The increasing power of the state meant that in some societies the prevalence of slavery and the exploitation of the poor reached higher levels than before.

While later preindustrial civilizations varied in scale and in economic, political, and ideological organization, they tended to be more powerful than early civilizations and better adapted to the transsocietal division of labour that characterized an *oecumene* stretching from Europe to East Asia. Ancient Egypt lost its political independence and then its distinctive political and religious institutions as it was absorbed successively into the late Roman and then the Islamic cultural sphere. Mesopotamian culture lost its distinctive characteristics following its incorporation into the Hellenistic world. In northern China the transition was internal and more gradual and did not involve such a spectacular break with the past, but it too came about as the result of centuries of competition among rival states. The disappearance of the distinctive features of early civilizations is evidence of their inability to compete with the institutions that characterized later preindustrial civilizations (Crone 1989; Gellner 1988; Hall 1986; Mann 1986).

In sub-Saharan Africa and the Americas, no indigenous societies had evolved beyond the level of early civilizations by the time of European contact. One possible exception was the Postclassic Maya (A.D. 900–1530), who built palaces and temples on a more modest scale than the Classic Maya and more structures serving public functions. Kings appear to have been less revered than previously, and at least one major centre, Chichen Itza, had a *multepal*, or joint government of nobles (Schele and Freidel 1990: 361). Maya art of the Postclassic period emphasized communal and social themes rather than the royal ones that had predominated during the Classic period. There is, however, no evidence of major changes in religious beliefs or other aspects of their social organization. It may be that what looks like an incipient development beyond the level of early civilization merely reflected highland Mesoamerican influences on the Maya of that period.

The Spanish conquests of Mexico and Peru were assisted by a smallpox pandemic that killed a vast number of indigenous people, and the subsequent consolidation of these conquests was aided by many epidemics of European diseases against which local peoples lacked immunity. Yet the rapid subjugation of Mexico and Peru, as well as the scarcely opposed British conquest of Benin, were a consequence not merely of superior European military technology but also of superior organization, discipline, and self-discipline and more aggressive ideologies, both religious and secular. These momentous events constitute further evidence of the superior organizational (but not ethical) achievements of later preindustrial and industrial civilizations.

ASIATIC SOCIETIES

The concept of 'Asiatic society' or the 'Asiatic mode of production' was prominent in discussions of early civilizations during the 1970s and 1980s, when Marxism briefly played a significant role in theoretical debates among anthropologists. Karl Marx (1964) had postulated that the traditional state structures of India and China consisted of egalitarian farming villages based on collective landholding that were dominated and taxed by a military elite. While the regional government structures created by this elite rose and fell as a consequence of military competition, farming villages remained unchanged over long periods. Marx viewed these arrangements as a primitive form of class society but one which, as a result of the village self-sufficiency on which it was based, had little potential for development. He believed that, because of this, the class societies of India and China were doomed to remain unchanged until European colonialism brought new and more dynamic economic factors into play. This concept introduced an element of multilinearity into Marx's thinking but also exhibited a strong Eurocentric bias. Marx himself was clearly ambivalent about the concept of Asiatic society and did not include it in his more dogmatic and unilinear versions of world history (Bailey and Llobera 1981; Dunn 1982; Krader 1975).

Some anthropologists identified Asiatic society as a form of the early state, while others equated it with early civilization and more specifically with what I will call early civilization's territorial variant. Marx equated it with later preindustrial societies as well as some early civilizations. In fact no early civilization appears ever to have had an egalitarian village base, all such communities having been hierarchized to varying degrees as a consequence of having existed in the context of class societies (Trigger 1985b). The concept of Asiatic society has generated some useful discussions, but its main features do not appear to correspond with any societies that have actually existed. It is a product of inadequately documented nineteenth-century speculation.

4 Evidence and Interpretation

For each of the seven early civilizations being compared, I compiled information regarding its environmental setting, population density and distribution, family and community organization, government, legal system, technology, land tenure, subsistence patterns, trade, manufacturing and distribution of goods, art, architecture, religious beliefs and practices, moral codes, specialized knowledge, and beliefs concerning the universe, the nature of the individual, and esteemed forms of behaviour. My goal was to ascertain how these elements were articulated in individual civilizations before attempting comparisons.

I sought to determine empirically the amount of research that was required by noting when I began to encounter a sharp and consistent decline in information that either supplemented or contradicted what I had already collected. Reaching that goal necessitated taking notes on as many as one hundred books and monographs dealing with each civilization as well as reading a large number of recent papers. After this stage was reached, I read mainly newly published works that provided general overviews of specific early civilizations or dealt with aspects that had been poorly covered in earlier studies. By doing the research myself, I sought to ensure comparability in the way data were collected and processed.

In the course of this research I became aware that there were many biases and limitations both in the sorts of data available concerning each early civilization and in modern interpretations of these data. Understanding the reasons for such variations and making allowances for them are vital for the success of any comparative investigation. This chapter discusses these problems and what I have done to try to minimize their negative influence.

SOURCES OF DATA

Because early civilizations are large and complex societies, the study of them is comparable to the proverbial blind men's investigation of an elephant. Both of the main sources of primary information regarding early civilizations – archaeological data and written records produced either by the civilization being studied or by outsiders – tend to be patchy and incomplete, and what is available varies considerably from one early civilization to another. By far the most valuable archaeological data come from the detailed settlement pattern surveys that have been carried out in southern Iraq (R. McC. Adams 1981), in the Valley of Mexico (Sanders, Parsons, and Santley 1979), and, in recent years, despite the great physical difficulties caused by extensive tropical-forest cover, in large stretches of Classic Maya territory (Culbert and Rice 1990). The least satisfactory settlement data are available for the Yoruba and for Shang and Western Zhou China. In China, historical archaeology, despite its professed Marxist orientation, has continued to concentrate on studying fine art. Much of the eastern part of the Shang homeland lies buried under the many metres of alluvium that the Yellow River has deposited over the past two thousand years (Jing, Rapp, and Gao 1997). Settlement surveys have been carried out in Egypt and highland Peru but on a local rather than a regional scale.

In the absence of extensive settlement data, much more tends to be known archaeologically about large urban centres than about farm villages and more about state-sponsored activities and the lives of the upper classes than about ordinary people. In Egypt differential preservation and recovery have also produced far more information about burial practices than about everyday life. Despite this variation, the archaeological data appear to have more comparability than the data from written sources. Also, while archaeological techniques change and evolve, because they are applied in a relatively uniform fashion they offer more standardized insights into early civilizations than written records. Archaeological data are generally believed to be more objective than written information, but Ian Hodder's (1982a) examination of material culture indicates that problems of objectivity and bias are inherent in them as well.

The written records produced by early civilizations never provide comprehensive or unbiased information. Literacy was severely restricted, and writings tended to reflect the interests and preoccupations of institutions, administrators, and the upper classes. Even when texts mention artisans or farmers, they describe them from above. The materials on which different sorts of messages were recorded and the ways in which they were curated influenced a text's chances of survival. The Classic Maya wrote on stone, ceramic vessels, and folded sheets of parchment and bark cloth. Only their writing on stone, pottery, and the walls of caves has survived in legible form; none of the books found in tombs is in readable condition. The messages recorded on ceramic vessels, mainly in association with religious themes, were different from the dynastic records carved on stone monuments. Even the general contents of Classic Maya books are unknown; the few surviving Maya books, dating from much later times, were divinatory manuals. While there is no direct evidence that the Maya used writing for administrative purposes, Maya art depicts scribes recording information for rulers.

Similarly, the only written records to survive from the Shang Dynasty are annotations on cattle scapulae and tortoise shells that were used for divination and brief inscriptions, recording mainly names and titles, on bronze ritual vessels. Epigraphic and historical evidence indicates that the Shang Chinese also wrote on strips of bamboo held together by string, but such records have perished. Studies of historical records and songs attributed to the Shang Dynasty that have survived in the Chinese literary canon appear, on stylistic and linguistic grounds, to have been forgeries composed during the succeeding Zhou Dynasty. The much longer texts commemorating significant historical events that were cast on early Western Zhou bronze vessels do, however, confirm the authenticity of the Zhou records that Chinese historians have preserved from ancient times.

A much wider range of texts has survived from ancient Egypt and Mesopotamia. These include business and administrative documents, personal letters, historical records and propaganda, royal proclamations, religious rituals, myths, divinatory literature, teaching materials, and collections of practical advice. At first these records tended to be terse, but by the late third millennium B.C. longer texts started to appear, some of which were clearly intended for enjoyment as well as to serve practical and religious ends. The Mesopotamians recorded official inscriptions on stone or metal but mainly wrote on clay tablets which, when baked (either accidentally or deliberately), became almost indestructible. Examples of even the humblest forms of documentation have therefore survived. In Egypt formal religious and government texts carved on stone and school texts and business records written on potsherds and limestone flakes frequently survive, as do religious texts painted on wooden coffins or papyrus scrolls preserved in tombs. Government administrative records and temple rituals written on papyri have mostly perished. Thus what we can learn about these early civilizations is determined by the range of what was recorded, which we sometimes know and sometimes do not, and by the extent to which texts of various sorts have been preserved and recovered.

The Aztec and other groups in the Valley of Mexico recorded ideas but not speech in bark-cloth books. Their subject matter was largely limited to divination, schematic ethnic histories, upper-class genealogical records, and tribute lists (Galarza 1997). Inka records consisted of knotted cords which, despite some claims to the contrary (Urton 1998), appear to have been used only for keeping accounts.

For descriptions of early civilizations that did not record the spoken word, we are dependent on the records produced as a result of European contact. Much information about the indigenous peoples of the Valley of Mexico (especially the Aztec and the people of Texcoco) and the Inka kingdom was recorded soon after the Spanish conquered these two civilizations. The earliest descriptions by Spanish conquerors tend to be of limited value because their authors had acquired only a superficial understanding of these cultures. Spanish settlers, government officials, and Christian priests gradually gained deeper insights into indigenous ways of life even as these were being radically transformed by European diseases and political and economic disruptions. Spanish officials recorded detailed information about indigenous patterns of land ownership, tax payments, and social organization in order to facilitate acquiring control over valuable local resources. Spanish priests in the Mexico City area collected detailed information in the Nahuatl language in order to identify and expunge indigenous religious beliefs (Durán 1971: 20–23). While analogous records of Andean culture are less abundant and sometimes influenced by existing descriptions of Aztec customs, their study is facilitating an improved understanding of indigenous Peruvian social organization, religious beliefs, cosmology, and ritual.

Despite the large amounts of information that were gathered in both regions, there is evidence that people deliberately concealed certain types of knowledge from Spanish priests and officials in an effort to protect traditional religious practices and avoid being interrogated by the Inquisition (Klor de Alva 1982). Further, Elizabeth Brumfiel (1991: 245–46) observes that these texts recorded normative accounts of human behaviour, usually from the point of view of upper-class male informants, that lack the flexible, adaptive, and dynamic qualities of real life.

Other important sources of information about Aztec and Inka culture were the descriptions produced by mestizo descendants of Spanish men and upper-class indigenous women and the data collected by educated Spanish settlers from their upper-class native wives and these women's families. These documents preserve valuable information about indigenous culture and oral history, but it is evident that native informants sought to make their ancestors seem as much as possible like Christians and Spaniards in order to win the approval of European readers. Indigenous historical accounts were also revised and new works created as ways to cope with national defeat and humiliation. The

Cantares Mexicanos, Aztec poems once thought to date from before the conquest, are now believed to have been composed in response to that cataclysmic event (Bierhorst 1985).

Information about the Yoruba and Benin peoples began to be recorded by European visitors as early as the sixteenth century. These sources became more abundant in the course of the nineteenth century and were supplemented by the writings of Yoruba converts to Christianity (S. Johnson 1921). In evaluating this material, the Europeans' limited understanding of Yoruba culture prior to the mid-nineteenth century and their pejorative attitudes towards African societies need to be considered, as well as the desire of Yoruba Christians to please European readers and enhance the status of their indigenous culture in the opinion of European co-religionists. In contrast to the other civilizations we have been considering, Yoruba culture continues to flourish despite radical economic and political changes during the colonial and postcolonial eras and widespread conversion to Christianity and Islam. Much has been recorded about Yoruba culture as a result of ethnographic research carried out by Yoruba as well as by European and American scholars during the twentieth century. These studies contextualize many categories of information about the Yoruba that were recorded only summarily in earlier times.

Four early civilizations that we are examining were composed of political units usually referred to as city-states. Adjacent city-states varied considerably in population, political organization, wealth, and relative power. In general, more is known about powerful and wealthy city-states than about smaller and poorer ones. It is therefore important to examine the full range of variation among states in each civilization in order to avoid exaggerating differences between city-state systems as a result of inadvertently comparing individual states that were at different levels of complexity. An internal comparison also provides information about how different aspects of specific early civilizations varied according to the size and power of individual states. It is clear that, as a result of interstate competition, the size and power of individual city-states changed radically over time. Therefore detailed information about a single state at one point in time does not shed adequate or reliable light on the full range of variations or transformations that characterized these civilizations. Interstate variation is documented most systematically for the Yoruba and to a considerable degree for the Valley of Mexico (Hodge 1984; 1998). Much information must be available for Mesopotamia, but most of it is not yet in a form that non-specialists such as myself can synthesize. The study of social and political variation among the Classic Maya states is only beginning. For larger territorial states, more records describe the highest levels of the ruling class and the central administration than deal with life in provincial centres and the countryside.

Probably more is known from both archaeological and written sources about the early sixteenth century in the Valley of Mexico than about a similarly brief period in the history of any other early civilization in our sample. This reflects the scholarly ability of Spanish priests and officials living in Mexico City and their Nahuatl informants' skill in communicating knowledge. Specialists have produced fairly comprehensive, although less even, knowledge concerning the Yoruba and less comprehensive information about the Mesopotamian, Inka, and Egyptian civilizations, in approximately that order. Written information about the Inka appears to be inferior both in quantity and in quality to that on the Aztec, perhaps because the centre of European intellectual life in Peru was Lima rather than the Central Andean heartland of Inka civilization. Much less is known archaeologically about highland Peru than about the Valley of Mexico as well. Despite the vast resources poured into the study of ancient Mesopotamia and Egypt, knowledge about any one period remains uneven. The more comprehensive archaeological surveys and the preservation of a wider range of written materials mean that more is known about ancient Mesopotamian civilization than about ancient Egypt, for which information tends to be focused more on the upper classes and on state-patronized culture. The two least well-known civilizations in our sample are Shang China and the Classic Maya. The main problem with the Maya is the restricted nature of surviving written information, which generally deals with the activities of kings. For Shang China a similarly restricted range of written texts is combined with limited archaeological data, which are also skewed towards upper-class culture.

SCHOLARLY BIASES

Understanding early civilizations necessitates knowledge not only of the limitations of data concerning the past but also of the biases that are inherent in modern scholarly interpretations of those data. Evaluating the modern scholarly literature requires comprehensive knowledge of what is known about each early civilization and the application of the standard techniques of historical source criticism to individual texts (Roberts 1996). The biases and skills of both original recorders and modern analysts must be considered.

In general, problems of interpretive misunderstanding are greatest when written information about an early civilization was recorded by outsiders. One of the best studies of such misunderstandings is Sabine MacCormack's (1991) work on the writings of Spaniards and Inka from the 1530s until the eighteenth century, which investigates how information about Inka religious beliefs and practices was recorded and how existing scholarly knowledge shaped interpretations of new information and reinterpretations of what was already known. Although it was not the main purpose of her study, MacCormack was able to make progress in distinguishing between early Inka religious beliefs and practices and the biased understandings of Spanish and mestizo interpreters.

The prejudices and academic allegiances of modern interpreters play a crucial role in determining what is available for comparative studies. Rationalists expect to find a high degree of uniformity, while relativists anticipate minimal similarities, except as a result of historical connections. Neither orientation is inherently bad provided that it is treated as a working hypothesis. What is unacceptable but occurs both consciously and unconsciously is the tailoring of data to accord with these preconceptions – assuming that less well-known civilizations will resemble better-known ones and ignoring data that do not accord with favoured theories. Identifying and making allowances for interpretive biases are vital to the success of any investigation that depends mostly on secondary sources.

Anthropological interests in early civilizations have altered significantly in recent decades as the focus has shifted from social behaviour to culture. Studies of early civilizations in the 1960s were dominated by a materialist perspective that highlighted subsistence patterns, craft production, exchange, settlement patterns, and political organization. Today there is increasing interest in religious beliefs and culturally determined perceptions, both as objects of interest in their own right and as significant determinants of social, political, and economic behaviour. While the idealist perspective that underlies much modern research is at odds with the materialism of an earlier era, the two approaches tend to be complementary and, when combined, produce richer and more nuanced insights into the nature of early civilizations than either by itself. Both have been enriched in recent decades by the critiques and new perspectives offered by feminist and gender studies.

Lack of awareness of the wide range of alternative arrangements possible in early civilizations tends to produce dogmatic misconceptions that lead to misinterpretation. The most striking example of such a misconception was Karl Wittfogel's (1957) notion of 'Oriental despotism', which he believed evolved as a result of leaders' self-interested extension of the authoritarian patterns needed to build and maintain extensive irrigation systems in arid lands to control all aspects of public life. This construct, which dominated the interpretation of early civilizations in the 1950s and 1960s, was effectively challenged only after Robert McC. Adams's (1965) detailed studies of settlement patterns in Iraq demonstrated that large irrigation systems in that region were a consequence rather than a cause of the development of complex societies. This freed scholars to ask questions they had ignored about the social organization of early civilizations and to formulate new theories about their development (Flannery 1972; E. Hunt 1972).

No less inhibiting were Karl Polanyi's dicta that profit-oriented exchanges did not occur in early civilizations and that exchange mechanisms evolved from reciprocity through institutionally directed redistribution to markets (Polanyi 1968; Polanyi, Arensberg, and Pearson 1957). This misconception, which required several decades of research to dispel, seriously distorted the understanding of the economic and social organization of early civilizations. It is now recognized that market exchange, which was often profit-oriented, appeared prior to and continued to exist alongside redistribution by government bureaucracies (Curtin 1984: 87–89).

Biases that influence the study of particular early civilizations also create serious comparative problems. Interpreters of Aztec culture have long been divided between those who view the Aztec upper class as brutal warriors appropriating human protein and other people's wealth (Caso 1958; Harner 1977; Soustelle 1961) and those who prefer to regard them as sensitive intellectuals disinterestedly probing the mysteries of the cosmos (León-Portilla 1963; 1992).

The study of ancient Mesopotamia has been shaped by the belief that this civilization crucially influenced both the ancient Hebrews and the Greeks and hence the origins of Western civilization. Many Assyriologists have been encouraged by this belief to make their interpretations of the behaviour of the ancient Mesopotamians conform as closely as possible to the values of modern Western civilization. Others insist that, if it is to be understood properly, ancient Mesopotamia must be studied independently from all other early civilizations (Landsberger 1976). Both approaches lead to an emphasis on the differences between Mesopotamia and other early civilizations (Bottéro 1992).

Egyptologists study a culture that Western civilization has traditionally regarded not only as a repository of arcane wisdom but also as the despotic and idolatrous antithesis of the Judaeo-Christian tradition. Yet Egyptologists find the civilization they study very different from this stereotype. To counter traditional biases, most have adopted the rationalist claim that all human beings have a common nature and seem convinced that they can automatically reproduce in their own minds the thought processes of an ancient Pharaoh. Even Barry Kemp (1989), who agrees with Henri Frankfort (1956) that certain highly distinctive themes shaped the development of Egyptian culture, assumes that most ancient Egyptian behaviour was influenced by concepts of self-interest and entrepreneurship that he considers to be shared by all human beings.

Most Inka specialists since the 1960s have argued that without paying special attention to the idiosyncratic principles of Andean culture it is impossible to understand Inka behaviour. They believe that the development of Inka society was shaped by postulates of reciprocity and community autonomy that were unique to the Central Andean world and make any comparison of Inka culture with non-Andean societies highly deceptive (Zuidema 1964; D'Altroy 1987a: 5). These studies are oriented very differently from Thomas Patterson's (1991) investigation of Inka dynastic politics, which emphasized the rational pursuit of political power and material resources by the various branches of the royal family and their supporters.

The cultural uniqueness of different early civilizations has also been emphasized by Dutch structural anthropologists. Rudolph van Zantwijk (1985) and Thomas Zuidema (1964; 1990) have drawn upon data recorded in the sixteenth century to reconstruct the cosmological beliefs of the Aztec and the Inka and demonstrate how these beliefs influenced social organization, architecture, ritual practices, and the use of agricultural land. Their intricate analyses, which integrate large amounts of esoteric religious and symbolic data that might otherwise have been ignored, suggest that extraordinarily elaborate cosmological ideas guided every aspect of Aztec and Inka life. Few scholars doubt that van Zantwijk and Zuidema have gained important insights into particular Aztec and Inka understandings of how the cosmos and their own societies functioned. Nevertheless, questions about the work of these two scholars remain unresolved. Their analyses assume that the principles which generated these ideas underlay and guided all Aztec and Inka perception and behaviour, but there is no way of knowing to what extent everyone shared these ideas at either a conscious or an unconscious level. Were these ideas alternatively elaborations by priests and officials of a simpler, more widely shared set of beliefs? Or were they developed symbolic interpretations created by and read into traditional ways of doing things by a small coterie of indigenous intellectuals? One must also consider whether van Zantwijk and Zuidema elaborated ideas to a greater extent than anyone in these early civilizations. Barry Kemp (1989: 4–5), commenting on some of the more elaborate and arcane interpretations of ancient Egyptian symbolism, has noted that, while these ideas may 'be quite true to the spirit of ancient thought', there is no way to determine whether such ideas 'ever actually passed through the minds of the ancients'. Kemp argues that it is possible for modern scholars to understand ancient concepts in such detail that they can pursue lines of thought that accord with the beliefs of an ancient civilization even though there is no evidence that such ideas ever occurred to any ancient person. The validity of interpretations of this sort is also hard to prove. Their questionable status is revealed when contrary postulates produce mutually contradictory interpretations of the same data. Although structural analyses provide valuable insights into early civilizations, studies of this sort risk giving rise to dangerous misunderstandings and must therefore be used carefully.

While my study seeks to be empirical, I do not subscribe to a narrow, positivist epistemology or deny that subjective elements influence the construction of knowledge and hence behaviour. Instead, I regard subjective elements, whether they are present in the original sources or in secondary interpretations, as challenges that must be indentified and understood if comparative work is to be effective.

EMIC AND ETIC APPROACHES

It is generally agreed that comparative research requires a standard set of categories to arrange and compare information about each society. There is the danger, however, that representing individual sociocultural systems with a single standardized terminology may be misleading. Faulty translations of indigenous concepts into such a nomenclature may bias and distort the results of comparative studies, usually in the direction of exaggerating the extent of uniformities among cultures. Such dangers can be countered by careful hermeneutic study. This view accords with the claim that an idea expressed in one natural language can be expressed in any other. General categories can be used for comparative purposes provided that it is established to what understandings each category refers in the various societies being compared.

Just as I have argued that anthropologists must understand early civilizations as holistic systems before they begin to compare analogous parts of them, so I would argue that, before making comparisons, anthropologists must attempt to understand each early civilization in the same terms as it was understood by its own people. While it is generally acknowledged that this sort of understanding is essential for comparing belief systems, even apparently utilitarian processes such as growing crops and working metals are enmeshed in complex systems of values and beliefs that may vary significantly from one culture to another (Lechtman 1993). The comparative study of early civilizations therefore requires both an *emic* and an *etic* approach to the understanding of culture.

This pair of terms is derived from linguistics, where *phonetics* refers to recordings of speech in which every sound variation that can be scientifically distinguished is noted. This amounts to several hundred sounds and intonation patterns, far more than can be distinguished in everyday speech. *Phonemic* recording notes only the two or three dozen sounds that are meaningfully distinguished by the speakers of any particular language. In English 'pin' and 'bin' are two different words, while in Arabic *p* and *b* are interpreted as the same sound. In English 'king' and 'queen' are believed to begin with the same sound, although *k* is velar and *q* uvular. In Arabic, however, *kalb* signifies 'dog' and *qalb* 'heart'. In anthropology *etic* refers to analysis in terms of cross-culturally applicable scientific terms and *emic* to the study of the terminology and underlying concepts that have meaning for the people who belong to a particular society. As Clifford Geertz (1979) has put it, an etic terminology employs 'experience-distant' concepts, while an emic analysis relies on 'experience-near' ones. It is frequently objected that etic concepts are merely the emic concepts of modern science and hence of Western civilization, which are ethnocentrically imposed on other cultures, but this does not have to be the case.

To limit imposing my own preconceptions on the data, I have attempted as far as possible to understand each early civilization on its own terms. I have done this by examining the terminology used in each early civilization for key concepts such as soil types, social classes, administrative titles, types of landholding, and religious beliefs. It is impossible to master all the languages required to understand seven different civilizations emically, but I have found a limited word-based approach helpful. Any emic approach, however, is time-consuming and has inherent limitations. In most cases, information concerning how people in early civilizations classified things is very limited. This is especially true for the lower classes, about whose beliefs little documentation survives. Emic studies depend on knowledge of a culture as expressed in its own language or languages. Yet a modern understanding of the ancient Egyptian language, which has had to be derived from ancient texts (assisted by knowledge of the Coptic language which is descended from it), remains limited despite almost two hundred years of intensive investigation. Often the number and variety of surviving texts are insufficient to support hermeneutic analyses that would reveal the exact meanings of many words. Hence what pass for translations of ancient Egyptian and Sumerian texts contain many approximate glosses rather than precise readings. The understanding of Classic Maya texts, which began to be deciphered only recently and survive in far lower numbers, is still more limited (Houston 2001).

The best-understood early civilization, from an internalist as well as other points of view, is that of the Valley of Mexico. The Nahuatl language is still spoken by a significant number of people, and in the sixteenth century very detailed descriptions of Aztec and Texcocan culture were recorded from indigenous informants in that language. This vast corpus of information has provided material for extraordinary studies such as Alfredo López Austin's *The*

Human Body and Ideology: Concepts of the Ancient Nahuas (1988). López Austin describes how the Aztec ascribed to each human being not one but at least three very different 'souls' or 'life-forces'. It is clearly misleading to gloss these concepts with a single etic term such as 'soul'.

Research of this sort in richly documented contexts also reminds us of the possible complexities of meaning that may underlie poorly understood concepts in other early civilizations. Ignorance of such complexities makes it easy unwittingly to impose our own understandings on other peoples. Realizing this reinforced my determination to learn as much as I could about how the people of each early civilization conceptualized their world before I attempted to translate such concepts into 'scientific' cross-cultural terminology. Where this exercise failed to produce positive enlightenment because the original terminology was not systematically preserved or inadequately understood, it helped to increase awareness of the limitations of the current understanding of particular early civilizations.

Emic approaches are essential for understanding belief systems. The ancient Egyptians had two words, *nḥḥ* and *ḏt*, that they frequently used together and that Egyptologists long translated as synonyms meaning 'forever'. Today it is understood that both words meant 'lasting as long as the cosmic order endures'. The word nḥḥ referred, however, to an entity's surviving by means of renewal that involved cycles of death and rebirth such as the daily setting and rising of the sun, the fall and rise of the Nile, and the death and birth of successive generations of plants, animals, and human beings. In the course of such renewals, vital forces were believed to pass from one manifestation to another. Certain human life-forces could, for example, after death unite with the sun in the underworld and be reborn with it each morning. The term ḏt, in contrast, referred to things' surviving by perpetually staying the same, the prime example being a mummified body preserved in its tomb. Humans looked to both forms of enduring to ensure the long-term survival of the various vital forces that constituted a living individual. Analyses of this sort supply information about the specific ways in which people living in particular early civilizations perceived themselves, their society, and the universe.

Not all emic studies are so productive. It was argued in Chapter 3 that 'class' is a crucial concept for understanding early civilizations, but if there was a generic term corresponding to 'class' in each early civilization it is not easy to identify. Its absence may not be particularly significant, however, since generic words are relatively infrequent in the languages of the early civilizations. There was no common term for 'religion' in ancient Egypt, any more than there was in Classical Greece (Vernant 1995: 9), but that does not signify that religion did not play a major role in both societies. Similarly, the absence of a word for 'law' in ancient Mesopotamia (Bottéro 1992: 179) does not mean that that civilization lacked a legal system or the lack of a Babylonian word for 'court' (Postgate 1992: 277) that there was no formal litigation. The absence of a word for 'religion' probably indicates that in ancient Egypt religion was so intertwined with daily life that it did not require a separate designation. In the same fashion, failure to designate 'class' may reflect a conception of social organization not as something distinct but as occurring in a broader context that embraced religious and other elements.

There were also considerable variations in the explicitness with which social hierarchies were terminologically expressed. The Egyptians used various terms for farmer, such as *sḫty* (marsh/country dweller), *mrt* (serf), and *nı͗swty* ('free peasant' or 'royal tenant') (Janssen 1978: 227). The meanings of these terms may have been exclusive or overlapping. Yet there is no evidence of a generic word denoting farmers as a class. The Aztec, in contrast, had a well-ordered class terminology. The upper class (*pipiltin*, singular *pilli*) was divided into three levels: *tetecuhtin* (singular *tecuhtli*) (high lords), *pipiltin* (ordinary hereditary nobles), and *quauhpipiltin* (nobles by achievement). Commoners were divided into *macehualtin* (singular *macehualli*), taxpaying members of collective landowning groups, and *mayeque*, rent-payers seemingly bound to land held by nobles in return for service to the state. There were also *tlacotin* (singular *tlacotli*) (slaves) (Berdan 1982: 46). For other early civilizations it has not been possible to work out a nested set of terms that precisely paralleled the social hierarchies indicated by their sumptuary laws and marriage patterns. Yet in the social and political spheres, the use of etic classifications may be analytically justified even if emic equivalents for such units are not always forthcoming. The situation is not markedly different in the class terminology of most modern societies, outside the specialized sphere of discourse influenced by the social sciences.

While the lexical approach is not as thorough as a detailed understanding of the languages spoken in each civilization would have been, together with a study of what is known about the beliefs of these societies, expressed in various literary genres such as hymns and myths, it helps to restrain scholars from unthinkingly imposing their own ethnocentric beliefs on the data and thus making the thoughts and behaviour of the people who lived in these societies appear more like our own and therefore like each other's than they really were. Because all behaviour is guided by beliefs, values, and expectations that are shaped to varying degrees by cultural as well as material considerations, it is vital that a comparative study of early civilizations take account of such ideas.

PROSPECT

It is clear that the 'facts' about early civilizations, especially those that are derived from secondary or heavily interpreted primary sources, are to a large extent consensually established rather than scientifically demonstrated. It is also clear that many interpretations are ideologically or theoretically driven. Much of the current literature about the Classic Maya is based on the belief that patrilineal extended families constituted the basis of Maya society, a claim that some eminent Mayanists reject as undemonstrated if not erroneous (Wilk 1988). Speculation based on such assumptions must be treated cautiously in a study of this sort. Scholars who regard a specific early civilization as unique will emphasize different facts from those who believe that cross-cultural regularities provide a reliable guide for understanding that civilization. Materialists and idealists will emphasize different data. I hoped, however, that by examining an extensive literature produced, over a fifty-year period that has witnessed many theoretical changes, by scholars with many different interests and theoretical orientations, I might partially neutralize the effects of these biases.

In the substantive chapters that follow, I have no doubt unwittingly adopted many specific interpretations that for one reason or another will not stand the test of time. I have also doubtless failed to note the contested nature of other interpretations and unconsciously permitted my personal views to influence what evidence I have and have not considered and how I have synthesized that evidence. I believe, however, that much of the information concerning the seven early civilizations that are being compared is sufficiently sound that my analysis can lay claim to a significant degree of objectivity. In illustrating major points I have tried to draw equally on all seven civilizations. In some instances, however, data are entirely lacking for some early civilizations, and in other cases there is much better documentation for one or two early civilizations than there is for the rest.

The following nine chapters compare various aspects of the sociopolitical organization of the seven early civilizations that have been selected for study. After that, five chapters deal with economic matters and nine more with knowledge, religious beliefs, and values. I could have started by examining either the economy or cultural features. An economic start would have implicitly privileged an ecological perspective and a cultural start an idealist approach to explaining human behaviour. After considerable experimentation, I concluded that beginning with a examination of sociopolitical features facilitated a more economical and generally more comprehensible comparison than starting with either of the alternatives. Such a conclusion accords with the traditional views of social anthropologists, who have maintained that all other aspects of a culture acquire their functional significance from the manner in which they are related to social organization. It also accords with classical Marxism, which, although materialist, attributes the key role in bringing about change not to ecological factors or technological change but, at least in class-organized societies, to universal calculations of self-interest that alter the social relations of production.

According priority to social relations also makes sense phylogenetically. Our primate ancestors were social creatures long before they developed technology and before their relations to the natural world and to each other were symbolically mediated (Mithen 1996). Thus social relations constituted the preexisting matrix that was radically transformed by the changing adaptive strategies and developing cognitive abilities of early hominids. Social relations were the core around which later developments accrued and in relation to which they acquired their functional significance. While social anthropologists and Marxists generally pay little attention to physical anthropology, the order in which different forms of human behaviour developed provides the most convincing argument for starting a general cultural comparison with an examination of social and political relations.

Sociopolitical Organization

5 Kingship

All the early civilizations compared in this study had kings. In modern political terminology this signifies that sovereignty, or supreme authority, was symbolically embodied in an individual person rather than in some collectivity of people such as all adults, all males, all property owners, or all nobles or some abstract concept such as God or Jean-Jacques Rousseau's General Will (Kamenka 1989: 7).

The terms used to designate kings had different meanings and connotations in the different civilizations. The Aztec word that is glossed as 'king' was *tlatoani* (plural *tlatoque*), which in Nahuatl meant 'great/revered speaker'. The Aztec and their Nahuatl-speaking neighbours applied this term to all hereditary heads of states, but they conceptualized political leadership in a dyadic fashion. The tlatoani shared sovereignty with the *cihuacoatl*, a hereditary official appointed from a junior branch of the royal family who could not become king. The cihuacoatl oversaw the courts and palace administration and when necessary acted as regent. Although his title meant 'snake woman', like the tlatoani the holder of this office was always a male. In Aztec thought, the tlatoani and cihuacoatl together symbolized lordship, just as the supreme deity Ometeotl, Lord and Lady of Twoness, was a dual entity that constituted the totality of existence. In practice, however, the Aztec tlatoani was a supreme ruler.

The Yoruba also had a generic title for their hereditary heads of state, *oba*. This title indicated descent from Oduduwa, the god who had created the world, and was traditionally restricted to the hereditary rulers of the significant Yoruba states and neighbouring Benin. Some subordinate local rulers also claimed the title of oba, although they did not enjoy many of the prerogatives of that office. In contrast to the English term 'king', 'oba' did not refer to the hereditary rulers of non-Yoruba states or to the heads of smaller Yoruba polities. Each Yoruba state also had a special title for its oba, such as the Oni of

Ife, the Alafin of Oyo, the Aleketu of Ketu, the Owa of Ilesa, and the Orangun of Ila. Among the Maya, the ruler of a city-state was designated *k'ul ahaw* (holy lord). Various Sumerian terms (*en*, *ensi*, *lugal*) designated the heads of Early Dynastic Mesopotamian city-states, but none of these terms was exclusive to a single city.

In Egypt the most important title used to designate the head of state was *nswt*. Only one legitimate nswt could exist in the world at a time, although the title was also applied to the king of the gods (*nswt nṯrw*). The nswt ruled by right not only Egypt but the entire world and was responsible for maintaining both the social order and the cosmic balance. He had to be Egyptian. If, during periods of civil strife or political division, more than one person claimed the title, it was understood that only a single claimant could be the true universal ruler. The kings of other countries were called *wr* ('prince' or 'great one') or *ḥq3* (ruler), terms which were also applied to subordinate officials or chiefs within Egypt.

Egyptian royal titles expressed many levels of cultural meaning. 'Nswt', in addition to signifying 'universal ruler', meant more specifically 'King of Upper (Southern) Egypt'. Rulers were also given the title *bỉty*, which meant 'King of Lower (Northern) Egypt'. According to the assymetrical dualism that dominated Egyptian thought, the term 'nswt' not only contrasted with 'bỉty' but also incorporated it. This usage reflected the Egyptian belief that at the dawn of history an Upper Egyptian kingdom had conquered and incorporated a Lower Egyptian one to create the Egyptian state. The king was also called *nswtbỉty*, 'King of Upper and Lower Egypt', which meant the same as 'nswt' in its inclusive form. After death kings were referred to only as 'nswt', which presumably designated the eternal, unchanging aspect of the monarchy: kingship as an eternal (ḏt) office and the dead kings who were identified with the god Osiris. The title 'bỉty' may have referred to the transitory, accidental, and renewing (nḥḥ) aspects of kingship: the king as a living individual. The titles *ḥm* ('Majesty' or 'individual in whom kingship is incarnated') and *nb* (lord) also designated the king as a mortal individual (Allen 2000: 31–32; Ray 1993: 70; Silverman 1995: 64–69).

The Inka ruler also had an exclusive title, *sapa inka* (unique Inka) (Rowe 1944: 258). The Shang ruler was titled *wang*. It is unclear whether the Shang rulers acknowledged the existence of other wang, ruling regions the Shang kings did not control.

Thus the terms for 'head of state' in different early civilizations covered only partially overlapping semantic fields. In general, city-states tended to designate kings generically, while territorial states acknowledged the existence of only one universal ruler. While 'king' may provide a reasonable gloss for these various words, a sound understanding of kingship in early civilizations can only grow out of a detailed comparative study of the concepts of kingship of particular early civilizations.

In recent years it has been suggested that some early civilizations may have lacked monarchs, but the proposed examples, which include the Teotihuacan state in the Valley of Mexico in the first millennium A.D. (Cowgill 1997) and the Indus Valley civilization (Possehl 1998), are archaeological ones for which there is no contemporary written documentation. The main argument advanced in favour of the absence of kings is the lack of representation of rulers in the iconography of these states. There is, however, a conspicuous lack of royal portraiture in the surviving art of Shang China and the Inka. For the Shang, there is no evidence that kings, who feature prominently in written records, were ever represented in art. We know, however, from historical sources that life-size statues of Inka rulers hammered from sheets of gold were objects of veneration. All these statues were melted down by European invaders in the sixteenth century. Likewise, in the Valley of Mexico, clearly identified royal representations appear to have been infrequent during the Late Aztec period and were associated mainly with larger and more centralized states. Hence a dearth of royal portraiture in some early civilizations does not indicate an absence of kings. Furthermore, each of the Yoruba states, in which much of the political power is known to have been formally shared among the heads of various leading families, had a divine king.

It therefore seems reasonable to conclude that all early civilizations probably had monarchs, even if kingship was defined somewhat differently and the actual political power exercised by such rulers varied considerably from one to another. While some small, non-state societies may have survived within or on the borders of city-state systems, republican forms of sovereignty within states, whether they took the form of despotisms, oligarchies, or democracies, arose from and replaced monarchies. The universality of kings in our sample suggests that in all early civilizations political power was represented in a personal manner. Hallpike (1986: 282) has observed that monarchs provided a concrete and hence easily understood way to represent supreme authority at the state level.

Early states also had kings. There are examples, in Hawaii and among the Zulu, of the evolution of kingship as the political power of certain chiefs increased (Flannery 1999). In the early civilizations, however, supreme power was less charismatic, more institutionalized, and more routinely transmitted from one generation to the next. As a result, the office of kingship grew ever more important by comparison with the particular incumbent of that office. Sovereignty nevertheless continued to be viewed as an attribute of an individual person. Even though kinship was no longer the only or even the most important principle structuring society, kings styled themselves fathers to their nations, a metaphorical status that combined concepts of benevolence and authority (Trigger 1985b). Kings were regarded as responsible for the general well-being of their realm, and their duties included maintaining internal order and prosperity, defending their kingdom from foreign enemies, and managing relations with the supernatural.

Kingship provided the ultimate level at which conflicts were resolved and decisions were made about general policy, although this was often done in the king's name rather than through his personal intervention. Maintaining public order required ensuring that farmers remained submissive to the state, produced food surpluses, and paid taxes and rents. It also involved mediating and resolving conflicts among the ruling classes that threatened the unity of the state. Kings were normally supreme military commanders. Although in Oyo and other Yoruba states military leadership was monopolized by a chief official from a leading non-royal lineage, Yoruba kings formally declared war and were held to be supernaturally responsible for the success or failure of military campaigns (R. Smith 1969: 120). It was believed that, if an army were defeated, the king had failed to perform his supernatural role, and regicide or royal suicide sometimes followed (Ajisafe 1924: 21). While the powers of kings varied, kingship constituted a focus that was essential for coordinating and managing matters of general concern.

QUALIFICATIONS FOR KINGSHIP

In all early civilizations male monarchs were preferred, and in at least five (Mesopotamia, China, the Valley of Mexico, Inka, and Yoruba) it appears that only males were allowed to rule. Among the Yoruba, references to female obas are confined to the early and largely mythological period (Denzer 1994: 8). The only female ruler reported in Mesopotamia was Ku-Baba, the reputed first ruler of Kish, who was also a goddess (Lerner 1986: 59). Occasionally female monarchs ruled Egypt, and the late Egyptian historian Manetho said that it had been agreed in very early times that women might rule. Nevertheless, female monarchs generally were installed only during dynastic crises, and their reigns were regarded as contrary to the normal order. They also contradicted Egyptian religious dogma, which viewed kingship as transmitted directly from the god Osiris to his son and reincarnation Horus. The goddess Isis, wife of Osiris and mother of Horus, was solely the means by which divine kingship renewed itself (Troy 1986). It is uncertain whether the female Maya rulers reported at Piedras Negras, Palenque, and Naranjo were monarchs in their own right or merely regents for juvenile male rulers (Graham 1991: 473).

A king symbolically embodied a polity's identity and reconciled the conflicting interests within it. The normal pattern of political and religious leadership in the Valley of Mexico was based on a principle of dual authority that reflected the primordial order of the universe. Yet the tlatoani, who represented the male cosmic principle, predominated and was the de facto paramount ruler of each city-state (Rounds 1983). In the 1960s some anthropologists theorized, on the basis of the Aztec example, that all early civilizations had two or more kings who shared power and reigned at the same time. Zuidema (1964: 127) suggested that the Inka had a pattern of dual kingship, with the leader of the dominant royal moiety acting as the primary ruler, but it is now clear that at the highest level the Inka specifically rejected the general principle of moiety co-leadership in favour of a single ruler (Gose 1996b). Some kingdoms in the Valley of Mexico and among the Yoruba simultaneously had multiple kings, but these were inevitably small, poorly integrated states made up of a number of groups each of which followed its own leader.

Kingship was hereditary in practice in all seven early civilizations and hereditary in theory in all except perhaps the Sumerian parts of Mesopotamia. This arrangement reflected the generally stable, institutionalized nature of leadership in early civilizations. Kingship tended to pass from father to son or from older to younger brother before descending to the next generation. In some states, such as the Asante kingdom of northern Ghana which developed as recently as the eighteenth century, royal office was inherited matrilineally. Yet, even in this matrilineal society, kings sought to marry in ways that would ensure that their sons or grandsons would succeed them (Wilks 1975). Because most kings had to play an active role in governing early civilizations, the inheritance of the royal office was rarely determined strictly by male primogeniture. Choice was required to maximize the likelihood that each king would be followed by a capable successor. Under these circumstances, various selection procedures were used to determine the succession. There was variation from one early civilization to another in defining both the group from which a successor might be chosen and how and by whom the selection was made.

Among the Classic Maya, kingship appears normally to have passed from a ruler to a son by his principal wife. Recent studies of Maya royal genealogies eliminate the suggestion that in the Early Classic period Maya kingship had rotated among a number of different patrilineages (A. Miller 1986: 41). The prestige of both parents' patrilineages played a role in establishing the hereditary status of an heir, thereby weakening the chances of succession by a king's sons born to women other than his principal wife. It is unclear, however, whether there was a preference for male primogeniture. The Maya practiced special heir-designation rituals, apparently in an effort to ensure a stable succession. This suggests the possibility that an eldest son's right to kingship might be called into question. It has also been argued that the custom of holding Maya rulers captured in battle as prisoners for long periods before killing them was intended to induce instability in their kingdoms by preventing their sons from formally succeeding them in the interim (Schele and Freidel 1990: 194).

In Mesopotamian city-states, kingship likewise regularly passed from a ruler to his son. Nevertheless, the succession had to be sanctioned by a city's patron deity, whose will was determined by oracles and divination. Urukagina of Lagash, who did not become ruler by inheritance, boasted that his city's god had selected him to be king from among thirty-six thousand male citizens (Postgate 1992: 268). Some early kings are also reported to have been selected or approved by popular acclaim. It was envisaged that a king could be unseated by an uprising of his own subjects, who were carrying out the wishes of their city god. J. N. Postgate (1992: 270) suggests that patrilineal descent was not an exclusive or adequate qualification for kingship and that Sumerian ideology did not admit of a hereditary right of royal succession (see also Mander 1999; Steinkeller 1993).

Both in Egypt and among the Inka, kingship was passed down from father to son, with the heir being designated by the ruling monarch. Ideally the heir was a son of the king's chief wife, but in exceptional circumstances such sons could be passed over in favour of a more capable son by a secondary wife. Even when an heir was designated well in advance, conflict over the succession might break out following a king's death, with different factions of the royal family and the upper classes supporting rival candidates. To further ensure a peaceful succession, Egyptian and Inka kings sometimes installed their preferred heirs as junior rulers during their own lifetimes. Often the junior king took command of the army as a deputy for his elderly father. Aged or weak monarchs in both civilizations were sometimes killed or deposed by ambitious sons seeking to prevent another brother or half-brother from being named as successor. In Egypt it was essential for a new king to perform his predecessor's burial rituals in order to validate his claim to the throne (Shafer 1997b: 283 n. 16, 287–88 n. 52). Among the Inka the previous ruler's choice of an heir was confirmed by a council of high officials, by oracles from the sun god that were delivered through the high priest of that deity, and by the oracle priests who spoke for previous kings (Kendall 1973: 72–73; Patterson 1991; Rostworowski 1999). In both states the transfer of royal office was regarded as an event by which both the cosmic and the political order were first threatened and then ultimately renewed.

The Aztec king was selected, often amidst considerable rivalry, from among the brothers or sons of the dead king by a council made up of the four highest officers of the state (van Zantwijk 1994). These officials were usually members of the royal family, and the new king was one of them. The cihuacoatl, acting as regent, also played a role in the selection. It is reported that in the formative period of the Aztec monarchy the election of a new king had been confirmed by all the men and women of the state (Durán 1964: 40–41), but later the people merely acclaimed the new ruler. As the Aztec state grew more powerful, succession shifted from a father-to-son pattern to one in which the kingship often passed from one brother to another before descending to the next generation. This change is believed to have been intended to increase the number of experienced adult candidates from whom a new ruler might be selected. The new procedure favoured the appointment of a member of the royal family who was already militarily and politically successful. As the Aztec state came to dominate more neighbouring kingdoms, such qualities were increasingly valued in a leader (Rounds 1982).

It has been suggested that in the Shang Dynasty kingship may have rotated between two patrilineal branches and ten matrilineal divisions of the royal clan (K. Chang 1976: 84). (Simpler rotations occurred among branches of royal families elsewhere, including Yoruba ones and that of the early medieval Scots [Whitaker 1976].) Yet there is no conclusive evidence that such a circulation of kingship occurred in Shang China (Vandermeersch 1977: 284–93). At first kingship appears to have passed from older to younger brothers of a single lineage before descending to the eldest son of the eldest brother. Later, kingship passed from father to son, with a strong preference for primogeniture (Chêng 1960: 216–17). This trend – the opposite of what happened among the Aztec – may have reflected a need to balance the strong emphasis on seniority as a source of higher status with a growing need for rulers who were in the prime of life as military leadership became more important. Strictly fraternal succession, with little possibility of passing over any but the most hopelessly incapable candidates, would have encouraged a rapid succession of aged rulers.

The Yoruba king was chosen from among the male descendants of previous rulers by hereditary officials who belonged to the most important non-royal patrilineages, acting in consultation with prominent members of the royal clan. Kingship frequently rotated among two or more lineages or branches of the royal family, so that a king was rarely succeeded by his own son. The state council could order an unsuccessful king to commit suicide or to be slain by his palace staff, but kings in turn had to confirm the appointment of new members to this council (Bascom 1969: 30–33; Pemberton and Afolayan 1996: 76–79). The obas of Benin, who had gone farther than any of the Yoruba kings in reducing the powers of their state council, also established a direct father-to-eldest-son inheritance of kingship, which accorded with the general Edo rule of inheritance. In contrast to Yoruba kings, the oba of Benin also could not be deposed by his chief councillors (Bradbury 1957: 40–41). Like the ancient Egyptian kings, a new king of Benin had to validate his succession by burying his father and performing elaborate installation rituals. Inability to fulfil these requirements might disqualify an incompetent elder son from becoming king. In Oyo and some other Yoruba states, the king's biological mother was killed or expected to commit suicide at the same time that her son was 'reborn' as king (S. Johnson 1921: 56) and was replaced by a woman who was appointed to be the official queen mother (*iya oba*) (Law 1977: 70–71). In Benin, the king's mother was not killed but installed in a palace at Uselu, just outside Benin city, where she wielded considerable power. She and her son, who was now a divine ruler, were, however, never allowed to meet again (Ben-Amos 1983; Bradbury 1973: 55).

Thus in early civilizations sovereignty was embodied in an individual, and the stability of kingship was both guarded and symbolized by the continuity of royal office within a single family. In more powerful royal families, kingship tended to be inherited either fraternally or generationally within a single lineage, but in some weaker ones it rotated among a number of lineages that claimed descent from a single remote ancestor. While such rotation has been explained as a device for holding together extensive kingdoms in the absence of centralized authority (Whitaker 1976), this cannot account for the practice in Yoruba city-states. Among the Yoruba, rotation perhaps mitigated competition among branches of royal families that might have torn states apart and resulted in the out-migration of defeated candidates for royal power and their supporters. The relatively low population density of the Yoruba facilitated such movement.

Because kings in early civilizations, unlike modern constitutional monarchs, had to be able to govern effectively and often provide personal military leadership, it was highly desirable that they be adult and competent males. For that reason, it was also desirable that a selection be made among a number of rival candidates. Where kings had more power, kingship was inherited according to male primogeniture or the reigning monarch decided which of his sons should succeed him. In other cases, decisions about the succession were made either by representatives of the royal family or by powerful members of the upper class. Even where the heir was specified by primogeniture, the need to perform various rites in order to become king ensured that a new ruler either could govern effectively or was controlled and supported by people who could.

THE SACRED CHARACTER OF KINGSHIP

Although individuals, families, and small communities often had patron deities with whom they communicated either directly or through the spirits of their dead ancestors, ordinary human beings had only limited contact with the supernatural. The king, standing at the apex of society, constituted the most important link between human beings and the supernatural forces on which the welfare of both society and the universe depended. These relations were mediated by rituals that only kings or their deputies were able to perform.

Only the Shang rulers were able to sponsor the scapulimantic divination rituals (divining according to the cracks that appear on burnt bones) that allowed them, through their dead ancestors, to communicate with their high god, Shangdi. These divinations also made possible the correct sacrifices that ensured good crops and the welfare of the realm (K. Chang 1983: 44–45). Maya kings sought, by ritually shedding their own blood or ingesting hallucinogenic substances, to enter into trance states that would permit them to communicate with the spirits of their dead ancestors and with cosmic deities. In Egypt official doctrine maintained that only the king could make offerings to the gods in temples throughout Egypt, to the royal ancestors, or even to dead commoners in their graves. The ritual formula that transferred offerings to the life-force (*kꜣ*) of a dead person described them as 'a gift that the king gives'. Thus, in theory, even the water that a farmer poured onto the grave of a dead relative passed into the spirit world as a gift from the reigning monarch, whose presence caused Egypt to prosper (Gardiner 1950: 170–73). It has been suggested that in Egypt prolonged natural catastrophes at certain periods may have led to the slaying or deposing of kings who were judged incapable of sustaining the cosmic order (B. Bell 1971).

Their being regarded as the embodiment of the strength and vitality of the kingdom led to an emphasis on the health and vigour of individual kings. Egyptian pharaohs, after a thirty-year reign and at frequent intervals thereafter, celebrated a Sed ritual (*ḥb sd*) in the course of which they symbolically died and were reborn. This ritual was believed to renew an aging ruler's physical and mental powers (Gohary 1992). Egyptians believed that a similar renewal took place when an old king died and was replaced by his son. In general, the iconography of kingship in early civilizations emphasized youth, prowess, and martial skills. Egyptian kings were rarely, if ever, portrayed as old or feeble.

Because of their close association with supernatural forces kings were ascribed various divine attributes. The most extreme claims about the divinity of kings were made in large territorial states, where direct contact between the ruler and most of his subjects was very limited. Because royal authority was necessarily mediated through multiple levels of officials, the ruler was perceived as a remote being who affected people's lives in much the same way as deities or natural forces (thought to be the same), and this made it easier for ordinary people to accept the notion of the divinity of rulers.

The Egyptian state placed special emphasis on the king's being the son or earthly manifestation of the solar-creator god and hence a universal ruler. Like the sun, the king experienced endless cycles of death and rebirth. Kings claimed to be the earthly manifestation of all the major Egyptian gods, each of whom was associated with a particular community in Egypt and identified in that place as the creator deity. By nourishing all these gods as a son nourished the spirits of his dead ancestors, the king played a key role in maintaining the cosmic order (Frankfort 1948; Silverman 1991: 56–71). Living kings, alone of human beings, were referred to as gods (*nṯr*) during their lifetimes (Hornung 1997: 301). It was as a direct result of the supernatural power of kings that the enemies of Egypt were defeated and the Nile River flooded each year. Yet kings appear to have been viewed as divine only in the sense that their bodies, like cult images in the temples, were receptacles which various gods could enter. An individual king became endowed with such power as a consequence of enthronement rituals which involved his purification, ritual rebirth, and crowning by the gods (L. Bell 1997: 140; Goebs 1998: 340). As a consequence of these rituals, each successive king represented the rebirth and earthly renewal of the previous monarch (and ultimately of Horus), while dead kings were identified with Osiris, the unchanging ruler of the realms of the dead. It may be as the earthly incarnation of divine power that the reigning king was referred to as *nṯr nfr*, which is conventionally translated 'beautiful god' but may have meant 'young' or 'reincarnated' god (Hornung 1982: 138–42; Malek 1997: 227).

Egyptian Kings were believed to be so charged with supernatural power that simply touching them or their regalia without taking ritual precautions could cause serious injury. Yet, while they regulated the cosmos, they were not expected to perform miracles. If a trusted adviser became ill, the king ordered a royal physician to attend him. An elaborate funerary cult was maintained for each dead king in the expectation that, as the unchanging (ḏt) form of supernatural power, dead kings could bestow supernatural blessings on Egypt. Despite many scholarly suggestions to the contrary, it is clear that even in the Old Kingdom all dead human beings became ḏt forms, even if only very minor ones. Thus the difference between dead commoners and dead kings was the extent of their supernatural power rather than a difference in kind (O'Connor and Silverman 1995).

Subjects of the Inka kings were taught that the king was a descendant and earthly manifestation or counterpart of the sun god, Inti, and perhaps of the older creator god, Wiraqucha, as well. The sun was regarded as the immediate source and repository of power for each Inka ruler. As in Egypt, the cosmic order was thought to be re-created with each successive reign (MacCormack 1991: 117). The transformation in the king's nature that resulted from his installation rituals required him to remarry his chief wife, who now became his queen (*quya* [*coya*]), a practice that led many Spanish chroniclers to believe that an Inka ruler married his chief wife only after becoming king (MacCormack 1991: 125). Two hundred or more boys and girls were sacrificed throughout the kingdom as part of the royal enthronement rituals (Kendall 1973: 197). If the king became ill at any time, four llamas and four children were killed and large amounts of cloth burned to ensure his recovery (Murra 1980: 58).

Both living and dead Inka monarchs were viewed as playing key roles in promoting agricultural fertility and military success, activities that were closely linked in belief and ritual. Dead kings were believed to be reunited with the sun, although their mummified bodies, which maintained their personal identities, continued to be clothed and offered food as if they were alive. Each dead king was a locus of supernatural power and an important source of oracular pronouncements on political matters. Living and dead kings were thus regarded, as was the sun itself, as a source of life and prosperity for their descendants and for the Inka state as a whole (Gose 1996a). As in Egypt, the dead ancestors of ordinary people also looked after the welfare of their descendants; what distinguished dead kings in this regard was the source and extent of the power.

In China, the Shang kings performed sacrifices to Shangdi. Whether the god was the apical ancestor of the Shang royal clan as many experts believe, as the senior living descendant of the royal ancestors – whose spirits alone were able to communicate and intercede with Shangdi – the king was uniquely qualified to manipulate supernatural power in order to promote the well-being of the whole nation (K. Chang 1983). Kings referred to themselves as *yü i ren* (I, the unique [foremost] man), using the status-neutral term applied to males (*ren*) of any rank (Wheatley 1971: 52). Later Chinese kings, including those of the Zhou Dynasty, did not claim divine status, although they bore the title 'Son of Heaven', *tian* (sky) having either replaced Shangdi or become a new name for him (Hsu and Linduff 1988: 320–21). The spirits of dead kings were regarded as extremely powerful and were consulted through divination. Their cults were aligned with that of the ten different suns that were believed to shine on the world on successive days in a ten-day cycle, each being identified with a particular sun. Dead kings were offered human and animal sacrifices just as were the spiritual forces inherent in the natural world.

Among the other civilizations in our sample, which were composed of much smaller states, there was considerable variation in the extent of deification ascribed to rulers. The Yoruba kings shared political authority with the title-holders of powerful non-royal patrilineages. Yet kingship was regarded as a divine office, and kings were believed to possess extraordinary supernatural powers that enabled them to ensure the fertility of their realm and the well-being of its people (Bradbury 1973: 74). Kings were venerated as the vehicles through which divine power was channelled into the human world, animating human beings as well as plants, animals, rivers, and the atmosphere. To protect people from their supernatural powers, kings were ritually secluded in their palaces. While each Yoruba state carefully remembered the names of its successive individual rulers, royal power was viewed as a continuous presence. Each successive ruler was endowed with an unbroken continuity of such power and spoke of what his royal predecessors had done as if their deeds had been his own (K. Barber 1991: 51). An oba's authority was described as 'unchallengeable' and his power 'like that of the gods' (Pemberton and Afolayan 1996: 1). In Benin asserting that the king performed human acts such as eating, sleeping, washing, or dying was an offence punishable by death (Bradbury 1957: 40).

Only Yoruba kings could perform the rituals that were crucial for the well-being of their land and people. The powers of dead kings were transmitted to their successors in rituals that involved the new king's ingesting small portions of his predecessor's body. Nevertheless, individual kings who grew senile or whose behaviour seriously displeased their councils might be slain. Many Yoruba still believe that gods take possession of ordinary humans for brief periods and speak and act through them as ordinary worshippers enter into trance in the course of rituals. Kings, it would seem, were believed, in the course of their installation ceremonies, to become possessed of the power of various deities, which remained with them for the rest of their lives or so long as they remained healthy and ritually pure. These rituals were accompanied by human sacrifices intended to increase the power of the king. While the spirits of all dead Yoruba were venerated by their descendants, who sought to benefit from their supernatural protection and support, the spirits of rulers were the objects of especially elaborate cults. Because their power benefited the living ruler, as did the power of cosmic deities, it helped to sustain the entire realm (Pemberton and Afolayan 1996: 73). The cult of royal ancestors was most elaborate in Benin, where each dead king was provided with a separate ritual compound (*ugha*) with its own altar (Bradbury 1957: 55). Yet here too royal power, although supernatural in origin, tended to be quantitatively rather than qualitatively different from that of other people.

The Maya term for 'ruler' that was commonly used after A.D. 400, *k'ul ahaw*, has been interpreted as signifying a leader with divine power or godlike status. Maya rulers wore the costumes and attributes of various gods and bore names that incorporated references to numerous deities. At Tikal these references often were to Kawil, a god of fertility and dynastic continuity; at Naranjo they were to Chak, the storm and rain god (Houston 2001; Martin and Grube 2000: 17). They may have been thought to receive supernatural powers in the course of installation or heir-designation rituals. There is, however, no evidence that they were believed to be gods. Dead rulers, in contrast, were identified with ancestral heroes and major cosmic deities, apparently while retaining their own personalities, and were worshipped in elaborate mortuary temples that each king had erected for that purpose (Freidel and Schele 1988a; Houston and Stuart 1996).

Finally, the Maya appear to have believed that, while rulers died, kingship was eternal. The succession of Maya rulers resembled the periodic deaths and rebirths of the gods who had presided over the universe in successive cycles since the beginning of time. Every Maya king symbolically re-emerged from the underworld at the time of his accession to direct the social order and passed back into the underworld, as the sun did at the end of each day, at the time of his death. The notion of royal sons' giving rebirth to the fathers who had engendered them has been described as the central mystery of official Maya religion (Freidel, Schele, and Parker 1993: 281). Yet, by Late Classic times this cyclical renewal was iconographically less important than chronicling the linear succession of specific rulers in each Maya city-state. This was made possible by the invention of the calendrical long count, which permitted short cycles of time to be viewed as segments of an endless, ongoing series (A. Miller 1986).

The Aztec and the other inhabitants of the Valley of Mexico believed that deities entered and possessed the bodies of their worshippers for varying lengths of time. At the installation of new kings, elaborate rituals were performed in the course of which the king was dressed in the regalia of major cosmic deities. These rituals were intended to ensure that the powers of these deities came to reside in the king and allowed him to ensure good harvests, lead armies to victory, and govern the state wisely (Clendinnen 1991: 78–81; Townsend 1989). The Aztec king was identified as the surrogate of Xiuhtecuhtli, the creator and fire god, who, as a manifestation of Ometeotl, controlled the central axis of the universe. Having this supreme ancestral deity as his patron did not, however, prevent the Aztec king from identifying with other major deities who were Xiuhtecuhtli's progeny (Heyden 1989: 39–41).

In this manner Aztec kings became divine (*teotl*) even if they were not regarded as gods. It was said that their lips and tongues became those of gods, since the gods spoke through them, and that they were the ears, eyes, and fangs of the gods (Townsend 1992: 205; López Austin 1988, 1: 398–99). Once installed, a monarch was expected to launch a military campaign that would demonstrate his newly acquired powers and produce a large number of prisoners for the sacrifice to the gods that would complete his installation. At their funerals, Aztec kings were again dressed in the costumes of leading cosmic deities, one on top of the other, in order to be identified with these gods prior to cremation (Heyden 1989: 41). The human sacrifices that are reported to have been made at regular intervals to strengthen King Mochtezuma II's *tonali* soul (the source of his vigour and rationality) may have been intended to nourish the special divine powers dwelling within him (Clendinnen 1991: 82). While Aztec kings were treated with great reverence, there is no evidence that they were thought to be different in essence from other members of the hereditary nobility (Read 1994). Instead, they were men in whom supernatural powers manifested themselves to a unique degree. Although the ashes of dead kings were interred in the platform of the chief state temple, there was no state cult of dead kings.

Mesopotamian concepts of kingship likewise were grounded in religion. The Sumerians believed that the gods had invented kingship as the most effective means for governing themselves and had then transmitted it to humans. Joan Oates (1978: 476) argues that the position of king (en or ensi) had evolved from a paramount male temple ritual office most commonly associated with female deities who were the patrons of city-states. In cities where the chief patron deity was male and therefore the en priest was female, kingship passed into the hands of a lugal (literally 'big man'), whose office may have been derived from that of a part-time military leader. Only after the Early Dynastic period did these titles begin to form a hierarchy in which lugal, now construed to mean 'hegemon', took precedence over ensi, meaning 'city ruler' or 'governor' (Hallo 1957).

Early Dynastic Mesopotamian rulers were viewed as human beings occupying much the same position in relation to a city's patron deity as the steward or foreman of an estate owner. The power that a ruler enjoyed as a result of the approval and support of the gods was symbolized by his being invested with the divine emblems of kingship – a crown, the throne of life, the sceptre of justice, and a mace to control the people – that were believed to have been sent to earth with kingship itself (Postgate 1992: 261–63).

It was the duty of Mesopotamian kings to ensure that deities were well fed, clothed, and housed. They risked divine punishment if they failed to carry out a god's wishes. A prudent king might, however, reasonably expect the favour and protection of his city's patron deity in return for his personal good behaviour and diligent conduct of his city's affairs. Kings received divine revelations and commands in dreams and visions. To avoid unwittingly offending the gods, they constantly sought through divination to ascertain the will of deities. The only inherently supernatural aspect of kingship was that kings, together with female priests or women of the royal household, impersonated major deities during the annual New Year's rituals that were associated with fertility and cosmic renewal. Presumably the power of these deities entered into the king and other participants during this brief period (Postgate 1992: 265–66).

Ironically, Mesopotamia, the civilization whose kings were perceived as most human, was the only one whose legends portrayed proud or impious kings taunting and insulting deities (Pritchard 1955: 84). These tales, however, illustrated that it was impossible for even the most ambitious humans to oppose the gods or acquire their powers. Mesopotamian rulers sometimes sought to escape divine wrath when they learned about it through divination by temporarily appointing a person of humble origin as a substitute king whose death might assuage the anger of gods. Such a substitute was slain after the danger had passed (Frankfort 1948: 262–65).

During the Akkadian dominance over Mesopotamia (2350–2190 B.C.) and again in the Ur III period (2112–2004 B.C.), hegemonic kings attempted to claim divine status. Their names were written after the classificatory sign (taxogram) that indicated a god, they were shown wearing horned headdresses like those of gods, and legal oaths had to be sworn in their names as well as those of deities. Some of these kings also established elaborate mortuary cults. It may have been in this context that some of the more celebrated rulers of the Early Dynastic period, such as Gilgamesh, who was claimed as an ancestor by the Ur III kings, began to be described as gods or demigods. Yet these claims failed to win widespread acceptance, and later, more powerful kings such as those of Assyria shunned such pretensions. Once the human status of kings had been established, it was impossible even for the most successful hegemons or hereditary rulers to transcend it (Engnell 1967; Frankfort 1948: 297–99; Postgate 1992: 266–67).

The rulers of early civilizations invariably claimed divine support, and most of them were believed to be endowed with divine powers. The most far-reaching claims were made in Egypt and among the Inka, both large states in which rulers tended to be remote from their subjects, but even here the human nature of the individual ruler was acknowledged. Strong claims of divinity in rulers were made among the Yoruba, whose heads of state were ritually secluded from their subjects. The weakest claims were found among the Mesopotamians, who in Early Dynastic times had become the most urbanized people in our sample and therefore the best able to observe their rulers at close range. The failure of Mesopotamian hegemons to achieve divine status suggests that historical as well as functional factors helped to shape the image of kings in these societies.

Kings also claimed to be the descendants of major cosmic deities. According to one version of Egyptian cosmology, at the beginning of time Egypt had been ruled by Atum or Re (the solar-creator deity), and he was followed in succession by his son Shu (air), Shu's son Geb (the earth), and Geb's son Osiris. Each of these deities had in turn withdrawn into a cosmic realm, leaving Osiris's son (or reincarnation) Horus to rule Egypt. All later Egyptian kings were linear descendants of Horus, who, after death, became identified with Osiris, the quintessential dead ruler (Meeks and Favard-Meeks 1996: 16–32). The Inka kings maintained that the sun god was the divine ancestor of their dynasty, his beams having engendered (either at Lake Titicaca or in the caves of Paqariktambo, near Cuzco) four pairs of males and females from one of which the Inka royal family was descended (Urton 1990). The Shang rulers belonged to the senior descent line of the Zi clan, which, according to a legend recorded at a later date, was descended from a mortal woman who had been made pregnant by a black bird that may have been Shangdi and was perhaps also identified with the sun (K. Chang 1976: 167). Yoruba kings each claimed to be descended from one of the sixteen sons of Oduduwa, the god who had lowered himself from the sky on an iron chain to create the world (Bascom 1969: 10–12). In Benin a descendant of Oduduwa replaced a previous dynasty of *ogiso* (sky kings) that had been deposed for misrule (Ben-Amos and Rubin 1983: 21; Egharevba 1960: 1–6). The Aztec rulers and the nobility in the Valley of Mexico traced their descent from an incarnation of the god Quetzalcoatl, who had ruled at the ancient city of Tollan (M. E. Smith 1996: 37–38). Maya rulers likewise traced their lineages back to one or more major deities of their pantheon (Houston and Stuart 1996: 290). The blood of Maya kings and of the descendants of kings was believed to be specially charged with supernatural power. Only Mesopotamian kings did not normally claim descent from the gods.

These claims established a genealogical affinity between kings and cosmic deities. They also implied that kings differed from commoners in origin and nature. Myths of this sort did not, however, clearly distinguish kings from hereditary nobles who were descended from earlier rulers. In the case of the Aztec and Inka nobility or the Yoruba royal clans, these descendants might be quite numerous. A Shang or Zhou king was further distinguished as the highest-ranking member of the senior lineage of the royal clan, which endowed him with indisputable genealogical superiority and ritual power. The Egyptians claimed that individual kings were fathered by the sun god, Re, who had taken possession of the reigning king's body at the time of their procreation. While rulers such as the New Kingdom Pharaoh Ramesses II might boast that their divine conception had set them apart from other humans even when they were still in the womb, the only proof that they had been conceived in a special manner was their eventual succession to the throne (Hornung 1982: 142). Claims like these generally emphasized not kings' uniqueness but their leadership roles, and they appear to have given kings powers that were greater than but not inherently different from those possessed by other humans. It was installation rituals that played the pivotal role in endowing kings with the supernatural powers that set them apart from other people. In the course of these rituals, which generally involved fasting, penance, and being invested with diverse regalia associated with deities, kings were identifed with various gods and acquired their divine powers. Egyptian and Yoruba rulers and perhaps others also became reincarnations of their predecessors. The sacred powers acquired in the course of these rituals were henceforth symbolized by the veneration with which rulers were treated, by the distinctive costumes they wore, and by the special regalia, such as crowns, staffs, and royal thrones or stools, that they alone were permitted to use. Like the kings themselves, these objects were often thought to be charged with supernatural power. While Mesopotamian kings were normally not believed to possess supernatural powers in their own right, even they enjoyed the special protection and support of the tutelary deities of their city-states. Installation rituals transformed kings into intermediaries between the human and the divine.

As individuals, kings remained human and mortal, but as incumbents of a sacred office they were set apart from all other humans as the result of having acquired unique supernatural powers. These powers enhanced their authority but also tended to delimit the scope of what they could do (Postgate 1992: 274). Supreme political power was universally understood and expressed in religious terms. Kings, like the cosmic gods, possessed powers to assist and harm human beings. To their subjects these powers must have resembled the immense forces that were inherent in the natural realm.

Some early civilizations emphasized possession of supernatural powers more than others. Those that most stressed such powers tended to be ones in which states were larger and kings more remote from most of their subjects. Yet the failure of increasingly powerful Mesopotamian kings to achieve recognition for claims to possess divine powers reveals that cultural traditions played a major role in determining to what extent kings were regarded as divine. Nevertheless, in Mesopotamia no less than in other early civilizations, political power was conceptualized in supernatural rather than simply political or economic terms.

RETAINER SACRIFICE

An interesting indication of how kings were viewed in early civilizations is the extent to which retainers and other human victims, willingly or unwillingly, were slain at the funerals of kings and high-ranking members of the nobility. There is evidence of retainer sacrifice in the early phases of both Egyptian and Mesopotamian civilizations. Hundreds of female and male servants, as well as artisans, were slain and buried around the Egyptian royal funerary complexes of the First Dynasty at Abydos and in smaller numbers around the tombs of the highest-ranking officials at Memphis (Edwards 1985: 23). Substantial numbers of retainers were interred in what are generally considered to have been Early Dynastic royal burials at Ur in Mesopotamia, although the female burials may have been those of high-ranking en priestesses rather than queens (Pollock 1999: 211). Some memory of this practice may survive in later Mesopotamian epic poetry, which speaks of servants' accompanying deceased rulers to the underworld (Kramer 1963: 130). Yet these sorts of killings do not appear to have persisted for long in cultures in which human victims were not regularly sacrificed to the gods.

Among the Aztec, Maya, and Yoruba, who regularly made human sacrifices to deities, human victims were slain in the course of high-status funerals. Human sacrifice was regularly part of the burial rituals of Yoruba and Benin kings (S. Johnson 1921: 44, 55). At Benin members of the oba's bodyguard were among those slain. In addition, wives and slaves of rulers committed suicide so that they could continue to serve them after death (Egharevba 1960: 76; Lucas 1948: 256). Human victims were also periodically sacrificed as part of the cult of deceased kings (Bradbury 1957: 39, 55).

The Shang interred up to several hundred humans in royal graves. While it has been suggested that most of these victims were foreign captives, archaeological data indicate that they represented a cross-section of royal retainers – women, officials, guards, and servants – as well as some prisoners of war. The latter were often decapitated or dismembered and had their hands tied behind their backs at the time of death (Keightley 1969: 369–77). Human beings were also sacrificed periodically, along with various domestic animals, and buried around the graves and ancestral temples of deceased members of the royal family. These practices appear never to have been extensive at the Zhou court, even during the Shang period, and died out completely during the succeeding Zhou Dynasty (Chêng 1960: 69–79; Hsu and Linduff 1988: 172).

It is reported that when an Inka king died, his favourite secondary wives, servants, and some officials were strangled, many of them voluntarily. In addition, one thousand boys and girls five to six years old, many of them children of the non-Inka provincial nobility (Betanzos 1996: 131–33), were assembled and buried in pairs throughout the kingdom. Among the Shang and the Inka, retainer sacrifice was practised on a much smaller scale at the burial of major officials.

Whatever the purposes served by the killing of humans in funerary contexts, it is clear that it was not a unitary phenomenon. Some killings appear to have been, like animal sacrifices, blood offerings intended to strengthen the soul of the dead person with the victim's life-force. This appears to have been the case with the humblest Shang and Inka funerary killings. At least some Yoruba human sacrifices made after the time of burial were charged with carrying messages and requests for supernatural assistance to the deceased (Connah 1987: 145), but these sacrifices also appear to have been intended to nourish and strengthen the spirit of the dead person. Sacrifices of this sort closely resembled those made to cosmic deities. In other cases it seems that household servants and officials were buried with, or near, a dead king or member of the upper class so that their souls might accompany and continue to serve that person. The killing of people, whether to nourish or to serve the dead, was a form of conspicuous consumption and thus a striking symbol of the deceased's high status, but its restriction to societies in which human beings as well as animals were regularly sacrificed to the gods suggests that it was associated with the equation of kings (including dead ones) with supernatural power. It is also significant that a more restrained form of retainer sacrifice was practised by high officials in societies where it was an attribute of royal burial practices, Mesopotamia being the exception. While kings were publicly recognized as being politically and symbolically unique, they were also identified in terms of ritual treatment as members of the upper classes.

VALIDATING POWER

Kings everywhere validated their claims to both temporal and supernatural power through their lavish lifestyles. Regardless of the extent of their power, kings, high officials, and their families lived in splendid palaces, wore magnificent clothes and elaborate jewellery, and were served by a large number of retainers. They also entertained lavishly and bestowed rare and valued presents on their principal supporters. The style and customs of the royal court set a standard that other people emulated to whatever extent they could afford and the law permitted. The wealth of kings provided visible evidence of their high social standing and the power of their kingdoms. At the same time kings were assiduous in their public and private devotions to the supernatural: building temples, making elaborate sacrifices to the gods, and presiding over lavish rituals that ensured the proper functioning of the universe and the welfare of society.

They also had to guard their personal authority in their relations with others. Their interactions with their subjects were heavily ritualized and governed by special etiquette. Among the Inka, for example, even the highest officials had to wear simple clothes, go barefoot, and carry small sacks on their shoulders when they were granted an audience with the king (Rowe 1944: 259). Among the Aztec and elsewhere, making eye contact with the ruler was forbidden. Kings tended to spend much of their time in the private apartments of their palaces, to which few people other than their servants had access, granting audiences to only a select few of their subjects and appearing in public only in connection with major rituals and communal festivities. Royal seclusion was carried farthest among the Yoruba, whose kings rarely left the inner quarters of their palaces and appeared in public only with their faces hidden by the beaded fringe of their crowns (Bascom 1969: 30–31).

To protect their supernatural powers and maintain their ability to communicate with and influence the supernatural, kings were expected to observe various taboos and penances. Major rituals sometimes required purification, fasting, sexual abstinence, and staying awake for long periods. Maya rulers subjected themselves to painful blood-letting to induce trances that facilitated communication with the supernatural (Schele and Miller 1986). Mesopotamian kings had their faces ritually slapped once a year by the high priest of their city's patron deity to remind them of the need for humility in their relations with the gods (Kuhrt 1987: 33).

Kings also had to be able to manage the political affairs of their kingdoms effectively. Many kings led armies into battle, and their ability to defeat foreign enemies both reflected and reinforced their political power. In centralized states powerful kings could, if necessary, use force to maintain public order and keep both officials and subject peoples under control. Where power was less centralized, kings had to rely more on their persuasive and diplomatic skills (Apter 1992). The political role of kings in preindustrial states was summarized in an observation that Arab writers attributed to the sixth-century-A.D. Persian monarch Khosrow I. He is supposed to have remarked that a kingdom could prosper only if its ruler had the skill to curb the rapacity of his officials so that agriculture and craft production might flourish and support the taxation system on which royal power depended (R. McC. Adams 1965: 71). Even an astute Yoruba king could transcend the severe physical and political limitations of his office to curb mutually destructive competition among rival members of the upper classes and enhance his own authority.

Finally, it is we, not the people who lived in early civilizations, who differentiate between political and sacred power. The Yoruba believed that a king who channelled supernatural energy into the human realm played no less a role in defeating foreign enemies than did the non-royal hereditary official who led the state's armies. The New Year's rituals that played a major role in Mesopotamian state religious observances, by reenacting and thus renewing the creation of the world and the establishment of kingship among the gods, affirmed the parallelism between the earthly realm and that of the celestial deities on which the prosperity of the earth depended (Hooke 1958). In Egypt the same verb (*ḫʿi*) designated the appearance of a king in glory upon his throne and the dawn, and the generational cycle by which a young king succeeded an older one complemented the daily birth, death, and rebirth of the sun and the annual Nile flood. Royal succession was as essential as these natural cycles because it renewed the cosmic power by which the gods and hence the universe, no less than Egypt itself, were maintained (Frankfort 1948: 148–61). In a culture in which kingship was perceived to be 'a power like that of the gods' and essential for maintaining the cosmic order, such parallels embraced both the central ideology and the practical role of kingship.

6 States: City and Territorial

A state is a politically organized society that is regarded by those who live in it as sovereign or politically independent and has leaders who control its social, political, legal, economic, and cultural activities. Two sorts of state appear to have been associated with early civilizations: city-states and territorial states.

The term 'city-state' has long been employed to describe the polities of Classical Greece, Renaissance Italy, and parts of ancient Southwest Asia (Griffeth and Thomas 1981). J. Eric Thompson (1954: 81–82) designated Classic Maya polities as city-states in the mid-twentieth century. More recently, city-states have been identified as the normal form of early state (Nichols and Charlton 1997) or as one of two types of state that prevailed from antiquity until the nineteenth century (Hansen 2000). City-states were relatively small polities, each consisting of an urban core surrounded by farmland containing smaller units of settlement. In territorial states a ruler governed a larger region through a multilevelled hierarchy of provincial and local administrators in a corresponding hierarchy of administrative centres. The distinction between these two types of states, as they are associated with early civilizations, rests not only on the size of territories but also on differences in the nature of their urban centres and in their economic and political organization. Each of the civilizations being studied consisted of city-states or territorial states but not both.

The distinction was foreshadowed when Childe (1928; 1934) first contrasted the development of civilization in Egypt and in southern Mesopotamia. He noted that in southern Mesopotamia monumental architecture, luxury crafts, and writing had developed within a network of small city-states, while in Egypt similar developments had occurred under the sponsorship of a single royal court, all the tiny chiefdoms and early states that had evolved along the Nile River north of Aswan during the late fourth millennium B.C. having been united under the enduring sovereignty of a divine monarch. He attributed this difference to variations in natural settings and in the techniques devised to extract surpluses from peasant producers. This distinction was adopted and extended by Henri Frankfort (1956) and more recently by Charles Maisels (1990).

Many anthropologists do not accept this dichotomy. The majority of these see civilizations as evolving in a unilinear fashion from something resembling Colin Renfrew's (1975) early-state module into city-states, territorial states, and finally empires (Allchin 1995; Renfrew 1997; D. Wilson 1997; Yoffee 1997). In this scheme, city-states and territorial states constitute successive stages in the development of larger and more complex polities rather than alternative forms of political organization that occur at the same level of complexity. Michael Mann (1986), who emphasizes the logistical problems inherent in controlling preindustrial societies, argues that small city-states were of necessity typical of early civilizations, although he acknowledges that ancient Egypt and China developed larger and more unitary states at an early period. It has also been argued that the hegemonic patterns in both Mesopotamia and the Valley of Mexico provide examples of city-state systems evolving towards territorial states (Sanders, Parsons, and Santley 1979: 163).

Marcus (1998: 92) maintains, in contrast, that the first states to appear in any region were territorial states, most of which later broke apart to produce clusters of city-states. She regards it as unlikely that a group of chiefdoms could evolve directly into a set of city-states. The development of extremely large urban centres at very early stages of civilizations such as Uruk in prehistoric Mesopotamia, Teotihuacan in the Valley of Mexico, and El Mirador in the Maya lowlands offers apparent support for this scenario. While much remains to be learned about how the earliest civilizations developed, the long persistence of both types in different regions of the world suggests that territorial states and city-states are stable alternatives rather than sequential stages in the development of more complex societies.

I agree that larger political entities must have evolved from small-scale beginnings. Yet it appears that the rate at which greater size and complexity developed differed significantly from one early civilization to another, as did the relations among political and cultural variables. In trying to impose a unilinear scheme on the development of Egyptian and Mesopotamian civilizations, Steward (1949) was forced, by the primary importance that he accorded to political criteria, to equate the Late Predynastic period, which immediately preceded the political unification of Egypt, with the Early Dynastic period that preceded political unification in Mesopotamia. Yet in Egypt the Late Predynastic period preceded the development of significant monumental architecture or an elite art style, while in Mesopotamia these features were already present long before the Early Dynastic period. Renfrew's early-state module, a political unit occupying approximately fifteen hundred square kilometres with a population averaging about ten thousand people and a principal settlement near the centre, resembles a small early city-state, but it fails to capture the considerable variation in size and political organization that was exhibited by the early states that European explorers encountered in places such as Buganda, South Africa, Hawaii, and eastern North America (Claessen and Skalník 1978; Cohen and Service 1978; Haas 1982). The evidence suggests much greater diversity in political organization than can be accounted for by a unilinear evolutionary model. The distinction between city-states and territorial states is an attempt to recognize that diversity.

CITY-STATES

Early city-state civilizations consisted of a network of adjacent, self-governing city-states. City-states rarely occurred in geographical isolation in early civilizations, although in later periods in the Middle East isolated cities such as Petra and Palmyra developed along trade routes. The territory controlled by a small city-state might be less than ten kilometres across, although exceptionally wealthy or powerful city-states might exceed one hundred kilometres in diameter. City-states also varied in the concentration of their settlement. Contrary to Anthony Giddens's (1981) claim that carefully delineated boundaries between polities are associated only with modern nation-states, boundaries between early city-states were clearly demarcated by natural features, artificial markers, or walled fortifications. Sentinels or armed guards were often stationed at such frontiers (McAnany 1995: 85–89). Most city-states had populations of between five thousand and twenty thousand people, but some hegemonic city-states were considerably more populous.

In our sample there are four examples of city-state civilizations: southern Mesopotamia, the Yoruba and Benin states of West Africa, the Valley of Mexico, and the Classic Maya. Agricultural settlement is documented in southern Mesopotamia by at least the fifth millennium B.C. (Redman 1978) (Fig. 6.1). For the Uruk period, between 3500 and 3200 B.C., there is evidence of increasing social stratification, organized warfare, urban centres, and a city-state system. There is also evidence of large public buildings, monumental art, bronze-casting, cylinder seals, and the earliest record-keeping. By far the largest city in southern Mesopotamia at this period was Uruk (Erech), which in the Late Uruk period occupied one hundred hectares and by Early Dynastic I times had expanded to four hundred hectares and may have had a

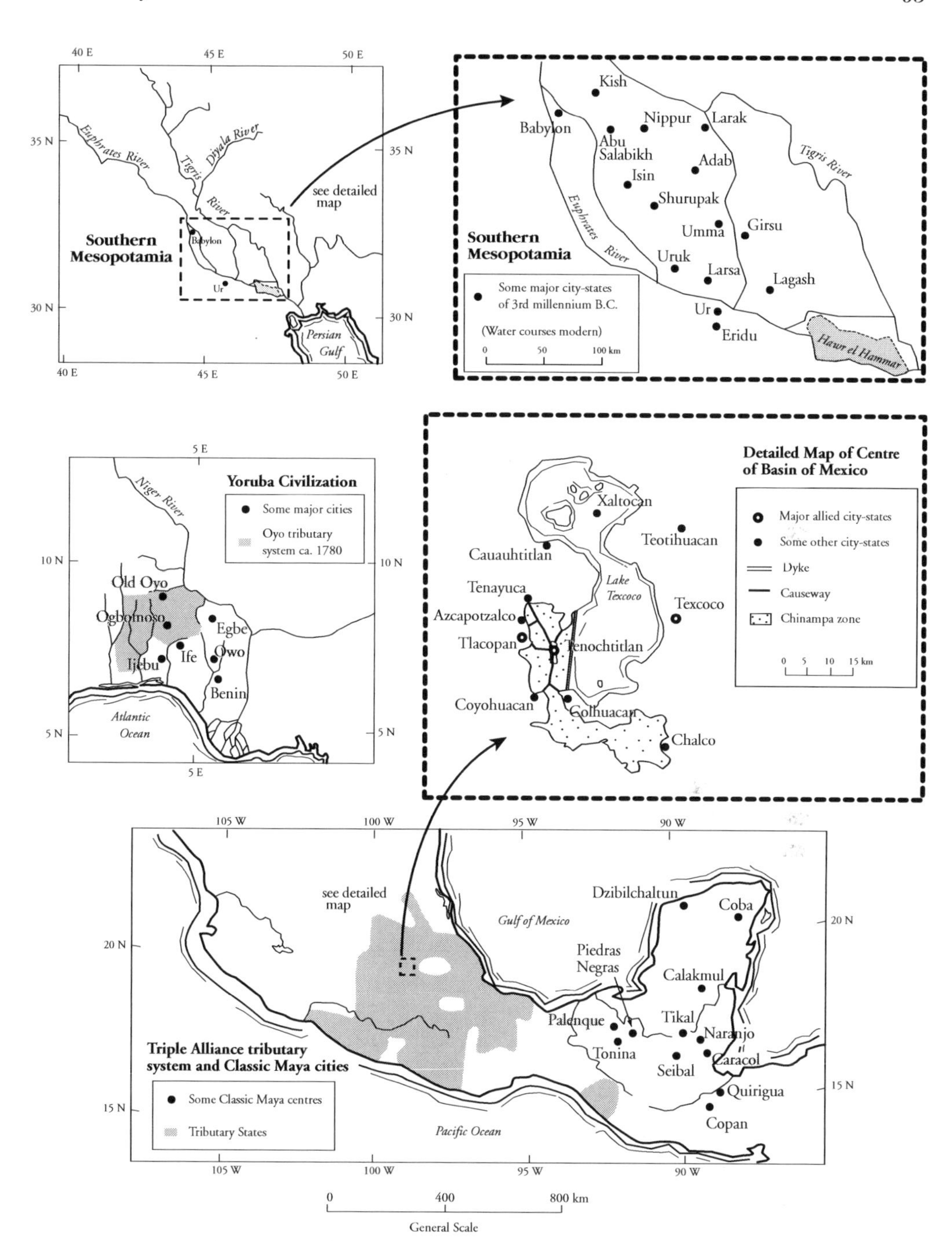

6.1. Maps of city-state civilizations at common scale (same scale as map 6.2).

population of forty thousand to fifty thousand people (R. McC. Adams 1981: 71, 85). The Uruk period thus witnessed the development of early civilization in southern Mesopotamia. While there has been some linguistically based speculation about ethnic changes prior to the Uruk period, there is striking continuity in the culture of southern Mesopotamia from Uruk times into the historical period. Yet archaeological data indicate that social and political organization may have altered radically at the end of the Uruk period, which some scholars interpret as a time of severe political disruption (Pollock 1999; Yoffee 1995: 286–88). A city-state system persisted in southern Mesopotamia for over fifteen hundred years, until lasting regional unification was brought about following the Old Babylonian dynasty.

Possibly beginning as early as the Uruk period, the inhabitants of some thirty city-states recognized southern Mesopotamia as a region (*kallam*) that possessed cultural unity, although it may already have been seen as divided into a largely Sumerian-speaking region (*kiengi*) in the south and an Akkadian-speaking region (*kiuri*) in the north. From early times the temple of Enlil in Nippur, a city that marked the division between these two territories, may have been, if not the centre of a league of city-states, at least a neutral location where representatives of these city-states could meet to regulate their affairs (Maisels 1999: 160–63; Postgate 1992: 34–38; Van De Mieroop 1999: 222–24).

Although the archaeological documentation is less extensive, Yoruba civilization evolved from a West African village society based on a largely indigenous agricultural complex. The origin of Ile Ife, which has remained the ritual centre of Yoruba civilization, appears to date at least from the ninth century A.D. Ife was at the apogee of its political power and prosperity from the eleventh to the fifteenth centuries. About this time another city, Oba, flourished to the northwest, possibly at the site of Esie. By the fifteenth century Owe rivalled Ife, and for two hundred years it was the cultural link between Ife and the emerging state of Benin (Edo), which, although Ewe-speaking, became in terms of its upper-class culture an integral part of the Yoruba sphere. In the sixteenth century, the city-state of Oyo, in the northwest, became dominant, exerting its power for the next two hundred years over Yoruba states to the south and east of Ife but never seeking to control Ife itself. In the south, Ijebu Ode controlled the coast between Benin and Lagos from the fifteenth to the eighteenth century (Pemberton and Afolayan 1996: 1–2). In the eighteenth and nineteenth centuries, Oyo and Benin were the most powerful states. Thus civilization has flourished in the Yoruba region in the form of a series of city-states for over one thousand years (Connah 1975; 1987; Ryder 1969; 1984; Shaw 1978; Willett 1973). Some Yoruba urban centres have persisted throughout that period, others have come into existence or disappeared, and still others have moved to safer locations. In historical times the Yoruba region had twenty or more kings and more than one hundred subordinate rulers of towns or groups of villages (R. Smith 1969: 8).

The pattern of city-states recorded in the Valley of Mexico in the early sixteenth century was the most recent of a series of city-state configurations beginning about 650 B.C. By that time the valley had a series of well-defined settlement hierarchies, the top level of which consisted of sites with several thousand inhabitants and civic-ceremonial architecture. By 350 B.C. Cuicuilco, in the southwestern quadrant of the valley, covered at least four hundred hectares, had a population estimated to have been about twenty thousand, and contained temple platforms up to twenty metres high. Teotihuacan, in the northeast quadrant, probably equalled or exceeded Cuicuilco in size and population. From this point on, periods in which one or a few powerful city-states dominated regional settlement patterns alternated with periods in which city-states tended to be more equal in size and power. Centralization was characteristic of the period between A.D. 100 and 750, when Teotihuacan was dominant, the period between 950 and 1150, when Tula was the leading centre, and the Late period, when the Aztec and their Texcocan allies became the most powerful and populous of some forty to sixty city-states in the valley (Charlton and Nichols 1997b; Hodge 1984). While the Aztec state of Tenochtitlan may have had a population of two hundred and fifty thousand, most other states had between five thousand and fifty thousand inhabitants.

It is not clear how much ethnic continuity there was in the Valley of Mexico over this two-thousand-year period. It is also unknown how long Nahuatl-speaking people have lived in the region. Strong cultural continuity resulted from new arrivals' assimilating local cultural traditions. The Aztec's own history of their city-state offers an official account of the evolution of Tenochtitlan from the time when landless Nahuatl-speaking immigrants established it as a semirural community in 1325 until it had become the dominant city-state in the valley in the mid-fifteenth century. While the Aztec claimed to have come from the north, they quickly adopted local institutions and cultural patterns. Similar but less detailed information is available concerning the older city-state of Texcoco. Despite varying degrees of hegemony and efforts by rulers to control and sometimes even to absorb neighbouring city-states, there is no evidence in the Valley of Mexico, any more than among the Yoruba, of city-states' being replaced by territorial ones. Nor does the extraordinary compression of population into one major urban centre during the Teotihuacan period support the idea that city-states developed from a primordial territorial state.

Classic Maya civilization grew out of a tradition of urbanism and monumental architecture that had become widespread in the Maya lowlands during the

Late Preclassic period (400 B.C.–A.D. 250), but some of its most distinctive features, such as its calendrical long count, stela complex, and increasing focus on kingship, first appeared in the Tikal area in the third century A.D. and gradually spread from there. Among the Maya a state was identified by the presence of a sacred king, but where an administrative centre lacks monumental art and hence official texts there is no way to determine whether its head was a minor king who lacked the resources or authority to erect stone monuments or a subordinate, non-royal official. Therefore it cannot be determined whether small centres remained kingdoms and were merely rendered tributary to powerful neighbours or whether they were organically incorporated into larger states. (A similar uncertainty would apply to the Valley of Mexico in 1519 were it not for extensive Spanish documentation.) In Late Preclassic times El Mirador was the largest Maya urban centre. In the Classic period Tikal appears to have been the most powerful city-state until A.D. 562, when it was encircled and defeated by an alliance of Calakmul and other city-states, including Caracol. Calakmul remained the most powerful state until A.D. 695, when it in turn was defeated by Tikal. After A.D. 750 power appears to have been shared among a growing number of smaller independent centres (Folan et al. 1995; Sharer 1996).

Assuming that each Maya site that had its own emblem glyph was a separate state, Peter Mathews (1991: 29) argues that in Late Classic times there were sixty or more Maya city-states, each controlling about twenty-five hundred square kilometres. Any larger units took the form of short-lived tributary systems in which defeated states remained self-governing. Marcus (1976; 1992b; 1993) has suggested that only polities much larger than this would have been true states, smaller ones having been de facto chiefdoms. While some Yoruba, especially in the northeast, lived in chiefdoms, documentary evidence indicates that many small political units, both among the Yoruba and in the Valley of Mexico, were organized as states. Marcus also argues that the large number of Maya kingdoms documented after A.D. 750 indicates not that existing kings were beginning to erect monuments but that the governors of outlying provinces of large states were declaring their independence and becoming kings in their own right.

R. E. W. Adams (1986: 437) has proposed that in Late Classic times there were only eight Maya regional states, each extending over about thirty thousand square kilometres. Other Mayanists have envisioned some thirty states, each averaging about eight thousand square kilometres (Chase and Chase 1996: 805). Some of the largest of these states had at least two levels of regional centres above that of villages. In the course of their development, dominant centres appear to have subordinated neighbouring minor polities by removing their sacred rulers or preventing their emergence. Less complete integration would have created states that were precarious unions of small polities whose rulers continued to nurture hopes of independence. The extraordinary flourishing of major Maya centres suggests that more complete integration was frequently achieved. This pattern was very different from the one associated with the growth of Mesopotamian city-states, whereby the populations of most surrounding communities were incorporated into evolving central urban complexes (Adams and Nissen 1972). The largest Mayan state was probably Tikal, which may have controlled 21,095 square kilometres prior to its defeat and the loss of some of its dependencies in A.D. 562 (Chase and Chase 1996: 805). This area may, however, have included some tributary states as well as the subordinate centres that were an integral part of the Tikal polity.

Although larger Maya centres fought with each another and sometimes reduced one another to tributary status, it seems that they did not try to incorporate each other to form still larger states. Instead they aimed to reduce rival states to self-governing but tributary status for as long as possible. After its defeat, Tikal, for example, continued to be ruled by its own sacred king. This may explain why victorious kings only rarely recorded their successes on monuments erected in the major polities they had defeated (Webster 1998: 317). The survival of sacred kings at centres such as Tikal during periods of subordination to other centres and the relative ease with which such states seem to have freed themselves from domination by powerful neighbours suggest that the control of defeated states by their victorious neighbours remained weak and indirect.

While Anne Pyburn (1997) is correct that, in terms of size, the distinction between city-states and territorial states may be arbitrary, Maya polities appear to fall into the general size range of city-states. They also resemble city-states far more closely than they do territorial states in terms of social, economic, and cultural criteria. Comparisons with other city-state systems are complicated by the unusually dispersed nature of Maya rural and urban settlement and by our very limited understanding of Maya administrative systems. In having a more dispersed population and therefore more secondary centres, Maya states resemble Yoruba ones more closely than they do the compactly settled city-states of the Valley of Mexico and Mesopotamia.

Each city-state usually had a centrally located capital city. The central location of the capital maximized the mutual accessibility of rulers and their subjects, made the capital most easily accessible to rural dwellers, and offered the city maximum protection against attacks from neighbouring city-states. Urban centres contained 20 to 80 percent or more of the total population of a city-state and ranged in size from a few thousand inhabitants to over one hundred thousand under exceptional circumstances. In some of the larger city-states and those with more dispersed populations, the capitals were surrounded by smaller administrative centres and both of these by numerous subordinate farming villages or hamlets. Benin is reported to have been surrounded by several hundred villages, some individually self-governing and others forming small political groupings or belonging to subordinate chiefdoms (Bradbury 1957: 15). Robin Law (1977: 9) suggests that in the Oyo kingdom the farming population had been more dispersed during the Old Oyo period than it was in the nineteenth century, when escalating warfare led people to seek the safety of the towns. As a result of this relocation, many areas of the countryside came to be occupied only on a seasonal basis. Elizabeth Stone (1997: 24) has noted the essentially urban character of the small communities that served as local administrative centres within city-states.

Where warfare was endemic, a large portion of the farming population of city-states lived in the main urban centres and worked land as close as possible to these communities. In Mesopotamia the average city-state was probably 40 kilometres in diameter, about the same size as Renfrew's early-state module. The capitals of adjacent Mesopotamian city-states were often visible from each other's ramparts. In the Valley of Mexico, city-state capitals averaged only 7 kilometres apart. Among the Yoruba, the centres of larger city-states, especially in the more populous south, were located about 40 kilometres from each other, but the centres of smaller polities (which were not always states) were much closer together. There was great variation in the size of Yoruba states. Stephen Houston (1993: 137–38) estimates that large Maya centres were 40 to 67 kilometres apart and that the mean distance between capitals and subordinate centres was 11.36 kilometres. He argues that city-states required secondary administrative centres wherever substantial populations were living more than a day's walk from a capital and that size alone accounts for the presence or absence of secondary centres within city-states. Hence, where individual city-states occupied a small territory or the population was clustered near the capital, there was no need for secondary centres. Thus, in Mesopotamia and to a considerable extent in the Valley of Mexico, city-states tended to consist of urban centres surrounded only by villages. Between 15 and 80 percent of the total population of city-states lived in urban centres.

Members of these societies identified with the city-state as a whole, not just with its capital. The Yoruba term *ilu*, which is usually translated 'city', included the surrounding farmland and designated the entire territory ruled by an oba (Krapf-Askari 1969: 25–27). The Nahuatl term *altepetl* or *huealtepetl* (big altepetl) likewise referred to an urban centre, its surrounding territory, and its ruler (M. E. Smith 1996: 163). Sumerian scribes used one word (*uru*; Akk.

ālum) to designate 'settlement' or 'city', but many terms to refer to different kinds of countryside (R. McC. Adams 1981: 137; Van De Mieroop 1999: 10). The Mesopotamian urban centre and its surrounding farmland were believed to constitute the estate of its patron deity. The basic geographical focus of allegiance was the territory that was ruled over by a king or by a tutelary deity.

Adjacent city-states were in regular contact with one another. While they were usually self-sufficient in food production, intercity trade was a regular source of the exotic raw materials needed to manufacture luxury goods and sometimes necessities and an important source of prestige items. The closer city-states were to each other and the smaller they were, the more readily regional economies emerged. Because of their proximity and economic interdependence, city-states also tended to be culturally interdependent and to share religious beliefs, artistic conventions, and symbolism, especially as these related to upper-class culture. In Mesopotamia, the city-state of Nippur, which never aspired to political hegemony, served as a neutral meeting place for representatives from other city-states (Postgate 1992: 34). Ife, in its symbolic role as the world's first city, served as a meeting place for people from all the Yoruba states; portions of the bodies of dead kings from Benin were brought there for burial in the place of origin of their divine ancestors (Egharevba 1960: 9). The rulers and the upper classes of neighbouring city-states also tended to intermarry, although such alliances did not prevent warfare as the upper classes of one city-state sought to enrich themselves at the expense of their neighbours. Warfare was waged over agricultural land, water rights, and more direct access to other resources but above all to force the rulers of weaker states to pay tribute to the rulers of stronger ones. These varied contacts, which either took place among the upper classes or were carried out for their benefit, constitute examples of what Colin Renfrew and John Cherry (1986) called peer-polity interaction.

Despite their cultural similarities, the inhabitants of adjacent or even single city-states did not always speak the same language. The Yoruba spoke a single language that had various dialects (Adetugbo 1973), but Yoruba civilization embraced the Ewe-speaking Edo people of Benin. The Classic Maya spoke two closely related languages that are ancestral to Cholan and Yucatec Mayan, currently spoken in the southern lowlands and the Yucatan Peninsula. These languages became distinct from other Mayan languages prior to 1500 B.C., and the southern lowlands appear to have been Cholan-speaking prior to A.D. 1000 (Henderson 1981: 50–52; Houston, Robertson, and Stuart 2000).

Nahuatl was the most widespread language in the Valley of Mexico in the sixteenth century A.D., being spoken in the dominant city-states of

Tenochtitlan and Texcoco and smaller neighbouring states in the southern part of the valley. Other states were composed of Otomi-speakers. While pejorative ethnic stereotypes abounded, wards of peoples speaking foreign languages or belonging to different ethnic groups lived amicably alongside the dominant local people in Tenochtitlan and many other highland Mexican cities. These enclaves often consisted of families of skilled craft workers who had been attracted to major centres by enhanced opportunities for obtaining exotic raw materials and selling their wares. The local upper classes welcomed such groups because of the special skills they brought with them (Brumfiel 1994; van Zantwijk 1985: 132–34).

Both Sumerian- and Semitic (Akkadian)-speakers lived in southern Mesopotamia during the earliest period from which readable records survive. In general, Akkadian appears to have been more commonly spoken in the north and Sumerian in the south, but speakers of the two languages lived alongside each other in most Mesopotamian city-states, with the linguistic mix differing from one state to another. Some southern city-states had rulers with Semitic names from earliest times (Postgate 1992: 35–38). The disappearance of Sumerian as a spoken language by about 1800 B.C. (Crawford 1991: 10) has been attributed to the gradual ecological decline of far-southern Mesopotamia, where most Sumerian-speakers lived. It may also be related to the problems that Sumerian-speakers encountered in reproducing themselves in the dense and probably unhealthy urban centres that most of them seem to have inhabited during the Early Dynastic period. Unlike the Akkadian-speaking urban dwellers, who were surrounded by Semitic-speaking agricultural and pastoral peoples to the north and east, the Sumerians do not appear to have been able to recruit large numbers of people speaking their language from rural settings (McNeill 1976: 55–57). The widespread presence of speakers of more than one language in Mesopotamian and highland Mexican city-states indicates that membership in a city-state was based primarily on loyalty to a ruler and to civic and local religious institutions rather than on ethnic criteria. Yet, in Mesopotamian mythology, the creation of different languages was one of the means by which the gods weakened humans by sowing discord among them (Kramer 1981: 357).

The more people lived in large urban centres, the greater was the incentive to reduce bulk transportation costs by growing as much food as possible nearby. When considerable numbers of full-time or part-time farmers lived in urban centres, agricultural production was intensified on adjacent land in order to reduce not only transport costs but also the time farmers spent travelling between their homes and their fields. There was also a tendency for farmers who maintained their principal residences in the city to live during periods of peak agricultural labour in temporary shelters or small houses near the fields they were cultivating. In the Valley of Mexico and among the Maya food was also grown within urban centres in kitchen gardens attached to residences. Even the Maya upper classes had their dependents grow food in gardens that surrounded their urban residences.

Full-time and part-time artisans tended to live in urban centres in order to be as close as possible to a large clientele and to suppliers of the exotic raw materials that many of them needed for their work. Potters, smiths, flint knappers, and practitioners of other crafts that were polluting or produced much waste material sometimes lived and worked in nearby rural villages, where the smoke associated with their activities was less bothersome, waste was disposed of with less trouble, and fuel was easier to obtain. Even these sorts of craft workers were, however, found in urban centres, especially if the materials they worked, such as copper, tin, or obsidian, had to be obtained from abroad or their products were intended mainly for a wealthy urban clientele (Schwartz and Falconer 1994; Stone 1990; 1997).

The presence of large numbers of artisans in a single urban community encouraged craft specialization. Urban markets expanded to facilitate the exchange of goods among craft workers, urban and rural farmers, and the urban upper class. Such markets also facilitated trade among neighbouring city-states and the exchange of locally manufactured goods for raw materials from less-developed regions. Market exchange made the products of craft specialists accessible to all who could afford them, except where sumptuary laws banned the possession of certain types of luxury goods by the lower classes. Making the products of craft specialization widely accessible encouraged further craft specialization, and this in turn may have promoted technological efficiency by making higher-quality implements more widely available.

City-states were generally small enough that all the leading people knew one another personally. While each city-state was headed by a monarch, royal powers varied widely from one civilization and one state to another. In general, power tended to be shared to varying degrees among different institutions, as well as among the heads of leading families and the wealthiest people, who were often the same individuals. Policies were decided and issues resolved in councils.

The divine powers ascribed to monarchs were generally less extensive in city-states than in territorial ones. Claims to possess such powers were heightened, however, not only by the greater effective power of individual rulers but, as among the Yoruba, by the extent to which rulers were secluded and therefore unable to exercise power directly. In Mesopotamia, however, a ruler's personal strengths and weaknesses seem to have been familiar to everyone.

TERRITORIAL STATES

In other early civilizations territorial states developed at an early stage in the evolution of social, economic, and cultural complexity (Fig. 6.2). Rather than quickly disintegrating, as most early states did, they became the focus for the development of civilizations marked by distinctive political and economic institutions and by a sharply demarcated upper-class lifestyle. Territorial states had to construct elaborate administrative hierarchies which were subject to a considerable degree of centralized control. Sometimes there was a close correlation between a single territorial state and a distinctive civilization, especially where the state had sharply defined ecological boundaries, as was the case with Egypt or the Andean highland core of the Inka kingdom. Where there were no clear ecological boundaries, however, it was possible for several coexisting territorial states to have generally similar cultures. This appears to have been the case in northern China.

In the centuries preceding the political unification of Egypt, a series of chiefdoms or small early states developed in the northern part of the Nile Valley. The most important of these polities were located in southern Upper Egypt, but there appear to have been others in Middle Egypt and the Delta. During the Late Predynastic period, Egyptian society was characterized by increasing social stratification, economic expansion, and trade, as well as by the development of rituals that would later play an important role in Egyptian kingship. These early states, with their capitals about twenty-five kilometres apart, probably resembled in many respects the city-states that had begun to develop in Mesopotamia in the Early Uruk period. Around 3100 B.C., however, the rulers of This, one of the major centres in southern Egypt, brought the whole of Egypt under their rule; a network of competing early states was replaced by a centralized government which divided Egypt into a series of provinces for purposes of local administration (T. Wilkinson 1996; 1999). Some unilinear evolutionists have described the later Egyptian provinces as continuations of predynastic city-states, but to call them city-states either before or after unification is misleading. Many provinces were created as administrative units long after Egypt had become a territorial state, and the older ones were thoroughly transformed by the imposition on them of a higher-level bureaucratic administration (Goelet 1994: 167).

If local ruling families survived unification, they were soon dissociated from their old territorial power bases and absorbed into the national upper classes. By Old Kingdom times it was normal for officials to hold offices sequentially in different parts of the country, with the highest positions to which they aspired being at the royal court. The only offices that may have remained

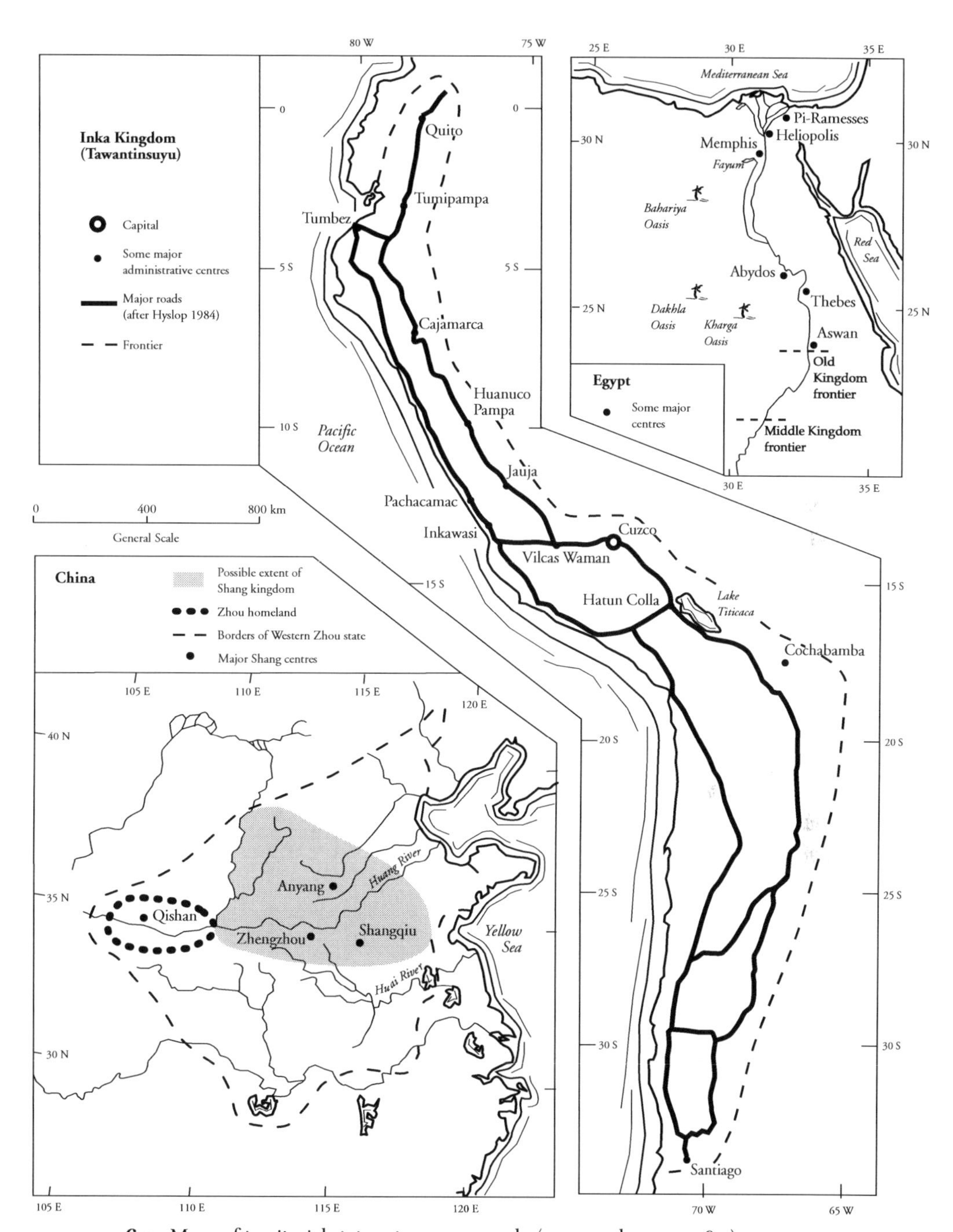

6.2. Maps of territorial states at common scale (same scale as map 6.1).

hereditary were those of village headmen. The royal court became the focus for the development of elaborate art, monumental architecture, literacy, and the distinctive behavioural patterns that characterized the Egyptian ruling classes (Frankfort 1956; Strudwick 1985). A common language appears to have been spoken throughout Egypt prior to unification, and this probably made it easier to promote a sense of national identity.

In the Andean region, chiefdoms and small states had developed along the Pacific seaboard by at least the second millennium B.C. and in the highlands somewhat later. More elaborate states were associated with the Moche civilization that flourished along the north coast of Peru during the first millennium A.D. The Chimu kingdom, which was centred in the Moche Valley, beginning in the fourteenth century A.D. controlled most of the north coast of Peru until it was conquered by the Inka in the 1460s. In the highlands, territorial states appear to have been established around centres at Tiwanaku and Wari between A.D. 600 and 1000. These states are believed to have sought to control mainly key resource areas and may not have been as complexly organized as the Chimu kingdom (Keatinge 1988; Lumbreras 1974).

When the Inka state developed, probably in the early fifteenth century, there appear to have been no societies at more than the chiefdom level in the Cuzco area or the central highlands of Peru. The Inka may have drawn on surviving remnants of Wari administrative practices, such as their revenue system (Keatinge 1988: 164), and on Chimu metallurgical technology and political skills. Their stonework appears to have been inspired by ancient stone buildings that Inka rulers had seen in the Tiwanaku area. Embarking on a fresh cycle of Andean state-building in a region that appears to have had no previous traditions of government on a large scale, the Inka quickly created not only the largest but the most integrated state constructed by any indigenous people in the Andean region.

The Inka imposed their administrative system over 984,000 square kilometres and perhaps eight to twelve million people who lived in pockets of arable land separated by mountains and deserts. They also created a new style of monumental architecture which, while highly distinctive and imposing, displays ample evidence of its derivation from traditional rural houses. In addition, they introduced their own distinctive style of urban planning. While the central highland core of the Inka state, between Ecuador and Lake Titicaca, bears the strong imprint of Inka culture, Inka cultural influence was less intrusive in coastal regions of Peru, where the highly elaborated forms associated with older cultures persisted, and in the far south, where only relatively simple facilities were installed to exploit the mineral resources of thinly populated regions (Earle 1994).

While the highland core was ethnically and linguistically diverse, this was the region that the Inka were most anxious to weld into a stable political unit. Nevertheless, even peripheral entities such as the Chimu state were radically transformed politically in the course of being absorbed into the Inka administrative system. Officials at all levels were required to use Quechua, which may already have been a lingua franca in the central highlands when the Inka rulers made it their administrative language (Carpenter 1992: 116–17; Rostworowski and Morris 1999: 807–9). Hence, while the distinction between core and periphery is of some heuristic value, the Inka were clearly seeking to construct an integrated state that stretched from Ecuador as far south as central Chile. They had been sufficiently successful that the Spanish scholar Bernabé Cobo (1979: 189), working with sixteenth-century written sources, described the Inka kingdom as 'a single republic'.

The Inka rulers divided the territories they conquered into more than eighty provinces, each ruled by an Inka governor. To produce more or less standard-sized provinces, they artificially combined small political groupings and divided larger states, including the Chimu kingdom, into smaller units. It was not difficult to dismantle most large states, since chiefdoms that had been recently incorporated into them had often preserved their sense of identity and were happy to be liberated. The upper classes of conquered chiefdoms and small states were co-opted into the new order by being recognized as officials at levels below that of Inka governor. For many of these leaders, the support they received from the Inka rulers meant an increase in their revenues and in the coercive power they could exert over their own people. For ordinary men and women, becoming Inka subjects probably meant producing larger surpluses than ever before. At the same time, especially in the highlands, the Inkas' suppression of local conflicts meant that people could often abandon their hilltop forts and settle near richer valley bottoms, where a wider range of crops could be grown (D'Altroy and Earle 1985).

In China, by the third millennium B.C. various Lungshanoid cultures of the Yellow River Valley were characterized by wheel-made pottery, increasing economic and political inequality, warfare, and the development of ritual practices such as human sacrifice and scapulimancy. Numerous towns surrounded by stamped-earth walls appear to have dominated smaller settlements spread across areas of several hundred square kilometres (Yan 1999). None of these towns exceeded twenty hectares. This suggests the development of complex chiefdoms or incipient states such as those of Predynastic Egypt or Early Uruk–period Mesopotamia. Such entities may have had the potential to develop in the direction of either one or more territorial states or a city-state system. There is no evidence of royal palaces until the Erlitou phase (2100–1800 B.C.), which has been identified with either the Xia or the early Shang Dynasty of recorded Chinese history. The oldest known bronze vessels date from this period (G. Barnes 1993; K. Chang 1986a; 1999; Maisels 1999: 260–341).

The cultural development of the central plain was significantly influenced by developments occurring to the north, east, and south. During the Erligang period, contemporary with the Shang occupation of Zhengzhou, a uniform style of bronze casting spread from the central plain over a huge area of northern and central China and apparently well beyond the borders of any one city- or territorial state. By the late Shang period, bronze industries very different from those of the central plain had developed in the Middle Yangzi region, Sichuan, and other parts of China (Bagley 1999: 208–21).

The Shang state has traditionally been described as a territorial state that had imposed its rule over the chiefdoms and small states of the central plain, but some scholars believe it to have been a city-state that had managed to subdue and extract tribute from a large number of adjacent city-states or a voluntary federation of city-states (Lewis 1990: 64; Stepugina 1991: 411; Yates 1997). It is possible that the frequent relocations of capitals ascribed to the Xia and early Shang Dynasties may be a later attempt to construe as a single, linear succession of kings various rulers who had held power simultaneously (Huber 1988: 75). We now know that later Mesopotamian king lists misinterpreted the contemporary rulers of various Early Dynastic city-states as dynasties that had ruled successively over the whole of southern Iraq (Postgate 1992: 26–32). The later Zhou rulers' allowing the descendants of the Shang royal family to continue to hold office as the dukes of Song so that they could offer sacrifices to their royal ancestors also suggests a city-state system (Hsu and Linduff 1988: 186).

There is, however, substantial evidence that the Shang kingdom was a territorial state that controlled about 230,000 square kilometres. One indication is the simultaneous use of multiple capitals. It is assumed either that the late Shang administrative capital was near Shangqiu, in eastern Henan Province, and that Anyang, some 215 kilometres to the northwest, was a royal ritual and burial centre (Keightley 1983b: 533; W. Watson 1979) or, as seems more likely given its more strategic location and its late foundation, that Anyang was the administrative centre and Shangqiu the ancestral cult site (K. Chang 1980: 210; Chêng 1960: 43; Li Chi 1977: 98–104). In either case the late Shang kingdom clearly had two major centres a considerable distance apart. The early Shang Dynasty also had two capitals, Bo and Xibo (West Bo), which some have identified with the walled sites of Zhengzhou and Shixianggou in Henan (Maisels 1999: 317–18). (Others have associated Shixiangguo with Tonggong, another early Shang secondary capital [Zou 1999].) Zou Heng maintains that throughout the Shang Dynasty kings had a number of separate residences which served as secondary capitals. This evidence suggests that the Shang ruled over a territorial state that had a core area at least several hundred kilometres across.

The late Shang rulers led a peripatetic life, travelling with their courts from one part of their kingdom to another. In the course of their journeys, they transacted business, sacrificed to local deities, hunted, feasted, and joined regional officials in putting down local rebellions and waging war against foreign groups (Keightley 1983b: 552), behaviour typical of the rulers of territorial states. Rulers of hegemonic city-states required the kings of tributary states to attend their courts periodically but did not visit tributary states, which they rightly regarded as dangerous enemy territory (Schele and Freidel 1990: 342). It also appears that writing, chariotry, and large-scale casting of magnificent ceremonial vessels flourished most spectacularly around the Shang royal capitals.

The oracle-bone evidence from Anyang and later historical records are generally interpreted as indicating that, until the rulers of a number of regional states each assumed that title during the Warring States period (481–221 B.C.), only one ruler was regarded as having the right to be called 'wang' (king). While the Zhou monarchs appear to have called themselves wang prior to overthrowing the Shang kings, this might indicate no more than that, as in Egypt, there could be rival claimants to the position of universal ruler. In the Western Zhou period various lords living in the Wei Valley referred to themselves as wang, suggesting that this title may have been used differently in that region than it had been in the Shang kingdom (Wang 1999: 242–43). Contemporaneous Shang inscriptions refer to the same Zhou rulers as 'hou' or 'bo', which were major titles but inferior to 'wang' in the Shang state.

It appears that, as new areas were incorporated, there was a tendency to appoint members of the Shang royal clan or other leading Shang families to rule over them. Populations from core areas were resettled in newly acquired territories. The establishment of garrison settlements among non-Shang peoples accords with a policy of policing and defending the borders of a territorial state (Keightley 1979–80: 27). Settlement of border areas may have promoted the linguistic as well as the cultural assimilation of these areas, resulting in the spread of the Chinese language into regions where it had not previously been spoken.

Evidence that Shang culture extended beyond the known borders of the Shang kingdom does not pose insuperable problems for the notion that it was a territorial state. In late Shang times, the predynastic Zhou rulers in the Wei Valley were sometimes subject to the Shang kings and sometimes independent of them. They appear to have derived much of their upper-class material culture from the Shang state and to have emulated the Shang rulers in many ways. It was later reported that writing was introduced to the Zhou court when Shang diviners defected there. Of the few sites that have yielded inscribed oracle bones, all appear to have been associated with the Shang and Zhou royal families (Hsu and Linduff 1988: 33–67; Rawson 1999: 375–97). This suggests that these two dynastic lines may have been of special importance in north-central China, much as later Chinese historians believed. If the Shang kings had ruled over a series of city-states, each state would have had its own king, and he in turn would likely have had his own diviners. Nor is there stylistic or other evidence that elaborate bronze vessels were being produced independently at numerous city-state capitals throughout the Yellow River valley. Western Zhou elite culture in particular displayed a high degree of uniformity at any one period. It is unclear whether ritual bronzes were cast in a small number of government workshops or produced in numerous secondary centres according to detailed prescriptions (Chêng 1963; Kane 1974–75; Rawson 1999; Thorp 1985).

Like the Shang, the predynastic Zhou rulers had multiple capitals. Both Shang and predynastic Zhou kings appear to have ruled over territorial states that, after the Zhou rulers broke free of their tributary status, existed briefly alongside each other until the Zhou conquered their Shang neighbours. The absence of sharp ecological boundaries to the south and west of the Shang state allowed more territorial states, such as that of Chu, to develop in that region. The evolution and functioning of both the Shang and the Western Zhou polity appear to have resembled the pattern of ancient Egypt more than that of ancient Mesopotamia. Northern and central China may in the second millennium B.C. have contained a considerable number of territorial states (Maisels 1999: 27, 312).

On the basis of the evidence from the early civilizations of Egypt, northern China, and the Inka, it is possible to identify features that territorial states had in common and that distinguished them from city-states. First, the total areas controlled by territorial states tended to be larger than those occupied by city-state systems. The Valley of Mexico, which was geographically and culturally distinct from other areas occupied by city-states in highland Mexico, enclosed some 7,000 square kilometres. Southern Mesopotamia, including both settled areas (never more than 12,000 square kilometres) and adjacent winter grasslands, covered about 120,000 square kilometres, while the Yoruba states, together with Benin, occupied about 130,000 square kilometres. The lowland Maya city-states were spread over 250,000 square kilometres, although most of the Classic Maya ones were concentrated in the southern half of that area.

In contrast, Old and Middle Kingdom Egypt controlled and utilized an area of about 333,000 square kilometres, of which only 19,000 square kilometres were not desert. The Shang state at its maximum may have controlled 320,000 square kilometres mainly of rich farmland, but its core was perhaps as small as 132,000 square kilometres. Finally, the Inka kingdom embraced 980,000 square kilometres, most of which was uncultivable desert, bare rock, or cold altiplano. Territorial states were able more effectively to control and exploit non-agricultural land than were city-states.

Second, the cities of territorial states were considerably less populous than those of city-states. Territorial states were held together by an upper class whose top stratum consisted of the royal family and the leading families of the core group that had created and governed the state. Lower-ranking functionaries were recruited from less prestigious members of the core group and by co-opting high-ranking members of conquered peoples. These rulers and officials, together with their retainers and craft workers, constituted the entire population of urban centres. Because the central government maintained order and defended the frontiers from external attack, there was no need for farmers to seek protection there. There is also evidence that the upper classes sought to isolate themselves geographically from farmers and the lower classes generally.

Third, the rulers of territorial states had at their disposal much larger surpluses than did those of city-states and were therefore able to create works of art and architecture on a more massive scale. Egypt's Great Pyramid was the largest single construction of the preindustrial era. The Inka erected elaborate stone building complexes at important provincial centres throughout the twenty-four-hundred kilometre-long core of their state. The Shang constructed massive, stamped-earth enclosure walls around royal residential complexes, as well as large palaces. Highly skilled and specialized artisans attached to the royal court crafted magnificent luxury goods and symbols of authority – bronze vessels in China, stone vessels and funerary sculpture among the Egyptians, luxurious cloth and ornaments made of precious metals in Peru. Everywhere luxury goods included valuable items of personal adornment. A monarch was able to derive great prestige and reinforce loyalty by bestowing such gifts on his relatives and officials.

Fourth, in territorial states the exercise of royal power required maintaining a considerable degree of centralized control over the economy. This included accumulating the surpluses required to support the upper classes, administration, army, and major construction projects and the production and distribution of the luxury goods that helped to ensure the loyalty of the king's supporters. The size of territorial states necessarily made central political control indirect, and therefore it could be challenged or subverted more easily than in city-states. The Inka and Egyptian rulers controlled foreign trade as well as all major mining and quarrying projects. While bronze tools were manufactured in Inka provincial centres, gold objects could not be transported away from the Cuzco area without official authorization. The central government also guarded the borders of the kingdom not only against foreign attack but also to stop dissidents from escaping and to control trade. The Inka, the Egyptian, and possibly the Chinese rulers fortified the borders of their kingdoms to control movement across them. In the early period of the Egyptian state its rulers also depopulated the regions lying immediately beyond their southern, eastern, and western borders, apparently resettling many of the foreign peoples who had lived in these regions in Egypt (Hoffman 1979). The control of borders 'caged' the subject populations of early civilizations and made them easier to control (Mann 1986: 38–40).

Fifth, there was much more continuity in agricultural life in territorial states. There is archaeological evidence that the unification of Egypt was accompanied by significant changes in settlement patterns, including the relocation of many small communities. Some of this relocation may have occurred spontaneously as a response to the greater security that followed unification; farming populations that had clustered around major centers, such as Hierakonpolis, may have dispersed, and many farmers may have moved, or been shifted, north as the Memphis area became administratively important and the hitherto sparsely populated western Delta was developed (T. Wilkinson 1999: 344–65). In highland Peru the Inka rulers ordered populations living in fortified communities on mountaintops to resettle in smaller, open settlements at lower altitudes and near better agricultural land (Hastorf 1990). There is also evidence of farming groups' being resettled in Shang and Zhou China as new lands became available. Because farmers continued to live in villages and close to the land they worked, however, they remained economically self-sufficient to a much greater degree and probably preserved the traditions of prestate village life to a much greater extent than urban-dwelling farmers in city-states and had less opportunity to develop a desire for goods manufactured in urban centres. While farmers were fully occupied with agricultural tasks during the sowing and harvest seasons, they could use the less busy intervening periods to manufacture the goods they needed (Weber 1976 [1896]: 108).

As a result, in territorial states there was a much larger economic gap between the upper classes and farmers. The upper classes used goods that were made by highly skilled, full-time artisans, often from valuable, imported materials. The rural population continued to use goods that part-time craft workers manufactured from traditional, locally available materials. These products were exchanged at local markets. The main economic transfers between farmers and the upper classes were the taxes and rents that farmers paid to the government and to landlords. Farmers had few reasons to visit urban centres or means to obtain luxury goods, except as rewards and gifts from officials and upper-class patrons. They also had less access to new technologies than farmers in city-states. Agricultural tasks were performed using wood and stone tools, although artisans who worked for the government were supplied with metal tools. By contrast, among the Yoruba and the Mesopotamians metal farming implements became common at approximately the same time that metal tools became available to full-time craft workers. It would also appear that, because in territorial states urban centres were smaller, farmers did not have the incentive to practice intensive agriculture in their vicinity that they did around major urban centres in city-state systems.

REGIONAL CONTROL

Since most of the arguments advanced against the distinction between territorial and city-states turn on the nature of city-state systems, it is necessary to examine more closely the political structures of such entities.

Confusion has been compounded by historians and political scientists applying the term 'empire' to two very different sorts of domination: integrated (or direct) and hegemonic (or indirect). Later preindustrial polities sought to administer conquered states directly, usually in order to exploit them more ruthlessly. The most ambitious and politically successful of these empires were eventually transformed into enduring regional states, while others expanded and contracted according to the power of the dominant state. Hegemonic empires ruled through indirect control, using a combination of force and persuasion to gain compliance and exact tribute payments from subordinate but still largely autonomous rulers (M. E. Smith 1996: 173–74). To avoid conflating these two very different types of political structures and encouraging anachronistic views, I will refer to hegemonic 'empires' as tributary systems.

Recent studies indicate significant variations in the sizes and populations of city-states within a city-state system as well as in particular city-states from one period to another (Hodge 1984). City-state systems frequently produced one or more city-states that dominated their neighbours militarily. These are often referred to as hegemonic city-states. In extreme cases the reallocation of wealth that such political domination brought about produced primate settlement patterns that resemble those found in later regional states. Yet, because of the differences in layout of the urban centres associated with them, such city-state systems can easily be distinguished archaeologically from the territorial states found among early civilizations.

The Aztec, together with their Texcocan and Tlacopan allies, constituted the so-called Triple Alliance, which they had established in the early 1400s. By the early sixteenth century this military alliance had come to dominate about 450 city-states, spread over the whole of the Valley of Mexico and much of central Mexico from the Gulf of Mexico to the Pacific Ocean. Tlacopan was a minor partner, perhaps included in the alliance primarily for ritual purposes (Spath 1973), and over time the Aztec came to dominate their Texcocan allies. Tributary payments were imposed on conquered city-states within the areas controlled by each of these three states, and tributary rulers were required to provision alliance armies passing through their territory and to convey tribute from farther away through their domains to hegemonic capitals. Yet, in general, the Aztec and their allies left local kings in place and intervened only occasionally in the routine administration of conquered city-states. States located beyond the Valley of Mexico tended to be governed internally as before. If a local king was especially troublesome, the Aztec might replace him with a more accommodating relative. Only rarely did they replace such a ruler with an Aztec governor. Even when they did, kingship was usually restored to the local ruling family as soon as an acceptable candidate, usually a son of the deposed king, was old enough to rule. Only a few very intractable city-states, located in crucial areas where alliances with powerful external enemies were possible, were dismantled. The men and women were killed, their children distributed for adoption among neighbouring city-states, and the emptied cities repopulated with colonists from the Valley of Mexico under the leadership of lords who were related to the Triple Alliance kings (Hassig 1988: 174–75, 207–8). Despite historical accounts of such resettlements, little in the way of Aztec art or cultural influence is evident beyond the Valley of Mexico. For the most part, life continued as before in conquered city-states, except that commoners had to either work harder to meet tribute payments or accept a lower standard of living and that it was more difficult to disobey local kings. The Aztec sought to control distant tributary states by spying on them, mercilessly crushing overt resistance, and imposing still heavier tribute upon reconquered states (Barlow 1949; Berdan et al. 1996; Hicks 1994; Hodge and Smith 1994; M. E. Smith 1986).

Within the Valley of Mexico, the Aztec and their allies intervened to a greater degree in the affairs of tributary city-states. They politically reorganized a few smaller and weaker states in order to facilitate tribute collection. These changes took the form of more effectively centralizing some states and amalgamating others. The Texcocans went farther than the Aztec by appointing the rulers of nearby tributary city-states to Texcoco's governing councils, including the highest-ranking one, which advised the Texcocan tlatoani. This arrangement did not, however, extinguish the formal independence of these states, which continued to be ruled by their own kings (Offner 1983). To a greater extent than outside the Valley of Mexico, the Aztec and Texcocan rulers married their daughters and those of high-ranking nobles to the kings of subordinate city-states. By doing so they ensured that eventually many of these rulers were related to their hegemons. Subordinate kings were required to attend major religious rituals, including coronations and victory celebrations, in Tenochtitlan and Texcoco. Land that was exchanged as wedding presents made rulers of tributary city-states increasingly dependent on property located outside their own city-states and therefore supportive of the larger order created by the Triple Alliance. Rulers of nearby tributary states were frequently called upon to supply soldiers for military campaigns outside the Valley of Mexico and labour and materials for maintaining palaces and undertaking major public construction projects in the Aztec and Texcocan capitals. The hegemonic states also used their power to rearrange interstate market cycles and trading patterns to their own advantage and turned much of the southern wetlands of the Valley of Mexico into food-producing areas for Tenochtitlan and Texcoco (Brumfiel 1983; Hodge 1984).

Yet the economic integration of the Valley of Mexico greatly outstripped its political integration. The most extreme example of political incorporation was the Aztec's annexation of the neighbouring city-state of Tlatelolco in the late fifteenth century. The capitals of these two states had been located alongside each other on the same island in Lake Texcoco, where both cities had expanded until they had physically coalesced. Growing rivalry had resulted in the Aztec's conquering Tlatelolco and suppressing its ruling dynasty. Yet Tlatelolco retained its civic centre and remained a highly prosperous fifth administrative division of the Aztec capital. The treatment of Tlatelolco suggests that groups living in the Valley of Mexico were very reluctant to suppress existing states (Charlton and Nichols 1997b: 203–4).

Events that occurred during the Spanish conquest demonstrate that even the Valley of Mexico, which was more politically and economically consolidated than the rest of the Aztec tributary system, still consisted of a series of city-states, varying in size and subjected, with varying degrees of willingness, to the Aztec and their allies. Kings of states located within a few kilometres of Tenochtitlan allied themselves with the Spanish in order to stop paying tribute to the Aztec. When the king of Texcoco died shortly before the Spanish arrived, the Aztec pressured their Texcoco allies to make his young son by the sister of the Aztec king their new monarch. This resulted in a civil war that divided Texcoco. An older half-brother of the new Texcocan king allied himself with the Spanish in a bid to seize the throne (Offner 1983: 238–41). It is thus clear that, while the Aztec interfered in the affairs of tributary and allied states for various political and economic reasons, their 'empire' remained a tributary system imposed on a large number of city-states that had remained self-governing. Whatever manipulations went on, there does not appear to have been any concerted plan to transform these states into a larger and more consolidated political entity.

Like the Valley of Mexico prior to the hegemony of Tenochtitlan, the Yoruba city-state system was dominated by a small number of powerful city-states. In the early nineteenth century, Yoruba polities varied greatly in size and power. When the more powerful ones conquered their neighbours, they did not suppress their governments or remove their kings, most of whom were believed to be fraternally descended from a single divine ancestor and therefore related to one another (R. Smith 1969: 109). They did, however, attempt to prevent subordinate community leaders (*bale*) from assuming the title of oba or minor obas from upgrading their status (Apter 1992: 21–22). In the Oyo tributary system, subordinate obas were not allowed to wear a beaded crown (*ade*) or to have eunuchs as retainers (Law 1977: 98–99). Yet, among the Yoruba, hegemonic states did not interfere routinely in the internal government of tributary states. Instead, they imposed tribute on their weaker neighbours and rearranged long-distance trade routes that passed through such states to their own advantage. Much of the wealth and power of the kingdom of Oyo was ensured by its controlling trade passing through subject states to the south. Hegemonic rulers installed *ajele* (agents) to observe and report the actions of the kings and governing councils of tributary states. Oyo ajele were inducted into the cult of Sango, the thunder god and son of Oduduwa, from whom the Oyo kings traced their descent. Such agents could, in emergencies, become possessed by Sango and, on that basis, claim supernatural authority superior to that of the local oba and his councillors. These agents reported to the Otun Iwefa, the chief Oyo palace eunuch in charge of religious matters, and to the Sango cult through the *ilari*, palace messengers and Sango priests (Apter 1992: 20–21).

In the Early Dynastic period southern Mesopotamia was a network of city-states, each with its own ruler. A number of city-states dominated all or most of southern Mesopotamia at various times, but there were also periods in which no single state dominated the region. Some states fought repeatedly with one another and imposed tribute and heavy reparations on their defeated neighbours, as well as making minor border adjustments. Hegemonic states grew richer and more populous and their urban centres expanded as a result of the wealth they obtained in this fashion. There is no evidence, however, that such states suppressed the governments of conquered city-states or interfered with their routine internal administration.

Efforts at regional control went much farther in Mesopotamia than they were to do in the Valley of Mexico as successive hegemons adopted different policies for maintaining long-term political and economic control. The first regional hegemony in Mesopotamia, apart from an early and perhaps mythologized one by the kings of Kish (Lamberg-Karlovsky 1996: 141–43; Steinkeller 1993), occurred when Sargon of Akkad conquered the other southern Mesopotamian states around 2350 B.C. He replaced their kings with his own followers and installed Akkadian garrisons in conquered cities. Local ruling families were, however, soon restored after the collapse of Akkadian power. A second (or third) round of centralization occurred during the Ur III period. The Ur III rulers subordinated or replaced rulers of conquered city-states, which they attempted to control by means of a civilian government largely composed of prominent local people and a military governor (*šagina*) who was related to the Ur royal family (Postgate 1992: 151–52). Building on Akkadian precedents, the Ur III rulers reserved the title ensi, which in the past had signified independent kingship, for the leader or governor of a subject city-state. These ensis, appointed by the king, were not allowed to enter into alliances or wage war on their own. Many of them were, however, former local rulers or close members of their families, and their posts could be passed from father to son. A subordinate city-state could construe the term 'ensi' as evidence of the continuity of its kingship. A third period of centralized rule was initiated by the Babylonian king Hammurabi around 1760 B.C. (Postgate 1992: 34–46, 151).

Cultural evolutionists have interpreted the recurrent cycles of unification that began in the Akkadian period as evidence of a transition from city-state to territorial state, but this interpretation does not account for the strenuous efforts by city-states to resist unification. The Akkadian rulers constantly had to suppress rebellions; the Ur III hegemony, although it was reinforced by regional economic controls, collapsed quickly; and Hammurabi's unification lasted for only two reigns (Yoffee 1991: 299–300). Elizabeth Stone (1997) argues that one of the major factors maintaining a city-state form of government in Mesopotamia was the reluctance of those who lived in these states to abandon a heterarchical pattern of political interaction. Norman Yoffee (1995: 290–92) has suggested that the earliest tendencies towards political unification were modelled on the tribal organization of society that prevailed in the Semitic-speaking areas of central and northern Mesopotamia and were resisted by the Sumerian-speaking city dwellers of the south. Elsewhere (1997: 258) he proposes that Mesopotamian city-states were 'never successfully absorbed into territorial states until non-Mesopotamian political systems and non-Mesopotamian ideologies of governance reformulated the social and natural landscapes of the area'. Hegemony was viewed as a power that the gods rotated from one city to another until Hammurabi claimed everlasting kingship for his capital city of Babylon (Jacobsen 1976: 189). The regional kingdoms that developed after the Old Babylonian period in Mesopotamia did not resemble early territorial states; urban centres retained their identity, administrative councils, and specialized economic functions within them (Maisels 1990: 172). Although fewer farmers now had reason to live in cities, their demands for manufactured goods and services continued to support large urban populations. Cities also retained numerous privileges and forms of self-government, although they were now permanently under the control of regional kings. Thus the cities of Babylonia during the first millennium B.C. did not at all resemble the administrative and court centres of early territorial states.

The longevity of city-state systems and their resistance to political unification is demonstrated by their persistence, despite hegemonic tendencies, for over a millennium in highland Mexico, among the Maya, and in West Africa until each of them was subjected to European colonization. In Mesopotamia, city-states, after successfully resisting incorporation into larger political systems for more than fifteen hundred years, were not transformed into territorial states but absorbed into regional kingdoms.

Unlike a hegemonic city-state system, the Inka 'empire' was organized as a series of provinces ruled by the Inka upper class. Governorships were not allowed to become hereditary. Provinces were governed from administrative centres which were not loci of population and often were new foundations. Local rulers, who in the central highlands were mostly descended from hereditary chiefs, administered largely rural populations. Their executive powers were subject to the approval of the provincial governor. To reduce the power of conquered groups, portions of large or potentially rebellious peoples were sent as colonists to far-off regions of the Inka state and replaced by reliable settlers from older parts of the kingdom (Patterson 1987). To construe as tributary city-states even administrative units composed of as many as ten thousand families is unrealistic, since they lacked the key features of such polities, including urban centres inhabited by craftsmen supplying a regional market.

While the Inka state was terminated by European conquest, the territorial states in Egypt and northern China evolved into regional states that, as the result of a process of convergence, shared many features with the urbanized regional states that had developed out of a city-state system in Mesopotamia. In Egypt this development began to occur in the late New Kingdom, when the central government lost control over foreign trade and the production of luxury goods. Administrative centres were transformed into loci of independent trade, manufacturing, and the exchange of manufactured goods with a rural hinterland. As a result, the number of urban dwellers increased. Rulers had to rely increasingly on the use of military force and develop the ability to tax an economy that they no longer directly controlled to any significant degree. In China it took almost a millennium for a territorial state to evolve into regional kingdoms in which monarchs ruled directly over family units and land was privately owned. While farmers continued in their spare time to manufacture most of the goods they required, large cities became centres of upper-class life and specialized production (Shen 1994). In the fourth century B.C., the various Chinese regional states were militarily united to form a single imperial state. Whether urbanized regional kingdoms in various parts of the world developed from city-states or territorial states, they had many features in common and were significantly different from both the city- and territorial states that had preceded them.

In the chapters that follow, the distinction between city-states and territorial states will provide an important framework for understanding functional patterning as it relates to variation in forms of social organization, economic behaviour, and culture in early civilizations. This distinction can help to explain features of early civilizations that were neither common to all early civilizations nor idiosyncratic.

7 Urbanism

Urban centres were features of all early civilizations (Bairoch 1988: 1–70). Contrary to a once fashionable belief, there is no evidence of a 'civilization without cities' (J. Wilson 1960), and this includes early civilizations in which, instead of cities, there were supposed to be 'ceremonial centres' inhabited only by a few priests, where people from the surrounding countryside assembled periodically for religious observances (J. Thompson 1954; Wheatley 1971). Nevertheless, the nature of their cities varied considerably.

Towns and cities were once defined as communities of non-food-producers with a minimum of 5,000 people or a population density of at least 386 people per square kilometre (Burgess 1926: 118), but such definitions have been abandoned. Some legally chartered 'cities' in medieval Europe had only a few thousand inhabitants, while 'farming villages' in Eastern Europe and Italy often had several times that number (Chisholm 1962: 60–61). In parts of China and Indonesia rural population densities have long exceeded 386 people per square kilometre (Cressey 1955: 15; Huntington 1956: 428). Finally, both in early civilizations and in other preindustrial societies, considerable numbers of farmers lived in urban centres. As recently as 1910, almost 10 percent of the population of Cairo consisted of full-time cultivators (Abu-Lughod 1969: 164). The key defining feature of an urban centre is that it performs specialized functions in relation to a broader hinterland (Trigger 1972). The largest entities of this sort in early civilizations were the capitals of city-states and the capitals and provincial administrative centres of territorial states, which normally had at least a few thousand inhabitants. Below these settlements were towns and villages that performed a more restricted number of specialized functions for smaller hinterlands. Yet cities, towns, and service villages are at best arbitrary units of a continuum of size and function, not structurally or functionally distinct entities. Definitions based on arbitrary quantitative divisions appear to bear little relation to concepts used in early civilizations and rarely contribute to a better understanding of urban phenomena (Vining 1955: 169). I will refer to relatively large, specialized settlements as 'cities', 'towns', 'urban centres', or 'administrative centres'.

Whatever else their function, cities were places where the upper classes of early civilizations lived, along with most people who did not produce food. They were the main locations of high-level political and administrative activities, specialized craft production, marketing, long-distance trade, higher education, artistic and cultural achievements, conspicuous display, court life, and religious rituals. With rare exceptions, important temples, palaces, and public buildings were located in urban centres. While these centres usually depended on food produced in the surrounding countryside, they contained all the institutions and produced everything that made the lives of the upper classes distinctive and worthwhile. Major cities impressed visitors by their scale, richness, and architectural magnificence and the grandeur of what went on in them. These attributes stressed the insignificance of the ordinary person, the power and legitimacy of the ruler, and the concentration of supernatural power (Rapoport 1993). It is therefore not surprising that the development of cities was strongly promoted by the upper classes, who used them to pursue their personal and collective goals.

Attributing the origin of all the cities of early civilizations to their religious functions (Wheatley 1971) is inconsistent with archaeological evidence, and it is not particularly helpful to trichotomize all preindustrial urban centres as regal-ritual, administrative, or mercantile (Fox 1977). The role of cities in early civilizations was to perform specialized functions in the context of a largely agricultural and relatively undifferentiated hinterland (Mabogunje 1962: 3–4). Concentrating a wide range of specialized functions in major centres made it possible to achieve significant economies of scale. If long-distance traders and skilled metallurgists lived in the same community, it was easy for metallurgists to obtain imported metal ingots and to sell or consign their surplus production to merchants for export. Metallurgists could also hope to find in cities the widest range of institutional and individual buyers for their products. Proximity was convenient for the upper classes, since it facilitated access to all the goods and services they required and enhanced their ability to monitor specialized activities in ways that increased their power and well-being (Garner 1967). The logistical and political considerations that encouraged the concentration of specialized functions in urban centres were the exact opposite of those that, under ideal circumstances, motivated subsistence farmers to live, dispersed in small groups, as close as possible to the land they worked.

The largest community in each city-state was usually located near its centre. Its central location minimized the cost of transportation and communication between it and the rest of the polity. Some city-states, especially if they were small or highly nucleated, had only a single administrative centre. Larger city-states and those with more dispersed settlement patterns had capital cities encircled at a distance of perhaps ten kilometres by smaller secondary administrative centres, each of which might in turn be surrounded by tertiary centres. Territorial states had numerous centres in nested hierarchies, with the larger ones being fewer and providing higher-level services for larger areas. Higher-level centres also contained the largest buildings and were inhabited by the most important people (Trigger 1972).

Major temples, palaces, and markets tended to be located in the centres of cities. Population was usually denser in the core than towards the outer limits, and the residences of prominent people tended to be concentrated there. Servants and retainers lived close to the people for whom they worked, which made the division of cities into different areas inhabited by rich and poor less clear than it is in modern industrial cities. Messy and polluting activities tended to be performed on the outskirts of cities if they were not banished to the countryside.

All cities faced problems of provisioning and waste disposal that they managed with varying degrees of rigour and success. In Egyptian and Mesopotamian cities, water was drawn from rivers, canals, wells, and cisterns and transported to homes that lacked their own wells either by hand or by donkey (Van De Mieroop 1999: 158–61). The Aztec capital of Tenochtitlan, located in the middle of a shallow saline lake, was supplied with fresh water by aqueducts that ran along the causeways linking the city to the mainland. In the Maya lowlands, where the porous limestone bedrock often left little surface water available during the dry season, many Classic Maya communities were forced to collect water and store it in underground cisterns (*chultuns*) and large open reservoirs. Many reservoirs in the centres of cities were established in abandoned quarries from which building material had been extracted. The large buildings and plastered plazas that the Maya constructed in urban centres were designed to collect rainwater and channel it into these reservoirs (Scarborough 1993).

Both the highland Mexicans and the Classic Maya recycled household organic waste onto garden plots near their houses, which they were able to multicrop in perpetuity. The large gardens that Maya households cultivated must have converted all their organic waste into fertilizer for their own use (Fedick 1996a). The Aztec, having much smaller garden plots, collected surplus household organic waste and conveyed it by canoe to agricultural areas outside the city. The movement of goods was facilitated by a network of alternating streets and canals that ran parallel to one another. Dwellings normally opened onto a street while their gardens faced a canal. Each canal was flanked by low dykes that protected nearby homes against small rises in lake level (Durán 1971: 231). The Maya appear to have collected inorganic waste near their houses and transported it periodically to the inner cities, where it was used for construction fill (Moholy-Nagy 1997). Aztec officials organized corvée labour to keep city streets and public spaces clean, but in Egypt as late as the New Kingdom garbage was dumped on vacant land between buildings (Kemp 1989: 300).

The dead were sometimes buried within communities. The Yoruba interred family members inside house compounds and the Maya in house platforms. In Mesopotamia major cemeteries sometimes were located in the central precincts of cities, but the dead were also buried in vaults beneath their houses. The Egyptians, Inka, and Shang Chinese normally interred their dead in cemeteries located outside their settlements.

Even in urban centres where attention was paid to hygiene, sanitary conditions must have remained well below modern standards. This likely created more serious health problems in larger cities than in smaller ones and more in crowded urban centres than in communities where houses were more widely separated. Many diseases, such as measles, rubella, smallpox, colds, and influenza, require interactive populations of three hundred thousand to five hundred thousand individuals to become endemic and therefore must have flourished in early civilizations as they had never done before (M. Cohen 1989: 49–50). Greater proximity to domestic animals enhanced the transmission of serious infectious diseases in Old World civilizations by comparison with New World ones (McNeill 1976: 45). Demographic data from selected Old World urban centres and from Teotihuacan indicate a relatively short life expectancy in both hemispheres (Storey 1985). While detailed demographic information is not available, it is possible that in at least some of these early civilizations large urban populations were unable to reproduce themselves – a situation that prevailed in many urban centres until the advent of modern preventive medicine (McNeill 1976: 55–57). Under these conditions, a continuing influx of rural people would have been essential.

URBANISM IN CITY-STATES

Each city-state normally had a single primary centre, which served as its capital. The atypical city-state of Lagash in southern Mesopotamia had three large centres: Lagash (El Hiba), Girsu (Telloh), and Nina (Zurghul), the first two of which served in turn as its capital during the Early Dynastic period (Falkenstein 1974 [1954]: 6–7). Multiple urban centres of this sort presumably arose as the result of a federation of two or more neighbouring polities. The capitals of city-states normally had from a few thousand to as many as fifty thousand inhabitants, although occasionally the capital of a hegemonic city-state might have one hundred thousand or more residents.

In city-states a high proportion of the population tended to live in the main urban centres. The extent of concentration varied from one early civilization to another and according to the political and economic circumstances of individual city-states. Because rural/urban boundaries tended to be fuzzy and the boundaries of states are rarely known, it is difficult to estimate what percentage of the population of any particular Maya state lived in urban centres. It has been estimated that 15 to 35 percent of the population may have lived in urban centres in most Maya city-states, although in some states this figure may have been as high as 50 percent (Chase, Chase, and Haviland 1990). Sanders, Parsons, and Santley (1979: 154, 162) have estimated that in most parts of the Valley of Mexico 30 percent of the population lived in urban centres; however, because of the large number of people living in Tenochtitlan and a few other large centres, the overall figure was 50 percent.

Fifty percent or more of Yoruba are reported to have lived in capitals (*ilu alade*, or 'crowned settlements'), where an oba who wore a crown with a beaded face-covering reigned, or in surrounding towns (*ilu oloja*, market towns) that were sometimes ruled by a subordinate oba (who could not wear this sort of crown). Most Yoruba extended families had their main residences in such centres, although some members of each extended family spent all or part of the time living in villages (*ileto*), hamlets (*abule*), or isolated homesteads (*ago, aba*) producing food. The Yoruba clearly distinguished 'town people' (*ara ilu*), who belonged to kin groups having rights of urban residence, from 'farm people' (*ara oko*), who were regarded as culturally inferior (Lloyd 1974: 32). Yet secondary towns, villages, and homesteads were all classified as *ilu ereko* (settlements on the fringe of farmland) to distinguish them from the main urban centres (Bascom 1969: 3–4; Krapf-Askari 1969: 25–28).

The highest concentrations of population in urban centres were achieved in Early Dynastic southern Mesopotamia, where, depending on the region, 70 to 80 percent of the population lived in cities and towns, from which many farmed the surrounding countryside (R. McC. Adams 1981: 90–94). At this time there were few permanent settlements of any sort in this region apart from city-state capitals. Although the rural population increased after the Early Dynastic period, rural settlements were abandoned again as a result of Amorite invasions around 2000 B.C. (Postgate 1992: 86).

The main reason so many people lived in urban centres was the greater protection these cities offered to houses and property where and when intercity conflict was prevalent. Mesopotamian and Yoruba cities were normally walled to protect them from attack. The mud-brick ramparts surrounding some Mesopotamian cities appear to have been intended not just for practical defense but to impress potential enemies with the strength and unity of the city that had constructed them; in the Gilgamesh epic the walls of Uruk – 9.5 kilometres in circumference, with bastions every 9 metres, and still 7 metres high (Huot 1989: 227) – were celebrated in these terms (Jacobsen 1976: 196).

Despite endemic warfare among city-states, walled cities were much less common in the Western Hemisphere (Sanders and Webster 1988). Tenochtitlan was approached by causeways with removable bridges, but most city-state capitals in the Valley of Mexico had no physical barriers around their perimeters. Guards appear to have been stationed on the frontiers of city-states to monitor travel and watch for invaders, and rulers were reported to have guarded their capitals day and night (Durán 1964: 61, 192). For the most part, however, highland Mexicans built walls around their ritual centres, other major buildings, and houses rather than around the city as a whole. Their chief defence appears to have been to lure enemy forces into the city, where they would be forced by the street pattern to break into smaller groups that could be fought from rooftops and ramparts. The final point of defence was the major temple platform in the city centre. Setting fire to the shrines atop such platforms symbolized the defeat of a city by its attackers (Hassig 1988: 62–105).

At an early period in its history the Maya city of Tikal constructed earth walls between swamps at its north and south ends, presumably as a form of protection (Culbert, Levi, and Cruz 1990: 115). The approaches to some other Maya cities were impeded by swamps and other difficult terrain. While Maya civic centres contained enclosed areas that could easily be defended, ordinary house groups, which were arranged on low platforms constructed around three or four sides of open courts, would have been relatively vulnerable to attack. A log palisade was constructed around the central plaza of the city of Dos Pilos during the final years of its existence (Schele and Freidel 1990: 505).

Since individual farmers in the early civilizations were able to produce only relatively small food surpluses, most people of necessity engaged in agricultural production. Where urban centres contained more than 15 percent of a state's total population, they must have been home to some full-time farmers. As we have seen, many Yoruba lived full-time in cities and worked land that their families owned nearby. Early Dynastic Mesopotamian cities appear to have housed the vast majority of full-time farmers; where 80 percent of the total population lived in cities at least 75 percent of urban dwellers would have been farmers.

As for Tenochtitlan, some argue that its island core was occupied exclusively by non-food producers, many of them craft specialists, fed by full-time agriculturalists from as far south as Lakes Chalco and Xochimilco (Calnek 1976; Sanders, Parsons, and Santley 1979: 154–55, 177–78) and by tributary states throughout the valley. Others maintain that many of its residents were full-time farmers who grew crops on the fringes of the city centre (M. E. Smith 1996: 195–201). The large dykes that the Aztec constructed to regulate water levels and reduce salinity in the area around Tenochtitlan would have had as one of their goals to support such agriculture. Economic specialization on the scale that would have been required for Tenochtitlan to have been a city of non-food-producers is attested for no other early civilization in this study, although it is known from some later preindustrial societies. Further, a predominance of craft specialists in Tenochtitlan is inconsistent with the extensive craft production and exchange documented for other city-states in the valley. I therefore tend to view Tenochtitlan as a city containing a considerable number of full-time farmers.

The urban centres of city-states frequently contained extensive areas that were not built over. I have already mentioned the kitchen gardens of Aztec and Maya cities. Mesopotamian cities had orchards as well as gardens inside the city walls, where fruit trees would have been safe from destruction by the enemy. These plots appear to have been privately owned, and therefore not everyone had access to their produce (Van De Mieroop 1999). Some Yoruba cities had thick forests just inside their walls that aided in defence and could be cleared to produce food in times of danger (Ajayi and Smith 1971: 24). Forests were left standing within the grounds of royal palaces to supply the wild plants that the obas needed to perform important rituals (Ojo 1966b: 22, 36).

The majority of full-time craft specialists tended to live and work in urban centres, where they produced goods for the upper classes and for sale to each other and to farmers living in the city and in the surrounding countryside. Workers specializing in a particular craft sometimes lived adjacent to one another in the same part of the city. Some urban farmers also worked on a part-time basis as craft specialists. Craft workers and urban farmers together constituted a large and easily mobilized pool of manpower for defending the city and waging war against its enemies.

Both in the Valley of Mexico and among the Yoruba, public markets located in special open spaces near the centres of cities played a prominent role in facilitating the exchange of goods. In Mesopotamia, shop-lined streets indicate vigorous commercial activity involving large numbers of people, and retailing there may have resembled the bazaars of modern Middle Eastern urban centres (Postgate 1992: 79). For the Maya, plazas may have provided market sites when they were not being used for religious rituals, but the apparent self-sufficiency of Maya urban families and upper-class control of access to exotic goods may have reduced the need for large public markets.

The layouts of urban centres in different city-state civilizations reveal flexible combinations of planning and unregulated growth, as well as a mixture of cross-culturally regular and culturally specific features. Mesopotamian cities were built along rivers or large canals and from Early Dynastic times on were surrounded with roughly oval walls of mud-brick. Sometimes branch canals ran though the cities (Gibson 1977; Stone and Zimansky 1995). The main temples were located near a city's geographical centre, often within a rectangular or oval enclosure wall. This temple quarter was called the *uruku* (sacred city) (Jacobsen 1970: 379), and a broad, straight avenue sometimes connected it to a principal city gate. Palaces were usually less centrally located than the main temple complex. The rest of the built-up area of the city consisted of a network of winding streets and alleys lined with one- or two-storey houses. Cities were divided into wards (*dagia*; Akk. *babtum*) that were often separated from each other by walls and had their own outer gates (Postgate 1992: 81–82). There was little difference in overall wealth among these residential areas, which seem to have been associated with ethnic or kinship groupings. Near the outer wall of the city were harbour areas (*kar*; Akk. *kārum*), apparently walled off from the rest of the city. These areas, which had their own administration, accommodated foreign merchants and perhaps the local traders who dealt with them (Fig. 7.1). Beyond the city walls were suburban areas containing orchards, fields, and country houses belonging to people who lived in the city (Stone 1990; 1997; Van De Mieroop 1999). During the periods of most intense urbanization, Early Dynastic II and III, at least eight cities in southern Mesopotamia occupied more than fifty hectares each, and two more covered more than four hundred hectares (Huot 1989: 158).

Yoruba cities and towns were surrounded by elaborate systems of earth ramparts, often planted with thorn hedges, and ditches. In the centre of the city was the walled *afin* or royal palace, surrounded by one or more market squares, the main shrines (both inside and outside the palace), and the house compounds of the principal members of the governing council. A number of streets, each about five metres wide, made their way from the centre of the city to one of the city gates and on into the surrounding countryside. Each of these streets tended to be associated with one of the wards (*adugbo*) into which the city was divided. These wards, which varied in number depending on the size of the city, were in turn composed of precincts (*ogbon*) inhabited by patrilineal extended families. In normal states there was only one palace in a city, but in smaller, less integrated communities several kings might reign

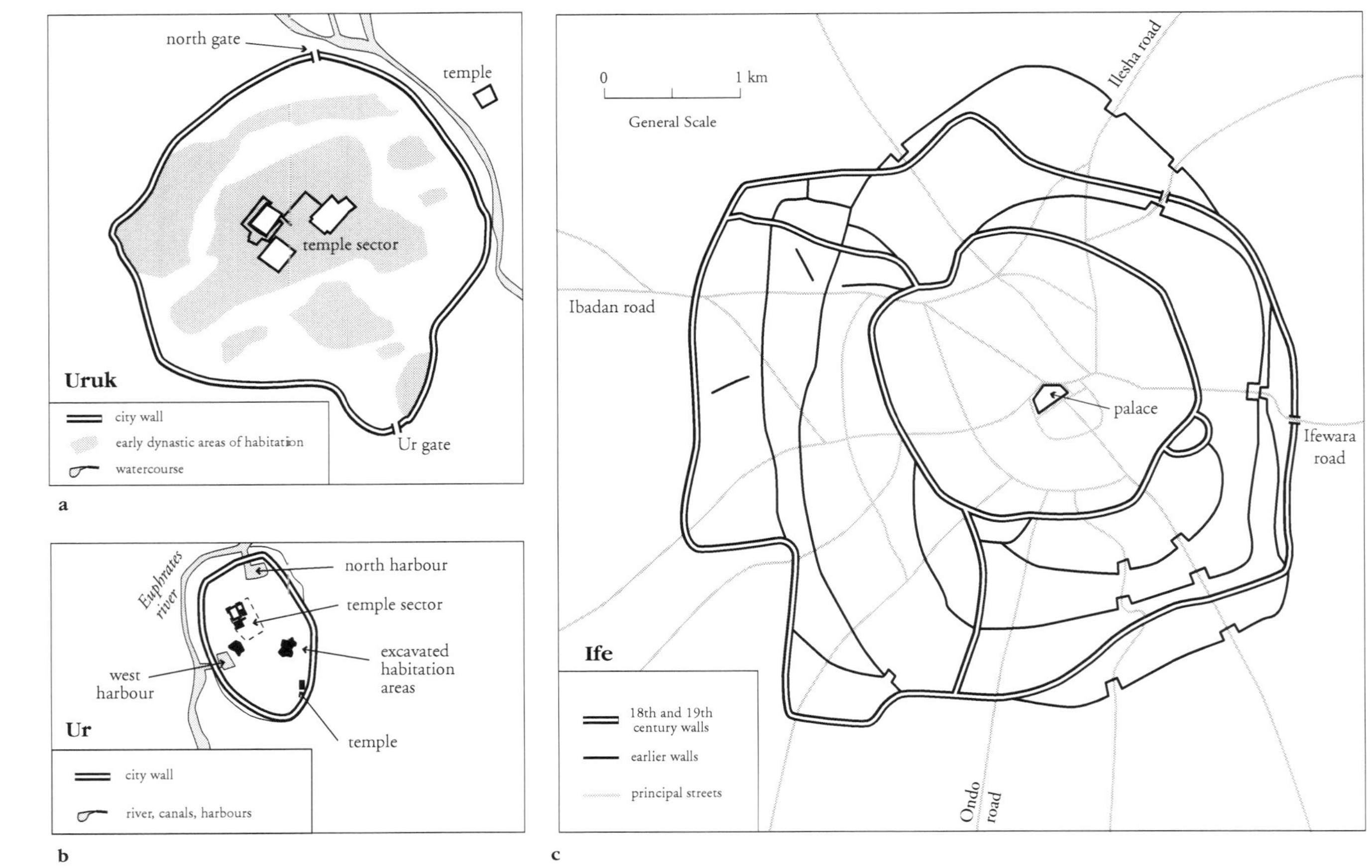

7.1. Urban centres in Mesopotamia and among the Yoruba: (a) Uruk, the largest urban centre in early Mesopotamia; (b) Ur, the capital of an important Mesopotamian city-state; (c) Yoruba city of Ife, showing walls of various periods and major streets. Sources: (a), (b) after Strommenger & Hirmer 1964: 408, 410; (c) after Shaw 1978: 146, and Willett 1967: 16.

over their own portions of the town, each from his own palace. Each of the lineages that took turns sharing the kingship of a whole community might have its own palace. Individual Yoruba urban centres had from about five thousand to perhaps seventy thousand inhabitants in precolonial times. Benin City had a population of fifty thousand. Then as now, the Yoruba were the most urbanized indigenous people in sub-Saharan Africa (Bascom 1969: 29–30; Krapf-Askari 1969; Mabogunje 1962; Ojo 1966b).

The urban centres of the smaller city-states in the Valley of Mexico had at their centres major temples, palaces, and markets, around which were arranged wards inhabited by endogamous corporate groups called *calpolli*. Each calpolli had its own centre, equipped with temples, meeting places, leaders' residences, and schools (Hodge 1984; M. E. Smith 1996: 187–96). Tenochtitlan, in 1519 the largest city in the valley with some one hundred thousand inhabitants, had at its centre a walled precinct containing the major temples and many other religious buildings (Fig. 7.2). Adjoining this precinct was a palace complex and a market area. From this central zone, four straight avenues stretched out in the cardinal directions, dividing the city into four quarters. A generally similar arrangement of public buildings and major streets had existed at Teotihuacan over a thousand years earlier. Each of the quarters had its own central temple and administrative complex, around which were arranged the many calpolli that composed the population of the city. A rectilinear pattern of streets and canals paralleled the main avenues, giving people access on foot and by water to all parts of the city. The city of Tlatelolco constituted a de facto fifth ward to the north of Tenochtitlan. Its centre contained a large temple complex and the main market that served the two cities (M. E. Smith 1996: 196–203; van Zantwijk 1985). Other large cities appear to have have been more dispersed and to have lacked Tenochtitlan's gridlike layout. Texcoco, the second-largest city, had a quadrilateral palace or ceremonial centre surrounded by a number of detached neighbourhoods (Hodge 1997: 211).

Maya cities were much less compact. At their centres were complexes of temples, palaces, paved plazas, and upper-class residences. Many of them had complementary paired precincts: a group of ritual buildings, at least partly devoted to the cults of dead kings, to the north and a royal palace complex to the south, with a ball court between (Ashmore 1989: 274). Around the centre of the city was a ring of moderately dense settlement which lacked large monumental structures, and beyond that was a zone of still less dense settlement. Throughout the urban zone, large multistructured residential complexes were surrounded by smaller, less elaborate residential units. The larger complexes appear to have belonged to powerful individuals or lineage leaders who exercised authority over their neighbours. Since shrines or temples of

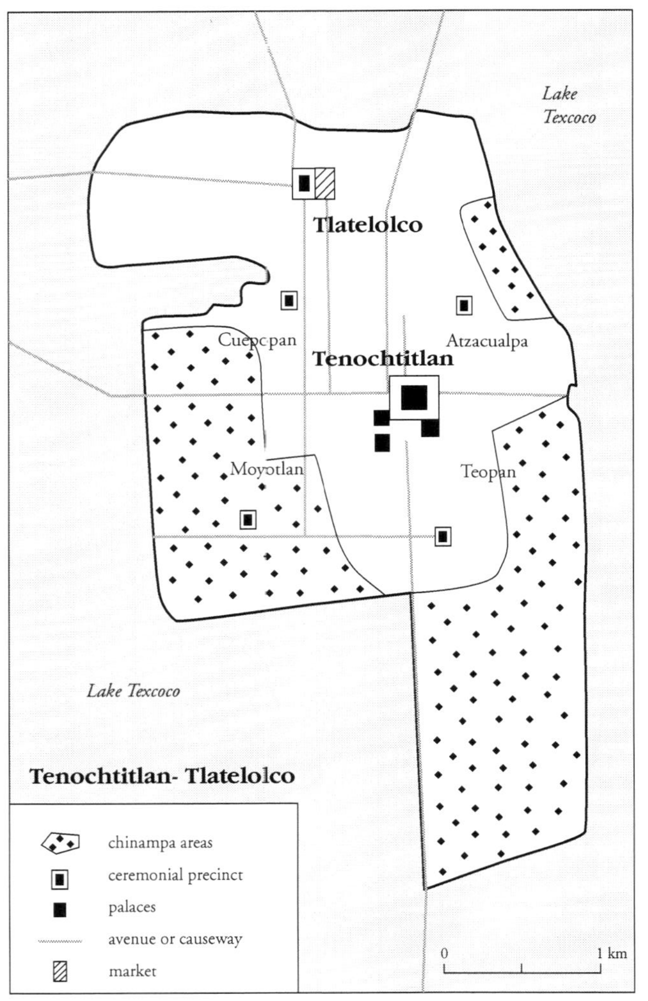

Lake Texcoco
Tlatelolco
Cuepopan
Tenochtitlan
Atzacualpa
Moyotlan
Teopan
Lake Texcoco
Tenochtitlan- Tlatelolco
chinampa areas
ceremonial precinct
palaces
avenue or causeway
market
0
1 km
a

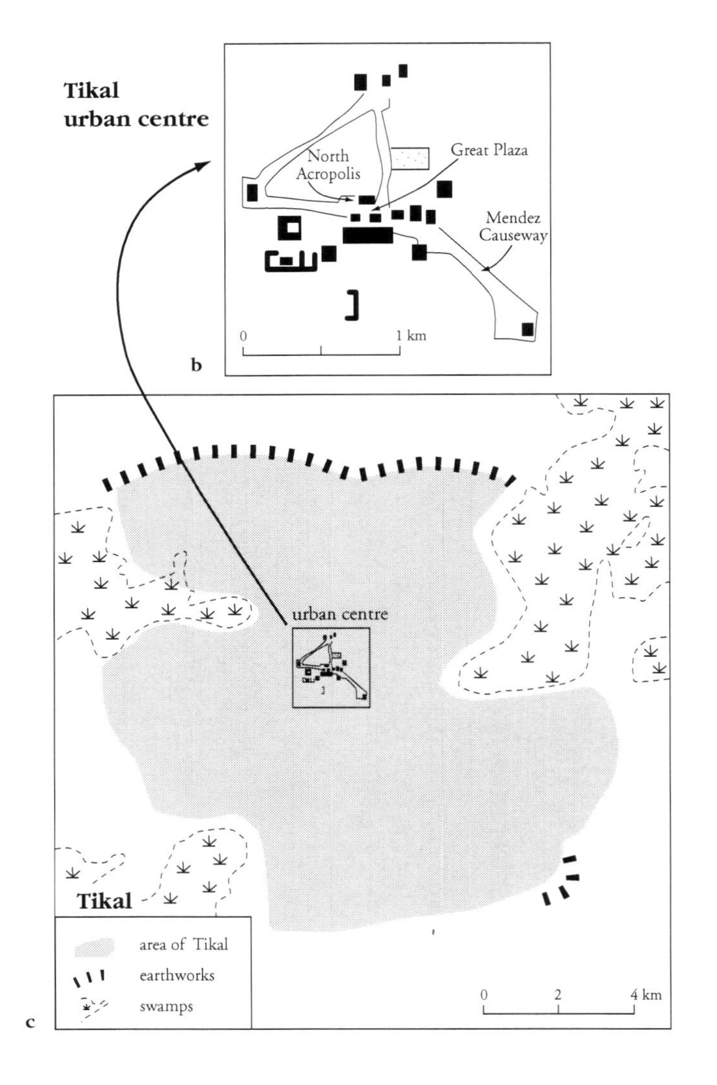

Tikal
urban centre
North Acropolis
Great Plaza
Mendez Causeway
0
1 km
b
urban centre
Tikal
area of Tikal
earthworks
swamps
0
2
4 km
c

corresponding degrees of elaborateness were associated with all residential complexes, a hierarchy of royal, upper-class, and commoner family cult centres extended throughout each city. In some urban centres, paved avenues joined upper-class ritual and residential complexes directly with the central parts of the city. Large Maya centres appear to have had from eight thousand to sixty-five thousand inhabitants. The central area of Tikal covered sixteen square kilometres and is estimated to have had a population of sixty-two thousand people. Calakmul appears to have been equally large. Caracol may have had thirty-five thousand to sixty thousand people living within three to four kilometres of its centre, while Coba, far to the north, had fifty-five thousand inhabitants. Small secondary centres were often located about ten kilometres from major urban centres (Andrews 1975; Ashmore 1981; Chase, Chase, and Haviland 1990; Culbert et al. 1990; Culbert and Rice 1990; Folan, Kintz, and Fletcher 1983; Folan et al. 1995; Pyburn 1997; Tate 1992; Webster 1997; Wilk and Ashmore 1988).

In all four city-state civilizations, the central public buildings of urban centres symbolized the unity of the city and of the surrounding territory it controlled. Mesopotamians and Yoruba used defensive walls to mark their cities' boundaries. In Mesopotamia walls separated different groups living within a city. Both in the Valley of Mexico and among the Maya, the marking of urban boundaries seems to have been much less important; their quarters, districts, and house complexes had at their centres ritual structures that expressed their individual identity. While the Yoruba and Mespotamians utilized barriers to demarcate cities and their subdivisions, Mesoamerican cultures used ranked systems of well-defined public buildings to identify such entities physically.

URBANISM IN TERRITORIAL STATES

Territorial states developed hierarchies of administrative centres at the local, district, provincial, and national levels, but the populations of those centres tended to be of modest size. Even national capitals, with perhaps fifty thousand inhabitants, were no more populous than the capitals of substantial city-states, although the populations that sustained them were many times larger. This was because these centres were inhabited almost exclusively by the ruling class and by administrators, craft specialists, and manual labourers who either worked

---

7.2. Urban centres in Mesoamerica: (a) Tenochtitlan-Tlatelolco in the early sixteenth century A.D.; (b) central four square kilometres of Tikal, a large Maya city; (c) the boundaries of Tikal as defined by structure density and location of earthworks, shown in relation to adjacent swamps. Sources: (a) after E. Calnek 1976: 293, and M. Smith 1996: 199; (b) after Blanton et al. 1981: 196; (c) after Culbert & Rice 1990: 118.

for the state or served the residents. Because the government protected the state as a whole against armed attack, farmers preferred for practical reasons to live in dispersed homesteads and villages near their fields rather than in urban centres. The houses of powerful officials sometimes had ornamental gardens, but these were mainly for enjoyment rather than to provide significant subsistence. Food was brought into the cities from the country estates of urban dwellers or as taxes and rents from rural villages.

Large territorial states sometimes had multiple capitals, which might shift location from one period to another. In Egypt the fortified palace and administrative centre founded, according to tradition, by Menes of the First Dynasty grew into the city of Memphis, which remained the primary administrative centre of Egypt throughout the Old and most of the Middle Kingdom. The main royal residences and burial places were located in its general vicinity, although the precise locations of both shifted from one reign to another. In the New Kingdom Memphis remained an important centre of government and court life but shared this role with Thebes, where the Egyptian kings were buried and had their main cult centre. As relations with the Near East became more crucial in the late New Kingdom, another royal residence was established at Pi-Ramesses in the eastern Delta. The sprawling remains of Akhenaton's short-lived capital at Akhetaton, in Middle Egypt, indicate how quickly a new capital could be constructed if a king wished to do so (Kemp 1989: 261–317). Equally significant was the speed with which the kings who united Egypt abandoned their original capital at This in Upper Egypt and the first ruler of the Twelfth Dynasty shifted his capital from Thebes to Memphis, perhaps recognizing that, because of communication difficulties, it was almost impossible to govern Egypt from a single capital located in the far south (Uphill 1988).

While the Inka regarded Cuzco as the cosmological centre of the world and their family seat, kings who had to remain away from it for long periods waging war and inspecting provinces established 'New Cuzcos' where they could perform essential state rituals. In these cities, as in major provincial capitals, streets, hills, plazas, and major buildings bore the same names as their prototypes in Cuzco, although they rarely closely resembled these prototypes in appearance (Hyslop 1990: 140, 172–76, 304–6). There is evidence that in the years preceding the Spanish conquest Inka rulers may have been deemphasizing Cuzco. Wayna Qhapaq, the last king to die before the Spanish conquest, may have intended to establish his mortuary cult in the city of Tumipampa (Tomebamba), in Ecuador, where he had resided for the last years of his reign, and the later Inka rulers promoted creation myths that traced their divine origin back to ancient ritual centres on Lake Titicaca (Urton 1990: 3).

While the frequent relocations of capitals historically recorded for the early Shang Dynasty have raised questions about the accuracy of these sources, they have generally been interpreted as motivated by military considerations related to expanding the Shang kingdom or maintaining its unity. Yoffee (1993: 70) has suggested that the rulers of territorial states may have sought to disembed political from social power by establishing new capitals where 'a formal separation from other elites allows for new policies to be implemented and new dependents to be recruited for the new enterprises'. It is therefore possible that the frequent shifts of capital cities of early Shang times were efforts to increase royal power.

In territorial states, kings spent much of their time travelling about their domains. Egyptian kings moved regularly from one part of the country to another inspecting provincial centres, collecting taxes, performing religious ceremonies, and hunting. In addition to their large palaces in the main administrative and ritual centres, they possessed a network of smaller residences throughout Egypt where they could stay while moving about (Kemp 1989: 218–23). Some of these were important centres for producing cloth and other goods for the court. The Inka kings travelled through their much larger kingdom inspecting administrative centres, performing rituals, hunting, putting down rebellions, and waging wars to extend or protect their frontiers (Kendall 1973: 67–68). They stayed in major provincial capitals and at rest stations along the main roads, where elaborate buildings were erected and equipped for government use. David Keightley (1983b: 552) suggests that by travelling about in their kingdom the Shang rulers renewed 'religious and kin ties (fictive or not) that bound the state together'. Rulers in all three territorial states were accompanied on these travels by armed escorts and large numbers of servants and officials.

Major urban centres took the form of dispersed settlements where rulers and the upper classes lived in special enclaves around which administrative and storage facilities, cult places, burial grounds, and settlements of lesser functionaries, retainers, craft workers, and supporting farmers were arranged. Elite enclaves, temples, and administrative centres were often enclosed by formidable walls, which not only protected their inhabitants against robbery and insurrection but also sheltered them from public view. Walled structures were therefore symbols of power and exclusivity as well as secure areas. Urban complexes in territorial states lacked outer defences, although entry to and exit from the capital area were controlled by official patrols and checkpoints. The dispersed nature of cities in territorial states was possible because there was little danger of external attack. The Inka 'fortress' of Saqsawaman, which was an imposing feature of the Cuzco landscape and a redoubt to which the upper classes and their supporters could retreat in time of rebellion or enemy attack, served storage and ritual as well as military functions (Hyslop 1990: 51–55).

The original administrative centre that had been established at Memphis came to symbolize the unity of Egypt. Its name, White Wall (*Inb ḥḏ*), signified an Upper Egyptian (hence 'white') presence in Lower Egypt, near the point where the two major administrative divisions of the country came together. This enclosure persisted in the form of a major administrative palace where the enthronement of Egyptian monarchs took place. For a king to circle this palace's outer walls symbolized taking possession of Egypt. Memphis's palace complex and the temple of Ptah to the south of it became the nucleus of a settlement that endured throughout Egyptian history. Bureaucrats, craftsmen, and others who worked for the state lived in the city, and high-ranking officials probably had official residences there as well (Fig. 7.3).

It appears, however, that the principal royal residence lay close to the pyramid complex of the reigning monarch and therefore was frequently located some distance north or south of Memphis. In the Old Kingdom, new royal residences seem to have been established in almost every reign. During the Middle Kingdom, the main royal residence appears to have remained at *Iṯi t3wy* (The Rightful Possessor of the Two Lands) about thirty kilometres south of Memphis. The palace of Djedkare-Isesi, a Fifth Dynasty ruler, is described as a rectangular structure about 640 by 230 metres that was called the 'Lotus Blossom of Isesi'. Nearby service towns would have been inhabited by skilled pyramid builders, palace servants, craftsmen, and later those who tended to the cult of the dead king. The settlement closest to Khufu's palace at Giza may have covered two hundred hectares. Residential palaces that were vacated when the court relocated may have been used for a time for administrative purposes, such as collecting and distributing resources, before being abandoned (Lehner 1997: 230–32).

Many features of these arrangements appear to have been retained in better-known New Kingdom capitals, such as Thebes and Akhetaton. On the east bank at Thebes, temples, an official palace, and various government offices were surrounded by the houses of officials, bureaucrats, retainers, craftsmen, and manual labourers. Only a few processional avenues imposed some degree of central planning on this agglomeration. On the west bank, at the edge of the floodplain, were a series of royal mortuary temples and the tombs of officials and kings. These were built and tended by workmen and priests who lived in nearby villages. Between these establishments were fields and a large number of farming villages, whose inhabitants probably worked part time as labourers and priests in neighbouring government and temple complexes. Kings appear to have located their main residential palaces on

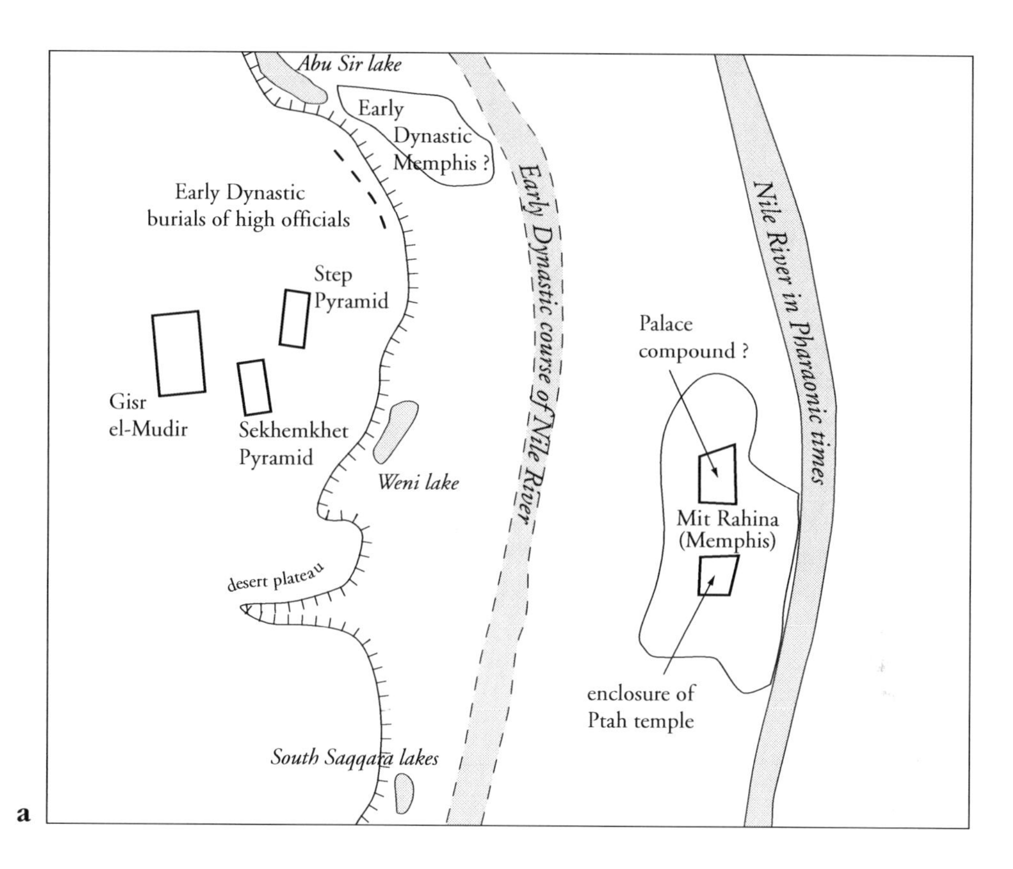

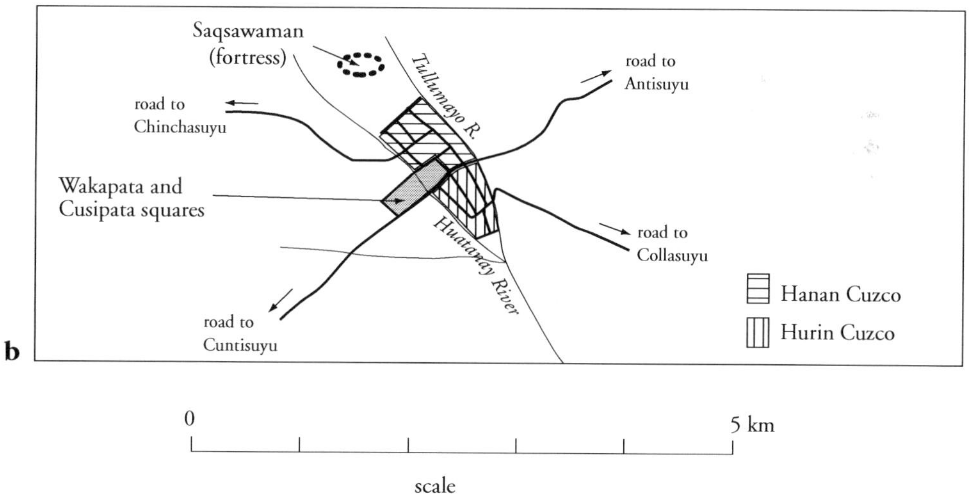

7.3. Urban centres in Egypt and the Inka kingdom: (a) the Egyptian Old Kingdom administrative centre at Memphis and some nearby royal burial sites; (b) the royal residential and ritual centre of the Inka capital at Cuzco – this area was surrounded by agricultural land and a ring of settlements occupied by people of lower status. Sources: (a) after Baines & Malek 1980: 135; (b) after Hyslop 1990: 30.

the outskirts of the urban area. Akhetaton displayed a similar combination of centrally located official palaces and temples and suburban residential palaces (Lacovara 1997; O'Connor 1995; 1998).

The Inka rulers used the resources of their kingdom to reorganize and transform the entire Cuzco Valley. At its centre was an urban zone of about forty hectares occupied by palaces, state buildings, and temples. This area was inhabited almost exclusively by members of royal lineages. Located on the site of the original town of Cuzco, this zone had been completely redesigned and rebuilt after A.D. 1438 by the Inka ruler Pachakutiq, who expelled all its non-Inka residents. The built-up area stretched from the fortress of Saqsawaman southeast between two small rivers, the Tullumayo and the Huatanay. Plans for the eventual expansion of settlement south of the Huatanay went unrealized. At the heart of this complex, marking the geographical and ritual centre of the Inka kingdom, were two adjacent squares, Wakapata and Cusipata, that were joined by wooden beams extending across the Huatanay River. Commoners from nearby communities frequently assembled in these squares to participate in major rituals and celebrations (J. Moore 1996). From these squares four roads ran outward to the main divisions of the Inka state. The road heading northeast divided Cuzco into upper (*hanan*) and lower (*hurin*) halves, which corresponded to the moiety arrangement found in all highland communities.

The rest of the city was traversed by three or four narrow streets that ran parallel to the rivers and a larger number of short intersecting side streets. The resulting roughly rectangular blocks, up to seventy-five metres long and forty-five metres wide, were occupied by the palace compounds of the reigning king and all the deceased ones. The dead kings' mummified bodies continued to be attended in their respective palaces as if they were alive. The palace compounds were located according to moiety affiliation: those associated with the earliest kings were located in Lower Cuzco and those of more recent kings in Upper Cuzco. Two royal palaces, belonging to Wiraqucha Inka and Thupa Inka Yupanki, contained the temples of the creator god Wiraqucha and the thunder god Illapa respectively (Kendall 1973: 115). Other compounds contained temples or housed special religious personnel. Still other compounds may have been used for administrative purposes. The main temple, the Qorikancha (House of Gold), was located at the south end of this urban complex. It faced onto another square where animals were sacrificed daily (Hyslop 1990: 36–47, 59–63; Kendall 1973: 112–15).

Central Cuzco was surrounded by a belt of farmland beyond which was a ring of planned settlements inhabited by officials who did not belong to the Inka royal family, provincial lords who were required to visit Cuzco periodically as proof of their loyalty, craft workers, permanent retainers who served the Inka elite, and conscripted labourers summoned from remote areas to work on government building projects in the Cuzco area. In this belt, as well as at Saqsawaman and in the central area, were located major storehouses for food, clothing, and other wealth belonging to the state. Representatives of every ethnic group in the Inka kingdom were said to have lived in these settlements, which were connected to central Cuzco by a radial set of trails that supplemented the four main roads that ran beyond the valley. Still farther from the centre, in the Cuzco and neighbouring Urubamba Valleys, were farming communities, but there too were the private estates and rural palaces of reigning and former kings and estates belonging to members of the nobility. The Cuzco Valley was covered by a network of shrines, some of which played a prominent role in state rituals. It has been estimated that fifteen thousand to twenty thousand people may have lived in central Cuzco, another fifty thousand in the surrounding ring of settlement, and a further fifty thousand to one hundred and ten thousand in other parts of the valley (Hyslop 1990: 64). Many of the inhabitants of the central area did not reside there full-time, however, and because numerous commoners lived and worked in different zones there may have been duplication in recording the population of these three areas. Thus the total figures estimated for the Cuzco Valley may be somewhat inflated (Hyslop 1990: 48–58, 63–67; Kendall 1973: 116–17; Zuidema 1964; 1990).

The dispersed layouts of Shang major centres resemble the capitals of other territorial states rather than those of city-states. At the Early Shang site of Zhengzhou a massive rectangular wall of stamped earth about 22 metres thick, 1,870 metres long, and 1,690 metres wide has been interpreted as an elite compound containing palaces and upper-class residences. Around this compound have been found small, isolated settlements once inhabited by bronze, bone, and pottery workers, an area of poorer houses, and various burial areas. The bronze workers lived in stamped-earth houses built on platforms which indicate a considerable level of affluence. The compound appears to have been surrounded by villages of craft workers and retainers who served the upper classes living within its walls. Still farther away would have been agricultural villages (An 1986; Bagley 1999: 165–68; K. Chang 1980: 263–88). The general arrangement of Zhengzhou resembles that of Cuzco. Another walled compound, about 2,150 metres square, has been identified just north of Anyang and tentatively dated to the beginning of the Middle Shang period (Tang, Jin, and Rapp 2000) (Fig. 7.4).

The late Shang royal centre at Anyang (Yinxi) has been described as a network of separate settlements spread over an area measuring six by four kilometres. Xiaotun, near the centre of the complex, contains a collection of large halls and temples facing south and appears to have been a royal palace

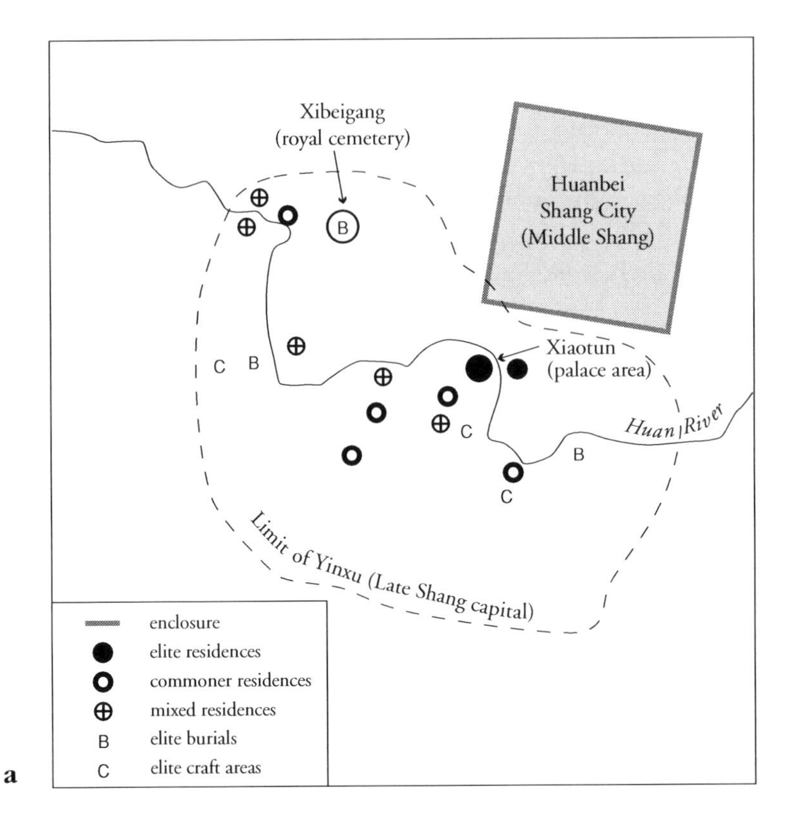

7.4. Urban centres in China: (a) Anyang, showing recently discovered Middle Shang administrative enclosure and major features of the Late Shang capital region to south; (b) Early Shang administrative enclosure at Zhengzhou and some surrounding settlements. Sources: (a) after Tang et al. 2000: 479; G. Barnes 1993: 128; (b) after K. Chang 1986a: 337.

complex. Around the major buildings were small houses probably inhabited by royal servants. It is not clear whether this central complex was walled, although the remains of an ancient ditch have been reported. There was another elite residential area nearby, and to the north at Xibeigang a large cemetery contained royal graves and evidence of ongoing mortuary rites. Interspersed throughout the area were settlements housing a mixture of wealthy and poorer individuals, sites inhabited exclusively by commoners, and various workshops (G. Barnes 1993: 126–29; K. Chang 1980: 70–135; Li Chi 1977).

The capitals of territorial states tended to be less compact than those of city-states, and their various components were often separated by areas of farmland. At least in part these arrangements seem to have reflected the desire of rulers to live in isolation from their subjects and perhaps even from most officials. While various central administrative and ritual structures were built near the centres of such agglomerations, at least some royal residences were located on the outskirts. By comparison with city-state capitals, the primary cities of territorial states tended to lack clearly marked centres or boundaries. While massive structures provided impressive displays of royal power, in territorial states it was the king and his court, wherever they might be, rather than any specific features of urban architecture that constituted the heart of the state.

To draw a complete comparison between city-states and territorial states with regard to urbanism, it is essential to consider the latter's provincial administrative centres as well as their capitals. In Egypt a network of administrative centres and government offices in smaller towns was necessary to serve royal funerary cults, levy and collect taxes, and control the countryside. Provincial centres would have required elite residences, offices, storehouses, barracks for police, and workshops where, for example, boats could have been built to transport surplus grain (David 1986; Wegner 2000). For the most part, these centres were small ones. Moreover, during the Early Dynastic period and the Old Kingdom, while the central government featured prominently in the construction of walled enclosures and temples at key ritual centres such as Abydos and Hierakonpolis, elsewhere most such construction appears to have been carried out by local officials. It was not until the Middle Kingdom that the central government began to play a systematic role in building temples throughout Egypt (Kemp 1977; 1983: 96–104; 1989: 65–83; Seidlmayer 1996). During the Old Kingdom, the main construction projects of the Egyptian state were focused on the Memphis area and in particular on royal tombs. This centralized symbolic affirmation of the unity of the Egyptian state would have been optimally effective if, in the course of corvée labour, most Egyptian men had seen and perhaps helped to build these monuments. Because they were also important regional cult centres, most of the provincial administrative centres endured throughout Egyptian history.

Inka provincial centres in the highlands invariably contained Inka-style cut-stone buildings constructed by local masons working to Inka specifications. In the lowlands Inka embellishments were often added to buildings of local styles. Administrative centres were established in every province, often away from indigenous settlements, as residences for provincial governors and places where food, clothing, and weapons could be supplied to government officials, soldiers, and farm labourers moving from one part of the kingdom to another. These centres also contained barracks in which large numbers of transient soldiers and labourers could eat and sleep. The full-time inhabitants of these centres included state functionaries, women charged with brewing beer, weaving cloth, and cooking for the state, and assistants attached to government officials. Food and other materials were brought from throughout each province to its administrative centre, where most of the bulk commodities were stored for government use. The workforces that built and maintained such centres were recruited locally, usually as corvée labourers. In contrast to the Egyptian kings, Inka rulers displayed their power not only in the capital region but systematically throughout their kingdom (Hyslop 1990: 69–101; Kendall 1973: 118–19; Morris and Thompson 1985).

Subsidiary centres of government in the Shang and Western Zhou kingdoms appear to have been much smaller than capitals. Each centre consisted of a walled enclosure containing the residence, ancestral temple, and other official buildings of the local ruler, as well as housing for his household servants and armed retainers. Both the words that later meant town (*yi*) and state (*guo*) appear initially to have referred to these walled residences (Hsu and Linduff 1988: 268–69). Thus *yi* probably originally designated a walled administrative centre rather than a more conventional town or city. The Chinese clearly viewed settlements of this sort as proper locations for the exercise of aristocratic power. There is no evidence that at this time secondary walled settlements were other than the seats of dominant lineages and their retainers (G. Barnes 1993: 136; K. Chang 1980: 158–83). This interpretation further calls into question the suggestion that the Shang rulers were hegemons ruling over a series of city-states.

In more secure areas, walls may have mainly protected the privacy of the local governing family, but in more exposed or unsettled territories they may also have sheltered a garrison, possibly related by blood to the presiding official, which cultivated land both inside and outside them. In times of enemy attack or local rebellion, such centres would have provided places of refuge for those in the region who supported the local ruler, together with their animals and movable property. They may also have attracted craft workers seeking work and protection. Thus these centres of regional government would have been smaller and simpler versions of royal court centres.

SOURCES OF VARIATION

Much of the variation in urbanism in the early civilizations is correlated with the distinction between city- and territorial states. Some of this variation was of a functional nature, such as the tendency for farmers to locate their homes in urban centres in city-state systems, where local warfare was common, but to live near their fields where a territorial state ensured their safety from attack. At the same time, the dispersed nature of major urban centres in territorial states suggests a pursuit of privacy on the part of the ruling class that, according to Peter Wilson (1988), is everywhere an important technique for enhancing the authority of rulers. In city-state capitals such privacy had to be ensured by limiting access to upper-class residences rather than by geographically isolating them. Whether or not different city-state systems constructed walls around their capitals may have been a simple alternative in their defensive strategies and the deployment of resources. It also gave rise to an Old World versus New World and hence perhaps a historically derived dichotomy. This particular difference seems to have been related to a more general tendency to distinguish social units by emphasizing boundaries in some societies and centres in others. In all early civilizations urban centres were viewed as exceptionally interesting places in which to live. They were the physical embodiments of political power and human achievement and the places in which humans came into closest contact with the supernatural powers that made the universe function.

8 Class Systems and Social Mobility

In early civilizations and other complex preindustrial societies, inequality was regarded as a normal condition and injustice as a personal misfortune or even an individual's just deserts rather than as a social evil (Weber 1976 [1896]: 258). Structures based on differential power were pervasive. Every child was born into and socialized by a family that was internally hierarchized in the image of the state. The subordination of children to their parents and, to varying degrees, of wives to their husbands went unquestioned, as did corporal punishment as a means of enforcing obedience and discipline (Trigger 1985b). Young people were expected to obey older people, especially older men. 'Father', 'king', and 'god' were often synonyms and metaphors for power. While most small farming communities were already hierarchized, they became even more so with the development of more complex societies. The most powerful and advantaged members of these communities strengthened their positions by acting as intermediaries between their fellow villagers and the state. The general pervasiveness of inequality ensured that its legitimacy went unquestioned. If egalitarian social organization was known to people in early civilizations, it was as a feature of small-scale and usually despised societies beyond the pale.

In all early civilizations richer and more powerful people cultivated a distinctive lifestyle. They controlled the major public institutions and used this control to protect and enhance their wealth and power. They also tended to marry people of similar status and to restrict and control vertical social mobility. Nevertheless, there were significant differences among early civilizations in the extent to which distinctions between classes were formally demarcated.

Ian Morris (1997) contrasts Ernest Gellner's (1983) model of 'agro-literate states' (large preindustrial kingdoms) with the ideal class structure of a democratic Greek city-state (*polis*) of the Classical period. In agro-literate states, horizontally segregated layers of the military, administrative, religious, and sometimes commercial upper classes were rigidly separated from laterally insulated communities of agricultural producers (Gellner 1983: 9–11; 1998). In democratic Greek city-states, male citizens were distinguished from female citizens, foreigners, and slaves. Morris argues that after 500 B.C., despite considerable real differences in wealth, the ideal of the equality of male citizens led to the disappearance in Greek urban settings of rich graves, elaborate funerary monuments, fancy houses, and elaborate clothes and jewellery (1997: 102–3).

No early civilization displayed that sort of ideologically driven symbolic equality. Kings, not a mass of sovereign citizens, stood at the head of society, and there were marked differences in way of life between the wealthy, powerful, and leisured minority that controlled society and the much poorer, hard-working, and ideally obedient mass of the population. Nevertheless, Gellner's and Morris's models indicate the need to consider how class was perceived and represented in early civilizations and to what extent differences in class and status were symbolically accentuated or disguised by lifestyles.

In early civilizations there was a need not only to protect the reality of power and authority from challenge and ridicule by the lower classes but also to ensure that the symbols of status were not encroached on by those of lower rank. Protecting the privileges and symbols of authority was one of the responsibilities of the monarch. In some early civilizations, sumptuary laws dictated what kinds of clothes, jewellery, and insignia could be worn by different classes. Among the Aztec particular colours and patterns of cloth were restricted to specific classes and ranks within classes. Every enemy soldier captured by an Aztec warrior entitled that warrior to wear a distinctive costume, ornaments, and hairstyle and to perform special honorific roles in public rituals. The state could punish and even kill people for infractions of these sumptuary laws (Clendinnen 1991: 120; Hassig 1988: 39–40; Soustelle 1961: 132–39).

The Inka government carefully regulated the kind and amount of goods that members of different classes could own. Inka officials distributed fancy clothes, women, male servants, metal ware, land, and minor public offices as rewards for service to the state. These gifts were carefully graduated to take account of the recipient's social rank. Rulers obliged individuals to wear their hair and dress in a manner that was distinctive of their ethnic group. This not only distinguished the ruling class from subject peoples but, when various ethnic groups were resettled in different parts of the kingdom, also distinguished such settlers from indigenous people. The Inka rulers were seeking not to create ethnic homogeneity but to preserve ethnic diversity so that they could play one subject group off against another. By carefully distinguishing hairstyles, dress, and ornaments they emphasized differences in class, ethnicity, and the favour of government officials (Kendall 1973: 33, 178; Rowe 1944: 262).

At the investiture ceremonies of regional officials, Western Zhou kings presented them with clothing decorated with symbols of office, special banners, elaborately crafted chariots and weapons, and jade ornaments. Gradations in these valuable presents reinforced an established hierarchy of privileges and prestige (Hsu and Linduff 1988: 177–78).

The Benin rulers claimed ownership of all the red coral beads in their kingdom. These beads were highly coveted royal honours. Kings assigned collars made of them to officials for their lifetimes, to be returned when the recipients died. The collars were also periodically recalled to the palace, where a slave was ritually sacrificed and his blood poured over them to renew their power. Special clothes bearing distinctive patterns were woven in the royal palace at Benin to be worn by the king and his major officials. The power of the king was displayed and reinforced by his ability to control luxury goods, both by regulating their manufacture and by determining who might own or use them (Bradbury 1957: 26, 46, 58). The aim of these regulations was to keep such goods scarce and therefore useful as status markers.

None of the early civilizations we are considering had orders – classes defined primarily by the type of work that each group did. Whereas in medieval Europe knights or professional warriors, priests, and manual workers constituted an overriding hierarchical framework, as the *brahmin* (priest), *ksatriya* (warrior, ruler), *vaisya* (trader, businessman), and *sudra* (farmer) orders (*varna*) still do in India, in all seven early civilizations both the priesthood and the army cut across class lines. The top levels of religious hierarchies were invariably occupied by members of the royal family and the upper classes. Middle levels were staffed by people drawn from the administrative class, while the physical labour required to maintain temples was usually performed by low-ranking priests drawn from craft workers and farmers. While major positions in religious hierarchies were generally filled by full-time personnel and less prestigious ones on a part-time basis, in Old and Middle Kingdom Egypt even high-ranking priests were government officials who took turns managing shrines and temples or performing religious duties. Military leaders were likewise drawn from the upper classes, while ordinary soldiers and militia conscripts were recruited from the lower classes. Full-time soldiers tended to be members of an intermediate specialist class.

PERCEPTION OF CLASS

In practice early civilizations appear to have had numerous social groupings – most of them highly localized, others geographically dispersed – each of which was aware of its social position in relation to other groups. Such units included families, localized occupational collectivities, and people who played specific types of leadership roles. While, inevitably, elaborate formal or informal gradations of status existed among these groups, there was also a tendency to generalize these gradations to form a small number of hierarchical divisions. Usually this involved distinguishing an upper class, free commoners, and slaves. Since slaves, if any, tended to be few, the bulk of the population was divided into two groups: upper class and commoners. Divisions of this sort provided a general framework for understanding the much more complicated relations of authority and deference that characterized interaction among individuals and collectivities. A dual distinction also reinforced the pretensions of the numerically inferior upper class by pairing it in a simple hierarchy with the vastly more numerous lower class.

While all early civilizations shared a general view of class hierarchy, the criteria and clarity with which these broad classes were distinguished varied. The Inka recognized an upper class that was entirely hereditary and divided into three main ranks on the basis of members' origins. The ancient Egyptians distinguished the *pꜥt* (hereditary nobility) from the *rḫyt* (defeated/subjected ones) or *nḏs* (small people) (Baines 1995b: 133; Malek and Forman 1986: 34). The hereditary nobles were, however, supplemented and increasingly eclipsed by a non-hereditary upper class composed of officials who held positions in the higher echelons of the civil service hierarchy. Throughout the Valley of Mexico, a hereditary upper class (*pipiltin*) traced their descent from the ruler of the ancient city of Tollan, who was believed to be a descendant or manifestation of the god Quetzalcoatl. Membership in that class could be acquired only through one or both parents. Among the Classic Maya hereditary *ahaw* (nobles) may have been differentiated from commoners (Freidel 1992: 130). In China a hereditary nobility was distinguished from ordinary men (*ren*) and dependent workers (*zhong*), and according to Léon Vandermeersch (1980: 18) the upper class was divided into two levels: *zi* (close relatives of the king) and *chen* (retainers). Other major upper-class titles suggest intervening grades of nobles.

In each of these civilizations the upper classes, or at least their highest levels, which traced their descent from former rulers, claimed a special supernatural origin. While in Peru the second major rank of the nobility was composed of ennobled commoners and in Egypt individuals of non-royal ancestry were raised to the rank of the hereditary nobility, in the Valley of Mexico an ennobled commoner could ensure that his descendants became hereditary nobles only by marrying a female member of that group.

The early Mesopotamians do not appear to have had a hereditary nobility, but their free population was divided into two groups with unequal political power and unequal rights before the law. The higher-ranking of the two thus constituted a formally recognized upper class (Diakonoff 1987; Maisels 1990: 273–74). J. D. Y. Peel (1983: 46) has proposed that the closest thing to a dominant class in Yoruba society was the entire body of male household heads. Yet, in addition to the royal clans, some Yoruba patrilineages were larger and more prosperous than others, and the most prominent male members of these lineages shared substantial power with the king. While these men and their families may not have constituted a formally recognized upper class, they formed a de facto one.

In territorial states there was a tendency for the distinction between the upper and commoner classes to be more overt, complex, and symbolically marked than in city-states. The upper classes were also more likely to be explicitly divided into multiple grades or ranks. This was done by means of ranked subclasses in Inka Peru, by tracing deep and unequal genealogical relations among descent groups in Shang China, and by using additional criteria such as civil service rankings in Egypt. Because territorial states extended over large areas, even members of the upper class could not all be expected to know one another personally. Fixed ranks and special insignia facilitated the recognition of authority that was essential for effective interaction among members of the ruling group.

In city-states, where prominent people tended to know each other personally, there was less need for a formal demarcation of status. There was also a tendency for power to be shared among the leaders of various groups and institutions, for the power of individuals and groups to be challenged, and for there to be more fluidity in which groups made various types of decisions. Under these circumstances, it must have been strategically advantageous to mute the expression of some types of social inequality in order to fend off challenges and reduce political tensions. At the same time, public attention had to be drawn to leading citizens to ensure that proper forms of deference were maintained. These contradictory objectives were not handled in the same way in all city-states. The peoples living in the Valley of Mexico and perhaps the Classic Maya had hereditary upper classes. Both the Mesopotamians and the Yoruba recognized general class divisions, but these divisions were not hereditary or socially emphasized to the same degree.

There are important similarities in class structure in all the civilizations in our sample, as well as similarities in the detailed criteria by which groups were ranked. Whether or not these criteria were terminologically marked, they appear to represent cross-culturally similar views concerning the appropriate correlates of prestige and status. Even an early civilization organized on the basis of orders such as that of Gangetic India would have conformed to this arrangement.

UPPER CLASSES

While symbolically the king stood above and represented all of society, he was also the leader of the upper classes. One of his most important functions was to unite that group and protect and promote its social and political interests. The upper classes in all early civilizations were small, amounting to no more than a few percent of the total population, but they controlled much of the surplus wealth of their societies and played key roles in decisions about policy and administration. They used their power to protect their economic and social privileges and reinforce their social position. Where the upper class was hereditary, it was normally composed of the king and other members of the royal family, collateral descendants of formerly independent rulers and leading provincial families, and administrators and soldiers who had been ennobled as a reward for their services to the state. Where the upper class was not formally hereditary, it was made up of the leaders of prominent lineages or ethnic groups, the administrators of major civic institutions, and wealthy landowners. Even in these societies kingship tended to be hereditary, and other offices were often controlled by the same families for long periods.

The luxurious lifestyle of the upper classes was supported by family or private ownership of land, by state salaries, which sometimes involved revocable assignments of land instead of actual payments, and by the opportunity to become the beneficiaries of bribes, fees, military booty, and economic control. Some members of the upper classes enjoyed these privileges simply as a result of belonging to upper-class families. They did little work, but their status put inherited land and other forms of wealth at their disposal. Other members played an active role in administering the state. The highest state officials belonged to the upper classes, and together with the king they made all the most important decisions. Members of this group also commanded the army and managed the major religious institutions. Less prestigious members of the nobility were minor officials, engineers, and sometimes high-ranking artists.

The Inka upper class was composed at the highest level by the reigning monarch, his immediate family, and the descendants of all previous Inka rulers. The latter were organized as *panaqas* (royal descent groups) each of which traced its origin to a particular king. Depending on how they were genealogically related to their founder, members of each panaqa (and perhaps also their dependents) were divided into three ranked groups called *qullana*, *payan*, and *kayaw* (Bauer 1998: 35–39). The members of a panaqa were collectively endowed with the dead king's palaces, personal wealth, and private land. Their chief task was to manage these properties and to feed, clothe, and care for the mummified bodies of the dead king and his chief wife. These two individuals were venerated as the founder deities of their panaqa, in the same manner as minor nature deities were regarded as the founding ancestors of commoner landowning groups (*ayllu*). Unlike ayllus, however, panaqas were not required to be endogamous.

It is often assumed that each new Inka king had to acquire his own wealth, everything that his predecessor had accumulated belonging to that king's descent group. This, it is argued, explains why each king strove to expand the borders of the kingdom (Conrad and Demarest 1984). If, however, it is true that the panaqa Qhapaq Ayllu always belonged to the reigning monarch, considerable wealth would have passed from each monarch to his successor, leaving only his palaces, personal lands, and private possessions to his other descendants (I. Farrington 1992: 369–70). It also appears that the panaqas of at least thirteen successive kings may have been assigned to only ten named divisions of the Cuzco terrain. This suggests that descendants of later kings had to share resources in the Cuzco area with descendants of much earlier rulers if their panaqas were assigned the same estates.

Panaqas were important political entities in the Inka state. The oracular pronouncements of each dead king, which his panaqa controlled, were an important source of political power for its leaders. Panaqas participated in policy-making and meddled in royal successions. Their leaders competed for high state offices, which were granted as a result of winning the king's favour, and sought to enhance their power by marrying their close female relatives to the king. The most recently formed panaqas appear to have been the richest. This may have been because the older ones had never possessed much land or wealth or because their wealth had had to be divided among a growing number of descendants of the original king. It is also possible that many of their resources had been reallocated to the panaqas of more recent rulers. All the members of this highest level of the Inka upper class claimed descent from the principal Inka deity, the sun god, Inti. Men drawn from this level occupied the highest offices in the Inka state (Gose 1996a; Patterson 1991).

The second rank of Inka nobility consisted of Inka-by-privilege (*ayllucusco*), who were organized into ten descent groups (ayllus). According to Inka traditions, they had originally lived in the Cuzco region, and their ancestors had supported the early Inka kings. In return, the Inka rulers had ennobled them when they found it necessary to recruit more administrators for their expanding bureaucracy. Unlike the true Inka nobility, these groups were derived, like ordinary humans, from minor supernatural forces, not from the sun god. The Inka and the Inka-by-privilege shared posts in the administration of the kingdom, although the latter generally occupied less important positions. Finally, conquered hereditary rulers and their descendants, down to the level of rulers of one hundred families, were often allowed to retain their land and privileges as members of the provincial nobility (Kendall 1973: 56, 101; Rowe 1944: 260–61). While their power was carefully circumscribed by Inka provincial overseers, their control over their own people was frequently enhanced rather than diminished by the political support they received from the Inka state.

In Egypt, the hereditary nobility were in theory descended from beings who had lived when the creator gods still ruled directly over the terrestrial realm (Morenz 1973: 47). They included descendants of kings and possibly also of cooperative local rulers whose territories had been absorbed into the Egyptian state at the time of its unification. Officials of commoner origin and their descendants were raised to this rank as a reward for especially meritorious service. Less prestigious honorary titles, such as *ḥ3ty* ʿ (notable), *smr wʿty* (unique friend of the king), *smr* (friend of the king), and *ḫtmt bỉty* (royal sealer), were assigned to favoured officials for their lifetimes (Allen 2000: 32). The hereditary title 'pʿt' was meaningful so long as an individual commanded sufficient wealth to live in an appropriate fashion. Such wealth was derived from administrative offices, land bestowed on individuals as gifts by the ruler, inherited estates, and land that was purchased using wealth accumulated from government stipends.

In contrast to members of Inka panaqas, the Egyptian hereditary nobility did not constitute a formally organized group or series of groups that enjoyed collective economic privileges or political advantages. Instead, individual title-holders had to look after their own interests. The most important and finely graduated Egyptian male status hierarchy consisted of the ranked positions that individuals might occupy in the state administrative system. These positions were an important source of power and wealth. The formal role that individual nobles played in relation to this hierarchy and in administering Egypt varied from one period to another. During the Fourth Dynasty, many of the highest state offices were occupied by sons and other close male relatives of the king. Later in the Old Kingdom such individuals were for a time excluded from these offices. Without private wealth or patronage and economic support from the king, nobles were in danger of lacking sufficient wealth to remain active members of the upper class. Both the non-corporate nature of the hereditary nobility and the role of the civil service ranking system in defining status reflected the importance of winning royal or official favour for preferment and career advancement (Baer 1960; Strudwick 1985).

Strong emphasis was placed at all levels of Shang society on the ranking of descent lines within clans and on birth order among siblings of the same sex. Power and authority passed from a man to his eldest son or from older to younger brothers within a specific descent line. Supreme power was vested in the senior line of the Zi clan. Males who were closely related to reigning or previous kings held important court offices or administered territories. Regional offices tended to remain hereditary in the senior male line of their occupants. As the state expanded, new territories were established where younger sons of officials might be installed. Thus officials of higher genealogical status tended to hold land closer to the centre of the state and participated in the functioning of the court while others lived farther away. As lineages expanded, it was increasingly difficult to find positions for younger sons that would allow them to maintain an upper-class lifestyle (Vandermeersch 1980: 81–122).

Territories were also assigned to leaders of clans that supported the Zi, while some conquered rulers were allowed to govern all or part of their former territories as Shang vassals. These officials were permitted to marry female members of the royal clan, and some of the most important of them married women of the royal lineage. The Shang upper class thus became a network of officials related directly or indirectly to the king. Officials who governed administrative territories bore the titles *hou* (archer lord?), *bo* (patriarch?), and *tian* or *dian* (field lord). While these positions normally were hereditary, successors, at least at the higher levels, had to be confirmed by the king, who could also promote or remove individuals from their offices (Chao 1972: 99–111). Officials who headed junior branches of a clan remained ritually and socially subordinate to the leaders of the senior branches from which they had split off, even when they lived far apart.

The Aztec nobility (pipiltin) traced their descent ultimately from the god Quetzalcoatl through the male or the female line or preferably both. In the centuries preceding the Spanish conquest, throughout the Valley of Mexico, the pipiltin had replaced or absorbed local elites that could not claim divine descent. According to tradition, all the Aztec had originally been commoners who had migrated into the Valley of Mexico from the north. Acamapichtli, the first Aztec king, had been invited to Tenochtitlan from the neighbouring city-state of Culhuacan, whose nobles claimed descent from the ruler of ancient Tollan. It was maintained that some of Quetzalcoatl's descendants had moved south to Culhuacan following the destruction of Tollan in the twelfth century A.D.

The hereditary nobles of the Valley of Mexico were divided into two groups: the tetecuhtin (lords), who were the king's main advisers and military officers, and the pilli, descendants of tetecuhtin who had not inherited their fathers' positions but served as government officials of lesser rank. Tetecuhtin headed *teccalli* (family groups) to which related, lower-ranked pipiltin belonged (Berdan 1982: 52–54). Pipiltin wore cotton clothes, sandals, feather work, and jade ornaments, lived in two-storey stone houses, ate the flesh of human sacrifices, drank chocolate and fermented beverages (in moderation) in public, kept concubines, entered the royal palace at will, could eat in the palace dining hall, and performed special dances at public rituals. They did not pay taxes (Clendinnen 1991: 120).

Because calpolli leaders were encouraged to marry the daughters of kings, powerful commoner families were drawn into the nobility and their primary loyalties transferred from their kinship and residence groups to the emerging upper class. As a consequence, class divisions cut across calpollis. Individual warriors who performed brave acts, especially those who captured at least four enemy soldiers in battle, were raised to the status of *quauhpilli* (eagle noble). Their position was not hereditary, but by marrying younger daughters of noble parents or daughters of nobles by their secondary, commoner wives they could ensure that their children inherited pilli status from their mothers.

The pipiltin appear to have been ranked in descending status according to whether they were members of the royal descent group, members of other prominent office-holding families, descended from pipiltin through both parents or only one, or had personally achieved that status. A noble's rank was further defined by the state offices to which he was appointed and by the finely graduated military honours that he won in recognition of his performance in battle. The main terminological distinctions were drawn between nobles who held high office, ordinary nobles, and eagle nobles. While the pipiltin were found throughout the Valley of Mexico, the difference between noble and commoner lifestyles was probably less marked in small city-states than in large and powerful centres such as Tenochtitlan and Texcoco.

Among the Maya, rulers and their families also appear to have belonged to a hereditary lordly class. It is generally assumed that large patrilineal extended families or clans played an important role in Maya social organization. These families are believed to have been stratified both internally and in relation to one another. Powerful ones may have increased in size and wealth by incorporating non-kin as low-status members or clients (Carmack 1973; 1981). It is unclear, however, whether the title-holders of major patrilineages formed a high-level governing group within each Maya city-state, as occurred among the Yoruba, or the most powerful local officials were consanguineal members of the royal family, as in China. If noble status was restricted to the senior lines of major patrilineal groupings, the situation was very different from that found in the Valley of Mexico. Some Mayanists question the importance of large patrilineal groupings in Classic Maya society or suggest that their importance varied from one Maya region and one class level to another (Chase and Chase 1992b: 307–10; Haviland 1992; Wilk 1988).

In each of the five early civilizations considered so far, there appears to have been a hereditary upper class, although in Egypt the importance of that group was eclipsed to a considerable degree by a ranking system based on honorary titles bestowed on individuals and personally achieved positions in the government administrative hierarchy. Insofar as these upper-class positions were hereditary, it seems appropriate to refer to the non-royal segment of the upper classes in these societies as a nobility or aristocracy. In two early civilizations, however, Mesopotamia and that of the Yoruba, there was an upper class but no hereditary nobility.

It is believed that in the initial stages of Mesopotamian civilization the leaders of major landowning extended families, who were sometimes also leaders of villages, wards, and ethnic groups, participated in the councils that governed early city-states, possibly in conjunction with a king. By the Early Dynastic period, kings, administrators of major temples, and important private landowners shared power. Rich private landowners occupied seats on city councils, and they and major temple officials advised the king and helped him to govern the state. Land that had once been owned collectively by patrilineal extended families fell increasingly under the control of palaces, temples, and wealthy families or individuals. As collectively owned land was transformed into institutionally and privately owned land, increasing numbers of ordinary people were forced to become clients of palaces, temples, and landowners in order to survive. This development accentuated the differences between a small privileged group and a much larger dependent stratum in Mesopotamian society. In the Old Babylonian period these two strata were designated *awilum* and *muškenum*. The awilum embraced the families of major office-holders and landowners and leaders of groups that possessed land communally. The muškenum were landless families under perpetual patriarchal authority or at best working conditional landholdings (Diakonoff 1987: 2; Maisels 1990: 262–74). Earlier the Sumerians appear to have drawn an analogous distinction between *dumugi* (property owners, citizens) and *guruš* (dependents). While both groups believed themselves to be descended from the same human ancestors and social mobility occurred, in the Early Babylonian period the two groups were marked by an explicit legal distinction between property owners, who were treated relatively leniently by the law, and poorer people, who were not.

There is no evidence of formal ranking within the Mesopotamian upper class. Power was both shared and contested by kings, temple administrators, and private and collective landowners. Only in a few hegemonic city-states and for limited periods was royal authority preeminent. Yet economic developments had produced deep economic and political inequality in Mesopotamian society. While various privileged elements, both individual and institutional, resisted centralization and struggled to control various spheres of activity, these same privileged groups cooperated in defending their privileges in opposition to lower-class discontent.

The Yoruba had a de facto upper class composed of members of the royal clan in each city-state, ward chiefs, leaders of important ritual societies, and rich and high-ranking members of the patrilineages that held seats on the state council. The generic term applied to such men was *olalá* (honoured) (Lloyd 1974: 49). Prominent members of the leading patrilineages engaged in fierce competition for their offices and titles. These patrilineages were invariably more populous, prosperous, and powerful than others. Their principal members owned many slaves who grew large amounts of food, and this permitted them to attract numerous clients, including soldiers who could capture more slaves for them in warfare and intimidate their rivals. A position on the state council enabled a man to share in the revenues of the kingdom and secure trading and other privileges that greatly enhanced his prosperity and that of his patrilineage. Over time titles might shift from one patrilineage to another, and the king could create new titles and offices. Nevertheless, the ability of office-holders to exploit their privileged positions to create wealth for their families tended to keep the upper class relatively stable. In Benin the kings had severely curbed the power of these leading families and developed an elaborate system of titles that rewarded individuals for their particular services to the monarch. Despite their loss of power, the leading non-royal lineages of Benin continued to enjoy affluence and social and ritual precedence (Bradbury 1957: 35–36; R. Smith 1969: 110–16).

The upper classes in early civilizations had many features in common. They controlled a disproportionate amount of the wealth of their societies, avoided physical labour, enjoyed an opulent lifestyle, and indulged in conspicuous consumption. They occupied the top administrative, military, and religious posts and constituted the highest levels of decision making and administration, either sharing power with the monarch or being the people most able to influence him. These upper classes were not always hereditary, and where they were not they might be defined either formally or informally. In territorial states upper-class status tended to be both hereditary and formally defined. The presence of hereditary nobilities in some but not all early civilizations refutes Charles-Louis Secondat, Baron de Montesquieu's (1689–1755) assumption that early despotic societies lacked them (Isaac 1993: 432). Yet to preserve upper-class status, individuals and families needed to maintain their wealth and access to high offices. The ability to do that became impaired as families slipped genealogically farther from major sources of power and fixed wealth became sub-divided over successive generations. An important way for members of the upper class to counter a loss of wealth and power was marriage into royal or other leading families.

COMMONERS

Commoners made up the vast bulk of the population in early civilizations, often constituting 90 percent or more. They rarely owned land individually and, if they did, only in small amounts. They depended for subsistence on the sale of goods they produced, worked for the state or other patrons, or formed collective landholding groups. Their political power was also severely limited. The lowest-ranking and by far the most numerous of them were engaged in agriculture. At the top of the commoner class were full-time specialists, more numerous than the upper classes but also amounting to no more than a few percent of the population. They are often claimed to have formed a 'middle class', but they did not derive their income from ownership of commercial and industrial enterprises within the context of a capitalist economy. Nor did they correspond to the professional bourgeoisie, the first form of the middle class to establish a place for itself in Western society. Specialists lacked significant political power and independent sources of wealth. Some may have owned small properties, but others either subsisted by selling their produce or received rations or grants of land in exchange for their services.

Many members of this group depended on the state or on members of the upper class for their positions and salaries. These might be called 'dependent specialists'. The principal exceptions were craftsmen and traders who made a living by selling goods to anyone who wished to buy them. Hence the term 'full-time specialists' seems preferable as a generic designation of this class. Specialists were divided into a number of different types of occupations of varying prestige. These occupations tended to be hereditary, and most were taught by father to son or learned through apprenticeship. In general, the less highly regarded the type of occupation, the more people practised it.

The most prestigious group of specialists was the lesser officials, who are often labelled 'administrators', 'bureaucrats', or 'scribes' (Egyptian *sš*, Sumerian *dubšar*, Aztec *tlacuilohqueh*, Inka *hampikamayoq*). Their principal duties were to see that the orders of upper-class officials were carried out, make the routine decisions required to do this (such as ascertaining how much tax individual farmers should pay), and keep track of the wealth and property of large institutions, rulers, and other members of the upper class. They were trained to read and write or to use whatever recording devices were employed by a particular civilization. In general, their work and style of life were more similar to those of the less prestigious members of the upper class than to those of any other group. It has been suggested, on the basis of very fragmentary surviving evidence, that among the Maya knowledge of writing may have been confined to certain members of the nobility (Fash 1991: 120). If so, those elite administrators must have been assisted by lesser officials who were not literate. It is possible, however, that some Maya officials of commoner rank were also literate. Those who designed fancy ceramic vessels and stone sculpture, both of which bore inscriptions, may have been the equivalents of master architects and engineers, rather than of craft workers, in other early civilizations. The Maya term *ah ts' ib* appears to have designated a writer and draftsman but not a painter or sculptor (Tate 1992: 20, 40–49).

The next rank of commoners consisted of full-time soldiers and police who were not members of the upper classes. In general, they and their families were well fed, housed, and rewarded for their services to the state. Their main tasks included guarding upper-class people and property, maintaining forts, and manning garrisons. In wartime they would be put in charge of other commoners who had been conscripted for military duty. Professional soldiers did not work with their hands, but their general deportment did not as closely resemble that of the upper classes as did the behaviour of lesser officials.

The third and lowest rank of specialists was full-time craft workers. They laboured with their hands and therefore resembled farmers more than they did soldiers or bureaucrats. Long-distance traders were part of this grouping. Craft workers were valued for their skills. Some were self-employed, others worked primarily for upper-class patrons, and still others were permanently attached to institutions such as palaces and temples. The state and the upper classes were the major consumers of the work produced by the most skillful artisans.

The servants of the upper classes formed an occupationally and socially diverse group. They were secretaries, guards, hairdressers, and other personal attendants, cooks and other types of skilled household staff, and unskilled workers who ground grain, hauled water, and disposed of waste. All these tasks were also performed by slaves, but skilled free staff would have been viewed as dependent specialists, equivalent to craft workers, while free manual labourers would have been equated with landless farm labourers.

The bulk of commoners, probably amounting to 80 percent or more of the total population, were farmers. Some farmers had legal rights to land, either as owners or renters; others were tied to land owned by others, while still others were landless labourers. Less secure rights to land generally correlated with lower social status.

Yoruba land was held collectively by patrilineal extended families, although such land reverted to the community if an extended family died out or moved away. In Inka society farmers belonged to ayllus, which were endogamous kinship and corporate landholding groups. In the Valley of Mexico, the macehualtin (tax payers) belonged to similar landholding calpollis. While ayllus and calpollis collectively owned their land, individual families could not permanently leave these groups without forfeiting their right to a share of it. In Mesopotamia collective ownership of land by patrilineal descent groups may have been widespread at an early period and private ownership of small plots of land may have resulted from the gradual breakup of such groups. Yet, as a result of growing debts, small farmers tended to lose their land. When this occurred, landless farmers had either to rent or sharecrop land owned by others or to work as hired labourers (guruš, *erin*). Some of these became dependents of temple estates while others did whatever jobs were available. Gangs of Mesopotamian labourers made their way north each spring helping to harvest the crops as they ripened (R. McC. Adams 1981: 145). The only other civilization for which free landless labourers are recorded is the Valley of Mexico, but these latter appear to have been immigrants from the north who were trying to insert themselves into local societies. Most appear to have found employment as burden carriers.

Some farmers were bound to land that was owned or otherwise controlled by the state or by members of the upper classes. These farmers did not pay taxes, but most of the surplus food they produced went directly to those who controlled the land; hence they were considerably less well off than landowning farmers. In the Valley of Mexico, the mayeque, who may have made up 30 percent of the Aztec population (van Zantwijk 1985: 271), were farmers who did not own land of their own or pay taxes, as the macehualtin did, but worked land owned by the crown. The produce of some of this land was intended for the upkeep of the palace, while other plots were assigned to the king, other members of the royal family, and nobles, including officials and honoured warriors. The mayeque fought as soldiers during military campaigns but do not appear to have been free to leave the estates on which they worked. They also would have been landless had they done so (Berdan 1982: 59–60; Hassig 1988: 30; Offner 1983: 133).

At least some Egyptian villagers appear to have possessed their own land, but it is uncertain whether this land was communally or family-owned. The Egyptian central government established large numbers of estates to support the royal court, royal funerary cults, and various officials. Most of these estates were located in less densely settled parts of Middle Egypt and the Delta. An estate consisted of farmers supervised by an official living in a large house that was also an administrative and storage facility. It is unclear whether farmers were legally attached to such estates or free men who had been attracted to them by promises of lower taxes (Kemp 1983: 85–92).

In China farmers belonged to corporate lineages whose members inhabited a settlement and worked adjacent plots of land. It is unclear, however, whether most agricultural land belonged to lineages or was assigned to government officials.

SLAVES

The conceptualization and practice of slavery differed significantly among early civilizations (J. Watson 1980b). It is often suggested that a continuum of lower-class people lived in various states of servitude to the upper classes (Pollock 1999: 121), and extreme Marxists have argued that in these 'slave societies' all the lower classes were slaves. Being bound to the land or to a particular workshop or patron did not, however, in itself cause a person to be regarded as a chattel. Individuals who were forced to work for creditors until a debt had been paid off were different from people sold into permanent and perhaps hereditary slavery because of indebtedness; they were in effect indentured labourers. Among the Aztec and Yoruba, temporary debt slaves often lived in their own homes and worked part of the time for themselves. Moreover, different members of a family often substituted for one another (Bascom 1969: 23).

Slaves were sometimes distinguished from the rest of the population by indelible brands or by distinctive clothing or hairstyles. They (and often their descendants) could be bought, sold, or reassigned as their owners wished, and they were generally excluded from membership in kinship groups. It was their owners who were answerable to the rest of society for their behaviour. Customary or statute law not only protected owners' rights to control and exploit slaves but also limited forms of mistreatment that might have provoked slaves to rebel. Slaves worked, normally without payment, as retainers, household servants, artisans, miners, construction workers, and farm labourers. They were not, however, called upon to undertake tasks that were not also performed by lower-class corvée labourers. Some slaves became trusted advisers and assistants of kings and high officials and thus acquired considerable informal power. Slaves in early civilizations tended to be few compared with those of Classical Greece and Rome.

Those who were enslaved included prisoners of war, criminals who had been punished by being deprived of their freedom, and individuals who had been sold to repay debts. Among the Aztec the latter included men who had bankrupted themselves as a result of gambling (Durán 1971: 281). Slaves were sometimes imported from less developed areas as tribute or merchandise. These slaves were usually ethnically different from their masters. The legal statuses of various categories of slaves differed, but these differences were never specified in as much detail as they were in ancient Athens (Westermann 1955). Temporary debt slaves enjoyed the most rights.

The Aztec generally sacrificed male prisoners of war and slaves delivered to them as tribute, since the high population density of the Valley of Mexico meant that there was little demand for additional labour. They appear to have employed slaves mainly as household servants, business agents, and concubines (Soustelle 1961: 74). The Shang rulers also appear to have sacrificed large numbers of military prisoners. Here population density seems to have been low, kept that way despite natural increase by expansion into enemy territory. The Inka did not enslave captives taken in battle; instead, dangerous enemy leaders were executed, while their followers, except for a few who were slain as human sacrifices in Inka victory celebrations, were sent home or resettled elsewhere in the kingdom (Rowe 1944: 279). In their wars with neighbouring city-states, the Early Dynastic Mesopotamians appear to have executed many male prisoners and blinded or castrated others before setting them to work performing repetitive forms of manual labour, usually on palace estates. Blinding was intended to make it more difficult for slaves to escape to their nearby city-states, while castration would have made it impossible for them to resume a normal life if they had returned. Numerous women captured in intercity wars were set to work as unpaid weavers for Mesopotamian temple and palace estates. The generic designation for a male slave was *arad*. Female slaves were called *géme*, but that term also designated a free but dependent female labourer (equivalent to the male guruš) (R. McC. Adams 1966: 102; Gelb 1973; Lerner 1986: 78–83; Maisels 1990: 156; Postgate 1992: 254–55; Siegel 1947).

In contrast, the Egyptians, with their low overall population density, enslaved large numbers of foreign captives (*sqrw ʿnḫ*). Male prisoners were employed as quarrymen, construction workers, household servants, and farmers, and whole families were settled as agricultural labourers. The Yoruba, who also had much surplus land, tended to employ large numbers of slaves, originally acquired as prisoners of war, as agricultural labourers, although others were used as household servants, tax collectors, and soldiers and bodyguards for prominent men (Goody 1980: 34–36). They sacrificed only a small number of slaves.

Buying and selling slaves was a significant activity in several early civilizations. Individual Mesopotamians preferred to purchase individuals who had been born as slaves and were therefore habituated to slavery or had been imported from distant lands and would have nowhere to which to escape. The word for 'slave' was written with the sign combination *nita* (man) + *kur* (mountain), suggesting that many of them came, either as prisoners of war or by trade, from the Zagros Mountains to the east (Goody 1980: 18; Postgate

1992: 106–7). In the Valley of Mexico there were specially designated markets in major urban centres where slaves could be purchased for human sacrifice or domestic service (Clendinnen 1991: 99). Slaves of local origin could not be sold for sacrifice unless they had flagrantly disobeyed successive owners. The exportation and sale of slaves captured in war was a major source of wealth for Yoruba military leaders and traders.

The treatment of slaves varied. Many of those owned by public institutions were little valued as individuals and were routinely overworked, underfed, and poorly housed and therefore suffered high mortality. Among them were the female slaves set to work in large weaving establishments attached to temples and palaces in Mesopotamia (Wright 1996b) and the gangs of men employed full-time in construction and mining projects by the Egyptian state. The latter included not only prisoners of war but Egyptians who had been sentenced to hard labour for evading corvée duty and other illegal acts (Hayes 1955; Kemp 1983: 83). Among the Aztec, debt slaves could accumulate earnings, own property, purchase their freedom, and marry, and their children were born free. The descendants of prisoners of war remained slaves for three generations and those of people enslaved as punishment for treason for four (López Austin 1988, 1: 402; Soustelle 1961: 74–78).

While there is no evidence of legal slavery among the Inka, there were two categories of people who resembled slaves in that the state took them from their ayllus as children and, if they were not soon slain as human sacrifices, assigned them to the perpetual service of high-ranking individuals or state institutions. The *aqllakuna* (chosen women) who were not distributed as concubines to the king and to men the king wished to honour were confined for the rest of their lives to closed houses (*aqllawasi*). There, as women consecrated to the service of the sun god, in addition to their religious duties they had to weave, brew corn beer, and cook food for the state. They were probably better fed and housed than most of the population but were forbidden to marry or to have unsupervised contact with other people (Kendall 1973: 192–93). The boys taken from their families became *yanakuna* (male servants), who worked for the king or were permanently assigned by him to particular nobles as household servants, craftsmen, or farmers. They could not be bought, sold, or given away by those for whom they worked. They were allowed to marry, probably initially being assigned young aqllakuna for this purpose, and their descendants inherited their status. They were not subject to any form of taxation, and the persons or institutions for whom they worked were responsible for seeing that they and their families were properly fed, housed, and clothed. Yet everything they produced belonged to their employers. The legal position of yanakuna probably differed little from that of farmers bound to the land or craftsmen tied to the service of particular institutions in other early civilizations, but their involuntary servitude in return for their keep resembled the economic role elsewhere played by slaves (Murra 1980: 165–77).

Shang records identify, in addition to tax-paying farmers, usually called *ren*, an inferior group of zhong who did not own land of their own. Their duties included agricultural labour, tending animals, military service, and constructing buildings – the same work that other commoners performed through the corvée – but they appear to have worked full-time for the king. Men of the same or analogous status were probably attached to aristocratic households. It is unknown under what conditions the zhong lived (Keightley 1969: 66–144), but it is not evident that they were slaves. In many ways they seem to have resembled yanakuna. In China prisoners of war may have been put to work as slaves until their fate was decided. Lin Chao (1972: 67–69) suggests that the term *chen* originally designated a slave, possibly of foreign origin, who personally served the king and only gradually came to mean a civil servant. David Keightley (1969: 357–79), however, finds no conclusive evidence of slavery in Shang China.

In Old and Middle Kingdom Egypt, foreign prisoners of war and tax defaulters became government slaves (*ḥmw nswt*), and some of them were assigned to high-ranking individuals. Yet in Egypt slaves were not numerous. There appears to have been relatively little private buying or selling of slaves or enslavement of individuals for debt. The terms *ḥm* and *b3k*, which later meant 'slave', appear originally to have designated free servants and retainers respectively (Wenke 1997: 47). Government slaves and their children seem to have been absorbed over a few generations into the commoner class. At the same time, many commoners were bound as agricultural and non-agricultural workers (*mrt*) to the service of nobles and officials (Loprieno 1997; Moreno García 1998). Thus in the three early civilizations where slavery was entirely absent or limited in extent, the bonding of commoners to the service of upper-class people appears to have placed some free persons in an analogous situation of servitude. All three civilizations in which this happened were territorial states.

SOCIAL MOBILITY

Social mobility was limited in early civilizations by the slowness of technological and social change and by a general lack of opportunity to gain access to knowledge from outside the social group into which a person was born. Most technical knowledge was transmitted from one generation to the next within such groups. In addition, in most early civilizations upward mobility either was regulated by the state or required recognition by the upper classes. This permitted members of the upper classes to dictate the terms on which their privileges and powers might be shared with others. The Yoruba positively valued social competition and, at least during the colonial era, expected families to rotate through cycles of commoner and upper-class status (Stone 1997). Yet their leaders tried to reinforce their own privileged positions and control social climbing. Leo Frobenius (1913, 1: 174–75) reports that in precolonial times the Ogboni society, to which all town and palace title-holders were expected to belong, could through divination justify judicially killing or offering up as human sacrifices individuals who were in the process of acquiring slaves and wealth. Such persons were charged with treason, and after they were executed their possessions were divided among the Ogboni and other officials. Frobenius noted, however, that such treatment was meted out only to upstarts who lacked influential relatives to protect them. This was therefore an effective way to restrict upper-class privileges to a small number of already powerful lineages. To consolidate their higher social standing, vertically mobile Yoruba also had to acquire titles that were controlled by the king.

Vertical mobility was most common in states that were expanding geographically or economically, where the need for more decision-makers and administrators resulted in the recruitment of new members to the upper and administrative classes. As the Inka state expanded, for example, the Inka rulers turned their earliest supporters into Inka-by-privilege, giving them hereditary upper-class status and making them junior partners in governing the kingdom. Upward mobility was most restricted in conquered states and chiefdoms, where resources were more limited than they might otherwise have been because of the need to pay tribute to a hegemonic power.

The Aztec illustrate the vertical mobility that occurred in a hegemonic city-state. As we have seen, warriors who captured four prisoners became eagle nobles. The state supplied them with food rations or the produce of a plot of land worked by mayeque, which allowed them to live as pipiltin, and when they married noble women their children by these women became hereditary nobles. Some young male commoners who displayed talents that would make them effective high-level priests or administrators were sent to the special schools (*calmecac*) where the sons of nobles were educated. As adults, they too were absorbed into the nobility. Influential nobles sought to have their sons by commoner secondary wives and concubines made pages at the royal court, where they would receive special training and make contacts that would help them achieve access to high office (Durán 1964: 222–23).

By the reign of Mochtezuma II, the Aztec tributary system was no longer expanding rapidly, and the king had adopted a policy of drawing the sons of favoured subject rulers from nearby city-states into the administrative hierarchy in order to establish Aztec hegemony, at least within the Valley of Mexico, on a broader, more cooperative basis. To accomplish this goal, Mochtezuma forbade sons of Aztec nobles to become pages unless their mothers as well as their fathers had been hereditary nobles. This decree debarred sons by secondary marriages, as well as the sons of eagle nobles, from high public office. It also created a major cleavage within the nobility by distinguishing an inferior rank of nobles, descended from only one noble parent, from a superior rank, descended from two. Mochtezuma is said to have dismissed and even executed nobles who were assigned to this new, lower status but had received high offices during previous reigns (Durán 1964: 223). In order to emphasize military achievement as the principal service to the state, from earliest times the Aztec had denied official offices to the sons of wealthy merchants and had not allowed them to marry noble women.

Requiring formal recognition for advancement was not, however, the only way of limiting vertical mobility. Beginning in the Old Kingdom, Egyptian writings extolled the ideal of the man who achieved success by winning the favour of his superiors because of his ability and hard work. Egyptian wisdom literature emphasized the importance of honouring such men for their achievements and not despising their humble origins (Lichtheim 1973: 66). Yet these same wisdom texts took the form of instructions prepared by an aged official for the benefit of his son and eventual successor. Even though each official had to work his way up through a series of lesser offices before taking over his father's position or a higher one, inheritance of high offices was regarded as normal. While the image of the self-made man expressed the official ideal of a royal bureaucracy, in reality positions tended to be inherited.

Another significant way to restrict vertical mobility was by strengthening class endogamy. Sometimes this involved discouraging or explicitly forbidding marriages between the upper and lower classes. Upper-class men were generally expected to marry within their own class, and primary marriages with lower-class women were thought inappropriate. In societies where it was accepted that lower-class women might be secondary wives or concubines of upper-class men, the children of these marriages were often subjected to social disabilities such as those imposed on them by Mochtezuma II. To an even greater extent, however, vertical mobility was restricted by various forms of personal self-interest favouring strategic intermarriage within both the upper and the lower classes.

In general, farmers who collectively possessed land sought to prevent its alienation by practicing endogamy within units such as ayllus or calpollis. While the patrilineal Yoruba did not do this, their laws forbade husbands and wives to inherit from one another in order to ensure that landholdings remained within the same patrilineage (Ajisafe 1924: 8). Farmers and craft workers each had their own local interests and, even if their lineages or communities were exogamous, preferred to contract marriages with groups of similar status that were close at hand. In this way, such groups could assure themselves of maximum local support in times of difficulty. Aztec who practised a particular craft, such as metalworking or feather working, belonged to a single calpolli. The children of Egyptian skilled workers who lived in the same community frequently married each other. Chinese crafts were generally lineage-based, but artisans belonging to different clans living close to each other probably intermarried.

Members of the upper class married over a much wider area than did the lower classes. In city-state systems, the royal families of different states frequently intermarried to reinforce political alliances. The Aztec kings married their daughters or those of leading nobles to major tributary rulers to encourage their allegiance and provide heirs to the thrones of these subordinate states who were close relatives (Hodge 1984: 138–39). Maya kings married their daughters to rulers of less powerful neighbouring states in the hope of creating enduring alliances that would be to their advantage (Schele and Mathews 1991: 245). In Shang China the king appears to have married the daughters of numerous subordinate lords and in turn used his daughters to consolidate a network of marital alliances with his more powerful subjects (Vandermeersch 1977: 275–77).

The ultimate assertion of political power was for a ruler to reject marital ties and hence obligations to other groups. Egyptian and Inka rulers married their sisters and half-sisters and, in the case of some New Kingdom pharaohs, their daughters and took female members of high-ranking families as secondary wives. With the Inka, these women usually came from powerful panaqas (Patterson 1991). Yet, because of the transcendant status of Egyptian kings, relatives of royal wives did not refer in inscriptions to the special relations to kings that such marriages created (Robins 1993: 28). Daughters of Egyptian kings also married members of the high nobility. From a male point of view these marriages had the disadvantage that a husband was expected to defer to his royal wife. In New Kingdom Egypt, Egyptian rulers married the daughters of foreign kings but refused, as a sign of their exclusive status, to allow their daughters to marry foreign kings (Desroches-Noblecourt 1986: 58; Robins 1993: 28, 32).

Marriages were also a way to construct networks of alliances uniting upper-class families. While in city-state systems such marriages, except at the highest rank, tended to be within state borders, marriage alliances joined high-level upper-class families over large areas. Lower-class alliances rarely extended beyond a single ward, community, or district. Especially in territorial states, this gave the upper class a considerable advantage in its efforts to control the lower classes despite its numerical inferiority.

Rulers and high officials often had children by numerous wives and concubines. If all of them had been able to claim a share of family privileges and resources, it could have undermined the power of the upper classes; hence it was desirable to prevent the undue expansion of the upper classes. Yoruba kings possessed large estates and numerous slaves, but these were inherited with the office rather than by their children. Obas' children could inherit only the wealth that their fathers and mothers had acquired personally in the course of their lifetimes. Hence those sons and grandsons of a king who had little hope of ever becoming kings themselves tried to insert themselves into their mothers' patrilineages and claim a share of their resources (Lloyd 1962: 44; Peel 1983: 59). As a result, after a few generations a Yoruba king had few identifiable descendants. The children of Inka kings other than their royal successors formed corporate descent groups that had to preserve their wealth and power by continuing to marry into the royal family and supporting successful candidates for the throne. In Egypt members of the hereditary nobility had to struggle as individuals to hold onto lucrative state offices, and those who were unsuccessful slipped into the scribal class. In China, where access to high office was channelled by kinship relations, junior branches of noble families likewise tended to move downward from a governing role to a lower administrative level (Vandermeersch 1980: 162). On occasion, as with the changes introduced by Mochtezuma II, the state intervened to debar lesser members of the nobility from access to major offices. While few of these actions prevented individuals from inheriting noble status, they did deprive junior or less successful individuals of the means to realize what was regarded as an appropriate lifestyle. As upper-class individuals declined into the lower administrative class, this process simultaneously forged closer bonds and some antagonism between the upper-class and administrative levels.

In Mesopotamia and elsewhere the children of purchased slaves belonged to their owners, but there appear to have been relatively few impediments to the absorption of slaves into the commoner class. Household slaves, for the most part, could earn or purchase their freedom, and their children were sometimes born free. Around A.D. 1505, the Aztec and Texcocans abolished hereditary slavery except for the descendants of prisoners of war and traitors (Offner 1983: 309; Soustelle 1961: 76–77). Egyptians frequently freed household slaves, and prosperous farmers and dependent specialists who were childless sometimes adopted their freed slaves and even arranged for them to marry into their families in order to ensure that they would care for their former owners in their old age (Robins 1993: 77). In Early Dynastic III Mesopotamian city-states, debt slaves were periodically freed in connection with general debt amnesties (Zagarell 1986: 416). Yoruba extended families also frequently freed slaves and adopted them as low-ranking lineage members who worked as farmers or professional soldiers (Akintoye 1971: 39–40, 52). In the early civilizations the upper classes relied principally on the productive capacity of free farmers, using slaves only as an auxiliary source of labour. Under these circumstances, the best way to control and motivate slaves was to keep their expectations of freedom relatively high. It is the limited utility of slaves as a source of labour that accounts for their frequent manumission and relatively small numbers.

Class systems in early civilizations were characterized by limited vertical mobility. Class membership was determined mainly by birth and, while vertical mobility did occur (especially in societies that were expanding politically or economically), promotion in the social hierarchy was decided in the final instance not by personal achievement but by royal or upper-class recognition, the criteria for which varied from one early civilization to another.

SIMILARITIES AND DIFFERENCES

All early civilizations had class systems. Yet, among early civilizations, there were significant variations in the extent to which class replaced kinship as the framework of social relations. In some early civilizations kinship relations occurred only within classes. In others, class divisions cut across functioning kinship networks. There were also variations in the extent to which the upper classes were formally delineated and membership in them was hereditary. Where both of these features were present, it is possible to speak of the upper classes as a nobility. Slavery, while not of major economic importance in any early civilization, appears to have been more prominent in city-state systems than in territorial states. There is no clear evidence of its presence in Inka Peru or Shang China.

In general, class divisions other than slavery appear to have been formally delineated more consistently in territorial states than in city-states. In highland Mesoamerica and probably among the Maya, class differences were hereditary; in Mesopotamia classes were legally distinguished but individuals had to achieve and maintain upper-class membership. Among the Yoruba, the upper class was defined by royally conferred titles and offices that certain kin groups sought to retain. In all these cases, the upper classes, for political and economic reasons, placed more emphasis on solidarity with unrelated members of their own class than with the lower-class members of the clans and lineage groups to which they belonged and whose support they frequently needed. Especially in territorial states, upper-class solidarity was much more extensive geographically than lower-class solidarity, which normally manifested itself at a local level.

The cross-cultural similarities in class structure were the expression of a fairly specific set of beliefs about the nature of status that were shared by all the early civilizations. It was agreed that giving orders was more prestigious than having to obey orders, that not having to work was superior to having to perform manual labour, that possessing specialized knowledge and skills was better than not possessing them, that wealth was superior to poverty, that having land was preferable to not having it, and that being free was better than being owned. Finally, although it was accompanied by greater risk of incurring the displeasure of the upper class or being unduly exploited by it, ordinary people saw more opportunities for bettering themselves in geographical and social proximity to the powerful than in remoteness from them. It was these propositions, which reflect considerable uniformity in human thinking about the nature of inequality in complex societies, that generated the multilayered social structures just outlined.

9 Family Organization and Gender Roles

Many different forms of kin relations were associated with early civilizations. While these relations were intimately connected with family life, residence patterns, marital practices, and the nurturing of children, they were also associated with broader sociocultural practices such as landholding, agricultural production, craft organization, inheritance of property, political and economic activities, value systems, and religious beliefs. They also constituted the primary sphere in which gender roles were defined, although class differences also affected these roles. Lower-class women in all early civilizations cooked, cleaned houses, cared for children, and spun and wove to provide clothing for their families, but the division of domestic labour among them varied according to the number of women who lived together and how they allocated household tasks among themselves. The division of labour and relations of authority between men and women also varied significantly from one civilization to another and according to class.

The seven early civilizations provide examples of kinship systems characterized by patrilineal descent groups (Shang and Zhou China, Yoruba-Benin, Classic Maya, Mesopotamia), endogamous descent groups or demes (Valley of Mexico, Inka), and non-corporate descent (ancient Egypt). The Egyptians did not have, beyond the nuclear family, any kinship unit that possessed land, political power, or a sense of corporate identity. In no two early civilizations was family organization precisely the same.

KIN AND GENDER RELATIONS

Family life in Shang China was structured by patrilineal descent. Each corporate descent group (*zu*) inhabited a single community, and its male members worked a tract of land or practised a particular craft. Among the upper classes, two or more generations of a family belonging to a corporate descent group lived, under the authority of its senior male member, in a house composed of living rooms, shrines, reception halls, and work areas arranged around a series of open courts. Commoners appear to have lived in smaller, possibly nuclear-family houses, but married sons remained subject to the authority of their fathers and uncles. Each corporate descent group traced its origin to a single male ancestor who was venerated by all his male descendants. Within the descent group patrilineal descent lines were hierarchically organized, with descent from elder brothers invariably ranking higher than descent from younger brothers. The oldest member of the senior line (*da zong*) was the group's leader and the sole person who could perform rituals honouring the group's deceased founder and chief guardian spirit. When a group had expanded until it contained over one hundred nuclear families (this was estimated to take seven generations), it split into two and the junior branch moved off to establish a new group.

It is generally assumed that already in Shang times all the patrilineal descent groups that could trace themselves back to a common ancestor shared a surname and constituted an exogamous clan (*xing*). Clans took the form of large ramages, which meant that their various descent lines (*zu*, *shi*) were ranked in terms of their genealogical proximity to the clan's founder. The descent groups which belonged to the same clan were often geographically widely separated from one another (Hsu and Linduff 1988: 148–50). The leading clan on the central plain of northern China during the Shang period was the Zi, and its senior branch (*wang zu*) supplied the Shang kings.

While this sort of clan organization was indisputably the basis of society in the Western Zhou period, Léon Vandermeersch (1977: 203) argues that, apart from the Zi clan, there is no evidence of clan organization in the Shang period. He maintains that only individual patrilineal descent groups existed and that the king alone practised an ancestral cult. Vandermeersch refers to high-ranking patrilineal descent groups as 'territorial houses'. Most scholars assume, however, that it is the documentation for clans rather than clans themselves that is lacking for the Shang period. Attempts by Kwang-chih Chang and Liu Binxiong to demonstrate that each Shang clan was divided into ten sections held together by cross-cousin marriage remain unsubstantiated (K. Chang 1978; Vandermeersch 1977: 284–93).

Shang rules of exogamy allowed marriage only between different descent groups and probably only between different clans. Commonly, two families appear to have been united over many generations by men's marrying cousins from their mothers' families, ideally mothers' brothers' daughters (Granet 1958 [1930]: 156–57). Women were not only required to live with their husbands' families but upon marriage forfeited membership in the lineage groups into which they had been born and joined their husbands' clans and ancestral cults. Thus a woman's position in Chinese society was determined in turn by that of her father, her husband, and her son. Women nevertheless played an important role alongside their husbands in the ancestral cult and other religious rituals of the family into which they had married. Moreover, women who bore sons could expect to be venerated after death in the ancestral cults of their husbands' families.

Most lower-class Shang Chinese were monogamous. To ensure the birth of sons, who would perpetuate their lineage, upper-class men frequently acquired secondary wives. In Zhou times these were often younger sisters or other close relatives of a chief wife who came with her as part of her marriage suite. If the chief wife died, one of her female relatives would replace her, thus maintaining the family alliance (Vandermeersch 1977: 311–12). The male heir of a man's position was normally the eldest son of his first chief wife.

Shang kings appear to have married many women, thus forging or renewing links between the royal family and leading lineages throughout the Shang kingdom. There is also evidence of royal endogamy within the Zi clan, to which both King Wu Ding and his consort Fu Hao appear to have belonged (P. Chang 1986: 130). In addition to bearing children, these women, and perhaps the wives of princes and other ladies living at the royal court, assisted the male relatives of the royal family in the work of administering the kingdom. They announced royal decrees, delivered formal messages, performed ancestral rituals and other religious rites, organized agricultural production, supervised the collection of taxes, raised troops, and on rare occasions led armies. Most important, they conducted royal business with their parental families and the regions where they had been born. They may have been the most effective links between the monarch and powerful families living in various parts of the Shang kingdom. Thus they performed many of the same court duties as were later performed by eunuchs, which are not reported before the Zhou period (Creel 1937: 293). In Zhou times one of the two chief royal stewards (*zai*) still had to receive instructions from and report to the queen (Hsu and Linduff 1988: 255). This practice may have been a vestige of the important administrative roles formerly played by women at the royal court. Mark Lewis (1990: 73) points out that in the Eastern Zhou period Chinese royal officials were regarded as having the same subordinate position in relation to the king as royal wives and concubines and treated these women as potential rivals. At least at the royal court, women appear to have played a different and more important role during the Shang period than in later times.

In southern Mesopotamia, a father and some of his sons or several brothers, together with their wives and young children, often formed a patrilineal

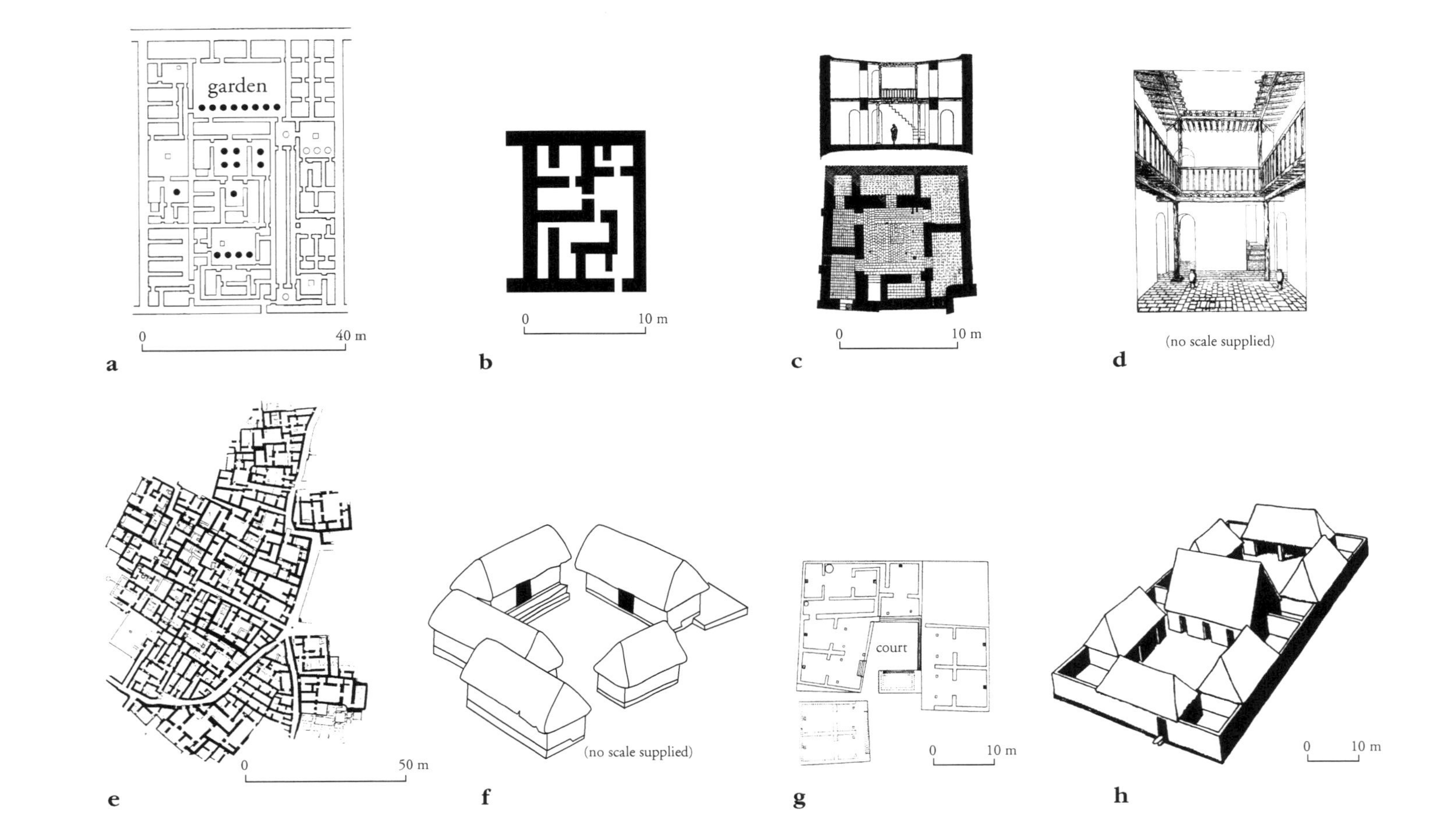
garden
0
40 m
a
0
10 m
b
0
10 m
c
(no scale supplied)
d
0
50 m
e
(no scale supplied)
f
court
0
10 m
g
0
10 m
h

extended family. These domestic units, as well as larger temple or palace estates, were called *é* in Sumerian and *bîtum* in Akkadian, words meaning both 'house' and 'household' (Pollock 1999: 117–18). In the countryside, a number of rooms, which housed nuclear families or were used for storage, were loosely arranged around an open compound. In urban centres, houses were arranged more compactly, with rooms opening off one or more interior courtyards (Fig. 9.1). In general, extended families appear to have been composed of fewer nuclear families in urban centres than in the countryside. Extended households in cities also seem to have diminished in size over time. Families that were patrilineally related sometimes lived in adjacent houses, but there is no evidence that city wards were kinship units. The governing of these wards by mayors and councils made up of the heads of leading households suggests that most of them were not (Crawford 1991: 93–95; Postgate 1992: 82–94, 310; Stone 1987; Van De Mieroop 1999: 104–6). Akkadian-speaking Mesopotamians seem to have formed larger kin groups than Sumerians, and wards of Semitic-speakers may have consisted largely of patrilineally related kin more often than was the case among Sumerian-speakers.

Sons inherited from their fathers land, houses, furniture, animals, slaves, and temple positions. Joint ownership of family property became less common over time, the normal practice being for brothers to divide their father's estate after his death. Either this division was into equal shares or the eldest brother was awarded between 10 and 100 percent more than the rest. In return, eldest sons were expected to care for parents in their old age and make offerings to their spirits after they died. The idea of extended families' holding property in common persisted to the extent that individuals wishing to sell their share of a house or family land had first to offer it to family members and obtain their approval (Postgate 1992: 94–101).

9.1. Houses in early civilizations: (a) plan of a large Middle Kingdom Egyptian official's residence at Kahun; (b) an ordinary house from Kahun – Kahun was established to house the mortuary priests of King Senwosret II; (c) elevation and plan of a Mesopotamian private house at Ur, from the Isin-Larsa period; (d) reconstruction of such a house; (e) street plan of a small section of Ur during the Old Babylonian period; (f) lower-class Classic Maya house group; (g) upper-class house from Chiconauhtla, near Texcoco, in the Valley of Mexico; (h) an Inka double-kancha enclosure at Ollantaytambo – while these particular structures were constructed by the government, it is unknown what class of people inhabited them (illustrations not to common scale). Sources: (a), (b) after Kemp 1989: 152, 158; (c), (d) after L. Woolley, *The Sumerians* (Oxford, 1928): figs. 26, 27; (e) after J. Hawkes & L. Woolley, *History of Mankind*, Vol. 1 (New York, 1963): 425; (f) after Wilk & Ashmore 1988: 133; (g) after G. Kubler, *The Art and Architecture of Ancient America* (Harmondsworth, 1962): 55; (h) after Gasparini & Margolies 1980: 190.

Daughters did not inherit property as such, but in any division of a man's estate land and property had to be set aside to provide dowries for unmarried daughters. Rich men often installed one or more of their daughters as priests in elite religious institutions. In Old Babylonian times some of these *naditum* lived as celibates in walled cloisters (*gagûm*) attached to major temples (Postgate 1992: 130–31). This arrangement required an endowment, equivalent to a dowry, for their support, but it was anticipated that these endowments would return to their brothers after they died. Thus making it impossible for some daughters to marry was a way of avoiding the alienation of family property.

Women were legally subject to their husbands, who were designated as their owners (*bêlu*) (Bottéro 1992: 186). In records they are often referred to not by their names but as the wife (*dam*), mother (*amma*), sister (*nia*), or daughter (*dumu*, *munus*) of their male kin (Glassner 1989: 82–83). Although women were not confined to their homes and appeared as witnesses and plaintiffs in lawsuits (Lerner 1986: 104), any property that married women possessed (mainly in the form of dowries) was controlled by their husbands, fathers, or brothers. Respectable women were required to avoid all extramarital sexual relations, while men were free to engage in them provided their female partners were adults and unmarried (Rohrlich 1980).

Marriages tended to occur among families of equivalent social standing and were arranged by adult males of these families, normally either the groom or his father and the bride's father. Upper-class families used daughters to create and strengthen economically and politically advantageous alliances. Girls were frequently betrothed in infancy but continued to live with their parents until their marriage. They sometimes began to have sexual relations with their future spouses prior to marriage. The groom was required to provide betrothal and bridal gifts and the bride's father a dowry, which could be substantial. The dowry was managed by the bride's husband and returned to her on his death (Lerner 1986: 107–13). With the approval of legal authorities, men were able to divorce wives they found difficult to live with. A divorced woman's dowry had to be returned to her unless she chose to continue to live in her former husband's home. When a woman died, her dowry passed to her sons or, if there were none, to her father or brother. Marriage contracts, written or verbal, could specify special terms for mutual separation, preclude wives from being enslaved for debts their husbands had incurred prior to marriage, and specify special property rights (107).

Marriage was predominantly monogamous. Only a few well-to-do men had secondary spouses (*aššatu*) or slave concubines (*esertu*). Such women were often supplied by a principal wife (*ḫîrtu*) who was unable to bear a child. Secondary wives or concubines were also provided for their husbands by certain high-ranking female priests, who were permitted to marry but required to abstain from sexual intercourse. In all these situations the principal wife was recognized as the female head of the family (Bottéro 1992: 186).

A king normally had a single wife and five to eight children. Some rulers of the Ur III Dynasty had more than fifty offspring, many of them apparently by royal concubines. The seclusion of royal women and the use of eunuchs to guard them appear to have begun in the Ur III period. Kings' wives and daughters were often educated and performed various political and economic administrative duties. Royal wives managed estates belonging to the palace and to temples, supervised various economic activities, and sometimes acted as regents and representatives of rulers. They frequently exchanged presents just as kings did (Lerner 1986: 61–69; Postgate 1992: 148–49; Silver 1986: 41–42). Although kings sometimes appointed daughters to be the high priests of city gods in an attempt to expand royal control over major temples (Postgate 1992: 26), their wives do not appear to have played a major role in state religious rituals, nor are they represented alongside their husbands in art. In state rituals the female counterpart of the king appears to have been a female priest. While kings sometimes married the daughters of foreign rulers, most royal wives were of local origin, perhaps reflecting the pressing need for most kings to consolidate alliances within their own city-states.

Other upper-class women played various public roles, mainly religious in nature. Where the principal city deity was male, the top-ranking cult priest was normally a woman (Oates 1978: 476). Such women were appointed by a male official (usually the king) and officiated in temples managed by males. There were other religious roles for women from wealthy families, such as high-status temple devotees, whose duties in Old Babylonian times included presenting offerings to deities on special occasions and tending to their sanctuaries (R. Harris 1975: 307–9). All these women, whether or not they led cloistered lives, were required to remain celibate. They could engage in business dealings, which augmented the endowments that supported them (Silver 1986: 42–44), and possessed their own seals. Other women, apparently of lower social status, worked for temples in less prestigious ritual capacities. Some of them joined associations of prostitutes that were connected to temples of the fertility goddess, Inanna (R. Harris 1989: 149). These associations included married women who had abandoned their husbands and women who had joined them as children (Bottéro 1992: 189–90).

While the legal rights of Sumerian women were limited, at least some women from well-to-do families held administrative posts, owned and bought property, engaged in business, and testified at legal hearings (Glassner 1989: 83; Oates 1978: 478; Van De Mieroop 1989). From Old Babylonian times there is mention of female scribes' serving cloistered female priests (R. Harris 1975: 196; 1989). At the lower end of the social spectrum, women ran taverns, engaged in freelance prostitution, and dabbled in witchcraft, living on the margins of society both socially and geographically. Many of them resided and carried on business in isolated locations near the city walls. Lacking families or protectors, they provided examples of an improper female lifestyle and were often brutally treated. It was maintained that prostitutes made poor wives because they were untrained and not disposed to look after a home and family (Bottéro 1992: 195). Also badly treated because they lacked male protectors were the single women, probably slaves of foreign origin, who worked alongside female members of debtor families in cloth factories belonging to palaces and temples. The women at the bottom of Mesopotamian society provided object lessons that to be secure and respected a woman needed a father, husband, brother, or son who was willing and able to protect her and defend her interests (Bottéro 1992: 193–98).

The Yoruba were organized as patrilineal extended families (*idile*) that owned residential property in a town or city and farmland in the surrounding countryside. In the southern Yoruba states, located in the tropical-forest zone, extended families tended to live in clusters of small multigenerational houses. On the savanna to the north, where there was greater need for formal military organization, entire extended families lived in single large compounds (*ile*) surrounded by stamped-earth walls more than two metres high (Lloyd 1962). More than two hundred people sometimes occupied a single compound. Within such a unit individual adults had single rooms of their own arranged around a series of open courtyards. These compounds also contained shrines, storerooms, reception rooms, and sometimes even a prison where family members could be confined.

Clans made up of a number of extended families (*agbo ile*, many compounds) that traced descent from a still more remote male ancestor (*orisun*, spring) sometimes lived adjacent to one another and formed wards or localities within a community. These groupings were also called idile. Each clan had its own oral history (*itan*), and its members shared distinctive personal names (*orile*), greetings, hairstyles, facial scars, food taboos, customs, and tutelary deities.

Every Yoruba extended family had as its head (bale) its eldest competent male member, regardless of his genealogical relation to his predecessor. Within the extended family, male seniority was reckoned by date of birth and female seniority by the length of time spent with the husband's relatives. The head of the idile was usually not one of the extended-family members who held the idile's town and palace titles. The bale was responsible for worshipping the extended family's gods and ancestors and for preparing supernatural 'medicines' that kept family members healthy and harmonious. He also dealt with government officials on behalf of the extended family and was responsible to them for his family's good behaviour. The bale had the power to punish members of his extended family for various forms of misbehaviour. This power was exercised by a court composed of the bale, elderly members of the family, and its titled office-holders (Bascom 1944; 1969: 42–45; Lloyd 1955).

Yoruba patrilineages were exogamous, and marriage was forbidden with maternal kinsmen over at least seven generations. Membership in an extended family was limited to the children of its male members (*omo ile*) and people who had been formally adopted into it. Wives (*aya ile*) remained members of their fathers' patrilineage, as did *ara ile*, strangers who were allowed to live in a compound but had not been adopted into its patrilineage (Bascom 1969: 43–44).

Edo (Benin) patrilineages were less elaborate than Yoruba ones. Only those of high-ranking families were more than two or three generations deep. Land tended to belong to communities rather than to kin groups, and titles were inherited by eldest sons if they were inherited at all. Edo families lived in both nuclear and extended-family residences (Bradbury 1957: 27–31).

The majority of older Yoruba men appear to have had more than one wife, the number varying according to a man's personal wealth. Multiple marriages were generally agreeable to first wives, who enjoyed seniority over junior wives and were relieved by them of many household chores. Women normally married only once, widows being inherited by their husbands' brothers or sons by other wives. Marriages were viewed as alliances between patrilineages and constituted a means by which such groups could secure allies for factional competition, trade, and warfare. Hence they were normally contracted between families of roughly equal social status. Women from the highest-ranking families married either the king (who had many wives) or men from families of equivalent status to their own (K. Barber 1991: 272), thereby reinforcing solidarity among the most powerful men in each city-state. Class endogamy was further encouraged by the increase in the bride-price with the status of the bride's family (Ajisafe 1924: 53; Lloyd 1974: 34).

Women married in their twenties and most men in their thirties, usually after a long period spent working for their fathers; however, if a man were wealthy his son might marry earlier. Girls were often betrothed in their infancy or even before birth but remained in their fathers' houses until they were married. For the betrothal of an adult woman her own consent was required. Marriage involved both a bride-price, normally paid in three installments by the groom or his father, and in ordinary families a period of labour service by the groom which compensated the bride's family for the loss of her labour. A husband had to provide his wife with a room of her own for herself and her children, adequate food and clothing, and some capital to begin trading. Divorce was rare but could be obtained on grounds of a wife's insanity, chronic illness, or infertility and a husband's laziness, indebtedness, or cruelty. A Yoruba woman could own property in her own name and manage it even if she were married (Bascom 1969: 59–65). Unmarried Yoruba women who became rich as traders might marry other women, whose children became their heirs (Denzer 1994: 18). As part of their continuing affiliation with their natal patrilineages, women regularly participated in religious rituals and celebrations at their fathers' compounds and were buried there (Bascom 1969: 60).

Use-rights to land, houses, and any other possessions of a patrilineage could be transmitted permanently only to a man's sons or, if he had none, to his surviving brothers. Yoruba spouses were forbidden to inherit from one another. This arrangement protected the collective possessions of a patrilineage against alienation. A woman had access to her family's agricultural land, houses, cult places, and financial help during her lifetime. Both men and women were able to pass along to their children the wealth they had earned personally. A man's property was divided in equal shares among the children of each of his wives rather than being bequeathed equally to each child (Lloyd 1962: 27, 292–307).

Women performed household chores under the supervision of the oldest woman in the compound. They also had the right to engage in business outside the home. This was done especially by older women or by senior wives in polygynous families, who could arrange for their children to be cared for by their husbands' younger wives. Many women engaged in local trade, selling family farm produce, crafts, and cooked food in the marketplaces. Other women engaged in long-distance trade, and the most successful of them came to own plantations and numerous slaves and even private armies. By being able to lend food, weapons, and soldiers to military leaders, some of them also became politically influential (W. Clarke 1972: 47, 86). They were rarely able, however, to convert their economic influence into political power for themselves and were often accused of witchcraft by rivals of men whose political careers they supported (K. Barber 1991: 232–35). Women also had a monopoly on producing certain types of manufactured goods, such as pottery, dyed cloth, palm and other vegetable oils, soap, mats, and beer (Denzer 1994: 7). Women who manufactured these products tended to organize themselves in community craft guilds. Some women fashioned influential roles as professional praise singers and leaders of religious cults (K. Barber 1991). Female palace officials, who were appointed from among the influential women in the community, helped to select and install new kings and were among their official advisers and agents. Some of them undertook diplomatic missions to other states on behalf of the ruler. They also conducted rituals for both living and dead kings. They had their own hierarchy of titles, and their public duties included supervising the marketplaces. At Ife and Benin high-ranking women were represented in royal art, though less commonly than kings. Most of the domestic labour within the palace was performed by less important female members of the king's household (Denzer 1994).

Royal wives were mostly of local origin. In Oyo new members of the state council (Oyo Mesi) gave a daughter in marriage to the king. The king also occasionally married royal women from non-Yoruba states such as Nupe and Dahomey (R. Smith 1969: 112). Yoruba and Benin rulers strengthened alliances by sending some of their children to live with neighbouring kings (Barnes and Ben-Amos 1989: 51). A king's many wives were able to engage in long-distance trade without having to pay the taxes that were normally imposed on the movement of goods. Their savings provided an inheritance for their children, who were unable to inherit land from their father because his official estates passed intact to his successor, usually not his son. An oba could transmit to his descendants only wealth that he had acquired prior to becoming king.

Maya families are generally assumed to have been patrilineal and patrilocal. Extended families spanning two or three generations appear to have lived in nuclear-family dwellings arranged around three or four sides of a courtyard. Poor families lived in houses constructed of wattle and daub, top-ranking ones in stone houses with poorer dwellings located nearby (Haviland 1968; Tourtellot 1988). Each such residential group had its own cult centre, and dead members were buried in the low earth platforms on which the main buildings were erected. Patrilineal extended families appear to have been exogamous, and immovable property and political offices were inherited patrilineally (Abrams 1994; McAnany 1995; Wilk and Ashmore 1988). It has been argued that patrilineal extended families were less important in major urban centres such as Tikal than in smaller urban centres or the countryside. It is unclear to what extent those who lived in a house cluster were members of a single extended family; the poorer residents may have been dependents or slaves (Gillespie 2000; Haviland 1988; 1992; Wilk 1988).

Upper-class women appear to have been of considerable importance, at least ritually and symbolically. Children inherited their status and names from both their fathers' and their mothers' patrilineages. This made marrying daughters to the rulers of smaller, neighbouring states or communities a potent means for a king to build political alliances. Female rulers, or at least regents, are recorded at various times. Royal mothers appear to feature more prominently than kings' wives in Maya iconography. Royal women are depicted participating alongside kings and royal heirs in religious rites, especially the accession rituals that stressed the continuity and importance of royal dynasties (Graham 1991; Joyce 1992; 2000: 54–89).

The Aztec emphasized patrilineal descent and had a kin terminology that stretched over seven generations, but, as did the Maya, they derived significant social status from their mothers' families. Ordinary Aztec families were monogamous, but wealthy nobles often had secondary wives and concubines, some of the latter having been acquired before marriage. Mochtezuma II was reported to have had two wives and many concubines, by whom he had a total of 150 children (Soustelle 1961: 178). The king of Texcoco was said to have had more than two thousand 'wives' by whom he had had 144 children, 11 born of his chief wife (Berdan 1982: 68).

Ordinary Aztec lived in extended-family houses constructed of stamped earth. These houses, which normally housed two to six patrilineally or bilaterally related nuclear families, had rooms arranged around two to four sides of a courtyard in which many domestic activities occurred. There also appear to have been special communal work areas for the women of the family. Each nuclear family had its own room or suite of rooms. Noble families lived in larger, often multistorey stone versions of such houses. In the countryside, extended-family houses were smaller, and there may also have been small, detached nuclear-family dwellings (Calnek 1972: 109–11; 1976: 298–300; Clendinnen 1991: 58).

Adjacent households belonged to the same calpolli or ward, each of which had from a few hundred to several thousand members. In more remote and rural parts of the valley calpollis tended to be small, were largely run by consensus, and had commoners as leaders. In urban locations they were larger and more hierarchical and their leaders had been co-opted into the hereditary nobility, with the result that they had access to additional land and resources from outside their kinship groups. Calpollis were endogamous, collective landowning groups. At least the larger ones had their own stone temples, commoner schools, and governing hierarchies. The Aztec believed that it was hard for persons to remain healthy if they remained for a long time out of sight of their calpolli temple (López Austin 1988, 1: 409). Because calpollis were endogamous, patrilineal descent did not play a particularly important role in regulating inheritance. This made marriage patterns of little consequence from the point of view of conserving communal property. Elderly women acted as go-betweens in arranging marriages between families. It appears that, even within calpollis, parents preferred marriages between families of equivalent rank and status. Both celibacy and divorce were discouraged, but men were allowed to divorce women who failed to produce children. Widows generally married one of their husbands' brothers. Men inherited their fathers' personal possessions and women their mothers'. Subject to some form of consent by calpolli members, public offices, including the leadership of calpollis, were inherited patrilineally, either from father to son or from elder to younger brother (M. E. Smith 1996: 145–51; Spath 1973).

Aztec women were expected to be virgins when they married and, while women were believed to continue to enjoy sex in old age more than men did, to remain faithful to their husbands (Clendinnen 1991: 166). They were, however, permitted to move about freely, engage in various part-time professions, and spend their earnings as they pleased. Many women were active in marketing, selling cooked food and cloth and the vegetables and handicrafts produced by their male relatives or retailing goods purchased from long-distance traders. In feather-working families women specialized in dying feathers. Other women embroidered cloth for temples, rich patrons, and market sale. Still others catered parties for their neighbours (Clendinnen 1991: 161–63). Wives of long-distance traders managed their husbands' business from home while the latter were absent and may have engaged by proxy in intercity trade (Clendinnen 1991: 135). Other women worked part-time as midwives, curers, and diviners, perhaps possessing knowledge that was not available to male physicians (Kellogg 1995).

Women also served as priests in local temples. Most of them did so on a part-time basis, but some remained celibate and functioned full-time for long periods as did many higher-ranking male priests. They never occupied the highest levels of priestly hierarchies, however, and they depended for their appointments on men (Kellogg 1995). For a woman to remain respectable she either had to be married or, in the case of celibate female priests, remain part of her birth family. Women who did not enjoy such protection were often forced into prostitution. Captive women were kept in state-controlled 'Houses of Joy', where they provided sexual entertainment for unmarried young warriors who had captured enemy prisoners. Aztec women who did not have families might work as prostitutes either on their own or under the supervision of a female protector, usually plying their trade in public marketplaces (Clendinnen 1991: 163–65). Although women played a significant role in Aztec military life by preparing the food that soldiers carried with them on campaigns, the state granted conquered land and tribute to male officials and successful warriors and not to women. Therefore women were unable to benefit directly from the vertical mobility that the development of tributary networks made possible (Nash 1978).

Aztec kings married the daughters of high-ranking Aztec nobles and rulers of friendly neighbouring states while bestowing their own daughters in marriage on such men. Land owned by royal families was exchanged as part of the dowries associated with interstate marriages, but it was managed by women's husbands and sons, not by themselves (Hodge 1984: 138–39). Royal women played no public roles in Aztec political and religious life, nor are they reported to have appeared in public with their husbands on any official occasion. Regents were appointed from the top ranks of hereditary male officials. Nevertheless, upper-class women played active roles in the political intrigues within and among the royal and noble families of city-states (Joyce 2000: 133–75; van Zantwijk 1994).

Most highland Andean nuclear families occupied one-room houses built of adobe or rough field stones. A small number of closely related nuclear families shared an enclosed compound (*kancha*), their individual houses being arranged around the inside of the wall (Kendall 1973: 123–27). A number of these extended families formed an ayllu or endogamous landholding group consisting of a few hundred people or more. It is debated whether ayllus were a primordial feature of Andean social organization or arose early in the Christian era as a form of resistance against developing state structures (Isbell 1997). Among the Inka and many other Central Andean highland groups descent was patrilineal, but in some other highland groups it was matrilineal. Inka kin terms reveal both patrilineal (Omaha) and matrilineal (Crow) tendencies, which may indicate an underlying pattern of parallel descent (Lounsbury 1986; Zuidema 1977). It has also been argued that the Inka had parallel inheritance, with some offices and property passing from fathers to sons and some from mothers to daughters. Supporters of this theory argue that noble women inherited fields from their mothers and female commoners inherited rights to ayllu land which they surrendered upon marriage (Silverblatt 1987: 7, 219). Yet ayllu land was assigned not to individuals but to nuclear families, and both land and herds were regularly redistributed in accordance with the changing number of children and other dependents that a couple had to support. In fact nothing was inherited except the right to a share of ayllu property. The office of queen was not inherited matrilineally but bestowed on the woman chosen to be the principal wife of the king. Finally, the endogamy of peasant groups ensured that marriage did not alienate property however it was inherited. These observations call into question the practical significance of parallel descent.

Each ayllu in a district belonged to one of two moieties, often designated hanan (upper) and hurin (lower). Ayllus belonging to the same moiety strongly supported each other economically and socially, while those belonging to opposite moieties cooperated politically and ritually. While each moiety had its own leader, it was agreed that the leader of the lower moiety was the helper of the leader of the upper one, who alone had the right to speak for both groups in their dealings with outsiders. Upper moieties frequently claimed to be descended from pastoralist invaders who had conquered the indigenous agricultural lower moiety. In reality, both moieties engaged in agriculture and pastoralism. In Cuzco the upper moiety embraced the descendants of recent rulers who had expanded the Inka kingdom, while the lower moiety embraced the decendants of earlier and apparently more peaceful kings (Gose 1996b).

To become an adult member of a community, each male commoner (*hatun runa*, 'big man') had to have celebrated a coming-of-age (or breech-cloth) ritual in which he received the name he would keep for the rest of his life. He also had to be married. Although ordinary people or their families no doubt decided among themselves who should marry one another, marriage was obligatory under Inka rule and was solemnized by rituals that government officials performed annually in each community for women between the ages of sixteen and twenty and men before they were twenty-five years old. This ritual symbolized the Inka king's control over the reproductive capacity of all subject women (Gose 2000). Since only able-bodied married couples were taxpayers, it was in the state's interest to ensure that all young adults were married. The king personally performed marriage rituals for members of the royal lineages at Cuzco. The next day royal officials married all other people of appropriate age in the Cuzco area. Ayllu members elsewhere were married by local leaders, in the presence of Inka administrators. The state provided each noble married couple with a home, while each ayllu built houses for its commoner newlyweds (Kendall 1973: 82–83).

The lower classes were monogamous, but a man could be given a second wife (normally from outside the community) as a reward for his services to the state. Upper-class males tended to be polygamous. A man's principal wife was a woman of his own class, but he also received from the king women captured in war and young aqllakuna as secondary wives or concubines. If a principal wife died a man could remarry, but none of his secondary wives was allowed to become his chief wife. The highest-ranking nobles were allowed to marry their half-sisters (Rowe 1944: 251–52).

Inka kings are reported to have had hundreds of secondary wives and concubines, who, unlike the quya or queen, were kept in seclusion. Provincial nobles regarded it as an honour for the king to take their daughters as secondary wives. These women and their daughters were often referred to by the name of the province from which the mother had come. Royal concubines were selected from among the young aqllakuna. The queen might be the king's sister or half-sister, although some were more remote relatives from powerful panaqas. Kingship was normally inherited by a son of the quya or, failing a suitable individual in that category, by the son of a secondary wife who belonged to the Inka nobility. A king often had older sons by concubines or secondary wives who came from the provincial nobility (Kendall 1973: 63–64, 72, 90; Silverblatt 1987: 87, 92).

It has been suggested that there was greater recognition of gender complementarity in Peru than in most other early civilizations. In agriculture this complementarity took the form of men's digging fields and women's planting tubers and seeds. It was manifested in mythology by the belief that men were descended from the sun and women from the moon, both of whom were children or manifestations of the creator deity, Wiraqucha (Kendall 1973: 182–83). Yet, even if it was the case in terms of ritual and ideology that the Inka queen ruled all women as the king ruled all men (Rostworowski 1960: 420), the administrative and military hierarchies of the Inka state were staffed exclusively by men.

Women were important in Inka religious observances but played different roles at different social levels. At the local level, elderly women as well as men presided over the cults of ayllu deities. The state cloistered large numbers of women, selected as children and ranked according to their social status, beauty, and skills, in houses of chosen women located in Cuzco and the provincial administrative centres. The high-ranking women among them, the *yuraq* (white) *aqllakuna*, became *mamakuna* and were in charge of other aqllakuna. Most aqllakuna, however, came from non-Inka ayllus, and those who were not sacrificed to deities, selected as concubines by the king, or bestowed by the king on lords and honoured commoners as concubines and secondary wives were classified as *yana* (worker) *aqllakuna* and remained cloistered for the rest of their lives. Because they were regarded as wives or concubines of the sun god, they were killed if they became pregnant or were discovered to have had sexual intercourse (Silverblatt 1987: 81–85). The creation of a substantial group of celibate women may have helped to limit population growth in areas of high population density.

Mamakuna were equal in rank to all but the most important male priests and played major roles in state cults. They presided over the worship of female deities and heard confessions of sins from other women but also participated in the worship of male deities. The aqllakuna from humbler backgrounds assisted them, cooking and brewing the beer that was offered to deities and to the men and women who participated in state-sponsored rituals and corvée labour and weaving *qumpi*, the elaborate and highly valued form of cloth that was burned as sacrifices to the gods, worn by the king and nobility, and distributed as rewards to commoners. Unlike the enslaved female weavers in Mesopotamia, the aqllakuna were socially revered and better housed and fed than most commoners.

Queens helped their husbands to govern the Inka state. They often travelled with the king, and the decision to create yanakuna was attributed to advice a queen gave her husband in the course of such travels (Murra 1980: 166). Alternatively, queens carried out royal duties in Cuzco during the king's absence and acted as regents for their young sons. They also participated in rituals alongside the king and alone presided over the celebration of a major state festival, Quya Raymi, which marked the beginning of the agricultural year in late September (Silverblatt 1987: 60–66). These ritual and political roles were validated by the Inka creation myth, which claimed that the Inka royal family had begun with four supernatural brothers and their four sister-wives; three of the brothers were transformed into *wakas*, natural embodiments of spiritual power, while the fourth and his divine wife became the first Inka king and queen (Urton 1990). Inka queens had their own palaces and farms. Metal statues of them appear to have been venerated alongside those of their husbands, and after death they were mummified and treated as deities just as kings were. Along with queen mothers and other prominent female members of the leading royal panaqas, they provided vital political links among the various branches of the nobility (Patterson 1991). Yet, despite all this, their positions in society were derived from and clearly subordinate to those of their husbands.

Although the ancient Egyptians kept track of lineal descent and recognized informal family groupings such as *ȝbt* (kindred?) and *mhwt* (household?), there were no formal corporate kin-based units apart from the nuclear family. There were no primary kin terms other than those which referred to the nuclear family – no specific designations for aunt, uncle, niece, nephew, cousin, or even grandparents and grandchildren. Grandparents and other lineal ancestors all were referred to as *ỉt* (father) and *mwt* (mother), children and all other lineal descendants as *sȝ* (son) and *sȝt* (daughter), while all collateral relatives were called *sn* (brother) and *snt* (sister). In the New Kingdom even the terms for husband (*hy*, *hȝy*) and wife (*ḥmt*) were largely replaced by *sn* and *snt*. These extensions of nuclear-family terms suggest little interest in distinguishing between immediate and more remote ancestors or descendants or between maternal and paternal relatives. Such usages accorded with a kinship system that was focused on the individual (O'Connor 1990: 6–11).

The clear distinction that was drawn between lineal descent and collateral relations was accompanied by an emphasis in Egyptian mythology on rivalry between a man and his male collateral relatives (brothers, nephews, and uncles). The most celebrated rivalries were those between the god Seth and his brother Osiris and later between Seth and Osiris's son Horus for the kingship. The ideal of individuals' being free of institutionalized family encumbrances also accorded with a state ideology that envisioned individuals as relating primarily to the bureaucractic hierarchy of the state. In everyday life, however, Egyptians identified closely with the villages and towns where they had been born or lived. Great emphasis was placed on achieving high social standing within such a community by performing generous acts, while people from other communities were viewed with suspicion and even hostility (Eyre 1999: 38–39; Janssen and Janssen 1990; 1996).

Ordinary Egyptian houses tended to be small, and it has been suggested, on the basis of New Kingdom evidence, that their public rooms were centres of female activity (Meskell 1998a). The homes of high-ranking people contained complexes of offices and storerooms, but at the centre was a courtyard off which opened spacious reception rooms and a series of living and sleeping rooms for the owner of the house and members of his family (Kemp 1989: 151–55). The Egyptian ideal was neolocal residence; a common expression for marriage was *grg pr* (to establish a house) (Watterson 1991: 60). Often, however, widowed parents, unmarried siblings, adult children, or even a married son and his family might occupy a house in addition to the owner, his wife, and their young children (Kemp 1989: 157–58).

Boys generally married between the ages of sixteen and seventeen and girls between twelve and fourteen. Families arranged marriages, but young people looked about for suitable spouses and romantic love was idealized. Male suitors sought to win the approval of a girl's mother prior to asking both her parents for permission to marry her. The vast majority of marriages were monogamous. Wealthier men, including some artisans, possessed concubines (*ḥb syt*) in addition to a wife, and some higher officials may have been married to two or more women although this is not certain (Allam 1981; Robins 1993: 60–62; Simpson 1974). Kings had one or more wives simultaneously, as well as many concubines. They could and did marry their sisters, but doing so was not essential to inherit the throne. In the New Kingdom kings also married their daughters, but this seems to have taken place only after the Sed rejuvenation ritual, which was usually first performed in the thirtieth year of a king's reign. This ceremony, which involved the ritual rebirth of the king, would have placed him in the same generation as his daughters, thus making father-daughter marriages equivalent to brother-sister ones (Troy 1986).

Egyptian men were supposed to love their wives and mothers and treat them well, but women were regarded as secondary to men (Robins 1993: 107, 191). Family homes were owned by the husband, although a wife was referred to as the *nbt pr* (mistress of the house) and it was her responsibility to care for and manage the house while her husband attended to other business (92). Also, with the exception of royalty, wives were normally buried in their husbands' tombs, where they were accompanied by fewer grave goods and ones of poorer quality than those buried with their husbands (Meskell 1998b). In the decoration of tomb chapels, women were represented less frequently and often on a smaller scale than their husbands. Nevertheless, individual royal and upper-class women were depicted more frequently in ancient Egypt than in any other early civilization (Robins 1993: 165–75). Kingship normally descended from father to son, and Egyptian religious beliefs indicated that only men could truly be monarchs.

Although the average Egyptian woman possessed less property than her husband, women were not confined to their homes or private quarters (*ỉpt*) and were fully recognized as legal entities. They could inherit, purchase, administer, and sell land, goods, and slaves in their own names. They could sign their own marriage contracts, make their own wills, and adopt their own heirs. They kept their own property after marriage, served as witnesses in court hearings, and initiated lawsuits against other people, including their own husbands and children. They could divorce a husband for impotence, adultery, or mistreatment. A widow had the legal right to one-third of her husband's estate, while her children inherited the rest. Yet, unlike her husband, a married woman was free to bequeath her own property to whomever she wished and could disinherit even her own children (Allam 1981; Leprohon 1999; Wenig 1969: 11–13). Women were required to provide corvée labour for the state, but this may have applied only to women who owned property (Robins 1993: 122).

Royal women derived their position and primary titles from their roles as a king's daughter, sister, wife, or mother. Some royal princesses accumulated all four titles. Royal wives performed rituals which usually complemented those of the king. Queen mothers sometimes acted as regents for their young sons (Troy 1986). Wives and daughters of nobles and officials who were present at the royal court bore the title *ẖkryt nswt* (royal ornament) and *nfrt* (beauty), according to whether or not they were married (Desroches-Noblecourt 1986: 77, 81; Robins 1993: 117). In the Old Kingdom many upper-class women, including queens, served as chief priests of major female deities, especially Hathor and Neith.

In addition to attending to or overseeing household chores, many women whose families belonged to the specialist class derived profit from performing various types of work outside their homes. In the Old Kingdom, female stewards, overseers, scribes, and physicians attended the wives of high officials and managed various aspects of their estates. Royal women may have been attended solely by female servants and officials. The wife of the Sixth Dynasty vizier Mereruka had a female staff consisting of a steward, inspector of treasure, overseer of ornaments, and overseer of cloth. Female singers, dancers, and acrobats worked in the royal palace, and women also served as mortuary priests (Robins 1993: 116). Some of these tasks required literacy (Desroches-Noblecourt 1986: 189–93; Robins 1993: 111–13). In general, however, women only oversaw other women, while males supervised subordinates of either sex. The mother of King Khufu was an exception; she served as the overseer of the butchers who prepared the meat offerings for her dead husband (Feucht 1997: 336–37). In the Middle Kingdom a few women may have continued to work as scribes and to oversee household tasks, but the administration of people and property had become almost exclusively male (Desroches-Noblecourt 1986: 192; Robins 1993: 116; Ward 1989). It is unclear to what extent in the Old Kingdom, professional women, such as scribes, worked full- or part-time and whether they were married.

Lower-class women derived incomes from a variety of part-time occupations, such as weaving, singing, dancing, playing musical instruments, midwifery, and professional mourning (Robins 1993: 119–20). While women were active as market traders in the New Kingdom, Old Kingdom scenes show men doing most of the selling (Kemp 1989: 255). There is no way to know to what extent this artistic convention reflected social norms. In the Third Dynasty, male and female millers, weavers, and washers worked in separate establishments in the royal palace, the women probably under female overseers. Women and men worked together baking bread and brewing beer in the palace kitchens, although it appears that only men cooked fish and meat (Feucht 1997: 336; Fischer 1989). Both married and unmarried women appear to have earned income as prostitutes. Men were warned against consorting with unknown prostitutes or promiscuous women so that they would not inadvertently become involved in quarrels with their husbands or fathers (Robins 1993: 69).

GENDER ROLES

The kinship systems of early civilizations have long been thought to display a patrilineal bias, and Victorian anthropologists viewed this an evolutionary advance over the matrilineal societies that they believed had preceded them; however, the bias of family organization in all the early civilizations was masculine but not always patrilineal. There is also no obvious correlation between their different forms of kinship organization and either territorial or city-states. Initially I hypothesized that the variations reflected the forms of kinship that prevailed in different regions prior to the rise of states. Important parallels have been noted between Inka kinship organization and that found among tribal peoples in central and eastern Brazil (Lounsbury 1986). Highland Mexican calpollis and Peruvian ayllus may have developed from some early form of endogamous kinship that was widespread in Central and South America, but if such an institution existed it does not appear to have been shared by the Maya. Cross-cultural ethnographic evidence indicates that considerably more variation in kinship systems existed at a prestate level, both on a regional basis and in relation to different types of economies, than is found in our admittedly small sample of early civilizations (Hallpike 1986: 141; Murdock 1949). While this difference could simply reflect sampling error, it suggests that kinship systems may have shifted in a particular direction as a result of the development of new and more convergent forms of social organization. Support for such a shift may be found in the kinship terminologies of early civilizations, which generally do not display a strong patrilineal bias. Those of the Yoruba, Inka, Maya, and Aztec appear to have employed a Hawaiian kinship terminology for designating cousins: both parallel-cousins and cross-cousins were referred to by terms that were identical or very similar to those used to designate siblings. According to George P. Murdock (1959a; 1959b: 29) such usage is found in 'bilateral societies with extended families or corporate kin groups but can also result from an incompletely assimilated shift from one rule of descent to another'. This interpretation suggests that not all these societies had been strongly patrilineal for a long time.

The degree and precise expression of a masculine bias varied from one early civilization to another, no doubt depending to some extent on the sort of social organization that had existed prior to the development of civilization in a region. The Asante state, in what is now Ghana, was of recent origin when it was first encountered by Europeans in the eighteenth century. Although Asante society was based on matrilineal descent, its rulers were already seeking to marry in ways that would ensure that male descendants would eventually inherit their offices (Wilks 1975: 371). The most important factor sanctioning a masculine bias appears to have been the growing importance of male-dominated political relations as these societies grew more complex.

Gender is commonly acknowledged to be a ubiquitous and fundamental component of social identity. It is also generally agreed that, while beliefs concerning masculinity and femininity are culturally constructed, prior to modern times all gender systems were based on the belief that men and women had different roles and responsibilities in social reproduction and maintenance. Men and women in every society dressed and behaved differently from each other (R. Wright 1996a), and in all preindustrial societies, crafts, or individual processes within crafts, tended to be segregated according to gender (Costin 1996; Murdock and Provost 1973). There is much evidence that women's interests were expressed primarily in relation to their families while men's concerns were expressed in relation to the broader sociopolitical sphere. Such focusing of expression does not signify that women or men did not exhibit a holistic interest in the forces that were affecting their lives.

Csilla Dallos (1997) has argued that, as individual identity had to be formulated in more communal and hierarchical terms as societies grew more complex, both men and women were forced to sacrifice their personal autonomy to serve the interests of the domestic group that was increasingly being pressured by society and the state. For men broad political considerations and for women the welfare of their families acquired increasing precedence over personal interests. It was as a result of these trends that the household and the nuclear family came to be viewed as a miniature kingdom, with its male head as its ruler and women, children, and dependents as his subjects. Under these conditions, gender relations grew increasingly unequal, and female identity was subordinated to complementing male gender roles.

One effect of this development was the separation of women in all early civilizations into two classes: those who were respectable and those who were not. To be respectable a woman had to be honourably attached to a parental family, husband, or appropriate institution, such as a Mesopotamian temple cloister or an Inka aqllawasi. Freelance prostitutes, innkeepers, and self-proclaimed witches were viewed as lacking honour and posing a threat to the moral order. Slave women held in Mesopotamian weaving establishments attached to palaces and temples were regarded as lacking anyone to protect their honour and appear to have been subjected to sexual abuse as well as harsh treatment (R. Wright 1996b). The captive women whom the Aztec kept as state prostitutes for the entertainment of young warriors likewise existed outside the normal moral constraints of society. Women who lacked the protection of male kin or responsible male officials were easy targets for robbery, intimidation, rape, and other forms of abusive treatment. Although such women were invariably few, their wretched lives, unsavoury reputations, and lack of legitimate redress stressed the importance of women's remaining respectable by continuing to depend on their male relatives. They also provided a negative example against which the behaviour of respectable women could be measured (Lerner 1986: 212–16).

Despite their general subordination to men and evidence of widespread resistance to such subordination in both the family and society in general, the position of women varied significantly from one early civilization to another (Nelson 1991; Silverblatt 1988a; 1991). Although little is known about the treatment of ordinary women in Shang and Western Zhou China, they appear to have been greatly disfavoured, both legally and economically, as a result of being fully absorbed into their husbands' patrilineages. The most favourably positioned women appear to have been those in the Yoruba kingdoms and in ancient Egypt. Yoruba women remained affiliated with their fathers' descent groups and therefore could rely on the ongoing active support of blood kin. The Yoruba also admired individual competitiveness and allowed that it could occur between men and women. Egyptian society had no lineage structure and even more strongly stressed individual achievement. In all early civilizations women as well as men participated in ritual activities. In general, however, the top positions in religious hierarchies were occupied by males. While men told women of equal or inferior social status what to do, women gave orders only to men who were clearly inferior to themselves. Yoruba, Aztec, and Egyptian women were active in market trade, though in Egypt it involved only the circulation of locally produced goods among the lower classes (Kemp 1989: 253–55).

In territorial states the need for loyal administrators and advisers to assist the king led to the involvement of upper-class women in administrative activities. Thus class dominated gender to the extent that upper-class women might give orders to lower-ranking men as well as women. Yet their administrative roles, like their roles in the economic and religious spheres, were largely restricted to assisting their husbands. In other spheres they tended to be limited to directing other women and male domestic servants. In city-state civilizations royal wives were often selected from leading families within the state, thus helping to forge alliances between the king and potential sources of significant internal opposition. Sometimes they were drawn from the royal families of neighbouring city-states, such marriages creating or reinforcing interstate alliances. Maya queens, perhaps most often queen mothers, were depicted playing important roles in royal and state rituals. Some Mesopotamian queens owned and seem to have managed their own and temple estates, but major ritual roles were played by female priests. Aztec and Yoruba royal wives seem to have been ritually and politically invisible. In these societies public rituals were performed by female office-holders who were not necessarily related to the king.

Where the documentation is sufficient, there is evidence that the status of women declined in early civilizations. Female rulers are mentioned for early times in the later traditions of the Yoruba and in Mesopotamia, but there is no contemporary evidence for these rulers, and no specific female rulers are attested for later and better recorded periods. It is therefore impossible to determine whether there really had been female rulers in the formative periods of these civilizations or they were later mythological creations that ascribed to earlier times practices that were different from those of the present. June Nash (1978) has indicated that among the Aztec the position of women declined as a combined result of increasing male specialization, an ideology that glorified warfare and male domination, and the benefits that the state showered on successful warriors and on men generally. Official Aztec myths stressed the ideological subordination of women, but life-sustaining goddesses continued to be honoured by commoners and the community as they had been in earlier times (Brumfiel 1996; Kellogg 1995; Nash 1978). The Aztec and their neighbours used women's tools as metaphors for subordination and humility; sending a present of raw cotton (used for spinning) to a foreign ruler constituted a gross affront (Nash 1978: 356).

Among the Inka, the growth of political power, which was primarily associated with males, reduced gender symmetry and enhanced the patriarchal character of society (Silverblatt 1987). In Egypt the gradual disappearance of female bureaucrats and chief priests, even if they had mainly served female members of the royal family and female deities, represented the removal of women from the political and administrative spheres and their confinement to the local economic realm and to subordinate ritual roles. The important roles played by royal women in Shang society eventually came to be performed by royal eunuchs, and women were confined to playing subordinate roles in sacrificing to their husband's ancestors. Yet, despite these growing restrictions, women in early civilizations do not appear to have been as disadvantaged as they became in some later preindustrial civilizations, such as those of Classical Greece and Rome.

SAME-SEX RELATIONS

What is known about male homosexual behaviour in early civilizations is mainly normative information that probably reflects the views of literate males, whose opinions may or may not have been congruent with those of other sections of society. Homosexuality in early civilizations was regarded as a kind of behaviour rather than the defining characteristic of a particular type of person (Somerville 1997). However, various distinctions relating to morality and character were drawn according to the circumstances in which individuals engaged in same-sex behaviour and the extent to which such behaviour precluded other forms of sexual activity.

In general, people in early civilizations considered reproduction the primary goal of sexual activity. Where lineages were important or property, power, and position regularly passed from one generation to the next, it was highly desirable to have descendants. It was also believed that only biological descendants could or would make appropriate offerings to the souls of dead family members. Further, people depended on their children to take care of them in their old age, and the domestic division of labour provided a strong incentive for both men and women to marry.

The state and the upper classes also had strong reasons to encourage a reproductively oriented sexuality among commoners. Larger populations meant increased tax revenues and more corvée labourers and soldiers. Therefore population growth became an upper-class ideal even where population density was high and where the lower classes did not share this ideal. The upper classes did not necessarily desire to expand their own ranks; rich Mesopotamian families sought to curb the division of landholdings and other family wealth by restricting the number of people among whom the family's wealth had to be shared, enrolling some female members in temples as celibate priests.

All the early civilizations also accorded great material and symbolic importance to fertility. Successful harvests and the reproduction of domestic animals were crucial for their survival and prosperity. This reinforced a reproductively oriented view of human sexuality. Human reproduction was clearly conceived as analogous to the reproduction of plants and animals. The ancient Egyptians and Mesopotamians viewed women as fertile fields and equated male sexual activity with ploughing and sowing such fields (Lichtheim 1973: 69). The Egyptians also imagined the divine power that had created the world as a form of male sexual energy (Robins 1993: 17). In Mesoamerica parallels were drawn between a woman's womb and the earth, and sexual activity was seen as a way of renewing all aspects of the terrestrial world (Townsend 1992: 132–36). Consequently, there was a tendency to regard sexual practices that did not lead to reproduction as contrary to the natural order of things.

It is clear that the Egyptians strongly privileged heterosexual relations and in particular heterosexual relations within marriage. Men who were unable for whatever reason to father children were regarded as pitiable or farcical (Parkinson 1995). Among forty-two moral and ritual offences that, according to the New Kingdom Book of the Dead, a dead man had to prove he had not committed in order to be admitted to the kingdom of the god Osiris were homosexual acts (Parkinson 1995: 61–62).

The Egyptians differentiated homosexual acts according to whether a man played an active (male) role or a passive (female) one, the active role being judged less compromising to an adult male's sexual identity. Sodomy was viewed as demonstrating the penetrator's power over another male, and sodomizing an enemy or having sex with a boy (willing or not) when women were unavailable did not call a man's virility into question. The god Seth was described as having this sort of intercourse with his nephew Horus in order to demonstrate that Horus was too young and weak to rule Egypt (Parkinson 1995: 65). Seth was a powerful deity who played a vital role in protecting the gods, but he also was a deity associated with confusion and disorder – with political crises, storms, and the dry, infertile lands beyond the Nile Valley. While his sexual appetite was easily aroused, his heterosexual activities were as unproductive as his homosexual ones. He had no children, and even his sister-wife Nephthys had become pregnant by the god Osiris, who was a brother to both of them.

A Middle Kingdom folktale portrays a high-ranking general named Sasanet as remaining unmarried and engaging in sexual activity, as the passive partner, with King Neferkare, who came every night to his house. Neferkare may have been King Pepi II, whose long reign marked the end of the Old Kingdom. While the tale is incompletely preserved, for any king to have engaged in this sort of relation equated him with Seth and called into question his ability to maintain the cosmic order (Parkinson 1995: 71–74).

Among the Mesopotamians, homosexuality was not an activity in which the gods engaged but a disability inflicted upon humans to prevent them from multiplying too quickly and disturbing the gods with their clamour (Postgate 1992: 295). The Code of Hammurabi, although containing numerous injunctions against sexual misconduct, did not explicitly refer to homosexuality. Some masters are reported to have sodomized their male servants, and there were guilds of male prostitutes (*assinnu*, *kurgarru*, and *kulu'u*) who played passive roles (*sinnišânu*) in sexual relations. They appear to have been connected with the cult of the fertility goddess, Ishtar (Inanna), who was believed to be entertained by their irregular sexual behaviour (*asakku*) (Bottéro 1992: 190–98). The *gala*, or male lamentation singers, attached to temples appear to have been transvestites, and transvestites or men who engaged in passive homosexual acts were attached to the royal court, apparently as servants and entertainers (Bottéro 1992: 197, 244; Postgate 1992: 126–27). Freelance male prostitutes, like their female counterparts, lived near the city walls and frequented taverns. They too were socially marginal, isolated, despised, and often mistreated. While transvestites and habitually homosexual men were assigned special roles in Mesopotamian society, it was generally agreed that by not marrying and having children, they had failed to realize the proper destiny of a man. They were probably included among the unclean and depraved persons who had to be expelled from cities whenever their main temple was restored, consecrated, and sanctified (Kramer 1981: 268). The gods had quixotically created such persons to be different from others and then had to provide special, anomalous roles for them in the social order (Bottéro 1992: 196–97).

The attitude towards homosexuality was more sharply negative among the Aztec and their neighbours. They viewed sexual intercourse as one of the few genuine pleasures of a painful and difficult existence, but they also believed that, by engaging in any form of sexual activity too frequently, young men impaired their physical and mental development and condemned themselves to impotence at an early age. There was therefore strong encouragement to restrict sexual activities to marital relations. Young, unmarried warriors were, however, provided with female companions as a reward for their military achievements. They were individuals believed to possess exceptional supernatural power. Men who habitually engaged in homosexual acts were regarded as weak, diseased, and withered. Passive homosexuality violated the military ideals that structured life in this part of the world. Homosexual or transvestite behaviour was punished by death or by being sold into slavery. Celibacy was also disapproved of except for ritual reasons (Clendinnen 1991: 169; López Austin 1988, 1: 303–6).

In the Inka kingdom marriage was obligatory and enforced by the state. In some Peruvian cultures, homosexual acts were associated with religious practices, being viewed as a way of transmitting supernatural power from one man to another in order to facilitate the performance of certain religious rituals. The Inka government vigorously attempted to suppress non-ritual homosexual practices within its domain. The punishment for sodomy involved the execution not only of those who committed it but also of their families and the burning of their houses (Classen 1993: 60–61; Kendall 1973: 88; von Hagen 1959: 179, 314).

While the degree of toleration of homosexuality varied from one early civilization to another, such behaviour was regarded at the very least as contrary to social ideals and at worst as a practice that violated the cosmic order and had to be punished by death. Even in the most tolerant early civilizations, those who publicly embraced a homosexual lifestyle were assigned socially marginal roles. There is no evidence in our sample that attitudes towards homosexual behaviour varied with formal political organization. Nor does growing land pressure appear to have encouraged greater tolerance of homosexual behaviour. The inhabitants of the Valley of Mexico, which had the highest population density in our sample, were among the most hostile to it. The desire of upper-class Mesopotamians to divide their landholdings among as few heirs as possible may, however, have encouraged a more relaxed attitude towards homosexuality. On the whole, family and state economic interests encouraged a negative attitude towards homosexual behaviour that both reflected and reinforced the increasing patriarchal tendencies in early civilizations.

DIFFERENCES AND SIMILARITIES

Early civilizations exhibited considerable variation in kinship organization, family residence arrangements, inheritance, the roles and status of women, and attitudes towards homosexual behaviour. There is no obvious correlation between these differences and various environmental settings, subsistence patterns, or forms of political organization, but there is some regional clustering in patterns of kinship organization. Endogamous descent groups were confined to indigenous civilizations of the New World. The two civilizations in which women had the most rights were located in Africa. The ones with the least hostile recorded attitudes towards homosexual behaviour were Egypt and Mesopotamia.

All early civilizations displayed varying degrees of masculine bias. It may be that the increasing importance of political relations for the functioning of complex societies led to a greater emphasis on male roles. If so, the transformation probably began during the early state period. The position of women appears to have been inferior to that of men in all the early civilizations, given the growing importance of male leadership roles, greater male access to wealth as a result of political manipulation and warfare, and the increasing domination of family life by society and the state. Patriarchal attitudes towards reproduction probably also encouraged more negative attitudes towards homosexual behaviour.

Nevertheless, the position of women varied significantly from one early civilization to another. In territorial states upper-class women generally enjoyed more political power and social visibility as a result of being drawn into secondary governing and ritual roles alongside their husbands. In city-state civilizations upper-class women appear to have had the greatest public visibility among the Classic Maya; in Mesopotamia and the Valley of Mexico they were limited to ritual roles, while among the Yoruba the chief public activity of kings' wives was trade. The distinction between territorial and city-states is far less useful for predicting the status of ordinary women. In Egypt men and women enjoyed considerable legal equality, and in highland Peru the complementarity of men and women in many productive tasks and in rituals was generally recognized. In Shang China, however, the legal and economic position of women seems to have been much less favourable. Although Aztec women possessed considerable economic and social freedom, they had very little role in public decision making. Women in Mesopotamia appear to have been even more restricted in terms of what they were allowed to do. The greatest degree of overall female economic and social freedom and participation in political decision making occurred among the Yoruba. While it might be argued that the position of ordinary women tended to be more favourable in territorial states than in city-states and that this reflected the higher status enjoyed by upper-class women in these societies, the sample is too small and the correlations too weak for this hypothesis to be supported. Moreover, the favourable position of Yoruba women stands strongly against this generalization. More important is the observation that, wherever the status of women can be traced over time, it appears to have declined rather than improved.

10 Administration

Weberian sociologists blandly define the state as a government that possesses a monopoly of the legitimate use of force within a specific territory. Marxists more cynically regard the state as a mechanism that deploys physical coercion to defend the property and privileges of the dominant social classes (Kamenka 1989: 7–11). While these definitions suggest what a state is, they are inadequate to describe, even from a purely political point of view, how a state operates. Physical force is never sufficient by itself to maintain order within society. Such order depends on most people's being prepared to accept the way things are being done. Social control is also inherent in communities, economic institutions, and the family, whose leaders exert their own forms of control through economic, social, and ideological coercion and by manipulating public opinion (Mann 1986). Within unified political entities, public order depends to a large degree on the extent to which those who control these other sectors of society are prepared to cooperate with the state and with each other.

The state can also be viewed as an administrative mechanism that extracts sufficient resources from society to maintain itself, defends the territory it controls from foreign aggression, and is responsible for maintaining the unity of its territory, if necessary by force. To do this it must uphold a social and economic order which convinces ordinary people that, despite the demands the state imposes on them, it makes their lives more prosperous and secure than they would be if the state did not exist. An enduring state thus has the dual task of protecting the privileges of the upper classes and ensuring that the lower classes are not exploited, impoverished, or disaffected to the point that their reactions undermine the social order.

To carry out these tasks the state must be able to collect taxes, administer the properties it owns, fund institutions such as armies, police forces, and public labour, and curb the dishonesty of officials and powerful people generally.

Such an administrative system is inevitably expensive and always in danger of becoming self-serving and thus undermining rather than helping to preserve public order (Tainter 1988). In early civilizations only the king, or perhaps the king and a small number of councillors, had an unequivocal vested interest in the equitable functioning of the bureaucracy as a whole. When they could get away with it, most officials sought to benefit themselves, their families, and their friends at the expense of the state through embezzlement and the shifting of tax burdens to others. As Ibn Khaldun noted in the fourteenth century A.D., where such behaviour got out of control it undermined the economy, encouraged social unrest, and eventually destroyed the authority and power of the state. Those who occupied the upper levels of the administration of early civilizations had to be sufficiently powerful and well-informed that they could control the officials under them and ensure that these officials served the state and not only their personal interests (R. McC. Adams 1965: 71).

At this point, however, a problem arose. In all early civilizations, rulers sought to enhance their control by projecting an imposing image of their power and authority. Yet the productive capacities of early civilizations were severely limited by comparison with those of modern industrial societies. Because of this, the ruling classes were disinclined to use more resources for managerial purposes than were minimally needed to perpetuate the system. Doing so would have reduced the wealth that they could use to provide themselves with abundant food, fancy clothing, jewellery, palaces, tombs, and numerous retainers, all of which made their lives more enjoyable and enhanced their public image (Trigger 1990a).

The most expedient way to reduce administrative costs was to delegate decision making from higher to lower levels in administrative hierarchies. In all early civilizations, families, wards, and small communities were permitted and even encouraged to manage their own affairs to a much greater degree than is characteristic of developed industrial societies. Aztec calpollis, Inka ayllus, Egyptian villages, and Yoruba extended families were left to regulate themselves, with the state intervening only when self-regulation had conspicuously failed to work. The most common limitation on the power of such groups was the requirement that death sentences be approved by higher officials and perhaps ultimately the king.

Effective administration depends on controlling subordinates, and this requires both knowledge and power. A hierarchical approach is essential for studying territorial states, in which leaders had to create effective ways to keep regions and localities linked to the central administration. Such an approach is also appropriate for understanding how villages and small administrative districts were linked to capitals in those city-states in which most of the population resided outside the main urban centre. It is less useful, however, for describing political processes in city-states where the population was largely concentrated in a single urban centre, political power was not strongly centralized, and the main problem was producing consensus among competing groups or interests. In some of these city-states kings had enough power to enforce order but not enough to subordinate the interests of other powerful groups entirely to their own. In less centralized city-states, kings served as a symbol of political unity, and experienced ones played a vital role in helping to broker consensus among competing political factions. Thus, when studying city-states, it is necessary to consider forms of administration that were heterarchical as well as hierarchical (Crumley 1987; Ehrenreich, Crumley, and Levy 1995).

CITY-STATE ADMINISTRATION

Elizabeth Stone (1997) has suggested that the large proportion of the population living in urban centres in early civilizations reflected the direct participation of large numbers of people in the government of such states. Yet there was no regular mass participation in government in the early civilizations comparable to that in the democratic city-states of Classical Greece. Political power may have been shared by members of numerous groups, but it remained the prerogative of a small minority of upper-class people, most of whom lived in the capitals.

Administrative relations between the urban centres and the rural hinterlands of city-states were shaped by the numerical dominance of the centre. Urban centres that contained more than 50 percent of the population dominated the hinterland politically, economically, and militarily as well as demographically. In Early Dynastic Mesopotamia only a small population appears to have lived in the countryside full-time. Among the Yoruba, many individuals shifted back and forth between city and countryside, and a substantial minority were politically associated with small towns or villages that enjoyed local self-government and whose leaders were connected as clients to politically important lineages in the capitals. Likewise, in the Valley of Mexico and especially among the Classic Maya, many city-state urban centres were surrounded by secondary administrative centres and rural communities whose leaders were affiliated with the political leadership in the capital.

Among the Yoruba, individual patrilineal extended families regulated their internal civil, religious, legal, and military affairs under the leadership of their bale, advised and assisted by a committee of elders. Leadership at this level was gerontocratic, but these officials exerted no significant influence beyond their own residential groups. When issues of major importance had to be discussed, meetings were held which all the adult residents of the group, as well as the (mainly female) members of the extended family living elsewhere, could attend. Genealogically related or neighbouring extended families also managed their collective affairs at the precinct (ogbon) and ward (adugbo) levels of Yoruba cities. Hereditary office-holders at both levels regulated the collective activities of these groups and presided over the public meetings that were held to discuss major issues (Bascom 1969: 30, 44–46).

Many political offices, including kingship, were hereditary in particular lineages, but since no exclusive rule of inheritance was specified they were the subject of fierce competition involving the eligible male members of the lineage. A number of the most important non-royal lineages in the capital had members who composed a small but very important state council, which shared power with the king. Often these officials were also ward leaders. Over time, an extended family that was in political decline might be deprived of its seat on the state council, while other important individuals or a representative of a newly important extended family might be appointed to it. The members of the state council, whose large compounds were often located adjacent to the royal palace, commanded the army, headed the cults of important deities, and played a major role in foreign affairs. They also collected a share of the fees paid for legal services, taxes on goods being transported from one community or state to another, and taxes and tribute levied on their own and conquered peoples. The leader of the state council of Oyo was commander in chief of the army and became regent on the death of a king. While the king had to approve the appointment of all new members of the state council, the council in turn selected a new king in consultation with spokesmen for the major royal patrilineages. The members of the state council could also, if they were in unanimous agreement, demand that a king abdicate or commit suicide (Law 1977: 73–74).

Yoruba life was also managed by age-grades and numerous voluntary associations (*egbe*) (Eades 1980: 99). The membership of these societies cut across lineage divisions and hence both promoted community integration and further decentralized political decision-making. The leaders of the more important voluntary associations played significant roles in the political life of their communities, especially in the smaller polities, where the power of both the king and the state council members was weak.

Voluntary societies included the Ogboni, some of whose leaders were those involved in electing and installing kings and leading officials. The initiates of this society judged some legal cases (Bascom 1969: 36–37). The main role of the Oro society was to clear communities of evil spirits, but its members also arrested criminals, settled quarrels, quelled civil strife, and executed kings who refused to commit suicide when ordered to do so by the state council (93). Age-grade societies, which bestowed titles on their members and collected initiation fees from them, performed various forms of corvée labour for the community, often under the direction of elderly compound heads. Craft associations not only organized and regulated various trades but, through their titled leaders, gave the members of different professions a voice at the higher levels of community government (Eades 1980: 85–86).

Despite the king's supreme ritual importance, his required seclusion enabled the members of the state council to derive vast political influence from their greater freedom of movement. Opportunities for the king to increase his power developed only if divisions arose among members of the state council or if he was able to forge an alliance with rising political leaders who were not yet members of it (Law 1977: 77–82).

Yoruba kings, as office-holders, possessed large amounts of land and numerous slaves, and therefore they were able to engage in foreign trade and supply horses and soldiers to military campaigns. In return, they received a large share of the booty collected in wartime, often in the form of slaves, and of the tribute that was paid by conquered states in peacetime. Kings used their share of this wealth to enhance their political importance in their kingdoms. Palace staffs, supported by the king's largesse, were made up of large numbers of officials, slaves, and household servants who bore palace titles and performed numerous domestic and political functions. Many royal officials who were eunuchs carried out administrative, military, judicial, and ritual roles outside the palace as the king's personal representatives (*ajele*). Slaves guarded the king and also acted as his agents in dealing with townspeople, village leaders, and rulers of foreign states. Slaves and eunuchs were valued because they did not have family interests that they might put ahead of those of the king. Women who bore palace titles also performed administrative tasks such as supervising and keeping order in the urban markets and among traders (Bascom 1969: 34–36; Law 1977: 233–42).

In theory the king ruled the capital through a hierarchy of state councillors and ward, precinct, and compound leaders and outlying communities through town and palace officials, leaders of outlying local centres, and bales. In reality his control over both the urban centre and the outlying communities was shared with quasi-hereditary leaders who belonged to non-royal lineages and with the office-holders of various voluntary, craft, and age-grade organizations. The revenues of the state were divided between the king and powerful state councillors, who created parallel administrative structures that vied with one another for influence in and beyond the capital (Bascom 1969: 29–30; Law 1977: 98–118).

Politically the most centralized state in the Yoruba cultural sphere was Benin. There the kingship and most other hereditary offices were inherited patrilineally through male primogeniture. Although the *uzama*, the hereditary leaders who were equivalent to the members of the state council in Oyo and other Yoruba states, provided military commanders in chief and played an important symbolic role in the installation of kings, their power had been radically diminished by comparison with that of their counterparts in Oyo and Ife. Moreover, most other titles had become non-hereditary and were in the king's gift. The palace title system was greatly expanded and opened up, so that any man able to afford the initiation fees could enter its lower grades. As a result, men personally loyal to the king were found throughout the kingdom. City officials represented a wealthy and influential section of the population that could exert pressure on the king, but with rare exceptions their titles too were non-hereditary, and the king could use his power to reassign them to attract powerful people to his service. The Benin state council was made up of the largely ceremonial uzama, the main palace and city officials, and a number of other military leaders. In Benin the king was the sole source of legislative and state policy, and military leaders were directly responsible to him (Bradbury 1957: 35–43).

Unlike Oyo, which was a relatively small city-state exerting hegemony over weaker, self-governing neighbouring kingdoms, Benin was surrounded by small communities directly subject to its king (Mercier 1962: 150–51). The territory ruled by the king was divided into a large number of tax units consisting of chiefdoms, villages, and wards. Each tax unit was controlled by a title-holder in Benin City, who acted as an intermediary in all dealings between its leaders and the royal court (Bradbury 1957: 42–43). Benin villages usually had as their head the oldest active man (*odiowere*), but some also had a hereditary co-ruler (*onogie*). These leaders and all the members of the oldest age-grade in the community constituted the village council (32–34).

It is unclear whether the political organization of Benin is better viewed as the most centralized variant of Yoruba kingship or as something different that resulted from the imposition of Yoruba ideas about political organization on an Edo society. Edo polities that were not influenced by Benin consisted of autonomous local communities. Yet, despite the control that the Benin monarch exerted over appointments to titled offices, the presence of influential city leaders meant that even in Benin City royal power did not go uncontested.

None of the Yoruba states had a broadly participatory form of government, but kings did share authority with the representatives of powerful lineages, voluntary societies, craft guilds, and age-grades. Those individuals participated in many types of decision-making that affected the administration of city-states. Despite the seeming fragility of these arrangements and occasional lapses into civic disorder, Yoruba cities endured for long periods. There is no evidence that a relatively decentralized state such as Oyo was politically less powerful than a more centralized one such as Benin.

Mesopotamian cosmological myths have sometimes been interpreted as embodying memories of a time when cities were governed by councils (*ukkin*; Akk. *puḫrum*) composed of elders and presided over by an en. This, it is suggested, was probably an office that elders occupied in rotation. Assemblies of all free males may have met occasionally to approve or reject proposals made by elders or ens, especially proposals that concerned waging war against other states (Jacobsen 1943; Van De Mieroop 1999: 133–39). Iconographic evidence has been viewed as indicating, however, that kings played a significant role as early as the Uruk period. If such assemblies ever existed, they were obsolete before the earliest records of contemporary political events. The Mesopotamians themselves believed, at least in later times, that kingship had descended from the sky world during the era of creation as a god-given model for conducting human affairs. In historical times kings and temple administrators played the major role in decision-making, although in each city councils composed of elders (*abba*; Akk. *šībūtum*), who were outstanding citizens or heads of powerful patrilineages, and even some ordinary citizens judged legal cases, discussed matters of common interest, and performed various administrative duties.

The internal affairs of each city ward were handled by a council composed of representatives of the leading households in that ward. The council made legal decisions, supervised land sales, and was responsible for maintaining law and order. It was headed by a *rubiānum* (mayor), who held office for a year and served as the main link between the constituency he represented and the king. In at least some cities, each ward official was aided by a policeman (*ukuuš*) (R. Harris 1975: 58; Postgate 1992: 81; Van De Mieroop 1999: 120–33).

In Early Dynastic times much of the population of southern Mesopotamia lived in urban settlements, and many people who had houses in nearby hamlets may have been city dwellers who inhabited these small settlements only while they were cultivating their fields. It is unclear how the growing number of people who lived year-round in rural settlements in later times governed themselves or were represented at the city-state level. If most of them worked land that belonged to kings, temples, or rich landowners, they would have had no direct role in government at the state level. By Old Babylonian times, however, the inhabitants of villages (*ālum*) administered their communities' affairs by means of councils of elders and must have enjoyed a status corresponding to that of the wards of capital cities (Postgate 1992: 83).

Kings may originally have been part-time military commanders, but by the historical period they were full-time leaders whose office was endowed with extensive agricultural land and herds of livestock. Kings alone were responsible for dealing with other states – maintaining and equipping professional soldiers, training citizen conscripts for military campaigns, coordinating the construction and maintenance of walls around cities, and conducting diplomatic relations with the rulers of other states. They also sought to control the internal affairs of their cities to varying degrees. In their capacity as the chief servant, or bailiff, of the city's patron deity, kings frequently claimed the right to review legal decisions made by lower courts. They required large administrative staffs to manage palace lands, purchase and store imported raw materials, manufacture the special equipment needed by the army, supervise public construction work, exchange gifts with rulers of other states, and coordinate economic, legal, and political activities with the leaders of wards, villages, and craft associations and with powerful landowners. Palace administrators in turn required the services of large numbers of scribes, who kept detailed records and oversaw the physical labour that was vital for the palace's economic functioning. In theory administrative and scribal positions were royal appointments, but in practice they often passed from father to son (Postgate 1992: 149–53).

Although temples existed in Mesopotamia long before any evidence of palaces, the rise of royal power appears to have been accompanied by the expansion of the temple estates that administered land viewed as the property of major deities. Temples were controlled by chief administrators or small groups of officials. These administrators were usually not the chief priests who served the deity, especially if those priests were women. The highest-ranking administrators directed the work of large numbers of priests (male and female), lesser administrators and accountants, and various craftsmen, tenant farmers, farm labourers, and slaves. Temple estates played a major role in looking after impoverished, sick, and crippled members of the community, many of whom were absorbed into the permanent temple workforce. Impoverished families often dedicated their children and other family members to temples. Temples lent grain to ordinary citizens at a lower interest rate than palaces, private landowners, or merchants. They also lent capital for the ransom of soldiers captured in battle (Postgate 1992: 117–36).

Temple estates appear to have expanded as much land that had been communally owned by patrilineal extended families passed into royal and private ownership. It is unclear to what extent their expansion was a form of corporate resistance to royal power or a response to the economic dislocation that resulted from the increasing privatization of land. While gods did not treat their tenants and workforce much more generously than other landowners, temples do appear to have looked after the poor and helpless better than other institutions were prepared to. Various kings sought to increase their wealth and power by assuming control over temple estates, but these attempts were not always successful (Kramer 1963: 79–83).

The competition for power among kings, temple leaders, wealthy private landowners, and the heads of patrilineal landowning groups created a fluid situation as power was negotiated at the ward and state levels. The king's role in government varied from one city to another and from one period to another in the same city. Mesopotamia is the only early civilization to produce detailed evidence of popular unrest as a result of economic exploitation and of efforts, usually by kings, to counter such unrest by freeing community members enslaved for debt and decreeing amnesties on debts that involved the pawning or loss of land (Postgate 1992: 195). Kings may have been more powerful in the northern, more Semitic-speaking parts of southern Mesopotamia than they were in the far south, and royal power may have grown as northern rulers came to control the south (Lamberg-Karlovsky 1996: 143–46). Nevertheless, in all southern Mesopotamian cities political power remained relatively decentralized as different groups competed for political control. J. N. Postgate (1991: 301) maintains that a form of administration based upon consensus survived the growth of hegemonic and later regional states in Mesopotamia. While political power generally appears to have been concentrated in fewer institutions than among the Yoruba, the structures of government in these two civilizations were very similar.

Tenochtitlan's extraordinary size, political power, and role as the centre of a tributary network that extended far beyond the Valley of Mexico made its political organization different in many respects from that of neighbouring city-states. All the city-states in the valley participated in a regional economy controlled to a large extent by the Aztec and were subject in varying degrees to Aztec domination.

The smallest unit of Aztec political organization was the calpolli. Tenochtitlan was said to have been composed of twenty large calpollis, each of which played a part in the city's complex ritual life (van Zantwijk 1985). For religious reasons there may have been resistance to increasing this number. In reality, by 1519 Tenochtitlan may have had four times that number of calpollis (called *tlaxilacalli*) (Clendinnen 1991: 33; M. E. Smith 1996: 312). Each calpolli or tlaxilacalli had one or two *calpollecs* (hereditary leaders). Their task was to manage the group's affairs with the advice and assistance of a council of elders drawn from member families. Together they oversaw the operation of the calpolli temple, the school where young commoners were trained as soldiers, and the military brigade. The leadership also settled internal disputes, collected taxes, and organized corvées to carry out public works, which included cleaning streets and dredging canals. Taxes in kind consisted largely of crops produced by young men working fields that remained the collective property of calpollis. This food was used to support corporate institutions and leaders and to pay taxes to the central government. Leaders were also responsible for keeping records, in particular concerning the assignment of land to members. They were assisted in collecting taxes and organizing corvée work by fiscal officers (*tequitlatoque*) who supervised groups of twenty to one hundred households (Berdan 1982: 59). It is unclear to what extent these officers were the same as the elders who sat on the calpolli council. Calpolli leaders had intermarried with the royal family soon after the establishment of the Aztec monarchy and thus had acquired noble status (M. E. Smith 1996: 145–51; Spath 1973). The power of the calpolli leaders in Tenochtitlan had been curtailed by the state administration. According to the Spanish, calpolli leaders had to report to the palace daily to receive orders from royal fiscal officers (Soustelle 1961: 41). Frederic Hicks (1982) suggests that in Texcoco, in contrast to Tenochtitlan, calpollis were no longer self-governing but organized and controlled by the upper classes.

At the top of the state administration were the king and the chief decision-makers, who bore the title *tecuhtli* (lord). In Tenochtitlan next in rank after the king among this group were the cihuacoatl and the members of the Council of Four. The cihuacoatl became regent when the king was ill or not in the capital, routinely supervised the priesthood, and was in charge of various fiscal and legal matters. Two members of the Council of Four were the commanders in chief of the army. Together the four were the king's chief advisers and administrators and may have governed the four quarters into which the capital was divided (Durán 1964: 40; Hassig 1985: 105; Soustelle 1961: 92).

The king and these five officials headed a hierarchy of administrative, military, and religious officials recruited from among the members of the royal family, other members of the nobility, and ennobled warriors. None of these offices was hereditary; individuals were appointed to them by the king. Appointment to the most important offices, however, depended on the high status of the candidate's forebears as well as on his own talents and achievements. High-ranking officials assisted the king in formulating major policy decisions and administered the palace law courts with the help of numerous secondary officials called *calpixque*. These lower-ranking members of the nobility oversaw the collection and distribution of taxes and tribute, the construction of state temples and public works such as causeways, aqueducts, and dykes to control water levels, the management of state land and royal property, and the amassing of the weapons, armour, and food supplies that were needed to provision the armies while on campaigns. Most officials worked in Tenochtitlan, but some were located in major towns throughout the regions that the Aztec dominated to supervise relations with subject states, oversee the collection of tribute, and ensure the delivery of food grown on fields that had been ceded to the Aztec as tribute. These officials were probably assisted by numerous record-keepers, the youngest and least recognized members of the hereditary nobility. All administrators and record-keepers would have required training in the schools where members of the nobility were educated (Soustelle 1961: 49).

Former commoners who had been ennobled as a reward for military valour but lacked special administrative training guarded the king and various public buildings, arrested and executed people on orders from the king and high officials, and trained young men to be soldiers in the commoner schools of the calpollis from which they came. The markets were regulated by *pochteca* (long-distance traders) who were empowered by the king to establish fair prices, control weights and the quality of goods being sold, and impose fines and other penalties on those who defrauded buyers (Berdan 1982: 42; Hassig 1988: 29).

In Tenochtitlan the power of the king and nobles was greatly strengthened by military success and royal control of the material resources received from the Aztec tributary network. In smaller and less powerful city-states the influence of calpolli and other community leaders remained stronger. Although the Texcocan king shared hegemony with the Aztec monarch, the much smaller Texcocan capital consisted of six wards, each with its own ruler and palace (Hodge 1984: 24–25; Offner 1983: 5–7). The Texcocan ruler had, however, gone farther than the Aztec king in integrating neighbouring city-states into a common political system. Fourteen small nearby city-states that were tributary to Texcoco participated to some extent in a common government. The tlatoani of Texcoco was advised by a high council attended by the kings of these neighbouring states as well as by the high-ranking Texcocan officials who presided over the councils of war, finance, religion, and justice. Commoners, palace officials, and other nobles from these subordinate city-states and from Texcoco served on these councils (Offner 1983: 147–49).

In some much smaller and weaker states there was more than one tlatoani, and decisions relating to the community had to be reached by consensus among these leaders. In small states with a single king, councils representing sectional interests such as those of quarters, calpollis, and communities played general decision-making roles that were much more important than the roles played by corresponding bodies in Tenochtitlan and Texcoco. Towns and villages located beyond city-state capitals were composed of one or more calpollis. While some larger communities had their own council and a subordinate ruler as their head, other communities had the same relation to the king as calpollis in urban centres (Hodge 1984).

While there was a vast amount of variation in the degree of internal centralization among the states in the Valley of Mexico, on the whole there appears to have been more centralization in this region than there was among the Yoruba or in southern Mesopotamia. At least in part this difference may be attributable to the sharp distinction between hereditary nobles and commoners (Stone 1997), which provided a basis for consolidating power structures that the other two city-state systems lacked.

Surviving texts reveal little about the officials and administrators who served the Maya's divine rulers. Except to a limited degree in Terminal Classic times, inscribed monuments were created solely to celebrate these rulers. Some of these texts mention officials with the titles *ahaw* and *sahal* (plural *sahalob*). Ahaw may have been close relatives of kings or simply nobles (Hammond 1991: 270); sahalob, mentioned in inscriptions only in the western lowlands, were hereditary officials at the royal court and governed secondary centres and rural districts (Hammond 1991: 280; Schele and Mathews 1998: 88–89, 339–40; Tate 1992: 20). The title *ah ch'ul na* (person of the sacred house/temple) appears to have been bestowed on some important court officials as well as on members of the royal family and occurs in the names of some royal spouses (Houston 1993: 130–34).

The distribution of high-status residences has been interpreted as evidence that Maya kingdoms may have been divided into small provinces ruled from local administrative centres by the hereditary leaders of the area's highest-ranking patrilineages. These districts, it is argued, were in turn composed of a number of communities or small districts governed by subordinate hereditary rulers. Comparisons have been drawn with the hereditary town and ward leaders that the Spanish encountered among the Maya in the sixteenth century (Marcus 1993). Alternatively, it has been suggested, that Maya political organization was more variable than this model suggests. While some Maya kings may have ruled over nested hierarchies of hereditary rulers, others may have created more unitary polities by replacing such rulers with their own specially appointed kinsmen or unrelated officials (Haviland 1992; Montmollin 1989). The claim that rulers at the district and local levels constituted an enduring hereditary element in Classic Maya political organization while particular kingdoms grew, broke apart, and sometimes ceased to exist requires further documentation.

The relatively dispersed nature of Maya settlement may have encouraged the development of hierarchical administrative structures that on a small scale more closely resembled those of territorial states than they did the administrative structures of any other city-state system in our sample. It remains to be determined how this affected Maya economic organization and beliefs. The Maya also seem to have resembled the highland Mexicans and differed from the Mesopotamians and the Yoruba in having a well-defined hereditary nobility. This, combined with the dispersed nature of Maya settlement, may have encouraged administrative structures to be segmentary and under the control of high-status patrilineal kin groups. What is not known is the extent to which kings were able to overcome the centrifugal tendencies inherent in such an administrative arrangement and replace it with a more centralized structure.

TERRITORIAL STATES

While city-states required systems to administer the territories beyond their urban centres, these territories were small, and a large proportion of the population, resources, and wealth of these states was concentrated in their capitals. Territorial states required much more elaborate regional administrations to deal with the serious problems of keeping large territories subject to some degree of centralized control. Egypt was divided into as many as forty-two provinces (*sp3t*). These administrative divisions mostly straddled short sections of the Nile Valley south of Memphis and consisted of areas of slightly raised ground bounded by Nile distributaries in the Delta. During the Old Kingdom a typical province had between forty thousand and seventy-five thousand inhabitants, while by the New Kingdom the average population of a province had probably risen to 112,000 people. The Inka organized their kingdom by provinces, each ideally containing forty thousand families or two hundred thousand people. The Shang state appears to have had at least a two-tiered system of regional government, with the units at both the provincial and local levels controlled by leaders of patrilineages linked in some fashion to the royal family.

Because of their size and numerous subdivisions, the governments of territorial states had to be hierarchical. Some of them were organized in a 'delegational' and others in a bureaucratic fashion (Kamenka 1989: 1–5; Weber 1968). Delegational systems have also been called 'segmentary' systems, and recent discussions of them are derived from Aidan Southall's *Alur Society* (1956) by way of Burton Stein's (1980) application of his ideas to the Hindu state of Vijayanagara (see also Southall 1988). The terms 'segmentary' and 'delegational' are in fact both problematic. 'Delegational' implies that effective centralized control existed over the whole of a territory before power was assigned to local officials to administer its parts; 'segmentary' suggests that larger political structures were created by linking together smaller chiefdoms whose rulers and local governments largely remained in place. In reality, both processes were involved in the creation of territorial states and often in the formation of the same state. The term 'delegational' is employed here mainly because 'segmentary' was originally developed to classify prestate societies and is therefore potentially the more misleading when applied to early civilizations (Marcus and Feinman 1998). 'Delegational' is also preferable because even minimal success in building territorial states required the creation of structures that would bind incorporated polities to the larger entities.

In delegational systems responsibility for all the affairs of a region located beyond the royal capital district devolved upon a single high-level official and his staff. This official ensured the maintenance of order in the region, was responsible for its defence, carried out public works, and collected taxes, a portion of which he remitted to the central government. Territorial states required multiple tiers of delegated authority. Officials at each administrative level were answerable to the king not only for their own conduct but also for that of all the lower-level district officials to whom authority within their jurisdictions had been delegated. Yet, in practice, higher-level officials often had no direct control over regions administered by subordinate officials and no direct access to their resources. The great attraction of such a wholesale delegation of plenipotentiary powers to regional and local leaders was that it constituted a relatively inexpensive way to administer a large state. The main challenge for the central government was to prevent a state administered in this fashion from disintegrating.

Kingdoms organized in this manner varied radically in the way in which the central government controlled regional officials. In some, rulers of formerly autonomous regions were retained as hereditary regional officials, with succession to office sometimes requiring royal approval. In such instances, the incorporation of conquered regions into a territorial state remained weak even if the local rulers were eventually linked to the king by marital ties. Alternatively, when a regional polity was incorporated into a larger kingdom, its former ruler was sometimes replaced by a governor selected from the king's family or entourage. In this instance the incorporation of the conquered territory was more secure, especially if older polities were dismembered or rearranged and new levels of regional control were established, but even here there was considerable variation in control. A king's powers were limited at the provincial level unless he regularly replaced regional governors or could remove them at will. While delegational systems were relatively simple to establish and inexpensive to operate, they placed little power to control local resources in the hands of the central government, and kingdoms tended to fall apart quickly if the central government faltered.

The alternative arrangement in territorial states was a bureaucratic administrative structure, in which central, provincial, and local governments were managed by officials who were individually responsible for specific aspects of administration. A province might be administered by separate military, legal, and fiscal officers, each of whom was assigned a particular sphere of responsibility and resisted encroachment on his domain. Officials were often transferred at regular intervals from one province and one branch of administration to another. With such arrangements, kings were better able to control what was happening at the local level and keep provincial officials closely tied to the central government. This form of administration was more expensive to operate and probably less efficient at the local level than a delegational form. Because officials were frequently transferred from place to place, they knew less about the regions they were governing than if they had remained in the same place for a long time. As a result, much de facto power remained in the hands of the indigenous population. The limited differentiation of early bureaucracies, by comparison with those found in modern industrial societies, and their more personal and less rule-bound style of governing suggest that rulers of large kingdoms were rarely willing or able to assume the full economic and administrative burden of controlling the lower levels of these administrative hierarchies. This difference led Max Weber to distinguish ancient patrimonial from more 'rationalized' modern bureaucracies and to view early administrative systems as extensions of the management of royal households (Kamenka 1989: 1).

After Egypt was unified, the rulers and members of some of the leading families of the small states and chiefdoms that had previously existed may have been allowed to continue as provincial administrators within their former territories, but within a few generations hereditary regional leaders had been entirely replaced by itinerant officials. In addition, some communities that had been capitals of significant rival polities prior to unification were replaced by new provincial administrative centres (T. Wilkinson 1999: 344–65). Village leadership may have remained hereditary, but the tombs of these leaders grew smaller as the power of the central government increased during the early Old Kingdom (Reisner 1932).

In its developed form, during the Old Kingdom, the civil service was headed by one or more viziers (*ṯ3ty*) who administered the country, or major divisions of it, in the name of the king. Under their supervision were government departments concerned with collecting surplus grain, administering royal estates and land registration, overseeing government supplies of linen, wood, wine, metals, and other valuable commodities, carrying out construction projects and supervising craft production in government workshops, and maintaining law and order and dealing with all legal matters that were of concern to the central government. Most of these departments were divided into parallel sections for Upper and Lower Egypt – a separation that may have been operational or largely symbolic (Strudwick 1985). The centralized administration of food offerings for royal funerary cults during the Fifth Dynasty suggests that many estates and sources of revenue officially assigned to individuals were managed collectively by a single bureaucratic organization (Eyre 1987a: 23).

The civil service was distinguished from the royal household staff, which included individuals of high rank who were the king's companions or managed his household and personal estates and numerous personal attendants of various ranks and with specialized skills. Some of these officials carried out special political commissions for the king. The regular government departments had their headquarters in the capital and branch offices in provincial centres as well as in smaller local centres within each province (Hassan 1993). The provincial units, at least in Upper Egypt, were of economic importance, since some of them had constituted maximal irrigation units since late Predynastic times (Butzer 1976). In the Old Kingdom the chief official representing the king or a vizier at the provincial level held a title such as *ỉmy-r wpt* (overseer of commissions), *ḥq3 sp3t* (ruler of a province), or *sšm t3* (leader of the land). Although he was responsible for ensuring that royal wishes were carried out, this official could not prevent officials working for other departments from reporting directly to their superiors at the capital. A single overseer of commissions was frequently responsible for several adjacent provinces (Baer 1960; Kanawati 1980).

At the top level of the administrative hierarchy, immediately under the vizier, were a number of *srw* (singular *sr*) (high officials). Those in the capital had easy access to the king, while the rest represented royal authority in the provinces. The srw and the high-ranking courtiers who attended the king and managed his household together would have totalled at most a few hundred individuals. Each government department was headed by a sr, who was designated as the overseer (*ỉmy-r*, 'giver of orders') of that department. Working under each sr were lesser-ranking overseers (ỉmy-r) and scribes (*sšw*, singular *sš*). The total number of literate Egyptians would not have exceeded 1 percent of the population during the Old and Middle Kingdoms (Baines 1983: 584). Ordinary overseers made low-level decisions but did not formulate general policies, while scribes were the record-keepers who carried out their orders. Many low-level officials were tax collectors and overseers of public works. Others were assigned more specific responsibilities, among them administering particular fortresses, dockyards, royal estates, and armouries and supervising particular groups of priests, soldiers, carpenters, and herdsmen (Kanawati 1977: 15–33; Strudwick 1985).

The ideal was for an administrator to occupy a series of posts of ever higher rank that would take him from one part of Egypt to another. He might in succession be a minor tax collector, in charge of a temple estate, manager of the food supply for the army, and then the civil administrator in charge of a province. His ambition was eventually to secure a high-ranking position in the central administration at Memphis and be buried near the pyramid of the king or the tomb of an important ancestor (near an older royal tomb). Sons of high-ranking officials aspired to take over their fathers' final and highest posts or to secure even more exalted ones, and many officials did in fact succeed their fathers. Yet the ideal of the Egyptian state – working one's way up the administrative hierarchy by earning the approval of senior officials and the king – also influenced career patterns. Egypt achieved the extreme in bureaucratic organization among early civilizations (Frankfort 1956: 99–103; Janssen 1978).

The civil service hierarchy was remodelled repeatedly during the Old Kingdom. In the Fourth Dynasty the highest state offices were held by close male relatives of the king under the joint supervision of the vizier, who collected taxes and oversaw the legal system, and the 'overseer of all the works of the king' (*ỉmy-r k3t nbt nt nswt*), who was in charge of public works. King Menkaure and his successors excluded members of the royal family from all high offices, including that of vizier. King Neferirkare of the Fifth Dynasty further abolished honorary court titles for close royal kin. At the same time, the number of administrative titles was increased, the tasks assigned to each official were more carefully defined, and positions were more precisely ranked. As a result of these changes, the civil service became separated from the royal family. The king now shared power not with the hereditary nobility but with a much larger number of individually more dispensable civil servants. Thus, contrary to what is generally believed, the king's control over his officials was increased.

King Djedkare-Isesi altered the ranking system to reduce the power of senior officials, dividing the vizierate into three: one each for Upper and Lower Egypt and one for the whole country. Viziers could once again be appointed from the hereditary nobility or even from among the king's sons. At the same time, the number of high titles that an official might hold at one time was reduced. Hereafter the organization of the civil service was modified in every reign but one until the end of the Old Kingdom. It appears that the kings repeatedly altered the way of doing things and the titles that accompanied government offices as one way of maintaining control over the bureaucracy (Baer 1960; Kanawati 1980; Strudwick 1985).

The Inka state has been described as 'proto-bureaucratic' (Gose 1996a: 21). Its rulers constructed a complex nested hierarchy of units organized as similarly at any particular level as local conditions permitted. Ten administrative levels extended from the monarch down to and often into the ayllu. The top three levels were staffed exclusively by members of the Inka nobility and included the central administration, the governing of the four quarters of the kingdom, and the governments of approximately eighty provinces. Five middle levels were governed by *kurakas*, or hereditary non-Inka officials who were members of various ethnic groups that had accepted Inka sovereignty, arranged in nested levels according to whether they governed approximately ten thousand, five thousand, one thousand, five hundred, or one hundred families. The kurakas in charge of at least the higher of these levels were recognized by the Inka as constituting a non-Inka nobility. In areas where leadership previously either had not existed at these levels or had not been hereditary, the Inka installed local notables as hereditary rulers. While the smallest group often coincided with the ayllu, larger or smaller ayllus may have corresponded with higher or lower administrative levels. The Inka further divided groups of one hundred families into units of fifty and ten families each under the supervision of non-hereditary foremen who were commoners of local origin. Low-level officials transmitted orders from their superiors and saw that they were carried out. The non-Inka nobility was responsible for maintaining order and ensuring that the local people performed their duties to the Inka state. The middle and lower levels of the Inka administration were allowed no role in the formulation of policy (Patterson 1987; Rowe 1944: 262–64).

Hereditary leaders from the *hunu kuraka*, the ethnic nobles governing ten thousand families, down to the ayllu level tended to be descended from families that had ruled an area prior to the Inka conquest. Because the Inka divided large polities or united small ones to create administrative units close to their ideal size, continuity in office-holding from pre-Inka times was far from complete. Moreover, while the leaders of these groups were hereditary, their succession to office had to be approved by the local Inka governor or the Inka monarch. Kurakas' loyalty to the Inka was reinforced by the increase in their personal incomes that was a result of state control and agricultural development (D'Altroy 1987b). Those at the highest levels were required to visit Cuzco periodically, and houses were provided for them and their retainers in the ring of settlements surrounding the elite centre. Inka officials replaced kurakas they suspected of disloyalty with more dependable members of their families or ethnic groups and sometimes rewarded conscripted soldiers for special acts of valour by making them foremen of fifty or ten families. They did not hesitate to intervene directly in the affairs of even small groups of their subjects. While they stressed loyalty to the Inka state, they encouraged rivalries and antagonisms among these small groups as a way of reducing the chances of their combining to oppose Inka rule. In addition to dividing ethnic groups and resettling portions of them alongside unrelated ones, they symbolically emphasized ethnic differences and encouraged ritual battles that kept alive memories of long-standing local disputes (D'Altroy 1992; Kendall 1973: 108–11; C. Morris 1998; Spalding 1984).

Provincial governors (*tukuyrikuq*) and all higher officers were appointed by the king from the various levels of the Inka nobility. A provincial governor lived in the administrative centre of each province but had to report regularly in person to the king. Governors were periodically transferred from one province to another to prevent them from acquiring a local power base, and their principal residences remained in or near Cuzco. Various itinerant inspectors and secret agents monitored their behaviour and reported on their loyalty to the king. A governor was assisted by a chief aide and a staff of priests, record-keepers, and officials in charge of corvée labour for public works. A rotating workforce of four hundred corvée labourers was always available at the provincial administrative centre, and larger corvées periodically repaired roads and erected buildings throughout the province, served in the army, and carried out mining operations. In general, military leadership was separate from the provincial administration, as were the overseers of crown estates and the officials who visited ayllus to select children to become aqllakuna and yanakuna (S. Moore 1958: 96–114; Rowe 1944: 269).

In the Cuzco area there was a similar range of overseers and administrators in charge of storage facilities, religious institutions, and state building projects. The construction of the fortress of Saqsawaman was directed by four master builders responsible to one of the king's many brothers. In addition, special government facilities were located at Cuzco, such as the schools for training the young men of the royal family and the sons of high-ranking administrators to be officials (Kendall 1973: 78, 130; Niles 1993: 161).

The most important offices of the central government were held by brothers, half-brothers, and other close male relatives of the king. The highest of these offices were the four *apukuna* or prefects of the quarters into which the Inka state was divided. These administrators helped the king to supervise the provincial governors in their quadrants. The king delegated many of his religious responsibilities throughout the kingdom to the high priest of the sun and his military responsibilities to top-ranking army officers, who served under a royal commander in chief (*apusquipay*). He was also assisted by a chamberlain, who routinely issued orders in his name and acted as an intermediary between him and other high-ranking officials. It is suggested that all these officials were viewed as substitutes for the king, who derived their power from speaking for him much as oracles spoke for gods and dead kings. None of these positions was hereditary. Yet together these officials extended the role of the king in governing the administrative, military, and religious spheres. While the higher administration of the Inka state was patrimonial rather than strongly bureaucratic, an effort was made to keep power under royal control by separating the military and the religious from the civil administration. By having a small number of close relatives act and speak for the king, it was also possible for a monarch who was largely reclusive for ritual reasons to maintain the appearance of infallibility (Gose 1996a).

While the Inka government was largely delegational within provinces, strenuous efforts were made to prevent provincial and higher government offices from becoming hereditary. The military was separated from the civil administration at the provincial level, and there was a tripartite division of administrative, military, and religious powers at still higher levels. Had the Inka state lasted longer, its administration might have become more completely bureaucratized.

In Shang China kin ties were used to structure political relations. The Shang kingdom was divided into a series of provinces or districts ruled by hereditary officials who bore the title hou or bo. Each of them, together with subordinate officials and retainers, occupied a fortified administrative centre (yi). The construction of such a centre appears to have required the consent of the king (Keightley 1969: 332). Each hou or bo controlled the population of the surrounding region, collected taxes, supervised agricultural production on state land, and commanded military units. It has been proposed that originally bo governed border regions while hou presided over more centrally located districts. Both types of officials are occasionally recorded as rebelling against the kings. While these titles may originally have denoted different functions, by the Late Shang period the functions had become blurred and the titles seem instead to have distinguished different ranks of the nobility and perhaps differences in the size or population of the territory they controlled. Both appear to have served as court officials as well as regional administrators. While this arrangement may have prefigured the five grades of lords who governed territories in Western Zhou times, there is no evidence that a five-tiered hierarchy existed during the Shang period (Chao 1972: 99–109).

These regional authorities belonged to a network of high-ranking lineages related to the Shang kings by blood or marriage. Some of them, including the earliest known Zhou rulers, appear to have been descendants of local leaders subdued by the Shang kings. Others were descendants of Shang kings or other high-ranking members of the Shang state who had replaced defeated local rulers. While the governors of provinces were granted hereditary control of them and peripheral provinces sometimes rebelled against Shang rule, Chao (1972: 115) maintains that the Shang kings were able to intervene actively in the management of these political divisions. Western Zhou kings dismissed or demoted regional officials whom they mistrusted, and so perhaps did Shang kings. Many regional officials appear to have been consanguineal members of the Shang royal family sent by the king to impose control over a region or to rule over conquered territories with the help of other members of their patrilineage. As genealogical relations between the heirs of such officials and the king grew more remote, their loyalty may have diminished (Shaughnessy 1999: 323). To counteract this tendency, such officials and their lineages appear to have been shifted from one location to another. A similar situation prevailed during the Western Zhou period, when, it is noted, these officials 'could migrate from one locality to another, and territoriality was of minor concern' (Hsu and Linduff 1988: 268). Court officials and regional rulers also looked to the king to establish their younger sons as rulers of new districts as the Shang state expanded. Those who did not secure such positions usually became landless officials working for their landholding kinsmen.

Hou and bo each controlled a variable number of tian, who ruled over small areas from their own more modest centres. Some tian were the heads of local ruling families who had accepted Shang rule. Like hou and bo, tian were hereditary rulers and, provided that they paid taxes and supplied military aid when called upon to do so, were probably left to manage the affairs of their district relatively independently (Chao 1972: 110–11). The available evidence suggests that the Shang state was governed by a nested hierarchy that had at least three major administrative levels. At the top a single hereditary king (wang) ruled from one or more capitals (*da yi*, 'big yi'), while under him hou and bo, and below them tian ruled from their own administrative centres.

The three top hereditary titles were *zi* (king's son), hou, and bo. The zi may have included some individuals who were honoured by adoption into the royal family as well as the actual descendants of Shang monarchs. All these were members of the royal clan (Chao 1972: 110; Chou 1968: 52–76). Many zi served as court officials, while others may have ruled over provinces and hence also been called hou or bo. Close kin of the reigning monarch appear to have lived near him, occupying high administrative posts and advising and supporting him.

The oracle-bone inscriptions reveal that a large number of official titles were used at the Shang court. Civil titles, each often divided into several grades, included *yin* (administrator), *chu* (fiscal officer, treasurer), *shi* (envoy), chen (retainer, courtier), *gong* (officer in charge of artisans or public works), and *zai* (steward in charge of household servants). Envoys carried messages between the royal court and provincial or foreign rulers, while courtiers, who were personal servants of the king, appear to have discharged many functions of public administration, both civil and military (Chou 1968). Written commands were issued by senior officials to officials of lower rank, who were often addressed collectively and solely by title. This suggests that court officials were hierarchically ordered (Keightley 1978b: 221). Yet the wide range of activities that the bearers of individual titles performed indicates limited bureaucractic specialization. It appears that younger sons of senior officials for whom provincial governorships could not be found slipped into courtier roles (Vandermeersch 1980: 41–43). The oracle-bone texts mention frontier guards (*shu*), who may have commanded border garrisons. It is not clear whether they were under the command of the governors of outlying provinces or directly under the authority of the king.

The administration of the Shang state seems to have been organized on delegational principles to a far greater extent than was Old Kingdom Egypt or the Inka realm. The Egyptian rulers sought to bureaucratize administration at all but the village level and rotated office-holders in order to maintain centralized political, economic, and religious control down to the local level. The Inka delegated most powers but rotated provincial governors and made some attempt to separate military, civil, and religious authority. The Shang kings and their Zhou successors tended to allow provincial and local control to become or remain hereditary, although they did occasionally move rulers and their lineages from one place to another. The strongly delegational nature of Shang territorial administration seems to have been linked to the important role played by patrilineal kin groups in Chinese society. The strength of such lineage structures may have inhibited the rapid development of bureaucratization such as occurred in Old Kingdom Egypt and appears to have been happening in the Inka state. Chinese rulers eventually succeeded in replacing a delegational state organization built around lineage structures with a bureaucratic form of administration, but this transformation required more than a millennium.

POLITICAL PROCESSES

The political systems of early civilizations were dynamic ones. In territorial states bureaucratic officials might aspire to become provincial rulers if they could avoid being moved from one place to another and combine a wide range of powers under their control. Delegational systems could be transformed into bureaucratic ones if the monarch could divide the powers that belonged to provincial governors among various officials responsible to the central government. These processes could result not only in major changes in administrative structures but also in the disintegration or territorial expansion of states.

The early growth of Tenochtitlan led its inhabitants, lacking nobles of their own, to solicit a foreign noble to become their king. As a result of this and subsequent marriages between kings' daughters and calpolli leaders, a noble class developed that cut across existing calpolli and ethnic divisions. Later Aztec military domination and exploitation of a growing number of neighbouring city-states increased the economic power of the Aztec nobility and promoted the expansion of this class as commoners who were successful warriors were recruited into it. The ability of the Aztec king to control the distribution of tribute resulted in an increase of royal authority beyond what was found in any other state in the Valley of Mexico. Calpolli leaders, while part of the noble class, were reduced to the status of minor officials who managed their own groups' internal affairs and carried out the orders of the central government. Decisions concerning the collective goals of Aztec society were made increasingly by the king and a small circle of hereditary members of the upper class (Davies 1980; Durán 1964).

Among the Yoruba the expansion of the Oyo tributary system increased the number of palace slaves and royal officials and might have resulted in an expansion of royal power if non-royal lineages in the capital had not seized power and made one of their own members the commander of the city's military system. The king now had to share with representatives of the dominant non-royal lineages not only political power but much of the tribute paid by conquered states. Despite this decentralization, Oyo remained the most powerful Yoruba kingdom until the nineteenth century. In the late eighteenth century, the oba Abiodun managed to harness military power in rural areas of his kingdom to defeat the non-royal urban lineages, but soon after this happened the Oyo tributary system disintegrated (Law 1977; R. Smith 1969: 32–50).

In the hegemonic city-state of Benin, royal authority was more centralized than in any of the Yoruba states. This had been accomplished by introducing royal primogeniture and making most public offices non-hereditary and subject to royal appointment. Even so, as a result of occasional civil wars over royal succession, episodes of royal control and urban prosperity in Benin alternated with interludes of political chaos and immiseration (Bradbury 1957: 20–21).

Within city-states realignments in political alliances and fluctuations in the extent of royal power could occur rapidly and frequently. Because of the complex ways in which economic, political, and military practices were articulated, it is not always possible to correlate periods of political centralization with political stability or hegemonic power.

In Old Kingdom Egypt, beginning in the reign of the Sixth Dynasty king, Merenre, there was an increase in the number of administrators assigned to each province. Overseers of commissions were replaced by provincial governors (*ḥry tp ʿ3*), each of whom had his own overseer of granaries and overseer of the treasury. Many officials were now buried in the provinces, and remaining in a single province became a desirable alternative to a career that culminated in holding high office at the royal court. It is unclear whether this change was initiated to improve the quality of provincial administration or to counteract the concentration of power in the hands of high officials at the capital or occurred because successive monarchs were for the first time unable to prevent the development of local and eventually hereditary power bases. In the late Sixth Dynasty the size and number of tombs of major officials in the Memphis area declined as fewer revenues reached the capital. At the end of the Sixth Dynasty Egypt split apart to form a number of independent provinces and competing small kingdoms (Fischer 1968; Kanawati 1977; 1980).

The Middle Kingdom rulers reunited Egypt but still had to cope with powerful hereditary provincial rulers in some areas, especially Middle Egypt. The kings of the early Twelfth Dynasty developed the Fayum area as a source of revenue and used part of this revenue to increase the military forces that were under their direct control. By the reign of Senwosret III the king was strong enough to abolish the remaining hereditary provincial rulers. He divided Egypt into three administrative districts, or *wʿrt*, each controlled by officials who were individually responsible to the vizier for legal matters, agriculture, finance, and general administration. Centralized control was thus reestablished. This completed a cycle of rebuilding the bureaucratic control that the central administration had lost in the late Sixth Dynasty (Grimal 1992: 166–68).

Despite a tendency for governments to fluctuate between more and less centralized control and between delegational and bureaucratic forms of administration, ideals concerning what was politically normal served as templates for action. In Egypt the ideal was that a single monarch should control a united Egypt and the world. When Egypt split apart to form a number of competing states at the end of the Old Kingdom, its rulers found themselves without a mechanism for securing and distributing the raw materials from abroad that were regarded as essential for upper-class burials and needed to produce luxury goods for the living. As a result, neither the most powerful rulers nor the wealthiest individuals were able to live in the style that, during the Old Kingdom, Egyptians had come to believe was normal for people of their station. Moreover, even powerful local rulers were severely limited in their ability to tax their subjects or control them, since dissident groups could threaten to declare their independence or switch their allegiance to competing leaders. Thus no ruler commanded the resources to build an elaborate tomb or produce high-quality art. Ordinary people appear to have had more possessions than under the Old Kingdom, but their lives were less secure because of endemic warfare (Seidlmayer 1987). This promoted a widespread desire for the reunification of Egypt and the reestablishment of a moderate degree of centralized royal power.

Elizabeth Stone (1997: 25) has argued that the city-state ideology of southern Mesopotamia prevailed over the regional-state ideology of northern Mesopotamia even though political unification became a regional reality. In Mesopotamia the city-state ideal endured into the first millennium B.C. despite the development of larger states and empires. Cities were still conceptualized as divine estates and the property of their patron deities, with consequent rights of self-government. Powerful Mesopotamian kings continued to be regarded as human servants of the gods as much weaker kings had been in early city-states. This too was a cultural template that Mesopotamian kings who wished to be regarded as divine found impossible to overcome (Baines and Yoffee 1998). In their art and in the political regimes they attempted to construct, the inhabitants of the Valley of Mexico in the Late Aztec period also appear to have been consciously modelling themselves on what they accepted were the traditions of the long-vanished hegemonic city-state of Tollan (Richards and Van Buren 2000).

The governments of early civilizations employed a mixture of bureaucratic and delegational administrative structures. Rulers sought to control officials, regions, kin groups, and institutions, while these groups sought to retain or establish their own full or partial autonomy.

City-states were characterized by perennial struggles between royal authority and more decentralized forms of political control. Those that lacked a hereditary nobility tended to exhibit more extreme heterarchical features, but no city-state found in early civilizations was governed 'democratically' by an assembly of its male citizens. Decisions were made by a relatively small number of leaders, who might include politically powerful individuals, representatives of powerful families, and the leaders of major institutions. In Aristotle's political terminology, such societies were not democracies but aristocracies. While the Aztec city-state grew increasingly centralized as its military power and wealth increased, successful Yoruba states such as Oyo combined military success with decentralized government.

Territorial states had to develop complex, multilevel administrative hierarchies. Bureaucratic features were strongest in Old Kingdom Egypt and weakest in Shang China. The apparently rapid development of bureaucratic structures in Egypt and Peru but not in China raises the question to what degree a strong emphasis on corporate patrilineages favoured the development and retention of delegational administrative structures in some territorial states and constituted a basis for resistance to centralization in city-states such as those of the Yoruba. Shifts in the degree of centralization and bureaucratization indicate considerable flexibility and the ability to conceptualize alternative political structures. There is also evidence of a tendency to idealize and preserve political arrangements over time.

11 Law

An important function of states is to maintain public order. One of the ways this is done is by legal action – settling disputes that might lead to violence, restraining and punishing those whose behaviour harms individuals or society, ensuring that government orders are obeyed, and validating certain controversial actions by individuals and groups (Postgate 1992: 275). Law frequently claims to serve the interests of society as a whole and actually does so insofar as public order benefits everybody. Yet, in early civilizations, the upper classes and the major institutions they controlled had far more wealth and privileges to protect than did commoners, and they relied on the law to do this.

The power to punish crimes, in particular with death, was an important manifestation of a ruler's authority. Among the Yoruba, the sword of state symbolized the exclusive and godlike prerogative of the monarch to execute criminals (Bascom 1969: 83–84). Laws were often claimed to originate with the gods, who transmitted them to humans through the proclamations of rulers. The Aztec term for 'laws', *nahuatilli*, meant 'a set of commands' (Offner 1983: 83, 242–45, 282). Laws were a means by which human society was not only regulated but also aligned with a cosmic order that was profoundly hierarchical. The Babylonian word *mêšaru* and the Egyptian *m3ˁt* referred both to the cosmic order and to legal justice (Bottéro 1992: 182). The Inka state claimed that subjects' commission of crimes such as murder, witchcraft, theft, and neglect of religious cults threatened the health of the king and considered them sacrilege (Rowe 1944: 305). Later evidence from China indicates that law (*fa*) was believed to have been created by superhuman beings in accordance with divine models and interests (Lewis 1990: 198). To promote order on earth, rulers sought to suppress blood feuds and punish murder, treason, theft, incest, and many other forms of misconduct.

Supernatural powers were believed to support the legal process by revealing guilt or innocence through oracles and ordeals and by punishing oath-breakers. The gods punished individuals whose crimes went undetected or unpunished by humans. The Babylonian king Hammurabi claimed to have assembled his law code at the command of the god Utu, or Shamash, who, because as the sun god he saw everything that humans did, was also the patron deity of justice (Pritchard 1955: 163–65). Promulgating this law code gave Hammurabi an earthly role analogous to that of Enlil, the chief executive deity of the Sumerian pantheon. The laws proclaimed by the Aztec ruler Mochtezuma I were described as 'flashes that the great king . . . [had] sown in his breast, from the divine fire, for the total health of his kingdom' (Offner 1983: 83). This claim referred to the divine powers that were implanted in the Aztec monarch at the time of his enthronement. The early Chinese believed that improper conduct was supernaturally punished.

Yet the coercive powers of the state were severely limited. Although exemplary and, by modern standards, often extremely cruel punishments were inflicted on criminals, they were in fact an indication of the weakness rather than the strength of law enforcement. Settlement patterns indicate that the maintenance of law and order was not as effective as the rulers of early civilizations would have wished. The upper classes normally lived in urban centres, many of which were walled or had their outskirts patrolled so that the movement of individuals in and out of them could be carefully monitored. Such arrangements protected urban dwellers against assaults by criminals and rebellious peasants as well as foreign armies. Within walled cities, temples, palaces, government offices, and storehouses were often surrounded by walls. In addition to emphasizing the importance and sanctity of such structures, these walls protected the people and goods inside them against thieves and casual intruders. Houses, especially those of wealthy families, frequently had a single, guarded entrance and no external windows, at least on the ground floor; rooms opened off interior courtyards. In New Kingdom Egypt upper-class houses were built inside walled enclosures, and Classic Maya houses faced inward from three or four sides of a courtyard. These arrangements suggest a concern for security as well as privacy (Flannery 1998; P. Wilson 1988). They also indicate that neither the state nor supernatural powers could ensure the safety of temples, palaces, and houses.

Significant state intervention at the lowest level of a polity was difficult where collecting information and conveying decisions were cumbersome and expensive. In keeping with their approach to administration generally, kings and government officials tolerated and encouraged self-regulation in legal matters at the local and family levels and by craft guilds and other local organizations.

In the Valley of Mexico and among the Yoruba, traders were assigned responsibility for policing urban markets. Among the Aztec, representatives of the pochteca were empowered to arrest, sentence, and punish petty criminals, dishonest traders, and tax evaders operating in marketplaces. In addition, the leaders of the pochteca could try and sentence members of their associations both in their native cities and on the road (Offner 1983: 156). By encouraging such groups to resolve problems, the upper classes spared themselves numerous difficulties and administrative costs and could devote more of the surpluses they controlled to conspicuous consumption. The state intervened only when lower-level controls failed to function or the interests of the upper classes were at risk.

Nevertheless, kings sought to give substance to their claim to be the supreme earthly legal authorities. They insisted on their right to hear appeals and to review the sentences of lower-level courts, in particular death sentences. In compact city-states, all capital cases were normally tried by palace officials or by the ruler himself; in city-states where there were substantial outlying settlements, the king or his officials tried all high-ranking people in urban law courts and reviewed sentences passed by community leaders on commoners in smaller settlements. Among the Yoruba, all public death sentences had to be approved by the king (Bascom 1969: 38–39), but the Egungun and Oro societies often secretly killed suspected witches on their own recognizance (40). The Yoruba kings also claimed the right to pardon or release any prisoner (Ajisafe 1924: 22). The Aztec king and other rulers in the Valley of Mexico reviewed most death sentences before they were carried out. Among the Aztec but not in Texcoco, the pochteca were granted the right to execute their own members without royal approval (Offner 1983: 156). In Mesopotamia there appear to have been legal limitations on the power of rulers to pardon capital offences; the king could spare the life of a male adulterer only if the husband of the woman involved decided not to kill her (Pritchard 1955: 171, law 129).

In territorial states problems of communication often resulted in regional officials' reviewing sentences in the king's name. In the Inka kingdom all regional officials below the rank of provincial governor had to obtain a governor's approval before a death sentence was carried out. Officials who failed to do so were subject to rigorous corporal punishment. The Inka ruler apparently had to approve all death sentences involving members of the nobility (Rowe 1944: 271–72). There were prisons throughout the Inka realm where individuals were held for interrogation and pending trial and the confirmation of their sentences. Incarceration was not, however, a form of punishment (MacCormack 1991: 157). In the early Zhou Dynasty, family or clan leaders had the authority to sentence their relatives to death. It is not known whether such sentences had to be approved by regional leaders before they were carried out (Creel 1937: 353).

LEGAL SYSTEMS

All early civilizations had a hierarchy of courts in which legal cases were heard and judgements rendered. Some of these were specially constituted bodies staffed by full-time or part-time judges; in other cases administrative assemblies or government officials performed legal duties as required. The lowest-level courts were associated with extended families, villages, or urban neighbourhoods. More important courts existed in city-states at the ward, city, and royal levels, although the last two were not always distinguished. In territorial states there were courts at various regional levels, the highest-ranking one invariably being at the royal court. Judgements at lower levels were usually made by the same authorities who coordinated other affairs at these levels. Low-level judges were usually commoners, while more powerful ones came from the upper classes. In the Valley of Mexico close relatives of kings served on the highest-level tribunals. Thus at the highest level both commoners and members of the upper classes were judged by representatives of the upper class. By contrast, upper-class individuals were never judged by tribunals presided over by commoners.

Yoruba extended households were self-governing in legal as well as in political matters, especially in the north, where single households often had several hundred members. The bale and other elders and titled male members judged cases that involved only members of the extended family. The bale had the power to fine, flog, or imprison family members for short periods and to sell them as slaves for various offences (Ajisafe 1924: 3). Cases were referred to ward and town leaders only if they could not be dealt with satisfactorily by the extended family (Bascom 1969: 44).

The lowest-level Mesopotamian courts mentioned in written records were councils made up of men from villages or town quarters, presided over by their mayor. The central government held the members of these local administrative bodies jointly responsible for unsolved robberies and the misconduct of those living in their area. The councillors collected information about local crimes, heard divorce cases, and cautioned owners to tether dangerous animals. It also appears that they adjudicated disputes and crimes within the group, but their decisions could be appealed to the next highest level if any of the litigants was not satisfied by a decision or the judges could not agree among themselves (Postgate 1992: 275–77).

The governing bodies of highland Mexican calpollis and Peruvian ayllus were likewise responsible for resolving internal quarrels and punishing crimes. In China lineage heads appear to have played an important role in settling disputes among family members (Creel 1937: 353). In Egypt, village councils (*d3d3t*, later *qnbt*) arbitrated disputes about property, sanctioned divorces, and tried to resolve internal conflicts. At least some of these councils were assisted by a scribe connected with the central bureaucracy, who offered legal advice and recorded the proceedings (Allam 1991; Eyre 1984: 100; 1991).

At this lowest level of legal deliberation there were no professional judges, and public opinion was generally relied on to enforce decisions. Nevertheless, a large Yoruba compound might contain a small prison, and both Yoruba and Chinese lineage leaders could impose severe punishments on family members. Decisions were based on a conventional rather than a specialized understanding of the law. In most cases, a litigant who was not satisfied could challenge a decision to a higher authority. In Egyptian local courts, disputes about property sometimes continued for decades and even generations (Bierbrier 1982: 103–4; Eyre 1984: 102–3). Because the legal authorities at higher levels were supported by increasing amounts of coercion, they did not have to rely on public opinion to enforce their decisions. Therefore cases could be decided more quickly and more arbitrarily than at the family or local level. Punishments also tended to be more severe in higher-level courts. Those who acted as judges generally possessed more detailed knowledge of laws as they were codified or understood at the royal court.

Yoruba disputes that could not be settled within extended families or that involved neighbouring families were taken to ward leaders, who were advised by the heads of the compounds within their district. If their judgement was not accepted, the case was referred to the ruler's court, composed of palace officials who met outside the royal palace daily and jointly with town officials every fourth day. Their decision was then communicated to the king for his approval. If no decision could be reached, the case was often referred to the Ogboni society, whose membership included other town and palace officials. Members of this highly secretive association used their supernatural powers to collect unpaid debts and resolve acts of violence. As judges, they specialized in cases involving murder. Their decisions too were referred to the king for his approval. Heads of outlying villages heard civil cases but referred ones involving capital punishment to the capital (Bascom 1969: 38–40). Members of the Oro society arrested criminals and brought them to court, as well as taking immediate action to halt violent quarrels (Ajisafe 1924: 92). All Yoruba officials who could render judgements had prisons or dungeons (*gbere*) where they could confine dangerous persons or condemned criminals for up to six months. After that time individuals had to be either freed or executed (Bascom 1969: 36–37).

The Yoruba king's bodyguard (*ogungbe*) acted as a police force and as executioners for the highest court. Another of their duties was to secure human sacrifices, many of them condemned criminals. Junior palace officials (*emese*) summoned people to the court, and the royal bodyguard arrested those who refused to present themselves willingly. Authorities from the ward level up, as well as the king, collected significant fees for hearing cases from both accusers and defendants (Bascom 1969: 35–36).

In Mesopotamia, cases that could not be resolved at the ward level were tried by members of the urban council of each city-state. A group of up to seven councillors acted as judges for each case, which was heard either in the council's assembly rooms or in a temple. At least by the Old Babylonian period, some judges were appointed by the king. Generally, the ruler of each city-state represented the ultimate level of appeal within the judicial system; however, during episodes of hegemony such as the Akkadian and Old Babylonian periods, the dominant ruler constituted a still higher level. Cases involving capital offences and other important ones which lower-level courts could not resolve satisfactorily eventually reached the highest level (Postgate 1992: 275–78).

Among the Aztec, above the level of calpolli tribunals there were separate courts for judging or reviewing cases that involved only commoners and for judging all cases in which nobles were involved. These courts were called *teccalco* and *tlacxitlan* respectively. The lowest courts of both sorts occurred at the district, quarter, or small-town level. The judges in these and higher courts were invariably members of the nobility. All criminal cases and unresolved civil cases were referred to the palace, where a high court consisting of thirteen judges, presided over by the cihuacoatl, met every ten to twelve days. It appears that death sentences passed against commoners at a lower level were simply reported to this court for approval, while nobles facing the death penalty or who protested judgements made against them at a lower level regularly appeared in person before it. All death sentences also had to be approved by the king (Berdan 1982: 104).

The state of Texcoco had constructed its legal hierarchy differently. Above the calpolli level, the Texcocan king established law courts in wards and settlements in which commoners were tried, sentenced, and punished, although capital punishment may have required royal approval. Depending on their nature, cases involving nobles were referred to one of the four advisory councils by which the affairs of Texcoco and nearby allied states were regulated. These councils met in the royal palace of Texcoco. As part of its business, the war council considered cases of treason, as well as offences and legal matters relating to the army, the finance council judged fiscal misdemeanours, and the religious council dealt with cases involving witchcraft, supernaturally mediated crimes, and offences committed on the open road. The legal council considered murder, assault, sexual transgressions, theft, drunkenness, sumptuary offences, and issues relating to slaves. Commoners as well as nobles served as judges on these councils, which were, however, presided over by close relatives of the monarch. Decisions and appeals from this level were transmitted to a supreme legal council, which met every ten to twelve days and reviewed the most difficult cases every eighty days. It was composed exclusively of high-ranking nobles, including the heads of the four advisory councils. The decisions of the supreme legal council were reviewed by two higher judges and then by the king, who, often after being advised by the rulers from allied cities, passed final judgement. All nobles from Texcoco and allied states were executed in Texcoco in a public ceremony that followed the royal review (Offner 1983: 147–55).

There is no evidence of special legal tribunals in Shang or early Zhou China. In the Western Zhou period local and regional officials appear to have performed legal functions as one of their regular duties, usually on their own but sometimes in conjunction with royal representatives. The presence of royal officials presumably allowed the king to punish disloyalty in regions that were remote from the royal court with the help of loyal provincial officials. Regional and local rulers generally had sufficient military force at their disposal to ensure that their decisions were carried out. At least in theory, a few types of offences, such as drunkenness among the Zhou nobility, were reserved for royal punishment (Creel 1970: 170, 192). Yet it appears that individuals were usually subject to the judgement and sentencing of their immediate superiors, with little if any effective right of appeal or requirement for royal approval even with regard to the imposition of the death penalty. When persons of high rank were executed, their extended families might also be killed or enslaved to prevent them from seeking blood revenge.

It appears that between men of unequal status, the more powerful was invariably deemed to be in the right, and therefore litigation could occur only between equals (Creel 1937: 352–55). Disputes between high-ranking officials about land and commercial transactions were mediated by their immediate common superior or by the king, who tried to guide them towards a mutually agreeable solution. There was no enforceable penalty for failure to carry out bargains. Theft was normally compensated by no more than a twofold repayment (Creel 1970: 188–89). The idea that just behaviour accorded with the cosmic order was already present at least by the early Zhou period, and the king's main jural role was to provide a model for proper conduct at all levels of society (Creel 1970: 163–64). The early Chinese legal system already seems to have anticipated the later distinction between punishment (*xing*), which was used to control the lower classes, and etiquette (*li*), which regulated relations among the gentry (Creel 1970: 331–36; Lewis 1990: 196).

At least some Egyptian villagers had their cases heard by government officials at the provincial level. State intervention of some sort was inevitable if written records that were kept in government archives had to be consulted, and may have been mandatory for cases to which the death penalty applied. Provincial officials seem to have had the power of life and death over ordinary people; only the wealthy and powerful would have been able to appeal their sentences to the central administration in Memphis.

During the Old Kingdom the Six Great Mansions (*ḥwt wrt 6*) appears to have been an entirely judiciary institution of the central government. It was concerned mainly with regulating the ownership and transfer of property. Many sorts of officials may have made judicial decisions (Kemp 1983: 83–84). Kings appointed high officials, including the vizier, to conduct special, often secret inquiries into crimes that seriously called royal authority into question – conspiracies against the king, royal tomb robberies, misconduct by women of the royal household, and thefts from temples. The commissions granted to these officials included the plenipotentiary right to try and punish those involved in such activities (Robins 1993: 137).

In the Andean highlands the non-Inka nobles were held responsible for maintaining order and curbing rebellion in their own territories. Ethnic officials, including ayllu heads, were permitted to impose minor penalties on those they governed. It is not known to what extent commoners or the non-Inka nobility could appeal from one level of the Inka administrative hierarchy to another. Inka officials acted in the king's name to enforce laws and apply them to the higher ranks of the nobility. Judges were not differentiated from general administrative officials.

LEGAL PROCEDURES

Legal hearings in early civilizations were conducted by judges, who heard testimony, weighed the issues, rendered a decision, and proposed a settlement or punishment. Especially at the upper levels, cases might be adjudicated by a single authority, but in other instances decisions were reached by a panel of judges working together. In the course of a trial, evidence was examined in detail: testimony was heard from opposing parties, witnesses were called, and, where applicable, documents relevant to the case were studied. Those presenting evidence were questioned by the judges, and litigants might be allowed to contest each other's statements. This was followed by a judgement, sentencing, and implementation of the sentence (Postgate 1992: 279). Upper-level courts were supplied with bailiffs and police and sometimes also with jailers and executioners (Berdan 1982: 104). The basic techniques for hearing cases and rendering verdicts were already present in prestate societies (Pospisil 1958, 1971), but in early civilizations they were adapted to the altered needs, values, and administrative practices of hierarchical societies, and, at least at the top end of the legal hierarchy, verdicts were enforced by the state rather than by public opinion.

Not only in societies such as Egypt and Mesopotamia, which had writing systems capable of recording speech, but also among the highland Mexicans, with their pictographic mnemonic devices, scribes were present to explain recorded evidence, cite relevant legislation, and record decisions (Postgate 1992: 281). In the early Zhou Dynasty litigants were occasionally represented by spokesmen, although they may have been simply individuals standing in for litigants who were unable or unwilling to attend a hearing (Creel 1970: 178). Friends or relatives might advise someone appearing before a court, but there is no evidence of professional lawyers.

Witnesses and litigants were often made to swear oaths, especially if the evidence was unclear or conflicting. Yoruba courts at all levels could administer a *kola* oath, which asked the ancestors to kill the person who swore it if he or she gave false evidence to the court. In higher-level Yoruba courts, witnesses could be asked to swear a still more powerful oath by the god Ogun while an iron object signifying the presence of the god was placed on their tongues (Bascom 1969: 40, 44). In Mesopotamia witnesses swore to be truthful on the symbol of a deity that was brought to the court from the god's shrine specially for that purpose. At various periods they might be asked to swear an additional oath in the name of the king. These oaths invoked divine (or royal) punishment if one lied (Postgate 1992: 287).

When the evidence was inconclusive, judges also had recourse to ordeals and oracles. Yoruba judges might ask accused persons to drink a toxic sass-wood brew in order to determine if they were witches (Bascom 1969: 40). In Mesopotamia ordeals were employed to discover the truth about sorcery, adultery, and homicide. Those accused of sorcery proved their innocence by staying afloat when they were thrown into the river. In Akkadian times ordeals were also used to resolve serious disputes regarding debts and ownership of property (Postgate 1992: 281). Finally, oracles were utilized to decide legal cases. In Egyptian villages councillors would consult the statue of the principal local deity to establish the guilt or innocence of a litigant, the answer being given by the god's statue's weighing more heavily on one side or the other of the frame on which it was being carried (O'Connor 1990: 16). These methods were based on the belief that supernatural powers might choose to reveal the truth to human petitioners. In Mesopotamia ordeals relating to economic issues gradually became obsolete as a consequence of the increasing use of written records to record business transactions. Eventually written records took precedence over any other form of evidence (Postgate 1992: 281–85).

Punishments for particular crimes differed in nature and severity from one early civilization to another. As in virtually all less complex societies, crimes such as treason, murder, and witchcraft tended to be punished more severely than theft or wounding. Yet in some early civilizations growing concern to protect property resulted in increasingly severe penalties for theft. The Yoruba punished witchcraft, poisoning, and violent murder with death; treason with death, exile, or loss of property; theft with death, amputation of hands, forced labour, enslavement, or wounding; highway robbery with death; repeated incest with castration or enslavement; assault with flogging; and manslaughter, rape, seduction, and adultery with fines (Ajisafe 1924: 29; Bascom 1969: 40). It was, however, possible for wealthy Yoruba criminals to escape execution by lavish gift-giving or providing a substitute human victim (Ajisafe 1924: 38). The Aztec punished treason or failing to report treason, adultery, kidnapping a child to sell as a slave, moving boundary markers, and disobedience to commands in battle with death and murder or theft with death or enslavement (Berdan 1982: 97–98). The Mesopotamians punished the murder of a free man, the kidnapping of another man's son, the harbouring of an escaped slave, and the purchase of stolen goods with death. Robbery was punished by multiple restitution or death, incest by death or exile, and wounding by retributive wounding or a fine (Pritchard 1955: 163–80). The Inka held witchcraft, treason, and various crimes against state property to be capital offences, while they punished adultery by death or flogging and all other crimes with various forms of execution and flogging or sent convicted persons to be labourers on royal cocoa plantations in the lowlands, where highlanders tended to die quickly from the hot climate and local diseases. They did not use fines, imprisonment, or enslavement as legal punishments (S. Moore 1958: 74–82). Punishments in ancient China included death (sometimes in cruel and exotic ways such as being boiled alive), the amputation of fingers, toes, feet, and noses, confinement in portable stocks, and fines (Creel 1937: 353–54). Surviving Egyptian records do not indicate standardized punishments for crimes such as murder and wounding, but individuals were beheaded, impaled, drowned, mutilated, exiled, and subjected to forced labour. Being burned alive was prescribed as a punishment for various forms of sacrilege (O'Connor 1990: 28; Robins 1993: 137–38; Strouhal 1992: 199).

All societies have rules for dealing with crimes such as treason, murder, injury, theft, and sexual misconduct. In early civilizations the lowest-level tribunals dealt with these offences by employing a mixture of customary local laws and the judges' awareness of how authorities at higher levels had modified such laws. There was also, however, an elaboration of laws, either by precedent or by legislation, to deal with problems specific to more complex societies. Their subject matter tended to vary from one early civilization to another.

The Mesopotamians developed especially elaborate rules relating to questions of property ownership, business transactions, and the conduct of business (Postgate 1992: 282–87). The Aztec had complex laws regulating the lifestyles of nobles and commoners, distinguishing the sorts of clothing and materials that people of different ranks and statuses could wear, the types of houses they could live in, and the conduct that was expected of them (Clendinnen 1991: 120; Durán 1964: 131–32). Inka law and Egyptian law, as far as it has been preserved, elaborated detailed regulations dealing with infractions, especially of a fiscal nature, against the state (Kemp 1983: 84). Inka law also included sumptuary regulations, which sought to limit the accumulation of wealth by lower-class families, as well as regulations that required each ethnic group to wear a distinctive costume (Kendall 1973: 33, 59). The Yoruba evolved elaborate legislation relating to debts and the use of royal or official regalia by ordinary people and fined people for ritual offences against the king such as bringing a corpse too near the royal palace (Ajisafe 1924: 22). Old laws could be altered and new ones introduced only after they had been discussed by members of the Ogboni society and approved by the king (Bascom 1969: 40).

LEGAL CODES

There were significant variations in the degree to which laws were codified and publicly promulgated in early civilizations. What are called 'law codes' began to appear in Mesopotamia in the Ur III period. The most completely preserved Mesopotamian law code is that of King Hammurabi, dating from about 1700 B.C. A prologue proclaiming that it was written to 'cause justice to prevail' and ensure that 'the strong might not oppress the weak' (Pritchard 1955: 164) was followed by 282 laws dealing with prices, trade, and commerce, marriage and divorce, criminal offences, and civil law, including slavery and debt. The laws took two forms: 'If crime *x* has been committed, the appropriate punishment is *y*' and 'If person N does *x*, person O must do *y* in return'. The code ended with an exhortation to all people to obey these laws and a curse upon future kings who ignored them.

Hammurabi's code treated manslaughter and accidental injury very differently from earlier codes. Following 'desert law', Hammurabi applied the principle of 'an eye for an eye' to such offences, while Ur III law had subjected them to fines. Jean Bottéro (1992: 161–64) suggests that these codes were not comprehensive sets of laws meant to be applied literally but generalized verdicts that provided models of sound legal judgement and represented Hammurabi and other kings as just rulers. Hence the spirit of these laws was more important than the letter. This might explain why the laws in the Hammurabi code are not always mutually consistent. Pritchard (1955: 166 n. 45) had earlier suggested that these inconsistencies reflected different stages in the development of Babylonian law.

Tenochtitlan, Texcoco, and perhaps other large states in the Valley of Mexico elaborated legal codes that, like the Mesopotamian ones, prescribed specific penalties for a vast number of offences. These codes had to be preserved by memory, although they may also have been recorded in mnemonic form in codices. The formulation of the first systematic legal code in Tenochtitlan was later described as part of King Mochtezuma I's (A.D. 1440–68) far-reaching reformulation of his state's legal system. This code probably incorporated customary laws but was mainly concerned with elaborating sumptuary regulations, distinguishing the rights of nobles from those of commoners, and compelling commoners to display more respect for the king and the nobility. In both Tenochtitlan and Texcoco, successive kings altered old laws and decreed new ones to take account of changing social conditions (Offner 1983: 81–85; Durán 1964: 131–33). The Yoruba distinguished between customary usage (*asa*) and formulated, or statute, law (*ofin*). Both types varied from one city-state to another (Lloyd 1962: 15, 26).

It has often been suggested that laws tended to be codified in a comprehensive fashion in multiethnic states such as those found in Mesopotamia and the Valley of Mexico in an effort to reduce friction among resident ethnic groups each of which had its own traditional laws (Offner 1983: 82). Yet similarly detailed law codes were not formulated for the Inka state, despite its extraordinary multiethnic composition, nor do legal codes appear to have been developed in Mesopotamia prior to the Ur III period. It seems instead that these codes were formulated in hegemonic city-states so that subject peoples would know what laws would be applied if they became involved in legal cases that would be judged by the hegemon or his courts (Postgate 1992: 289–91). This would have been necessary if laws varied significantly from one city-state or one hegemonic regime to another.

In other early civilizations, legal codes appear to have been less systematically elaborated and less publicly proclaimed by rulers. In Egypt, for example, it is unclear whether there was any central body of written laws to guide the actions of government officials. The term *hp* meant both 'law' and 'custom', and, while occasional references to a 'hp of the king' were probably to laws, they did not necessarily refer to written ones (Bontty 1997). Village courts were able to take account of local customs and precedents, which would be drawn to the attention of officials if cases were referred to higher courts (McDowell 1999: 167, 188). C. J. Eyre (1984: 92) asserts that there is no direct evidence of codified law until after the New Kingdom. Nevertheless, a late Middle Kingdom papyrus detailing what to do with people who attempted to evade corvée duties cites precise variations of offences, and this suggests the possible existence of a legal code relating specifically to corvée that has not survived (Kemp 1983: 84).

The Inka formulated numerous laws dealing with the way in which ethnic nobles and commoners were to be treated by the state, perhaps to provide guidance to provincial officials (S. Moore 1958: 74–85). While the early Zhou kings are said to have greatly admired the legal practices of their Shang predecessors and to have promulgated their own distinctive laws, there is no clear evidence of general law codes in China at this period (Creel 1970: 165–66, 192). Royal judgements appear to have been viewed as providing general principles rather than specific prescriptions for punishing misdeeds and resolving disputes. The absence of specific legal codes accords with the later Chinese view that precise laws encourage rather than prevent wrongdoing (Creel 1937: 350–51). It thus appears that, in general, there was less concern for promulgating explicit legal codes in territorial states than there was in hegemonic or rapidly changing city-states.

LAW AND SOCIAL HIERARCHY

Hammurabi's code proclaimed that one of its chief goals was to defend the weak against the strong. Yet in early civilizations there was no concept of equality before the law. On the contrary, social inequality was expressed and defended in many ways by legal systems.

Law that was administered by the state generally punished crimes committed against kings, government institutions, deities, and temples more severely than crimes committed against other individuals. Hammurabi's laws sentenced to death even upper-class persons for theft from the king or from temples. The theft of livestock, which was treated separately, from king or temples required a thirtyfold restitution, with death as punishment if the fine could not be paid, whereas a similar crime committed against a private person called for a fine or a tenfold repayment (Pritchard 1955: 166, laws 6–8). Texcocan law punished crimes committed within the royal palace more severely than crimes committed elsewhere (Offner 1983: 159). Among the Inka, theft from individuals or ayllus was punished at worst by flogging, but anyone who stole from government fields or storehouses or from temples or refused to perform labour service was executed. Death was also the punishment for breaking into houses where chosen women lived, setting fire to suspension bridges, and (for commoners) attempting to seduce upper-class Inka women. Inka law stressed the sacred status of the Inka royal family and permitted the king to execute subjects and confiscate their property more or less as he wished (S. Moore 1958: 74, 81–85). In Egypt the law sentenced people who robbed government institutions and temples either to be killed or to be mutilated and condemned to lifelong slave labour. The same sentences were imposed on individuals who evaded paying taxes or performing corvée labour and on officials convicted of having been corrupted by bribes (O'Connor 1990: 28–29). In cases of theft from individuals, in contrast, injured parties received only two- or threefold compensation for their losses and even this limited compensation was often hard to collect (Eyre 1984: 93; O'Connor 1990: 29).

Crimes committed against upper-class people also tended to be punished more severely than crimes against commoners. Hammurabi decreed that, if someone belonging to the upper-class was found guilty of having knocked out an upper-class person's eye or tooth or broken a bone, the same should be done to him. If he had injured a commoner in the same ways, he had only to pay financial compensation. If an upper-class man assaulted a woman of his own class who was pregnant and caused her to miscarry, he had to pay three times more damages than for injuring a commoner in the same manner. Even within the upper class, a man who struck someone superior in rank to himself was given sixty lashes in the presence of the city council, while for striking an equal he would have merely had to pay a fine (Pritchard 1955: 175, laws 202, 203).

S. F. Moore (1958: 79) maintains that the Inka punished most crimes differently according to rank; nobles received light sentences for crimes for which commoners were executed. Such treatment was justified by claiming that public ridicule or loss of office was as harsh a punishment for members of the nobility as corporal punishment, exile to the tropics, or execution was for commoners (75). Whatever a man's class, the punishment for committing adultery with a noble woman was death, while committing it with a commoner was punished relatively lightly (Rowe 1944: 271). The Inka also had two classes of prisons where individuals were interrogated, held for trial, or punished – ordinary prisons for commoners and more spacious and comfortable ones for nobles. Yet, regardless of class, traitors, witches, those who stole state property, and people who insulted the king were killed by being incarcerated in royal dungeons filled with snakes and wild felines (Kendall 1973: 133; Rowe 1944: 471).

In the Valley of Mexico the legal punishment of different classes was more complex. The law discriminated against commoners in the sense that adultery by male nobles with commoner women was punished less severely than commoners' adultery with noble women. Texcocan law punished theft with strangulation or enslavement, the severity of the penalty depending on the value of what had been stolen, where the crime had been committed, the thief's previous criminal record, and the damage caused. Yet the ability to avoid such penalties by making restitution payments greatly advantaged wealthier, upper-class offenders (Offner 1983: 278–79). Aztec law, however, punished drunkenness in members of the upper classes more harshly than it did drunkenness in commoners. Male nobles were strangled for severe public intoxication and forfeited their titles and positions even for a minor offence (Berdan 1982: 97). Commoners had their hair cut off and their houses levelled for a first offence and were executed after a second conviction. The reason for this was the belief that nobles, as descendants of the god Quetzalcoatl, possessed stronger spiritual powers that gave them a natural right to dominate and lead commoners, but these same powers made it easier for them to resist temptation. Upper-class drunkenness represented a failure to live up to claims that justified the privileged position that nobles enjoyed and dissipated the special powers they possessed.

Priests and young commoners undergoing military training were also executed for single acts of drunkenness. Many priests were nobles, but those who were not and young commoners training to be soldiers were subject to special discipline because their service to the gods and to the state necessitated their conserving as much supernatural power as possible. Priests were executed if they were discovered breaking their obligation to be celibate (Berdan 1982: 97, 131–33; Offner 1983: 268–69). A similar attitude appears to have existed in early Zhou China, where death was prescribed for officials who participated in alcoholic drinking bouts or sought to alter prescribed ways of doing things (Creel 1970: 190). The Zhou (and perhaps the Shang) nobles, like those living in the Valley of Mexico, believed that they were set apart from commoners by a superior nature that endowed them with greater vitality and power (Lewis 1990: 32–33).

The state sought to reinforce parental authority and hence the context in which habits of obedience to all levels of authority were learned. Texcocan law executed individuals who injured or attacked their parents (Offner 1983: 204), while the Hammurabi code stipulated that a son who struck his father should have his hand amputated. If the adopted son of a married Babylonian priestess (who was not permitted to bear children of her own) denied his obligations to his adoptive parents, he could be sentenced either to have his tongue cut out or to be blinded (Pritchard 1955: 175, laws 192, 193, 195).

The ambivalent attitude towards slaves in early civilizations is reflected in legislation concerning them. In Mesopotamia killing someone else's slave was a much less serious offence than harming any free person. It was compensated by replacing the slave or paying a stipulated fee to the slave's owner. At the same time, a free person of whatever rank who concealed a runaway slave or helped such a slave to escape from the city was executed (Pritchard 1955: 166–67, laws 15, 16, 19). Yoruba law permitted owners of slaves to execute them or offer them as human sacrifices. Presumably such powers of life and death were used mainly to intimidate and control slaves soon after they had been captured in battle. Killing another's slave required twofold restitution (Ajisafe 1924: 28, 65). In Middle Kingdom Egypt royal slaves, many of whom were prisoners of war, could be condemned to death if they misbehaved but only after a hearing by a royal tribunal (Loprieno 1997: 200).

Most early civilizations, including the Yoruba, had laws protecting household and debt slaves and allowing them to be emancipated and even adopted or married into their former owners' families. In the Valley of Mexico laws protected obedient and well-behaved slaves against being executed, used as human sacrifices, or sold against their will (Offner 1983: 141). Both Aztec and Yoruba slaves who took refuge in the royal palace were freed by the king. It was illegal for anyone except their owner and his family to try to impede their flight (Ajisafe 1924: 22; Offner 1983: 140). In their mixture of harshness and leniency, laws relating to slaves reflected both the need felt in early civilizations to maintain control over this tiny, oppressed minority and a willingness to absorb them over time into the free labouring classes.

Among other classes, inequality was reinforced by the practice of justice as well as by the nature of the laws. In the middle and upper tiers of the judicial system all decisions were made or controlled by authorities who were members of the upper classes. Despite formal orders that they should dispense justice impartially and the severe punishments that were prescribed for failing to do so, upper-class judges tended to favour members of their own class in disputes with commoners. The upper classes also had more wealth and wider social connections, which allowed them to bribe judges more effectively than lower-class litigants (W. Clarke 1972: 253). Since in many law courts litigants were expected to pay judges for hearing their cases, the distinction between fees and bribery was often far from clear. The Hammurabi code ordered that a judge who altered a decision in someone's favour should be fined twelve times the amount that was involved and permanently lose his right to hear cases (Pritchard 1955: 166, law 5). That such severe penalties were thought appropriate suggests that the corruption of justice was widely perceived to be a serious problem. Given the close ties uniting the upper classes, this does not mean that such penalties eliminated the problem or were very often imposed.

The control of the justice system by the upper classes also meant that lower-class litigants were more likely to be subjected to painful and dangerous ordeals in the course of a trial. They were not only more likely to lose lawsuits but also, because of the nature of the laws, faced harsher penalties: flogging, torture, mutilation, forced labour, being sold as slaves, and painful forms of execution. While a person of any status who incurred the Inka king's anger risked being penned up with his lethal menagerie, lower-class people ran far greater risks of being severely punished by the law than did members of the Inka nobility. Finally, extremely unpleasant penalties were often inflicted on the families of individuals convicted of serious crimes, and these too were most likely to be applied to members of the lower classes. Among the Aztec, all the members of a traitor's household were enslaved for four generations (Offner 1983: 225). In Egypt the wives and children of men evading corvée duty could be enslaved (Robins 1993: 137), as could the families of Yoruba men convicted of certain kinds of theft (Bascom 1969: 40). The Inka exterminated entire families of persons found guilty of witchcraft, probably because it was feared that other members of such families might also be witches (Rowe 1944: 314).

Thus, while Aztec commoners were reported to have litigated among themselves like quarrelling turkeys (Offner 1983: 135, 259), most lower-class individuals avoided taking their social superiors to court. On the contrary, the threat of litigation was a way to intimidate commoners and reinforce the power of the upper classes. Law courts were used to collect debts from people who were equal or inferior in status to their creditors; defendants were most often poor men and women accused of theft and not paying their debts (Robins 1993: 137). The Middle Kingdom 'Tale of the Eloquent Peasant', which describes how the king, after a long delay, vindicated a poor farmer who protested after being robbed and beaten by a powerful official, is overtly about justice being done to an ordinary person. Yet justice was finally rendered in this case only because the verbatim recordings of the farmer's verbose pleas for justice had entertained the king (Lichtheim 1973: 169–84). Eyre (1984: 104) observes that, because of their power to bribe, socially manipulate judges and witnesses, and ignore public opinion, powerful Egyptians had no fear of the courts. Under these circumstances, the principal goal of the weaker party was to pacify and win the favour of his superiors, not to oppose them. A powerful husband might seek justice against a socially inferior adulterer, but a lower-class husband would not accuse a powerful official of seducing or raping his wife. H. G. Creel (1937: 354; 1970: 190–91) observes that in early Zhou China members of the nobility were punished far less often than commoners. It was not easy for the king or regional leaders to impose severe penalties on individuals who were supported by powerful kinsmen and many armed retainers.

Far from being a means of securing justice for the weak, the upper levels of the legal system were a powerful instrument of intimidation and control in the hands of the upper classes. The courts provided a way to coerce less powerful individuals and reinforce the power and privileges of the upper classes and of major institutions. This use of the legal system is archetypally represented in the biblical account of how the Israelite Queen Jezebel obtained royal possession of a vineyard that its owner, Naboth, did not wish to sell to the king; she had Naboth condemned to death on a false charge of blasphemy and his vineyard confiscated by the crown (I Kings 21). This account of the use of legal systems conforms to Aztec descriptions of the law as a wild beast, a trap, or a snare, an overpowering force to be feared because people could be punished by it for crimes they did not commit (Offner 1983: 243–44).

Even the use of the legal system for litigation among the upper classes was discouraged. The Hammurabi code stipulated that, if an upper-class man brought charges of murder or witchcraft against another upper-class man and failed to prove them or was found guilty of giving false testimony in a case involving a capital offence, he could be executed (Pritchard 1955: 166, laws 1–3). Such laws not only discouraged illegal behaviour but indicated that considerable risks were involved in undertaking even legitimate legal actions of these sorts.

These arrangements suggest that in early civilizations governments were not anxious to expend time and resources regulating aspects of human relations that could be controlled in a less formal manner. This in turn implies that an important function of the legal system was to reinforce the power and privileges of the state and the upper classes. While the legal system had to be protected from being totally discredited as a result of too obvious corruption and oppression, it functioned, behind claims of impartiality, as a not very subtle means by which powerful individuals could coerce less powerful ones.

LAW AND SOCIAL ORDER

The legal systems of early civilizations appear to have grown out of the seemingly universal legal practices of smaller, more egalitarian societies. These practices involved the recognition of local authorities as having the right to hear disputes and render verdicts in accordance with generally accepted principles, which in turn were enforced by public opinion (Pospisil 1971: 39–96). With the development of early civilizations, these arrangements were transformed into multitiered, hierarchical legal systems staffed at the higher levels by upper-class judges whose decisions were enforced by the power of the state. The king was universally acknowledged to be the supreme legal authority, and the laws upheld by the state were often treated as royal or divine pronouncements.

There was, however, considerable variation from one early civilization to another in the extent to which legal authorities and offices were differentiated from general administrative ones. There were also marked differences in the degree to which laws were codified and those relating to different general categories, such as commerce, administration, and class privileges, were elaborated. In general, variations in such categories reflected the different preoccupations of the upper classes in particular early civilizations.

In most early civilizations law was described as a powerful force maintaining order in an equitable, if unequal, fashion in the social realm. Yet, because at all but the lowest levels of the legal system laws were made, cases were decided, and punishments were determined by the upper classes, the legal system was a potent instrument for intimidating individuals of lower status. Chinese law appears to have differed from that of other early civilizations only in that, in theory as well as in practice, litigation was possible only between equals. No efforts were made to idealize the legal system as a means by which justice was provided for all. Early Chinese realism with respect to law appears to have had long-term consequences for the development of Chinese civilization, which never evolved a strong sense of either private property or individual legal rights. Elsewhere, in due course some people were inspired to try to realize the ideals embedded in representations of their legal system as an instrument of social justice as well as social order.

12 Military Organization

Military force played three important roles in early civilizations. It secured and defended the frontiers of states; it enriched powerful rulers by enabling them to exploit peripheral areas that contained valuable natural resources, control lucrative trade routes, and impose tribute on conquered peoples; and it maintained internal order – suppressing rebellions, ensuring the collection of taxes, maintaining social peace, and protecting the power and privileges of the upper classes. No clear distinction was drawn between military and police forces. Because order and prosperity were important for everyone, military strength was endowed with great political and religious significance.

Armed conflict was invariably destructive of human life and property, but wherever it occurred in early civilizations it was preferable to belong to a strong and disciplined polity than to a weak one. Military success offered opportunities for personal enrichment and prestige to kings and commoners alike. Warfare was surrounded by elaborate rules of conduct which sought to limit unforeseen consequences, but these rules were often disregarded in extreme situations or when fighting enemies who did not understand them. The Aztec and Inka both requested the target of a planned attack to submit peacefully. Aztec ambassadors invited rulers to become friends of the Aztec king, allow trade, and pay nominal tribute. If this offer was not accepted, a short time later their Texcocan allies would threaten the targeted state with severe punishment if it did not submit. Finally, the Tlacopans, the third members of the Triple Alliance, would call upon the warriors of the threatened state to surrender and save lives. These preliminary encounters were believed to be essential to justify a military campaign (Berdan 1982: 106).

Rituals linked warfare to the cosmic order. Offerings were made to supernatural beings to win their favour or induce them not to assist the enemy. The Inka rulers consulted oracles before starting a war, sought to win the favour of the enemy's deities or to weaken them, and dedicated a portion of any territory they captured to the service of the gods (Kendall 1973: 99–108). The Shang kings sanctified war as a hunt for human prey to be sacrificed to their ancestors and the gods. Major Chinese military campaigns began at the earth altar and ancestral temple of the king or of a major provincial lord, where the war was announced to the ancestors and their help requested. Tablets inscribed with the names of these ancestors were carried into battle. After a successful campaign, prisoners were sacrificed or severed enemy ears and heads were brought from the battlefield and presented at the ancestral temple (Lewis 1990: 23–25). Before a military campaign, Aztec soldiers gathered at temples to offer their own blood to the gods and receive weapons. Armed priests carried images of the gods into battle (Hassig 1988: 9). The Aztec justified war as an opportunity to collect prisoners who were sacrificed so that their blood and flesh could nourish the gods. Mesopotamians believed that wars were fought at the command of the patron deities of city-states, whose will a king was supposed to be able to interpret (Mikhaeli 1969: 78). At the start of a military campaign, Yoruba soldiers offered sacrifices to their war standards and covered themselves with charms that they believed would protect them in battle (Ajayi and Smith 1971: 29).

Ultimately, it was kings who were held ritually and operationally responsible for warfare. Peter Gose (1996b) has observed that among the Inka war was the key to royal power. Kings normally led armies in person or delegated command of them to close relatives or high officials. Inka kings also initiated wars, although only after consulting with high-ranking military and civilian administrators. At an early period, to begin a war Mesopotamian leaders might have needed the consent of a council of leading citizens and an assembly of men of fighting age (Postgate 1992: 81). The Aztec ruler sought the support of a council of high-ranking veteran soldiers (Hassig 1988: 47–48) and of the calpolli leaders who had to call up and provision most of the troops. Neither Yoruba kings nor any member of Yoruba royal patrilineages normally led armies, and in some states, such as Oyo, kings were forbidden to do so. Just as did rulers who actually led or commissioned armies, however, Yoruba kings bore the ultimate responsibility for victory or defeat because of the supernatural powers that they commanded (R. Smith 1973: 227). They also profited economically from war as did kings in other early civilizations; in some cases receiving one-third of the slaves and other booty (Peel 1983: 45).

Kings often began their reigns with shows of military force. Aztec rulers needed to capture the large number of prisoners that had to be sacrificed to complete their enthronement rituals. King Tizoc, who ruled from 1481 to 1486, may have been poisoned when he failed to do this (Hassig 1988:

198). The Maya similarly appear to have treated warfare as an integral part of royal succession ceremonies; heir designates were required to capture one or more enemy soldiers of high rank for human sacrifice (Schele and Miller 1986: 116–17). New Egyptian kings could demonstrate their prowess in many different ways, including big-game hunting and erecting large buildings, but many of them led military expeditions (Hornung 1997: 306–8). Shang kings were active as both soldiers and hunters, moving about their kingdom to join regional officials in attacks against rebels or foreign enemies (Keightley 1979–80).

Given its importance, documentation of warfare is surprisingly limited, sporadic, and equivocal for most early civilizations. Archaeological evidence of warfare sometimes occurs in the form of city walls or frontier fortifications, but city walls were not just for protection against foreign attack. Moreover, while fortifications were not common in the Valley of Mexico or among the Maya, literary sources reveal that warfare was prevalent in both regions. Among the Shang Chinese and the Inka, warfare did not receive explicit iconographic attention. Egyptian generals regularly depicted themselves as officials wearing civilian dress rather than military uniform. In works of art, New Kingdom Egyptian rulers and Mesopotamian kings were represented on a much larger scale than the armed forces they led, while the Old and Middle Kingdom Egyptians, Maya, and Aztec often depicted military action in the form of the king alone smiting one or more enemies. Yet we know from reliable literary sources that the Egyptians and Aztec fielded large armies. This discrepancy suggests that the general lack of representation of large armies in Classic Maya art does not signify that large armies were never assembled. What it does indicate is that the discussion of warfare in early civilizations requires documents as well as iconographic evidence.

MASS ARMIES

In most early civilizations wars against neighbouring city-states and foreign peoples were waged mainly by conscript armies composed of farmers and craftsmen led by officers who belonged to the upper classes and the bureaucracy. The rest of the time many of these officers were engaged in various forms of civilian administration. Military campaigns usually began after the main harvest had been collected. This period also frequently corresponded with the dry season, in which travel was easier. Militias were trained to varying degrees and fought either with weapons that ordinary people used for hunting and defence against wild animals or with more specialized weapons provided by the state. In some civilizations conscripts were fed and clothed by the government while they were on campaigns; in others they were expected to provision themselves.

The Aztec and their allies waged war to control trade routes and collect tribute from city-states they had subdued over much of central Mexico. Throughout the Valley of Mexico, warfare was valued as a source of individual social mobility and an activity that was essential to maintain the cosmic order. While the Aztec idealized warfare even more than most of their neighbours, their views about it were based on concepts that were shared by all the peoples of the region.

At birth every Aztec male child was formally dedicated to the military, in token of which a warrior undertook to bury the child's umbilical cord on a field of battle during the next military campaign. The Aztec took more care to educate young men to be citizen-soldiers than any other early civilization. Every calpolli had a *telpochcalli* (school) in which young commoners were taught to be warriors by members who had been elevated to noble status as a reward for multiple acts of valour in warfare. Graduates of these schools were incorporated into their calpolli regiment, which fought alongside others in military campaigns. Normally each calpolli supplied four hundred soldiers under the command of its own officers (Townsend 1992: 197).

Boys began to attend such schools at puberty. Younger boys were under the control of older trainees who had already participated in military campaigns. All of them continued to eat at home but were required to sleep in the school buildings and to avoid drunkenness and sexual licence. They grew food on fields that belonged collectively to the calpolli and performed corvée labour – dredging canals, repairing streets, and cleaning public places under the direction of calpolli elders. They were also instructed in the special lore and traditions of their calpolli. Together with the young women of their calpolli, they attended sessions in the *cuicacalli* (houses of song), where they learned the songs and dances they would perform as adults at major religious festivals (Clendinnen 1991: 112–18; Hassig 1988: 30–34).

Yet the young men's training was principally as soldiers. About the age of twenty they first accompanied older warriors to battle as shield-bearers and observers. In the next campaign they were allowed to fight in small groups under the supervision of seasoned veterans and began to rise in the warrior hierarchy by capturing enemy soldiers for human sacrifice. Those who failed, even as part of a group, to capture a prisoner were not allowed to cut off a youthful lock of hair, which remained a lifelong source of humiliation for them. Whether or not they were militarily successful, men were allowed to marry and withdraw from the telpochcalli by their mid-twenties (Hassig 1988: 36–40).

Sons of nobles received a more intensive administrative and religious education in special schools (calmecacs) that were attached to temples. They too began to receive rigorous military training when they were about fifteen years old. A young noble's reputation and chances of being appointed to a major state office could be ruined by his inability to succeed as a warrior (Clendinnen 1991: 121–22).

The Aztec fought with clubs, *atlatls* (throwing sticks) and darts, and slings, but their principal weapons were swords and spears. While Aztec soldiers were trained and drilled with wooden weapons, they fought with swords edged along two sides with obsidian blades and with obsidian-tipped darts and spears. These weapons, which had great cutting power, were distributed to ordinary soldiers in wartime and stored between campaigns in armouries near the temples at the centre of the city and perhaps also in or near calpolli temples (Hassig 1988: 61, 75–94). Leading soldiers wore heavily quilted cotton armour. Tribute-paying city-states along the routes armies travelled were required to supply the soldiers with food as they passed by. Between harvest time and the start of spring planting, the Aztec calendar was filled with rituals relating to war (Clendinnen 1991: 295–97).

In addition to wars of conquest, highland Mexican city-states engaged in *xochiyaoyotl* (flowery wars), which consisted of carefully prearranged, 'friendly' battles between rival states. Soldiers were killed in these battles and prisoners taken, but military action was restricted to the battlefield and the overt political status of the participants was not altered, at least in the short run, by the outcome. The rationale for these contests was to capture prisoners for sacrifice to the gods. Flowery wars were said to be waged when not enough wars of conquest were occurring. In addition to training soldiers and permitting individuals to win military honours, these contests served to deflect formidable nearby rivals while states were expanding elsewhere and to reduce the strength of rival states too powerful to be conquered in a single campaign. The Triple Alliance repeatedly challenged the Tlaxcalans, east of the Valley of Mexico, to flowery wars in an effort to weaken them, but they were unable to incorporate them into their tributary system (Hassig 1988: 129–30, 172; M. E. Smith 1996: 184–85).

Mesopotamian city-states fought over water rights, agricultural land, and trade routes. Wars were a source of wealth for rulers in the form of tribute and female slaves, who could be employed as weavers. Military action was also necessary to defend Mesopotamian states against incursions by Semitic-speaking pastoralists from the northwest and the peoples of the Zagros Mountains to the east, who appear to have grown increasingly dangerous in the course of the third millennium B.C. The Ur III ruler, Shu-Sin, built a wall where the

Tigris and Euphrates Rivers came closest together to hinder the southward movements of Amorite bands (Crawford 1991: 27).

Glyptic representations of battles and bound prisoners occur as early as the Uruk period (Collon 1987: 162), but for Early Dynastic I times there is still no clear evidence of standing armies. Kings or prominent citizens appointed by city-state councils may have led armies raised from among the free men of the community. Such levies continued in wartime long after kings assumed permanent control of military affairs. Conscript soldiers were armed with metal axes, spears, incurved swords or daggers, and stone-headed maces that were either owned by them or produced and stored at palaces or temples and issued to them in wartime. These arms were heavy and specialized compared with those used in neighbouring Egypt at the same period. There is no evidence in the Early Dynastic period of archers or lightly armed fighters. The bow and arrow were introduced in Akkadian times (Huot 1989: 225; Jacobsen 1943).

It is not known how or by whom soldiers were trained. In Sumerian, *erin* meant both a dependent labourer and a soldier, which suggests that many soldiers were recruited from the paid labour forces of temple estates. The term *nubanda*, which later became a military rank, was originally the title of a temple administrator. Military service must also have been required of those who owned or rented land. In all cases, it would have been perceived as a form of corvée labour. Defeated cities frequently had their walls breached or levelled, and their temples were sometimes plundered, although this was believed to provoke the anger of the gods and draw divine retribution upon kings who allowed such an offence to occur (Gelb 1973; Mikhaeli 1969; Postgate 1992: 241–56).

Egyptian kings fought wars to defend their borders, control foreign trade routes, and obtain prisoners to augment agricultural production. Commoners were recruited for military service as one of many forms of corvée labour that did not require specialized skills. Soldiers were referred to generically as *ḏ3mw* (recruits) or *nfrw* (young men), and in the Middle Kingdom the term *ʿnḫ n nỉwt* (community dweller) in practice meant a soldier (Eyre 1999: 38). The term *mšʿ* was applied equally to an army and a mining crew. In the Sixth Dynasty, the courtier and high official Weni led five consecutive armies, composed of men conscripted from all over Egypt, into Canaan (Grimal 1992: 82–85). Like other corvée labourers, soldiers were fed and cared for by the state while they were away from home. Farmers fought with bows and arrows, clubs, and spears, presumably the same weapons they used for hunting and defence against wild animals in their home villages. Workers attached to specific temples and mortuary cults were granted permanent immunity from all forms of corvée, including military service (Andreu 1997: 21–23).

12.1. Inka battle scene depicting the storming of an Andean fortress (*pukara*), from the lavishly illustrated manuscript *El primer nueva crónica y buen gobierno* (New Chronicle and Good Government of Peru), written by the Andean provincial noble, Felipe Guaman Poma de Ayala, probably finished in 1713 or 1715. Source: after F. Guaman Poma de Ayalla, *Nueva Crónica y Bien Gobierno* (Paris: Muséum National d'Histoire Naturelle, Travaux et Mémoires de l'Institut d'Ethnologie, 23, 1989), 63.

The Inka state resorted to large-scale warfare to extend its control over the peoples of the Central Andes (Fig. 12.1). Later expansion appears to have aimed mainly at gaining control of more remote areas that were rich in natural resources, especially metals, and at securing defensible boundaries. Inka officials used corvée labour as a source of soldiers, every male between the ages of twenty-five and fifty being liable for military service. In each settlement or ayllu, instructors were responsible for teaching teenage males how to fight. Military contests involving young men from neighbouring communities were among the activities encouraged by the Inka state. Members of the Inka nobility were educated at special schools in Cuzco where, in addition to being taught how to be administrators, they received a rigorous military education and were encouraged to fight enthusiastically for the Inka king. The individual strength and military skills of young Inka nobles were tested in the course of an elaborate set of coming-of-age ceremonies in which their ears were pierced and the king presented them with insignia of noble status. These ceremonies included races and individual and group combat in the course of which some contestants were killed (Bram 1941; Grou 1989).

Ordinary Inka conscripts were organized in groups of ten, one of their number being responsible for seeing that the rest were armed, fed, and had the necessary supplies (Kendall 1973: 98). These in turn were incorporated into groups of fifty, one hundred, five hundred, and one thousand (Hyslop 1990: 147). If conscripts were away from an ayllu during the growing season, its remaining members had to plant and harvest their fields for them. Some soldiers may have been accompanied by their wives, who helped to cook and carry equipment. Food and clothing were provided by the state from depots located at provincial administrative centres and government rest places located along the main roads. Small units might pass the nights in large public halls at such places, but large armies lived mainly in tents provided by the state (Murra 1980: 99). Inka soldiers did not wear uniforms, and most fought with the slings, bolas, bows and arrows, spears, and clubs that they had been trained to use in their home villages (Hyslop 1990: 147). In the celebrations and rituals that followed a conquest, defeated soldiers were made to wear women's clothes as a sign of submission, and the Inka king walked over the prostrate living bodies of his enemies (Classen 1993: 56–57).

The Yoruba waged war to control trade routes and obtain slaves. Military service was obligatory for all free and able-bodied Yoruba men. If a person refused to fight, his crops might be plundered and he himself be severely beaten. The heads of extended families were required to train and arm their followers and organize them into a fighting force that could join their city-state's army when required. Extended-family units were aggregated under ward and quarter leaders. The principal weapons were iron spears, double-edged (*ida*) and single-edged (*adedengbe*) slashing swords, daggers for stabbing, and bows and arrows. Extended families supplied both food and arms for military campaigns, although once out of their own territory armies tended to live off the land (Ajayi and Smith 1971).

The available data on Maya warfare deal almost entirely with the behaviour of kings and high-ranking officials, and it is unknown to what extent commoners were summoned for military service during wartime. Maya epigraphic and pictorial evidence documents numerous episodes of the capture and eventual sacrifice of the kings and nobles of one city-state by the rulers of another, and the capture of large images of deities that accompanied military expeditions was one of the most celebrated accomplishments of Maya kings (Harrison 1999: 155–56). This and the absence of fortifications have led some Mayanists to conclude that Maya warfare involved small bands of upper-class warriors engaging in heavily ritualized and perhaps prearranged conflicts on the borders of their respective states. Such battles, it is argued, established the relative prestige of individual rulers and members of the upper classes and provided upper-class victims for a sacrificial cult (Schele and Miller 1986: 209–40). Other Mayanists have suggested that some wars were fought to create regional superstates (Demarest 1978; Webster 1993: 429–30). Still others deny that territorial gain was a significant motive for Maya warfare; they maintain that warfare among city-states was concerned mainly with establishing tributary networks and controlling trade routes (Culbert 1991b: 336; Freidel 1986; Houston 1993: 137–38). Competition of this sort involved the efforts of major kingdoms, such as Calakmul, to form alliances with far-off states that would encircle mutual rivals or threats such as Tikal and, by gradually severing their trading networks, weaken them economically prior to a major military confrontation (Drew 1999; Martin and Grube 2000; Sharer 1996).

In fact, warfare was directed not only against the borders or outlying administrative centres of city-states but also against their capitals. The defacement and smashing of stelae in the centres of major cities such as Tikal suggest that enemy armies penetrated them. In its final phase an attempt appears to have been made to fortify the centre of Dos Pilos against such an attack by erecting palisades and fortifications built of stone blocks wrenched from existing buildings. Similar emergency fortifications have been identified in some other urban centres (Houston 1993: 46). Yet, while victorious rulers no doubt sought to humiliate defeated cities, imposed tribute on them, and sometimes installed individuals of their own choosing as their kings, there is no evidence that efforts were made to incorporate one large city-state into another. Nevertheless, known patterns of warfare would have required large military forces, even though such forces are not documented in Maya art and inscriptions. The general lack of specialized weapons and military technology suggests that most soldiers were farmers or craftsmen conscripted for short military campaigns. Most battles probably dissolved into individual combats, and kings and high-ranking officials were no doubt special targets for attack and capture. There is no proof, however, that Maya kings deliberately exposed themselves to capture in battle or that kings taken prisoner were necessarily captured in hand-to-hand combat by other rulers. They may simply have taken personal credit for every ruler and many nobles captured by their armies.

Inferential evidence suggests that the lower classes did participate in military campaigns, but it is not known how they were trained, called up for military service, or commanded.

The numerous references to warfare in Shang divination texts suggest that warfare was of great importance to the Shang kings (Keightley 1979–80). Warfare appears to have been much concerned with occupying and settling peripheral lands, with protecting Shang settlements against attacks by pastoral peoples living to the north and west, and with maintaining the unity of the state. Shang oracle bones refer to the king's levying farmers and state labourers for military campaigns, the farmers in units of one thousand and the labourers usually in multiples of one hundred. It is not clear what role these conscripts played in military campaigns or to what extent they constituted the bulk of a military force (Keightley 1969: 66–144). In Shang and Western Zhou times continuous liability to military service may have been limited to the retainers of nobles who lived near the capital or alongside regional officials in their fortified administrative centres (Lewis 1990: 53–64). Some of these retainers may have farmed the surrounding countryside but been available for military campaigns whenever they were needed. Most royal armies must have been composed of local rulers and their retainers assembled by regional officials and by the king, who had their own larger forces. It appears that at each level officials were responsible for arming and training their own followers. If soldiers had to abandon their crops to accompany their lords on military campaigns, other workers must have been available to cultivate their fields. These may have been full-time farmers, who were not normally called upon to fight but may have been requisitioned as porters in wartime to assist armies that passed through the regions where they lived (Lewis 1990: 55).

While conscript armies could be used to defend a state or wage war against others, they were not a source of internal power for kings or members of the upper classes. It has been suggested that the rulers of territorial states, especially multiethnic ones, could have used conscripts to suppress uprisings in remote parts of their kingdoms or played rivalrous neighbouring groups off against one another. The Inka rulers may have been pursuing this sort of policy when they moved portions of recently conquered ethnic groups nearer the centre of their kingdom and replaced them with settlers drawn from peoples who had long demonstrated their loyalty or when they encouraged ritualized competition among neighbouring groups. These arrangements did not, however, supply rulers with a reliable source of physical coercion. The injudicious application of such a policy might have created anarchy rather than increased the power of the state.

OFFICERS AND PROFESSIONAL SOLDIERS

Arguing that conscript armies were the only military force available to the rulers of early civilizations, Elman Service (1975) concluded that these were not true states in the sense that the legitimate deployment of physical force played a significant role in ensuring their viability. Rather, he suggested, extending the now-discredited view that chiefdoms were held together only by supernatural sanctions, early civilizations were large, chiefdom-like theocracies in which authority was sacerdotal and all sanctions were supernatural (91 n. 9). Without addressing in detail the nature of armies in early civilizations, Maurice Godelier (1986: 31–32) also maintained that in such societies the power of rulers resulted from the belief on the part of most of their lower-class subjects that powerful supernatural forces supported them. Godelier argued that, because the people in the Andean region thought that the Inka monarch was divine and kept the universe functioning, they believed that they owed their lives to him and accepted that this gave him the right to dominate and exploit them – that if they did not obey him supernatural powers would punish them and the well-being of the cosmos would be endangered (159–61).

Godelier was correct that Inka monarchs, like other Andean rulers and rulers in most other early civilizations, promoted a belief in their own divinity. Yet numerous subject peoples had only recently been incorporated into the Inka state, and many people who belonged to these societies would have remembered that, before they were ruled by the Inka king, their world had functioned perfectly well without him. Moreover, there is no evidence that subject groups anywhere accept theocratic claims easily or uncritically and much evidence that they generate their own counterideologies to oppose those of their rulers. If fear of divine sanctions alone were an effective control, why did all ancient states have to guard temples, palaces, and government storehouses from thieves and threaten robbers with drastic physical punishments? Why were Egyptian and Inka divine monarchs assassinated as a result of court intrigues? Why was the threat of violence needed to collect taxes in ancient Egypt and other early civilizations? Why did protests occur when, as happened in New Kingdom Egypt, governments could not pay their employees' wages? Why were there peasant revolts? Morton Fried (1967) strongly disagreed with Service's views and argued that physical force played an important role in managing early civilizations.

Service and Godelier were correct only to the extent that force alone is never sufficient to make a society work. Farmers in early civilizations depended on governments for defence from external attack and the maintenance of internal order and were prepared to tolerate and at least minimally support any regime that could do this. Capable rulers took care not to alienate most of the population by allowing rapacious officials to overtax and abuse them and won support by functioning as a source of prestige, status, and material rewards. Nevertheless, the rulers of early civilizations needed trustworthy and capable soldiers to guard them and their families, nobles and government officials, government storehouses, and tax collectors. They also frequently needed soldiers to garrison control points and frontiers and to wage wars that took men away from their homes for months or even years at a time. Some of this work could have been done by military corvées, but many tasks were better entrusted to professional soldiers, whose loyalty was reinforced by their socially and economically privileged status. As more complex forms of weapons and more sophisticated techniques of fighting developed, the need for more specialized training also encouraged the professionalization of the armed forces. These factors suggest that, contrary to Service, conscript armies were rarely if ever adequate for all the military and policing tasks that had to be performed in early civilizations.

The Inka, long considered to have had no career soldiers, are now acknowledged to have been in the process of building large professional armies (Grou 1989; Murra 1986). Rotating corvées of farmers called up for short periods of military service produced large armies that could overwhelm adjacent territories or intimidate the rulers of small polities into submitting to Inka rule. Yet armies of this sort were inadequate for wars that continued for years such as those that the Inka king Wayna Qhapaq was waging in Ecuador early in the sixteenth century. Inka rulers discovered that career soldiers could be more highly trained and better armed and hence produced more effective fighting forces. Well-trained and loyal soldiers were also needed to garrison administrative centres and protect Inka governors. Large numbers of full-time soldiers were settled near Cuzco both to protect and maintain order in the capital region and to be ready to move in any direction to suppress rebellions in the provinces (Hyslop 1990: 318). Prudence dictated that armies of conscripted subject peoples not be assembled within striking distance of Cuzco (Kendall 1973: 99). As the Inka state reached its ecologically sustainable boundaries, there was also a growing need for soldiers to defend its borders against incursions by tribal peoples living to the north, east, and south. This required establishing fortified garrisons that did not have ethnic affinities to local groups living on either side of the border they were guarding.

Full-time soldiers to perform these special tasks were recruited from subjugated ethnic groups that were noted for their martial skills. These groups, which were otherwise a potential threat to Inka control, were transformed into supporters of the Inka state by assigning them a privileged position within the kingdom's social and economic hierarchy. Individual farmers who distinguished themselves in battle while performing military corvées were also recruited as full-time soldiers, while instructors who trained young commoners to fight may also have channelled the strongest, bravest, and most skillful into military careers. Inkas-by-privilege may have been selected on the basis of their personal performance to become middle-level officers, commanding units of one hundred, five hundred, or one thousand soldiers (Grou 1989).

These recruits were specially trained and armed with shields, helmets, and round metal plates to protect their bodies, and they fought with metal axes, metal-tipped spears, and heavy stone maces. They and their families were exempt from any form of taxation. Career soldiers were frequently granted land owned by the king for their support. It is unclear if the garrisons of frontier forts took turns working this land and guarding forts or if the land was worked for them by local populations as part of their labour tax (Hyslop 1990: 148–72). Extensive government farms were created to feed the royal armies. The Cochabamba Valley in Bolivia was a particularly important centre of maize production that freed the full-time soldiers stationed near Cuzco and elsewhere from having to grow food to feed themselves and their families (La Lone and La Lone 1987; Wachtel 1982). The loyalty of seasoned regiments of full-time soldiers and their commanders, who had served Wayna Qhapaq in Ecuador, assured his son Atawalpa of victory over the larger armies, made up mainly of peasant conscripts, that fought for his half-brother Waskar when the two princes struggled to succeed their dead father.

The Inka king was surrounded by a palace guard of two thousand soldiers and a personal bodyguard of one hundred high-ranking officers. These units were composed of nobles and men recruited from special ethnic groups such as the Cañaris, who were renowned for their military ability. The Cañaris and their families had been resettled in the Yucay Valley, near Cuzco, where they had been granted tax-free land. The king's guard, Inka nobles, and full-time soldiers formed the core of any major Inka army. Such armies were officered at the highest levels by Inka nobles, who commanded units of twenty-five hundred and five thousand soldiers. An entire army made up of a number of such units was led either by the king or by a close royal relative who served as its commander in chief (Kendall 1973: 98). Some of these officers performed military duties only as one of a number of high-level administrative functions. Others, however, spent their careers leading armies (Grou 1989).

When the Egyptian kings abandoned their early policy of depopulating adjacent regions (Hoffman 1979) for one of constructing forts along their frontiers to control the movement of people and goods, these forts were probably manned by full-time soldiers. Middle Kingdom forts in Nubia were garrisoned by rotating military units until the end of the Twelfth Dynasty, when these garrisons were replaced by settlers from Egypt. At least during the Twelfth Dynasty, grain was sent in bulk from Egypt to the Nubian forts rather than grown locally in that infertile region. The garrisons were also supplied with standard military equipment, such as hide shields and stone-tipped spears, some of which may have been manufactured at the large Egyptian forts in Lower Nubia (S. Smith 1995; Vila 1970). Royal palaces, provincial administrative centres, and government warehouses were probably also guarded by full-time soldiers. Beginning in the First Intermediate Period, companies of forty lightly clad archers or spearmen were depicted in the service of regional officials. Similar squads of soldiers were associated with provincial governors in the early Middle Kingdom (Andreu 1997: 19–21). These were probably the same sort of full-time soldiers or police that had been employed by the central government in the Old Kingdom. Beginning at that time, large numbers of Medjay pastoralists from the Eastern Desert, as well as Nubians and Libyans, were recruited as soldiers and settled in Egypt with their families. One of their tasks was to assist government officials to collect the grain tax from recalcitrant Egyptian farmers, whom the soldiers would arrest, flog, and imprison until they delivered what bureaucrats had estimated was the government's share of the harvest. In the Sixth Dynasty, companies of these foreign recruits, as well as conscripted commoners, were led by high-ranking officials on military expeditions against Canaan (Strouhal 1992: 202–3; Trigger 1976a: 54–63).

Senwosret III boasted that increasing royal revenues during the Middle Kingdom permitted him to expand the number of soldiers in his service and increase their remuneration (Lichtheim 1973: 199). It is uncertain whether such soldiers performed their military duties full-time. They may have been given land to work themselves or have worked for them by tenant farmers. There is no evidence of specialized weaponry, apart from large shields and battleaxes, prior to the introduction of chariots, compound bows, and new and more effective types of bronze swords and daggers from southwestern Asia during the Second Intermediate Period. Nevertheless, professional soldiers appear to have been specially trained to move in formation and fight as units (Andreu 1997: 23–25). They may also have played a leading role in the attacks on fortified Canaanite towns that are depicted in tombs of the Fifth and Sixth Dynasties. These assaults involved the undermining of town walls and the use of wheeled siege ladders by soldiers armed with axes. Large armies are recorded as being led by government officials during the Old Kingdom and by kings' sons, who were sometimes junior co-rulers, in the Middle Kingdom (Andreu 1997: 21–23). There is no evidence that these leaders, who were titled *ỉmy-r mšʿ* (overseer of an expedition) or *ṯsw* (commander), were full-time military personnel. If there were full-time officers, it was probably at a lower rank than is documented in tombs and funerary texts. Professional soldiers increased in numbers and were far more complexly organized in the New Kingdom (Schulman 1964).

Because of the crucial importance of warfare in Shang and Western Zhou China, military organization appears to have been professionalized to a considerable degree. Among those employed full-time may have been some military officers, troops who were trained to handle special equipment such as chariots, and numerous soldiers who protected the upper classes and helped to enforce their authority. Many different types of army-related offices are mentioned in Shang texts. General categories include *ya* and *shi* (officers, commanders), *ma* (chariot officers), *she* (archery officers), *chuan* (dog officers), and *shu* (garrison commanders). Dogs may have been used in military and police actions, as well as for hunting, which was viewed as a form of military training (Chao 1972: 14–15, 74–86; Chou 1968: 276–320; Vandermeersch 1980: 66–68). Each of these categories was subdivided into various ranks. While some offices may have been entirely military, others seem to have been of a mixed nature. Chariot and dog officers may have been responsible for breeding horses and dogs as well as for their military training and use. *Yang* (sheep officers) appear to have been agricultural officials who were involved with military campaigns on which animals were likely to be captured as booty (Keightley 1969: 88). *Kung* (artisan officers), whose concerns were not primarily military in nature, perhaps accompanied military expeditions to attend to the provisioning and repair of military equipment (24–27). The distinction between military and non-military offices does not appear to have been closely drawn, and it may not be correct to speak of a specifically military as distinguished from a civil administration. There also appears to have been much overlap in function among the holders of different military titles.

Next to ritual vessels, elite weapons such as dagger-axes, knives, and arrow and spear points, along with helmets, shield bosses, and chariot fittings, were the most important products of the Shang bronze industry (Chêng 1960: 156–76). Horse-drawn chariots were costly to manufacture and use but were produced in large numbers, which suggests that they were manned by commoners as well as by aristocratic army leaders. This impression is reinforced by the large numbers of chariots, together with their horses and personnel, that were buried in ritual contexts at Anyang and elsewhere (Lu 1993). Chinese tradition maintains that chariot drivers were menials until the Spring and Autumn period (722–481 B.C.) (Creel 1970: 276–80). Chariots appear to have been used not only as mobile raised platforms for directing battles but also to break the ranks of enemy foot-soldiers. Since considerable experience was needed to drive and fight from a chariot, only well-trained, probably career soldiers could have used them. Each chariot carried a driver, a dagger-axe man, and an archer. Chariot burials suggest that there were two crews for each chariot and that every chariot was accompanied by about one hundred foot-soldiers. Chariots were deployed in basic units of five and larger units of twenty-five. Two of these larger units would have been made up of three hundred men (Chao 1972: 79–81). The infantry was organized in squads of ten men, each under the command of a better-armed leader. Ten of these squads formed a company and three companies a combat unit. Archers were also organized in units of three hundred men (Chou 1968: 279–84; Hsu and Linduff 1988: 27).

The Shang king appears to have been able to mobilize many soldiers, whom he sometimes led himself. Otherwise, he appointed generals, who were often princes and in two recorded cases women (*fu*) of the royal household. Princes had their own officers and soldiers under their command. Individual royal armies appear to have numbered from three thousand to five thousand soldiers organized into right, centre, and left divisions. The king sometimes sent royal forces to help provincial administrators suppress rebellious local officials, carry out punitive raids against foreign enemies, and annex new territory and to man border garrisons and facilitate the settlement of new areas (Keightley 1979–80; Vandermeersch 1980).

The entire Western Zhou male ruling class was trained as warriors (Lewis 1990: 243). Zhou kings were personally protected by their 'tiger guards' (*hu chen*) and had a large standing army six divisions of which were located near their old capital in the Wei Valley and eight more around the eastern administrative centre they established at Chengzhou (Chêng 1963: 294; Hsu and Linduff 1988: 241–45). Each of these fourteen armies was divided into a right and a left half. Regional and local officials in charge of fortified strongholds or walled administrative centres had their own smaller armies or armed retainers. These forces guarded against enemy attack and controlled the surrounding countryside. Weapons were stored when not in use in or near the leader's ancestral temple (Hsu and Linduff 1988: 268–69; Lewis 1990: 23, 260). Regional and local officials led their soldiers to join the royal army when ordered to do so (Lewis 1990: 261).

The divisions of the royal standing army are said to have been self-supporting (Keightley 1969: 267–78). Hence some or all of these soldiers and their families may have grown crops around the centres where they were based. Alternatively, full-time farmers may have been assigned to produce food for these regiments. If such soldiers were engaged in warfare during the growing season or had to accompany the king on lengthy military campaigns, they and their families must have depended on surplus food produced by others (Lewis 1990: 261–69). The relative proportion of military as opposed to other forms of labour appears to have increased from conscripted soldiers through armed supporters of provincial rulers and the standing armies of the king to full-time armed guards, charioteers, and military officers.

The later development, during the Warring States period (481–221 B.C.), of mass conscript armies composed not only of retainers (*guoren*) living in and around administrative centres, but also of country people (*yeren*) was accompanied by the symbolic division of the year into seasons of growth (spring and summer) and seasons of death (autumn and winter), the latter being the time for interstate wars. Mark Lewis (1990: 65) suggests that before that time the elite and their retainers hunted and waged war in every season. It was also not until late Zhou times that armies were legally and ritually distinguished from the state and it became possible for generals to commend, reward, and punish soldiers independently of rulers (Lewis 1990: 126–27; Maisels 1999: 309–11).

The Aztec and other polities in the Valley of Mexico linked male political and administrative careers to military service as well as to status at birth. All military achievement was individual and calculated according to how many enemy warriors a soldier had captured alive in battle. Combat was therefore primarily a personal enterprise. Every prisoner captured entitled a soldier to be promoted to a higher rank in the warrior hierarchy. Each rank was associated with a different costume, insignia, and privileges. The king publicly conferred these distinctions on soldiers at annual religious celebrations. Nobles who had captured four prisoners would join the eagle (*caucuauhtin*) or ocelot (*ocelomeh*) orders, which had their meeting places in the royal palace (Hassig 1988: 45). Membership in these orders was a prerequisite for holding any significant military or civil administrative position. The capture of more prisoners led to membership in still higher military orders, the *otontin* (Otomies) and *cuahchicqueh* (shorn ones), which qualified a noble to hold the highest military positions (Hassig 1988: 45–46). The two principal army leaders, the *tlacateccatl* (he who commands warriors) and the *tlacochcalcatl* (the man of the place where weapons are stored) were close relatives of the king, and one of them usually was chosen as his successor. The king, as supreme head of the army, bore the title *tlacatecuhtli* (lord of warriors) (Soustelle 1961: 44).

Warfare opened a narrow path for commoners into the nobility (Clendinnen 1991: 120). As we have seen, commoners who had captured four prisoners were made eagle nobles. Such men were granted either the produce of a plot of land in some conquered city-state or a supply of maize from the palace, the two being effectively the same in that palace officials oversaw the growing of corn in tributary states and its transportation to Tenochtitlan. This would also explain why it was said that, while eagle nobles were granted land, unlike hereditary nobles they were not also granted bound labourers (mayeque) to cultivate it (Hassig 1988: 29). Nevertheless, such revenues made eagle nobles, like hereditary ones, independent of their calpollis (Hassig 1988: 145–46). An eagle noble no longer had to earn a living with his hands or perform corvée. Eagle nobles who captured many enemy soldiers could join the higher military orders, but their lack of hereditary nobility and of an upper-class education debarred them from holding major administrative offices (Berdan 1982: 103).

Ennobled commoners trained young men to fight in calpolli schools, spent part of each year guarding the royal palace, and arrested and executed people on the orders of the king and of palace judges and administrators. They watched over the central armouries where lethal weapons were kept out of the hands of commoners during peacetime. They also provided experienced middle-level leadership and highly skilled fighters for military campaigns. In this way the Aztec state recruited career soldiers who lacked the administrative training a hereditary noble would have had to provide leadership for the army as well as a police force which ensured that the decisions of the king and palace administrators were carried out. Eagle nobles and hereditary nobles who commanded the army constituted a substantial body of full-time soldiers at the disposal of the state (Berdan 1982: 64–65).

In Mesopotamia the key responsibility of the Early Dynastic kings was to protect their city-states from attack by neighbouring states or nomadic groups. Armed attendants were killed and buried with rulers at Ur (Postgate 1992: 241), and there are depictions of uniformed soldiers wearing metal or leather helmets, leather armour, and cloaks, carrying shields, and armed with bronze spears, maces, daggers, sickle-shaped swords, adzes, and blades mounted on wooden handles. Soldiers of this sort were trained to fight in phalanx-like formations that would have allowed them to cut through the ranks of less well-organized adversaries (Fig. 12.2). The infantry was accompanied by a primitive 'chariot' force using heavy wooden carts with four solid wheels, each pulled by four onagers. These carts transported two fighters armed with spears, javelins, and axes. As in China, such vehicles were used as observation platforms to direct a battle. On level terrain they were also employed as assault vehicles (Mikhaeli 1969; Postgate 1992: 245–50). Thus there appears to have been in each Mesopotamian city-state a core of full-time or nearly full-time soldiers, employed, trained, and equipped by the king. One of their roles may have been to curb pastoral intruders at times of the year when most people were engaged in farming and city-states would normally have been at peace with each other. In return for their military service, these soldiers were assigned the use of land that belonged to the palace. In many cases the use of such land was inherited from one generation to the next, along with the military duties

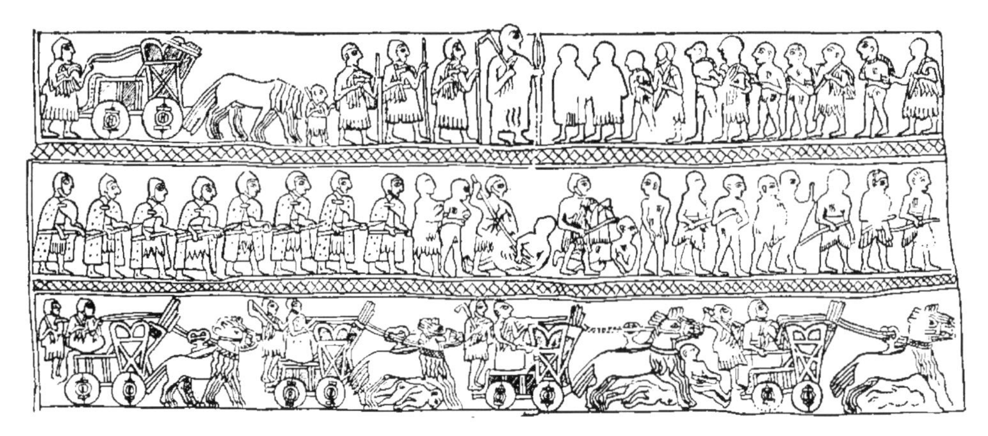

a

b

12.2. Mesopotamian battle scenes: (a) one side of the so-called Royal Standard of Ur, a box-like object from royal tomb PG 779 in the Royal Cemetery at Ur – from bottom to top, it portrays a chariot charge cutting down the enemy, followed by infantry, the taking of prisoners, and presenting these prisoners to the king. The 'standard' is a mosaic of lapis lazuli and other stones, shell, and ivory set in wood. Early Dynastic period, ca. 2700 B.C., height 20.2 cm; (b) the Stela of the Vultures, carved in limestone, commemorates a victory of King Eannatum of Lagash over the neighbouring city of Umma. This panel portrays enemy corpses being trampled under foot by heavily armed infantry fighting in a phalanx formation, from Telloh (Girsu), Early Dynastic III, ca. 2450 B.C., height of panel ca. 85 cm. Sources: (a) after C. L. Woolley, *The Sumerians* (Oxford 1928), 51; (b) J. Oates, *Babylon* (London, 1979), 27.

associated with it. Mesopotamian career soldiers were bound to kings who were not only their military superiors but also their landlords. Other palace land produced surplus grain that supported economic activities related to the army. Metal was obtained from long-distance traders in return for grain or cloth produced by palace dependents, and some of this metal was turned into weapons perhaps in palace workshops or, alternatively, by artisans working for the palace in their own homes (R. McC. Adams 1966: 143).

Career soldiers were trained and officered by high-ranking palace officials. In peacetime these soldiers guarded the palace and royal properties and ensured that the king's orders were carried out. Control of a standing army was a significant source of political power in a city-state, where even a small amount of force could alter the internal balance of power and hence the pattern of government significantly. Thus the influence of kings tended to increase at the expense of temples and rich landowners. In wartime, career soldiers provided a trained core for an army still made up largely of conscripts (Postgate 1992: 241–42).

Mesopotamian kings generally appear to have had palace staffs of about five hundred people, many of whom were probably soldiers. Sargon of Akkad claimed that over ten times that number ate bread in his palace daily, and his total standing army must have been considerably larger. Shulgi, a hegemon of the Ur III dynasty, recruited a regiment of spearmen among the citizens of his capital (Postgate 1992: 242; Van De Mieroop 1999: 34). Prisoners captured in battle were held for ransom, killed, or put to work as labourers for palaces and temples. In Hammurabi's time, soldiers were generally ransomed by their families (Postgate 1992: 254–56). If their families lacked the resources to pay for this, ransoms were sought (as loans?) from temples and, as a last resort, from the king (Pritchard 1955: 167, law 32). Hegemonic rulers used their military power to try to subdue resource-rich areas to the northwest and east of Mesopotamia and south along the Persian Gulf. Control over these areas appears invariably to have been fragile and transitory.

A Yoruba state had no single standing army, but that did not mean that there were no full-time soldiers. Kings had armed attendants who not only protected them and their palaces but also arrested people, brought them to court, and executed criminals. The kings of Benin recruited and armed a large number of young men who acted as their bodyguards, policed the palace, conveyed messages, and enforced their wishes throughout the state. For as long as they served the king, these young men were forbidden either to wear any clothes or to marry, observances which betokened their childlike devotion to the monarch. When they left his service, the king clothed them and gave them valuable presents (Bradbury 1973: 61; H. Roth 1903: 24).

Titled members of the main extended patrilineages in Yoruba capitals and smaller towns, in addition to having numerous male kin who followed them into battle, were attended by a permanent entourage composed of as many as 150 well-armed kinsmen, mercenaries, and slaves. Supporting these retainers, who were full-time soldiers, consumed a major portion of these leaders' resources. These soldiers did not wear uniforms but were supplied with padded jackets, as well as single- and double-edged swords, spears, lances, and javelins made of iron. Unlike conscripted soldiers, they did not fight with clubs and slings. In the northern and central woodland-savanna region, most full-time soldiers were horsemen armed with thrusting spears, while infantry, equipped with leaf-shaped swords that were better suited for close fighting, predominated in the forested south. Maintaining horses was difficult even in the northern Yoruba regions and added greatly to the cost of outfitting retainers. It also made the distinction between full-time and part-time soldiers much more important in the north than it was in the south, where armies were composed almost entirely of infantry and only major leaders rode horses. Rulers of powerful northern states such as Oyo, who were precluded from leading soldiers into battle, invested in horses which they supplied to lineage leaders in return for a larger share of the booty from military campaigns (R. Smith 1973).

By owning large numbers of slaves, leading Yoruba could produce enough food to support many full-time soldiers. Promising slaves were also recruited as full-time soldiers (R. Smith 1969: 119). In peacetime these supporters constituted an armed guard and were a major source of political power for their patrons. They also enabled the Yoruba leadership to keep the lower classes under control. In wartime they formed the well-trained and equipped nuclei of the larger units that came together to form a city-state army. The full-time soldiers who were members and followers of each extended family rallied to that family's ward and quarter leaders.

In Oyo the state army was led by the seven Oyo Mesi, who constituted the state council that governed the kingdom in collaboration with the king. Each of them led the forces from his section of the city as well as the armed fighters sent by his dependents in the countryside. The army as a whole was commanded by the *basorun*. Special military titles were bestowed on important office-holders, cavalry leaders, and leaders of the vanguard, which was made up of young fighters. In addition, there was an elite group of seventy mounted warriors called *eso* who ranked militarily immediately below the Oyo Mesi and served as subordinate commanders under them. The Oyo Mesi conferred this title on individuals with the approval of the king. All but one of these warriors lived with their followers in a special section of the capital called Oke Eso. The one exception, the *are ona kakamfo*, had a military base near the border and was usually not allowed to visit the capital because the Oyo Mesi feared that he might conspire with the king against them. An unsuccessful campaign by the rural military force he commanded was customarily cause for his execution. The Oyo army was divided into a centre and two wings and engaged in skirmishes, raids, set battles, and sieges but rarely attempted to take a town by direct assault (Ajayi and Smith 1971: 13–55; Law 1977: 74–75; R. Smith 1969: 120–29; 1973).

In Benin, despite the greater power of the king, the army was usually led by the *ezomo*, a hereditary official whose position corresponded to that of the basorun in Oyo. He and his fellow councillors lacked the power of the Oyo Mesi, however, and he was clearly subordinate to the king. Alternatively, the king could appoint as army commander the *iyase*, who was the chief town official of Benin city and the oba's main rival for power. After he had commanded an army, the iyase was required to leave Benin and settle in a town or village outside the capital and a new iyase was appointed; thus by conferring army leadership on an iyase the king could eliminate a dangerous rival (Bradbury 1957: 36, 43–44). Presumably, the wealth that could be acquired from leading a successful military campaign was the main reason that an iyase would accept such a command.

Among the Maya, even if armies were mainly conscripts, kings and nobles would at the very least also have had guards and armed retainers. A few representations suggest that some kings had armed retainers, perhaps of foreign origin, supplied with specialized weapons, such as obsidian-tipped spears. (Henderson 1981: 137). The upper classes and their retainers would have provided leadership for Maya armies.

CAREER SOLDIERS AND CIVIL AUTHORITIES

In early civilizations, armies did not develop, as they did in the Roman Empire and some other later preindustrial states, into separate institutions whose commanders possessed power independent of the state and were therefore able to challenge or dominate civil authorities. The highest-ranking leadership of military forces was always drawn from the upper echelons of the general power hierarchy. Yet in all six well-documented early civilizations some soldiers were better trained and armed than the farmer and artisan conscripts who might periodically be assembled to attack neighbouring states or defend their own, and the poorly documented Maya do not appear to have been an exception to this pattern.

Some of these more specialized soldiers appear to have been engaged in military activities full-time. Others combined farming and soldiery but were exempt from taxation and corvée labour. Where there was a need to defend the state against external enemies who were not tied to an agricultural cycle, there may have been a greater need for soldiers who were wholly disengaged from agricultural production. Yet full-time soldiers provided the cores of mass armies in all early civilizations and were essential to the support of civil authorities within each state. In most cases, the ultimate control of military and police forces lay with the king. Among the Yoruba, control was shared by non-royal officials who belonged to a small number of powerful lineages, but even these were able to use their armed retainers to control slaves and intimidate the lower classes. Career soldiers could be provided with more elaborate equipment and, because they were better trained and disciplined, could make better use of it. Chariots were advantageous for directing battles and smashing through poorly coordinated infantry lines. Metal weapons were more deadly than ordinary stone or bone ones. Shields and armour, whether made of metal, thick leather, or padded cloth, protected combatants. On the whole, however, technology was less important than the discipline and fighting style most evident in the phalanx techniques of Mesopotamian soldiers and the military formations of Chinese ones.

Professional soldiers were recruited in various ways. For Aztec commoners it was as a reward for valour. For Yoruba slaves it was a way to escape from agricultural drudgery and a move towards eventual emancipation. Mesopotamian kings recruited regiments from among the free men of their own cities, presumably those who were seeking to better themselves economically. Inka officials recruited career soldiers from among ethnic groups and individuals who displayed a conspicuous talent for military life. Career soldiers were paid with grain allotments or given the use of land which they or their families could work themselves or rent to full-time farmers. The economic benefits that they and their families enjoyed were inducements to support their patrons, since continuing service depended on their patrons' military and political success.

Professional military forces were larger in territorial states than in city-states, but it is unclear whether a higher percentage of the population was so employed. Career soldiers always represented a small fraction of the total population. Most states relied on temporary conscripts to form the bulk of their armies. In the Valley of Mexico all free men were subject to military service and had been specially trained for it. In Shang China military service may have been limited to some of the farmers and labourers who lived in and around administrative centres, many of whom might better be described as soldiers who farmed in their spare time than as farmers who also served as soldiers. While there is no direct evidence of conscript armies among the Classic Maya, there is no direct proof of career soldiers either. Denying the existence of conscript soldiers would suggest that Maya warfare was a ritual game mainly played by kings and nobles, a view that does not accord with what we know about it.

In city-states professional soldiers were key in asserting the power of kings and ruling groups over rival factions and the lower classes. The wealth that the leaders of hegemonic states extracted from neighbouring polities augmented the ability of rulers to support more soldiers and maintain their political dominance. Yet the decentralized military and political leadership of Oyo demonstrates that hegemony did not inevitably increase the political power of kings. Nevertheless, even where kings did not control the army, military success reflected favourably on the role they played as the ultimate intermediaries between the human and the divine realms.

13 Sociopolitical Constants and Variables

The development of early civilizations appears inevitably to have produced monarchs; even in societies with patterns of dual leadership at lower levels there was a single preeminent ruler. The unity of the state seems to have been conceptualized by imagining the political, economic, legal, military, moral, and cosmological dimensions of society to be embodied in the person and will of a single human being. Kingship was viewed as inherited within kin groups; the Sumerians may have believed that it was conferred on individuals by the gods, but even for them kingship was hereditary in practice. The powers of kings, the roles they played, and the ways in which kingship was conceptualized varied considerably from one early civilization to another. In Egypt monarchs could exercise great personal influence, although doing so required considerable skill. Among the Yoruba, in contrast, kings had to share power with the leaders of important kin groups and sometimes were no more than figureheads. Kings were present in all early civilizations not so much because they were practically necessary as because kingship was a master concept in terms of which other, less comprehensible political relations could be understood and negotiated. The unity of states had to be achieved not only politically but also symbolically.

All early civilizations were based on the idea of social and economic inequality, which not only informed the understanding of society as a whole but also pervaded the family. As a consequence, ideas of inequality and obedience to authority were inculcated in everyone from earliest childhood. As children grew older, the concept of obedience was reinforced in schools, social life, and relations with government officials. In each early civilization a small number of privileged people were supported by a large number of taxpaying farmers. This upper class governed society and controlled much of its wealth and surplus labour. Beneath it were various groups of specialists ranked according to how much they resembled the upper classes in not having to engage in hard manual labour. Ordinary bureaucrats normally ranked above professional soldiers and they in turn above specialized craft workers and household servants. The highest grade of farmers possessed land, either individually or collectively; of lower status were farmers who had to rent land, farmers who were tied to land owned by others, and landless manual labourers. At the bottom of the class hierarchy in many early civilizations were slaves: temporary debt slaves, who could hope to regain their freedom, hereditary household slaves, and prisoners of war or criminals, who were often condemned for the rest of their lives to labour under extremely wretched conditions. Slaves tended to be most common in city-state civilizations. In territorial states they were often replaced by individuals who were bound to the service of government institutions or individual members of the upper class but could not be bought and sold. Both slaves and such bound individuals were relatively few.

There was some vertical mobility in all early civilizations, but it varied considerably in degree. Slaves were absorbed fairly easily into the lower free classes. Upward mobility was possible for commoners in states that were expanding either economically or militarily, but it was impeded by the difficulty of acquiring the appropriate skills and generally subject to the approval of the upper classes.

The rich and powerful strengthened their social position by contracting marital alliances with members of their own class. Rulers often married their younger daughters to officials or client rulers to consolidate the support of such individuals, and upper-class families might maritally co-opt promising young men. While peasants married within the same village or landowning group and artisans often married among themselves, the upper classes forged marital links within their own class that often extended across whole states and sometimes united families of equivalent status in neighbouring polities. These far-reaching ties helped them to cooperate in controlling the rest of society.

In all the early civilizations for which we have adequate documentation, the privileges of the upper classes were protected by armed forces and the legal system. While lower-class conscripts were generally used to fight foreign wars, professional soldiers served as a police force to protect the upper classes, government property, and officials. Commoners were encouraged to settle their own disputes, provided that this did not disadvantage the upper classes, but the legal system invariably had higher levels at which decisions were enforced by the punitive power of the king. This system was used to intimidate the lower classes and protect the privileges of the wealthy and powerful.

FORMS OF STATE

The early civilizations in our sample exhibited only two varieties of political organization: city-states and territorial states. These types of states were differentiated on the basis of numerous organizational principles not only from each other but from later regional urbanized kingdoms, later city-states, and true empires. City-states in early civilizations controlled small territories and often had a single urban centre surrounded by farming villages, although the geographically largest of them and those with the most dispersed populations also had small towns that served as secondary administrative centres. These secondary centres caused the general arrangement of settlement units of those city-states to resemble superficially the arrangements of territorial states. Other aspects of their settlement patterns were, however, very different.

City-states frequently had numerous farmers living in their urban centres and intensively working the land nearby. This arrangement reduced the cost of transporting food to the city and offered farmers' homes maximum protection against attacks by neighbouring states. It also encouraged the broader participation of the well-to-do in political life. Cities were centres for the production and marketing of goods. High-quality raw materials imported from abroad were sold publicly by long-distance traders (the Maya being a possible exception). Full-time craft workers manufactured goods not only for temples, the government, and the upper classes but also for other craft workers and for farmers. Markets made such goods more accessible to ordinary people, and this increased the demand for manufactured products and supported more specialists and the production of better-quality goods.

Territorial states had one or more royal capitals and numerous regional administrative centres. These urban centres tended to be inhabited only by administrators, full-time craft workers, and labourers employed by the government and by government officials. Farmers lived in villages in the countryside and, in addition to growing food, produced handicrafts from locally available raw materials and exchanged these products at local markets. Full-time specialists generally worked for the government, often in government workshops, where they were provided with exotic raw materials obtained by the state. Relatively little of what they produced was accessible to ordinary people and then only as gifts from members of the ruling class.

Archaeological evidence makes it clear that neither the ancient Egyptian nor the Inka territorial state evolved from a city-state as defined here. Egypt's development involved the political unification of a series of chiefdoms or small early states, and the Inka united a large number of chiefdoms. In China, the Yellow River floodplain was probably a zone of chiefdoms resembling those found in Predynastic Egypt and the central Andean highlands rather than of city-states prior to the emergence of territorial states. Nor did the city-states in our sample eventually become territorial states. Mesopotamia moved toward a definitive regional unification in the mid-second millennium B.C., but large urban centres continued to play a crucial role in the economic, cultural, and religious life of the region rather than coming to resemble the administrative centres of early territorial states. In Egypt after the New Kingdom and in late Zhou China, territorial states evolved more populous and economically more important urban centres, economies that were less controlled by the central government, and administrations that were increasingly based on the centralized control of military power. Rather than city-states' evolving into territorial states (or, alternatively, developing from the breakup of such states), in Egypt, Mesopotamia, and China civilizations of both types evolved into a single later form: the urbanized regional kingdom (Trigger 1985a).

Elizabeth Stone (1997: 25), following Eisenstadt, Abitbol, and Chazan (1988: 186–92), has suggested that it would have been much easier to create territorial states where existing hereditary nobilities could be absorbed into expanding power structures than where expansive rulers had to rely wholly on military power. Mesopotamia and the Yoruba, the early civilizations that she treats as quintessential examples of city-states, did not have hereditary upper classes. In them a heterarchical sharing of power resulted in large urban centres where there was political competition, a moderate amount of social mobility, a high degree of entrepreneurship, and broad access to goods produced by full-time artisans. Kings were not embedded in a hereditary nobility through which they could dominate the rest of society. Instead, they shared power with other sections of the upper class and played a mediating role in city-state politics. While they were regarded as essential for placating the gods, they reigned with the consent of their more powerful subjects.

All the rulers of the city-states in the Valley of Mexico, and probably the Maya kings as well, belonged to a hereditary nobility that was coterminous with the upper class. The mutual recognition that the Aztec monarchs and the rulers of tributary states all belonged to the same, genealogically related regional upper class may have provided a basis for closer relations between them. The Aztec used marital alliances to establish more intimate ties with the rulers of some subject states, and this may help to explain how they were able to create a tributary network far more extensive than any Yoruba or Mesopotamian one. It also might be argued that, because of their hereditary nobilities, the Aztec and Maya had greater potential for creating regional urbanized kingdoms than did the Yoruba and the Mesopotamians. Evolutionists who do not distinguish between territorial states and regional kingdoms might also argue that the

Aztec and Maya represented an intermediate level of political development between the Yoruba and the Mesopotamians, on the one hand, and territorial states with hereditary nobilities, such as those of the Inka and Shang, on the other.

Yet the claim made in the Valley of Mexico that all kings and nobles were descended from the god Quetzalcoatl was paralleled by the claim of Yoruba and Benin rulers that they and all the members of Yoruba royal clans were descended from the god Oduduwa. While the Aztec quickly expanded the descendants of their first kings, traced through either the male or female line, into a sizable nobility, the Yoruba curbed the expansion of their royal clans by restricting membership to male descendants and creating economic conditions that encouraged most kings' sons who had no hope of becoming kings to seek adoption into their mothers' patrilineages. Hence the potential for creating a larger hereditary aristocracy, which was actively pursued in the Valley of Mexico, was rejected by the Yoruba. This calls into question the proposal that the presence or absence of a hereditary nobility can by itself account for the major political differences between the Valley of Mexico and the Yoruba. It is also noteworthy that the Mesopotamians, who appear to have lacked any arrangements predisposing them to develop a hereditary elite, repeatedly created hegemonic city-state systems and that Mesopotamia, after remaining a city-state system for almost two millennia, was transformed into a regional kingdom. There is no convincing evidence that this was about to happen either in the Valley of Mexico or among the Maya. The chief source of power for both Mesopotamian and Aztec kings was their control of the army and the distribution of tribute. The Yoruba kings, by contrast, did not control the army and had to share foreign tribute with their chief councillors. While it has been argued that the expansion of royal power in Mesopotamia resulted from foreign ideas imposed on the region by Semitic-speaking pastoral leaders, the increasing military power of Sumerian rulers allowed them to bring about an unprecedented degree of economic centralization within the hegemonic city-state system they created during the Ur III period. The Yoruba rulers were prevented from doing this by being forced to share military power with other leaders.

Both the Inka and Chinese territorial states had hereditary ruling classes, and incorporating the hereditary rulers of numerous small polities into a national upper class may have played a significant role in the unification of Egypt. In Egypt hereditary nobles were, however, quickly eliminated as major powerholders, and thereafter, at least in theory, the power of officials depended entirely on royal favour. Thus hereditary nobilities were not essential for the governance of all territorial states, and the preexistence of a hereditary nobility does not appear to have influenced whether early civilizations developed as city-states or territorial states. There is also no evidence that the presence of a hereditary upper class accelerated the rate at which city-states were transformed into regional kingdoms.

Why some early civilizations developed as city-state systems and others developed as territorial states is unclear. The limited variation in our sample suggests that viable early civilizations could be organized in only a limited number of ways. Perhaps only two general forms of political organization functioned well enough to endure for a significant length of time. Once city-state systems or territorial states arose in a region, there seems to have been little prospect of the development of the alternative form of political organization. Either type of state seems eventually to have been able to evolve into a regional kingdom.

The central governments of early civilizations preferred that small groups, such as extended families, landowning collectivities, and craft associations, be self-regulating. Higher-level authorities intervened only when their interests were threatened by specific forms of non-compliance, such as refusal to pay taxes in kind or to supply corvée labour, or by the breakdown of local order. Otherwise, letting local groups manage their own affairs reduced the cost of government.

In city-states, rich landowners, powerful lineages, temple corporations, merchants' associations, and influential voluntary groups had their own forms of self-government and were represented in various ways on councils at village, ward, or city levels. These councils, which exercised both legislative and judicial functions, shared power with or organized their activities around a king. Administrative procedures were less formal than in territorial states because communication could be more direct and decision making more decentralized. In some city-states, especially hegemonic ones that administered tributary networks, kings were able to use their control over the army and the distribution of tribute to enhance their power and move towards a more centralized form of government.

In territorial states and hegemonic city-states, high-level administration appears to have originated within the royal household, and a distinction between the royal household and the state developed only slowly. From Old Kingdom times on, the Egyptians differentiated between the officers and revenues of the royal court and those of the various branches of government, but into the New Kingdom royal estates were used to support both the royal family and the state. This reluctance to distinguish clearly between the royal household and the state was reflected in a similar reluctance to assign mutually exclusive and precisely defined duties to individual officials. High-ranking officials seem to have been viewed as officers of the king's household and therefore bound to do whatever the king ordered. Max Weber called this a patriarchal form of government. Eventually, however, these states came to display two types of administration – either delegational or bureaucratic. In delegational systems a king, while keeping an area around the capital under his direct control and receiving a share of the taxes collected by officials in every part of the realm, delegated a full (or nearly full) range of powers over more distant provinces to subordinate officials. Central control could be strengthened by relocating subordinate officials from time to time. The bureaucratic approach strengthened the power of the central government by dividing authority to administer different activities, both at the capital and in provincial and local centres, into a sufficient number of parallel structures that no single official had enough power to challenge the central authority. While delegational states were harder to hold together, bureaucratic ones were often less efficiently governed, especially when officials were moved at frequent intervals not only from one province to another but also from one branch of administration to another, unfamiliar one.

FORMS OF FAMILY

Family organization among early civilizations varied, although it generally had a masculine bias. The Yoruba, Chinese, and people in the Valley of Mexico lived in patrilineal extended households. So did the Mesopotamians, although over time the number of families living together appears to have grown smaller and even to have given way to nuclear families, especially in urban centres. The Classic Maya are generally believed to have lived in patrilineal extended-family groups, but this is denied as a general principle by some Mayanists and considered inapplicable to some major urban centres by others. Andean highland peoples lived in extended-family units, although in some areas these groups were matrilineal rather than patrilineal. In Egypt the ideal household was a nuclear family, although often at least parts of two adult generations lived together. There was no correlation between different types of family organization and the distinction between city-states and territorial states.

To some extent, different types of family organization may represent a survival of various forms that had existed in particular parts of the world prior to the development of early civilizations. The special emphasis placed on endogamous landholding units and dual leadership at lower social levels in the Valley of Mexico and highland Peru may have resulted from historical connections between these two regions, which shared crops of Mesoamerican origin. Yet Mesopotamian extended families appear to have declined in importance in urban settings as ownership of land and property shifted from a collective to an individual basis. Among the Yoruba coresidential units were much larger in the north than in the south, probably because of the need in the north for a more integrated form of military organization to cope with the greater military threat from adjacent non-Yoruba states. Thus family organization seems to have been shaped to some degree by the functional requirements of particular early civilizations.

Patrilineal extended families could be interpreted as encouraging the development of a delegational form of government in Shang and Eastern Zhou China and of a more heterarchical form of government among the Yoruba. Conversely, the most bureaucratized form of government emerged in ancient Egypt, where there was no extended family. Nevertheless, the growing military power of kings among the Aztec and the Mesopotamians made it possible for them to construct modest bureaucracies that operated without sharing power with extended families or endogamous landowning groups. The Inka kings, while favouring their close relatives for high offices, selected officials from among the various levels of the hereditary nobility without primary reference to specific panaqa or ayllu membership. In these societies extended families, while socially important, played a political role that was more modest than in China or among the Yoruba. It is therefore impossible to determine whether large extended families encouraged the development of delegational or heterarchical forms of administration or more centralized and bureaucratized forms of government promoted the breakup of large extended families. While in Mesopotamia the declining importance of large extended families appears to have accompanied the growth of royal power, it is not clear that there was a direct connection between these two trends or, if there was one, which was cause and which was effect.

In all early civilizations women appear to have been significantly disadvantaged by comparison with men. This disadvantage reflects, at least partly, a pervasive tendency to model family relations on those that characterized the state. Families were conceptualized as miniature kingdoms in which the father had the same relation to his wife (or wives), children, and other dependents that a monarch had to his subjects. Since all early civilizations had male heads of state and female ones were regarded as exceptional or not allowed, this arrangement either encouraged the development of patriarchal relations within families or reinforced existing ones. While women had played important decision-making roles in many small-scale societies, men had generally acted as spokespeople in conducting public business. This form of behaviour may have been related to strategies that sought to protect the reproductive capacity of small groups by exposing males rather than females to greater risk of loss of life in encounters with potentially hostile neighbouring groups. The exposure of males to greater danger is found not only in human hunter-gatherer societies but also among higher non-human primates (DeVore and Hall 1965). As human societies grew more complex, the increasing regulatory importance of the public domain may have enhanced the political role traditionally played by men and, along with it, their authority to make decisions relating to all aspects of public life. Through status emulation, such patriarchal attitudes influenced the nuclear and extended family. While suggesting why patriarchal tendencies were nearly universal in early civilizations, this explanation does not imply that these attitudes were in any fashion biologically innate.

In everyday life the position of women varied considerably from one early civilization to another. In general, Yoruba and ancient Egyptian women possessed more freedoms and explicit legal rights than did women in other early civilizations. They did not, however, have an equal role with men in the political and administrative spheres, and married women were subordinated to their husbands in many ways. Inka farm women played a significant role in religious activities, and their special role in growing crops was symbolically acknowledged. Women in the Valley of Mexico could move about communities freely and engage in local trade, but their participation in political and administrative activities was extremely limited by comparison with that of men. Mesopotamian women were even more limited in their freedom to move about and manage their own affairs, and ordinary women in ancient China appear to have been totally integrated into their husbands' extended families. In many early civilizations, slave women and prostitutes provided examples of the humiliation and dishonour that could befall women who did not have male kin to protect them. There is no evidence that overall the status of ordinary women was different in city-states from what it was in territorial states, but for upper-class women the situation was somewhat different. In territorial states royal women appear to have played significant roles in government, and, as members of a small ruling group, upper-class women were viewed as suitable to direct the activities of lower-class males as well as of subordinate females.

EXPLAINING REGULARITIES

There was considerable cross-cultural uniformity in the sociopolitical institutions of early civilizations. The similar general conceptualizations of kingship, similar class and legal systems, and the use of full-time police and soldiers to support the upper classes recurred in every early civilization for which there is adequate documentation. In addition, there were only two basic forms of political organization (city-states and territorial states) and only two systems for administering extensive territories (delegational and bureaucratic). Further, despite variation in family organization and gender roles from one early civilization to another, male dominance appears to have increased as a result of the development of early civilizations. These findings do not accord with the basic tenet of cultural relativism – that human behaviour is shaped primarily by cultural traditions that are not constrained to any significant degree by non-cultural factors. They certainly do not confirm the argument that universals, if any, are insignificant (Geertz 1965).

It might be objected that the early civilizations examined in this study shared many sociopolitical features only because these traits are the ones I employed to assign societies to this general category. Yet the recurrent and correlated features are too numerous and complex for this objection to carry significant weight. The societies at this level of complexity that are alleged to have displayed radically different features are not well enough documented to be certain that these features are not the anthropologists' own inventions. Increasing information about the Maya has made this early civilization, once believed to be radically different from any other, closely resemble other city-state systems. The principal challenge in terms of sociopolitical features is therefore to explain cross-cultural similarities and limited variation.

Many uniformities may reflect functional requirements. For societies to grow more complex they may have to evolve specific forms of organization. Information theory suggests that the number of decision-making nodes and of decision-makers must increase as societies grow in scale and complexity. An increasing number of nodes at any one level in turn requires the creation of more higher-level nodes to coordinate them, which produces increasingly multilayered decision-making hierarchies (van der Leeuw 1981). Such hierarchies also require more resources to facilitate communication between levels and provide the compulsion that ensures that higher-level orders will be carried out. For complex societies to function, decision-makers must be able to determine courses of action for others without undue delay. This requires the setting of strict limits on the amount of consultation and explicit personal consent required to establish and implement public policy. Decision-making in early civilizations was inevitably associated with what people in small-scale, egalitarian societies would have regarded as unacceptably arbitrary power (Flannery 1972).

Information theory offers a functional explanation for the development of institutionalized systems of unequal political power. The repeated independent evolution of early civilizations that possessed class systems, administrative hierarchies, hierarchical legal systems, and military and police forces suggests not only that these features corresponded to functional needs but also that human beings can repeatedly transcend the intellectual constraints of traditional cultures to create structures that can satisfy new functional requirements.

Neoevolutionists have argued that, because arrangements at the preceding chiefdom level were already so similar, they facilitated the development of cross-culturally similar institutions in early civilizations. This argument, which reflects the neoevolutionist passion for unilinear change, diminishes the importance of the functionalist causality which neoevolutionists also cherish. It is also not a position that is supported by archaeological evidence, which indicates considerable variation in the types of societies that gave rise to early civilizations (Yoffee 1993).

A functionalist or adaptationist argument does not, however, explain why in early civilizations the unity of the state was symbolically expressed by a monarch. Nor does the presence of a king in each early civilization correspond with the relativist-romanticist belief that peoples coping with similar problems have virtually limitless specific ways of conceptualizing solutions for these problems. It does, however, correspond with the nineteenth-century evolutionist assumption that people at a particular level of social complexity who face similar problems will tend to devise similar solutions for them. This was a view to which Franz Boas (1963 [1911]: 154) subscribed, despite his commitment to cultural relativism, when he drew attention to the detailed and far-reaching cross-cultural similarities that characterized fundamental human ideas. Varied cross-cultural similarities, especially those of a cognitive variety, that cannot be explained simply by functional arguments suggest that certain ways of thinking and behaving may in some manner be 'hard-wired' into the human psyche even if they are not realized in the same way in societies at different levels of complexity. This embeddedness may also explain why social scientists habitually treat many regularities in sociopolitical organization as commonplaces, but the existence of these regularities requires explanation.

Limited variation, such as the differences between city-state systems and territorial states, appear to reflect functional alternatives that correspond equally well with human needs and perform equally as long as these two sorts of societies are not competing with each other or with any more complex societies (Hallpike 1986: 75–76). More idiosyncratic variations in family organization and gender roles, although still relatively limited, may partly reflect differing cultural heritages from an earlier stage of development. Even these differences seem to have been modified convergently in the context of early civilizations as families became internally more hierarchical and patriarchal and the public role of women was increasingly restricted.

In drawing attention to cross-cultural regularities in many major features of sociocultural organization in early civilizations and to the limited range of differences in other features, I am not seeking to impose undue uniformity on the data. Kingship had a different specific meaning in every early civilization, as did slavery and the concept of an upper class. Yet these differences cannot be allowed to obscure the great similarities in sociopolitical organization that early civilizations came to share as a result of convergent development. To ignore these similarities out of loyalty to hoary dogmas of cultural relativism or historical particularism would be as misleading as to ignore cultural differences in the name of unilinear evolutionism.

Economy

14 Food Production

Gordon Childe (1928), Karl Wittfogel (1938), Julian Steward (1949), and many other social scientists believed that early civilizations originated in river valleys located in arid or semiarid regions where, as a result of irrigation works, rich, easily worked soils fed large rural populations, produced surpluses that supported many full-time craft specialists, and allowed a ruling class to live in luxury. Many Old World prehistorians continue to hold this view (Hassan 1997: 51). Yet primary civilizations evolved in many different kinds of environments: river valleys in warm, arid regions (Egypt, Mesopotamia), tropical forests and tropical forest-savanna borderlands (Maya, Yoruba), mountainous valleys of different sizes, shapes, and elevations (Peru, Valley of Mexico), and temperate rainfall zones (Shang China). Early civilizations are associated with vast differences in temperature, rainfall, elevation, topography, soil fertility, and microenvironmental diversity. In addition, very different assemblages of domesticated plants and animals constituted the basis of food production in different parts of the world, with no significant overlap between the Eastern and Western Hemispheres. These domesticates, often considerably transformed from their wild ancestors, and knowledge of how to care for them were part of the cultural heritage from earlier phases in the development of each region. Early civilizations are found in temperate or hot climates rather than in cold ones (Northern China, where the average temperature in January would have been close to the freezing point, and highland Peru were borderline cases) and in areas with light, easily worked soils and without dense, deeply rooted grasses. Yet not all regions with these characteristics produced early civilizations. There is no basis for theories that attribute the rise of civilization to the influence of a single type of environment or climatic event.

Childe (1930) also maintained that the development of early civilizations was a consequence of the invention of metallurgy and, in particular, of bronze-working, which encouraged the manufacture of implements that permitted more productive agriculture and the growth of cities and more hierarchical societies. Others have argued that agriculture was impossible in tropical forests such as those of West Africa prior to the development of iron tools. Yet agricultural implements tended to remain simple in most early civilizations. The Classic Maya and the peoples of the Valley of Mexico manufactured all their agricultural implements from wood and stone. The Maya used stone axes and adzes to cut down or girdle trees and simple wooden digging sticks to till the soil and plant crops. The Aztec had a somewhat more elaborate wooden digging stick (*huictli*) with an enlarged base that could be pressed into the earth with the foot and used as a spade (Donkin 1979: 6). Both lacked tools capable of turning over soil impregnated with deeply rooted grasses. The highland Peruvians employed agricultural implements made of wood with stone, bone, and rarely bronze cutting edges. Their most important implement was the *chaki taklla* (foot plough), a wooden digging stick with a heavy stone blade and a firmly attached crossbar that could be pressed deeply into the soil with a foot. These were used to turn over the shallow-rooted grasses of the Andean highlands. All the Shang or early Zhou agricultural implements appear to have been manufactured from wood, bone, shell, and stone, and two-pronged hand ploughs managed by two men were used to turn over grass-covered soil. Alternatively, these have been interpreted as foot ploughs or digging sticks equipped with a foot bar that two men might have employed to lever up clods of earth (Hsu and Linduff 1988: 351).

The Yoruba, by contrast, employed an extensive array of iron implements to till the soil, including heavy short-handled hoes and machetes with sharp cutting edges. Yet Maya success in cultivating similar tropical forest and savanna environments far more intensively indicates that metal implements did not provide the crucial advantage that is often attributed to them. In southern Mesopotamia, little stone was available on the floodplain. In the Ubaid period the Mesopotamians manufactured sickles and sometimes mullers, hammers, and even axes from heavily fired clay. The sickles had sharp, vitrified cutting edges but shattered easily, and by the start of the Early Dynastic period they had been replaced by wooden sickles with cutting edges made of imported flint and some agricultural tools were already being made of copper. By the Akkadian period copper sickles had become more common, and by the Ur III period copper sickles, hoes, and axes were standard (Edens 1992: 125–26; Pollock 1999: 85). In Egypt during the Old and Middle Kingdoms, agricultural implements and all other tools used by farmers continued to be made of stone, bone, and wood; only in the New Kingdom did metal farming implements become common (Andreu 1997: 107; David 1986: 169–70). The failure to manufacture copper and bronze farming tools in most societies where these metals were known reflects the relative scarcity of copper and tin throughout the world. By contrast, the abundance of iron ores made iron an appropriate material from which to manufacture farming implements once it was known how to smelt them.

Egypt and Mesopotamia were the only early civilizations in our sample that supplemented human agricultural labour with that of domestic animals. Oxen- and donkey-drawn ploughs were present from an early period. Draft animals are estimated to have resulted in a 50 percent reduction in the human labour needed to grow grain, and this permitted small groups of men to work large, monocropped fields (R. Hunt 1991: 148). Special skills were required to construct and maintain ploughs, and draft animals had to be fed, harnessed, and trained to pull them.

Animal-drawn ploughs were used not to cut deeply into the soil or to turn over heavy turf but to loosen the surfaces of fields to help conserve subsurface moisture and cover seed. Ploughs were equipped with wooden blades, which in Mesopotamia were sometimes sheathed with copper. Mesopotamian ploughs were also equipped with a 'drill' or funnel which dropped seed into the furrows as the plough moved along (Postgate 1992: 167). This form of sowing was more economical of grain than the broadcast method employed in Egypt. Because ploughs were expensive to manufacture and used to work large fields, they either belonged to large estates or were owned communally. Small independent farmers had to rent ploughs and teams of oxen or pay to have their fields ploughed. Animal-drawn ploughs were not used until the late Zhou period in China, although animal traction was employed routinely for military purposes in Shang times. The absence of ploughs in New World civilizations can be explained by the lack of domestic animals that could have been used to pull them; the Peruvian llama was unsuitable as a draft animal, although it was used to carry light packs. The Yoruba kept a few cattle, but ploughing was not well adapted to their root-crop agriculture. Even the Egyptians and Mesopotamians did not use their ploughs, as Iron Age Europeans were to do, to cultivate rich and fertile but heavy and therefore hard-to-work soils. Instead, they worked lighter soils that could otherwise have been cultivated using hand implements.

There is therefore no basis for viewing the rise of early civilizations as being closely linked to improved agricultural implements. The development of such technology was related to historically contingent factors such as whether draft animals were available and whether metallurgical techniques were capable of mass-producing farm implements. Moreover, the Maya, using digging sticks, were able to support a civilization that was at least as complex as that of the iron-using Yoruba in a generally similar environment.

Efforts have also been made to correlate the development of civilization with the segmentation of different forms of agricultural production – the separation of gardening from grain production or of agriculture from animal husbandry. It has been suggested that more complex segmentation of agricultural activities would have produced a greater division of labour as individuals and groups specialized in performing different tasks and that this in turn would have promoted the development of expertise and higher levels of food production (Fussell 1966). It has also been maintained that increasing agricultural specialization influenced gender relations by making agriculture a male occupation. In reality, however, women in early civilizations appear to have performed many agricultural tasks, such as herding animals and tending kitchen gardens near their homes. Where major reliance on a few crops created short peak periods of agricultural labour, women and children also joined in activities such as winnowing grain. Such labour fluctuations reached extremes in societies that worked fields with animal-drawn ploughs. The highland Andean civilization was the only one in our sample that recognized and ideologically justified the cooperation of men and women in producing food (Silverblatt 1987: 10–15). In other early civilizations, the ideological celebration of men as food producers served to reinforce patriarchy. Although the symbolic differentiation of male and female tasks exceeded their real separation, a growing division of labour in complex societies resulted in men's increasingly specializing in food production while women specialized in food processing and other household tasks.

In the past it would have been argued that Aztec, Maya, and Yoruba gardening represented the simplest form of agriculture associated with early civilizations. These economies would have been followed by that of the Shang Chinese, who appear to have kept more domestic animals and sowed grain in hand-ploughed fields as well as tending kitchen gardens. Next would have come the Inka economy, with its altitudinally varied plant complexes and specialized herding sector. Egypt and finally Mesopotamia would have represented the most elaborate forms of agriculture, with their complex associations of gardening, ploughed fields, farm animals, and specialized herding. Yet, as we have already noted, much of this variation was fortuitous. The lack of any indigenous large domesticable animals in Mesoamerica and of suitable draft animals in Peru precluded various forms of specialization. The presence of adjacent pastoral peoples in China, Mesopotamia, and (to a much lesser extent) Egypt created additional possibilities for articulating complementary forms of food production. More important, however, there is no evidence that organizational specialization of this sort corresponded with increased productivity. The Yoruba kept a few large domestic animals, but their agricultural system, while highly sophisticated and well adapted to their environment and to a low population density, was much less productive than that of the Aztec or the Maya, who did not. Specialization in food production was important, but it does not account for overall productivity. To understand productivity, intensification of production and labour must be considered.

Many evolutionary theories treat population pressure as the driving force behind more intensive food production and the development of more hierarchical societies, including early civilizations (Boserup 1965; M. Cohen 1977; P. Smith 1976). These theories assume that population pressure characterized all early civilizations and that people submitted to taxation and political authority only if they had nowhere else to go. This ties in with the argument that early states and civilizations developed only in regions where fertile soils were circumscribed by far less productive areas, with the result that, as populations expanded, people could not easily evade political authority by moving elsewhere (Carneiro 1970b). Using Michael Mann's (1986: 38–40) terminology, these populations became 'caged'.

Agricultural land was naturally circumscribed in the Valley of Mexico, Peru, Egypt, and Mesopotamia. In highland Mexico and Peru, arable land, located mostly in valleys, was limited, and relocation from one valley to another would have been socially and politically difficult for farmers. Moving to the lowlands would have required ecological knowledge that was not easily obtained. Escape from Mesopotamia necessitated a major change in lifestyle (one that has been undertaken in the Middle East by marginal and oppressed farmers who become pastoralists [A. Cohen 1972: 7]). The areas immediately adjacent to the Nile Valley in Egypt had little sustaining power in historical times. Pedro Cieza de León observed that in Peru the population was easy to control because most of the region consisted of wasteland that offered no refuge to dissidents (Salomon 1986: 20).

The Classic Maya, Yoruba, and Shang Chinese civilizations had no such natural boundaries. The Maya could have expanded farther south into Central America (McAnany 1995: 146), and the low overall population density of the Yoruba gave people considerable room for movement and colonization within their existing territories. Shang and Zhou expansion was ecologically restricted by the cold and arid terrain to the north and west, but vast amounts of desirable farmland lay to the south. People in these civilizations had large areas of less densely inhabited arable land into which to escape from authority.

Another intensification argument is that, as population densities increased and suitable land was developed to sustain higher levels of production by means of drainage, terracing, and irrigation, such land became an investment that its owners would not willingly abandon. They would submit to authority and taxation if necessary to retain possession of their farms and supported rulers who offered their holdings protection against claims by neighbours who lacked such good soil or intruders from elsewhere (Linton 1933; 1939). Theories of circumscription thus assume that coercion depended either on increasing population density without any outlet for excess population or on the growing appeal of staying in one place.

Estimates of population sizes and densities without modern census data depend largely on archaeological settlement patterns and written records. Even if archaeologists can date houses and farming hamlets to specific periods, it is notoriously difficult to determine how many buildings were occupied simultaneously, how many nuclear families inhabited each structure, and how large the average nuclear family was. Written information is frequently even less reliable. Early European visitors to Mexico, Peru, and West Africa recorded their own and what were purported to be indigenous estimates of the populations of specific cities or regions, but they seem often to have exaggerated population size to impress European readers. In Mexico and Peru, reliable census data are available only after the Spanish conquest, when European diseases had destroyed much of the aboriginal population. For the Yoruba and Benin, census data are available only after European colonization had resulted in major economic and political changes. There are reports by Greek and Roman writers on the population of Egypt, but because of the intensification of agricultural production that occurred during the Ptolemaic period (Butzer 1976: 50) it is difficult to apply these figures to earlier times.

Despite these limitations, the intensification of food production does appear to be closely correlated with increasing population density. The investment of more labour in agricultural production is indicated archaeologically by hydraulic works, including various forms of irrigation, which were intended to bring more land under cultivation and would have permitted more abundant crops to be grown in most areas than rainfall agriculture alone. Drainage schemes also brought more land under intensive cultivation. Agricultural terraces vary from simple works designed to limit soil erosion in areas of rainfall agriculture to serried banks of carefully irrigated and drained artificial fields such as those that lined the steep lower slopes of the Andes. Most of the labour needed to construct and maintain irrigation works, terraces, and wetland fields could have been performed at the village or district level. Other promotions of intensive agriculture took the form of state-directed projects intended to increase royal revenues.

AGRICULTURAL REGIMES

Yoruba territory extends from the swampy coastal plain along the Gulf of Guinea north through tropical forests to the southern edge of the savanna.

The terrain, which mostly lies below five hundred metres, rises gradually to the north, where a flat plain is interrupted by massive outcrops of metamorphic rock rising as high as nine hundred metres. A number of small rivers flow south into the Gulf of Guinea. It is a region of red lateritic soils. In the far south, around Lagos, the mean temperature is 27.2 degrees C in January and twenty-five degrees C in July; around Ibadan these figures are lower only by a degree or less. Dry, hot harmattan winds blow south from the Sahara Desert between December and February, while moist winds blow north from the Gulf of Guinea at other seasons. The coastal region receives significant rainfall year-round, but in the north rains sufficient to grow crops last for only six months, with peaks in June and again in September and October. The dry season in the north lasts from December to February. Two hundred and thirty centimetres of rain fall each year around Lagos but only 111 centimetres around Ibadan. Agriculture is therefore more seasonal in the north, and farmers who live there are more likely also to engage in other forms of labour (Bascom 1969: 4; Ojo 1966a: 24–26, 66).

Despite their iron agricultural tools, the Yoruba had the least intensive subsistence pattern in our sample. They practised swidden agriculture, which involved girdling large trees and cutting underbrush and small, second-growth trees during the dry season and then, when the wood had dried out, subjecting the area to a controlled burn. Finally, the soil was broken up and hoed, and tubers and seeds were planted between the stumps in April. Prior to A.D. 1500, the main crops were yams, which were West African domesticates, and sorghum and pearl millet from the Sahel, but, since their introduction from the New World, maize has largely replaced sorghum and cassava is common. Beans, melons, oil palm, kola nut, and other fruits and vegetables were also cultivated prior to European contact. African cotton was grown to make cloth. Yams were planted in low mounds of loose soil and, after they were dug up, dried to make flour (Law 1977: 100). A wide variety of crops were grown together in a manner imitating natural plant growth in tropical clearings, a practice that minimized both erosion and the need for weeding. Successive yam crops began to mature in July, November, and December. Groves of oil palms were planted on community and lineage land (Bascom 1969: 18–20; Bradbury 1957: 23; Forde 1934: 151–56).

Cities were surrounded for up to thirty kilometres by belts of farmland. An extended family usually had holdings near the city (*oko etile*) and at varying distances farther away. This land was divided among the patrilineage's adult male members. Farmers commuted between their houses in the city and nearby farms but lived in houses or cabins on these farms for weeks at a time when agricultural work was at its peak. Other members of the same extended family lived year-round in agricultural hamlets farther from the city (*oko egan*) but sometimes moved into their patrilineage's urban compound when they grew older. In general, younger and less prestigious members of urban lineages tended to live and work farther from the city (Krapf-Askari 1969: 39).

Three years of cropping were followed by seven to twenty years of fallowing, during which time the soil's fertility was renewed. The land was then recleared of trees and crops were planted once again. Because population density was low, there was usually enough land around agricultural hamlets for an extended family to occupy the same farms and houses indefinitely, cultivating adjacent patches of land in rotation. Although land close to cities and occasionally small plots of land inside cities may have been cultivated more intensively than land farther away, the Yoruba made no use of infields (specially tended and artificially fertilized land) near their residences. In the north, only some onions and other garden vegetables were hand-watered during the dry season.

Farming was viewed as men's work. Wealthier and more powerful extended families had male slaves to help cultivate their fields and release male family members for other tasks. Women might help to carry seed yams to a farm and harvest some crops, and they transported surplus food to market and sold it. They were not, however, asked to help clear fields or hoe crops (Bascom 1969: 20). Ideally their tasks were homemaking and marketing. Less affluent farmers were routinely helped by their unmarried sons or engaged in balanced labour exchanges (*aro*) with neighbours. They also invited other relatives, friends, and age-mates to attend bees (*owe*) when they needed extra labour to clear fields. Such assistance was reciprocated while in progress with food and drink and in the long run with return labour.

Yoruba families kept a small number of goats, sheep, dogs, chickens, and a few diminutive cattle for sacrifices and eating, although only the wealthy consumed meat regularly. Meat was mainly a ceremonial and celebratory food and was sometimes preserved by drying (Law 1977: 99–100). Horses were kept for military purposes. Farmers who had a specialized knowledge of wild animals, plants, and medicines and belonged to hunters' associations hunted in the forest reserves during the dry season and guarded the borders of the state against surprise attack. Males in Epe and other coastal communities supplied smoked fish to traders coming from as far away as Oyo, Ife, and Ado-Ekiti (50). Animals were not employed for ploughing. Their skins were used to make leather, but no use was made of secondary animal products such as milk and wool (Ojo 1966a: 30–50).

Gender relations with respect to agriculture appear to have been more flexible in Benin. Richard Bradbury (1957: 23–24) reports that, while the people of Benin regarded growing yams as a male occupation, women helped to plant, weed, and harvest the crop. They also cultivated their own fields, where they grew various other crops to feed their families and to sell. Young men who helped to work their fathers' yam fields also grew crops on adjacent land, which they sold for profit.

No reliable population statistics are available for the Yoruba during the eighteenth and nineteenth centuries. The population at that period has been estimated to have been between five and ten million. More recent figures indicate that the Yoruba generally have a population density of 30 to 60 persons per square kilometre. This may be higher than in previous centuries as a result of the introduction of European medicine. The population varies, however, from Ife, near the center of Yoruba territory, with 135 people per square kilometre, and Ekitu, northeast of Ife, with 60 per square kilometre, to Ondo, southeast of Ife, Oyo, and Benin, each with about 30 per square kilometre (Bascom 1969: 2; Bradbury 1957: 4; Eades 1980: 82; Lloyd 1962: 53). These are low population densities compared with those of other early civilizations. They confirm that for all lineages and individuals who were trying to accumulate food surpluses in order to increase their political power, securing labour was a much greater problem than acquiring land. This problem was widespread in sub-Saharan Africa.

The successive Shang and Western Zhou kingdoms were centred on the central plain of northern China, much of which is less than forty-five metres above sea level. Enormous deposits of light, easily worked soil were carried down the Yellow River from the loess plateau to the north and deposited on this plain. River channels were often higher than the surrounding plain and changed course over time, sometimes dramatically (Jing, Rapp, and Gao 1997). Numerous lakes and marshes existed in low-lying areas north and south of the levee backslopes. The plain was originally covered with temperate forest, including oak, pine, cypress, tamarisk, and mulberry, and was home to wild animals such as cattle, bears, tigers, leopards, and panthers.

The present climate of northern China is strongly seasonal. The average temperature is zero degrees C in January and twenty-eight degrees C in July. Winds blow mainly from the north in winter and from the southeast in summer. Rainfall is highest in midsummer but totals only seventy-six centimetres annually and as little as fifty centimetres in the lower Yellow River valley. There is also considerable variation in rainfall from one year to another, with precipitation being uncertain in the spring and sometimes excessive in July. Strong winds, heavy downpours or prolonged droughts, crop diseases, and insect pests threaten the crops. Snow falls in winter, and crops can be grown only from spring to autumn.

It has been suggested that northern China may have been a few degrees warmer and the overall precipitation somewhat greater in Shang times than at present, but the climate would still have been continental rather than tropical or subtropical. The Shang oracle-bone records, which include divinations concerning the weather, suggest only limited climatic change (Chêng 1960: 83–88; Keightley 1999a; Wheatley 1971: 22). These texts indicate royal concern that there be enough rain to grow food and fear that heavy summer rains may spoil the crops (Keightley 1979–80: 29).

Wheat was the preferred cereal of the upper classes, and broomcorn millet (*Panicum miliaceum* [*shu*]) was generally preferred to foxtail millet (*Setaria italica* [*chi*]) (Hsu and Linduff 1989: 345–55). Barley, sorghum, hemp seed, and numerous varieties of protein-rich beans (including soybeans) and peas were grown as food crops. Clothing was produced from hemp, linen, and wool. The upper classes already wore silk. A character that later means 'rice' (*dao*) appears in the oracle-bone texts, but it is not known if wet rice was grown in the Yellow River valley in Shang times. Producing it would have required irrigation, for which there is no evidence (Bagley 1999: 178; Chêng 1960: 197; Hsu and Linduff 1988: 365). Domestic animals included pigs, dogs, water buffaloes, sheep, and oxen, as well as horses.

Fields initially had to be cleared of forests. Their fertility was maintained by fallowing, burning weeds and brush as fertilizer, and manuring (Hsu and Linduff 1988: 354–55). Fields were surrounded by low earth walls inside ditches which prevented the subsoil from becoming waterlogged as a result of excessive summer rains or high water tables in low-lying areas (H. Sugiura, cited in Isaac 1993: 452–53). Idealized descriptions of later times suggest that individual fields were surrounded by shallow ditches, blocks of nine large fields by deeper ones, and one hundred such blocks by still larger trenches (Vandermeersch 1980: 221–22). Each cultivator was assigned approximately 6.6 hectares of good land for cultivation and more for fallow, allotments being larger where the land was poorer.

The culturally approved view of country life had men working the land while women cooked, looked after children, tended the family house, and wove. Men worked in teams. In spring, grass was burned from the fields and the root-impregnated soil was turned over with two-man hand ploughs. The clods of earth were then broken up by pounding them with clubs or ordinary hoes. Large grain fields appear to have been monocropped, and men worked in large groups to harvest them (Granet 1958 [1930]: 140–46).

Farmers planted orchards and vegetable gardens near their houses, while grain and hemp fields were located farther away. There appears to have been considerable antipathy towards pastoral peoples who lived to the north and west and, when driven by hunger or attracted by the prospect of easy plunder, harassed settled regions. The Shang and Zhou people relished meat but shunned milk and dairy products because of their associations with pastoralists (K. Chang 1977: 29).

No population figures are available for Shang or Western Zhou China, and there are as yet no comprehensive settlement pattern data. The earliest surviving census, for A.D. 2, suggests a population of forty to sixty persons per square kilometre on the central plain, but by then China had an agricultural economy based on iron tools and private ownership of land (Barraclough 1984: 80). If Shang and early Zhou agriculture depended entirely on rainfall, population density was probably relatively low. Yet patrilineages appear to have been multiplying rapidly, and the apparent expansion of Shang and Zhou populations into adjacent regions suggests considerable natural population increase (Pokora 1978: 193, 209).

The Lower Mesopotamian alluvial plain, which constituted the heartland of southern Mesopotamian civilization, is located in a desert or semidesert region. Between ten and twenty centimetres of rain fall each year during the winter, mainly in November and December, and again in March and April. This is sufficient for winter grazing but not for agriculture in the regions beyond and between the floodplains of the Tigris and Euphrates Rivers. Southern Mesopotamia was more or less cut off by extensive marshes to the east of the Tigris from the Susiana plain and the forested valleys of the Zagros Mountains. The average temperature of southern Mesopotamia is sixteen degrees C in January and twenty-eight degrees C in July, with large diurnal variations and low humidity (Postgate 1992: 6–20).

Settled life depended entirely on water from the rivers. The Tigris, which received numerous tributaries from the east, was a turbulent river but too deeply cut into the floodplain to be a useful zone of settlement in ancient times. It was first substantially harnessed for irrigation purposes in the Hellenistic period (R. McC. Adams 1981: 244). However, its major tributary, the Diyala, was an important area of settlement. The Euphrates River flowed across the desert farther west. Incised into the plain to the north, it formed levees in southern Mesopotamia, where it was also divided into a series of braided channels. It carried less flood water than the Tigris and flowed more slowly and was therefore easier to control. Its various branches were, however, subject to both gradual and abrupt shifts. The Euphrates carried a vast amount of silt, most of which was deposited on the flat delta north of the Hammar Swamp. Channels were bordered by low, easily breached levees composed of coarse deposits beyond which broad, gentle backslopes composed of fine silts sloped down to the desert. The levees and backslopes were covered with willow, poplar, and tamarisk trees and licorice shrubs. It is uncertain whether, in the third millennium B.C., the Persian Gulf reached almost as far north as Ur and Lagash or whether lagoons, swamps, and marshes stretched south, as they do today, to near the present shoreline (Pollock 1999: 34–35; Postgate 1992: 14–20). Both the Tigris and the Euphrates flooded in the spring, reaching their highest level in April.

Irrigation was essential for growing crops (Fig. 14.1). Water was drawn from the Euphrates through canals that ran south along the levees and was then distributed by gravity flow through smaller channels that flowed down the backslopes. Controlling the flow of water required diverters, head regulators, and dykes. Water that was not absorbed by the soil accumulated in brackish ponds and lakes on the edge of the desert. Around 2500 B.C., small, shifting distributaries were replaced by more extensive and permanent canals (Maisels 1999: 86–87; Postgate 1992: 174). Considerable engineering skills were required to build even these medium-sized systems, which were replaced by still larger irrigation complexes in the first millennium B.C. Water was distributed through small feeder canals to fields (*ikum*) approximately sixty metres square and surrounded on all four sides by low banks. As more agricultural land was required, dykes were constructed to reclaim some of the marsh land along the lower margins of the backslopes. At least one canal built in Ur III times was forty-five kilometres long (Postgate 1992: 182). An elaborate and carefully administered system of allocation was required to provide every field with four waterings during the course of the growing season. Because of the terrain, large-scale irrigation systems were generally more difficult to construct in the northern part of southern Mesopotamia than in the south (R. McC. Adams 1974b; 1981: 1–10; Liverani 1996; Oates 1996; Walters 1970).

The main crops were barley, wheat, legumes, and flax, which was used to produce both oil and cloth. Sesame was grown for oil after 2300 B.C. Wheat and barley were winter crops, grown on the backslopes. Fields were prepared in July and August. They were weeded and harrowed, using oxen-drawn ploughs, and then flooded. Ploughing loosened the surface of fields in order to minimize evaporation. Crops were sown in August and September, watered and tended over the winter, and harvested in March and April. The Mesopotamians also maintained year-round kitchen gardens, vineyards, and orchards along the levees. In the orchards a three-tiered pattern of cultivation was practised. Fig trees, apple trees, and pomegranates were planted in the shade of high date palms, while vegetables such as onions, garlic, cucumbers, and lettuces were grown beneath the shorter trees. Some of these gardens and orchards were located inside the city walls. The Euphrates and the Tigris were lowest in winter, when water was needed for agriculture, and highest in

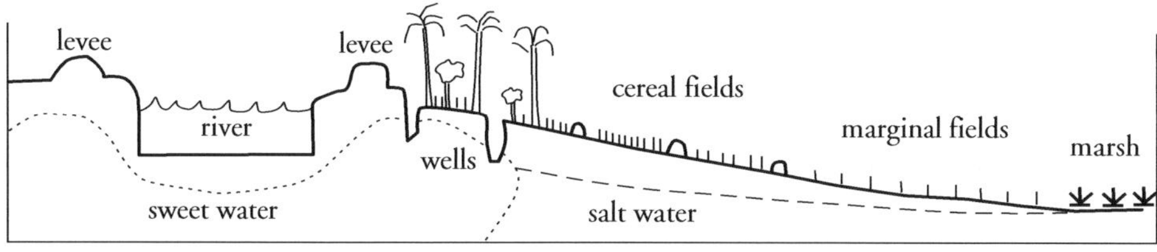

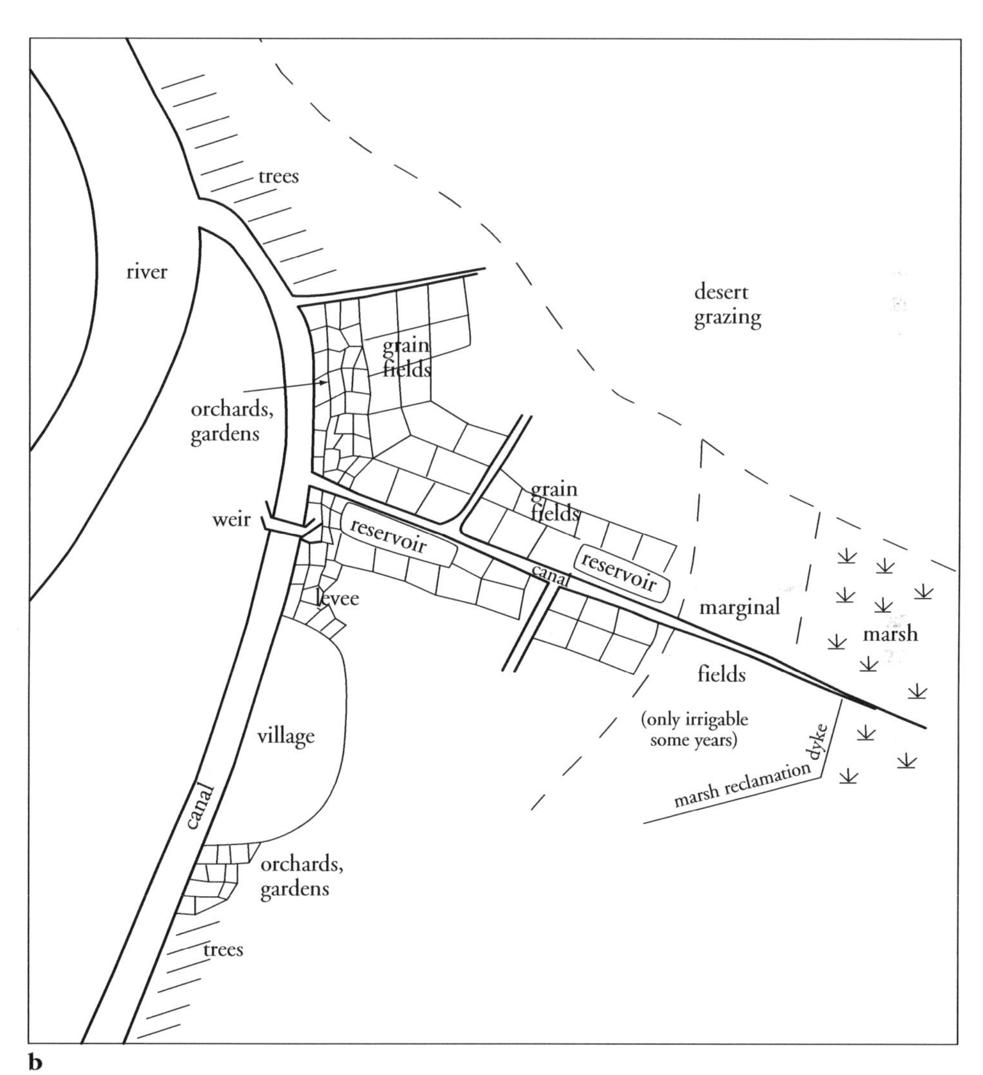

14.1. Mesopotamian irrigation system – hypothetical reconstruction in (a) cross-section and (b) plan of one irrigation unit. Sources: (a), (b) after Postgate 1992: 175.

spring, when their floods threatened the ripening crops. Much effort had to be expended in strengthening the levees to hold the flood waters within their banks (Maekawa 1984; Postgate 1992: 167–82).

Soils along the levees were higher, coarser, and well-drained, and therefore salt from river water quickly made its way back into the river and the arable land remained fertile. On the more fine-grained, heavier soils of the backslopes, poorer drainage meant that irrigation water tended to remain near the surface, and the accumulation of salts there eventually destroyed the fertility of the soil. Fallowings every other year allowed deeply rooted weeds to dry out the upper soil, after which accumulated salts were flushed deeper with heavy applications of fresh water. This meant that only half the available grain fields could be cultivated at one time (Gibson 1974; Jacobsen 1982; Powell 1985). Despite the strenuous efforts made in ancient times to slow or prevent salination, modern experiences suggest that in many areas fields would have become uncultivatable after fewer than fifty years (Fernea 1970). Although debates continue concerning the historical importance of salination (Pollock 1999: 37–38; Yoffee 1995: 296), it has been suggested that, around 1500 B.C., the sedentary population of southern Mesopotamia declined rapidly as massive salination forced ever more people to move north. The short life-span of backslope fields, together with high interest rates, may also explain the low price of land in ancient Mesopotamia (Postgate 1992: 184). Opening new fields required not only constructing new canals but also clearing trees, which were a source of charcoal for cooking and industrial operations.

The Mesopotamians herded sheep and goats on a large scale and apparently kept and ate large numbers of pigs. Cattle were bred in smaller numbers, mainly for milking and ploughing, and were given names similar to those of humans. Donkeys and oxen were used to draw ploughs, and donkeys and asses pulled carts and carried burdens. Sheep, goats, and cattle spent the summer and autumn eating the stubble and wild growth from the fields and fertilizing them with their droppings as they did so. In the winter, cattle were fed grass that farmers had accumulated or were pastured in the marshes. Sheep and goats fed on the wild vegetation that grew in the adjacent deserts or in the foothills of the Zagros. In the deserts the vegetation was limited, but flocks of sheep and goats could graze over large areas. These animals were herded both by shepherds who lived in urban centres and agricultural villages and by pastoral tribesmen independent of any city-state. The latter kept in contact with agriculturalists, and many grazed their flocks on the stubble of fields after the desert pastures had dried up. Fishing, which was an important source of protein, was carried out at least in part by full-time specialists (Postgate 1992: 158–66; Zeder 1991).

Farm work, especially grain cultivation, which involved using animal-drawn ploughs, was always represented as a male occupation. Commercial texts reveal, however, that large numbers of poorer women were employed to winnow and carry grain, break up clods on ploughed fields, tow boats, and press oil (Van De Mieroop 1999: 64). In Old Babylonian economic texts from Sippar, some female slaves were described as trained ox drivers (R. Harris 1975: 256–57, 337). The use of ploughs and draft animals favoured the development of large institutions and wealthy landowners as corporate extended families declined in size and importance. Landless labourers moved from one city-state to another, helping to harvest grain each spring as the crops ripened from south to north (Maisels 1990: 183).

Robert McC. Adams (1981: 90) proposes that 107,000 people occupied 4,100 square kilometres of arable land in southern Mesopotamia in the Early Dynastic I period, and Susan Pollock (1999: 65) suggests that there were 200,000 people in Early Dynastic III times. Adams's figure represents a very low density of only 26 persons per square kilometre. An estimate for the Ur region at this period suggests a population density of 66 persons per square kilometre of arable land (H. T. Wright in R. McC. Adams 1981: 327). This is about as high a population as could be sustained if 1.5 hectares of arable land were needed per person. Adams (1981: 149, 251) estimates a population of at least 500,000 for Mesopotamia in the Ur III period. If the expansion of irrigation had brought the extent of arable land close to the sustaining capacity of water from the Euphrates (12,000 square kilometres, half in fallow), this would indicate an overall population density of 42 persons per square kilometre. Richard Hunt (1991: 145) has estimated a maximum sustaining capacity for agricultural land in Mesopotamia of between 123 and 208 persons per square kilometre, depending on crop yields. This suggests that a city of 100,000 could have been fed using the agricultural land located within a radius of 12.4 to 16 kilometres, although the linear arrangement of arable land along river channels in Mesopotamia would rarely have permitted such an ideal arrangement. More detailed research is needed on population size and population density, both of which appear to have been low by comparison with most other early civilizations. A low population density accords, however, with a subsistence pattern that produced only one grain crop per year and had only a little more than 50 percent of arable land under cultivation at any one time.

Ancient Egypt, which was called the Black Land (*kmt*), was the floodplain of the Nile River north of Aswan. This plain varied in width from a few hundred metres in the far south to 22.5 kilometres in Middle Egypt. The Delta to the north, where the Nile broke into a fan-shaped series of distributaries, extended 160 kilometres from south to north and was 240 kilometres wide at the Mediterranean coast. Even if winter rainfall was somewhat higher in the Old Kingdom than it is today, it would have been insufficient to grow crops or even to graze animals outside the Nile Valley, except near the coast. Currently 18 centimetres of rain fall annually at Alexandria but only 2.54 centimetres at Cairo and one-tenth that amount at Aswan. Humidity also diminishes from north to south. The Egyptian climate is biseasonal. The average temperature from the north to the south of the country is seventeen to twenty-two degrees C in January and twenty-seven to thirty-three degrees C in July. Between March and June strong winds bring hot temperatures and dust storms from the Sahara Desert. The rest of the year, cooler winds blow from the north. In ancient times the north winds were used to push sailing boats upstream against the northward current of the Nile River.

Life in the Nile Valley depended on the annual Nile flood, which arrived at Aswan in mid-August and persisted there until early October. The higher waters took a month or longer to reach the north of the country. The average inundation covered two-thirds of the rich alluvial soil of the Nile Valley, which amounted to about 17,000 square kilometres. Floods varied in volume, however, from year to year and over longer periods. Unusually high floods were as harmful to agriculture as very low ones. In prehistoric times, the valley south of Cairo was covered not with forests but with seasonally inundated grasslands. There were permanent swamps only in restricted, low-lying places. Water was also temporarily impounded on the floodplain behind fossil levees that had been abandoned as a result of lateral shifts in the course of the river. The Delta was a region of raised sand islands and grass-covered floodplains. Only its northern third was covered mainly by swamps, brackish lagoons, and salt marshes (Butzer 1976).

The ancient Egyptians planted only one cereal crop each year, in the autumn after the Nile flood had subsided. Barley and wheat were their main food crops. Beans and chick-peas were also grown in large quantities, along with linen to make cloth. These were all domestic plants that had come to Egypt from the north and were ideally suited for growing during the relatively cool Egyptian winters. The Egyptians also had gardens and orchards, which were located close to their houses and were walled or fenced for protection from animals. To lessen the chances of their being flooded, houses were constructed on high ground – on the tops of levees that ran along either side of the Nile and its side channel, the Bahr Yusuf, and on abandoned levees that ran parallel to the river. In gardens cabbages, asparagus, cucumbers, radishes, onions, lettuce, and other vegetables were grown year-round on plots hand-watered with buckets filled from wells, reservoirs, or the river (Eyre 1994). No labour-saving devices were employed to help raise water, the *shaduf* (weighted water hoist) being unknown before the New Kingdom. Date palms, with their deep roots, could reach the water table year-round from the tops of levees.

The Egyptians constructed lateral earth banks or dykes between levees or other natural elevations on the floodplain and built up levees where necessary to create agricultural basins (Fig. 14.2). These basins, enclosing between nine and one hundred square kilometres, were smaller and easier to build in the far south, where the floodplain was narrower. Canals conducted water from the river into the basins as the Nile flood reached its peak. The canals ensured that even basins located on high ground could be filled almost every year and water impounded in them long enough to moisten the soil sufficiently to produce a crop. Basins were equipped with 'siphon canals' that drained the remaining water into progressively lower basins until it returned to the Nile after the flood had subsided. Systems of interconnected basins extended along the Nile Valley for twenty-five to thirty-five kilometres each, the length of an Upper Egyptian province or administrative district. Building and maintaining basin systems did not require direction at higher administrative levels. The central government did, however, play an important role in maintaining the boundaries between provinces and thus ensuring that adjacent basin systems did not encroach on one another (Butzer 1976).

Each basin was divided into square plots. As in Mesopotamia, light ploughing served not to turn over deep furrows but to loosen the surface of the soil and cover seed, which was broadcast rather than planted with a seed drill. The soil was sufficiently moistened by the Nile flood that no further irrigation was necessary for crops to grow and ripen. The crops were harvested in the spring. This left a long summer period when only kitchen gardens and livestock required tending. This cycle was not altered until sorghum was introduced in the third century B.C. Sorghum was drought-resistant and even when planted after the barley and wheat harvest would grow without irrigation.

The lower water table following the recession of the Nile after the annual flood drew salt deep into the ground, clearing the fields of it. Therefore salination was not a problem. It used to be claimed that the annual deposits of Nile silt renewed the fertility of the soil, but Nile silt is not particularly rich in nutrients. Egyptians fallowed their fields or alternated legumes with cereals to fix nitrogen. Most important, they pastured domestic animals on crop stubble and fallow grasses so that animal droppings would fertilize the soil (R. Hunt 1987). The numerous cattle, sheep, goats, pigs, fowl, and donkeys that they raised were thus vital for crop production. In addition to providing meat, sheep and goats produced wool, while cattle yielded milk and pulled ploughs. Donkeys were used as pack animals. These animals had to be fed during the inundation. During the Old Kingdom, the upper classes also kept gazelles, oryx, ibex,

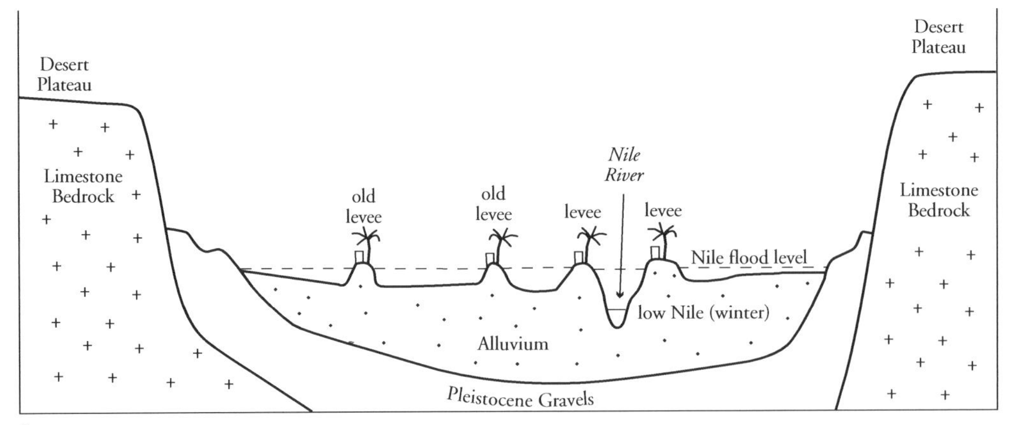

a

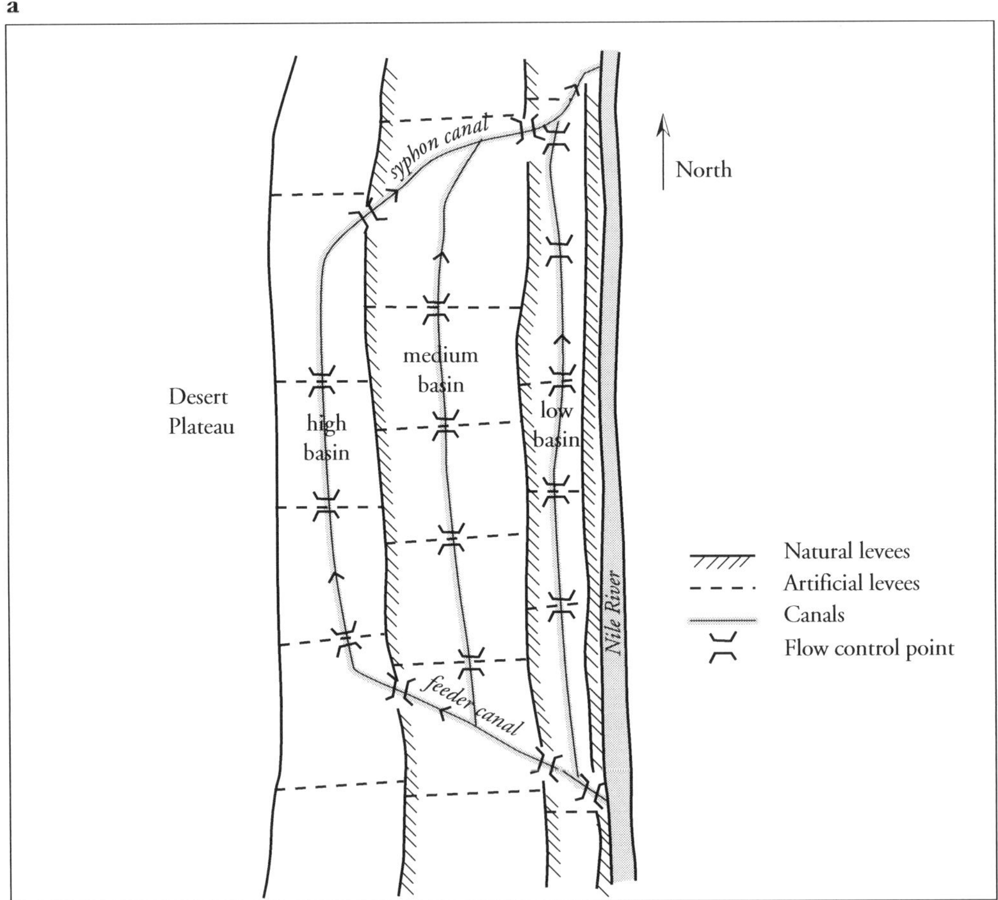

b

14.2. Egyptian agricultural basin system: (a) cross-section of the Nile Valley in Upper Egypt; (b) plan of a basin system on the west side of the Nile River. An Upper Egyptian province normally contained two such systems, one on either side of the Nile. Sources: (a), (b) after Butzer 1976: 15, 42; L. Krzyzaniak, *Early Farming Cultures on the Lower Nile* (Warsaw, 1977), 35.

addax, and hyaenas as semidomesticates and ate them. Cats were the only indigenous wild species of animal to be domesticated in historical times (Butzer 1976: 15, 91). Fishing and hunting contributed significant protein to the diet.

Men from the same community worked together to plant and harvest crops. They shared draft animals for ploughing. Most families probably kept sheep, goats, fowl, and perhaps pigs. Cattle were owned by more prosperous farmers and by estates. Large herds of cattle were tended by herdsmen, who led a harsh, itinerant life. They fed on wild grasses near swamps, especially in the Delta and Middle Egypt, and some were driven long distances in the course of a year in search of pastures. As the human population expanded, the use of the floodplain for pasturing cattle declined, although this was not a significant development during the Old and Middle Kingdoms. While farming was considered men's work, women and children helped with the harvest, gleaning, winnowing, and sieving grain and pulling up flax. Women probably also tended household animals and kitchen gardens (Feucht 1997: 318–19) but were not recorded as having ploughed, reaped grain, fished, fowled, hunted, or herded cattle.

Butzer (1976: 83) estimates that in the Old Kingdom, Egypt had a population of 1.6 million, with an average population density of 93 persons per square kilometre, and that in the Middle Kingdom its population was 2 million, with an average density of 108 persons per square kilometre. Other estimates for the Old Kingdom have ranged as low as 1 million and as high as 3 million (Strouhal 1992: 134–35). If the population in 150 B.C. was about 4.9 million, even allowing for the more intensive cultivation practised at that period, it seems possible that there may have been 3 million Egyptians as early as the Old Kingdom. This would have produced an overall population density of 165 persons per square kilometre of arable land. Population density varied, however, by region. During the Old Kingdom, it was higher in the far south and around Memphis and lowest in Middle Egypt and the Delta. Later the population increased more rapidly in the Delta than in Upper Egypt, so that by the New Kingdom most of the population lived in the north (Butzer 1976: 83, 101). T. K. Park (1992) has stressed variability in access to water as a major factor promoting class stratification in ancient Egypt. While this may have been important in some densely populated regions, Park may have underestimated the buffering effect of low population density.

The Central Andes, the heartland of the Inka state, is an extremely mountainous area traversed by numerous unnavigable rivers flowing west into the Pacific Ocean and east into the Amazon drainage. Arable land is scattered in highland basins and steep-sided river valleys. Along the fog-shrouded Pacific coast, average temperatures vary from 15 degrees C in August (winter) to

22 degrees C in February (summer). At Cuzco the mean July temperature is 10 degrees C and the mean January temperature 13.5 degrees C. In the still higher Lake Titicaca basin, the mean varies from −2 degrees C in July to 5 degrees C in November. Throughout the highlands, daily temperature fluctuations are more extreme than seasonal ones, on most days amounting to from 11 to 17 degrees C. Rainfall generally decreases from north to south. About 80 centimetres fall each year around Cuzco. The dry season in the high Andes lasts from April to November, while rain falls from December to March.

The principal highland administrative centres of the Inka state were located in the *quechua* (temperate region), between twenty-three hundred and thirty-five hundred metres above sea level, a rolling landscape with a moderate climate and rich volcanic soils. Above it, the *suni*, a rough, barren region, has frequent frosts and thinner soils. Still higher, the *puna* (altiplano), between four thousand and five thousand metres, consists of vast tablelands too cold for trees to grow but covered with thick grasses that are foraged by cameloids. Still higher, the *janca* region consists of rock and snow-covered peaks without vegetation.

Below twenty-three hundred metres is the *yunga* (hot region). On the western side of the Andes, numerous river valleys lead down to the arid *chala* (coastal plain), which except in El Niño years receives less rainfall than the Sahara Desert. Where this plain is crossed by rivers are narrow, once forested valleys. In the valleys that descend steeply from the mountains, rain is frequent, but there is little arable land. On the eastern slopes of the Andes, valleys covered with deciduous and evergreen forests run down into the Amazonian lowlands.

Aboriginal Andean farmers lived in a challenging environment. Throughout the highlands, arable soil constituted only a small part of the total land surface. Pockets of such soil were usually sharply delineated and separated from each other by vast stretches of inhospitable terrain. Under these conditions, possessing land and holding onto it were matters of vital importance. Because of the steep topography, many ecological zones, none of which was totally reliable for human subsistence, occurred in close proximity to one another. Highlanders confronted extreme diurnal temperature fluctuations, low annual temperatures, irregular rainfall, and steep valley sides with insufficient soil cover (Burger 1995: 12–25). In the midst of this diversity, groups as small as ayllus aspired to self-sufficiency in food production.

Farmers expanded arable land by terracing the hillsides, especially the steep and semiarid lower sides of valleys, where maize and other temperate crops grew best. Building terraces (*pata*) required constructing large numbers of well-anchored stone retaining walls and filling them with gravel and topsoil brought up from the valley bottoms. Channels were often constructed both to drain the terraces, so that saturation from excessive rainfall would not cause them to collapse, and to irrigate them in times of drought. Irrigation systems were also developed in the valley bottoms. The fertility of terraced fields was maintained by applying fertilizers, including llama, human, and bird droppings (Donkin 1979; Rowe 1944: 210). Land at higher altitudes did not require irrigation or fertilizer but had to be fallowed for seven years after every four years of cropping (Kendall 1973: 141).

To reduce the danger of crop failure as a result of frost and crop diseases and to increase the variety of its diet, each family planted many different species of plants and many varieties of each species. Andean highlanders are said to have grown more than two hundred different varieties of potatoes (Kendall 1973: 140). They also planted crops with different maturation periods in order to have a staggered harvest (Zimmerer 1993: 24–25). Fields were prepared in August and maize was sown mostly in September so that crops would be ready for harvesting beginning in January. Most potatoes were also planted in September. While the largest potatoes were harvested in June, more rapidly maturing varieties were ready to be dug up between January and March, and there was another harvest in May (Kendall 1973: 149–50; Rowe 1944: 212).

For each family to be able to grow as many different crops as possible, the ideal location for a farming settlement was about thirty-five hundred metres above sea level. Below, terraced and irrigated land produced maize, beans, squash, and other crops that had been domesticated in warmer regions. Maize was especially valued as a luxury food and as the main ingredient for alcoholic beverages (Murra 1960). The colder and wetter zone above produced locally domesticated tubers such as potatoes, meshua, olluco and oca, grains such as *quinoa*, and *tarwi*, a nutritious legume. Some communities also established colonies at still lower altitudes to grow chillies, cacao, cotton, lima beans, and other tropical crops, although these items were also carried into the highlands for sale by itinerant herders. The desire of Andean groups to be economically autonomous led them to support the Inka state in return for the state's protecting arrangements that enabled them to control dispersed eco-niches extending from high-altitude grazing lands to the tropical forests (Kendall 1973: 140–41; Masuda, Shimada, and Morris 1985; Rowe 1944: 210). Herders (*punaruna*) appointed by each ayllu tended large flocks of llamas and alpacas on the grasslands above four thousand metres. These animals provided meat and wool for making clothes. Wild vicuñas were also fleeced of their fine wool in the course of annual roundups. Ideally, each nuclear family possessed ten llamas. Fresh meat was more regularly provided by guinea pigs, which roamed free inside farmhouses (Rowe 1944: 219). Dogs and ducks were also kept and occasionally eaten. To buffer crop failures, Andean farmers developed elaborate storage systems, freeze-drying llama meat and tubers to produce *ch'arki* and *chuño* and constructing rodent-free but well-ventilated granaries (*qollqa*).

When fields were cultivated, men turned over the grass-covered soil with their foot ploughs and women smashed the clods of earth. At planting time, men dug holes or loosened the soil while women placed the tubers or seeds in the ground. Because the earth was regarded as the mother of crops, it was thought appropriate that women rather than men should place her children in her womb (Kendall 1973: 142; Silverblatt 1987: 29).

The Inka state controlled 980,000 square kilometres and has been estimated to have had a population of between eight and fourteen million people (Earle 1987: 65; Rostworowski and Morris 1999: 771). Some have raised this figure as high as thirty-seven million (Schaedel 1978: 293–94). If the Inka kingdom consisted of about eighty provinces with an ideal forty thousand families in each, it would have had a population of sixteen million. A conservative estimate of twelve million suggests an overall population density of 12.2 persons per square kilometre. This estimate means little, however, since the total area includes huge stretches of desert, barren mountains, and puna that were scarcely inhabited. Today only 2 percent of Peru is estimated to consist of arable land. Assuming generously that one-tenth of the surface area was habitable, this produces a population density of 122 persons per square kilometre of arable land. The fertile area may well, however, have been considerably smaller in the Central Andean highlands and the population density correspondingly higher. As a result of herding, the puna was also used to produce food, although it was not inhabited in a sedentary fashion.

Thus the pressure of population on the relatively small amount of arable land in the Central Andean highlands and the danger of crop failures led to the elaboration of a complex and intensive system of agriculture. The Inka state greatly benefited highland farmers by abolishing local warfare, thus permitting them to leave their hill-forts and resettle near the thirty-five-hundred-metre line where they could grow the widest possible array of crops (Earle and D'Altroy 1989; Hastorf 1990; von Hagen 1959: 118, 169). In addition, the Inka state made it easier for highlanders to establish agricultural colonies in lowland regions, which had come under Inka rule. Both of these developments helped ayllus to realize more completely their aspiration to be self-sufficient in food production.

Apart from the Maya Mountains in Belize, the Classic Maya inhabited a flat to slightly rolling and porous limestone plateau. The region remains hot throughout the year, averaging twenty-two degrees C in January and twenty-eight degrees C in July. The northern area of Maya settlement, in the Yucatan

Peninsula, currently receives 178 to 229 centimetres of rainfall annually, while the southern lowlands receive up to 300 centimetres. These rains fall between June and December, although the rainy season is shorter in the north than in the south. The dry season starts in January and reaches its climax in April and May (Hammond 2000: 197–204; Henderson 1981: 41–44).

The Yucatan Peninsula was originally covered with scrub forest, including palm, palmetto, oak, and pine trees. Because surface water is rare, caves and sinkholes were important locations for human settlement. The southern lowlands have deeper soils and are naturally covered by a canopy of mahogany, wild fig, and ceiba trees over 50 metres high. Maya farmers avoided patches of grassland with stunted trees because they indicated poor soils, but they periodically burned these areas to open them up and attract deer and other browsing animals which they hunted (Atran 1993; Fedick 1996a).

There is no more than sixty metres of topographic relief in the southern lowlands, which has numerous swamps, a few permanent lakes, and many natural, clay-lined seasonal waterholes. Rivers flow down from the highlands along the western edge of the region and from the Maya Mountains in the southeast. In most areas the Maya constructed cisterns and elaborate systems of catchments and reservoirs to collect and store rainwater for drinking and gardening during the dry season. These systems frequently utilized plazas as collecting areas and stone quarries as reservoirs (Lucero 1999; Scarborough 1993). The southern Maya lowlands are dominated by deep mollisols, which are naturally more fertile than most other soils found in tropical forests (Fedick 1996b: 341; Fedick and Ford 1990: 28). In the north, fertile soil is shallower and more discontinuous.

The Maya were long thought to have depended on swidden agriculture to grow maize, beans, squash, and less important crops. The modern Maya grow one to three crops each year in this manner. In December they cut the trees, leaving the branches to dry over the winter. In April they burn the fields, prepare the soil, and plant maize between the charred stumps of the bigger trees. The corn is weeded once or twice, in June and July, and harvested in September or October. In September they sow a second crop, usually beans, between the cornstalks. This crop matures in December and January. Two years of cultivation are followed by seven to ten years of fallow (Atran 1993; Henderson 1981: 41–46).

Archaeological data show, however, that Classic Maya population density was considerably higher than could have been supported by swidden agriculture in its present form (Fedick 1996a; Flannery 1982; Harrison and Turner 1978; Pohl 1985). It appears that, like the Yoruba, the Classic Maya grew various root crops, such as manioc and sweet potatoes, together with corn, beans, and squash. The root crops produced several times as much food per hectare as did maize (Bronson 1966; Sanders 1973: 339–40), and this diversity helped to maintain soil fertility even if it did not eliminate the need for fallowing. The Maya preferred rich, well-drained soils when these were available. In clearing the forest they preserved wild fruit-bearing trees, especially breadnut (*ramon*), which is a highly productive food source, although the Maya consumed it mainly as a famine food (Atran 1993: 683–86). The Classic Maya also made extensive use of the wild plants that flourished on their fallows and grew cocoa and cotton.

In some hilly regions there is evidence of extensive dry-wall terracing on sloping terrain. Such terraces would have helped to retain soil and moisture. In other areas, the Maya piled up muck from the bottom of shallow swamps to create raised fields separated from one another by narrow waterways (Dunning 1996). They also dug grids of ditches back from rivers to create similar fields. These two sorts of fields absorbed groundwater and could be watered using buckets. Their fertility was maintained by periodically piling on top of them vegetation dredged from adjacent canals. Raised fields constructed in swamps might produce three or more crops each year, while fields on a floodplain, which would have been inundated between June and November, produced two (Culbert, Levi, and Cruz 1990; Harrison 1990; Levi 1996: 97). In the north, cacao and fruit trees, as well as two food crops per year, were planted in large, natural sinkholes. Terraces and raised fields now appear to have been less extensive than was once believed. Terraces are most widespread on the Vaca Plateau around Caracol and raised fields in northern Belize and the Candelaria area. In other regions either fluctuations in water levels were too great or the soil was too poor to permit intensive agriculture (Fedick 1996b).

An important source of food was the gardens attached to Maya houses. Clusters of houses belonging to different extended families were widely separated, even in urban centres, to provide space for these gardens, which were sometimes enclosed by stone walls (Graham 1999). Gardens were associated with upper-class residences as well as with the homes of ordinary people. A study at Sayil indicates that the largest gardens were attached to the most elaborate residential complexes (Dunning 1996: 60). Gardens contained fruit trees and probably were used to grow condiments as well as staples, especially root crops. These gardens appear to have been fertilized with kitchen and human waste and probably were kept moist with water drawn from urban reservoirs and household tanks. Kitchen gardens could thus produce three or four crops each year over an indefinite period. It appears likely that these infields were a major source of food for families in both urban centres and the countryside.

Swidden agriculture was used to grow food during the wet season on fields some distance away from urban centres or permanent rural settlements. Some of those who cultivated swidden land constructed seasonally occupied houses near these fields; however, these living quarters had no accompanying burials or provisions for storing water for the dry season (Santley 1990: 333; Dunning 1996: 61). There is growing evidence of regional variability in Maya agriculture and of variation in intensity from one region to another. The most serious problems appear to have been securing water and controlling labour in a region where arable land was not strongly circumscribed.

The Maya depended heavily on fishing and hunting as sources of animal protein. Their few domestic animals were dogs, turkeys, and ducks. They also kept some semidomesticated peccaries.

The Classic Maya were once believed to have had low population density, although this made it difficult to understand how they had constructed so many impressive urban centres. Recent studies of settlement patterns indicate that large areas had an overall population density of about 180 persons per square kilometre (Rice and Culbert 1990: 26). In some regions, such as Río Bec, the maximum population density may have reached 282 persons per square kilometre, while in the Tikal and Calakmul regions it seems to have been as low as 120 per square kilometre (B. Turner 1990: 321–23). Overall population densities were low in areas where there were extensive seasonal swamps that were unsuitable for agricultural development or too little water to support intensive agriculture.

The Valley of Mexico is an elevated plain separated from other regions of highland Mexico by rugged mountain ranges on its eastern, southern, and western flanks but by only a few broken hills from the Meseta Central to the north. Until the eighteenth century, when drainage to the outside was artificially established, the Valley of Mexico was a closed hydrological basin of seven thousand square kilometres with a series of large but shallow and seasonally fluctuating lakes at its centre. These lakes were fed by rivers and streams descending from the mountains and from artesian springs. Only two rivers flowed year-round. The central lakes, which were all interconnected when they were at their fullest, stood at altitudes between 2,238 and 2,245 metres. The largest of these bodies of water, Lake Texcoco, was also the lowest and most brackish (Hassig 1985: 41–46).

The Valley of Mexico is located in what modern Mexicans classify as *terra fria*, the cold rather than the temperate or tropical zone. Winters are dry and cool, averaging eleven degrees C. Frosts occur regularly in most parts of the valley between November and the end of January and exceptionally between September and March. Summers are warm, with an average temperature of twenty-one degrees C, and rain is abundant at that time. While scattered showers occur from November until the end of April, 80 percent of the annual rainfall takes place between June and October, with July and August constituting a drier interval. Rainfall varies between 45 centimetres in the north and 150 centimetres in the south (Sanders, Parsons, and Santley 1979: 81–83).

Back from the lakes, a broad, gently sloping lower piedmont rises to twenty-five hundred metres before giving way to a steeper upper piedmont. Soil is generally fertile and easily worked, although it tends to be shallower in the upper piedmont than it is lower down. Above twenty-seven hundred metres is a rugged sierra, where agriculture is impossible. In the sixteenth century, the upper rim of the valley was covered with forests of oak, cypress, and alder, with pine at higher altitudes. The rulers of the various states in the valley were able to regulate the use of these forests sufficiently to preserve them as a source of timber and for curbing soil erosion (Hassig 1985: 207–8; Sanders, Parsons, and Santley 1979: 84–89).

The Aztec and their neighbours grew corn and amaranth as their main cereal crops, along with *chía* (*Salvia*), squashes, tomatoes, chillies, avocados, and many other food plants. Hemp was grown to make cloth, but cotton had to be imported from the hotter lowlands. Maguey was cultivated for its sap, which was fermented, and its fibres, which were used to manufacture textiles.

While some swidden agriculture was practised in the higher and the more northerly portions of the Valley of Mexico, it does not appear to have been of great economic importance. Irrigation schemes were developed in the middle and lower piedmont regions, using water from the mainly seasonal streams flowing down the sides of the valley. Because of the sloping terrain, high water tables and salination were much less of a problem than they were in Mesopotamia. Until around A.D. 1400, these schemes generally sought to irrigate areas of only ten to one hundred hectares, but after that time more extensive systems with complex feeder canals were constructed. Creating these more extensive systems required larger workforces and skilled hydraulic engineering (Doolittle 1990). Vast numbers of short, irregular terraces were constructed to control soil erosion (Sanders, Parsons, and Santley 1979: 243–48). The number of crops grown each year was limited by seasonal frosts, but in lower and more southerly areas two crops could be grown annually.

In 1519, the main agricultural area was located in the southern part of the central lakes (Fig. 14.3). There, in the fifteenth century, a series of major dykes had been constructed to impound fresh water and control water levels in various parts of the lake system. The largest of these was the Dyke of

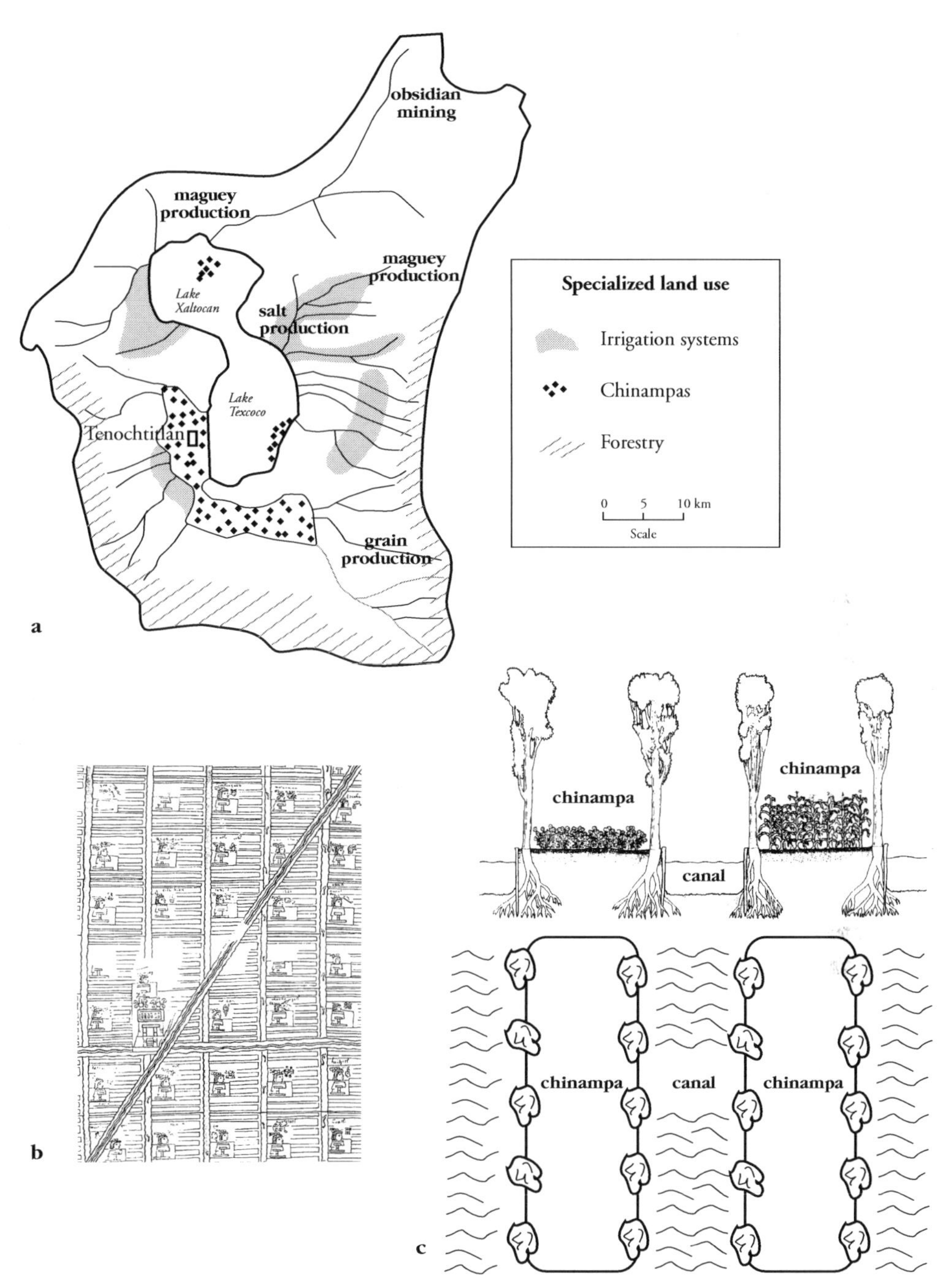

14.3. Agriculture in the Valley of Mexico: (a) map showing specialized forms of land use – the rest of the valley was used for rainfall agriculture, which was more productive in the south than in the north; (b) detail of Plano en Papel de Maguey, ca. 1523–25, showing a chinampa district; (c) cross-section and plan of a chinampa field. Sources: (a) after Sanders & Price 1968: 192; (b) after A. P. Maudslay, *The True History of the Conquest of New Spain*, Vol. 3 (London, 1910); (c) after M. D. Coe, The Chinampas of Mexico, *Scientific American*, July 1964.

Nezahualcoyotl, a multistate construction built around A.D. 1450. It created a large zone of fresh water around the Aztec capital. Within this zone and in Lakes Chalco and Xochimilco to the south, twelve thousand hectares of *chinampas* were constructed. Like the Mayas' raised fields, these were long, narrow fields constructed of layers of mud, dredged by hand from the shallow lake bottoms, and waste vegetation. They were raised high enough above the lake level that roots did not become water-logged, and their edges were reinforced by planting trees around them. The fields were fertilized with fresh mud and floating vegetation, as well as with human excrement brought by canoe from urban centres. The lakes provided year-round moisture for growing crops, as well as protection against frosts. This permitted three or four crops to be grown each year, with fallow periods amounting to no more than a few months every three or four years while the fields were being repaired and fertilized. By germinating plants on floating rafts it was possible to shorten the growing season for each crop. The exceptional fertility of the soil ensured a very high yield. Produce was transported to cities located around the southern edge of the lakes by canoe (Calnek 1972; 1973; Hassig 1985: 46–53; Parsons 1976; Sanders 1976: 131–36; Sanders, Parsons, and Santley 1979: 273–81).

Commoners had substantial garden plots (*calmil*) adjacent to their houses. These gardens, while not as big as Maya ones, were intensively cultivated, weeded, and fertilized with domestic refuse. Men are recorded as cultivating fields; it is not known to what extent women were responsible for working or helping to work garden plots (R. McC. Adams 1960: 287; Berdan 1982: 12–13; M. E. Smith 1996: 77–78, 189, 195).

Dogs, turkeys, rabbits, and ducks were the only domestic animals kept in the Valley of Mexico, and all these species were eaten. There was heavy reliance on beans and other vegetable sources of protein. The lakes were a significant source of meat protein in the form of fish, migrating waterfowl, and other aquatic life.

Systematic archaeological surveys of the Valley of Mexico indicate a total population in the Late Aztec period of more than one million people. This meant an overall population density of two hundred persons per square kilometre in the Late Aztec period and of five hundred persons per square kilometre in relation to arable land (Sanders, Parsons, and Santley 1979: 162, 219, 378–80), the highest population density in our sample. Despite a challenging climate and the lack of large domestic animals, a population of this density was fed through a combination of irrigation and chinampa agriculture. While there had been severe famines in the fifteenth century, the subsequent development of hydraulic works appears to have buffered climatic variations and allowed a general increase in food production that was able to support a rapidly growing population.

INTENSITY OF FOOD PRODUCTION

Early civilizations developed in many different geographical settings, some of which did not naturally or easily support a dense population. Ancient Egypt and Mesopotamia both depended on irrigation agriculture in a desert zone, but their hydraulic systems were radically different because each region had its own, environmentally determined requirements for effective water management. While the Egyptians relied on controlling annual floodwaters, the Mesopotamians, because their natural watercourses were elevated, depended on gravity-flow irrigation, which made agriculture much more labour-intensive. Different species of domestic plants and animals were available to various early civilizations, and their specific potentials and requirements resulted in radically different patterns of agriculture and diverse combinations of agriculture and animal husbandry. Some early civilizations, especially those of Mesoamerica, depended for subsistence primarily on domestic plants. Others incorporated caring for animals into routine farm life, while yet others developed herding as a specialized branch of farming or exchanged produce with independent herding peoples living along their frontiers. These variations were largely determined by the various sorts of plants and animals that had been domesticated prior to the rise of civilization, the patterns of caring for them inherited from an earlier period, and the different ecological settings in which these civilizations had developed. Success stemmed from the care with which agricultural systems were adjusted to the needs of different sizes and densities of populations. The result was nearly idiosyncratic variation. The primary shared requirement of subsistence patterns in early civilizations was that they be able to feed relatively dense, sedentary farming populations and produce a surplus that could support an effective government administration and an upper class. A wide range of subsistence patterns could meet these requirements in many different types of environments.

The early civilizations of our sample may be rank-ordered in terms of the intensity of food production (as measured by population density), from least to most, as follows: Yoruba, Shang China, Mesopotamia, Egypt, Inka, Classic Maya, and Valley of Mexico. (I acknowledge the speculative nature of the population estimates on which this ranking is based, especially those for China and Mesopotamia, but they are the best that available data and current methods permit.) The higher population densities in the early civilizations of the Western Hemisphere seem to correlate with a relative absence of communicable diseases compared with the Old World and the higher productivity of local cultigens such as maize and potatoes. Therefore these estimates are probably accurate enough, at least relative to one another, to permit some theoretical propositions to be examined.

The intensity of food production did not correspond with the number of food sources exploited. The peoples living in the Valley of Mexico and the Maya had very weakly developed animal husbandry yet sustained the highest population densities of our sample. This may have been possible at least partly because humans were not competing with domestic animals for plant food. The Yoruba, however, also raised few large animals, but their largely vegetable-based subsistence economy was the least intensive. The highland Peruvians grazed llamas and alpacas in areas that were unsuitable for crops, but their population density appears to have been less than that of the Maya and Aztec, who kept no large domestic animals, and greater than that of the Egyptians and Mesopotamians, who combined the herding of animals in areas not used for agriculture with grazing domestic animals on the stubble of their fields.

The least (Yoruba) and the most (Valley of Mexico) densely populated early civilizations were both city-state systems, with other city-state systems and territorial states falling between them in random order. This arrangement casts doubt on the widely held belief that the development of large, densely settled urban centres by itself promoted more intensive agriculture (Netting 1969). Greater intensification as a result of urban growth seems to have occurred with the development of chinampas to feed Tenochtitlan and Texcoco, but kitchen gardens were associated with country as well as city life among the Maya and in the Valley of Mexico, while no intensive agriculture is documented for the Yoruba. Despite its extremely high degree of urbanization, especially in Early Dynastic times, southern Mesopotamia had neither a particularly high population density nor a particularly intensive form of agriculture.

Metal tools were employed in agriculture only by the Yoruba and in Mesopotamia; that both were city-state systems accords with the suggestion that city-states favoured the production and dissemination of more complex tools. Yet among the Maya and in the Valley of Mexico wooden digging sticks supported a more productive subsistence economy than Yoruba iron implements. Moreover, despite the labour savings that resulted from using ploughs and draft animals, the early civilizations that employed animal traction for grain production (Mesopotamia, Egypt) supported less dense populations than some that did not. That agricultural tools generally remained simple in all early civilizations does not, of course, mean that the introduction of more efficient tools might not alter the ways in which particular peoples worked the soil. The

Maya and Aztec probably would have performed agricultural tasks differently if they had possessed iron hoes and machetes as the Yoruba did. Yet, while reducing labour, having iron tools did not independently enhance productivity.

The least intensive system was that of the Yoruba, who lived in a region of tropical forests and savannas, but the Maya, who lived in a similar environment (albeit one with unusually rich soils), used a combination of raised fields, irrigation, kitchen gardens, and swidden to support a much denser population than was achieved by hydraulic agriculture in Egypt and Mesopotamia. The inhabitants of the Valley of Mexico and of highland Peru, both using a combination of rainfall and irrigation agriculture, were near and at the top in terms of productivity despite the severe climatic and topographical limitations of their environments.

The civilizations that occupied the most clearly circumscribed productive areas were Mesopotamia, Egypt, highland Peru, and the Valley of Mexico, and all of them had medium to high population densities. The Yoruba, Shang Chinese, and Maya, each occupying only part of a more extensive fertile agricultural region, had low to high population densities. The Yoruba were surrounded either by powerful states or by small-scale societies denser than their own; so it is not surprising that in times of crisis Yoruba groups tended to relocate within their own territory rather than trying to expand it. Thinly settled adjacent territory did not, however, attract Maya settlement, while the Shang and Zhou populations maintained a relatively low population density by militarily expanding into adjacent regions.

Elizabeth Stone (1997) has proposed that, where population densities do not preclude relocation and agricultural land lacks substantial labour investment or is quickly exhausted, the control of labour is more critical than the control of land. The ability of families or small communities to relocate beyond the range of a leader's power may, she suggests, explain the prevalence of heterarchical rather than centralized governments among the Yoruba, where traditions of politically disgruntled factions moving to other states or founding new ones abound, and in Mesopotamia. Within the Valley of Mexico, however, because of the development of chinampas and forms of irrigation that were less susceptible to salination than those of Mesopotamia, developed land acquired high, long-term value, and its owners became increasingly subject to political control. The Maya's heavy reliance on kitchen gardens may have made their owners more susceptible to coercion. While the special vulnerability to salination of fields in southern Mesopotamia may to some extent have inhibited the local development of more centralized forms of government, it appears that in all other city-state systems land ownership became more important and people were more easily coerced by governments as population densities increased.

By encouraging the development of more intensive food production, denser populations increased the vulnerability to political coercion of all those who possessed land with potential for development. The primary basis of centralized power was the ability of rulers to punish uncooperative landholders by confiscating their land. The principal differences between more centralized and heterarchical city-states thus appear to relate to the presence in hierarchical states of higher overall population densities and the ability to cultivate plots of land intensively and on a long-term basis.

Territorial states offered alternative solutions to the control of land and labour. Because of its scarcity and high maintenance costs, fertile land became a contested resource everywhere in the Andean highlands. The Inka state, by suppressing intergroup conflict, was able to guarantee its highland subjects not only secure tenure of fertile fields but also conditions under which the maximum expansion of arable land was possible. Egyptian farmers were still moving from the south into less densely settled areas of central and northern Egypt throughout the Old and Middle Kingdoms. The emergence of a single state guaranteed landowners' control over farm labour while eliminating the possibility that defeated political opponents and their followers would find refuge elsewhere, and these may have been among the most important considerations encouraging the development of a territorial state that embraced the whole of Egypt (R. Allen 1997). Thus, where control of either land or labour was a problem, territorial states offered alternative solutions to those offered by the development of city-states. While the development of more centralized or heterarchical city-states may have an ecological explanation, it appears necessary to account for the development of either city- or territorial states politically.

The most obvious correlation is between intensity of food production, with its attendant higher labour inputs, and population density (Boserup 1965), but it is not clear whether intensity of food production was the result or the cause of higher density or the two stimulated each other's development. It was long assumed that population increase was an independent variable leading, especially in ecologically circumscribed regions, to more intensive food production and the development of early civilizations. Today experts are less certain. The Ibo, who live next to the Yoruba, had double the Yoruba's population density but never developed states or cities. Thus population density does not explain the development of Yoruba civilization (Bascom 1955: 452).

It is now clear that, even prior to the development of modern methods of birth control, birth rates were subject to some limitation through infanticide and abortion and the alteration of patterns of procreative behaviour. In all five early civilizations for which data are available, the prolonged nursing of infants is reported: two to four years among the Yoruba (Bascom 1969: 57), two to four years in the Valley of Mexico (Clendinnen 1991: 155; López Austin 1998, 1: 449), three years in Egypt (Robins 1993: 89) and Mesopotamia (R. Harris 1975: 330, 357–58), and for as long as a woman could produce milk while avoiding sexual intercourse in Peru (Kendall 1973: 75). The Yoruba believed that children would die if nursed for less than two years, and to ensure the production of milk Yoruba women avoided sexual intercourse as well. While in some societies, including ancient Egypt, upper-class women hired wet-nurses to feed their babies, most mothers in early civilizations seem to have breast-fed their own children for long periods and practised birth-spacing.

Lengthy nursing of infants is a pattern that anthropologists usually associate with mobile hunter-gatherer societies and regard as contrary to the desire of farmers to produce large numbers of children as farm labourers and to support them in their old age. Prolonged nursing alone increases the interval between births, although sedentary women regain body weight and hence the ability to become pregnant faster than hunter-gatherer women (Howell 1979; Lee 1972). The lengthy nursing of infants in early civilizations suggests that population increase in these societies may not have been as rapid or families as large as is generally believed. It also indicates that rapid population expansion cannot be attributed to specific economic interests that supposedly were universally shared by the farmers who made up the vast majority of people in all early civilizations. Behaviour that limited family size appears to have been as characteristic of early civilizations as it was of hunter-gatherers. Postgate (1992: 295) suggests that the numerous measures the Mesopotamian gods were supposed to have taken to slow human population growth reflected a Mesopotamian belief that increased population posed a potential threat to the stability of their society.

Since population increase is not an independent variable, various different reasons may explain why it and more intensive forms of food production occurred in specific settings. Ecological changes may occasionally have necessitated new forms of food production which required more labour input, and this in turn may have encouraged farmers to have more children. The development of larger markets for farm produce could also have resulted in population increase. Perhaps the most important incentives for population increase, however, were political competition and warfare. Where such competition occurred, greater numbers meant more security. Under these circumstances, families, communities, and whole societies may have been anxious to outnumber their competitors even if feeding more people required investing greater effort in producing food. For farmers the benefits of larger families had to outweigh the extra labour needed to feed and care for children.

There is evidence that controls on reproduction can be relaxed quickly and for short periods when the costs of population increase are low or ordinary people judge it to be desirable (Warrick 1990). For kings and members of the upper classes in early civilizations, larger numbers of farmers usually meant increased productivity and hence more grain surpluses, corvée labour, and soldiers. Almost invariably, they valued having more people under their control.

Thus, as long as larger numbers of people could be fed without reducing available surpluses, the ruling classes had a vested interest in seeking to increase their support base by encouraging higher levels of reproduction. Such strategies might have been frustrated by rising mortality rates or, if there was inadequate circumscription, by emigration. There is no indication that rulers understood how to influence, except by exhortation, rates of reproduction among their subjects. An alternative option, expansion into neighbouring regions, might have kept the overall population density relatively low but increased the wealth of rulers by giving them control over more people and natural resources. This appears to have been the course followed in Shang and Zhou China. Such an option would not have encouraged the development of new and more intensive forms of food production.

Egyptian kings sought to increase the population by settling prisoners of war from Nubia, Libya, the Sinai Peninsula, and Canaan in less populated areas of Egypt. They also welcomed peoples from these lands as refugees in times of famine and actively recruited them as mercenaries. The Egyptian government wanted foreigners as additional sources of labour and of military power. Throughout ancient Egyptian history there was always room in Egypt for voluntary or involuntary newcomers (Eyre 1999: 35). Wealthy Yoruba sought to increase their labour forces by acquiring many prisoners of war, whom they put to work as slaves on their farms. Semitic-speaking pastoralists also appear to have been welcome to settle in southern Mesopotamia, while the immigrants who moved as individuals and groups into the Valley of Mexico, attaching themselves to existing states and sometimes founding new ones, were often viewed as a means of increasing the wealth and power of local rulers.

When population density exceeded the limit sustainable by the existing system, food production became more intensive. This frequently required investing more labour. Population growth locked a people into a new system of food production even if more energy was required for each unit of food that was produced. This process occurred most quickly where geographical circumscription made it hard for people to move elsewhere and where investment in agricultural land made its occupiers especially vulnerable to government demands (Boserup 1965; P. Smith 1976).

When required, intensification of food production seems to have occurred relatively easily. In most cases, the knowledge possessed by local farmers was deployed to devise more efficient systems. This was so even where the state had to intervene in order for major objectives to be achieved. The vast expansion of chinampas in the Valley of Mexico, which was grounded in long-standing experience of wetland agriculture in Mesoamerica, occurred quickly, even though it involved undertaking hydraulic projects on a hitherto unprecedented scale. Mesopotamian irrigation schemes grew more elaborate over time as the population and state demands for surpluses increased, but each innovation was based on previous experience. Sometimes, however, expertise was borrowed from elsewhere. When the Egyptian rulers of the Middle Kingdom wished to increase their personal revenues by expanding agriculture in the Fayum, they appear to have employed settlers from the Middle East. The agricultural expansion of the Fayum required gravity-flow irrigation systems that were well known in Mesopotamia and the rest of the Middle East but were totally different from the basin irrigation practised in Egypt. It is probably no accident that many people of Semitic descent (*ʿ3m*) lived and worked in that area in the Middle Kingdom (Butzer 1976: 41–47; David 1986: 41, 190–93; Grimal 1992: 166).

LABOUR AND SURPLUS PRODUCTION

The agricultural systems of early civilizations were particular heritages from a regional past modified to meet the requirements of expanded populations and demands for surplus production by the government and the upper classes. Therefore the way in which each civilization organized food production exhibited many idiosyncratic features. At least two crucial features of food production were shared by all early civilizations: the production of surpluses that were in large part appropriated and utilized by the upper classes and the dependence of agriculture on human labour, only supplemented in some cases to a limited degree by animal traction. Where technology was limited and production depended mainly on human labour, the agricultural surpluses that any one farmer could produce were small. Increasing the number of persons supported by each unit of cultivated soil usually required increased labour input for each calorie of food produced, and therefore an increase in population density did not necessarily result in per capita increases in food surpluses. It appears that, regardless of the agricultural regime followed, between 70 and 90 percent of the labour input in early civilizations was, of necessity, devoted to food production. This means that all early civilizations had to remain predominantly agricultural. It also means that the surplus resources available to the upper classes were never large in relation to total production and had to be used carefully. Because of this, strategies for increasing revenue had to be mainly political (R. McC. Adams 1960): increasing the number of farmers controlled, creating situations in which ruling groups shared available resources more disproportionately among themselves according to rank, or persuading farmers to surrender marginally greater amounts of surplus production without increasing the cost of the mechanisms needed to ensure social control.

15 Land Ownership

In early civilizations surplus crops and, to a lesser extent, livestock were the most abundant sources of wealth, and controlling these resources was the key to political power. The study of the production and control of food surpluses in early civilizations is complicated by vague and conflicting scholarly definitions of key concepts, in particular those relating to land ownership. Some analysts term 'private' any land that was not owned by the monarch or the state, whether it was possessed collectively or individually and whether or not it could be sold. Stricter definitions restrict 'private' to land owned by individuals that could be sold to any buyer. To reduce these ambiguities, I propose to differentiate three broad categories of land ownership in early civilizations: (1) collective ownership by kinship groups or communities, (2) ownership by institutions such as temples or the state, including landholding by individuals or groups as benefices from such institutions, and (3) private ownership. Because of lack of relevant information, the Classic Maya are excluded from this discussion.

One of the most persistent myths about early civilizations, which can be traced back to Montesquieu, is that of 'eminent domain' (Isaac 1993: 432). This is the notion that in early civilizations rulers owned all the land in their kingdoms and prohibited alternative forms of ownership, making everyone the tenant or slave of the ruler. The evidence that has been interpreted as supporting this claim appears to be metaphorical and political in nature. A Yoruba ruler was often said to own his kingdom, but in reality ownership of all but the palace and the royal farms was vested in communities and patrilineages (Pemberton and Afolayan 1996: 58). In the Valley of Mexico, high officials asserted that the land utilized by calpollis belonged to the king and the nobility, who only permitted commoners to use it in return for their services to the state (Offner 1983: 125). This claim appears to reflect the ideology of the ruling classes rather than what members of calpollis believed. In practical terms, the concept of eminent domain seems to have been no more than an assertion of sovereignty equivalent to that made by all modern states. Its primary significance was that individuals or groups could not sell or give land to foreigners in ways that extinguished or diminished the ruler's authority to treat that land as part of his kingdom. Among the Yoruba, land could not be sold, given, or bequeathed to foreigners without the king's permission. The new owner had to agree to pay taxes and recognize the ruler's continuing sovereignty over the land. A Yoruba king did not, however, have the right to appropriate or decide what should be done with land that belonged to specific communities or kinship groups.

COLLECTIVE OWNERSHIP

While many anthropologists are inclined to regard collective ownership of land as evolutionarily 'primitive', its main feature is that it is relatively resistant to economic exploitation by people who do not produce food, whether acting together or individually. Producers who are constituted as corporate landowning groups have more freedom to define their relations with the state and the upper classes than producers acting individually, especially those who lack the most important means for supporting themselves: land.

Collectively owned land was common in some early civilizations. In the Valley of Mexico, the most extensive category of land was *calpollalli*, which belonged jointly to members of calpollis. Calpollis were, first and foremost, landholding groups. Part of the calpolli land consisted of common fields that were cultivated by internal corvée labour. The produce from these fields supported the calpolli leaders and their families, sustained the calpolli temple and other communal activities, and was used to pay taxes. The rest of the land was divided among all the families that belonged to the calpolli, whether their adult male members were full-time farmers or had another profession. Full-time artisans, traders, and administrators were allowed to rent their holdings to landless workers and thus continued to derive at least part of their subsistence from them. Calpolli land could not, however, be rented to members of the same or another calpolli, since such an arrangement would have contravened the legal equality and exclusivity of rights to land that defined calpolli membership (Berdan 1982: 89). In many parts of highland Mexico, calpolli lands were regularly reassigned to reflect changes in family size and ensure that each family continued to have a share that was proportional to its needs. In the southern part of the Valley of Mexico such periodic redistributions did not occur, which suggests that over time considerable inequalities in land ownership may have developed. This development may have been offset to some degree by the expansion of arable land that resulted from the construction of chinampas. Since calpolli land could not be sold, if a family died out or moved away its holdings reverted to the collectivity and were available for redistribution (Berdan 1982: 55–57; Offner 1983: 124–26).

The highland Peruvian ayllu was also an endogamous landowning group. Each nuclear family received a share of the various kinds of ayllu land that were required to produce all the basic foodstuffs it required. Every family had to cultivate parcels of land at different altitudes. A local ayllu leader oversaw the annual reallotment of land as part of the process of crop rotation and fallowing. This reallotment ensured that, despite its changing membership, each family continued to have an equitable share. Ayllu members assisted one another in cultivating their land and also cultivated land assigned to members of the ayllu who were sick, crippled, orphaned, or called away for long periods of corvée labour. Land that was set aside to support ayllu leaders and religious cults was also cultivated collectively by ayllu members. Those who worked such land were entitled to allotments of food equivalent to their subsistence needs during the time expended to perform this task.

Yoruba farm land belonged collectively to extended families. However, the ownership of any land unclaimed by extended families or abandoned if an extended family died out or moved away reverted to the community. A king could dispossess an extended family of its land only by banishing that family from his kingdom. Land could not be sold or alienated in any other fashion at either the individual or the family level. Royal lineages held their land on the same terms as others.

Some Yoruba farm land, called *ajoyeba* (title land) was worked collectively by members of patrilineal extended families to support their lineage's head and corporate activities (K. Barber 1991: 162). The rest was assigned among the individual, often polygynous, families that made up the extended family. The amount of land cultivated by families varied according to their size, wealth, and status. Large families had to cultivate more land than small ones in order to support themselves. The most important factor that enabled wealthier or more powerful men to cultivate proportionately more land was the number of dependents, debtors, and slaves they could assign to agricultural tasks. Prestige depended on being able to support many armed retainers who had to be fed. Major officials usually had large tracts of lineage land under cultivation close to the urban centres where they lived (Peel 1983: 57). Women also invested wealth they acquired from trading in buying slaves, whom they used to cultivate land belonging to their patrilineage (W. Clarke 1972: 86). Thus collective ownership of land did not preclude the use of land for economic and political competition among individual Yoruba. In most Yoruba states population density was sufficiently low that individuals could bring as much land as they wished under cultivation. Where there was pressure on land, extra farm land was assigned to the title-holders of patrilineal extended families so that they could maintain their political power and the prestige of their group. Lineage heads also rented unused extended land to strangers on a permanent or short-term basis as a source of income (Lloyd 1962: 83, 89).

Rights to farm holdings were inherited by the sons and daughters of deceased male members of an extended family. Land could not, however, be alienated from the patrilineage by further inheritance through female members. The slaves that individual men and women acquired during their lifetimes became the personal property of their heirs, male and female, and this made it possible for these heirs to bring land under cultivation regardless of its lineage affiliation. The only farm land that a king could transfer to his children was the part of his lineage's holdings that he had cultivated prior to becoming king (Lloyd 1962: 18–37).

In Mesopotamia during the late fourth and early third millennia, patrilineal extended families appear to have collectively owned extensive tracts of farm land. By the time the oldest readable texts provide detailed information about economic transactions, all or part of such holdings could be sold to non-kin, subject to the agreement of all the male members of an extended family. In the third millennium B.C., a rapid increase in institutional land appears to have greatly reduced the amount of collectively owned land. Poor harvests and other economic and ecological crises may have forced less affluent extended families to pledge their communal lands, as well as the personal freedom of family members, in return for loans (Diakonoff 1974: 15; Maisels 1990: 151–52; 1993: 172–75; Van De Mieroop 1999: 203–6).

While statewide royal cancellations of debts (*amargi*), which are recorded as early as the reign of Entemena of Lagash (ca. 2400 B.C.) and were sometimes proclaimed to celebrate royal accessions or the thirtieth year of a king's reign, helped to counteract the growing economic and social inequality that resulted from indebtedness, it is uncertain whether early acts of this sort did more than free persons enslaved for debt. It is not until the Old Babylonian period that debt cancellation is clearly recorded as returning land sold under duress to its original owners, and even then there were many exclusions (Hudson 1996: 46–49; Postgate 1992: 194–98). This left a long period during which collectively owned land may have passed into the permanent possession of creditors while its former owners became tenant farmers or landless labourers, perhaps often after having been temporarily enslaved. The alienation of land possibly began through the fiction of adopting a potential buyer into a family (Yoffee 1988). He could then purchase a piece of land on the same terms as a single family member might have bought the rights of multiple heirs to a plot that had become too fragmented for further subdivision.

As a result of these processes, collectively owned land was transformed into institutionally and privately owned estates. Land ownership became concentrated in the hands of an ever-smaller number of institutions and individuals. In the course of this transformation, leaders of some extended families may have become the heads of major institutions or wealthy estate owners (Ellis 1976).

It is agreed that in China land was not bought and sold before the Spring and Autumn period (722–481 B.C.) (Ke 1989: 52). In Shang and Western Zhou times blocks of land were occupied and worked by extended families, but it is unclear whether these families collectively owned the land they cultivated or whether it belonged to the king or some regional or local official (Wheatley 1971: 66). Government decrees which moved extended families from one part of the kingdom to another and assigned them to serve new lords suggest that at least some extended families may have had hereditary access to land but did not own it. Extended families also tended to split after they grew too large to be supported by the land that was available to them. At this juncture, junior branches, with the approval of high-ranking officials, went off to occupy land elsewhere. Regional rulers sent to occupy new territory assigned the land around their headquarters to their officials, household retainers, and soldiers (Vandermeersch 1980: 43, 131–33). This suggests that land ownership may have mattered less to descent groups than access to agricultural land through lineage-mediated political relations, which could be interpreted as evidence that in Shang and Western Zhou China all land was in some sense regarded as institutional. Massive relocations of ayllus by Inka rulers did not, however, undermine the status of ayllus as collective landholding units. It is therefore possible that some or all rural extended families regarded the land they worked as their collective possession. Senior lineages, which remained in one place for a long time, may have come to venerate a specific locale because their ancestors were buried there. It is also not impossible that, in a fashion analogous to what happened in parts of the Valley of Mexico, Chinese officials regarded all the land within their domains as their institutional holdings, while commoner patrilineages simultaneously viewed the land they farmed as their collective possession.

For Egypt it is difficult to study matters that existed beyond the purview of the state. It is unknown to what extent, in the late Predynastic and Early Dynastic periods, villagers collectively owned the land they worked and whether these arrangements remained intact into later times in areas that were relatively unaffected by the government's creation of agricultural estates (*ḥwt*). These unaffected areas would have included the far southern parts of Egypt that were already heavily populated in Early Dynastic times. It is unclear whether the creation of estates extinguished the rights of existing farming communities to own land or these communities were incorporated into estates with their ancient land rights intact although they were henceforth required to pay rents to the estate owners. The latter arrangement seems possible if the term *nỉwt*, which denoted some small rent-paying unit, also referred to a farming community. The continuation through the Old Kingdom of the titles *ḥq3 nỉwt* (overseer of a village) and *ḥq3 ḥwt* (overseer of an estate) suggests the enduring importance of farming villages as fiscal entities (Eyre 1987a: 34; 1999). One archaeologically well-studied small settlement in Middle Egypt, Naga ed-Deir, displayed remarkable social continuity through the Old Kingdom, although it became both less egalitarian and poorer as the economic demands of the state increased during the Third and Fourth Dynasties. Its wealthiest family clearly had close relations with the provincial administration. During the Early Dynastic period its leader had been able to obtain some items of gold jewellery manufactured at the royal court (Reisner 1932: 185–92). It is unknown to what extent these possessions were rewards for loyal service to the government or were purchased using wealth derived from private holdings or from the disproportionate amounts of land and labour that would have been available to the head of an established landowning community.

In most early civilizations collectively owned land could not be bought or sold; it was the common and inalienable possession of a kinship group or an endogamous community. Evidence of increasing sales of collective land in Mesopotamia during the Early Dynastic period suggests that in this early civilization collective ownership was in sharp decline. Some collective landowning groups, such as those found among the Yoruba, in rural areas of the Valley of Mexico, and in highland Peru, were managed by traditional community leaders supported by public opinion. Sometimes these leaders were the oldest male members of a group; others belonged to specific descent lines. Larger landowning groups tended to be more hierarchical. They were managed by councils on which various extended families were represented by hereditary officers. The leaders of such groups were often co-opted by the upper classes.

Differences in the size of collective landowning groups influenced attitudes towards land and surplus production. Small-scale units generally strove for group self-sufficiency, while their members enjoyed relative economic equality and were committed to supporting one another. In larger units, the land and labour of the group tended to be treated more as a resource belonging to the group's leaders. Inequality was justified as necessary for representatives or leaders to be able to perform essential acts of hospitality and worship on behalf of their followers. Maintaining membership in a collective landholding group remained essential for having inalienable access to land. In cases where the distribution of land within such groups grew less equitable, richer members could use prisoners of war or debtors to enlarge their personal productive labour force, or portions of collectively owned land might be sold to outsiders to cover individual members' debts. These situations created circumstances that eventually might permit all collective land to be transformed into institutional or private land. An alternative threat to collective land, when its co-proprietors were not powerful, was expropriation by politically dominant leaders.

INSTITUTIONAL OWNERSHIP

Institutionally owned land in the early civilizations was not public property (*res publica*) as defined by Roman law. Rather than being established for the enjoyment or benefit of the community as a whole it was set aside to provide revenue for the state, religious cults, office-holders, and socially privileged individuals. Conceptually it was closely related to those portions of collectively owned land that were cultivated by the whole group to support its leaders and finance group activities. Yet those who jointly owned collective land agreed about what would be done with the common surpluses they produced, while those who benefited from the surplus production of institutional land had rights to that surplus independent of the wishes of its cultivators.

Institutional land was not individually owned and therefore could not be bought or sold. Individual use of a plot of institutional land may or may not have been hereditary, but inheritance of benefits from it was accompanied by the transmission of related duties or roles from one generation to the next. Institutional land assigned to individuals in return for service is often referred to as prebendary land. In medieval Europe, such land was set aside to produce rents to support administrative personnel. To avoid the overly specific connotations of this medieval terminology, I will call such land 'office land'.

Among the Yoruba, the only institutional land was the title farms belonging to the king. This land consisted of farms cultivated by palace servants, royal slaves, and sometimes corvée labourers. Like other agricultural land, title farms were usually located outside cities; however, at Ode Onde such a farm lay within the sixteen-hectare enclosure of the palace (Lloyd 1962: 72, 112). The produce of royal farms was used to feed the king, his family, and his large palace staff, to offer hospitality to citizens and to strangers, and to subsidize royal rituals. This land was passed down not from father to son but from king to successor.

In the Valley of Mexico, kings held *tlatocatlalli*, fields and estates that could be inherited by their children. Such land was exchanged among rulers of different city-states when their children married. Major lords and probably most if not all members of the hereditary nobility held *pillalli* (nobles' land). These two sorts of land provided rulers and hereditary nobles with a source of income that made them to varying degrees independent of the taxes paid by commoners. Modern scholars often refer to holdings of these sorts as 'patrimonial land'. Such land was set aside for the use of kings and nobles within the city-state to which they belonged. As a result of conquest and royal intermarriage, however, variable amounts of such land were held by kings and nobles in other city-states (Offner 1983: 129–38).

Jerome Offner (1981; 1983), who maintains that there was a thriving market in land, asserts that this patrimonial land was private. Pedro Carrasco (1981) and John Gledhill (1984) assert, in contrast, that the alienation of such land was highly restricted and therefore it was institutional. It seems to be generally agreed that such land could not be transferred to individuals who were not members of the nobility. As a result of divided inheritance, land of this sort would quickly have become fragmented, although blocks of it could also have been consolidated by means of strategic marriages among the nobility. Even so, efforts to maintain or assemble manageable units of land would have necessitated that nobles exchange holdings, and such exchanges may have given the false appearance of buying and selling. Because there is no evidence that patrimonial land could actually be sold, it seems likely to have been institutional rather than private. Patrimonial land existed to support the upper classes and in their view remunerated them for the political and military leadership they provided. Yet a numerically expanding hereditary nobility meant that the amount of land and income available to individual members of this class would have declined in each generation.

There was, in addition to calpolli, nobles', and royal land, land that was owned and operated by the state. It was given various names according to the specific use that was made of it, but all of it was controlled and administered in much the same fashion. Palace land (*tecpantlalli*) was used to pay for the operation of the royal palace and therefore to feed and otherwise support the king's numerous retainers, attendants, and servants. Office land (*tlatocamalli*) supplemented the incomes of hereditary nobles and provided salaries for eagle nobles, who did not possess patrimonial land of their own. Other state lands provided income that kings could direct to temples (*teopantlalli*), use to subsidize the operation of the army (*milchimalli*), and bestow as royal gifts upon calpollis and commoners. Normally all these types of land were located within the borders of a city-state. Yet hegemonic city-states appropriated fields in tributary states located near enough that it was economically feasible to transport bulk produce. The Aztec acquired their first state land in another jurisdiction following their defeat of the hegemonic state of Azcatpotzalco (Hassig 1988: 145–46). Tributary states were responsible for delivering food at specified intervals. Such land was called *yaotlalli* (land captured in war) (León-Portilla 1984: 23; Offner 1983: 126–39; Soustelle 1961: 80–81). States also acquired land by sponsoring major reclamation projects. While the chinampa land around Tenochtitlan appears to have belonged to individual calpolli, the chinampa fields in the Chalco-Xochimilco region probably belonged to the Aztec and Texcocan states.

Office land constituted a major source of revenue for the nobility, all of whose active male members were involved in some sort of state service. Individual office-holders in hegemonic city-states were often allocated specific fields in tributary states. Such grants stiffened the determination of these officials to ensure that their city-state remained militarily dominant. Most of this land, both at home and abroad, was worked under the supervision of government fiscal officers (calpixque) (Soustelle 1961: 41, 49). In the case of high officials, storable surpluses were probably conveyed directly to the residence of the individual to whom the produce of the land had been assigned. In other instances it was transported to the royal palace, where accountants apportioned it among lesser officials who had rights to a share of it. Beneficiaries of state lands received much more food than they and their families could eat. They invested the surplus in long-distance trade or used it to buy whatever they wished at city markets. State land could not be inherited and was reassigned at the king's pleasure. While patrimonial land appears not to have been private, state land definitely was not.

Both patrimonial and state lands were worked by mayeque (tenant farmers), recruited from landless families, rather than macehualtin (collective-landowning commoners). In conquered city-states some macehualtin may have been transformed into mayeque when foreign conquerors reassigned their land to produce tribute. The portions of the harvest that tenants had to surrender to their landlords were much higher than the surpluses that the collective-landowning commoners had to produce for communal use and to support state projects. While, among the Aztec and their closest allies, calpollis retained possession of their communal lands and may even have extended them, it appears that in many adjacent parts of the Triple Alliance tributary network an increasing amount of land was being used to subsidize the Aztec and Texcocan states and their officials.

Nobles may have tried, where possible, to convert their office land into patrimonial land in order to benefit their families. This appears to have been done on a massive scale after the Spanish conquest in an effort to prevent state lands from being sequestered by the Spanish government. Such manoeuvres may have considerably coloured an understanding of the nature of landholding at an earlier period (Gledhill 1984: 139). Deception would have been easiest with office land that, as a result of sons' inheriting their fathers' offices, had remained in the same families for several generations. Prior to 1519, such a tendency would have been resisted by strong kings, who derived much of their power over the nobility from their control of office land. However, kings must have endowed eagle nobles who married into the hereditary nobility with land to ensure that their children might enjoy the same privileges as did those of other minor hereditary nobles. The patrimonial land assigned to such nobles probably came from state land.

After the incorporation of a region into their kingdom, Inka officials insisted that each local ayllu work plots of land set aside to support the state and various state and local religious cults that the Inka kings patronized. While fields designated for state and religious purposes were cultivated independently of one another, both were managed by government officials. In order to reduce the resulting hardship for the local population, at least some of these fields were created by new terracing and hydraulic works rather than sequestered from existing ayllu landholdings. State, temple, and ayllu lands were not established in equal proportions. Because the food surpluses that it was technologically possible for each farmer to produce were modest, state and temple fields represented only a small portion of the total land that an ayllu cultivated (S. Moore 1958: 24–38; Murra 1980: 31–34).

While farmers preferred to grow many different crops on their land, it was the policy of the Inka government to produce only a small number of crops on state and temple fields. Its preference for corn rather than potatoes and other root crops may in part explain its emphasis on constructing agricultural terraces in annexed territories. Maize, which the Inka symbolically associated with the sun because of the yellow colour of its kernels, was used to produce highly prized food and beer that was distributed to work parties and local people on festive occasions (Murra 1960; Zimmerer 1993: 24). Farmers were obliged to cultivate state and temple lands before they worked their own plots, but they were provided with seed from government and temple storehouses and were fed and provided with tools while they did so. In return, the entire harvest produced on state and temple fields belonged to these institutions. Ayllu members were also drafted to tend the llama and alpaca herds that belonged to the state and to temples (Rowe 1944: 265–67).

The Inka kings further increased the revenues of the state and of the highest ranks of the Inka nobility by creating large estates which they assigned in perpetuity to themselves and their descent groups, to other prominent members of the nobility, and to the army. Unlike ayllu land, these estates were exempt from taxes. Wayna Qhapaq established the largest army estate at Cochabamba, a rich, low-lying maize-growing valley in Bolivia. The original population of the region was resettled elsewhere and replaced by fourteen thousand labourers. Most of these were corvée workers who came in rotation to Cochabamba to work for a single growing season, but a smaller number of workers were settled there permanently to supervise the storage of maize and its transportation to Cuzco. Another, smaller army estate in the low-lying valley of Abancay employed one hundred to two hundred families (Wachtel 1982).

The large royal estates, such as those of kings Thupa Inka Yupanki and Wayna Qhapaq in the Yucay Valley, near Cuzco, consisted of elaborate villas which served as country retreats for the Inka rulers and elaborate agricultural terraces. After the king died, his mummified body continued to visit his estates, and their agricultural produce helped to feed his descendants, who were responsible for maintaining his mortuary cult. Smaller estates assigned to members of the royal family such as kings' brothers, uncles, mothers, sisters, wives, and concubines and to other high Inka officials were inherited by these people's descendants. They could not, however, be sold, transferred, or divided, and therefore the well-being of the group ultimately depended either on their numbers' not increasing unduly or on their finding additional sources of revenue. Estates were also assigned to major temples (Murra 1980: 34–42).

The ayllus whose traditional lands were converted into estates were allotted collective land elsewhere. They moved to their new holdings and were replaced by permanently assigned labourers (yanakuna). The use of such labourers on personal estates permitted a larger portion of the crops to be retained for upper-class or government use than could be extracted from ayllus by means of a labour tax. There is evidence that estates and government farms were increasing rapidly in number and importance in the final years of Inka rule (Wachtel 1982). They supported an expanding army and an upper class that needed more resources to finance its growing numbers and various projects. While many royal and official estates were located in the vicinity of Cuzco, Wayna Qhapaq founded royal estates near Tumipampa, in Ecuador. Royal estates were also established in the lowlands to grow cacao and tropical fruit.

The Inka rulers granted small allotments of tax-free land to members of the lesser nobility and commoners to reward them for valour, bridge building, permanent garrison duty, and various other services to the state. Like the larger estates, these lands were inherited by all of an individual's descendants and could not be sold, divided, or alienated (Kendall 1973: 145). Hence they cannot be categorized as private holdings.

The Shang kings are recorded as owning large plots of agricultural land near Anyang. These fields or estates were given names such as *da tian* (large field) or *zhung tian* (centre field) and were worked either by corvée labour provided by commoners or by landless workers who permanently served the king (zhong). At least some of these workers were supplied with tools by their overseers. Presumably all the food produced on such land belonged to the king. It seems probable that princes and other high-ranking nobles possessed land of this sort. As with Inka upper-class estates, possessing such fields must have greatly increased the amount of food at the disposal of their owners (Keightley 1969: 109–11).

Later tradition affirms that each block of arable land that was worked by a lineage contained a central field that the members of that lineage cultivated for the king or lord who controlled the region or for some other designated beneficiary. It was called the *gong tian* (lord's field) (Vandermeersch 1980: 217). While it is uncertain whether a nine-field system ever actually existed (Creel 1937: 313), the proportion of eight to one falls within the range of agricultural land that might have been assigned to taxpaying cultivators and upper-class beneficiaries in an early civilization.

The state was divided into jurisdictions which various lords or officials controlled and from the tax fields of which they were entitled to collect revenues in the form of crops. Each lord could assign the revenues from one or more of the tax fields he controlled to a subordinate official, courtier, soldier, artisan, or retainer. In this way, the upper classes and their dependents obtained a major portion of the resources that they required to support themselves and their families and to carry out the functions for which they were responsible. It is unclear if all the produce of tax fields belonged to officials or their appointees or some of it went to the head of the lineage that worked it. Alternatively, the lineage head may have been supported by a share of the food produced on the attached fields (Vandermeersch 1980: 210–17, 227). Exchanges of lords' fields are recorded for the Western Zhou period. Such exchanges may have been essential in a kingdom in which officials occasionally were transferred from one region to another. These fields could not, however, be sold by those who benefited from them, since they belonged either institutionally to some level of government or collectively to the lineage that worked them (Hsu and Linduff 1988: 275–79). Because Shang divination appears to have been ascribed an important supernatural role in making crops grow, royal exhortations that officials make sure that farmers diligently cultivated the soil need not be interpreted as administrative orders as opposed to ritual pronouncements intended to encourage the growth of crops. Such admonitions may, however, have referred to the cultivation of fields that produced crops specifically reserved for the king and government officials.

Institutional land played an important role in the economy of southern Mesopotamia during the third millennium B.C. Most temples, as distinguished from small shrines, were endowed with land that was regarded as constituting the estate of the presiding deity. In Lagash there were more than twenty temples of this sort. The main temple and the largest estate were usually associated with the patron deity of the city. It has been estimated that 30 percent of the working population of the state of Lagash was employed by or rented land from these temples (Tyumenov 1969: 122–24). The temples in Lagash are estimated to have owned two hundred to three hundred square kilometres of agricultural land, or about one-tenth of the arable land belonging to the city-state (Diakonoff 1969b: 174). Royal estates were divided into the personal land of the king and land belonging to the palace (*égal*, 'great house') (Maisels 1990: 171). As among the Aztec and the Inka, this was a division between institutional land that supported the ruler and his family and lands used to pay for administering the state (Gelb 1979: 5).

Temple and royal estates were organized in a similar manner. Both institutions appear to have been able to acquire land by purchase and seizure for indebtedness, while temples also received land through donations. While both institutions may have been able to sell as well as buy and receive land, the dominant trend was towards accumulating more land, thereby fostering the growth of what constituted a divinely or royally owned trust. Both temples and palaces became major centres for the production and storage of agricultural produce. By the time the earliest readable documents appear, about 2500 B.C., much land that formerly had been owned collectively by patrilineal kin groups appears to have fallen under the control of kings, temples, and wealthy estate owners (Diakonoff 1969b: 177; Maisels 1993: 172–76; Yoffee 1988).

Temple estates derived income or services from their land in at least three different ways. The *nigenna* land, which was used to maintain the temple, was cultivated by labourers who received rations (*šeba*) of barley, wool, and oil. These workers were either slaves or free but landless labourers. If the latter were full-time employees of the temple, they and their families were generally supported by a combination of food rations and small plots of temple land that they cultivated in their spare time. In the Ur III period, these sorts of labour were increasingly supplemented and replaced by individuals' working solely for wages (Postgate 1992: 237). Casual, often itinerant, agricultural workers were hired for the annual peak labour periods (Maisels 1990: 194). All the food produced on this land belonged to the temple. It must have provided the bulk of the agricultural produce that the temple used to feed and pay workers, buy raw materials and manufactured goods, and support its ritual activities.

Gankur land was assigned in varying quantities to year-round manual labourers, minor officials, and major temple administrators as a source of income.

The labourers and their families were expected to grow their own food, but officials were assigned sufficient land to support farmers as well as the officials and their families. The highest-ranking officials derived enough income from the land assigned to them to maintain a comfortable lifestyle and engage in commerce. Wealthy individuals often hired stewards (*iššakku*) to manage their office land as well as any land that they owned outright. Sometimes a single steward worked for several officials (R. Harris 1975: 166). This land could be neither sold nor inherited by the people who benefited from it, although it might pass from fathers to sons together with specific temple administrative positions. By Ur III times, temple offices had become saleable commodities (Postgate 1992: 314). While landholdings were transmitted with the offices, the land remained the property of a temple.

Ganaru land was let by the temple on a rental or sharecropping basis both to farmers who lacked their own land and to commercial entrepreneurs, who in turn sublet it to farmers. Rentals, which were usually for a period of two or three years, gave a farmer the right to cultivate a plot of land in return for a fixed annual payment, normally in grain (Steinkeller 1981). With sharecropping, the landowner contributed to the costs of production and shared the risk of a bad harvest but received a larger share of the crop. In good years renters profited more from their work than did sharecroppers; in bad years sharecroppers suffered fewer losses. Sharecroppers were therefore generally landless farmers who could afford to risk less than could tenant farmers. Holders of office land derived revenue by renting it, sharecropping, or working it using paid labourers. All temple allotments were subject to yearly rotation or redistribution. Fields which were worked or sharecropped by the temple were supplied with seed, draft animals, ploughmen, and equipment from central facilities. Workers on temple estates were subject to the state corvées that constructed and cleaned major irrigation systems, built and repaired city walls, and performed military service (R. McC. Adams 1966: 107–8; Diakonoff 1969b: 176; Ellis 1976; Falkenstein 1974 [1954]; Foster 1982; Frankfort 1956: 65; Maisels 1990: 151; Postgate 1992: 126; Van De Mieroop 1999: 146–58).

Royal estates were run on similar principles except that the tenants were mainly officials, artisans, and professional or semiprofessional soldiers in the service of the king. Ordinary landholders either cultivated their small allotments or had them worked by other members of their families, while high-ranking officials rented or sharecropped their larger allotments. By the time of Hammurabi many royal soldiers could 'sell' their right to allotments, but this transfer required that the 'buyer' legally agree to perform the same services for the king as the previous allotment holder (Diakonoff 1969b: 197; Yoffee 1977).

It has been observed that both temple and royal estates tended to specialize in growing grain, while private citizens preferred to invest in orchards and kitchen gardens (Stein 1998). Grain was easily stored and relatively durable and therefore a suitable commodity for the commercial transactions of large institutions. Moreover, because of their large size and abundant resources, temple and royal estates were better equipped than small-scale cultivators to manage large irrigation systems, own the equipment and animals required to plough fields, and cope with the complicated crop rotations and anti-salination procedures that were necessary to grow grain crops on the backslopes of river channels (Postgate 1992: 188–90).

There is much controversy about the order in which various Mesopotamian institutions developed. Temples are identified long before palaces in the archaeological record, and by the middle of the fourth millennium B.C. some appear to have evolved significant bureaucracies that were concerned with crops, domestic animals, crafts, allotting fields, procuring raw materials, issuing rations to workers, and constructing large buildings and irrigation works (Nissen, Damerow, and Englund 1993). Yet it is not clear to what extent temples already possessed large estates at that time. Palaces do not appear until the Early Dynastic period and from the beginning seem to have possessed land the main purpose of which was to provide kings with the revenues required to maintain and equip the armies that were needed to defend city-states. The palace also had to support a large administrative staff that increasingly came to constitute the central government of the city-state. Kings sought to increase their revenues by buying or appropriating (often by compulsory purchase) more land (R. McC. Adams 1966: 142–48; Postgate 1992: 184).

Kings also sought to control temples and their revenues. King Shulgi, of the Ur III dynasty, placed major temples at Lagash and perhaps elsewhere under the control of palace officials, and Hammurabi assigned state accountants to temples (Postgate 1992: 300). Under public pressure, however, Urukagina, a ruler of Lagash in the 24th century B.C., seemingly restored to various gods the ownership of temple estates that had been sequestered by his predecessors and abolished royal taxes on these estates (Diakonoff 1969b: 189–90). Some Assyriologists see royal estates, during the course of the third millennium, as competing with and gradually replacing temples as the most powerful economic and political force in society (Postgate 1972). Others argue that temple estates expanded as a reaction to increasing royal power and the erosion of collectively owned landholdings (B. Foster 1981; Huot 1989: 153; Nissen 1988: 147–48). This view is a development of Max Weber's (1976 [1896]: 188) suggestion that ordinary people turned to priests for protection against the despotic power of kings.

It is now argued that spiralling debts may have caused individuals and groups to donate their land and themselves to temples in return for protection against creditors and royal administrators. High taxes and the economic hardship that small groups faced as a result of poor harvests may have encouraged the gradual disintegration of collective landholdings. Loans made at high rates of interest often had to be paid off by selling, with the approval of all the male co-owners, portions of collective land that in earlier times might or might not have been alienable. As a result of these sales, the poorest and politically weakest members of landowning groups would have found themselves unable to subsist on what remained of their extended family's collective landholding, and some may have decided to donate themselves and what remained of their land rights to temple estates. Other landless individuals may have sought the protection of temple estates. *Arua*, the term for free-will gifts to temples, included chattels, *ex voto* objects, prisoners of war (donated by kings), and ordinary people, many of them widows, orphans, and other impoverished individuals (Maisels 1990: 154–55; Postgate 1992: 135). While temple estates do not appear to have been indulgent institutions, they did provide economic security for marginalized members of society. Thus palaces and temple estates both may have expanded as rival institutions as collective ownership of land declined in importance. This development would have sustained the heterarchical nature of Mesopotamian, and especially Sumerian, society despite the growing centralization that was resulting from the increasing power of kings.

Egyptian kings had begun to establish royal estates (ḥwt) long before the Old Kingdom, and throughout the period they continued to create large numbers of these institutions. Estates varied in size from one to over fifty hectares. While the revenues derived from estates were assigned to specific individuals and institutions, they remained the property of the government unless their ownership was specifically relinquished. Many estates were intended to support the monarch and close members of his family. Others (*ḥwt k3*) financed the funerary cults of kings, female members of the royal family, and high-ranking officials. The revenues from still other estates were assigned to temples or provided officials' salaries (Eyre 1987a: 22–23). While officials received income from royal estates as payment for the work they did for the government, the successful transfer of specific official positions and associated lands from father to son over several generations blurred the distinction between office land and land that may have belonged privately to officials.

Each large estate and perhaps clusters of small ones had a manager (*ḥq3 ḥwt*), whose substantial residence served as the estate's administrative centre and storehouse. At least during the late Old Kingdom, a centralized bureaucracy with its headquarters in Memphis collected grain and other foodstuffs from estates throughout Egypt and distributed them to the various royally endowed funerary cults in the Memphis area (Eyre 1987a: 23, 34; Roth 1991b). This eliminated the need for individual cults to provision themselves from their widely scattered landholdings. It also gave the central government considerable control over these estates and their produce. By appointing government officials to well-paid but part-time positions supervising the various royal funerary cults, it was also possible to return to the royal administration some of the revenues that had been dedicated to these cults, thus making them less of a threat to the central government's control of the economy than Egyptologists used to believe. Funerary cults also provided income for the artisans who worked part-time for them as priests. While it has been argued that in the Early Dynastic period the central government provisioned officials from the palace, as the bureaucracy expanded increasing numbers of officials were provided with estates instead of a salary (Eyre 1987a: 23). In at least some cases the holders would have managed these estates, thereby reducing the administrative load of the government bureaucracy.

The central government was particularly active in establishing estates in less densely populated regions, especially in the Delta and Middle Egypt (Kemp 1983: 91). Many estates in the western Delta were devoted to wine production and raising cattle. These estates were settled by farmers from more densely populated regions of Egypt and with foreign families who had been captured in war and were gradually transformed from slaves into free farmers. It is not clear to what extent Egyptian farmers were permitted to move freely from one region to another or could be forced to do so. Many individuals may have been happy to relocate from densely populated regions where land was becoming scarce to regions that were developing rapidly. In parts of the country experiencing economic growth, competition for labour may have resulted in more favourable working conditions. The distribution throughout Egypt of estates assigned to support specific government institutions, major religious cults, and royal funerary cults must also have given officials who derived their living from working for these institutions a vested interest in keeping Egypt united.

PRIVATE OWNERSHIP

Private land is owned by a single person or by two or more freely associated partners and can be bought and sold as these individuals wish. It is frequently subject to taxation by the government and following an owner's demise may be inherited, like other personal possessions, according to socially prescribed rules. Owners can also dispose of such property during their lifetimes and often can bequeath it to whom they wish. Both unilinear evolutionists and substantivist economists believe that private property is a recent innovation (Polanyi, Arensberg, and Pearson 1957), but since the right of individuals to possess goods is recognized in much simpler societies the existence of private land in early civilizations should not be ruled out. There is, however, no evidence that such land existed in most early civilizations. It has been claimed that in the Valley of Mexico land granted to individuals could be sold by them (Offner 1981; 1983), but there is no proof that this was so even with the patrimonial land that was inherited in noble families. In Peru hereditary estates and those who worked them could not be sold or exchanged. Among the Yoruba there is no evidence that land was privately owned, although successful warriors and traders who invested in large numbers of slaves could bring large amounts of collectively owned land under cultivation for their personal benefit. Because of the Yorubas' relatively low population density, wealth was derived from private ownership of the human means of production rather than land. In China, rights to the produce of fields that were collectively worked were assigned to various officials and their retainers, but these fields were owned either collectively by extended farm families or institutionally by the government. That leaves Mesopotamia and Egypt as early civilizations in which some land might have been privately owned.

It is believed that in Mesopotamia prior to the third millennium B.C. most land was owned collectively. In the course of the third millennium, as communal land rights were pledged for debts, increasing amounts of land fell under the control of temples or palaces, but some of it appears to have become the property of individual creditors. The sale of perhaps 263 hectares of land in four lots, recorded on the Obelisk of Maništušu, which dates about 2500 B.C., has been interpreted as evidence that at first collectively owned land could be sold only to a king, but this is far from certain (Maisels 1990: 151–57; Postgate 1992: 41, 94–99). At the beginning of this transformation, leaders of landowning patrilineages were probably in a privileged position to transform collective holdings into private estates. The senior branches of these lineages may have accumulated wealth and power at the expense of junior branches, and eldest sons may have bought out the inheritance rights of younger siblings either while their fathers were alive or after their deaths. Initially the transfer of land to non-family members probably required fictional adoptions and the consent of the extended families of the sellers (Postgate 1992: 182–84). Such legal fictions grew less necessary as the pawning, buying, and selling of the use of land and then of land itself continued. Eventually land came to be treated like other forms of private property. It is also possible that high-ranking officials who made their positions hereditary managed to convert their large personal grants of temple or palace land into permanent and eventually disposable holdings (Crawford 1991: 46).

Small privately owned farms that resulted from the breakup of collectively owned land were extremely vulnerable to ecological or economic crises and to sickness in a family; hence they were easily lost as a consequence of indebtedness. This probably facilitated the development of large private estates, tracts of which the owners either rented to tenant farmers or sharecropped with them. In Akkadian times, such an estate might employ several hundred agricultural workers and their families (R. McC. Adams 1966: 107). Although the extent of privately owned land at any one period is uncertain and it developed slowly, unsteadily, and in diverse ways out of collective forms of land ownership, it increased over time and probably included most of the best orchards and gardens.

To possess arable land was the primary goal of all Mesopotamians (Postgate 1992: 183). Collective or private ownership of land made an individual a citizen (dumugi) and an integral member of a Mesopotamian city-state in a way that was not open to those who were either landless or worked another's land. Declining collective ownership of land would have made individuals anxious to acquire land in their own name as a way of retaining their status as landowners. The goal of prosperous Mesopotamian individuals, such as traders, appears to have been to invest in enough farm land and urban property that they and their families could live on the revenues derived from renting and sharecropping (Maisels 1990: 228; Oppenheim 1969: 11). To be supported in this manner was to imitate the life of the gods.

Yet, as the amount of institutional and privately owned land increased, the number of people who possessed land constantly declined, and the economic and social gap widened between those who owned land and those who merely worked it. Palace and temple estates emerged as the richest institutional landowners, but considerable amounts of land were either collectively or privately owned at any period. Wealthy officials probably invested much of their surplus income in land. At the same time, the direct transfer of some land from collective to private ownership limited the power of temple hierarchies and kings and thus helped to maintain the broad, heterarchical nature of political power in southern Mesopotamia.

It is less certain that private land existed in Old Kingdom Egypt. Christopher Eyre (1987a: 33) maintains that there is no evidence that a clear distinction was drawn between privately owned land and office land, which implies that there was no concept of privately owned land. Barry Kemp (1983: 81) asserts that private ownership of land is well documented for the Old Kingdom. Texts of this period refer specifically to fields or estates that were inherited from a parent (Malek and Forman 1986: 80–81). At least some of this land could be alienated from its possessors' heirs in a variety of ways, including using it to endow personal funerary cults. Much of this land appears, however, to have been bestowed on individuals by the king, and it is frequently difficult or impossible to distinguish between an outright gift and a bestowal that would eventually have reverted to the king. It is especially difficult to distinguish privately owned land from office land that was held by successive generations of a family that performed the same or equivalent services for temples or the state. Possessors of such land had powerful reasons for trying to make their rights to it appear to be those of permanent ownership. Especially under weak central administrations, efforts to do this would have created much ambiguity about the legal status of many parcels of land. Even records of sale, which became more common in later periods, do not resolve whether freeholds or use rights were being transferred from one individual to another (Robins 1993: 136). It is also impossible, for lack of evidence, to know whether private land was being created through the sale to individuals of collectively owned land. Nevertheless, it does seem as if something closely resembling private land was already being transferred by sale in the Old Kingdom (Malek and Forman 1986: 82).

Revenues from these different categories of land circulated in highly complex ways. For example, the mortuary cult of a high official might have received food supplies from royal estates or from a plot of land specially set aside for this cult by the king. It might also have received endowments from a private funerary estate established by the deceased or through the endowed purchase of reversions, or reuse, of food offerings from nearby royal funerary cults, temples, or more lavishly endowed tombs. This income would have supported low-ranking officials who, among their other duties, would have made regular food offerings at the dead person's tomb (Kemp 1983: 85–107).

LAND OWNERSHIP AND POLITICAL AND ECONOMIC VARIATION

Land owned collectively either by patrilineal descent groups or by endogamous communities played a major role in food production among the Yoruba, in the Valley of Mexico, and in highland Peru. In Mesopotamia there is circumstantial evidence that collective ownership had been important at an early period, but by the time the first detailed records appear land was being sold by the collective agreement of extended families to the king and possibly to other individuals, as well as being donated to temples. In Egypt collective village ownership of land, which antedated the development of royal estates, may have continued into later times. In Shang and Western Zhou China agricultural land may have belonged either collectively to the patrilineages that worked it or institutionally to officials who were able to assign the surplus production of such land to themselves and their supporters and retainers. In the Valley of Mexico and Peru, land was owned collectively by endogamous groups, among the Yoruba, the Mesopotamians, and perhaps the Shang and Western Zhou Chinese by patrilineal extended families, and in ancient Egypt by communities.

Institutionally owned agricultural land was important in the Valley of Mexico, highland Peru, Mesopotamia, and Egypt. Among the Yoruba it appears to have been limited to fields belonging to the office of kingship. In Mesopotamia it was divided between the palace and various temples, and the rivalry between them helped to preserve the heterarchy of this society. In the Valley of Mexico institutional land was shared by the king and the hereditary nobles, but the king's control of palace lands enabled him to subsidize the entire nobility and thus promoted political centralization. Inka royal estates, state farms, and gifts of land produced income for the king, his close relatives, high officials, royal descent groups, and the army. In Egypt the government developed unused or underused land as estates that could be assigned to support various institutions, government officials, and other privileged individuals. In China at least the king possessed office land that was worked by corvée and by landless labourers who were bound to royal service. Local and regional officials expanded their income mainly by increasing the number of cultivators whose communal labour produced food surpluses that were at their disposal.

Thus in many early civilizations the upper classes derived revenues from lands set aside to provision rulers, temples, leading families, and officials. A considerably higher percentage of the food produced on this land went to its beneficiaries than was collected in taxes on equivalent amounts of collectively or privately owned land. The Inka was not the only early civilization to use corvée labour to produce food for the state and its designated beneficiaries on institutionally owned land. Such labour was also employed in the Valley of Mexico and probably in China, and these states, together with ancient Egypt and Mesopotamia, also attempted to increase the share of the crops that went to state institutions and the upper classes by creating special forms of labourers who were required to work some institutional land on a full-time basis. The Inka differed from other early civilizations only in the extent to which taxes were collected in the form of labour.

There is no evidence of private ownership of land among the Yoruba, Inka, Shang Chinese, and the peoples of the Valley of Mexico. Individual Yoruba who commanded extra human labour were able to develop large farms on patrilineally owned land that provided them with the resources required to promote their political careers. In Mesopotamia, privately owned land appears to have grown increasingly common as the collective ownership of land declined. Old Kingdom Egypt displayed a complex mixture of collectively, institutionally, and (probably) privately owned land, its most striking difference from Mesopotamia being that most institutional land was ultimately controlled by the king or by the state. Royal control of institutional land appears to be a general characteristic of territorial states.

A final question is whether there was a developmental sequence from collective to institutional to private ownership of land. There is some evidence that might be interpreted as supporting this claim. In Mesopotamia it appears that collective land gradually was transformed into institutional and privately owned land, and in Egypt a similar development may have occurred. In China, over a much longer period than we are considering, collective and most institutional land was transformed into privately owned land, although rights to private property were never guaranteed in China to the same extent that they were in countries that adopted Roman law (Ke 1989; Shen 1994). In the Valley of Mexico institutional land existed alongside collectively owned land and tended to expand as hegemonic states exploited their weaker neighbours. The Inka kingdom appears to have been energetically creating institutional land in a region dominated by collectively owned land in order to increase the amount of food available for government projects and the wealth at the disposal of the upper classes. In contrast, the Yoruba had experienced only very limited development of institutional land.

Increasing proportions of institutional and privately owned land might be used to arrange these civilizations in a hypothetical evolutionary hierarchy. The replacement of collectively owned land by increasing proportions of institutional and privately owned land is correlated with compelling farmers and farm labourers to produce and surrender increasing amounts of surplus food. While the state and the upper classes were able to appropriate crop surpluses for their own use from farmers who cultivated land that they owned collectively, the amount was limited compared with what could be extracted from landless farmers who cultivated institutional and private land as bound labourers, sharecroppers, or tenant farmers.

Yet care must be exercised in advocating such an interpretation. The long-term survival of collective and institutional ownership of land in all early civilizations and the relatively limited development of private ownership in all but one early civilization suggest that all three forms of land ownership were compatible with early civilizations as a general type of society. All of them supplied the food surpluses that were necessary to support the upper classes and those specialized workers who supplied the upper classes' particular wants. It is also clear that specific combinations of land ownership corresponded functionally with more general political and economic variations among early civilizations. In Mesopotamia heterarchical power encouraged the development of rival landowning institutions; in Egypt, the Valley of Mexico, and Peru the development of institutional land ownership was one device among many for reinforcing royal authority. In territorial states, the king or government claimed paramount control over institutional land. Finally, among the Yoruba, where arable land was relatively abundant, wealthy and powerful individuals used slaves and debtors to work large portions of communal land and kept all the surplus production for themselves. This arrangement increased the crop surpluses being accumulated by members of the upper classes as institutional or private ownership of land did elsewhere. In dealing with land ownership, we are considering an aspect of social organization in which historical particularities played a significant role alongside a limited range of strategies that were deployed by the upper classes to encourage the production of larger crop surpluses and ensure their appropriation of them. These strategies must have been devised independently as each early civilization developed.

16 Trade and Craft Specialization

Evolutionary archaeologists used to believe that increasing social complexity and intellectual progress resulted primarily from the development of more complex technology, in particular increasing dependence on metallurgy. This view rested on the assumption that in early civilizations metal was used primarily to manufacture cutting tools. Yet it has long been recognized that the development of metallurgy was not as crucial to the evolution of various early civilizations as this view suggested (Childe 1951: 26–27).

The Yoruba were the only civilization in our sample that forged iron on a large scale. It is generally believed that, because of its greater technical complexity, iron forging began much later than the working of gold, silver, and copper. It has also been assumed that knowledge of how to work iron spread to Africa from the Middle East during the first millennium B.C. Nevertheless, radiocarbon dates which indicate that iron-working was well established as early as 700 B.C. in Uganda and West Africa and may have been practised there in the preceding millennium raise the possibility of the independent invention of iron-working in sub-Saharan Africa. The use of iron appears to have reached southern Nigeria early in the Christian era (Connah 1987: 113, 141; Holl 2000: 14–15; Shaw 1978: 69–99). Raw materials needed to make iron, in the form of laterites and iron-rich shale soils, were abundant in Yoruba territory, although they were more common in the north than in the south (Ojo 1966a: 96–98; Peel 1983: 22–23). Beginning in the sixteenth century A.D., iron as well as brass ingots were purchased from European traders operating along the Gulf of Guinea. Because of the abundance of locally produced iron, Yoruba were able to manufacture heavy agricultural implements, tools, ornaments, and ritual objects from this metal. According to archaeological evidence from Ife, they also beat or cast ornaments and ritual objects from gold and copper or copper alloys (mainly brass) beginning around A.D. 1000. Casting was done using the lost-wax method (Connah 1975; Dark 1973; Forman, Forman, and Dark 1960; Shaw 1978; Willett 1967).

In southern Mesopotamia during the third millennium B.C., copper, silver, lead, and gold were used to manufacture bowls, statues, ornaments, and jewellery. Gold objects first became abundant in the context of growing royal power during the Early Dynastic III period (Huot 1989: 115). While arsenic-copper and other alloys had been used still earlier, by Early Dynastic III times bronze was being cast as well, using tin that came from Afghanistan and possibly also from Anatolia (Yoffee 1995: 298). Weapons such as spearheads and daggers, as well as axes, adzes, and more specialized carpenters' tools, were also being manufactured from copper and bronze. Mesopotamian metalworkers were skilled at using single and two-part moulds and the lost-wax casting technique as well as at hammer-shaping metal. They also produced metal wire and decorated metal objects with gold leaf, metal granules, and cloisonné. During the third millennium B.C. an increasing number of agricultural tools came to be made of copper and bronze. Christopher Edens (1992: 126) argues that, by the end of the Akkadian period, copper had become an 'industrial' as well as an ornamental metal. By Ur III times the standard bronze alloy contained 17 percent tin, although different amounts of tin were being added to copper for specific purposes (Crawford 1991: 131–37; Moorey 1985; Postgate 1992: 225–29).

The Inka created numerous luxury goods and religious objects from gold, silver, copper alloys, and platinum, including jewellery, decorations for clothes, metal cups and other tableware, and statues. Lead was used as a decorative inlay. The alloying of copper and tin to make bronze had been invented in Bolivia about A.D. 700 (Kendall 1973: 167). Metals were mined or panned from rivers and smelted using crude but effective and quickly learned techniques (Franklin 1990: 114–15). Many mines occurred in the southern, sparsely settled part of the Inka kingdom, in modern Bolivia and Chile. Rivers in Ecuador produced platinum that was mixed with gold dust to reduce its high melting point. Skilled Inka craft workers were familiar with many techniques for working metal but generally hammered gold and silver objects from sheet metal and cast bronze ones (Rowe 1944: 246–48). They knew how to gild and plate metal but preferred to create alloys and then treat their surfaces in ways that would increase the abundance of the more highly valued metal. Inka weavers likewise preferred to weave complicated multicoloured designs into cloth rather than to decorate it by embroidery or dyeing, and Heather Lechtman (1993) argues that the two Andean crafts exhibited a unique approach to technology. The Inka also manufactured numerous weapons, especially battleaxes, from bronze, as well as crowbars, chisels, knives, and other implements for working soft stone and wood that were made available to workmen engaged in state enterprises. Some foot ploughs were provided with bronze blades, but this treatment was probably limited to ceremonial implements. Other tools were made of stone, bone, and wood (Rowe 1944: 247–48).

The ancient Egyptians worked gold, silver, copper, and electrum, a naturally occurring mixture of gold and silver. Bronze remained virtually unknown during the Old and Middle Kingdoms. Jewellery, vessels, and statues were usually made by beating sheets of metal into shape, although some statues were made of carved wood covered with gold foil and small ones might be cast. Weapons such as daggers were regularly cast from copper (Andreu 1997: 68–69), but as late as the Middle Kingdom government forces were supplied with spears and arrows tipped with expertly worked flint points (Vila 1970). Whereas carpenters and sculptors who worked for the government were provided with copper tools, in the remains of Kahun, the town attached to the funerary complex of the Middle Kingdom ruler Senwosret II, surviving flint tools outnumbered metal ones (David 1986: 93). Granite and much limestone were worked using naturally occurring nodules of diorite (a much harder stone) as hammers. Agricultural tools were generally manufactured from stone and wood.

The Shang Chinese were superb metalworkers and had easy access to copper and tin. They cast ritual vessels by pouring bronze into multisectional moulds, which allowed them to produce extremely complex shapes. The purpose of sectional moulds does not seem to have been to turn out multiple copies of the same vessel, since no two vessels appear to have been precisely the same. Lead was sometimes added to the bronze alloy to alter its colour and fluidity. Shang metallurgists also manufactured bronze buckles, bells, other musical instruments, weapons, and fittings and ornaments for chariots and horse harnesses. The surface of the metal was often extensively worked after casting and sometimes inlaid with gold and silver (Chêng 1960: 156–76). Metal was not commonly used, however, to make jewellery. The Chinese preferred to wear smooth, cool stones, such as jade, believing that they promoted calmness; because of its association with fire, direct contact with metal was considered disturbing (Franklin 1983: 95; Franklin, Berthong, and Chan 1985). Few if any bronze tools and no metal agricultural implements have been identified, although moulds for making bronze hoes and picks appear to have been found in one workshop at Zhengzhou. Royal artisans manufactured more arrowheads from bone than from metal (Keightley 1969: 40, 92). This pattern of metal use continued during the Western Zhou period. Iron – cast rather than forged – was used extensively only in late Zhou times, and only then did metal farming implements and household tools become common.

Craft workers in the Valley of Mexico worked gold, silver, and copper by hammering, open-mould casting, and lost-wax casting. They used these metals principally to make jewellery, including small bells that were sewn onto clothes. Copper was frequently combined with gold to produce an alloy called *tumbaga* or covered with gold leaf. While they also manufactured some drills, chisels, awls, axes, sewing needles, and fishhooks from copper, the vast majority of their tools and weapons were made of wood and bone edged with obsidian blades. A large obsidian-edged sword (*maquahuitl*) could cut a human body in two (M. E. Smith 1996: 171). Some small bronze tools were reaching the Valley of Mexico from towns located adjacent to Tarascan territory, in western Mexico, where a knowledge of bronze-working had been introduced from Peru about A.D. 1200 (96–98). No one in the Valley of Mexico knew how to manufacture bronze objects. Agricultural tools were not made of metal.

There is no evidence that the Classic Maya worked or had significant access to metal, although imported metal figurines are occasionally found in ritual caches (Baudez 1994: 59; Schele and Freidel 1990: 434). That they erected impressive stone buildings and carved magnificent limestone stelae employing only stone and bone tools demonstrates that metal tools were not a prerequisite for creating or sustaining an early civilization.

The evidence suggests that in early civilizations copper was used first to manufacture ornaments and ritual objects and only later to fashion weapons, craft tools, and finally agricultural implements. Copper and bronze tended to be used only to manufacture luxury goods, weapons, and craft workers' tools until abundant supplies of copper and tin became available with the development of more efficient mining and more cost-efficient transportation. Iron is far more prevalent in nature than either copper or tin, and once it was known how to refine iron ore it became possible to produce a wide range of tools. The economic and social potentials of copper-bronze and iron technologies were therefore radically different (Heichelheim 1958). While substantial iron-working developed considerably later than bronze-working in southwestern Asia and China, in sub-Saharan Africa there is no evidence of a Bronze Age prior to an Iron Age.

Early civilizations were associated with a wide range of cutting-tool technologies. There was no obvious correlation between the formal complexity of these technologies and significant measures of social complexity such as population density or the division of labour, and therefore the development of metallurgy cannot have been a key factor shaping the development of early civilizations. Stone tools long continued to be used for agricultural and construction work where specialized craft workers were being supplied with metal tools. Finally, because obtaining stone to make cutting and hammering tools sometimes presented the same logistical problems as did procuring metal or metallic ores, the general impact of the use of metal on the division of labour in early civilizations was not much different from that associated with the use of stone. Stone tools persisted not as a result of cultural inertia but because societies were not convinced that it was worth making the various organizational changes necessary to adopt a new technology.

What stimulated increased economic interdependence and political integration in early civilizations seems to have been the trade and craft specialization encouraged by the politically motivated demands of the upper classes for prestige goods and by expanding markets for better-quality mass-produced commodities as population densities increased.

TRADE

In early civilizations, most of the goods that people used in everyday life were produced and sold locally. Long-distance trade differed from local trade in scale and organization, and because rulers were concerned with its political ramifications they related to it differently in city- and territorial states. In most city-states the decentralized nature of political power encouraged the development of intercity trade as an independent enterprise. Because city-states were often at war with one another, major economic advantages were also derived from conducting such trade at arm's length from political authority. In territorial states, government control of long-distance trade and of exotic goods generally was an important source of power for rulers.

In Mesopotamia intercity trade and trade with more remote regions were conducted by professional merchants. The merchants in each city-state belonged to one or more merchants' associations (*damgar*). The head of the merchant association (*gal damgar*) was either its highest-ranking member, who had also been granted a palace title, or a palace official who acted as the king's chief liaison with the merchants. Traders received allotments of temple land and were exempt from performing corvée labour (R. McC. Adams 1974a; Leemans 1960b; Postgate 1992: 211; Silver 1986: 132–33).

It used to be believed that long-distance traders were originally employed full-time by palaces or temples, which provided them with a fixed income in the form of an allotment of land. Polanyi (1957) argued that the economy was so deeply embedded in the political organization of early civilizations that what modern scholars wrongly imagined was 'foreign trade' was in reality gift exchanges among the rulers of city-states, who did not seek to derive any economic profit from these exchanges. While few experts would now accept this interpretation as accurate for the late third millennium, some argue that this was probably the form that intercity exchanges took in Early Dynastic times (Crawford 1991: 25; Foster 1981). The still later Ur III government may have engaged in some long-distance sea trade, but even this is uncertain (Lamberg-Karlovsky 1996: 160–63; Postgate 1992: 220–21).

The earliest available evidence indicates that, already by the Early Dynastic period, intercity and interregional trade was being carried on for profit and that merchants acted as independent agents. By the Old Babylonian period merchants were establishing joint-stock companies (*naruqqu*, 'sacks') in which a number of merchants invested capital for a fixed period, specified a division of profits and losses, and appointed a particular merchant to conduct the trade (Silver 1986: 88; Van De Mieroop 1999: 197–202). Merchants traded goods owned by temples, kings, wealthy landowners, and kin groups on a commission basis and bought and sold goods on their own account. An important export from Mesopotamian cities was food staples such as grain and dates. A temple in Lagash arranged to have a merchant transport over thirteen thousand fish caught by its workers to Nippur and sell them there (R. McC. Adams 1974a: 248). Merchants also traded wool, cloth, and other Mesopotamian manufactures with far-off regions in return for metals, wood, semiprecious stones, and other raw materials. In pre-Akkadian times foreign trade was mainly conducted to secure raw materials for making luxury goods, but with the growing use of copper agricultural tools foreign trade also became essential for food production (Edens 1992: 126–32). Only small amounts of manufactured goods were imported from abroad.

Mesopotamian merchants established trading posts near foreign towns in what is now Turkey and perhaps also in Iran and around the Persian Gulf. There resident Mesopotamian merchants could trade with the local people on a regular basis while their subordinates managed the transport of goods. Long-distance merchants also cultivated good relations with merchants in other Mesopotamian city-states. Intercity trade was important for securing goods from abroad, since specific raw materials entered southern Mesopotamia from different directions and hence came first to different city-states (R. McC. Adams 1974a: 246–47; Lamberg-Karlovsky 1996: 157; Van De Mieroop 1999: 185–93). Intercity trade also facilitated more specialized production in individual city-states. Isin, for example, was a major centre of leather production, while Lagash became a centre for the slave trade (Crawford 1991: 124–25). Hegemonic Mesopotamian cities used their political power to ensure that their own merchants could trade with foreign regions, unhampered by intervening city-states.

Merchants belonging to different Mesopotamian city-states developed complex commercial relations with each other. Instead of paying for all goods as they were received, they built up credit and incurred debts with each other. A merchant living in Ur could have what he owed to a merchant in Lagash paid by a third merchant in Nippur who was indebted to him. The successful operation of such a credit system required elaborate record-keeping, including detailed contracts and receipts. Given the lack of a single unit of account, it also required complex accounting techniques. No less important was the need for mutual trust among trading partners; it was essential that their good relations survive even wars between their respective city-states (Larsen 1976; Leemans 1950; 1954; 1960a; 1960b; Snell 1982; Van De Mieroop 1999: 212).

It is also clear that a profit motive was active in long-distance trade. A Mesopotamian merchant could sell cloth he had purchased in his home town for several times its original value in Turkey and buy silver there that he could sell back home for three times what he had paid for it (R. McC. Adams 1974a: 246). Such increases in value more than covered the cost of transporting goods by river, sea, or donkey. Grain prices also fluctuated according to scarcity, both on a seasonal basis and depending on the size of the annual harvest. Efforts by governments to control rising prices by decreeing maximum amounts that could be charged for goods were only partly successful (Silver 1986: 78–79).

No obvious market-places have been identified in Mesopotamian cities. Commercial transactions appear to have taken place near the city gates, in small shops, and along a 'street of purchases'. The city of Sippar had a square (*ribitu*) where taverns, which functioned as male social clubs, and shops that sold luxury goods were located (R. Harris 1975: 17; Postgate 1992: 79, 192–93). Specialists may have produced goods in or near their homes and sold them there to farmers and other craft workers. Merchants also may have sold imported goods from their houses, although they no doubt delivered bulk consignments directly to temples, palaces, and the homes of rich clients.

In the Valley of Mexico and adjacent parts of central Mexico, long-distance traders (pochteca) were excusively male, although female members of their families invested in trading expeditions and looked after their husbands' businesses while these men were abroad trading. The pochteca in each major city-state were organized into one or more traders' associations, each of which was also a calpolli. Membership in such a calpolli was hereditary, although individuals could join it by adoption. Male pochteca were stratified by age and wealth. Each pochteca group had its own school (telpochcalli), where its young men learned to bear arms so that they could defend themselves while travelling abroad. The pochteca did not, however, serve in the army. Instead they risked their lives travelling into foreign and even hostile regions to trade for exotic goods (M. E. Smith 1996: 120–23). Some boys from trader families attended nobles' schools (calmecacs), where they learned to keep accounts (van Zantwijk 1985: 144).

Pochteca were highly rivalrous among themselves. Individual traders sought eminence by investing some of the profits they derived from successful long-distance trade in lavish, competitive feasting of other pochteca. Once a year all the traders displayed their wealth at their calpolli temple and each boasted of his accomplishments, resourcefulness, and bravery. The long-distance traders also taunted local market traders for their lack of courage and initiative (Clendinnen 1991: 138–39). Yet they attributed their success to their plain living, hard work, solidarity among themselves, generosity to other long-distance traders, and respect for foreign trading partners (van Zantwijk 1985: 171).

Each pochteca calpolli had two headmen (*pochtecatlatoque*) who represented their fellow traders in dealings with the king (van Zantwijk 1985: 143). Only medium-sized and large cities had resident groups of pochteca, and the largest cities often had several. There were twelve cities with resident pochteca in the Valley of Mexico, but the traders from only five of these cities, including Tenochtitlan and Texcoco, were permitted to trade beyond the tributary system of the Triple Alliance. Pochteca from different regions traded with one another over the whole of central Mexico and when travelling would stay at each other's homes. Farther south, where there were no traders' associations, they exchanged goods with rulers and their representatives (Townsend 1992: 190). Goods were transported by human bearers (*tlameme*), who were usually free but landless men from outside the valley.

Long-distance traders usually travelled in groups and were armed to defend themselves. Because of the many uncertainties and dangers they encountered, trading expeditions were the foci of numerous religious observances. Divination was practised before leaving to ascertain unsuspected dangers and the chances of success. Merchants did not wash their bodies until they returned to their homes, arriving at night to conceal the quantity of goods they had purchased abroad. They celebrated each successful trading expedition by hosting a communal feast but only after having visited their calpolli temple to thank their patron deity for their safe return (van Zantwijk 1985: 158–60).

Pochteca did business abroad for kings and nobles on a commission basis but also exchanged wares with local market traders over a large area. They brought into the Valley of Mexico exotic raw materials that artisans needed. For the elites of Tenochtitlan and Texcoco, their most important task was to obtain exotic luxury goods from outside the tributary network that their states controlled, especially quetzal feathers. In city-states that did not have access to tribute, rulers and commoners alike depended wholly on pochteca to supply foods and raw materials from warmer ecological zones and luxury products from distant cities. Trading practices among long-distance merchants were simpler and more direct than in Mesopotamia because record-keeping, if employed at all, must have been limited to recording ideographically the type, number, origin, and destination of goods. Merchants had to commit details of contracts to their memories.

Cities in the Valley of Mexico had large central markets (*tianquiztli*). Those in the main urban centres (Tenochtitlan, Tlatelolco, and Texcoco) met daily, with a larger assembly occurring every five days. The Spanish estimated that forty thousand to fifty thousand people attended the Tlatelolco market on peak days. In the various quarters of large cities and in smaller cities and settlements, markets usually met every five days, with a larger and more varied market being held every twenty days. The biggest market-place in any city was located near its centre, close to the main temples and the royal palace, and was usually surrounded by a wall that was colonnaded on the inside. Market days were arranged so that neighbouring markets did not coincide, giving both buyers and sellers an opportunity to do business at a number of them. This arrangement also gave local traders a chance to transport goods from larger markets to smaller ones (Hassig 1985: 73–84). It has been argued that the Aztec and Texcocan rulers altered the locations and operation of markets to reduce the wealth and power of subordinate rulers and increase the size of the main market in their own capitals. If so, such actions reinforced changes in marketing patterns that were already being brought about by the collection of large amounts of tribute by these two cities and by their increasing wealth and population (Berdan et al. 1996).

At urban markets, buyers exchanged mainly maize and cloth for more perishable foodstuffs, beverages, raw materials such as wood, hides, and salt, goods manufactured locally or in nearby parts of the Valley of Mexico, and exotic raw materials and manufactured items imported from more remote areas by the pochteca. Female traders played an active role in the operation of local markets, where they sold food and manufactured goods produced by their male relatives or purchased wholesale from long-distance traders (van Zantwijk 1985: 131–32).

Some markets were noted for particular specialties: Alcolman for dogs, Azcatpotzalco for slaves and birds (which were valued for their feathers), and Texcoco for clothes, pottery, and painted gourds (Hassig 1985: 73). Markets were also frequented by barbers, porters, craft workers, and prostitutes seeking customers. Kings and nobles, through their agents or officials, used the markets to exchange the large amounts of food and cloth they received as tribute and from their estates for any items they needed or wanted. It was illegal for individuals to buy or sell goods elsewhere than at a public market, where the state imposed a tax on all transactions (Townsend 1992: 173).

Different sections of markets were reserved for particular categories of goods. This arrangement made it easy for buyers to compare what was being offered for sale. While Aztec sumptuary laws determined who could publicly wear or display certain products, every kind of goods could be sold at public markets. The markets were patrolled by officers and presided over by judges who maintained order, settled disputes, and punished theft and fraud. At the great market at Tlatelolco these powers were delegated to the city's pochteca (Hassig 1985: 67).

Yoruba itinerant or long-distance traders (*alajapa*) were less formally constituted than were the pochteca. Long-distance traders came from many different classes. They included the wives and sons of kings who were seeking to acquire wealth from trade because royal children could not hope to inherit much from their fathers. Royal traders' goods were free from transport and sales taxes, and they could expect to be provided with free lodgings and food wherever they travelled. Yet anyone was free to become a long-distance trader, the main prerequisite being the ability to amass enough capital to get started. Women played a major role in Yoruba trade at both the intercity and the local level. Because they were not as likely to be attacked by soldiers, it was less dangerous for women than for men to engage in intercity trading during wartime. Thus women could ensure that essential commodities continued to circulate among states. Capital to begin trading was often provided by a woman's husband (Bascom 1969: 65). Slave trading and trading beyond Yoruba ethnic territories tended to be done by men, some of whom were organized in special associations (Law 1977: 210).

To travel more safely through dangerous regions, merchants formed caravans and hired soldiers to protect them. They bought slaves or engaged porters to carry their goods or carried them themselves. Each trader could join or leave a caravan at any point along the way. While many traders, especially female ones, travelled relatively short distances, a single caravan might journey from the Guinea coast as far north as the Nupe and Hausa markets, transporting slaves, horses, and natural produce from one region to another. The circulation of manufactured goods encouraged specialization in weaving and dyeing, pottery manufacture, and gold and silver working in Yoruba cities or regions (Hodder and Ukwu 1969: 46). By transporting goods from one place to another, traders could increase the value of these goods by up to fivefold (Falola 1991). Long-distance traders bought and sold goods not at urban markets but through local brokers (*alarobo*), and this allowed them to handle goods in bulk quantities. Foreign merchants sometimes were explicitly forbidden to trade at local markets. Government officials, associations of local merchants, and commercial brokers provided lodging and storage facilities for traders from other towns (Falola 1991: 131).

Yoruba cities normally had several markets (*oja*). The main market was located in the centre of the community, usually in front of the royal palace. It was referred to as the *oja oba* (king's market), and it normally met twice daily or every second day. Smaller markets, each controlled by a local official called a *bale oloja*, met in various wards of a city and in smaller communities every eight or sixteen days. In general, local products predominated at neighbourhood markets, while both local and imported goods were traded at the central urban markets and at other major ones that developed along important trade routes, especially near the borders of states and at transition points between ecological zones. The establishment of a new market had to be approved by the local king (Bascom 1969: 25–26; Hodder and Ukwu 1969: 19–96).

Much food, both raw and cooked, was sold at Yoruba markets. Because of the remoteness of many farms from urban centres and the problems involved in storing most Yoruba agricultural produce for long periods, it was probably expedient for families to sell much of their farm produce in bulk through the markets and to buy fresh food as they needed it (Krapf-Askari 1969: 155). While most of this food was sold by women, a woman normally turned the profit over to her husband on the ground that he had grown it (Bascom 1969: 25). Because of the long time and the large amount of fuel required to cook many types of Yoruba food, even poor people found it more economical to buy such food already cooked (Hodder and Ukwu 1969: 103). Local market women bought goods at main markets in order to resell them at smaller community markets and kept these profits for themselves.

Markets were policed by the local traders' association. The woman who headed this association often had the palace title *iya oja* (market mother) and served as the chief palace liaison with all the craft associations in the city (Hodder and Ukwu 1969: 55). Minimum sale prices were established each market day among the sellers, but how much each item actually sold for was determined by haggling. Food and other goods were sold by number or container size rather than by weight.

The king of Benin, unlike neighbouring Yoruba rulers, controlled his people's trade with Europeans at the seaport of Ughoto (Gwatto). He claimed a monopoly there over all trade in slaves, ivory, palm kernels, and pepper. Officials and commoners could trade other goods with Europeans but only after senior palace officials had finished conducting the king's business (Bradbury 1957: 25).

The Maya rulers and nobles of historical times controlled interstate trade (Coe 1993: 170), and it may be significant that 'God L', who was associated with the western Maya region in Classic Maya times, is iconographically identified as a merchant of royal status (Taube 1992: 79–88). Archaeologists have failed to identify market-places in Classic Maya urban centres. If considerable food was being grown around house clusters in urban centres as well as elsewhere, there may have been less stimulus for exchange between the urban nobility and craft specialists, on the one hand, and farmers, on the other, than there later was in highland Mexico. This, combined with the more dispersed distribution of Maya urban centres, might have encouraged classic Maya rulers to control interstate trade (Schele and Freidel 1990: 93). Trading networks were able to distribute substantial quantities of obsidian originating in Central America throughout the Maya lowlands, where it was transformed into blades that reached farmers as well as the urban elite (Sidrys 1979). This broad distribution of imported raw materials differs from distribution patterns in territorial states.

Among the Mesopotamians, the people living in the Valley of Mexico, and the Yoruba, long-distance traders derived substantial profits from transporting various types of goods from regions where they were abundant and relatively cheap to places where they were scarcer or did not naturally occur. In the Valley of Mexico, pochteca were able to exchange the surplus food and cloth that the upper classes derived from their lands, taxes, and tribute for rare, exotic items that these people highly prized. They also acted as spies and agents for their king, observing political and economic conditions in the various states they visited both within and beyond the Triple Alliance's tributary system. In return, the Aztec king undertook to avenge traders from his own state who were killed or molested by foreigners; attacks on pochteca travelling abroad provided him with a good excuse to declare war on hostile or uncooperative states. Pochteca also were exempt from corvée labour (Berdan 1982: 31).

Yet relations between merchants and other Aztec males were characterized by antagonism. The Aztec believed that social mobility or confirmation of high status was legitimate only as a reward for outstanding military service. The profits merchants derived from peaceful, long-distance trade, usually with real or potential enemies, were stigmatized as ignoble. Whereas individual warriors proclaimed their high status publicly and proudly, however rich a merchant became and however close his semiclandestine dealings with the palace and the king, he was required to appear in public as a simple commoner, barefoot and dressed in maguey-fibre clothes. Merchants who flagrantly disregarded this regulation risked confiscation of their property or execution (Clendinnen 1991: 136; Soustelle 1961: 64). Merchants were also forbidden to hold public office or marry into the noble class. Successful merchants sought to acquire public prestige by ritually sacrificing foreign slaves they had purchased. Sponsoring such a sacrifice was necessary to become a slave trader or the head of a pochteca calpolli. Yet a long-distance trader could carry out this sacrifice only if he could secure the cooperation of a high-ranking warrior, and this required feasting and giving many costly presents to the warrior and his friends (Clendinnen 1991: 136–40; van Zantwijk 1985: 148). Thus even this ceremony dramatized the social and political superiority of warriors over traders. Despite their wealth, the pochteca were effectively deprived of an autonomous public role in Aztec political and community life.

In Mesopotamia there is evidence of an analogous though much less marked prejudice against merchants. Long-distance traders had close relations with temple administrators and palace staffs, but they worked and may have lived in walled-off 'harbour' (*karj*; Akk. *karum*) areas located along the outer walls of cities rather than inside the city proper. These 'harbours' were centres of foreign trade, where visiting merchants from other city-states and foreign lands were lodged. They had separate legal status and their own courts and enjoyed a degree of administrative independence under an 'innkeeper of the harbour' who looked after and may have been held responsible for the behaviour of foreign traders. As in the Valley of Mexico, the close contacts that long-distance traders had with merchants in other, often hostile, communities rendered them suspect among their own people. Mesopotamian merchants invested their profits in land and houses, and when they could live comfortably from such investments and lending their surplus wealth they seem to have abandoned trade and moved into the city (Oppenheim 1969: 6, 11).

Among the Yoruba no stigma appears to have been attached to being a trader. Traders included the wives and sons of reigning kings. In towns where there were no merchants' associations, local notables frequently acted as brokers and landlords for long-distance traders. Successful traders, no less than successful military leaders, were able to invest their profits in slaves and develop an agricultural base for supporting retainers. Yet a large number of long-distance traders were women, and male traders came from a broad social spectrum. Successful trading appears to have been a less certain way to seek political power and obtain titles than was military prowess. Thus the social situation of Yoruba traders may not have been so different from that of traders in Mesopotamia and the Valley of Mexico.

If interstate trade among the Maya was directly controlled by the upper classes, their arrangements were significantly different from those found in other city-state systems. Benin demonstrates, however, that direct control of some aspects of trade by rulers occurred in other city-states.

Territorial states appear to have replaced long-distance commercial trade with the controlled acquisition of key resources by the central government. In these states monopolistic control of exotic raw materials and of the production and distribution of coveted luxury goods were important for reinforcing government authority.

In Old and Middle Kingdom Egypt, foreign trade was carried on by the government. Large government ships were sent to Byblos, in what is now Lebanon, to purchase commodities such as silver, which, because it had to be imported, was worth more than gold in Egypt. They also obtained at Byblos lapis lazuli from Afghanistan and local Lebanese cedar wood and tree resins. Olive oil was imported overland from Canaan. In the Old Kingdom, Egyptian officials led donkey caravans south into the Sudan to obtain ivory, ebony, gold, and animal skins from local rulers, while ships sailed south along the Red Sea to Punt, in the Horn of Africa, to trade for myrrh for religious rituals and embalming and many other African products. Cattle may have been purchased from the Libyans. While the state paid for the goods it obtained from neighbouring peoples, all exchanges were subject to the threat that the more powerful Egyptians might attack these peoples if they did not cooperate. The government also sent expeditions to quarry various kinds of stone and to mine gold, electrum, and copper in the eastern and western deserts adjacent to Egypt and Lower Nubia and copper and turquoise in the Sinai Peninsula. In the Middle Kingdom, Nubian traders coming from the south were compelled to unload their cargoes and exchange them with officials at border fortifications near the Second Cataract. Asian merchants appear to have brought goods to Egypt, but they too had to pass border control points and trade with Egyptian officials. Only later, in the New Kingdom, do Asian traders appear to have done business with Egyptians who were not government officials (Frankfort 1956: 118–19; Kemp 1989: 172–78).

When the central government collapsed at the end of the Old Kingdom, the privileged classes lamented their inability to obtain the cedar wood needed to manufacture coffins to bury their dead properly (Lichtheim 1973: 152). Control of materials that were valued because they were used to manufacture luxury goods and perform rituals was a source of power for rulers. By monopolizing foreign trade and the procurement of exotic raw materials, the government was able to restrict access to these materials to artisans in its own employ.

Internal trade was limited to everyday objects that part-time craft workers made from local materials. Such trade occurred in villages, small towns, and provincial capitals. Markets (*mryt*) appear to have been small, informal assemblies at quaysides that were of little concern to the government except perhaps as a minor source of tax revenue. In depictions of Old Kingdom markets, the traders were mostly men (Kemp 1989: 255), but in the New Kingdom female traders were frequently shown. The main items that were traded appear to have been cooked food, drinks, vegetables, fruit, fish, and household goods such as mats, baskets, and pottery (Eyre 1987a: 31–32). Some low-value goods from settlements bordering the Nile Valley may also have been sold at these markets. Natron, which was mixed with water for daily ablutions and used to embalm the dead, was brought into the Nile Valley from nearby oases at least partly by ordinary farmers who were also entrepreneurs (Lichtheim 1973: 170). In the New Kingdom traders (*šwty*) travelled along the Nile exchanging agricultural products for other goods needed by temples and private persons. They appear to have worked for temples or for one or more individuals, but it is not clear whether they were paid employees, operated on a commission basis, or kept a share of the profits. They were neither wealthy nor high-status persons, and some may have been slaves (Kemp 1989: 257–59). There is no evidence that such traders had existed before.

The Inka rulers reluctantly allowed entrepreneurs to continue trading beyond the borders of their kingdom, especially to the north (Salomon 1986; 1987). Some of this trading involved voyages on large balsa rafts northward along the Pacific coast. These traders obtained goods that were not available within the Inka kingdom, such as spondylus shells, which played an important role in religious rituals (Gose 1993), and they provided the Inka rulers with intelligence that helped them to expand the kingdom. One of the main places where these long-distance traders interacted with the government was the northernmost Inka administrative centre of Quito. Llama herders continued to trade produce in the course of their travels between the southern highlands and the coast as they had done in pre-Inka times (van Buren 1996), but in general the government appears to have discouraged interregional trade within the Inka kingdom. Inka officials monitored the transport of luxury goods from one region to another at provincial administrative centres, official rest stops, and bridges. The movement of people and goods into and out of the Cuzco district was carefully controlled. Individuals had to have official authorization to travel from one province to another. All gold that was mined had to be sent to Cuzco, and removing gold objects from the city without official permission was a capital offence (von Hagen 1959: 148). Interregional trade was further discouraged by satisfying the traditional desire of highland ayllus for economic self-sufficiency – extending zones of cultivation down valley sides and providing highland ayllus with secure access to plots of land at lower altitudes (Earle 1987; Rowe 1944: 233). Large areas south of Lake Titicaca that had little agricultural potential but were rich in gold, silver, copper, and tin were annexed, and mining and refining in the state-owned mines were supervised by local leaders who forwarded the metal they produced to provincial administrative centres (D'Altroy and Earle 1985; Earle 1987: 74).

While it has often been asserted that the Inka had no markets, both Thupa Inka Yupanki and Wayna Qhapaq were reported to have ordered or sanctioned their presence in all provinces and towns. A market was held every five days in Cusipata, one of the two main squares in central Cuzco, while another market five leagues from the city centre occurred every nine days, probably to serve the ring of service settlements that surrounded the upper-class urban core. The Spanish described the goods that were exchanged at these markets as being trifles of low value that people purchased in small quantities. Most sales were made by women, and no market tax was collected (Earle 1985; La Lone 1982; S. Moore 1958: 86, 133; Murra 1980: 142–47). In modern times Andean women tend to barter within communities and men in broader contexts (Urton 1981: 21). Presumably these markets, like Egyptian ones, were places where ordinary people exchanged food and local handicrafts and hence were a vital aspect of village life.

Very little is known about trading in Shang and Western Zhou China, although in later times merchants were called *shang ren* (Shang people) (K. Chang 1980: 241; Creel 1937: 316). Raw materials such as the turtle shells used for divination appear to have been imported from beyond the borders of the Shang kingdom. Men who belonged to certain lineages seem to have worked as commercial agents, although it is not clear whether they were independent traders or government officials. As in highland Mexico and Peru, long-distance traders are said to have acted as spies for the government (Creel 1937: 317). Cowrie shells were used to store wealth, for gift-giving, and to pay for the manufacturing of valuable objects.

Exchanges between individuals in early civilizations were done by barter. Although the buyers and sellers in each early civilization must have possessed roughly equivalent understandings of the relative value of most goods, the value of food varied according to scarcity, both seasonally and from year to year. Skilled or highly reputed artisans demanded more for their wares than ordinary workers. Individual exchanges involved haggling and were complicated by the need for the buyer to provide items that the seller was willing to take in exchange. Often the purchase of an item involved the seller's accepting a variety of goods, measured by number, size, or weight, in exchange (Kemp 1989: 248–50).

To simplify exchanges, 'currencies' were used to pay for items. In the Valley of Mexico, hollow quills filled with gold dust, T-shaped copper bars, standard pieces of cotton cloth (*quachtli*), and cacao beans, singly or in bags, provided units of exchange of different values. Depending on their size and quality, pieces of cloth used in commercial transactions were equivalent to between sixty-five and three hundred cacao beans. These 'currencies' were used to even out differences in the value of goods that were being exchanged (Berdan 1982: 43; M. E. Smith 1996: 124–26; Soustelle 1961: 81–82). The Yoruba and the Chinese employed cowrie shells to pay for purchases. In Benin brass bracelets and pieces of cloth were also used (Bradbury 1957: 46). In Mesopotamia pieces of copper and silver stamped by the king to certify the quality of the metal were used in trading, but these were still weighed individually to determine their value, and pieces of metal could be broken off to cover a lesser amount. In early times, Mesopotamian traders calculated the value of goods in relation to barley, copper, or tin, depending on the worth of the transaction, but by Ur III times silver had replaced copper as a significant measure of value. In the Old Babylonian period merchants were using silver as their primary accounting unit in dealings among themselves and with major institutions. The government, for its part, sought to convert surplus wool into silver, even though this involved selling wool in bulk to merchants at less than its market value (R. Harris 1975: 49). Yet, while prices were often calculated and quoted in silver, payments in this metal appear to have been rare. Most silver made its way into and stayed in palace and temple treasuries (Oppenheim 1964: 87; Postgate 1992: 200–204). In the Old Kingdom the Egyptians used the unidentified *šʿty* as a standard unit in connection with bartering (Kemp 1989: 255). It has been suggested that in the New Kingdom this unit was a silver disk weighing about 7.5 grams (Strouhal 1992: 198–99), but this seems unlikely to have been the case earlier; a Fifth Dynasty market scene indicates that a single piece of cloth was worth six šʿty (Kemp 1989: 255). Most of these 'currencies' (cacao beans being a conspicuous exception) were not only a means for facilitating exchanges but also a way to store value. There is no evidence that in any early civilization a single commodity came to be used as the sole measure of value for everything else that was bought and sold.

Long-distance trade was embedded in political processes to varying degrees. In the two adequately documented territorial states, both foreign trade and the mining of stone and mineral resources were controlled by the central government. In three well-documented city-state systems, foreign trade was carried on by individuals or groups operating independently of the state, and therefore trade was possible among states that were hostile or even at war. Political power was the principal way to acquire wealth, while wealth was essential to maintain political power. Wealth acquired from trade could not easily be translated into power. The Aztec value system stigmatized as dishonourable wealth that was not acquired through warfare. Mesopotamians downgraded merchants by comparison with property owners. Even the Yoruba limited the political role of successful female traders to supporting male aspirants for high office, while such men sought to distinguish themselves as soldiers. If Classic Maya rulers monopolized long-distance trade, their political prominence facilitated such control; it did not result from it. In city-states merchants were able to acquire wealth but were to varying degrees politically constrained; in territorial states, long-distance traders were largely replaced by government officials.

COMMUNICATION NETWORKS

Intercity trade depended on transport. Yet, in general, the transport of goods continued, like agriculture, to rely on relatively simple and labour-intensive means. In Egypt and Mesopotamia boats played a significant role in transporting goods by river and sea and donkeys were used to carry loads overland. While wheeled vehicles were constructed in Mesopotamia, there is no evidence that carts played a significant role in long-distance trade. Although the Egyptians were familiar with the principle of the wheel as early as the Old Kingdom, no wheeled vehicles of any sort were used in Egypt until after the Middle Kingdom. In highland Peru llamas carried loads of medium weight, and in Mesoamerica canoes were used wherever possible. Yet, in highland Mexico and among the Maya and Yoruba, human carriers transported most goods over long distances. Mountainous and swampy terrain and the absence of large domestic animals (or the problems involved in breeding them in unfavourable climates) explain the heavy reliance on human carriers in these regions. Human labour was also important for transporting goods in Peru. In Mesopotamia and China, rulers and some soldiers drove chariots, and among the Yoruba leaders and elite soldiers rode horses. In other early civilizations, upper-class people travelled either on foot or in boats and litters.

In most early civilizations relatively little effort was expended on the construction and maintenance of roads or footpaths. In central Mexico, despite the importance of trade and the absence of navigable waterways (except for the large lakes in the centre of the Valley of Mexico), there was little emphasis on road construction. The causeways leading into Tenochtitlan from the adjacent mainland were impressive feats of engineering. The wooden bridges that could be taken up at various points along the causeways served a defensive role as well as allowing for essential water flow and canoe traffic. Yet, while the streets of Tenochtitlan and other major cities were broad and straight, even the main thoroughfares were paved only with compressed earth. Corvées drawn from various calpolli kept streets clean and in good repair.

In the highland Mexican countryside, roads were nothing more than beaten paths that varied in width according to how much they were used. Local authorities, who were responsible for such care as was taken of roads, probably feared them as avenues of invasion as much as they valued them as a means to facilitate trade. Despite such fears, all settlements were connected by roads to neighbouring communities. Rather than running straight, each major road linked a maximum number of urban settlements. There was no main road directly linking any community on the Gulf of Mexico with Tenochtitlan but rather a series of alternative routes running through different intervening urban centres. This arrangement was adapted not to the needs of an empire or even of a hegemonic system but to those of warring city-states. It permitted alternative routes to be used for trade and communication if any particular segment of the road system was blocked by intercity conflict. Travellers spent each night in closely spaced urban centres (Hassig 1985: 171; Santley 1991).

All Yoruba roads were unpaved. The principal roads, along which most trade moved with the permission of local rulers, ran north-south through major urban centres. These roads were linked to smaller communities by east-west feeder routes which also joined larger communities to one another. Along the main roads were caravanserais (*aroje*) where traders spent the night if they were unable to reach the next town (Falola 1991; Hodder and Ukwu 1969: 27–29).

In Mesopotamia most goods were probably transported from one city to another by water, but urban centres were also linked by dirt roads. Shulgi, a king of the Ur III dynasty, boasted of having created a system of messengers and road stations as part of his increasing bureaucratic control over the whole region (Postgate 1992: 42). Private travel between cities appears to have been infrequent and dangerous, and even the sending of personal letters was uncommon (Oppenheim 1964: 120).

The Egyptians depended largely on the Nile for travel and transport. The river was connected by canals and loading basins to major temples and palaces and, at least during the flood season, to the royal pyramids, which were located just beyond the edge of the floodplain. Canals also permitted water transportation into the heart of major cities such as Memphis and Thebes. In addition, trails located in the adjacent deserts cut across bends in the Nile Valley, joined the valley to the western oases, the Red Sea coast, and desert quarries and mining sites, and probably ran parallel to the Nile the whole length of Egypt. These trails permitted messages to be conveyed more quickly by runners than by water and would have allowed government soldiers to approach communities from the desert as well as from the river.

The most complex road system in any early civilization was constructed by the Inka, in part by incorporating already existing roads. This network ran from Quito in the north to the Mendoza River in Chile in the south and is estimated to have consisted of a total of forty thousand kilometres of roads. Of these, twenty-three thousand kilometres were part of the main lattice, while the rest led to specific communities. Although the Inka conceptualized four main roads extending from Cuzco through the primary divisions of the kingdom, there were in fact two major roads running north-south that were connected by a series of shorter east-west roads. The main road through the highlands was strategically more important than the one that ran parallel to it along the coast. The Inka rulers regarded it as the artery that allowed them to dominate both the highland and lowland portions of their kingdom. The widest and best-constructed portion of that road ran between Cuzco and Quito.

Roads were built and maintained by local corvée labour under Inka supervision. While only short sections of roads were paved, the Inka rulers made an effort to keep the entire system passable during all seasons. Roads were regularly cleared of stones and were provided, where required, with drainage channels and stairways. Rope bridges were used to cross deeply incised rivers and balsa rafts to cross unfordable coastal ones. In general, the Inka sought to build roads that were as straight as possible and to do that skirted irregular terrain. The principal roads also avoided mountain passes that rose above five thousand metres. Where possible, the main north-south route ran through major highland administrative centres.

The main purpose of the Inka roads was to transport state information, government troops and corvée labourers, and government supplies (Gose 1993: 483); they were not intended for private use. Government inns (*tampu*), well stocked with food and clothing, provided overnight lodging for soldiers, corvée labourers, and officials travelling on government business. Whether located in administrative centres or in the countryside, these service centres were one day's journey apart. In addition, runners' stations (*chaskiwasi*) were established every three to six kilometres along the main roads, and runners stood ready there to relay messages or goods. In addition to facilitating government business, the royal road (*qhapaq ñan*) was a substantial and pervasive symbol of the Inka state (Hyslop 1984; von Hagen 1959).

For Shang and Western Zhou China, oracle-bone inscriptions suggest that travel by kings, officials, and armies over an extensive road network played a major role in maintaining the integrity of the state (Keightley 1979–80). Roads are said to have been kept in good repair and provided with rest houses for the use of government officials (Creel 1937: 316).

Important as intercity trade may have been in some city-state systems, it did not encourage the development of complex transportation and communications systems. The value of such systems for trade was counterbalanced by the fear that they would facilitate attack by neighbouring states. Only a hegemon seeking to unify a region might attempt to construct a more efficient road system. In contrast, government activities in ancient Egypt and China and especially in the Inka kingdom led to considerable investment in the construction and maintenance of transport systems. In the Andes, the controlled movement of people and goods was essential for maintaining the unity of the state.

CRAFT PRODUCTION

Many everyday goods used in early civilizations were produced by farmers in their spare time. Farm labour was often seasonal, and during slack periods farmers and their families manufactured tools, baskets, sandals, clothing, furniture, and ornaments for themselves and to exchange with their neighbours. If individuals or families concentrated on manufacturing a single type of product, they could hone their skills and produce higher-quality goods. The development of part-time specialization required broader exchange networks, with exchange usually occurring at markets located in villages and small towns.

Still better-quality goods were produced by full-time specialists. Full-time metalworkers might manufacture bronze or iron tools that other people needed but lacked the equipment, raw materials, and technological knowledge to make for themselves. Other full-time craft workers might produce pottery, basketry, or leatherware superior to what part-time craft workers could manufacture but inexpensive enough that most people could afford them. These goods were sold at village and city markets, and both the volume of goods produced and the degree of specialization increased with population density and the size of urban centres. Full-time craft workers functioned as individuals or in family groups. Some potters and leather workers and a larger percentage of metallurgists might be employed full-time by temples, palaces, and private patrons.

At the top of the craft hierarchy were the elite craft workers who specialized in producing goods of exceptional quality and high value for the state and the upper classes. These goods were frequently manufactured from imported raw materials. Teams of full-time specialists possessing a variety of complementary skills often worked together to create these objects. The intrinsic value of the raw materials from which such goods were made and the time-consuming labour needed to manufacture them made possession of such goods a sign of high status or royal favour. Some elite craft workers sold such goods on the open market, and others combined independent production with working part-time on commission for upper-class individuals or institutions. Still others were employed full-time by governments, temples, or wealthy patrons and, though treated with considerable respect, were bound to their employers in much the same manner as were less skilled craft workers or household servants (Trigger 1968: 54).

Cross-cultural studies indicate that in preindustrial societies particular crafts were performed either by men or by women but not by both. When men and women worked at the same craft, they usually performed different tasks. The same craft was not, however, practised by the same gender in every culture (Costin 1996; Murdock and Provost 1973). In early civilizations, both cross-cultural regularity in the gendering of crafts and male professionalization appear to have been more pervasive than in less complex societies. As most crafts grew technologically more complicated and were practised in workshop settings rather than in the home, they tended to become male activities. In manufacturing ceramics men generally replaced women as mass production and the use of the potter's wheel increased. Men also dominated tasks that did not have a domestic origin, such as metallurgy. Large numbers of women continued to be involved in domestic tasks such as brewing and baking when these became full-time occupations within palaces, temples, and state institutions. Such tasks provided employment for lower-class women in Egypt and were among the duties assigned to chosen women in Peru. In Egypt, however, men soon became professional brewers and bakers and monopolized specific forms of food processing, such as the drying and cooking of fish and meat (Feucht 1997: 336–37). Among the elite feather workers (*amanteca*) in Tenochtitlan, women cleaned and dyed feathers while men sewed and glued them onto cloth or wood to produce costumes and decorations (M. E. Smith 1996: 100–102).

Craft knowledge tended to be passed from generation to generation within families. Girls learned from their mothers and aunts, boys from their fathers and other older male relatives. There was little chance for outsiders to learn crafts, although apprenticeship occurred, sometimes in the guise of adoption. Most craft workers could not read or write, and therefore knowledge relating to their work was transmitted orally, sometimes as trade secrets. Because of this, much of the specific craft lore even of literate early civilizations has been irretrievably lost.

The production of cloth was a major activity in all early civilizations and played as great a role in the lives of most women as agriculture did in men's (E. Barber 1994). It remained a domestic task but also underwent considerable specialization. It was one area of production in which women played a significant role in 'industrial' as well as household production, although men as well as women became involved in the production of cloth for commercial and other special purposes.

While large amounts of ordinary cloth were needed for clothing and other domestic purposes, high-quality cloth became an important status symbol. Cloth of this sort was woven from valuable raw materials, such as silk in China or cotton, which had to be imported from the lowlands, in the Valley of Mexico. It could also be richly ornamented with special colours and designs, very finely woven, or woven in complex patterns. Among the Inka, fancy cloth (qumpi), decorated with complex patterns and bright colours and finished on both sides, was manufactured for the government. The Maya upper class, especially women, are shown wearing richly patterned robes, while upper-class Egyptians prized very finely woven linen.

Cloth also had ritual significance in some early civilizations. The Inka burned cloth as offerings to the gods and used large amounts of it to wrap and periodically rewrap the bodies of their ancestors (Murra 1962). Egyptian priests were allowed to wear linen but not woollen clothing while serving in temples. Clothing of special patterns or styles emphasized the divine qualities of kings, and particular types of vestments were regarded as appropriate to be worn while performing particular rituals. Because cloth weighed little, was highly variable in design, and required much labour to produce, it was also a major commodity in long-distance trade. While every woman knew how to produce ordinary cloth, the production of fancy cloth required special training, time, and often access to better-quality materials. It also encouraged an enhanced division of labour.

In all early civilizations cloth was manufactured from plant fibres. Linen was used in Egypt and Mesopotamia, maguey fibres, hemp, and New World cotton in the Valley of Mexico, hemp and cotton by the Maya and the Inka, Old World cotton by the Yoruba, and hemp and linen by the Chinese. Woollen cloth was woven from sheep and goat hair in Egypt and Mesopotamia and from llama, alpaca, and wild vicuña wool and even bat hair in Peru (Rowe 1944: 240). The Chinese produced silk from insect cocoons. All forms of cloth production required considerable labour to grow or collect the raw materials and to process, spin, dye, and weave them.

Women generally produced the ordinary cloth that was worn by their families (Fig. 16.1). In most societies the role of women as domestic cloth producers was the symbolic counterpart of the primary role claimed by men as food producers. In Inka society, where women were acknowledged to play an important role in agricultural production, elderly men helped to spin thread (Rowe 1944: 241). Although they did not join in many other forms of household labour, upper-class women supervised and even participated in the production of clothes for their families.

The Inka required all the married women of commoner families to spin and weave fixed quantities of wool that were assigned to them each year from state and religious herds. Producing ordinary cloth was a form of labour tax. The state issued this cloth to soldiers and other corvée labourers who were away from their homes for long periods (Murra 1980: 68–70). The Egyptian government may have collected one-tenth of the cloth produced by each

16.1. Female weavers in early civilizations: (a) Inka woman weaving on a backstrap loom (from Guaman Poma de Ayala); (b) bird's eye view of Egyptian women using a ground loom, tomb of the Middle Kingdom provincial ruler Khnumhotep II at Beni Hasan (BH 3); (c) a seven-year-old Aztec girl being taught to spin by her mother (Codex Mendoza); (d) a fourteen-year-old Aztec girl learning to weave using a backstrap loom (Codex Mendoza). Sources: (a) after Pomo de Ayala, 215; (b) after P. T. Nicholson & I. Shaw (eds.), *Ancient Egyptian Materials and Technology* (Cambridge, 2000), 277; (c), (d) after J. Cooper-Clark, *The Codex Mendoza* (London, 1938).

household as a tax, and estate owners had tenants' wives weave cloth that the owners could sell. It is unclear whether this weaving constituted part of the payment for renting land or these women were remunerated for their work (James 1962).

In addition, the state and large institutions in some early civilizations developed weaving as an industry. In Mesopotamia as many as 750 women were assigned to individual workshops belonging to temples, palaces, and private estates to weave both ordinary and high-quality cloth. Many of these women were slaves; others belonged to indebted families. They usually worked in teams of twenty under a male or female supervisor. Weaving shops were recorded as early as the Early Dynastic period, and in Ur III times, six thousand weavers were working in such establishments, many of them under very poor conditions, in the city of Girsu alone (Postgate 1992: 235; R. Wright 1996b). The cloth they produced was distributed to temple and palace staff and used for foreign trade. Among the Inka fancy cloth was woven by the chosen women and by full-time male specialists (*qumpikamayoq*) attached to the state or the upper classes (Costin 1998b). Whereas ordinary cloth was produced by farm women using backstrap looms, fancy cloth was woven on vertical looms (Kendall 1973: 179–80). In Egypt, secondary royal wives, concubines, and their female servants, who lived in royal palaces scattered throughout the country, wove cloth for the king, sometimes on a large scale (Kemp 1989: 222). Many smaller estates belonging to Egyptian officials also had weaving shops. In the Old and Middle Kingdoms weaving was done both at home and in workshops by women using horizontal looms. In the New Kingdom, following the introduction of the vertical loom, men gradually replaced women in workshops (Andreu 1997: 71–72). David Keightley (1969: 48–49) believes that in Shang China high-quality textiles, especially those made of silk, were produced by specialized artisans working in royal workshops.

Finally, many Aztec and Egyptian women wove cloth at home and sold it in public markets. Yoruba men and women produced cloth for sale on both a part-time and a full-time basis. Yoruba men used horizontal or belt looms to weave narrow bands of highly decorated cloth, while women wove wider sheets on vertical looms. The Yoruba believed that if men or women used each other's looms they would change sex. Male involvement in commercial weaving was most common in the northern part of the Yoruba country, where farm labour was more seasonal (Ojo 1966a: 86–87).

Thus in all the early civilizations, the manufacture of cloth was an important aspect of domestic production. In addition, it was a widespread household industry. In some early civilizations, weaving was also the most 'industrialized' form of production in terms of the number of people working in a factory setting.

The rulers of early civilizations are often said to have sought to control the production of luxury goods in order to increase their political power (G. Stein 1998: 21–22). It has been assumed that they did this by requiring craft specialists to work for them and by monopolizing the supplies of raw materials that craft workers required. Childe (1965 [1936]: 212–13) further argued that the role played by palace and temple officials in setting production targets and evaluating production stifled innovation and inhibited the further development of craft skills. This view is, however, partial and misleading. Relations between craft workers and officials varied considerably among early civilizations, especially between city- and territorial states.

In Mesopotamia there were many different types of full-time craft workers (*giškinti*). Ordinary craft workers, such as woodworkers, basket makers, rope makers, house builders, boat builders, leather workers, and potters, have to be distinguished from more highly skilled smiths, stone carvers, and ivory and wood carvers (Moorey 1994; Postgate 1992: 232). Different categories of workers worshipped particular patron deities and seem to have had spokespeople who represented their interests, but it is unclear if, like the merchants, they belonged to formal associations (Postgate 1992: 229; Van De Mieroop 1999: 183–85).

Mass-produced wheel-made pottery already predominated in southern Mesopotamia by the start of the third millennium B.C., and copper and bronze tools slowly replaced stone ones over the course of the next thousand years. In the third millennium, ensuring the production of specialized weaponry became the responsibility of palaces, while temples employed increasing amounts of metal cult equipment. Both palace and temple estates needed large numbers of metal implements and agricultural tools. Groups of smiths (*simug*) frequently worked for temples and palaces under the direction of a foreman who was responsible to the general overseer of the institution. Among the foreman's duties was checking the weight of the metal supplied to smiths against the weight of the objects that the smiths produced. In the Old Babylonian period some smiths and stone workers were full-time employees of temples, but it is not clear if this had been the case in earlier times. Gold workers were employed on a part-time basis and sometimes recruited from other cities (Postgate 1992: 229). The only clearly documented manufacturing by workers wholly controlled by palaces and temples was that performed in weaving factories. Major institutions may not have tried so hard to control labour that supplied fluctuating needs as opposed to producing goods they used or sold on a regular basis.

Archaeological evidence indicates major workshops in residential areas of Mesopotamian cities. While the largest potteries and stoneworking sites were located on the leeward side of cities, in order to reduce smoke and dust pollution, copper and gold workers, who used already smelted metals, had workshops along streets near urban centres. There is also evidence that each ward had resident potters, smiths, and lapidaries who supplied local wants (Silver 1986: 119; Stone 1997: 20). This indicates that all urban dwellers had access to most if not all major types of craft specialists working in their own neighbourhoods. It also suggests that ordinary people could obtain manufactured goods directly rather than having to purchase or receive them as payment from temples. Since there is no evidence that the people who worked for a particular temple or for the palace were residentially segregated in Mesopotamian cities, it appears unlikely that these craft workers were the full-time employees of a temple or palace. Independent craft workers would have been able to purchase supplies of copper, tin, and other imported raw materials directly from long-distance traders (Van De Mieroop 1999: 176–83).

J. N. Postgate (1992: 225–29) maintains that temples, with their great corporate wealth and demand for luxury goods, played a major role in encouraging technological development in Mesopotamia. Robert McC. Adams (1966: 140–43) has argued that the growing need of palaces for more effective armaments had the same effect. It remains to be determined whether these institutions exerted their influence mainly as purchasers or as the actual organizers of production. Except for hegemonic states such as Akkad and Ur III, whose rulers patronized the production of outstanding works of art, the quality of stone carving and metalwork does not suggest a sharp division between elite craft workers labouring exclusively for major institutions and full-time specialists producing for a broader market. State efforts to control production may have been focused on palace workshops and on the role of supervisory personnel. Yet, while many ordinary Mesopotamian craft workers may have worked full-time for institutions and institutions may have provided the major market for more specialized goods, it seems unlikely that most craft workers were legally or contractually tied to these institutions (R. Wright 1998).

In the Valley of Mexico utilitarian goods such as pots, reed mats, woodwork, leather goods, and canoes appear to have been produced both by full-time craft workers in urban centres and by farmer-craft workers in rural as well as urban areas. Elite craft workers lived almost exclusively in urban centres, where they could most easily obtain exotic raw materials and sell their products to the upper classes and the pochteca at large central markets. The most skilled craft workers tended to gravitate towards Tenochtitlan, which, being the valley's largest and wealthiest city, provided the most buyers for their goods.

Craft specialization was organized by calpollis. In some calpollis all men specialized in a particular craft; in others some worked as full-time craftsmen while others were farmers or combined farming and part-time craft work (Brumfiel 1998). The urban calpollis that produced luxury goods may have been composed largely of elite craft specialists. These producers of luxury goods were called *toltecca*, implying that their skills were derived, like the institutions of nobility and kingship, from the ancient city of Tollan, where they had a supernatural origin. These specialists included goldsmiths, who produced jewellery, feather workers, who manufactured fans, shields, warriors' costumes, capes, headdresses, and tapestries, and lapidaries, who ground lip and ear plugs, beaded necklaces, bracelets, and other ornaments from jade, obsidian, and other attractive stones (M. E. Smith 1996: 99–107). Sons of gold workers and feather workers received some training in the schools for nobles or at their own versions of such schools to familiarize them with the details of Aztec religious iconography (Clendinnen 1991: 132). Also included among these specialists were mural painters and sculptors, who carved stone both in the round and in relief (Berdan 1982: 153).

While most Aztec elite craft workers obtained raw materials and sold their products in market-places, the most skillful were also commissioned to produce goods for the king, sometimes in special workshops in royal palaces. Most stone sculptors and mural painters probably worked for the king most of the time, since there was little other demand for their specialized products. In hegemonic states, especially Texcoco and Tenochtitlan, royal patronage encouraged the carving of stone statues, ritual bowls, altars, cult objects, and decorative plaques, some of which were works of great size. These arts achieved exceptional levels of refinement. Kings presented such objects to major temples and used them to adorn their palaces (Townsend 1979). They also distributed to the nobility and to outstanding warriors luxury goods that other craft specialists sold to or manufactured for the palace. Skilled craftsmen were lavishly rewarded for their services to the king (Brumfiel 1987).

Luxury goods were also produced in smaller cities, and there was some regional specialization. Azcatpotzalco, for example, was renowned for its silversmithing, while the best-quality pottery came from Cholula, outside the Valley of Mexico; the Aztec king would use no other. Craft workers in still smaller centres tended to specialize in utilitarian crafts. Masons from Coyoacan and carpenters from Xochimilco were in much demand for major construction projects in Tenochtitlan (Berdan 1982: 176). The production of household pottery, obsidian blades, and textiles was carried on in rural and urban settings throughout the Valley of Mexico. Elizabeth Brumfiel (1980: 466) argues that increasing craft production in urban centres in Late Aztec times resulted in a decline in craft production and a growing emphasis on food production in rural areas.

Among the Yoruba, particular crafts were practised by extended families. Depending on demand, craft production might be full-time or part-time, but all extended families included full-time farmers. Specialists who practised the same craft in a particular city but belonged to more than one patrilineage formed craft associations that set standards, established prices, and regulated other matters of common interest. There were associations of brass-workers, iron-workers, wood- and ivory-carvers, calabash-carvers, mat-weavers, leather-workers, drum-makers, and potters, as well as of doctors, hunters, and traders (Eades 1980: 85–86; Ojo 1966a: 80–102; R. Smith 1969: 118). Most were associations of male craft workers, but potters' associations and those of the broadcloth weavers were female. The distinction between luxury and utilitarian crafts was less marked than in the Valley of Mexico and more resembled the situation in Mesopotamia. Each craft association had its patron deity, and its leaders were in contact with palace officials about matters of mutual interest. In Benin, each craft association was located in a separate ward of the 'town', as distinguished from the 'palace', district of the city (Bradbury 1957: 34).

While most skilled Yoruba craft workers laboured in urban centres, crafts such as smithing, potting, and mat-weaving were also practised in villages (Peel 1983: 74–75). Ritual and utilitarian pottery was brought to Benin from villages to the north and west (Bradbury 1957: 26). Craft specialization also occurred regionally: the Ijebu area was noted for its gold and silver work, Oyo for its leather and calabash-carving, Ogbomoso for its dyeing and weaving, Ilorin for its pottery, and Ife for its brass-casting and production of glass beads (Ojo 1966a: 102). Most craft work was done within family compounds, but kings sometimes commissioned famous metalworkers and wood-carvers to carry out special projects at their palaces. The royal palace at Old Oyo was famous for the one hundred brass-covered posts that hold up a roof running around the four sides of one of its courtyards or long corridors. In Old Oyo there was also a group of craft workers whose sole employment was to sew and embroider with beads crowns, staffs, robes, and leather work for the palace (S. Johnson 1921: 45, 153, 258). The role of blacksmiths in forging weapons created close economic relations between them and kings, high officials, and other military leaders, but these links did not prevent them from producing identical weapons for general sale.

The king of Benin had special relations with members of the city's brassworkers' association. During the installation of a new ruler, these specialists were required to come to the palace, where, with the ritual assistance of the new king, they cast brass portrait heads and other regalia that would be used in the cult that was being established for the previous ruler. Creating these objects required an exceptionally high level of skill in making moulds and casting and polishing metal. The smiths were forbidden to cast similar ritual objects for anyone else; other families had to use less prestigious wooden or ceramic heads for their ancestral cults. The same craft workers also produced elaborate brass plaques and other decorations for the royal palace. Their largest castings weighed as much as twenty-two kilograms and required many crucibles of molten metal (Garrard 1983: 19). The king lavishly rewarded these craft workers with farms, slaves, cowrie shells, and other gifts. The brasssmiths' slaves and other dependents worked farms that provided them with food and an income that was independent of their craft work (Bradbury 1957: 34). The smiths also manufactured jewellery and other goods in their own ward for general sale. While the work they were permitted to do was limited by the king's insistence on monopolizing their finest creations, royal financing supported a division of labour and levels of expertise that could create works of exceptional quality whenever required.

The king of Benin also regulated all ivory-carving, which could be done only for him. He distributed ivory staffs to office-holders, including village leaders, who in the absence of his special favour had to be content with wooden ones. In addition, the ruler of Benin employed weavers from the Onwina Nido ward of Benin City to produce cloth with special patterns that could be worn only by the king and high-ranking officials. This work was done both in the weavers' ward and at the palace (Bradbury 1957: 26).

Maya craft specialization appears from archaeological evidence to have been associated with residential groups and therefore perhaps with extended families. As among the Yoruba, it seems that not all members of a residential group were craft workers; craft specialists may have lived with upper-class patrons or with kinsmen, servants, or retainers who produced food for them. There is evidence that at least some elite craft workers were attached to and supported by high-status households, including those of kings. Some elite craft workers, such as master vase-painters and stela-designers, are inferred from their titles to have belonged to royal lineages, although these titles may have merely signified royal support or patronage. Less skilled craft workers seem to have belonged to commoner extended families (Aldenderfer, Kimball, and Sievert 1989; Haviland 1974; Inomata 2001; McAnany 1993: 71; Reents-Budet 1998; Tate 1992: 20, 47).

The known distribution of different craft specializations in Maya urban settings does not suggest a geographical clustering of specific occupations. Nor do particular craft specializations correspond to the differential elaboration of houses in residential clusters or the locations of house clusters in relation to urban centres. While utilitarian crafts may for the most part have been part-time ones, upper-class patronage would have allowed many forms of elite production, such as jade carving and the production of the most elaborate painted pottery, to have developed into full-time occupations (Becker 1973; Moholy-Nagy 1997).

Smaller Maya communities, such as Colha, in Belize, specialized in producing stone tools for export (Hester and Shafer 1994). Individual workshops produced different stages or types of tools (King and Potter 1994). Utilitarian pottery was made in small villages on the peripheries of urban centres, especially in agriculturally less productive areas. This pottery appears to have circulated directly to the area around its production site rather than through nearby urban centres. Maya potters specialized in making particular styles of pottery rather than a limited range of functional categories (Ball 1993: 244–45; Potter and King 1995). This, together with the lack of concentration of elite craft production near the centre of cities and the absence of any physical evidence of market-places, casts further doubt on the existence of a hierarchical market system among the Classic Maya.

There is finally the question of whether some Maya artisans worked exclusively for the king. Except near the end of the Classic period, only kings appear to have erected carved stone monuments, which were clearly the work of master designers and master stonemasons. Some stelae are inscribed with the names of several craft workers. Master craftsmen seem occasionally to have worked in more than one polity and may have been free to move from one state to another. Alternatively, they may have been despatched by royal patrons to produce monumental works for friendly rulers or been carried off by victorious kings (Schele and Miller 1986: 219; Tate 1992: 40–49). While palaces controlled the work of some craft workers in other city-state systems, upper-class control of elite production among the Maya would have been greater overall if kings and nobles had monopolized long-distance trade and the acquisition of luxury raw materials.

In at least three of the four city-state civilizations we have examined, craft production was closely linked to markets and long-distance trade, which provided exotic raw materials and a means of selling surplus produce to buyers over a large area. In general, market prices determined what products were available to people of differing means. In the Valley of Mexico and Benin and perhaps among the Maya, rulers imposed sumptuary regulations on certain luxury goods or directly controlled their production and distribution. Because of their abundant wealth and their ability to sponsor highly skilled craft workers, hegemonic rulers were especially effective patrons of the arts. Public markets encouraged more ordinary full-time production, which made better-quality goods available to most people. City-state systems gave farmers easy access to such goods. Rulers in city-state systems that had powerful hereditary class systems (Valley of Mexico, Maya) seem to have intervened more directly in the production and distribution of craft products, especially luxury goods, than the rulers of city-state systems that lacked them (Mesopotamia, Yoruba). In Benin, however, there was considerable royal intervention despite the absence of hereditary classes.

In territorial states there tended to be two tiers of craft production. During their spare time, farmers used locally available materials to produce what they and their neighbours needed, with each household aiming at self-sufficiency or producing for a local market. Mass-produced and specialized goods were manufactured in royal workshops by artisans who worked full-time for the state. Their royal employers supplied them with raw materials, and in return they were expected to produce weapons, tools, and storage vessels for people who performed special tasks for the state, as well as luxury goods for the use and enjoyment of their upper-class patrons. The cost of producing luxury goods was of less concern to elite craft workers' patrons than the quality of those goods. The ability of kings to display and distribute status symbols that no one else could emulate was a major source of prestige and power. While only a few of these coveted goods trickled down to local leaders as rewards for their loyalty to the state, the possibility of such rewards reinforced that loyalty.

In Egypt the most skilled craft workers (*ḥmwt*) worked for the king, usually near the royal court (Andreu 1997: 58–69). Some groups of goldsmiths, sculptors, painters, and elite carpenters were assigned to a *wꜥbt* (pure place), which was, or had attached to it, a workshop, for producing funerary goods. Craft workers laboured in teams under the supervision of two 'great controllers of craftsmen' (*wr ḫrp ḥmwt*) and a hierarchy of overseers (Eyre 1987a: 26–27) to decorate tombs, carve statues and stone vases, and manufacture jewellery and fine furniture for the upper classes, as well as cult objects for temples. Dwarfs and hunchbacks were responsible for either manufacturing gold objects or caring for them. Sometimes artisans of the royal residence were despatched to work on the tombs of high officials.

The most skilled craft workers were rewarded with minor part-time palace or temple offices, land, servants, slaves, cattle, and other material goods (Strouhal 1992: 167). While few of these craft workers were buried in tombs as large and substantial as those of some doctors, hairdressers, and manicurists who personally attended the king, they were invited to participate in upper-class banquets and hunts. Some artists were permitted to portray and name themselves among an official's valued retainers when they decorated his tomb (165–66). In better-documented examples from the New Kingdom, royal tomb-builders and the sculptors who carved colossal royal statues received state housing, substantial salaries, living expenses, and servants to fish, grow crops, and grind grain for them and their families. They were also allowed to work for private clients in their spare time (Eyre 1987b: 168–83). In the Old Kingdom the monarch was able to reward high officials with luxurious presents produced by elite craft workers: stone coffins, statues, inscribed doorways, and other fittings for their tombs, as well as personal jewellery and high-quality furniture (Eyre 1987a: 21–22). The consistently high quality of the art and jewellery produced by royal craft workers during the Old and Middle Kingdoms testifies to the sustained achievements of these royal artisans and of the institutions in which they worked.

Also labouring for the government in provincial administrative centres as well as at the royal court were the full-time craft workers who manufactured utilitarian goods for the state. They included coppersmiths, who cast chisels, knives, and other metal tools for government craftsmen; carpenters, boat-builders, tanners, and leather-workers; and potters and bricklayers (both designated *qdw*) (Strouhal 1992: 141). The boat-builders constructed large royal ships and seagoing vessels as well as the barges used to haul government grain from one part of Egypt to another. In the Middle Kingdom, government boat-building near This, in Upper Egypt, was closely supervised by the vizier who resided in far-off Memphis (Kemp 1989: 130). Craft workers of this sort were also attached to private estates, temples, and pyramid towns, where they worked part-time as priests of the local royal mortuary cult and supported themselves as coppersmiths, carpenters, and other craft workers or by farming (David 1986: 165–70).

The most esteemed luxury goods in the Inka kingdom were produced by full-time specialists (*kamayoq*), the most skilled of whom lived and worked near Cuzco. Most of them were bound to the service of institutions and high-ranking individuals. When the Inka conquered the north-coast state of Chimor, which was noted for the excellence of its metallurgy, its most celebrated metalworkers were resettled near Cuzco and ordered to produce goods in the Inka style. The output of elite gold- and silversmiths included statues of kings and gods and life-sized replicas of llamas and plants that were placed in temple and palace 'gardens' as fertility symbols. Skilled metallurgists also produced gold and silver cups, tableware, and jewellery, which the Inka king distributed as royal gifts to members of the nobility and occasionally to commoners who served the state well. Even small gold or silver bangles and pins used to fasten garments (*tupu*) were treasured indications of royal favour (Earle 1987: 73; von Hagen 1959: 214). A royal monopoly of gold bullion facilitated concentrating the working of this precious and symbolically charged metal in the Cuzco area, while silver was worked at Cuzco and other centres such as Hatunxauxa (Earle 1987: 73–74; Kendall 1973: 171–72; Murra 1980: 157; von Hagen 1959: 107). The main Inka potteries at Sanyo, near Cuzco, turned out handmade polished cups, plates, and bottles decorated with repetitive geometrical patterns and stylized animals. This pottery was a highly valued though less prestigious substitute for metal vessels (Kendall 1973: 174–77).

The decorated pottery and fancy cloth produced near Cuzco were copied at government workshops throughout the Inka kingdom. Fancy cloth was woven by chosen women, who resided in all the provincial administrative centres, and by yanakuna, who served government officials. Male and female dwarfs, hunchbacks, and cripples, who were unsuited for agricultural labour, were also set to work as full-time weavers. Standard Inka-style pottery was produced at provincial centres and elsewhere both by specialists and by corvée labourers (Costin and Hagstrum 1995). Yanakuna likewise manufactured bronze tools and weapons at Cuzco and in provincial centres (von Hagen 1959: 157). Throughout the kingdom craft workers alloyed bronze according to a standard formula (Earle 1987: 74).

State-directed craft production was assigned to specialist communities of artisans as well as to yanakuna. Specialist communities, while continuing to be organized as ayllus and feeding themselves, were exempted from the agricultural labour tax and other forms of corvée. They were also fed from state supplies for as long as they worked on government projects. At Millerea, on the north shore of Lake Titicaca, one thousand Aymara weavers wove cloth for the Inka army (Earle 1987: 72). These production enclaves permitted the government to control the design and quality of goods, which were intended to be copies of what was being produced under high-level supervision at Cuzco.

These arrangements ensured that state officials controlled the production and distribution of all luxury goods, as well as of specialized weapons and tools, while the king personally controlled the distribution of the most valued prestige objects. While local rulers had weavers and smiths attached to their households, they depended on the king and on provincial governors to provide them with more highly valued luxury goods. At the village level, part-time craftsmen specialized in producing different types of goods which were exchanged among nearby households or at local markets. Because of government curbs on interregional trade, the raw materials used by local craft workers must have been of local origin.

Most of what is known about the organization of craft production in Shang China comes from only a few archaeological sites and relates to the production of luxury goods. Bronze vessels, which were used to offer sacrifices to ancestors, were among the most treasured possessions of the upper classes; less privileged families had to make do with ceramic or wooden vessels. Bronze-workers, like other producers of luxury goods, lived in their own small communities, each of which was probably inhabited by a single patrilineage and its retainers. Communities of this sort were located near the royal administrative compounds at Zhengzhou and Anyang. The bronze-workers lived in comfortable houses built, like upper-class ones, on stamped-earth platforms. They appear to have been divided into master craftsmen, assistants, and apprentices and were probably assisted in menial tasks by humbler retainers and slaves. Many different skills were required to produce high-quality bronze objects: processing ores, creating and decorating sectional moulds, assembling the moulds, casting the vessels, and finishing them. Carrying out such projects required numerous specialists to work in teams and therefore a high level of economic support. It is estimated that about three hundred people had to cooperate to cast an eighty-seven-kilogram ritual vessel (Franklin 1990: 20–24; Hsu and Linduff 1988: 18–19; Treistman 1972: 85–92).

The demand for bronze weapons and ritual vessels among the upper classes was constant. Groups of bronze vessels hidden in times of crisis suggest that family shrines contained a current set of ceremonial vessels, together with some earlier vessels that were especially esteemed. Less valuable earlier sets and single vessels that had particular personal significance for the deceased were buried with the dead, presumably so that they could use them to continue sacrificing to their ancestors. Vessels interred with women of high status were generally less elaborate than those buried with men (Rawson 1993).

Bronze-casting appears to have been carried out across northern and central China in Shang times. It is widely assumed that the best-quality bronze vessels were made in one or a few royal centres. Some modern experts claim to be able to distinguish vessels produced at Anyang from contemporary but clumsier and more old-fashioned ones made in less important centres (Kane 1974–75: 80). Robert Bagley (1980: 98) states that, while Zhengzhou-period vessels were uniform in style and therefore perhaps were produced at only a few royal workshops, those dating from the later Anyang period that are found in outlying regions differ in type, style, and motifs from those produced at Anyang. Robert Thorp (1985: 54–55) cautions, however, that few stylistic differences are exhibited by vessels produced within the known borders of the Shang state and therefore presumably by specialists working for different lineages of the Shang ruling class. Gina Barnes (1993: 124) suggests that only a small number of Anyang-style bronzes were produced at Shang royal capitals and the rest were local copies. It is possible that craft workers trained at Anyang were sent to work for various regional officials.

In the Late Shang period, the Zhou rulers produced bronze vessels that initially copied Shang prototypes. Soon, however, their vessels acquired their own distinctive style (Hsu and Linduff 1988: 41–42). To date, the early Zhou capitals are the only places except Anyang where abundant traces of writing have been recovered. These Zhou texts date from the Late Shang period. While the Shang writing system was used in both societies, surviving examples of Zhou writing are distinguished by the smaller size of the characters and by different calendrics (46–49). Thus both writing and bronze-working exhibit a rapid divergence from Shang prototypes. By contrast, the relative stylistic unity of bronze vessels within the core of the Shang kingdom seems to reflect political control similar to that which the Inka central government exerted over the production of luxury pottery and cloth.

Pottery was also produced in specialized communities near the great administrative compound at Zhengzhou and probably near provincial administrative centres throughout northern China. Much of the Zhengzhou pottery consisted of high-quality utilitarian wares, fashioned with only limited use of the potter's wheel but fired using elaborate kilns in which the furnace was separated from the baking oven. A small amount of the pottery produced at Zhengzhou constituted luxury wares, including heavily decorated ritual vessels made of white clay and water-resistant stoneware vessels covered with a glaze that had to be fired at a minimum temperature of twelve hundred degrees C (Chêng 1960: 137–55). Still other communities of craft workers around Zhengzhou consisted of stone- and shell-carvers, stoneworkers, and carpenters. The stoneworkers not only manufactured jade and marble luxury products but also mass-produced stone arrowheads for the army and stone knives and sickles for state labourers.

An important craft that could have been practised only with upper-class patronage was the production of chariots, which began in the thirteenth century B.C. Sophisticated carpentry was needed to produce eighteen-spoke wheels that were 125 to 140 centimetres in diameter and therefore considerably larger than those made in the Middle East in the Late Bronze Age. Zhou rulers are recorded as presenting elaborately decorated chariots as gifts to regional officials (Lu 1993). The large numbers in use suggest that they must have been manufactured in regional centres as well as at the royal court.

The artisans who worked for the royal court were supervised by a large number of full-time artisan officials (gong), who also performed court rituals and accompanied military expeditions, perhaps to oversee the maintenance of equipment. It is unknown to what extent these artisan officials coordinated specialized production throughout the kingdom and whether similar administrators worked for regional and local officials (Keightley 1969: 8–65). What is known about the Shang court suggests that it managed elite production much as it was managed in Egypt and Inka Peru.

SPECIALIZATION IN CITY- AND TERRITORIAL STATES

In territorial states the goods used by the upper classes and the government tended to be made by full-time and elite craft workers employed by the state. These goods circulated separately from goods made and used by commoners. In this manner, the central government created a monopoly of high-quality goods that reinforced its political control. The most luxurious goods were produced, often from exotic raw materials, at or near the royal court, and distributing them was a prerogative of the king. Less valuable luxury goods and utilitarian items required by the state were produced both around the royal court and in provincial administrative centres. Farmers generally had to rely on goods manufactured from local raw materials by part-time rural craft workers.

In city-state systems only the rulers of hegemonic states possessed economic resources that approximated those that were regularly available to the rulers of territorial states, and their power fluctuated and was often short-lived. Full-time craft workers tended to sell most of their products publicly, and exotic raw materials were available to artisans from long-distance traders and at local markets. This meant that better-quality goods of all kinds were available to anyone who could afford them. If the quality of the luxury goods produced in city-state systems rarely matched the best that was created in territorial states, the overall quality of goods available to everyone was higher. In city-states that were divided along hereditary class lines and in some other hegemonic city-states, the upper classes attempted, by enacting sumptuary laws and controlling long-distance trade, to regulate the distribution of goods in ways analogous to those found in territorial states, where goods circulated at the commoner and the upper-class levels but only rarely passed from one level to the other. Among the Classic Maya, upper-class control of interstate trade may have constituted a mechanism of political control that resembled those found in territorial and some hegemonic states, but exotic goods such as obsidian were widely distributed in Maya society.

17 Appropriation of Wealth

A defining feature of all early civilizations was the institutionalized appropriation by a small ruling group of most of the wealth produced by the lower classes. Economists commonly define wealth as the stock of goods and claims that individuals or corporate groups can give away or use to purchase goods and services. In modern industrial socictics, where almost everything can be bought and sold, any sort of asset constitutes wealth (Polanyi 1944). In early civilizations, however, some types of goods did not circulate freely. Communal land, which could be inherited but not alienated, was clearly a source of wealth that economically advantaged its owners by comparison with groups that were landless. Agricultural workers who lacked their own land had to pay to use other people's, usually by surrendering a substantial portion of their production to its owners. Yet, while inalienable communal land constituted a source of wealth, it was not a form of wealth. In Peru the king gave gold objects to individuals as testimonials of his esteem for them or as rewards for service. Although these objects could be inherited, they could not be bought or sold. Thus, while they were valuable social assets, they too were not commodities, and hence did not constitute wealth. Palaces, temples, and tombs, which expressed the power of the upper classes, also fell into this category. In some early civilizations, such as Egypt, Mesopotamia, and the Valley of Mexico, metal bullion and cloth were commodities that were easily stored for long periods and facilitated exchange; hence they constituted important forms of wealth, as did many exotic raw materials. Nevertheless, the most common and economically important forms of wealth in early civilizations were agricultural surpluses.

Farmers and artisans did not accumulate large amounts of wealth, although they created virtually all the wealth that existed in these societies. Most of them lived only slightly above the subsistence level and had to depend on their own sustained labour to support themselves. Food is reported to have become scarce in the month prior to the annual maize harvest among many of the poorer families living in the Aztec capital of Tenochtitlan (Clendinnen 1991: 66). Some merchants accumulated great riches as a result of their trading activities, but they generally lacked political power and therefore had to cultivate the goodwill and protection of rulers and officials. Most of the wealth produced in early civilizations was controlled by powerful individuals, families, and institutions.

Producers, as far as they could, sought to benefit by personally disposing of their surplus production. Some ancient Egyptian farmers habitually tried to conceal part of their harvest to avoid having that portion taxed by government officials. Tax collectors, for their part, sought to stop such evasion by calculating harvest yields as accurately as possible and forcing farmers who claimed to have produced less to reveal their hiding places (Lichtheim 1976: 170–71). Farmers must have disliked having to produce more surplus grain than they and their families required only to have most of it appropriated by landowners and government officials. At the same time, the upper classes and the government would have liked production to increase so that they might have still greater wealth at their disposal.

Members of the upper classes competed among themselves for the control of surplus wealth, and this competition gave rise to many different types of appropriation. One of the main forms of obligatory wealth transfers in early civilizations was taxes, which had to be paid to the state. Surplus wealth was transferred to individual members of the upper classes as rents paid to owners for the use of land and as fees and bribes offered for various services, such as rendering legal decisions. Corvée, indentured, and slave labour were yet other means by which the state or upper-class individuals could enrich themselves at the expense of the less powerful. Other important wealth transfers in early civilizations took the form of payments that rulers of weaker states were compelled to make to rulers of more powerful ones. Many scholars, when dealing with early civilizations, use the terms 'taxes' and 'tribute' interchangeably or refer to the obligatory transfer of wealth both within and between states as 'tribute'. The latter usage is exemplified by expressions such as 'tributary mode of production' (Amin 1976). The unjustified implication of this usage is that in early civilizations both forms constituted a surrender of wealth by subjects to rulers that was fundamentally different from the payment of taxes in modern societies. I will use the term 'tax' in the conventional manner to refer to obligatory wealth transfers from individuals or groups to states and 'tribute' to designate wealth transfers between states. While the two were not necessarily terminologically differentiated in all early civilizations, Egyptian officials of the New Kingdom distinguished between the tribute (*ìnw*) paid to them by conquered Syrian and Canaanite principalities and the taxes (*b3kw*) collected within Egypt and Nubia, which was by then an extension of the Egyptian state (Priese 1974). Whether or not it had an emic referent in each early civilization, the distinction between taxes and tribute is a heuristically useful one.

TAXES, CORVÉES, AND RENTS

It used to be argued that the appropriation of foodstuffs in early civilizations was achieved as a result of the control that the upper classes exercised over arable land. Some scholars surmised that farmers were bound to the land much as peasants were in medieval Europe. Others believed that, by owning all the agricultural land, the upper classes forced peasants either to rent it from them or to enter into sharecropping relations, thus ensuring that they would receive most of the surplus (Weber 1976 [1896]). The alternative concept of the Asiatic society postulated that members of egalitarian farming communities owned the land collectively and the upper classes used the threat of force to extract surplus production from them in the form of taxes or tribute (Isaac 1993). It is now clear, however, that land ownership in early civilizations was considerably more complex than either of these models and that, when it came to transfers of wealth, it was economically less important than the right to appropriate agricultural production and the surplus labour of the lower classes.

The ways of appropriating food surpluses were varied. Taxes might be paid to the state by farmers who collectively owned and worked the land or by institutional or private landowners. They could be levied in kind on all types of agricultural produce or only on grains and other easily stored crops. They might be paid entirely or in part with something of equivalent value such as metal bullion or cowrie shells. A fixed amount of tax might be collected annually for a particular amount of arable land, a different rate might be set annually depending on varying crop yields, or a fixed percentage of the total yield might be levied. Privately or institutionally owned land was taxed in some early civilizations but exempt from taxation in others.

Privately, institutionally, and even collectively owned land might be worked by slaves or by farmers who were bound to the soil in return for their subsistence. It might also be cultivated by landless labourers for a fixed daily wage (often paid in foodstuffs), rented to landless farmers for a fixed amount, or sharecropped with tenant farmers. Each of these arrangements resulted in the return of a substantial share of the crop to the landowners.

Commoners could also be required, as a form of labour tax, to work plots of land that were assigned to local officials, temples, or the state and to provide corvée labour for government mining operations, build temples, palaces, and royal tombs, clean and maintain public thoroughfares, provide domestic service for kings and lords, and participate in military operations. Taxes were frequently collected on handicraft production, market sales, and goods being transported from one place to another. Sales taxes could either be collected in addition to or substituted for direct levies on production. Taxes of all sorts were paid to various levels of government and sometimes by the same people to more than one level.

In Shang China, if later traditions are correct, rural lineages handed over approximately one-ninth of their agricultural production to the upper classes by cultivating fields to produce harvests that were assigned either to the king or to regional governors, local leaders, and various stipendiaries who worked for these officials (Vandermeersch 1980: 215–17). After the annual harvest, they may also have had to perform a month of non-agricultural corvèe labour for their lord (Hsu and Linduff 1988: 349). Oracle-bone texts reveal that kings and perhaps other high-ranking lords mobilized ordinary people to perform various forms of corvée labour for themselves or the state: preparing agricultural land, planting and harvesting millet on special estates, building fortifications and palaces, assisting at hunts, performing military service, and helping the army to transport supplies. These were the same forms of public works that were performed by landless labourers who worked full-time for the king. Both types of labourers served under officers with 'military' titles, which suggests that no distinction was drawn between military service and other forms of corvée labour. All the food produced by these workers would have belonged to the king or high-ranking lords (Keightley 1969: 66–144; 1999b: 281, 284). Thus Shang commoners appear to have paid taxes mostly in the form of labour. There is no evidence, however, that payment in kind was ruled out or regarded as inappropriate.

Subjects of the Inka ruler were unique in our sample in that they paid all taxes in the form of labour rather than goods. In addition to cultivating their own fields and ones that supported the corporate activities of their ayllu and its leader, farm families had to work separate plots of land that belonged to the Inka state and to religious cults sponsored by the Inka government. The seeds and tubers sown in these fields and perhaps the tools that were used were supplied by the institutions to which the harvest belonged. Working this land was justified as reciprocity for the king's permitting ayllus to keep most of their land following their incorporation into the Inka kingdom (Kendall 1973: 145–46; Murra 1980: 31–33). Despite the integral involvement of women in agriculture, the Inka state also represented agriculture as a form of permanent bride service owed to the Inka ruler, who claimed control over all women. A similar logic was applied to fish and other natural resources by claiming that they belonged to the king, who granted ordinary people the right to use them provided that they supplied these items to government officials whenever they were asked to do so (Gose 2000: 85). By accumulating resources only through the appropriation of labour, the Inka monarch avoided having anything given to him by his subjects, which would have implied that he was inferior to the givers. Farmers had to transport the produce of the state and temple lands they cultivated to government and temple granaries located as far away as their provincial administrative centre. Ayllu, state, and temple land constituted the basis of three separate systems of production, each of which depended on the same people's labour. All the food produced on government land belonged to the state, while all the food grown on temple lands was devoted to the service of the gods (LeVine 1992).

Farmers also had to provide the corvée (*mit'a*) labour required to tend state and temple herds of llamas and alpacas, construct and repair government roads, mine and refine metals, erect buildings, manufacture various sorts of goods, and perform military duties. Hereditary lords and governors had a right to the labour of one person from every hundred families under their control, this labour being provided by each family in turn. A governor could summon four hundred workers from all parts of his province to labour at the administrative centre; a *hunu kuraka* (head of ten thousand families) could call on one hundred of his subjects to perform domestic and agricultural tasks, a *waranka kuraka* (head of one thousand families) on ten subjects, and a *pachaca kuraka* (head of one hundred households) on one subject (Julien 1988; LeVine 1987). Rotating corvée labour produced grain on large state farms to support the army and the upper classes. Far more grain was produced for the upper classes on these farms than on an equivalent amount of farm land worked by members of ayllus for themselves, the government, and temples (S. Moore 1958: 49–53, 61–67). Married women each year had to spin and weave fixed amounts of raw materials supplied by the state.

While no goods were actually transferred from farming communities to the state, farmers produced large amounts of surplus food that, along with corvée labour, belonged to the government, state-sponsored religious cults, and the upper classes. Officials reciprocated with hospitality in the form of cooked food, maize beer, and entertainment and, if the workers were away from home for a long time, clothing. These exchanges were modelled on the traditional usages of Andean agriculture. Farmers regularly called upon neighbours, relatives, and friends to help them accomplish major tasks on the understanding that they would reciprocate whenever the latter needed help, and the women of the group for whom the work was being done supplied all the workers with food, drink, and entertainment for the duration of their toil (Murra 1980: 90–91).

Corvée labour done for the state and for state-sponsored temples differed from local reciprocity mainly in the highly asymmetrical nature of the exchange and the emphasis laid on the special obligations that subjects owed the king. Much more labour was supplied by commoners to the state than went into providing them with food and entertainment. Moreover, all the food, drink, and clothing that were distributed to labourers had been produced for the state by unpaid male and female workers. Token reciprocity facilitated the production of large amounts of goods for the use of the upper classes (Morris and Thompson 1985).

Inka officials' appropriation of a small number of girls and boys from each ayllu was yet another form of tax. The king eventually made some of the young women who were not used as human sacrifices his secondary wives and concubines and bestowed other women as extra wives on nobles and commoners who had served him or the state well. The majority of these women spent the rest of their lives secluded in the houses for chosen women, where they assisted in religious rituals, wove fancy cloth, and cooked and brewed for the state. The food they prepared was not only offered to the gods and distributed to participants in religious festivals but also supplied to corvée labourers working for the state or travelling from one part of the kingdom to another (Kendall 1973: 192–93; Zuidema 1990: 58–59). The boys who were not sacrificed were bound hereditarily to the king and other officials as household servants, craft workers, specialized retainers, and farm labourers. Their ranks were swelled by whole groups of conquered peoples subjected to this form of service. They had to turn over all their produce to the official for whom they worked and by whom they and their families were fed, clothed, and housed. While some came to enjoy positions of trust, they kept a much smaller portion of the food they produced than did members of ayllus. Estates constituted a small enough portion of all agricultural land that the government did not have to tax their production to protect its own fiscal structure (Murra 1980: 168–75). This resulted in higher returns for individual members of the Inka nobility who had been granted such lands. Estates and their bonded labourers greatly enhanced the revenues of the king, of royal descent groups, and of other individuals on whom they were bestowed.

In Egypt many individual farmers or farm communities paid a portion of their crops as rents to men and women who owned estates or had been granted the use of them by the government. Estate-holders included government officials, funerary cults, nobles, temples, the king, and the central government. In dealing with their landlords, villagers were represented by their headmen. Unless estates belonged to the king or the state or had been declared tax-free by the king, their owners or managers had to pay taxes to the central government.

Farm villages that were not attached to estates seem to have paid taxes directly to the government (Andreu 1997: 109).

During the Old Kingdom, a nationwide biennial cattle count provided the basis for the government to levy a tax in kind on living animals and the hides of dead animals belonging to individuals, communities, and institutions (Kees 1961: 87–90). Systematic records were also kept of what land was held by different institutions and individuals and who was responsible for paying the taxes on the crops that each plot of land produced (Kemp 1983: 82). To assess the productivity of land, the presence of ponds, canals, wells, trees, and swamps, and anything else that might enhance or reduce its value was recorded (Eyre 1987a: 6). Already in the Old Kingdom, the amount of the grain tax appears to have been determined in some general fashion by the level of the Nile flood, which was carefully recorded each year. If the flood rose too high and destroyed irrigation works or was too low for crops to be grown on higher ground, the tax rate was reduced (Andreu 1997: 106–8; Eyre 1999: 45). The produce of trees was also taxed (Kees 1961: 80). In addition, the government sought to collect a tax on goods produced by part-time craft workers and by the wives of commoners, of which cloth was probably the most important item. This tax may have consisted of one of every ten items produced (Kees 1961: 53; Kemp 1983: 82–83).

Government officials collected grain, dates, domestic animals, and manufactured goods as taxes in the countryside and conveyed them to provincial administrative centers, where they were placed under the control of the local overseer of the granaries (*ỉmy-r šnwt*) and the overseer of the treasury (*ỉmy-r pr ḥḏ*). Much of what was collected remained stored at the provincial administrative centres and was used to pay resident officials and their assistants, sustain government-employed craft workers, support local government projects, feed corvée labourers in transit from one part of the country to another, and provision royal visits. Other goods were forwarded as needed to the national capital (Hassan 1993: 564–68; Strudwick 1985: 276–99). Temple estates were usually located near the cult centre to which they belonged, but those of an important one might be scattered throughout Egypt, as were those assigned to royal funerary cults. Kings derived revenues from personal estates, state-owned land, and taxes. Goods passed as rents from farmers to estate-holders and as taxes from landowning farmers and estate-holders to the government.

Egyptian farmers were also required to perform corvée labour. Tasks included constructing and maintaining irrigation systems, erecting buildings (including royal tombs), quarrying and mining, transporting goods, and participating in military expeditions. Some of this work was done near where farmers lived; other corvées were performed away from home, often near the royal capital and sometimes outside the Nile Valley. Military and mining expeditions and pyramid-building might require groups of men to be away from their villages for three months or more at a time. Corvée workers were organized into units of one hundred men, divided into groups of ten, each with its own leader. Expeditions, some composed of over seventeen thousand men, were sent into the Eastern Desert to quarry stone under the leadership of expedition commanders (*ỉmy-r mšʿ*) or royal (literally 'divine') treasurers (*sḏ3wty nṯr*). In addition to corvée labourers, state craftsmen (*ḥmwt pr ʿ3*), millers, and brewers accompanied such expeditions. Still larger groups of labourers were assembled to help construct royal pyramid complexes (Andreu 1997: 29–36; Eyre 1987a: 10–20; Kemp 1989: 129). Corvée labourers were fed, housed, and clothed when they were away from their homes for long periods. The selection of individuals for successive tours of duty must have been worked out between low-level government scribes and village leaders. Severe punishments were inflicted on people who attempted to evade corvée duty or deserted their work parties. In the Middle Kingdom, they and their families were confined to government prisons (*ḫnrt*) and might be condemned to perpetual slave labour on government estates or those belonging to government officials (Andreu 1997: 27–28; Kemp 1983: 83–84).

Aztec calpolli members had to cultivate land specially designated for the support of calpolli officials, temples, schools, and regiments. Urban calpollis, in particular, tended to be larger and less egalitarian than were Peruvian ayllus. Their leading families and most successful warriors were usually members of the nobility; hence collective labour helped to support the upper classes within calpollis as well as those organizations' corporate activities. Members of calpollis also had to provide corvée labour for the state, helping to construct public buildings and to clean and repair streets and public places as well as serving as soldiers. It has been suggested that calpollis were required to surrender one-third of their harvest to the state (López Austin 1988, 1: 75), but it is unclear whether this was a direct tax or included all the food resources that calpollis expended training their regiments, supporting military campaigns, and performing other state duties. Nor is it even certain that a harvest tax was levied (van Zantwijk 1985: 283). Public institutions, the king, nobles, and successful warriors were granted land worked by landless farmers who were allowed to keep only enough of the food they produced to feed themselves and their families. No tax appears to have been paid on these lands or their produce. Goods sold in public markets were subject to a tax that may have amounted to 20 percent of the value of what was sold and could be paid either in kind or with cloth or cacao beans. Because of the high volume of market exchange, this tax greatly enriched the palace and enhanced the power of the king (Berdan 1982: 42).

In Mesopotamia much institutionally and privately owned land was rented, sharecropped, or worked by wage labourers, and all these arrangements ensured that most of the food produced belonged to the land's owners or designated beneficiaries. Kings controlled the revenues from palace lands and taxed cultivated fields, crops, and herds belonging to individuals, kin groups, and sometimes temples. Various kings attempted to increase their control over temples and temple revenues, but some of these attempts were unsuccessful (Diakonoff 1969b: 189–90; Postgate 1992: 185–87, 300).

In addition, kings and possibly city councils imposed various taxes on the sale and movement of goods; the city administrators may, however, have been acting only as agents for the king. There are references to taxes on goods leaving and entering cities (which were collected at the city gates), taxes on land, an annual tax that in Old Babylonian times was paid in silver by well-to-do people, including merchants, priests, and officials, and an annual tax collected in kind on grain and animals from officials, merchants, shepherds, soldiers, scribes, tavern keepers, and cookshop operators (R. Harris 1975: 40–45). Taxes were also levied on burials and divorces. These taxes were collected by a wide variety of officials, including gatekeepers, city administrators, and judges, in return for a commission. The right to collect taxes, rents, and dues was also sold to entrepreneurs in return for a portion of their value, usually paid to the government in silver. These same entrepreneurs often made loans at a high rate of interest to farmers and others who were experiencing short-term financial difficulties and had problems meeting tax payments. The king also had the right to call on all free men to perform corvée labour. In later times, corvées, including military service, appear to have been commutable by payments in silver or grain (Diakonoff 1969b: 189–90; R. Harris 1975: 40–45; Van De Mieroop 1999: 203–6).

Kings, temples, and landowners accumulated substantial wealth as the result of their ability to appropriate crop surpluses. Although kings had to bear most of the costs of managing the state, their large landholdings and their ability to collect a wide range of taxes made them the wealthiest and most powerful individuals in each city-state.

The Yoruba acknowledged that they owed taxes and corvée labour to community leaders and kings but viewed them as payments for the services, both natural and supernatural, that leaders provided for their community. A lineage that refused to pay such taxes would have been expelled from a community (Lloyd 1962: 63). Relatively little food was collected as a direct tax on land or produce. Each household presented a few yams as token offerings to local officials and the king at the beginning of the annual harvest (Law 1977: 229; Lloyd 1962: 128). It is possible that no greater effort was made to collect harvest taxes because yams and other Yoruba crops could not be stored for as long as the grain crops of other early civilizations (Bradbury 1957: 23). Large areas were brought under cultivation using hereditary slaves, prisoners of war, and debtors, all of whom laboured in return for basic necessities while the kings and wealthy men and women who controlled their labour lived in luxury and supported numerous armed retainers. In addition to offering token gifts of food to the king, Yoruba men were required to perform corvée labour, which was deployed to build and repair the royal palace and city walls, to tend sacred groves, and sometimes to work palace farms. Such labourers expected to be provided with food and drink by the officials responsible for these corvées (Ajisafe 1924: 25; Ojo 1966b: 63–66).

Most taxes were probably collected on market sales (Hodder and Ukwu 1969: 108). Taxes were also levied on craft production and on the movement of goods between one state and another and in and out of cities. The tolls that were collected on food being brought into cities (Bascom 1969: 37) constituted a more important source of revenue than did the agricultural produce presented as gifts to the king at harvest time. These taxes were paid either in goods or in cowrie shells to gatekeepers who kept a portion of what they collected as payment for their work. The rest was shared by the king and a small number of leading non-royal officials such as the members of the state council in Oyo. Each such official was authorized to collect taxes, together with the king's agents, at different city gates and along different roads. This prevented the palace from appropriating too much wealth at the expense of those with whom the king shared political power.

The king and a much greater number of officials shared the many fees that were levied for hearing legal cases and the fines that were imposed at various levels. Officials received presents and bribes for helping to settle disputes and assisting petitioners in various ways. The king and the chief officials of militarily successful Yoruba states also shared a large portion of the booty, including prisoners, captured during military campaigns. Whether these prisoners were kept as labourers or sold as slaves, they constituted an important source of income. The king also received fees for permitting certain rituals to be performed at shrines he controlled, collected death duties on the properties of wealthy citizens, and received payments for sanctioning the installation of officials and agreeing to bestow titles on individuals (Bascom 1969: 37; Law 1977: 229–31; Lloyd 1960: 229).

The king of Benin was supported by a more robust and centralized version of the Yoruba tax system. The palace organization and state rituals were funded by presentations of palm oil, meat, and livestock twice each year by all ward and village leaders. These contributions were assembled by local leaders from every household in their ward or community. In addition, the king could call on taxpayers to help repair and extend the royal palace and for extra levies of goods when special sacrifices were deemed necessary for the good of the nation. The king also derived considerable revenue in return for granting the numerous titles that were under his exclusive control, exerted considerable control over revenue from legal fines, and claimed ownership of all prisoners taken in war, although he returned most of them to their captors (Bradbury 1957: 41–43).

Almost nothing is known about how the Maya upper classes extracted surplus wealth from commoners. The vastness of state projects and the opulent life of Maya rulers suggest, however, that the Maya upper class, and kings in particular, did it very effectively.

In all early civilizations a small privileged class appropriated, in ways that were deemed to be socially acceptable, a disproportionate share of the available wealth. Ownership of land was not the key to this process. In most early civilizations, agricultural produce and manufactured goods were appropriated by the state in the form of taxes in kind, while surplus labour was appropriated by imposing corvées. While the more intensive forms of appropriation associated with institutional or private ownership of land were practised only to a limited extent in most early civilizations, they appear to have predominated in Mesopotamia and Egypt and to have been rapidly increasing in the Inka kingdom and at least some of the more powerful states in the Valley of Mexico.

The amount of food available for appropriation would have varied according to the environmental settings and the differing overall productivity of the agricultural regimes of various early civilizations. Yet, as a result of the general simplicity of the technology and the predominant role played by human labour in every sector of agricultural production (except Egyptian and Mesopotamian grain production, for which cattle traction was also used), the per capita range of variation in intensity of food production was not great. Nevertheless, the appropriation of even slightly larger amounts of food produced on institutionally or privately owned land would have substantially increased the food resources available to a minuscule upper class.

Substantial amounts of food and manufactured goods were also appropriated by imposing market, sales, and transportation taxes and charging fees to use state services such as the legal system. Such taxes and fees appear to have been especially common in city-state systems, where trade and marketing were important aspects of the economy. It also may have been more practical to tax foodstuffs in this fashion in societies where food was produced continuously over much of the year, as was the case with chinampas and kitchen gardens in Mesoamerica, rather than where there was a single annual grain harvest, as in Egypt and Mesopotamia. The Mesopotamians appear to have taxed grain being brought into cities as well as fields and crop yields. Increasing the range of taxable items and the diversity of ways in which revenue was collected disguised the total amount that was being appropriated from the producer and probably facilitated its extraction.

Some of these strategies may have been more appropriate than others in particular ecological settings, and some combinations of strategies may have been generally more effective than others. To the extent that resources flowed into the hands of various segments of the upper classes, the power of the monarch was limited. The Yoruba, whose taxation arrangements ensured that most of the resources available to the central government would be shared by the king and a few high-ranking non-royal officials, had a much less centralized government than the Aztec, whose monarch controlled substantial revenues derived from patrimonial and office lands and market taxes. Even the king of Benin did not succeed in controlling wealth and its distribution to the same extent as the most powerful rulers in the Valley of Mexico. The Egyptian and Inka bureaucracies made it possible for central governments to collect and store goods for their own use in capitals and administrative centres in all the regions they controlled. In China regional officials appear to have controlled the collection and distribution of surplus resources in regions that were under their direct control and, like the king, probably received tax payments from officials who ruled smaller areas subject to their authority. Yet, because of the delegational nature of political organization, they had to cede economic control of various subregions to these subordinate officials.

Because of their low per capita productivity, early civilizations did not have the capacity to monitor and tax resources as is done today. The government of Old Kingdom Egypt appears to have gone farthest in keeping detailed registers of land ownership and rights to benefit from its produce, but there is no evidence of detailed reckonings of the total revenue received by the central government (Strudwick 1985: 251–300). The Inka organized taxation in accordance with a decimal system based on multiples of one hundred nuclear families. Among the Yoruba, assembling revenues from different social groups, especially those living outside the capital, was a complex, decentralized operation. In the kingdom of Ife five officials who lived in towns some distance from the capital collected contributions from the heads of nearby settlements, which they subsequently shared with the king (Bascom 1969: 29). The king of Benin collected taxes through agents living in Benin City who were responsible for dealing personally with the representatives of various communities scattered in different parts of the kingdom. The agents kept a share of these taxes as a commission and forwarded the rest to the palace (Bradbury 1957: 42–43). In Mesopotamia and the Valley of Mexico, different kinds of agents collected different sorts of taxes. Although high-level officials established targets for tax collection, the manner in which specific sums were collected appears to have been determined by highly specific personal and political considerations, including bribery.

There is no evidence that even states which developed elaborate systems of food storage, such as those of ancient Egypt and the Inka, assumed major responsibility for public welfare in times of famine. The Egyptian government may have lowered taxes on grain when harvests were poor, and local officials occasionally claimed to have shipped food from areas of plenty to nearby areas where people were starving. There is, however, no indication that food was stored with the specific intention of eventually using it for famine relief. Even the biblical folktale of Joseph, often interpreted as evidence of such storage, says that Joseph, as a royal official, accumulated surplus grain for seven years so that the king might become rich by selling it to his subjects at a high price during a time of famine. Letters from the early Middle Kingdom speak, perhaps rhetorically, of people in one part of Egypt being driven to cannibalism while people in other regions had sufficient food to eat (James 1962: 33; Lichtheim 1973: 87). In the devastating famine of A.D. 1450–54, the Aztec king was able to provide only minimal food relief. In order to survive, many Aztec had to sell themselves or their children into slavery to traders bringing food from outside the Valley of Mexico. The later expansion of wetland agriculture in the Valley of Mexico and the subjugation of warmer, maize-producing areas outside the valley may have been intended in part to improve the long-term food supply and protect the Aztec against the recurrence of such famines (Davies 1980: 92–93). There is no evidence, however, that Aztec kings ever contemplated the need for the state to stockpile food for this purpose. The main reason the Aztec state appropriated food was to enable the king and his officials to enjoy a luxurious lifestyle and subsidize his efforts to enhance his power.

Sharecropping and rental rates suggest that under optimal conditions a hard-working farm family might have been able to produce up to 50 percent more food than was required to meet its minimum subsistence requirements. Taxes collected directly from free farmers always seem to have been considerably lower than that, amounting to roughly one-tenth to one-fifth of the total amount of food produced. The suggestion that an Aztec calpolli surrendered as much as one-third of its crop yield seems unlikely and may have been invented to justify higher exactions during the colonial period. While in some early civilizations farmers consumed extra food of their own while performing local corvées, in

Peru corvée labourers were always fed by the state, and in Egypt they were fed at least while they were away from home. Elsewhere at least some corvée labourers expected food and entertainment from those who directed their work, so even in these cases corvée labour was not the direct equivalent of an additional transfer of food resources from taxpayers to the state. It would appear that about ten farm families normally were willing to support one or at most two non-food-producing families without subjecting the social and political order to undue strain.

Farmers must have appreciated the protection from external attack, the maintenance of local order, and the water-management systems that governments provided. In return, they would have been prepared to pay taxes if they believed these taxes were not extortionate and were imposed reasonably equitably. An effective ruler had to curb abuse of the tax system by his officials and keep his own expenses and those of the upper classes within reasonable limits. To collect increasing amounts of taxes would have required more coercion, which would have increased the cost of managing the state. By comparison with some later preindustrial societies, such as the Roman Empire, early civilizations seem to have kept both taxes and expenses low. Max Weber (1976 [1896]: 63–64) observed that hereditary rulers generally preferred a 'prudent and durable rate of exploitation' and security of revenues to trying to maximize capital accumulation. Other forms of economic exploitation were also kept under control. Slaves were relatively few, and their treatment was only rarely characterized by the brutality associated with Late Republican Roman Italy or early modern colonial plantation economies. The most widespread form of exploitation was that of landless farm labourers, who were generally compelled to surrender a higher percentage of their production to landowners than were farmers who owned their own land. The many forms of appropriation that were practised simultaneously and the widespread private ownership of land suggest that the economic exploitation of landless people may have been harsher in Mesopotamia than in any other early civilization. Even there, however, government interventions, in the form of periodic cancellations of some debts, seem to have kept economic inequality and exploitation within socially manageable limits.

That it was less important who owned land than who had a right to appropriate agricultural production and control surplus agricultural labour explains why a variety of landowning and landholding practices and many different techniques for taxing goods were able to support systems characterized by generally similar levels of sociopolitical inequality. The material asymmetry of these transfers justifies the suggestion that all these societies shared a 'tributary' mode of production (Amin 1976: 9–16), so long as it is understood that the term 'tributary' refers to the payment of all forms of taxes. The key features of this mode of production were the ability of the upper classes to extract substantial surpluses from commoners and the significance of the control of surplus wealth as opposed to the ownership of property. Because most wealth was produced by farmers, who constituted the vast majority of the population, the amount of wealth available to the upper classes tended to be directly proportional to the number of people they could exploit.

TRIBUTE

The upper classes in some early civilizations were further enriched by tribute extracted from weaker neighbouring states. This was accomplished by the use or threat of military force. While some of this wealth was widely distributed within dominant states, encouraging broad support for a policy of hegemony, its dispersal was directed by the king or whoever controlled the military. The ability to distribute these resources increased the authority and power of such leaders. Most of the wealth that was received as tribute was distributed among members of the upper classes, thus increasing their power in relation to commoners.

In territorial states most of the wealth that supported the upper classes was produced internally. In Egypt tribute appears to have been of economic and political importance only in the New Kingdom. The rulers of subject city-states in Canaan and Syria supplied the Egyptian king with slaves, manufactured goods, olive oil, and wood without receiving payment in return. Nubia, which, unlike Canaan and Syria, was colonized and directly administered by Egyptians, was important economically as a place where Egyptians could mine gold and trade for ivory, ebony, and other products coming from south of the area of Egyptian domination (Trigger 1976a: 110–14). Shang rulers may have imposed the payment of tribute on states located beyond their borders, such as that of the Zhou rulers, whom they forced for a time to acknowledge their dominance but were unable to incorporate into the Shang state. The Inka do not appear to have collected tribute from any groups living beyond the borders of their kingdom, probably because such groups were too poor and often too mobile to be worth trying to dominate.

In contrast, in city-states tribute played a major role. The more powerful militarily a ruler was and the more states he dominated, the more surplus wealth he controlled. The more wealth a ruler possessed and the more soldiers and retainers he could support, the more powerful he was. Tribute allowed a ruler to increase his general revenues and sometimes to obtain goods that were not available in his own kingdom. It was also a way to gain control over interstate trade routes and markets and rearrange these to the economic advantage of a hegemonic state. While dominant city-states interfered to varying degrees in the internal government of tributary states, for the most part weaker states were allowed to remain self-governing. This meant that, if hegemonic power declined, a tributary system could disintegrate very quickly. When either a hegemonic ruler's wealth or his power started to diminish, the feedback loop linking the two unravelled and hegemonic status was gravely threatened.

The Aztec and their partners in the Triple Alliance controlled the largest and best-documented tributary system in our sample. They had compelled the whole of the Valley of Mexico and large areas of central Mexico from the Gulf of Mexico to the Pacific to pay them tribute. Different sectors of control were assigned to each of these three city-states, with Tenochtitlan controlling the largest and most diverse region. Beyond the Valley of Mexico, the Triple Alliance's power had spread along major trading routes and embraced city-states in all ecological zones from the temperate highlands to the tropical lowlands. They did not bother to subjugate some poorer and more isolated states and were unable to subdue some stronger ones. The Tlaxcalans, living to the east of the Valley of Mexico, although unconquered, were completely encircled by the Triple Alliance, and all interstate trade with them in salt and exotic luxury goods had been cut off (Barlow 1949; Berdan et al. 1996; Hassig 1985).

Tributary states in the valley supplied the Aztec, Texcocans, and Tlacopans with food and cloth as tribute. The nearest states also provided labour for building projects as well as stone and gravel, which were in short supply in the marshy setting of Tenochtitlan. States within an eighty-kilometre radius of the valley supplied large amounts of maize, which had to be carried to Tenochtitlan and Texcoco by human bearers. The high cost of transportation made hauling bulky items, such as food, from farther away uneconomical (M. E. Smith 1996: 174). Beyond that radius some states did not pay regular tribute but were required to provide military service and present Triple Alliance leaders with gifts at irregular intervals. These states were exempt from regular tribute either because it was hoped that they would provide defence against common enemies located beyond the tributary system or because Triple Alliance control was not yet strong enough to incorporate them fully into the system. Other city-states were forced to pay tribute in amounts that varied according to their political relations with the Triple Alliance. Weaker states located near the centre of the tributary network tended to be taxed more heavily than stronger or more distant ones that could rebel more easily. States that had submitted without fighting might pay only token tribute, while other states paid larger amounts according to how hard they had resisted the alliance or how often they had rebelled (Barlow 1949; Berdan et al. 1996; Hassig 1988: 174–75; M. E. Smith 1996: 175–82).

All the tribute from distant city-states consisted of valuable, low-bulk material, much of it exotic. Raw cotton, sheets of fancy cloth, finished clothing, elaborate suits of armour made of quilted cotton, and ornate shields were standard items of tribute. Tributary states also supplied copper and bronze objects, pieces of gold, jade, turquoise, and ornaments made from these substances, chocolate, rubber, incense, feathers, live birds, and exotic animals. Some of these goods originated outside the Triple Alliance's sphere of control, and the states that supplied them had to obtain them by trade (M. E. Smith 1996: 178–82).

Stipulated amounts of tribute were collected by the rulers of subordinate city-states and forwarded every eighty days to a pair of Aztec or Texcocan fiscal agents stationed in each of thirty-two city-state capitals that served as centres for tribute collection. Located between and beyond these tributary units were twenty-three more centres for supervising relations with subordinate states that did not pay regular tribute. In areas nearer the Valley of Mexico, fiscal agents and their assistants also supervised the cultivation of fields that had been ceded to the Triple Alliance and arranged to have the surplus produce of these fields transported to their alliance capitals. Transport costs were borne by subordinate states as an additional form of tribute (Hassig 1985: 105–10; M. E. Smith 1996: 175–80). In each of the Triple Alliance capitals the tribute became the property of the king and was stored in the royal palace. Successive Aztec kings built new palaces, and the abandoned ones may have been used for storage and administrative purposes.

Tributary networks gave the city-states of the Triple Alliance access to vast amounts of raw material and manufactured goods that they otherwise would have had to purchase or do without. The tribute collection area of Coayxtlahuacan, in the modern state of Oaxaca, annually forwarded to Tenochtitlan 4,000 textiles of various specified designs, 2 feathered warrior costumes, 2 strings of jade beads, 800 quetzal feathers, 40 bags of cochineal dye, 20 gourd vessels filled with gold dust, and a royal feather headdress. Each year the Aztec received a total of 665 warrior costumes, 147,200 pieces of cloth or items of clothing, and 4,400 loads of raw cotton (M. E. Smith 1996: 178–81). Tribute provided a major economic stimulus for Tenochtitlan to become the largest city in central Mexico. This wealth economically subsidized upward social mobility, provided skilled craft workers with cheaper raw materials, and directly or indirectly benefited all of Tenochtitlan's inhabitants. It was no accident that the Triple Alliance's tributary network expanded along major trade routes.

The Aztec rulers used tribute to help provision the army, reward valiant soldiers, pay public officials, subsidize lavish public works, and support temples and public rituals. Every day the king fed hundreds of lords, officials, armed retainers, priests, artisans, pages, servants, and visitors at the royal palace. He paid and rewarded officials and professional soldiers with pieces of cloth that they could use to purchase anything they wanted at public markets. He exchanged some of the maize and cloth that he received with the pochteca in return for the highly esteemed luxury goods that they obtained from beyond the farthest zone of tribute collection. He also distributed food and clothing to ordinary people at a festival that occurred just before the annual harvest, where commoners had to line up and wait patiently for their share of gruel and tamales while the upper classes feasted and danced. Even this public display of royal generosity emphasized the deference and submission that the Aztec nobility expected from commoners (Clendinnen 1991: 66–67).

The Aztec king's control over the distribution of tribute greatly enhanced his power amongst his subjects. They looked to him for material rewards and social advancement. He used his wealth to support and expand state institutions, feed a large palace staff, and reward and win the support of officials and warriors (Berdan 1982: 12, 39–40). Conversely, having to pay tribute weakened subordinate rulers. They could not reward warriors or patronize craft workers to the same extent as they had before, and to cover the cost of paying tribute they had either to lower their own standard of living or to increase taxes. Very often tributary rulers had to rely on their Triple Alliance overlord to keep them in power by quelling local opposition. Conquered states became politically more factionalized and less able to resist foreign domination (Hodge 1984).

In Early Dynastic Mesopotamia, defeated city-states had to pay tribute or indemnities to victorious neighbours and cede disputed border lands and water rights to them. This resulted in the transfer of considerable agricultural potential. Entemena, the ruler of Lagash, exacted over 10,800 metric tons of grain from the neighbouring state of Umma as reparations for a 'rebellion' (R. McC. Adams 1966: 149). Booty, reparations, tribute, ransoms, and prisoners of war greatly increased the wealth and power of successful Early Dynastic Mesopotamian kings, even if they shared much of this wealth with their soldiers and with temples, as thanks offerings for the supernatural support they had received.

The tribute that had to be paid to Sargon of Akkad on a monthly or yearly basis allowed a vast expansion of that hegemon's palace staff and military forces (R. McC. Adams 1966: 143; Jacobsen 1970: 191). Ur III rulers sought to control and unify key sectors of the economy throughout the region they controlled. By contrast, the Old Babylonian hegemons apparently encouraged economic decentralization but used many different techniques to collect revenues from the city-states that fell briefly under their control. The extraction of wealth from subordinate city-states brought great wealth to Mesopotamia's hegemonic cities. Leo Oppenheim (1964: 117) stated that 'real prosperity came to a Mesopotamian city only when it had in its midst the palace of a victorious king'. While ordinary cities were poor and fell prey to victorious armies, the sanctuaries and palaces of dominant cities were sumptuously adorned, and traders, craft workers, and retainers flocked to them to serve their kings.

Tribute was delivered to Oyo, which had created the largest of the Yoruba-speaking tributary systems, by subordinate kings and other community heads who gathered with their followers at several tribute-collecting centres before attending the *bere* festival held at Oyo each January. The tribute consisted of bere grass (which was used to rethatch the palace), cowrie shells, live rams, dried meat, yam flour, and a fixed share of taxes collected on goods passing through the gates of tributary cities. This tribute was presented to the king through titled officials in Oyo city who were appointed to act as patrons (*baba*) for particular groups of tribute bearers. In return for doing this, these officials were allowed to keep a share of these payments. Besides collecting tribute on a regular basis from this ring of subordinate city-states, the king of Oyo occasionally demanded and received tribute from more distant states. After Oyo defeated Dahomey in 1730, Dahomey was required to send a portion of its annual booty, including slaves, cowrie shells, and coral beads, to the ruler of Oyo (Law 1977: 99–109; R. Smith 1969: 40–43). Within Oyo, tribute, like taxes, was shared between the king, who supernaturally ensured military victory, and the seven officials who composed the state council and controlled the armed forces. The king of Benin personally benefited to a far greater extent from Benin's hegemony than the king of Oyo did from Oyo's preeminence. He appears to have carefully monitored the collection of taxes throughout the entire region he or his predecessors had conquered and maintained a monopoly over the trading and sale of ivory and certain other commodities. These monopolies greatly augmented the wealth that was available to the king and increased his political power.

In all city-state systems, conquests resulted in the transfer of wealth from weaker states to dominant ones. This wealth enhanced the power of the top-ranking officials who received it. In the Valley of Mexico, Mesopotamia, and at Benin, the recipient was the king. In Oyo, as in other Yoruba states, tribute, like war booty and taxes, was shared by the king and the non-royal members of the state council who controlled Oyo's army. The key factor in determining who benefited most from receiving and hence controlling the distribution of tribute appears to have been control of the army.

APPROPRIATION AND POLITICAL ORGANIZATION

In early civilizations the upper classes appropriated wealth from commoners in many different ways. Invariably these appropriations involved some form of corvée labour. The transfer of wealth was also accomplished by assigning prime agricultural land to upper-class individuals or institutions, charging rents for the use of land, sharecropping, imposing taxes on land or agricultural produce, taxing the sale or transport of goods, and levying fees for rendering legal decisions and other services. Using various combinations of these appropriations to collect revenue, the upper classes in all early civilizations succeeded in transferring most of the surplus wealth produced by commoners to themselves. The differing impacts that these transfers had on social organization were determined by the extent to which wealth was controlled by the king or passed directly to a broader spectrum of the upper classes. In delegational politics much wealth fell directly under the control of regional officials, forcing the king to rely on them for support.

Among territorial states control of wealth may have been less centralized in Shang China, with its delegational administration, than it was in Old Kingdom Egypt and Inka Peru, with their more bureaucratic forms of government. Nevertheless, the Shang kings carried out vast construction projects (Keightley 1969: 126–40). Among city-states, the Yoruba king was forced to share state revenues with the titled representatives of leading non-royal lineages, whereas the Aztec kings derived much greater power from their ability to control the collection and distribution to their subjects of most of the wealth derived from taxes. The ruling classes in powerful city-states further increased their revenues by forcing rulers of weaker states to pay them tribute. Tribute was a transfer of wealth from one segment of the upper class to another, and it usually resulted in pressure on commoners in weaker states to work harder and pay more taxes. It strengthened the control exercised by the highest-ranking military leaders in powerful city-states, since it was they who were able to distribute it. In the more centralized city-states the king distributed tribute among his followers; among the heterarchical Yoruba, kings shared the right to collect tribute with other leading officials.

18 Economic Constants and Variables

A general precondition for the development of early civilizations was the upper classes' ability to ensure that farmers produced substantial agricultural surpluses and that most of these surpluses be at the disposal of a small ruling group. Because agricultural surpluses constituted the main form of wealth in early civilizations, this control resulted in marked economic inequality.

The early civilizations were all low-energy societies, human labour being the principal and often the only source of energy for agricultural production. Further, while the Yoruba employed a wide range of iron agricultural implements and the Mesopotamians increasingly used copper and bronze ones, farmers in the other early civilizations made all their agricultural implements of stone, bone, and wood. The complexity of tool technology was not correlated with the intensity of food production or with the densities of population supported in the various early civilizations. The main factors determining intensity of food production were the farming techniques employed and the amount of labour invested in producing crops. The general simplicity of agricultural technology meant that early civilizations were confined to areas that had light, easily worked soils.

Unexpected variation has been found amongst these societies, however, in environmental settings, population density, intensity of agriculture, and the geographical mobility of people. Some, such as Egypt and Mesopotamia, developed in river valleys located in zones of low rainfall, where all but the simplest agriculture depended on some form of irrigation. They also developed in temperate river valleys such as that of the Yellow River in northern China, in mountainous areas such as the Valley of Mexico and the Andean highlands, and in tropical forests and savannas, as did the Yoruba and the lowland Maya. All except the Yoruba used hydrological works to some extent, but the archaeological record disproves the claim that early civilizations invariably began in arid regions where agriculture relied wholly on irrigation and only secondary civilizations developed in other ecological zones (Sanders and Price 1968; Wittfogel 1957). There were, however, important differences in the nature of hydrological works even in environments that were generally similar in type.

Most early civilizations developed in regions that remained warm to temperate throughout the year. Such climates did not require a heavy investment in providing substantial shelter, heating, and warm clothing for the entire population, and this greatly reduced the ecological cost of supporting early civilizations. Nevertheless, northern China has cold winters, and living in the Andean highlands requires warm clothes and substantial housing. Thus, while the higher costs involved in sustaining human beings in colder climates may have inhibited the development of early civilizations, they did not confine them to tropical and subtropical regions.

The many different environmental settings in which early civilizations developed imposed specific requirements and limitations on subsistence patterns. An important example of such limitations was the absence of any large domesticable species of animals in Mesoamerica. Most of the domestic plants and animals that early civilizations relied on and most agricultural practices were continuations of what had been present in each region at an earlier stage of cultural development. Cross-cultural parallels in subsistence patterns reflected general biological similarities in the kinds of plants and animals that were suitable for domestication and how they were handled. The numerous specific differences in agricultural practices from one early civilization to another indicate that practical and locally adaptive knowledge concerning agriculture, often acquired long before the development of civilization in a region, remained important despite significant sociopolitical change. Regionally specific agricultural knowledge was among the most valuable forms of cultural capital that early civilizations inherited from the smaller-scale societies out of which they developed. Because this knowledge had been developed to cope with specific local conditions, it was effective and therefore resistant to change unless crops or technologies that turned out to be locally more productive were introduced from elsewhere (Boyd and Richerson 1985).

INTENSITY OF PRODUCTION

Average population densities in our sample ranged from perhaps sixty persons per square kilometre among the Yoruba to five hundred persons per square kilometre in the southern part of the Valley of Mexico. There appears to have been a close correlation between population density and the intensity of agriculture, as measured by the elimination of fallowing and the increasing number of crops grown on the same plot of land each year (Boserup 1965), but the causal direction and precise nature of this correlation have not yet been determined.

It is frequently assumed that farming groups in preindustrial societies were characterized by a high rate of population increase because a sedentary lifestyle facilitated women's becoming pregnant at short intervals and farmers welcomed children as a source of labour (Lee 1972). Yet data on nursing in five early civilizations in our sample suggest that the rate of population increase in early civilizations was not as high as often has been assumed. In all of them children were nursed two to three years or longer and in some women avoided sexual intercourse to ensure that they did not become pregnant while they were nursing. This reproductive restraint may have conflicted with the desire of rulers for population growth among the lower classes to expand the tax base and increase the supply of soldiers and corvée labourers. Because they had multiple wives and concubines, many upper-class men had numerous children (Betzig 1986), but upper-class women do not seem to have had more children than lower-class ones.

Natural population growth was not, however, the only source of increasing density. In the southern and politically most dynamic part of the Valley of Mexico, a rapidly growing population partly fueled by immigration from other parts of Mexico encouraged increasingly intensive agriculture that culminated in the chinampa development of the fifteenth century. Feeding the expanding city of Tenochtitlan encouraged more intensive agriculture in order to reduce the cost of transporting large amounts of food to that megacity. Yet, despite claims to the contrary (Netting 1969), there is no obvious correlation between the development of large urban centres and generally higher population density.

Intensification could occur quickly if additional labour was available and there was a growing demand for food. While governments played a leading role in developments such as the multistate dyke-building projects to control water levels and concentrate fresh water in the southern lakes of the Valley of Mexico, productivity ultimately depended on the knowledge, labour, and skills of individual farmers. Their thorough familiarity with locally effective agricultural techniques and the local environment allowed these farmers to increase productivity fairly easily when social conditions required them to do so or rewarded their efforts. Traditional agricultural knowledge provided a basis for its own elaboration and development. Still more radical changes may have been accomplished by rulers' importing farmers or agricultural experts who brought new farming techniques with them. Gravity-flow irrigation, for example, may have been introduced to the Fayum in Egypt during the Middle Kingdom by settlers from the Middle East (Butzer 1976: 36–37, 47, 51).

There is no evidence that specific types of environment alone determined population densities or the intensity of agricultural production in early civilizations. Although the Classic Maya and the Yoruba both lived in tropical forest and savanna, the Maya had high overall population density and intensive agriculture and the Yoruba had low population density and swidden agriculture. Also, the Yoruba developed cities and kingdoms while their Ibo neighbours, with much higher population density, did not (Bascom 1955: 452).

There was also no clear tendency for naturally circumscribed early civilizations to have higher population densities as Carneiro (1970b) once suggested. Agricultural land was circumscribed by barren terrain in Mesopotamia, Egypt, individual valleys in highland Peru, and the Valley of Mexico, but there were no obvious ecological barriers circumscribing the Maya, Yoruba, or early northern Chinese civilizations. The lowland Maya, who could have expanded into adjacent areas of Central America, had a higher population density than did the naturally circumscribed ancient Egyptians.

Beyond this, circumscription is a political phenomenon as well as an ecological one. Egyptian rulers built walls and massive fortresses along their frontiers and sometimes dispersed or deported neighbouring peoples in order to create uninhabited wastelands, the better to control the trade in exotic goods and cage their subjects (Hoffman 1979). The Shang and Zhou states, lacking natural frontiers, gradually conquered neighbouring chiefdoms and settled them with loyal populations who ensured that they were controlled and eventually assimilated. Inka kings resettled subject populations on a large scale and controlled trade and human movement across their well-marked borders. In general, it appears that the need to control internal populations and foreign trade led the rulers of territorial states to establish boundaries whether or not these states were ecologically circumscribed. In city-states there appears to have been little effective government control over movements across state boundaries in peacetime, and the possibility of refugees' being offered a friendly reception by nearby city-states made it harder for rulers to suppress dissent. While in each early civilization, ecological conditions provided a context for political manipulation, the specific ways in which borders were defined and populations controlled cannot be understood without taking account of political factors. Because both the ecological and the political factors were highly variable, there is no simple cross-cultural correlation between circumscription and territorial or city-states. The relation between culture and environment is better comprehended by a possibilist approach than by an ecologically deterministic one.

There may, however, have been a correlation between the political decentralization of Yoruba and Mesopotamian city-state systems and the fact that arable land (apart from that planted in oil or date palms) was not an enduring asset in those societies (Stone 1997). In such situations control of land was perhaps less important than control of labour, and this may have made it harder for rulers to coerce landowners. Powerful Mesopotamian rulers sought to settle nomadic groups on newly irrigated land and to compel them to pay taxes, perform corvée labour, and provide military service, but farmers could avoid royal exactions by moving away. Yoruba extended families were able to relocate, often over long distances, because population density was low. Had it increased significantly, they would have had to develop more intensive forms of agriculture, and this would have made specific plots of land more valuable and reduced their owners' mobility.

The problems of Mesopotamian agriculture probably encouraged the development of large-scale land management in order to cope more easily with the effects of salinization. This favoured the growth of major landowning institutions, although it does not explain why privately owned land also replaced collective ownership by patrilineages. The higher population densities among the Classic Maya and in the Valley of Mexico may have facilitated greater centralized control in these civilizations, but, as already noted, it is not clear why the Maya did not expand territorially more than they did. In each case both political and ecological factors seem to have been involved.

APPROPRIATION

Collective ownership of land by farming families predominated in the Valley of Mexico, highland Peru, and among the Yoruba, but governments were able to appropriate substantial surpluses from these groups. In all early civilizations, alongside collectively owned land, there was land owned by institutions – the king, the state, or religious cults. In Mesopotamia and Egypt institutional land was of great economic and political importance, and it was rapidly becoming more common in the Valley of Mexico and the Inka kingdom. In Mesopotamia collectively owned land was transformed into institutional and privately owned land to a greater extent than in any other early civilization. The division of institutional land between temples and palaces reflected and reinforced the heterarchical nature of power. In Egypt, Inka Peru, and the Valley of Mexico all such land was managed by state officials, including land that was devoted to supporting cults. That arrangement reflected the greater centralization of political power in those early civilizations. For the upper classes the great advantage of institutional or privately owned land was that it facilitated the appropriation of a much larger share of the crops than could be extracted from equivalent amounts of collectively owned land.

No unilinear evolutionary sequence in which collectively owned land was gradually replaced by institutional and then by private holdings can be identified. It is impossible to demonstrate that all land in early civilizations was originally owned collectively. Moreover, the ability of wealthy and powerful Yoruba to use the labour of privately owned slaves and debtors to derive large agricultural surpluses from land collectively owned by their lineages demonstrates that changes in the nature of land ownership were not the only or even necessarily the most effective way for individuals to appropriate larger shares of agricultural production. The long-term survival of collective land alongside institutional land and, in the few examples where it actually developed, private land indicates the lasting utility of the first two types.

There was no obvious correlation between types of landholding and territorial or city-states. Among city-state civilizations, Mesopotamia had the largest amount of private and institutional land and the Yoruba the least. In the Valley of Mexico most land was collectively owned. Among territorial states, collective ownership predominated in Inka Peru and perhaps in China but appears to have been superseded to a significant degree by institutional and private ownership in Egypt.

There also appears to have been no correlation between types of land ownership and population density. Collective ownership was a prominent feature of the most (Valley of Mexico) and least (Yoruba) densely populated societies in our sample. The survival of collective ownership may be associated with the presence of lineages or endogamous collectivities in some societies, but it is not clear what caused such forms of social organization to persist or diminish. Forms of social organization may to some extent have been random inheritances from the past that persisted as long as they were not incompatible with changing social needs. While endogamous groups seem to have flourished in both rural areas and urban centres in the Valley of Mexico and the Inka kingdom, patrilineal extended families appear to have diminished in size and importance in the urban centres of Mesopotamia.

Taxes were not the only, or the most effective, way to extract agricultural surpluses from farmers. Rents and sharecropping substantially increased the amount of food surpluses that individual landowners or the state could collect from landless farmers. The use of slaves, serfs, debtors, and hired labourers to work the land resulted in entire crops' being handed over to landowners, who could treat as profit everything but what was needed to feed the workers and pay estate managers. Yet, because it was hard to control and motivate such workers, these more exploitative forms of cultivation also remained the most restricted types in early civilizations.

Some states imposed taxes on the transport or sale of foodstuffs. Yoruba kings and high officials derived more revenue from taxing the movement of food into cities and its sale at urban markets than they did from taxing land or agricultural production, which amounted to no more than levies voluntarily paid on the production of food.

Another source of revenue for the state was taxes levied on craft production and on the movement and sale of such goods. The greater role played by market exchange in city-states encouraged more taxing of the movement and sale of goods, while in territorial states the main emphasis was on taxing agricultural production.

In territorial states most tax revenues remained within provincial jurisdictions. Some goods were transmitted to the capitals of territorial states for use by the king and the royal court. In most city-states, the revenues that the state derived as taxes belonged to kings and reinforced their authority. In heterarchical Yoruba polities, revenues were divided among the king and major office-holders. Yoruba officials also collected substantial fees for hearing legal cases as well as the fines that were imposed as forms of punishment. In other early civilizations reparations to injured parties tended to be more common than fines.

MANUFACTURING

The growth of early civilizations expanded the market for manufactured goods, which in turn facilitated craft specialization and the production of higher-quality merchandise. There was also a growing demand for luxury goods to denote upper-class status. Luxury goods were often made from rare and expensive raw materials that could be obtained locally only with great effort or had to be imported from abroad. These goods were manufactured by highly skilled workers who often laboured in teams to produce small numbers of exquisitely crafted objects. So much care and effort had to be invested in fabricating these goods that less lavishly supported artisans could not produce them.

Thus hierarchies of craft workers evolved in early civilizations. The least specialized were men and women who produced goods within a household for that household's own use. Next were part-time craft workers who manufactured a particular sort or range of goods when they were not engaged in farming. They or other members of their families exchanged these goods at local markets. Still more specialized were full-time craft workers who employed a particular technology to produce goods for everyone in a community. A single bronzeworker, for example, might manufacture everything from sickles to jewellery, depending on what his clients wished to purchase. At the top of the hierarchy were elite craft workers who produced luxury goods exclusively for the upper classes and the state.

Interpretations of the economies of early civilizations were long distorted by Karl Polanyi's claim that in these societies trade and production were completely 'embedded' in political organization. According to Polanyi and his followers, governments played the key role in securing exotic raw materials, organizing production, and seeing that each individual received what he or she required. Prices were controlled by the government, and land and many other necessities were not regarded as commodities. Polanyi contrasted such an administered economy with those of modern industrial societies, where almost anything can be bought and sold (Polanyi, Arensberg, and Pearson 1957). Polanyi's views and still earlier ones influenced by European corporatist thinking exerted an especially strong influence on the interpretation of ancient Mesopotamian civilization. Palace and temple estates were viewed as controlling all aspects of trade and production, and every individual was imagined to have been employed by these institutions (Falkenstein 1974 [1954]).

Polanyi was correct to the extent that in all early civilizations most land was owned collectively or institutionally rather than privately and therefore could not be freely bought and sold. Nevertheless, as the result of a more realistic appreciation of the problems involved in processing information, it has become impossible to imagine any early civilization as possessing the resources needed to administer an entire economy or any ruler as wishing to do so. The highly complex government administrative records of the Ur III period in Mesopotamia or of state-directed boat-building in Middle Kingdom Egypt were focused on particular aspects of the economy that were of special interest to governments. Most of the everyday economic activities that kept people alive appear to have gone on independently of the state. There is growing appreciation of the considerable variety of ways by which goods were produced and distributed in early civilizations. Many of the most important differences appear to correspond with the distinction between city-states and territorial states.

In Mesopotamia and the Valley of Mexico as well as among the Yoruba (the three well-documented city-state systems in our sample) long-distance exchange was managed by professional merchants who traded goods with their counterparts in nearby city-states and with far-off regions. Traders obtained exotic raw materials from abroad and transported raw materials and manufactured goods from one city-state and one region to another. They had close relations with kings, major institutions, prosperous landowners, and craft workers in their own city-states but operated largely independently of these individuals and institutions. It has been argued that Akkadian and Ur III rulers tried to develop state-controlled trade alongside or in addition to that of independent traders, but it is uncertain how far this process was carried.

Craft workers produced goods both in urban centres and in the surrounding countryside, purchasing exotic raw materials from long-distance traders and selling what they manufactured at urban markets. In the Valley of Mexico the purchase but not the sale of certain types of goods was limited by sumptuary laws. Renowned Yoruba artists were invited to carry out commissions for kings and sometimes worked at the royal palace. In Benin elite bronze-casters were forbidden to produce certain ritual objects for anyone but the king and were lavishly rewarded for their work. In the Valley of Mexico, expert stone sculptors and mural painters may have worked exclusively for rulers. Yet it does not appear that in these societies full-time craft workers were mainly employees or servants of kings. In Mesopotamia some specialists may have worked full-time for temples or palaces, but many of these were probably ordinary craft workers who manufactured goods that institutions required in large quantities. Some more highly skilled artisans may have manufactured goods, such as military chariots, for which there was no demand except from the king. Yet metallurgists, potters, and stone carvers lived and worked in various city wards and sold at least some of their products to ordinary people, including temple and palace employees. This suggests that these institutions did not allocate to their employees the manufactured goods that these employees needed, as Polanyi imagined. Urban craft workers probably sold their goods to individual purchasers as well as to temples and palaces.

This sort of economy accords with the crucial role played by markets in facilitating exchange in city-states. The presence of many farmers in or near urban centres created a demand for goods, and the craft specialization that this encouraged made higher-quality manufactured goods available to all. The vast majority of full-time craft workers produced goods for the entire population rather than only for the government and the upper classes. Wealthy hegemonic rulers alone had the resources to employ considerable numbers of elite specialists to produce goods of superlative quality. The distinction between ordinary full-time craft workers and elite specialists tended to be a fluid one.

In territorial states farmers manufactured goods from local raw materials in their spare time and exchanged these goods within villages or at local markets. Royal and government workshops employed groups of full-time specialists to manufacture tools, weapons, and other items used by workers performing special tasks for the state and elite specialists to produce numerous luxury goods. Many worked under close surveillance by government officials. The craft workers who manufactured luxury and display goods for the use of the upper classes were lavishly supported by the government. Control of exotic raw materials, elite craft workers, and the luxury goods they manufactured constituted a major source of power for kings and officials.

This system created a two-tier economy in territorial states, with the upper classes receiving luxury goods as gifts from the king and farmers fabricating what they needed in their spare time. Part-time craft workers lacked both access to exotic raw materials and the time, training, and incentives to produce high-quality products. Elite craft workers were more lavishly subsidized and better provided with exotic raw materials than were the vast majority of full-time craft workers in city-states and therefore could produce extremely high-quality luxury goods. The only important economic link between the realm of production and consumption of farmers and that of the upper classes was the appropriation of food surpluses by the state and by landlords.

It has been suggested that Classic Maya kings or upper classes may have controlled interstate trade and markets may not have played a significant role in the Maya economy. Yet exotic goods, such as obsidian, were widely distributed within Maya city-states. This suggests that the Maya upper class may have had more control of external trade than was the case in other city-state systems without the emergence of a two-tier economy.

Rulers of hegemonic city-states extracted tribute and reparations from weaker neighbours and used their political control to reroute long-distance trade and alter marketing patterns to the advantage of their own polities. These city-states grew large and prosperous by comparison with militarily less powerful neighbouring states. Skilled artisans were attracted to them by the low cost of materials and increasing local demand for their products. Elite craft workers developed in them. Military leaders, who controlled the distribution of tribute, found their authority greatly enhanced. In most city-states the main political beneficiary of hegemony was the king, although among the Yoruba the non-royal title-bearers who commanded the army controlled much of the tribute. Thus, while tribute did not inevitably increase the authority of the monarch, it did enhance the power of those who controlled the state. Tribute played the same role in increasing the power of rulers in hegemonic states as royal control of exotic raw materials and elite craft workers in territorial states.

PRODUCTION AND CONSUMPTION

Systems of agricultural production, land ownership, and the techniques by which surplus production and lower-class labour were appropriated by the upper classes varied significantly from one early civilization to another. At least some of these differences contrast with the more limited variation exhibited in sociopolitical organization. The environmental settings of early civilizations and their technologies were especially variable. Forms of production and distribution of goods differed radically between city-states and territorial states, although there may have been more variation within each of these two types than has so far been delineated. Nevertheless, the variation between city- and territorial states indicates that the development of early civilizations was shaped to a significant degree by sociopolitical factors. Subsistence economies were largely a heritage from earlier stages of development in various regions, but as population densities increased, regionally and locally, food production intensified. The development of craft production was influenced to a large degree by the various political frameworks in which it occurred.

A question rarely asked in studies of early civilizations is why the acquisition of greater political power was always accompanied by the appropriation of a disproportionate share of surplus wealth by the upper classes. It can be argued from a functionalist viewpoint that effective decision-making in early civilizations required that a small number of leaders possess sufficient political power to ensure that the orders that were necessary to regulate large-scale societies were carried out. To do this, leaders needed to control a disproportionate share of resources to be able to pay for police and military backing and reward loyal supporters with generous gifts and hospitality.

This answer, however, does not account for the lavish lifestyle of the upper classes. In complex societies, conspicuous consumption is indeed universally understood and admired, if not always morally approved. It is recognized as a deliberate violation of the principles of least effort and the conservation of energy which shaped human relations with the natural environment in all low-energy societies and were therefore implicitly familiar to everyone living in early civilizations (Trigger 1990a; Zipf 1949). These principles could be deliberately ignored only by individuals who controlled a disproportionate share of natural and human resources. The conspicuous waste of such resources served not only to manifest power but also to reinforce it. In complex societies political power is accompanied by a humble lifestyle (usually a conspicuously humble one) only in very exceptional circumstances often religious in nature.

In small-scale societies, where people know one another, gossip, ridicule, and fear of being accused of witchcraft compel hard-working and capable individuals to behave in a manner that is simultaneously generous and humble, even though their personalities might incline them to act differently. Only in response to such socially sensitive conduct are they accorded de facto leadership roles (Lee 1990; Trigger 1990b). Once those who make decisions in larger societies are able to exert political power and control communication networks, they can disable the traditional mechanisms that maintain social and economic equality. The neutralizing of such mechanisms invariably leads powerful individuals to assign to their own use much of the wealth produced by the lower classes instead of continuing to share the products of their own labour with others. Ostentation and conspicuous consumption replace personal restraint, generosity, and humility. The rich use their political power and administrative control to silence the protests of those who object to these changes. The fear of witchcraft ceases to be a device for encouraging social and economic equality and becomes a technique of intimidation exercised by the wealthy and powerful against politically weaker individuals. These developments raise many questions about human nature and the role it may have played in shaping early civilizations.

Cognitive and Symbolic Aspects

19 Conceptions of the Supernatural

The Egyptians had no word for 'religion'. Religion was inseparable from daily life. They did, however, have a rich vocabulary referring to priests, deities, and worship. All aspects of state activity, everyday life, and material culture in ancient Egypt were coloured by religious beliefs and symbolism. Drama was religious in nature, tombs and temples were viewed as microcosms of a supernaturally animated universe and decorated accordingly, and mundane activities such as the netting of birds and the hunting of hippopotamuses symbolized the curbing of supernatural forces that threatened the cosmic order (Lustig 1997b). Analogous religious symbolism permeated the other early civilizations.

Marshall Sahlins (1976: 211–12) has argued that each stage in the development of society has a dominant source of symbolic production that supplies the major idioms that permit social relations to be understood and publicly discussed. He maintains that in early civilizations religion was this source. Once societies grew too large for kinship and other personal relations to provide the basic metaphors that guided thinking about social relations, religion supplied the concepts that were needed to consider and shape the moral order. Only much later, in increasingly commercial and industrial societies, did political and economic concepts supplant religious ones in this key role.

Clifford Geertz (1973: 90) has described religion as a symbolic system that establishes powerful, pervasive motivations by formulating a general order of existence and a model for perceiving the world. This useful characterization reflects his more general view that human behaviour is governed by 'systems of significant symbols' (1965: 112). He does not explain, however, why forms of religious thought are a feature of all cultures. Conceding universality to religion comes oddly from an anthropologist who maintains that variability is the essence of human behaviour and that universals are classificatory 'fakes' (1965: 101).

In recent decades, the term 'ideology' has often been treated as synonymous with concepts such as religion, worldview, belief system, and cosmology. Robert McC. Adams (1992: 208–9) has correctly observed that ideology is analytically of no significance if employed in this diffuse manner. It more usefully designates a set of beliefs or propositions that are consciously or unconsciously used to promote social cohesion and unity by masking the inequality and exploitation that are present in a particular society. Ideology seeks to represent the self-interested behaviour of politically active groups within a society as being altruistic. In this manner, it not only sustains but helps to increase the power and privileges of ruling classes. Such a program is most successful when the aggregate of beliefs and images being conveyed defines and appears to satisfy the collective aspirations, objectives, and ideals of whole societies (Giddens 1979: 193–96).

In early civilizations much if not all ideology was religious in nature because political thought tended to be religious. Stephen Houston and David Stuart (1996: 289) observe that the rulers in early civilizations sought to link themselves to an immutable divine order so that the power and mystery of divinity might sanction and reinforce their worldly authority. Religiously grounded ideology was used to justify and promote the activities of the upper classes. In the sphere of law, supposedly innate differences between various social groups were used to justify inflicting less severe penalties on upper-class individuals than on lower-class ones who had committed the same crimes. Wars, from which the upper classes were most likely to profit, might be validated by claiming that they were necessary to safeguard society as a whole or to preserve the cosmic order. Most studies tend to concentrate on ideology as a political practice and therefore focus on its functional and pragmatic aspects. This approach fails to explain how particular ideologies became 'the driving force behind expansionist states' (Fash 1991: 75). To do that for early civilizations, it is necessary to understand their religious beliefs.

RELIGION IN EARLY CIVILIZATIONS

One of the greatest obstacles to understanding the religions of early civilizations has been a tendency to impose on them beliefs associated with later transcendental religions. Christianity, Judaism, and Islam all assume the existence of a single, all-powerful, universal, and moral god who does not depend in any way on his creation but upon whom the entire universe depends for its being and preservation. It is often accepted that the religious beliefs of early civilizations were similar to those of later transcendental religions except that the idea of a single deity had not yet been developed. Instead, early civilizations postulated the existence of multiple gods who often acted at cross-purposes to one other. On the basis of the work of Edward B. Tylor (1871), it used to be assumed that still earlier there had been an animistic stage when the universe was believed to be pervaded by a supernatural power that did not yet manifest itself in the form of specific deities.

The religious concepts of early civilizations differed far more radically from those of later transcendental religions than nineteenth-century anthropologists assumed. Like band and tribal societies, early civilizations do not appear to have distinguished between what we perceive as the natural, supernatural, and social realms. Beginning in the first millennium B.C., the Greeks, the Hebrews, the Zoroastrian Persians, and various Hindu and Chinese philosophers differentiated the natural world, made up of plants, animals, and inanimate objects, which possessed only limited or no consciousness; the social world of humans, whose behaviour was guided by goals, reason, and moral considerations; and the supernatural world of the gods, who for the first time were seen as existing apart from and independently of the natural and social realms. Supernatural beings possessed intelligence and emotions, but they were less subject than humans to the constraints of the material world, which they had created. In Greece, a small number of materialistic philosophers effectively denied the existence or at least the relevance of the supernatural, leaving only the social and natural realms as matters of human concern. This did not, however, prove to be a popular view. The greatest and most lasting discovery of the later preindustrial societies of Eurasia was that the behaviour observed in the natural world was fundamentally different from that encountered in the social realm and that, because of this, relations with plants, animals, and inanimate objects had to be very different from those with human beings. The philosopher Karl Jaspers (1953) labelled this dramatic shift in human outlook, which he believed marked the beginning of modern society, the axial era (Eisenstadt 1986).

In early civilizations, it was assumed that the natural world, of which humans were a part, was suffused with and animated by supernatural powers. There was no distinction between the natural and the supernatural: everything was alive, conscious, and interrelated (Townsend 1979: 28–31). Humans lived in a realm composed only of other beings; there were no things (J. Allen 1988: 8). Nature functioned because it was animated by powers that behaved much like human beings but were usually much stronger and therefore could determine human destiny. These powers are variously referred to in the anthropological literature as 'gods', 'goddesses', 'deities', or 'spirits' (Swanson 1960: 6–31).

Deities possessed reason, will, a full array of human emotions (including love, anger, jealousy, ambition, and compassion), and the ability to communicate with each other and with human beings. They also possessed enhanced powers that enabled them to do what ordinary humans could not. They lived longer, were able to change shape, moved instantaneously from one place to another, could be present in many places at the same time, and travelled back and forth between the terrestrial realm and the extraterrestrial ones. Human souls could also move about in dreams and shamans could visit the realms reserved for the gods, but for humans these were special capacities rather than normal attributes. The gods, or at least the mightiest of them, also possessed the power to create and sustain the universe. Deities in early civilizations in many ways resembled those found in polytheistic post-axial cultures, although the latter were anthropomorphized more systematically and clearly distinguished from natural phenomena.

People who lived in early civilizations believed that, because the natural world, which they inhabited and were part of, was animated by spirits, it was possible for them to interact with the natural/supernatural realm in much the same way that they interacted with other human beings, especially very powerful ones. They hoped, by communicating with the deities who pervaded the natural world, to win the favour or at least avoid the anger of the powerful supernatural forces that controlled the cosmos. This meant that what we identify as the natural and the supernatural were regarded not as separate from but as intimately linked to and interpenetrating the social realm. Human beings could communicate with a supernaturally animated natural realm much as they communicated with one other. It follows from this that the axial-age distinction between culture and nature, to which Claude Lévi-Strauss has attributed universal relevance, meant no more to people living in early civilizations than it did to hunter-gatherers (Ingold 1996: 117).

The refusal of people in early civilizations to distinguish the social, natural, and supernatural realms has tended to be interpreted as the manifestation of a 'primitive' or 'prelogical' stage of intellectual development. Yet the distinction between this outlook and later ones was clearly ontological rather than epistemological; it had to do not with perception and logic but with the manner in which the universe was assumed to operate. Christopher Hallpike (1979) and others have demonstrated that the people who lived in early societies were as fully aware of causality as we are. They understood that water habitually flowed downhill, that specific types of stone could be shaped using particular techniques, and that clay became harder and more waterproof when it was fired. The difference between early views and modern ones was that, when it came to conceptualizing the nature of the universe, early peoples used the understandings that were most familiar to them, those that concerned the way human society worked. The universe was presumed to be animated by powerful forces that possessed human-like personalities.

This process was encouraged by what J. S. Kennedy (1992) has characterized as humanity's compulsive anthropomorphizing, a form of thought that is prevalent in all societies even if it has been somewhat curtailed in modern science and engineering by trying to account for the behaviour of natural phenomena other than in terms of the understandings and purposeful interventions of actors. Stewart Guthrie (1993) argues that humans are innately predisposed to view the natural world as social. Sahlins (1976: 53–54), echoing Marx and Engels, maintains that explaining the world in terms of social understandings was accompanied by a reciprocal assumption that the social order mirrored that of the natural/supernatural realm.

As a result of the pervasiveness of human-centred explanations, it was assumed in early civilizations that there were no instances of the operation of cause and effect that could not be suspended by the gods if humans could only persuade them to do so. Therefore the powerful human-like forces that animated nature could be appealed to when human beings needed supernatural help to cope with insurmountable natural and social dangers. If supernatural powers ensured that water normally ran downhill, people might hope that in times of crisis or special need these same powers might be persuaded to make it flow uphill. Conversely, flint-knappers or potters might request that appropriate supernatural forces ensure that the laws of nature, on which they depended, not be abrogated in the course of their work (Childe 1956a; 1956b: 170). The belief that nature was controlled by supernatural forces that were inherent in it was no more detrimental to the recognition and use of concepts of cause and effect than was the medieval European belief in miracles. It provided people in early civilizations with reassurance that by addressing the gods they could do something effective to cope with the many natural challenges that their technology and medical knowledge were ill-equipped or entirely unequipped to handle.

THE NATURE OF DEITIES

Despite intensive study of the religions of early civilizations and a massive data base, there is little agreement about how deities were conceptualized. Prominent Mayanists such as Tatiana Proskouriakoff have expressed doubts that the Maya recognized actual deities as opposed to vaguely personified and mutable natural forces (Taube 1992: 7). Some Sinologists maintain that the Chinese venerated primarily if not exclusively ancestral deities (Allan 1991: 19–20), and some experts on the Yoruba believe that most of their deities were human beings who, because of their special qualities, were treated as divinities after they had died (K. Barber 1981).

Resolving such issues is difficult even for the best-documented early civilizations, but special problems are encountered with at least three of them. The Yoruba have been exposed for several centuries to Christianity and Islam. This contact may have modified indigenous religious concepts or at least the way in which these concepts are explained to foreigners. Much of what is known about early Chinese religious beliefs has reached the present filtered through Confucian humanism. During the Warring States period, this movement appears to have reinterpreted cosmic deities and nature spirits as a succession of human ancestral heroes beginning with Huangdi, the Yellow Emperor. Such changes may have misleadingly enhanced the apparent importance of ancestor worship in early Chinese religion (Allan 1991: 19–20; Lewis 1990: 167–68, 195). Similarly, religious concepts of highland Mexican origin may have altered lowland Maya religious beliefs in Postclassic times. There is, for example, growing evidence that the idea of 5,126-year cycles of creation and destruction of the universe may not yet have been present in Maya culture during the Classic period (Bassie-Sweet 1991: 251; Schele and Mathews 1998: 106–7; Reents-Budet 1998: 78).

Concepts of deity seem to have varied significantly from one early civilization to another. This would accord with a widely accepted particularist view of religious phenomena. Yet, while not denying that specific delineations and classifications of deities, the myths concerning them, and the extent of their anthropomorphization varied considerably from one early civilization to another, certain features appear to be cross-culturally recurrent. In each early civilization people viewed deities as a series of manifestations of the forces of nature, which, whether or not they assumed human form, were aware of human beings, as people in industrial societies believe the physical universe is not. Deities possessed individual personalities which inclined them to treat human beings well or badly. Yet human beings could never be certain of a particular deity's continuing goodwill, even if that deity were a benevolent one and they had served it assiduously. Dealing with deities was no less problematical and potentially dangerous for humans than dealing with kings and upper-class people was for the lower classes or dealing with the natural environment could be for all human beings.

The deities did not, however, exhaust the varieties of supernatural power in early civilizations. The Aztec and their neighbours believed that a numinous divine power was diffused throughout the universe. This force animated natural phenomena, human beings, and humanly fabricated objects, as well as the gods. The Aztec referred to this diffuse power, as well as to specific deities, as *teotl* (Townsend 1979: 28). They are reported to have believed that everything in nature had a soul – including plants, animals, and stones – and for this reason apologized to trees when they cut them down (López Austin 1988, 1: 346). Yet, while teotl manifested itself in maize, which it caused to grow, individual cobs of corn were not regarded as deities because they possessed only a limited power to nourish humans (Broda 1987: 75). Likewise, an Aztec prisoner of war contained divine power that could nourish the gods if he were sacrificed to them, but this did not make him a god in the same sense that the divine forces that controlled rain, sunlight, or success in warfare were gods. The divine energy that pervaded the universe was of the same substance but different in degree and in the way it behaved from the deities that determined how the cosmos would function. Inga Clendinnen (1991: 248) has described the Aztec gods as clusters of sacred forces engaged in complex interaction.

The Classic Maya used the same root to refer to sacred entities or deities that possessed wills and personalities of their own (*k'u*) and to the cosmic power (or soul-force) (*k'ul*) that they believed hallowed and activated the entire universe. K'ul has been described as a vital, impersonal, natural force that animated all things, including the gods (Houston and Stuart 1996: 291; Schele and Mathews 1998: 413; Sharer 1996: 153). It was the power that made plants grow, animals reproduce, and people live and it kept the cosmos functioning. It also sustained objects that human beings had made, including ceramic vessels and sacred buildings, and enabled those objects to perform their social functions. The amount of k'ul that was concentrated in a temple increased as a result of the building's being repeatedly used and had to be ritually released when the temple was abandoned if it were not to become dangerous. K'ul appears to have been closely associated with blood, and was also present in plant secretions (*itz*) such as the sap and gums (used for incense) associated with the cosmic tree that held up the universe. They were believed to transmit supernatural powers from one level of the cosmos to another and used to practise witchcraft and divination (Freidel, Schele, and Parker 1993: 234, 448). Yet only in certain instances did these supernatural powers come together to form deities.

The use of a single term to designate supernatural energy and deity is not documented in the other civilizations in our sample. In highland Peru, however, *kamaquen* or *kamaq* (from *kama*, 'existence') referred to the enduring supernatural essence or soul-power that energized and shaped matter, made deities flourish, and provided all that was necessary to sustain different forms of life in the natural and social realms (Gose 1993). As a result of possessing this power, deities, including animal spirits and the ancestors of human groups, were able continuously to fashion, energize, and sustain their living descendants. Being dry and unchanging, kamaquen produced life by combining their own life-shaping power with the animating force of water, which was believed to come from the Pacific Ocean and was considered essential to produce life. Diviners or shamans (*kamasca*) were believed to be infused temporarily with the kamaquen of a particular deity (Salomon 1991: 16).

The Yoruba concept of *ase* signified life-force and authority and also the energy that was associated with the act of procreation. This force existed everywhere, brought all things into existence, and opposed chaos and decay. While ase was most notably present in deities (*orisa*), it could be accumulated by individual human beings. By acquiring sufficient ase, anyone or anything could become a deity (H. Drewal 1989: 258). Some of the ase of a god could be incorporated into a potion and transferred to a devotee of that deity by being rubbed into his or her head (M. Drewal 1989: 203–7). The ase of a king, who had the power of life and death over his subjects, was second only to that of deities, who created life (Pemberton and Afolayan 1996: 89–90). Like the power of life and death, ase was composed of contrasting qualities such as heat and cold, violence and peace, danger and safety, red and white (Apter 1992: 84). Ase, as energy, manifested itself differently in different people or deities. The ase of the war god Ogun was violent, that of the creator deity Orisala (Obatalla) wise and peaceful (H. Drewal 1989: 240–41, 258).

Although there is no direct evidence for China from as early as the Shang or Western Zhou periods, a similar concept, first recorded in the Han Dynasty, may have been *qi*, which is interpreted as referring to the formless but configuring primal energy present in everything that existed. Qi was associated with wind, breath, life, vapours arising from cooked grain, the human spirit, strong emotions, and sexual arousal. This concept may originally have referred to a primordial life-force emanating from the waters under the earth and animating everything in the cosmos, while *shen* denoted both individual celestial gods and the spirit force, associated with the sky world, that created form and order out of chaos (Lewis 1990: 140, 162, 213–18).

In Egypt the creation narrative associated with the solar cult at Heliopolis identified the primary energy promoting the establishment and functioning of the universe as male sexual drive and sunlight. In New Kingdom temple rituals performed throughout Egypt, the sexual arousal of male deities by female singers and dancers played a vital role in the daily rites of cosmic renewal (Robins 1993: 153). In other Egyptian creation narratives, creative power was identified with supernatural power or magic (*ḥk3*), creative utterance (*ḥw*), and supernatural insight (*si͗3*). These powers seem to have represented a more abstract and analytical understanding of the forces that had created and sustained the universe (J. Allen 2000: 156–57, 171–73). Associated with these powers was cosmic order (*m3ʿt*), which prevented both deities and the universe from lapsing into primal chaos or cosmic disorder (*i͗sft*) (Englund 1989b: 19).

Etymologically, ḥw was associated with *ḥw*, (food) (the vowels may have been different) and m3ʿt with *m3ʿw* (food offerings). The cosmic order was thus closely aligned with the creation and nourishment of life.

The Egyptians viewed divine power as animating and sustaining the universe. The hieroglyph for god (*nṯr*) has been interpreted as a banner blown in the wind, indicating the presence of an invisible force. The adjective *ntry* may refer to this power. Yet, while all natural phenomena were believed to be animated by divine power, natural phenomena were not regularly equated lexically with deities. *Rʿ* was the ordinary word for the sun as well as the name of the sun god, Re. Yet the earth god (Geb) and the sky goddess (Nut) were not designated by the common terms for earth (*t3*) and sky (*pt*). The Nile River, which was identified with the earth god or with Osiris, the god of fertility and death, was never an object of worship in its own right and was referred to simply as *ỉtrw* (the river), while the Nile flood was associated with a minor deity, Ḥʿpy. This suggests that the ancient Egyptians believed natural phenomena to be animated and controlled by divine power or manifestations of divine power rather than divinities in their own right.

In the past, Tylor's followers interpreted such diffuse supernatural power as the 'mana-like' vestige of an animistic stage of religious belief. This view overlooked the lack of evidence of a belief in some general supernatural force in small-scale human societies without an accompanying belief in behaviourally and often physically anthropomorphized spirits (Trigger 1990c: 107–10). The concept of an abstract supernatural force represented an attempt to describe the power that animated the universe, including human beings. The idea of deity sought to identify and establish relations with delimited manifestations of that force that were vital for the survival and welfare of human beings. These manifestations were associated with various aspects of nature, such as sunlight, moisture, fertile soil, food, geological formations, and the powers associated with various meteorological phenomena. Supernatural force manifested itself in human beings in forms such as body heat, the ability to think and move, male sexual drive, and female reproductive capacity. Thus, any one of these forces or any combination of them could have been used to conceptualize supernatural power in a generic sense.

This general analytical framework was shared by all societies that understood the cosmos using the same concepts they employed to analyse social relations. The main difference between more egalitarian societies and early civilizations was the differing understanding of society that was brought to the analysis. In egalitarian societies, people saw themselves relating to other human beings and to spirits as individuals who for various personal reasons possessed differing degrees and sorts of power.

In all early civilizations, deities were believed to participate in the control of natural processes and the shaping of social life. Some of these deities were manifestations of what we perceive as natural forces; others represented surviving and often supernaturally empowered aspects of deceased humans. Ancestors were linked by their reproductive powers to the creative forces of the natural world, and it is often difficult to distinguish ancestral deities from spirits or gods associated with the natural realm.

It is indicative of the extent to which human behavioural characteristics were projected onto the cosmos that not only the spirits animating living beings but also those controlling what we would regard as inanimate phenomena were gendered. The vast majority of deities were either male or female; the rest were bisexual or took both male and female forms (Clendinnen 1991: 168, 249). Deities became the foci of myths or sacred narratives that recounted their deeds and in the course of doing so described their personalities and special qualities, thus enhancing their resemblance to human beings (Taube 1992: 8).

In early civilizations, deities differed from one another in the extent of their powers and the aspects of nature they controlled. Some exercised a general cosmic function or controlled (or were) natural phenomena that were of great importance to human beings, such as rainfall, sunlight, or reproductive capacity; others were associated with the functioning of more geographically delimited aspects of the natural world, such as particular rivers, lakes, or hills. Minor deities occurred in large numbers and were regarded as subject to the authority of more powerful ones.

Although deities regulated (or were) aspects of the cosmos, they also acted as patrons of kingdoms, cities, families, craft associations, and individuals. They were venerated by their clients, who expected them to look after their interests. In general, major cosmic deities were the patrons of territorial or city-states while less powerful forces of nature, or divinized ancestors, were the patrons of smaller social groups. Ayllus, calpollis, and patrilineages worshipped ancestral spirits, local gods, or cosmic deities according to their own rites and at their own cult places. Humans also sought to placate hosts of minor spirits that might inflict illness or bad luck on them, often by seeking help from the more powerful deities who controlled such spirits. The relations between deities, the natural world, and the spirits of human ancestors were complex and expressed in culturally specific ways.

Thorkild Jacobsen (1970: 21; 1974) estimates that there were three thousand to four thousand deities in the Mesopotamian pantheon; ancient lists record the names of more than two thousand of them, mostly in Sumerian forms (Bottéro 1992: 216). About fifty were major deities, seven of whom possessed the power to determine annually the fate of all human communities and individuals.

Lower in rank were the *igigi* and below them still lesser spirits and demons, some of which caused illness. All these supernatural beings were descended from An, the sky god. While the principal deities constituted a well-defined family extending over four or more generations, minor supernaturals were classified in groups according to function and lacked individual genealogies.

High-ranking deities included Enlil, the storm god, Enki, the god of fresh water and fertility, and Ninhursaga, the goddess of barren ground. Among the younger generations of deities were Nannar, the moon god, Utu, the sun god, Inanna, the goddess of storehouses and fertility, and Erishkegal, the goddess of death and the underworld (Jacobsen 1976: 121–22). The principal deities were associated with various aspects of nature and have been described as the 'motors' driving the natural world (Bottéro 1992: 215). At the time of creation they had also become the patron deities of specific city-states (Oates 1978: 474), and these assignments mirrored the economic geography of southern Mesopotamia. In the far south, the chief urban deities were patrons of fresh water and marsh life; along the lower Euphrates River they were associated with orchards and cattle breeding; in the north they were patrons of sheep herding; and to the west they were connected with grain farming (Jacobsen 1976: 25; Maisels 1990: 310–12). In addition to controlling various natural forces and being associated with particular urban centres, these deities presided over specific functions of the social realm. Utu, the sun god, was the god of justice, Enlil the god of kingship, and Enki responsible for craft production. Individual humans looked to minor deities to promote their personal well-being. These deities acted as intermediaries between individual humans and higher-ranking deities.

Richard Townsend (1979: 31) observes that in the Valley of Mexico cults addressed natural phenomena such as rain, fire, sun, wind, and air through the deities that animated them. H. B. Nicholson (1971b) has assigned most of these deities to three thematic complexes: celestial creativity and divine paternalism; rain, moisture, and agricultural fertility; and war, sacrifice, blood, and death. Normally two deities were singled out for special reverence by each city-state. The Aztec's principal deities, whose main shrines were located atop their largest temple platform, were Tlaloc, the chief god of water, rain, and fertility, and Huitzilopochtli, a solar war god who was their patron deity.

Variation in the way in which major deities were conceptualized and named in different city-states provided distinctive patron deities for the hundreds of city-states that existed across central Mexico. Townsend (1979: 29) suggests that variations in the names of gods were kennings, or descriptive titles, that differentiated local aspects of a limited number of deities. It is also possible that numerous originally separate gods were being systematically ordered by identifying them as variants of a smaller number of deities. Scholars have assigned at least eleven deities to the Tezcatlipoca complex – four of them clearly different forms of Tezcatlipoca and the others either closely related deities or alternative names for him (M. E. Smith 1996: 211–15). Historical evidence suggests that the Aztec had upgraded their once humble patron deity, Huitzilopochtli, by identifying him with the Tezcatlipoca of the south, who was a deity of major cosmic importance. Gods also tended to be arranged in sets of four, one for each direction, with perhaps a fifth deity for the centre.

The major gods in the Valley of Mexico were the foci of elaborate myths concerning their cosmic functions, relations with each other, and dealings with human beings. These myths provided them with distinctive personalities and identified them with human leaders who had played a major role in the founding and early history of particular city-states. Quetzalcoatl, a major cosmic deity associated with creation, fertility, and the planet Venus, was identified as the ruler of the former city of Tollan, from whom all members of the nobility in the Valley of Mexico claimed to be descended. This equating of gods and ancient ethnic leaders has encouraged the view that all Mexican gods were deified heroes and ancestors. As in Mesopotamia, in addition to their identification with the forces of nature and with particular cities, gods were assigned specific social roles. Huitzilopochtli was a god of war, Quetzalcoatl the principal deity of priests, and Tezcatlipoca a patron of kings.

Ranking below the principal deities were numerous nature spirits. These included the calpolli deities (*calpolteotl*), to whom members of calpollis attributed their corporate existence and well-being. These deities had led their human followers to their historical places of settlement and continued to live nearby in hills, caves, and other natural features. Minor supernatural beings were believed to be present in inanimate objects made from stone, clay, and other materials and capable of emerging from them to harm human beings during periods of cosmic breakdown (López Austin 1988, 1: 70, 246, 252–53). The term *teotl* seems to have been applied to the dead only in its broad sense of any numinous power. There is no evidence of ancestor cults in the Valley of Mexico, regardless of how high the status of the person, and the human personality was believed not to endure long after death. Deities appear to have been forces of nature that were drawn into human affairs and were often identified with legendary political leaders.

The Yoruba revered an elaborate hierarchy of deities who were referred to as *orisa*, *ebora*, or *imole* (Bascom 1969: 77). These deities were believed by traditional religious specialists to number between four hundred and seventeen hundred. Their names, interrelations, and gender varied from one place to another (Apter 1992: 154–55). The most senior was the creator god, Olorun, who lived in the sky, while the rest either lived exclusively on earth or shifted between earth and sky. A number of deities associated with various aspects of nature, such as particular hills, rivers, trees, the earth, lightning, and diseases, were worshipped in one form or another throughout the Yoruba region. Minor bush spirits that manifested themselves in trees and ponds tended to be friendly and inclined to help humans, but the forest was also a realm of ghosts, monsters, and demons who sought to harm people (Bascom 1969: 77; K. Barber 1981; 1991: 316). The most powerful deities had already existed prior to the creation of the world, but their natures were defined only later as a result of their achievements in the terrestrial realm (Apter 1992: 151). Many deities were created through the fragmentation or division of existing ones, and each new deity was assigned its own taboos, songs, and personality (K. Barber 1981: 732–33).

Many powerful deities were equated with important historical personages who had lived near the time of creation. The thunder god, Sango, was identified with the fourth king of Oyo, who committed suicide after inadvertently destroying his palace with his powerful lightning charm. Such individuals had been transformed into deities by sinking into the ground, rising into the sky, or becoming a rock or a river. Despite their continued supernatural presence in the terrestrial sphere, they were immortal beings of heaven (*ara orun*) instead of simply mortal beings on earth (*ara aye*) (Apter 1992: 151). Thus, like the Aztec, the Yoruba viewed their major deities as natural forces while simultaneously equating them with major historical figures. While Bascom (1969) and others interpret these deities as ancestors (*agbanle*) who became gods, Apter (1992: 150–52) regards many of them as nature deities on which the personalities of specific human beings have been superimposed. The goddess Ayelala, however, began as a slave who was sacrificed in the nineteenth century in a ritual that marked the conclusion of a war between two Yoruba states and quickly evolved into a regional deity whose main function was to punish oath-breakers (Awolalu 1979: 41–44). It was therefore possible for humans to become deities, as well as for deities to be woven into human history. For humans to become or to be identified with a deity they had to depart from the human world in some ritually significant manner.

Yoruba kings or royal lineages claimed a special relation with one or more major deities, making these gods the patron deities of their city-states. The king of Oyo supported the cult of Sango, whom he claimed as his ancestor and whose most important shrine was located in the royal quarter of the Oyo capital. Other deities were associated with the heads of quarters and lineages. Such patronage did not prevent these deities from having other, less important cults in other quarters of the same city and at still lower levels in the social hierarchy (Apter 1992: 21). Extended families often venerated one or more major deities as their patrons or protectors. Sacrifices were also offered to ancestral souls by their living patrilineal descendants in the expectation that such souls would promote their family's welfare among the gods. Despite their interventionary powers, however, dead ancestors were not designated as deities, and the worship of the gods greatly overshadowed that of ancestors (Bascom 1969: 77).

Shang kings and nobles focused great attention on reporting to lineage and clan ancestors and petitioning and sacrificing to them at their tombs and at special ancestral shrines and temples. In their pursuit of supernatural support to ensure good weather, abundant harvests, productive hunts, successful journeys, and health and well-being for themselves and their families, Shang rulers approached their principal god, Shangdi, through the mediation of their ancestors (Eno 1990). While the most remote ancestors were regarded as the most potent intermediaries and the ones whose sphere of operation affected society as a whole, it was recently deceased ancestors who were directly appealed to for intercession. Because of fear that they might be malevolent as well as well-intentioned, they were carefully placated (Allan 1991: 50–52; Keightley 1978b: 218).

Shangdi has been variously identified as the apical ancestor of the Shang royal clan, a dead king, the collective embodiment of all dead kings, and a nature deity unrelated to Shang royalty. While the king communicated with Shangdi through the deceased Shang rulers and more remote non-royal ancestors, Shangdi issued his commands not to living kings but to the forces of nature (Chao 1972: 143–44). Fragmentary legends have been interpreted as suggesting that Qi, the hero-ancestor of the Shang royal clan, was the offspring of Shangdi, who, in the form of a black bird, had caused the wife of the mythical emperor Diku to become pregnant by swallowing an egg. The black bird has also been identified with the sun (*ri*) (Allan 1991: 39). This myth suggests that Shangdi may have been a major nature deity who commanded other nature deities and had the power to inflict disasters as well as blessings on the Shang kings and their subjects. Each noble clan may have had its own hero-ancestor descended from a nature deity (Keightley 1999b: 252–53).

The early Chinese worshipped many deities identified with the forces of nature. Trees and groves were locales of popular cults, and earth altars (*she*) were the foci of community and state agricultural rituals addressed to the deities that ensured the fertility of the soil. They also venerated spirits associated with rivers, lakes, forests, winds, rains, astronomical bodies, and mountains and offered sacrifices to the cardinal directions (Creel 1937: 180–81; Lewis 1990: 215). Stellar deities, as well as ones associated with the winds and rain, were probably viewed as having their primary locus in the sky, while others, perhaps originally presided over by the god Huangdi, were associated with the Yellow Springs, or underworld (Allan 1991: 66; Granet 1958 [1930]: 153). Deities such as the Dragon Woman and the Eastern and Western Mothers were yet other objects of cults associated with natural forces. While it has been suggested that only the royal and noble families venerated their ancestors, every extended family may have had an altar to its ancestors and to the soil (Granet 1958 [1930]: 246).

Maya deities have been described as manifestations of natural phenomena (Schele and Miller 1986: 42). Gary Gossen and Richard Leventhal (1993: 210–11) maintain, in contrast, that at all levels Maya religion was based on ancestor worship and that state cults were addressed to royal ancestors as well as to nature deities. These characterizations are not necessarily contradictory. Regionalized manifestations of nature deities had tutelary relations to polities or to royal and other high-ranking families, and in this context nature deities and royal ancestors became identified with each other (Houston and Stuart 1996: 292, 302; Taube 1992: 9). While major deities in different centres may have had the same names and been recognized as part of a common overall structure of belief, their ritual significance, specific meanings, and myths appear to have varied significantly from one city-state to another. Because of this variation, it has been questioned to what extent Maya deities constituted a clearly defined set (Taube 1992: 7).

It has been suggested that Maya gods were less personally characterized than those of other early civilizations (Baudez 1994: 267; A. Miller 1986: 21), tending to occur in multiple forms relating to each of the four directions and exhibiting young, old, and dead manifestations. Yet their apparent lack of characterization may simply be a consequence of the scarcity of known Classic-period myths. Sons' engendering or giving rebirth to their fathers may have been the central mystery or metanarrative of Maya religion (Freidel, Schele, and Parker 1993: 281).

The most powerful Classic Maya deity appears to have been K'awil, an aged, omnipresent deity associated with rulership, scribal arts, the four quarters, the world tree, all levels of the universe, the principal bird deity, and maize. His counterpart in the Postclassic period was the paramount deity Itzamna, whose power was based on his command of witchcraft and other forms of esoteric knowledge (Taube 1992: 31–42, 78). It is not clear, however, that K'awil enjoyed a paramount position among his fellow deities during the Classic period. The majority were identified with the sun, rain, weather, and crop fertility, as well as with human activities such as rulership, subsistence, and trade. Maya deities were articulated within the framework of a 260-day sacred calendar, while the timing of their rituals was determined by the roles they played in annual natural cycles (A. Miller 1986: 22).

Maya rulers traced their descent from major deities, and dead kings were identified with one of the Hero Twins who had defeated the gods of death and risen temporarily out of the underworld as the sun or Venus. Long-dead royal ancestors were also identified with sun gods and moon goddesses and recently dead kings with the young maize god and K'awil (Houston and Stuart 1996: 297). These were all deities whom rulers impersonated while alive. Kings also erected elaborate funerary monuments where they were venerated after death as manifestations of various celestial deities who sank into the underworld and rose again.

Much attention also appears to have been paid to the mortuary cults of non-royal ancestors. William Haviland (1968: 112) maintains that in Late Classic Tikal only elite compounds had identifiable ancestral shrines, but this does not mean that ancestral cults were limited to the nobility. Such cults may have played an important role in religious life at all levels of Classic Maya society.

Among the Inka supernatural power was manifested in *wakas*, visible objects animated by deities who communicated with humans through dreams, oracles, and supernatural signs and provided them with life, food, health, fertility, and whatever else they required. The most powerful deities had as wakas the sun, moon, ocean, stars, and meteorological phenomena such as lightning. Most deities were, however, associated with less powerful and more localized wakas – mountains, lakes, springs, caves, rock outcrops, trees, shrines, ancient ruins, and effigies (MacCormack 1991: 338). Field wakas were usually stones that served as boundary markers (*saywa*) or field guardians (*wanka*) (Rowe 1944: 296). Living humans who had waka status were referred to as *willka*. In addition, numinous objects called *conopa*, including unusually large or curiously shaped corn-cobs, were kept and venerated in houses. Such objects are variously referred to as minor domestic deities or talismans (MacCormack 1991: 406). Deities could be persuaded to move into new physical embodiments if their old ones could not be transported to a new location or had been destroyed. From this it is clear that wakas were physical manifestations of divine power rather than the essence of such power.

Many wakas were revered as *rumapkamaq*, creators and sustainers of local human groups. Each such waka traced its origin to a deity whose body had turned to stone but whose enduring supernatural power was a source of fertility and protection on which the survival and well-being of an ayllu depended. Through its power to shape matter, such a waka was able to create new members for the ayllu. Wakas could speak through oracle priests and afflict ayllu members with famine and disease if they became displeased with their behaviour (Gose 1993). After death the power that had shaped and sustained a human being returned to the waka from which it had come, but the mummified body (*mallqui*) also became a waka. Mummified ancestors constituted links between creator wakas and the living people they supported. The mummified bodies of dead kings were important wakas, kings having been created by and embodying the power (*kamaquen*) of the sun. The body of Manqu Qhapaq, the first Inka king, was preserved only in the form of a stone. The bodies of some children who had been ritually sacrificed by royal command also became wakas, some of which were venerated as oracles in the communities where they had been born (Rowe 1944: 295–98).

Egyptian deities (*nṯrw*) were the forces that animated the various aspects of the natural world: sun, earth, water, sky, moon, stars, winds, geological formations, and wild and domesticated plants and animals. Each deity had its own name and attributes, and the most important of them were the tutelary deities of particular Egyptian towns and localities (J. Allen 2000: 43–45). Each major Egyptian temple had not only its own presiding deity but also its own creation myth and place of creation. While gods who bore the same name sometimes presided over a number of widely dispersed localities, it is difficult to determine whether these deities represented syncretisms of once distinct gods or had been transplanted from one place to another. If the latter, each local manifestation acquired its distinctive attributes. The principal male deity in each locality was viewed as the creator god, whose power had brought the universe and human society into existence and sustained both. Through his female counterpart, this god continually renewed himself by being reborn as his own son. During their lifetimes, kings were the earthly manifestation of the living version of each creator god; in death they became identified by means of mummification with the older and unchanging (dead or Osiris) form. Offerings were made at the graves of ordinary people, and the term nṯr was applied to dead commoners as well as to living kings and nature spirits. Nṯr appears to have signified any entity that received cult offerings. The extent of such an entity's supernatural power seems to have corresponded to the volume of offerings received (Meeks and Favard-Meeks 1996: 33–37). Egyptians must have believed the supernatural powers of dead commoners to be very limited by comparison with those of dead kings or major deities.

In all early civilizations deities or personified natural/supernatural powers were thought to play a major role in the operation of the natural and social realms. Tutelary deities were identified in various ways with human ancestors. The Chinese, Inka, and perhaps the Maya looked to dead ancestors for significant protection against natural and social calamities. The Aztec and Yoruba identified early historical figures as human manifestations of gods, while in ancient Egypt gods were believed to have ruled on earth prior to giving rise to the first mortal kings. The Mesopotamians, while occasionally identifying early heroic rulers as the children of gods and mortal women, generally saw little in common between the gods and human ancestors.

Divine power was identified most essentially with the forces of nature. Even ancestral spirits, to whom great powers were attributed, were, because of their fertility, regarded as forces of nature. Gods associated with natural phenomena sometimes bore the common or generic names of those phenomena. Other gods were given names that alluded to one or more of their characteristic natural aspects. The Aztec sun god was called Huitzilopochtli, 'hummingbird of the left side', a kenning reference to his being a solar deity who had cosmic associations with the Tezcatlipoca of the south (the left-hand side of the sun's daily course across the sky) and hence with the directional colour blue, which was associated with hummingbirds. Some Sumerian deities were referred to as the lord (*en*) or lady (*nin*) of the element they animated, such as Enlil (Lord Wind), Enki (Lord [moistened] Earth), and Ninhursaga (Lady of the Stony Ground).

The whole of nature was believed to be animated by a primordial divine power that manifested itself to varying degrees in different entities. Major natural forces and in some civilizations deceased ancestors possessed much more of this power than did living humans. Human destiny was seen as determined to a large extent by divine powers that manifested themselves in nature or were nature and thus played a major role in shaping the social order.

MANIFESTATIONS OF DEITIES

Deities were believed to have personalities that resembled those of powerful human beings, but they were not invariably anthropomorphized (Fig. 19.1). Sometimes they combined human and animal attributes. Deities could also manifest themselves as natural phenomena such as animals, plants, rocks, and stars, in effigies and ritual objects, and in living human bodies, which deities might occupy while humans were in a trance state.

There is considerable uncertainty about the extent to which anthropomorphic portrayals of deities were intended to be iconic or were believed to represent their actual forms. Egyptologists debate whether Egyptian deities were thought to exist primarily in human form or as immaterial forces that animated the universe (J. Allen 2000: 43–45; Bonnet 1999 [1939]; Silverman 1991: 15–16). Most Egyptian deities were depicted either entirely in human form or with anthropomorphic bodies and animal heads. Sometimes the same deity was portrayed in both fashions. Egyptian texts indicate that deities were

19.1. Deities as depicted in early civilizations: Egypt – (a) Min, (b) Seth, (c) Horus, (d) Isis; Valley of Mexico – (e) Tonatiuh, the sun god, (f) Huitzilopochtli; Maya – (g) Young Moon Goddess, (h) Itzamna, (i) Ix Chel, Old Moon Goddess and Goddess of Medicine, (j) Death God, all from the Post-Classic Dresden Codex; Mesopotamia – (k) Gudea, King of Lagash, being presented to his city god Ningirsu (seated) by two other deities, on a cylinder seal from Telloh (ca. 2144–2124 B.C.). Sources: (a) – (d) from Gardiner 1961: 215; (e), (f) from Eduard Seler, *Gesammelte Abhandlungen zur Amerikanischen Sprach – und Alterthumskunde* (Berlin, 1902–1904); (g) – (j) from G. Zimmermann, *Die Hieroglyphen der Maya-Handschriften* (Hamburg, 1956), pls. 6, 7; (k) from Woolley, *The Sumerians*, 89.

thought to have imperishable bodies made of gold with lapis lazuli hair (Meeks and Favard-Meeks 1996: 57), but sometimes they passed surreptitiously among humans in forms that were indistinguishable from those of mortals (Lichtheim 1973: 220). Major deities entered the body of the king when he procreated the heir to the throne. It was believed that beholding a deity in his or her full glory could cause a human being to catch fire. Gods therefore most often appeared either enveloped in or in the form of natural phenomena such as earthquakes, storms, or fires (Morenz 1973: 32). These apparitions were accompanied by dazzling radiance or a sweet aroma and created powerful sensations of reverence or terror in the humans who witnessed them. During such encounters, the presence of an invisible deity was sensed, and the deity could be heard speaking in one's heart (Hornung 1982: 132–35). The primary form of an Egyptian deity may have been a numinous power that could take many forms (*ḫprw*), although these transformations did not include changes of gender.

An Egyptian deity existed simultaneously as a *b3* (free life-force) or *3ḫ* (illuminated spirit) in the sky, as the special power in a cult statue (*ẖnty*) or in cult objects in his or her temple or in living humans, animals, or trees on earth, and as a mummified body (*ḏt*) in the underworld (Hornung 1982: 132–35; Morenz 1973: 151). Different gods could temporarily combine with one another to increase their power without compromising their individual personalities or independence. Such deities were referred to in both the singular and the plural. These combinations often endowed local gods with the cosmic functions of the sun god, Re (Morenz 1973: 140–46). Parts of deities, such as eyes, could act independently of the god to whom they belonged or become another deity. While gods behaved in a human fashion, their personalities were only occasionally clearly distinguished from one another.

Egyptian gods were drawn down from the sky into cult statues to activate them for daily rituals that nourished the gods and ensured that they performed the acts necessary to renew creation (Morenz 1973: 88). When occupied by a deity statues could make oracular pronouncements if questions were put to them by appearing to tilt in one direction or another. In addition, priests might sense the god present in the statue speaking to them in their hearts. Gods communicated with ordinary Egyptians by means of dreams, visions, and spirit possession (Baines 1991a). They also entered into trees, individual wild or domestic animals, and even whole herds or species, and the behaviour of these animals provided oracular responses to questions put to them. The Apis bull of Memphis, who was associated with the Egyptian creator god, Ptah, indicated by his actions the answers to questions that priests addressed to the god incarnate in him (Morenz 1973: 103). Yet, the Egyptians also believed that the gods had made animals for human benefit. They did not hesitate to work, castrate, kill, and eat animals or to offer them as sacrifices to the gods. Prohibitions against killing or eating animals that were sacred to specific deities were observed only locally. Hence divine power was manifested in nature and made it work, but nature itself was not regarded as divine. Rocks and animals were no more deities than cult statues were; instead, they were places where divine power might manifest itself.

Major Mesopotamian deities were conceptualized in human form, although this did not extend to lesser spirits, demons, or even a son of the solar god, Utu, who was depicted as a bull (Oppenheim 1964: 184). Gods were also represented anthropomorphically in the cult images that were the foci of temple rituals. These statues, made of precious materials attached to a wooden base, were manufactured in special workshops and endowed with life by means of 'opening of the mouth' rituals. So important were such statues that the names used to designate particular years sometimes commemorated their creation. These images stood or sat in the inner chambers of temples, although in some cases, when doors were open, they could be glimpsed from temple courtyards (Oppenheim 1964: 185–86; Postgate 1992: 118). Mesopotamian deities had distinct personalities, and some male ones were described as engaging in sexual relations with human women. Most encounters between deities and humans were, however, accompanied by a divine luminosity that filled humans with paralysing fear (Jacobsen 1976: 12; Oppenheim 1964: 176).

Thorkild Jacobsen (1976) suggests that before the Early Dynastic period Sumerian gods were conceptualized less in human form than as natural phenomena. The female deity Inanna may have begun as a date palm and only gradually evolved into an anthropomorphic fertility deity. As natural manifestations were replaced by anthropomorphic ones, the older forms became the symbolic attributes of deities, and the gods retained their natural associations. Nannar continued to be identified with the moon, Inanna with date palms and the planet Venus, Utu with the sun, and Enlil with storms. In addition to animating cult statues, the gods entered into portable holy symbols on which oaths were sworn (Postgate 1992: 280). These symbols were also carried into battle and paraded around the countryside to encourage the payment of tithes. Deities appeared and spoke to people in dreams. They also conveyed messages through natural events such as earthquakes, the shapes of the livers of sacrificed animals, and the changing positions of the planets, all these manifestations being objects of divination (Oppenheim 1964: 210–27).

Yoruba deities were conceptualized as existing in human form but were only infrequently so portrayed (Frobenius 1913, 1: 196). Often more abstract cult symbols hosted the presence of a god. The door to almost every Yoruba household and the gates of most Yoruba towns had a shrine to the god Esu, represented by a block of laterite or a crude clay statue. Esu was important because he conveyed sacrifices to the other gods (Bascom 1969: 79). Living animals, among them snakes and crocodiles imported from the coast and kept in walled ponds, were also venerated as incarnations of deities (Ojo 1966a: 168). Yoruba gods communicated with humans by temporary spirit possession during rituals, controlling the movement of their bodies and speaking through their mouths. These human 'horses' or 'mounts' of deities were said to be permanently altered by such episodes (Bascom 1969: 78). Costumed members of the Egungun society provided vehicles that permitted the souls of the dead to return temporarily to the human world by possessing their bodies.

In the Valley of Mexico deities were portrayed in human form in codices, and distinctive human personalities were ascribed to the most prominent of them in myths and legends. Numerous local forms of deities had to be distinguished by minute differences in their costumes, which dominated the portrayal of most deities. Because deities represented sacred forces interacting with each other, it was possible by adding a few ornaments to incorporate one god into another without either deity's losing its identity (Clendinnen 1991: 248). Earth deities frequently incorporated reptilian and crocodilian body parts. The power of deities entered into cult statues in temples, which appear to have been three-dimensional renditions of the images represented in codices. These statues played an important role in temple rituals. Sacred bundles containing portable statues and other objects associated with deities were an important focus for concentrating divine power (van Zantwijk 1985: 38).

As a result of hallucinogens and dance-induced ecstasy, people became possessed by deities, who spoke and acted through them. Such individuals temporarily ceased to be themselves and became 'mirrors' of deities (Clendinnen 1991: 259). Deities were also drawn into the human world for solicitation and invocation by means of *ixiptlas*, images made from amaranth dough, which worshippers consumed, elaborately dressed images erected on pole frames, and costumes worn by kings, priests, or less prestigious god impersonators during religious ceremonies. Captives used as god impersonators were slain as human sacrifices at the end of the ritual as a means of empowering the deity they represented. While the purpose of ixiptlas was normally to draw deities closer for more effective communication with human beings, the effect of a king's wearing the costumes of many high-ranking deities was to endow him permanently with their power (Clendinnen 1991: 249–53; Townsend 1979: 28). Gods, like sorcerers and other powerful humans, could transform themselves into animal shapes (*nahualli*), and therefore some animals were really deities travelling about the human realm (Clendinnen 1991: 55; López Austin 1988, 1: 364–71).

The Maya generally depicted deities in human form. Some deities had a few animal features, such as square eyes or animal markings. Other supernaturals were portrayed as a combination of human and animal features or were composed of parts of animals that lived in different environments. Still other deities were shown as animals behaving like people, such as the rabbit scribes who assisted the Lords of the Underworld (Schele and Miller 1986: 42–43). Deities also manifested themselves in natural phenomena such as the sun, stars, or rain. Some gods were portrayed in only one form, others in young, old, and dead variants, in different anthropomorphic and zoomorphic versions, and in different colour and directional forms. Deities were also represented in the form of their animal co-essences or spirit familiars (*way*).

Kings and other humans were intermittently possessed by various deities and appropriated their powers by wearing the costumes of these deities. This behaviour involved the same principles as the Aztec use of ixiptlas (Houston and Stuart 1996: 306; Taube 1992: 8–9). By means of appropriate costuming and spirit possession, one person could become consubstantial with many deities (Schele and Miller 1986: 66). Through painful forms of self-bleeding and hallucinogens administered both orally and rectally, members of the royal family entered into trance states that drew their divine ancestors back into the human realm. Finally, cult images, at least some of them carved from wood, kept in Maya temples served as receptacles of divine power. These images appear to have been activated by re-enacting the circumstances that had led to the birth of the deities they represented (Houston and Stuart 1996: 302–6).

Among the early Chinese, the character for Tian (sky), the Zhou deity who replaced Shangdi as supreme god, appears to represent an anthropomorphic figure, and Shangdi may have been conceived in human form as well (Eno 1990: 3). Ancestral souls were probably visualized in human form. The souls of the dead were drawn into the bodies of ritual impersonators (*shi*), usually their young grandchildren, so that they could participate in sacrificial meals and bless their living descendants (Allan 1991: 157; Creel 1937: 336). In contrast, lineage ancestors and the spirits worshipped at the altars of the soil were from an early period represented by inscribed tablets rather than by images (Granet 1958: 239–40; Laufer 1913). Various nature spirits may have been represented by the birds, tigers, snakes, turtles, and *taotie* monsters cast on Shang ritual vessels (Allan 1991: 130–72). Yet there appears to have been no more obvious representation of gods in Shang elite art than there was of kings.

Andean conceptualizations of deity tended to be mainly aniconic and abstract. While major deities were often represented anthropomorphically, most deities were associated with natural objects (waka). Inti, the sun god, was worshipped both in human form and as a solar disc. Wiraqucha, the creator god, was represented by an anthropomorphic gold statue in his main temple in Cuzco; in other cult centres he and other deities took the form of poles covered with human clothing (Cobo 1990: 23–26). Deities appeared to humans, often in times of crisis, in the form of imageless radiance, and therefore it was not always obvious which deity was being encountered. Deities could also change their form: Inka legends reported that stone wakas had turned into superhuman warriors when Cuzco was attacked by its enemies and become stones again after the Inka had won the battle (MacCormack 1991: 287–89, 328–29). Every deity that was venerated, including dead kings, had one or more oracle priests through whom the deity could regularly address human beings (Gose 1996a). Gods also spoke to humans through dreams and apparitions.

While most deities could, on special occasions, manifest themselves almost anywhere and to anyone, especially in dreams and visions, in early civilizations they regularly did so only to priests and officials at appropriate temples, shrines, and cult places. Some deities were restricted to one cult centre. The vast majority of Andean deities were each associated with a single dawning place (*pakarina*) where they had first appeared at the time of creation. Yet the Inka rulers constructed temples for the worship of Inti, their ancestral sun god, in provincial centres throughout their kingdom. These royal solar temples symbolized the unity of the Inka state and the acceptance of Inka authority in far-off regions. Major Egyptian deities such as Ptah, who was worshipped as the creator god at Memphis, had modest 'guest temples' in major temple complexes elsewhere in Egypt. In city-state systems the same major deities or local variants of them were worshipped in many places. Tezcatlipoca and Quetzalcoatl were venerated in various forms throughout highland Mexico, often as the tutelary deities of different city-states. The Maya built large mortuary temples in each of which a particular dead king was identified with a local variant of a major cosmic deity.

The most important deities – the animators of major cosmic forces and the patrons of states, large cities, and rulers – received offerings at major cult centres. These temples were the earthly abodes of deities rather than places of public worship. Deities of lesser importance had smaller cult centres that were maintained and controlled by villages, corporate landowning groups, extended families, nuclear families, and voluntary ritual societies. Local leaders or part-time priests officiated at smaller temples or at open-air shrines such as those associated with Andean ayllus. In the Valley of Mexico each calpolli maintained a temple for its tutelary deity, while every household had a shrine containing clay statues of maize goddesses and sometimes the cloth-wrapped thigh bones of sacrificed prisoners who had been captured by family members (Brumfiel 1996). Ordinary Egyptian household shrines were a focus for the veneration of dead ancestors as well as deities of fertility and childbirth, such as Taweret and Bes, who did not have major temples anywhere in Egypt. These cults sought to ensure the fertility and general well-being of the family (Demarée 1983; Robins 1993: 75–76). Rituals for dead relatives were also performed at their tombs or graves, located in cemeteries outside settlements. The Chinese honoured ancestors in household shrines that varied in importance and elaboration according to the antiquity of the patrilineal descent group and hence the social status of the head of the household (Granet 1958: 246). Mesopotamians honoured household and personal deities in their homes and performed rituals for their dead ancestors, who were sometimes buried in vaults under houses (Postgate 1992: 99–101).

In all early civilizations the universe appears to have been conceptualized as a manifestation of supernatural power, which supplied it with life and activity. The most potent manifestations of that energy were deities of varying degrees of importance who pervaded different aspects of the natural world and made them function. While there was considerable variation in the extent to which the representations of deities were anthropomorphized, the idea of groups of deities with human-like mental qualities animating the universe and in this and other ways controlling human existence appears to have been shared by all the early civilizations.

ONE OR MANY?

Some anthropologists have maintained that in early civilizations all deities were recognized as particular manifestations of a single god; others have argued that religions in early civilizations were polytheistic. This debate has been labelled the problem of 'the one and the many' (Hornung 1982). The claim that all gods are manifestations of a single deity was part of a belief in 'primitive monotheism' advocated long ago by Christian anthropologists of the Vienna school. In its most strident form, primitive monotheism maintained that all early peoples possessed the (divinely revealed?) knowledge of a single god. Various forms of evidence have been cited in support of this notion.

The first type of evidence is belief in a single creator deity. The Egyptians maintained that all things came into existence as the result of the activity of an original creator god who gave rise to the other gods and to all else that exists and, as the sun, re-created the universe each morning. The Aztec and their neighbours maintained that all the gods were in some fashion emanations of Ometeotl (The Lord and Lady of Two-ness), an undifferentiated form of cosmic power that continued to exist in the highest celestial sphere. It was Ometeotl who sustained life and sent each new child into the world (León-Portilla 1963: 84–106). While the initial 'transformations' of both the Egyptian creator god and Ometeotl created multiple deities out of a single or dual one, they do not appear to have altered or diminished the original divinity. In the Heliopolitan creation myth, the Egyptian creator god, Atum, produced the next generation of deities by mixing together his semen and spittle. Ometeotl did so through a process of non-reductive duplication whereby cosmic power manifested itself in individual forms in different spheres, creating time and space. In both Egyptian and Valley of Mexico mythology, later generations of deities were produced by sexual reproduction, a process that by its very nature created new beings without altering existing ones. Both creator deities continued to play an active role in the universe they had brought into existence.

The Yoruba believed that their supreme god, called Olorun (owner of heaven) or Olodumare (one of superlative greatness?), created the other major deities and all human souls, which could not exist without his continued support. While Olorun received sacrifices only through the gods he had created, he heard people's prayers, intervened directly in terrestrial affairs, and personally determined the fate of each human being prior to that person's rebirth. Unlike the other gods, Olorun could not behave badly, and ultimately all the other gods were accountable to him for their actions (Awolalu 1979: 1–20, 50; K. Barber 1981: 729). Deities could, however, divide or be separated to form new gods and be created by sexual reproduction, while humans could become gods. Thus not all of them were direct manifestations of Olorun.

In the Andes Wiraqucha, whose name may have meant 'ocean of fat' or 'boundless vitality' and who was either a single creator and fertility god or a complex of such deities, was believed to have vanished into the Pacific Ocean after fashioning the world and the ancestors of all people, animals, and plants. Yet he continued to appear to Inka rulers at times of crisis and, as Pachakamaq (creator/animator of the world), was a very influential lowland waka and oracle. While various lowland myths stated that Pachakamaq had created the sun, the Inka claimed that Inti, their solar deity, was Pachakamaq's father. Wiraqucha was the direct recipient of prayers but not usually of sacrifices, which, except on special occasions, reached him only through the other gods. He also lacked land and flocks of his own. He appears to have been viewed as the main deity of the lower half of the cosmos, while the sun was the principal deity of the upper half (Cobo 1990: 23; MacCormack 1991: 59–61, 343, 350–51; Sullivan 1985).

While the role that the powerful Chinese celestial deity Shangdi played in the creation of other gods is unknown (Eno 1990), he continued to control the universe. Mesopotamian religious lore mentions a primordial female deity, 'The Mother who Gave Birth to Earth and Heaven', who may have been the goddess Tiamat (Frankfort 1948: 283–84). Mesopotamian deities were produced by successive generations of sexual reproduction beginning with a mating between sea water (Tiamat) and fresh water (Apsu). The original Mesopotamian creator gods were slain by their descendants, who represented a more differentiated and active universe, leaving An as the oldest living god; the younger gods used the corpses of their primordial ancestors to create the current cosmos.

Although people in most early civilizations believed that all deities were in some manner created or engendered by a single primordial deity or pair of deities, there is no evidence that later gods were regarded merely as manifestations of specific attributes of that deity. Whenever enough is known about individual deities it is clear that, instead of representing selected attributes of a single being, each deity had a complex nature that was complete in itself. Each represented one or more of the conflicting forces that were observed to be present in the natural and social realms. Primordial creator deities did not always rule over younger gods, who were sometimes at odds or even in open conflict with them. While the details of the creation of the gods differed from one early civilization to another, they were usually seen as having been produced in a way that did not diminish the substance of the original deity.

A stronger argument that all the gods in each early civilization might be manifestations of a single supernatural force has been found in the ways in which many gods could absorb one another and turn into others. Both Egyptian and Aztec solar deities defeated the stars each dawn and incorporated their essences into their own being only to release them in the evening (Goebs 1998). The Egyptian sun god, Re, is described as devouring the other gods every morning and vomiting up their bodies in the form of fish and their b3-spirits in the form of birds every evening (Troy 1989: 131). While Egyptian gods combined with or 'inhabited' each other without impairing their individual identities (Bonnet 1999 [1939]), Aztec, Maya, and Yoruba deities assumed distinctive local or otherwise spatio-temporally restricted forms without losing their generic identities. While these actions, which went beyond single deities' merely altering their appearance or entering the bodies of animals or oracle priests, may indicate that all deities were believed to be manifestations of a single divine power, they do not constitute evidence that all deities were manifestations of a single supernatural being. In early civilizations the anthropomorphization of natural/supernatural forces does not appear to have reached the point where people began to think of deities as multiple expressions of a single god.

THE MORAL ORDER OF THE GODS

There is no evidence that in any of the early civilizations, except perhaps that of the Yoruba, people believed that a unified moral order pervaded the universe. Among the Yoruba that order was associated with the overlordship of the morally transcendent though not omniscient Olorun. Although it is possible that this aspect of their religious beliefs reflected their long exposure to Christianity and Islam, even within Olorun's overarching moral order deities competed with each other and championed opposing tendencies and causes. The Aztec conceived of the universe as having a highly complex but unstable structure within which major gods competed ruthlessly for power and control. Their behaviour, determined by the roles they played in the functioning of the cosmos, resembled that of the forces of nature more closely than it did human interactions based on moral or ethical considerations. The Egyptian concept of m3ʿt, conventionally translated 'truth', 'right', or 'justice', referred to the fragile natural order that kept the universe functioning and prevented it from lapsing into disorder. It also designated the traditional order prevailing in the social realm, which paralleled the order that the creator god had first established to control the cosmos. In both realms m3ʿt was based on a balance between opposites in which order prevailed over but could not eliminate disorder. This delicate balance was seen as providing the conditions necessary to support life (J. Allen 2000: 115–17). In the other early civilizations, relations among the gods also largely reflected those obtaining in the natural world.

Only the Mesopotamians, at least by the time the creation epic *Enuma Elish* was composed during the Old Babylonian period, saw relations amongst the gods as governed by considerations that fundamentally resembled those prevailing in human societies. The slaying of the primordial deity Tiamat and her confederates by younger gods symbolized the triumph of social values over older, natural ones. The deities descended from An were represented as reluctantly having accepted one of their number to be their king in order to ward off the threat of physical destruction posed by the primordial gods. The original motto of the new regime was 'safety and obedience', meaning 'security in return for obedience'. Following the destruction of the older gods, this motto was replaced by 'benefits and obedience', meaning 'prosperity in return for obedience'. After defeating the older deities, the new supreme god, Marduk, refashioned the universe in a manner that rendered it beneficial to his fellow deities while at the same time subjecting all that was in it to his personal domination. Yet, while the *Enuma Elish* implies that the deities agreed to adopt a centralized political regime for pragmatic, self-interested reasons, it does not suggest that doing this made all of them of one mind (Jacobsen 1976: 173–80). Whether the Mesopotamian gods were governed by a natural or a pragmatic political order, their relations were not characterized by an overarching moral order or even by a moral consensus.

In the early civilizations gods often fought with each other. In the Valley of Mexico, the four sons or emanations of Ometeotl struggled with each other to control the universe, with one of these gods and then another achieving supremacy and briefly presiding over a new cosmic order. Mexican gods also wounded and killed each other (Caso 1958). Huitzilopochtli decapitated his sister Coyolxauhqui when she tried to murder their mother, who had become pregnant out of wedlock (Matos Moctezuma 1988: 39–42). The Egyptian god Seth murdered his older brother Osiris to become king of Egypt and battled his nephew Horus to keep that position. Rebellious subjects, deities as well as humans, had driven the still earlier generations of Egyptian gods from the earth when these gods had grown old and feeble (Meeks and Favard-Meeks 1996: 23–33). In Mesopotamia the older gods had attempted to destroy the younger and more active generations of deities to silence the noise these gods were making. Erishkegal, the Mesopotamian female deity of the underworld, killed her sister Inanna, when Inanna attempted to usurp her realm (Jacobsen 1976: 55–57).

Deities also raped, seduced, and committed adultery with one another. The Egyptian god Osiris fathered the god Anubis by his brother Seth's wife, and Seth in a display of sexual dominance sodomized his young nephew Horus. The Mexican god Tezcatlipoca stole Xochiquetzal, the first wife of Tlaloc, the rain god (Caso 1958: 42). Both the Mesopotamian storm god Enlil and the fertility god Enki seduced and raped various goddesses (Jacobsen 1976: 104, 112–13).

In addition, gods deceived, robbed, and betrayed each other. According to one version of the Yoruba creation myth, when the god Orisala became too drunk to carry out Olorun's command to create the earth, the god Oduduwa stole the equipment Olorun had given Orisala to perform this task and carried out the work himself. This led to a fight between Oduduwa and Orisala in which various other deities took sides. Finally Olorun accorded Oduduwa the right to rule the earth but bestowed on Orisala the privilege of fashioning bodies for human babies (Bascom 1969: 10). The very existence of the Mesopotamian deities was threatened when a rebel deity stole their charm of supremacy (Oppenheim 1964: 269). The Egyptian goddess Isis created a poisonous snake and had it bite the sun god in order to force Re to tell her his secret name so that she could use it to cure him. Re's disclosing of his name constituted sharing his power with Isis (Meeks and Favard-Meeks 1996: 98–99). The Mesopotamian goddess Inanna, in a fit of anger after she discovered that her husband, the pastoral fertility god Dumuzi, had been carousing while she was trapped in the underworld, condemned him to be her replacement there. A major ecological disaster on earth was averted only when Dumuzi's sister, the vineyard deity Geshtinanna, agreed to alternate with her brother in the underworld for six months of every year (Jacobsen 1976: 26–71). During a visit to Eridu, Inanna stole various divine powers that were essential for the operation of the social order and carried them off to her own city, Uruk (114–15). The Maya Hero Twins used trickery and deceit to outwit and slay the gods of death and escape from the underworld. When the Mesopotamian god Enlil decided to destroy humanity for making too much noise, Enki, who disapproved of this policy, secretly warned a human family what was about to happen and advised them to build a large boat so that they might save themselves (120).

Deities were easily offended and capable of great severity in their dealings with human beings. The Inka god Wiraqucha called down fire upon people living near Cuzco who had hurled stones at him while he was travelling through the Andes (Rowe 1944: 316; Sullivan 1985), and the Egyptian sun god Re ordered the ferocious lion goddess Sakhmet (identified with his fiery eye) to devour humanity when their behaviour displeased him (Meeks and Favard-Meeks 1996: 26). While, in these examples, the gods relented before everyone involved was destroyed, their actions, like those of the forces of nature, killed and injured innocent and guilty people alike. Moreover, while gods might punish individuals, ethnic groups, or all humanity for immoral or disrespectful behaviour, they attacked them for more trivial reasons. Mesopotamian kings dreaded that some inadvertent mistake they made in performing rituals might result in tutelary deities' abandoning their city-states to their enemies. They were also apprehensive that deities would quarrel with each other, bringing undeserved misfortunes to their peoples (Postgate 1992: 263–69). Jacobsen (1976: 120) describes Mesopotamian gods as treating humans in a selfish, ruthless, and unsubtle manner.

While the deities of the early civilizations possessed human-like personalities, they often dealt with human beings in ways that seemed to be more inherent in the natural world they animated than part of the social realm. In many myths their behaviour was transparently that of natural forces: floods, storms, droughts, and volcanic eruptions afflicted humanity without warning. An attack launched by Enlil against a Mesopotamian city was described as the approach of a devastating thunderstorm (Pritchard 1955: 455–63). The complex hierarchies of deities presiding over different sectors of the universe also resembled the unequal but multiple and conflicting forces of nature to a greater extent than they did the political organization of even heterarchical city-states. Apart from the Mesopotamian gods, who at least in later times explicitly recognized the authority of a single leader, various groups of deities formed competing and often shifting factions. Even Mesopotamian deities continued to struggle for power within the general political framework they had established.

Paramount deities tended not to be the patron deities of states. Wiraqucha was not the patron god of the Inka, nor was Olorun the chief deity of any Yoruba city-state or Ometeotl the principal deity of any Mexican one. Powerful, active deities tended to be associated with kingdoms and rulers, while less powerful ones were associated with smaller communities, less prestigious descent groups, and individuals. The Inka kings recognized local deities as the gods of conquered peoples but attempted to integrate regional and local deities into a state pantheon by establishing asymmetrical kinship relations between these deities and leading Inka ones (Silverblatt 1988b). In a totally different fashion, in Egypt the deity of every provincial centre continued to be recognized as the creator of the universe, while the king claimed to be the earthly incarnation, son, and priest of each of these gods (Frankfort 1948: 41–42). The Shang rulers claimed a unique relation to the god Shangdi, and the worship of Shangdi may have been restricted to ancestral temples in royal palaces.

In Early Dynastic Mesopotamia, the chief executive of the gods was not An, the father of the gods, but his son Enlil, the patron deity of the neutral city-state of Nippur, who was later replaced by the Old Babylonian dynasty's patron deity, Marduk. Mesopotamian city-states were each presided over or owned by one or, in the case of Uruk, two high-ranking deities. In the Valley of Mexico each city-state especially honoured two gods, one of whom was its patron or protector. The Maya linked their cities to local versions of major deities from whom their royal families claimed descent. The chief ritual focus of a Yoruba city-state was the king, whose clan claimed descent from Oduduwa and other major deities.

Thus in some early civilizations either there was no paramount deity or that deity was not associated with any one state or dynastic lineage. City-states usually claimed a close association with one or more high-ranking deities, while the rulers of territorial states either forged special relations with the deities of the numerous localities they ruled or established the worship of a particular dynastic god as the focus of a state cult. The cult of that god could either be imposed on subject peoples or retained as a prerogative of the royal family. The resemblances between the organization of the gods and the loose hierarchical relations of natural forces appear to have been closer than those between the organization of the gods and that of the human political realm.

THE POWER OF THE GODS

Whereas in monotheistic religions, deities are believed to be eternal and all-powerful, the deities of early civilizations were born or created, died or were killed, and sometimes grew old or lost power to other deities. Caution is, of course, needed not to interpret these statements too literally. The Egyptians referred to creating cult statues as giving birth (*msi͗*) to the gods. Although the primary referent of msi͗ was to a woman giving birth, the Egyptians also used this verb to refer to creator gods' bringing the sun or anything else into existence by non-sexual means. The Maya also used the verb 'to give birth' (the upended frog glyph) to refer to acts that caused existing deities to manifest themselves in the human realm (Bassie-Sweet 1991: 152; Schele and Miller 1986: 183). The Egyptian gods who had ruled on earth at the beginning of time slowly grew old and feeble and eventually withdrew into the sky realm where they could rejuvenate themselves. The highland Mexicans and the Maya believed that the sun grew old and died each day and was rejuvenated each night in the underworld. After the Egyptian god Osiris (the elder Horus) was murdered, he remained confined to the underworld but was reborn on earth as his son Horus or as the sun god Re (Meeks and Favard-Meeks 1996: 32–33). Classic Maya deities were born on specific days, some of the most important close to but not precisely at the start of the most recent long-count cycle in 3114 B.C. These gods may have died and been reborn repeatedly at various points in the much longer cycles of Maya time (Schele and Miller 1986: 48).

The notion of cycles of death and renewal of the gods, which paralleled or were extrapolations of various natural cycles, affirmed rather than denied the collective power of the gods. Nevertheless, at least the peoples in the Valley of Mexico, the Maya, the Egyptians, and the Inka appear to have believed that at some time in the future the existing gods would perish and the cosmos would lapse into disorder, either to begin a new cycle of existence or to cease to exist forever. The Aztecs and their neighbours believed that if the sun god were not regularly nourished with human blood the universe would quickly dissolve into chaos.

Major Egyptian deities, instead of being all-powerful and self-reliant, were protected and served by retinues of supernatural guards and retainers. Because they shared power, no deity was omnipotent. Re suffered from severe pain and illness as a result of being bitten by a serpent. Even semi-transcendent deities such as Olorun or Ometeotl had to carry out their works through subordinate deities. The Inka observed that their solar god, the most powerful deity in the upper world, could not prevent himself from being covered by clouds, which, because of their connection with rain, were presumably associated with Wiraqucha, the principal deity of the lower realm (Cobo 1979: 134–35).

Gods could also be indecisive and cowardly. The Egyptian tribunal of deities that was charged with deciding whether Horus or Seth should rule Egypt was, like many a village court, unwilling to render a decision for fear of offending one of the contestants and his supporters (Lichtheim 1976: 214–23). At the most recent re-creation of the universe, a major Aztec god hesitated to sacrifice himself for the purpose, provoking a minor god to cast himself into the divine hearth in his place (León-Portilla 1963: 44–45; Townsend 1979: 53). Gods were also capable of short-sighted and injudicious behaviour that they later regretted. After the flood, the Mesopotamian gods who had ordered the destruction of humanity grew hungry and began to regret that there were no humans left to provide food for them (Pritchard 1955: 95).

Deities were also not omniscient. They cheated and deceived one another, and sometimes even humans outwitted them. The Mesopotamians believed that temporarily appointing a substitute to replace a king who had angered the gods would divert their anger to a socially insignificant victim (Bottéro 1992: 139–53). It was also widely believed that protective amulets and incantations could prevent deities from learning about displeasing things people had done or render them incapable of harming individuals. The Egyptians believed that, armed with the right spells, the dead could conceal from the gods knowledge of major wrongdoings they had committed during their lifetimes (Pinch 1994: 61–160).

Thus, while deities were believed to live longer and be more powerful than human beings and to affect their lives in crucial ways, people perceived far fewer differences between themselves and the gods than the adherents of modern monotheistic religions. Deities were not thought to be omniscient or omnipotent and were rarely believed to be changeless or eternal. As supernatural powers animating the natural world, they were caught up in cycles of growth and decay that often seemed unlikely to continue forever. While they possessed great powers, humans could use spells to deceive them, influence their behaviour, and appropriate their powers to a limited extent and for varying periods of time. The gods thus reflected human characteristics, which had been projected onto a natural order that humans found difficult to control and very threatening. The main precondition for this transposition of ideas from the social to the natural realm was recognizing the vast powers inherent in nature, the specific impacts these powers had on human beings, and the relative autonomy from one another of various sorts of natural forces.

RELIGION AND SOCIAL LIFE

The deities of early civilizations were viewed as supernatural beings who animated (or were) the natural world and therefore exerted great power over humans. Gods had mental faculties and gendered personalities that resembled those of human beings, but they could transform themselves, move rapidly about the earth, and pass between it and the realms above and below in ways that human beings could emulate only in dreams and trances.

In early civilizations as in earlier small-scale societies, the natural, supernatural, and social realms were not categorically distinguished. Nature was believed to be impregnated with supernatural powers that possessed human-like intelligence and motivations. This was not an analytical failure but reflected a particular ontological position. People living in early civilizations acted on the world technologically as far as they were able, but their technology, most crucially their agricultural and transport technology, was rudimentary, and they remained heavily dependent on the vagaries of the natural environment. When their technology was insufficient, they sought to control natural phenomena in the same way they tried to influence the behaviour of powerful human beings. In doing this, they applied to the natural realm what appears to have been humanity's oldest and most highly developed skill: understanding of social behaviour (Mithen 1996). It was, however, a skill that could appear effective only to people who believed that nature was controlled by forces that behaved more or less as humans did. Where technology did not suffice to control nature, people sought to make nature conform to their purposes as they would have done other people: by persuasion, magic, and spells. What they did not perceive was that the non-human world, both animate and inanimate, operated on fundamentally different principles. Major insights into this distinction were not achieved until the first millennium B.C. The religious beliefs of early civilizations were therefore products of a different set of analytical categories from those that scientists in modern societies use. They were not the results of a defective or 'primitive' intelligence or of an inability to understand causal relations.

The principal difference between the religious beliefs of early civilizations and those of still earlier, more egalitarian societies was that the various forces controlling nature had come to be viewed as more unequal in power and more hierarchized as human society itself had acquired these characteristics. Yet it was not believed that nature totally resembled states. In Mesopotamian society, at least by the Old Babylonian period, supernatural forces had sworn obedience to a single divine leader. In other early civilizations either there was no single supreme deity or such a deity was not concerned with dominating the others. This reflected a perception of the cosmos as composed of forces that, while unequal, were not arranged in a single, all-embracing hierarchy.

The views of the cosmos that prevailed in early civilizations call into question the suggestion that early civilizations were the first societies in human history to insulate themselves from the natural world (Renfrew 1972: 13). Because the divine was seen as manifesting itself in the natural world, people sought not to be separated from nature but rather to establish good relations with the supernatural powers inherent in nature that could help to ensure their well-being. Under these circumstances, a desire to be insulated from the natural world was inconceivable. People living in early civilizations not only felt less cut off from nature by a massive intervening technology than we do but actively sought to insert themselves, as individuals and societies, into the natural order which they believed was simultaneously a supernatural one.

As society expanded and kinship declined in importance as a factor unifying social life, religion replaced kinship as a source of concepts for analysing and discussing the social order. Myths concerning a supernaturally animated cosmos permitted a detailed analysis of ideas and strategies that could be used to promote, sustain, and change the sociocultural order as well as to criticize specific policies. Such religious understandings supported the political claims of the upper classes by identifying them with the organic powers of reproduction and the hierarchies that were believed to be inherent in a cosmic order that was simultaneously natural and divine (Bauer 1996: 327). Having interpreted nature in terms of familiar social categories, the leaders of early civilizations used the understanding they derived from this operation to justify the unequal social order they had created.

20 Cosmology and Cosmogony

In early civilizations ideas about the structure and origin of the universe were articulated in the form of myths or sacred narratives. Such an approach was inevitable given that the universe was believed to be animated and controlled by supernatural forces. Because of this, it is impossible to divorce the investigation of ancient cosmologies from the study of religious beliefs.

John Baines (1991b) has suggested that the ancient Egyptians did not record myths systematically because myths and dogmas were not as central to Egyptian religion as cults and rituals. Inadequate recording and preservation of myths are serious problems in the study of all early civilizations. Yet myths that are reasonably well recorded also tend to be highly variable. Within early civilizations, beliefs relating to the structure and creation of the universe varied from one period and from one state, city, cult centre, and family to another. Adherence to alternative versions reflected not only local traditions but also rivalries, factionalism, and resistance to centralization. Rationalized corpuses of mythology were developed for literary purposes only after myths had ceased to have major religious and political significance. Much of the seeming unity of modern versions of Greek and Roman myths is the product of harmonization that occurred during the Renaissance (Grant 1973). To compare concepts relating to cosmology and cosmogony in different early civilizations, it is necessary to focus not on the surface detail but on the basic structures of myths.

While the shape and size of the earth were first correctly approximated by the Greek astronomer, Eratosthenes of Cyrene, in the third century B.C., astronomical knowledge has expanded rapidly since the invention of the Galilean telescope in the seventeenth century A.D., creating a vast divergence between ancient and modern understandings. People in early civilizations believed both the earth and the cosmos to be very small by modern standards. Each early civilization was thought to be located at the centre of both the terrestrial plane and the universe and regarded as cosmologically privileged in its relations with the forces that had created the universe. The cosmography of early civilizations was not only anthropocentric but also ethnocentric (M. Wright 1995).

In city-state systems, every capital city claimed a privileged position in the cosmos. In the Valley of Mexico, however, by 1519 few people would have openly disputed the hegemonic city of Tenochtitlan's claim that it was the centre of the world (D. Carrasco 1987). In early Mesopotamia a privileged position was accorded to Nippur, a centrally located cult centre that avoided direct involvement in the wars that pitted other Mesopotamian city-states against one other (Postgate 1992: 33–34). The Yoruba believed Ife to be the place where the world was created, the world's first city, and their religious and cultural centre. The Maya seem to have recognized four major cities (*can caanal*, 'the four on high') as playing special roles in relation to the four quarters of their civilization. The four cities varied from one period and perhaps one city-state to another (Marcus 1993: 149–52).

Much of the research on the views that people in early civilizations had of the universe since the 1950s has been strongly influenced by the publications of Mircea Eliade (1954), a specialist on Siberian shamanism. Eliade maintains that all early humans sought to understand the workings of the supernatural in relation to an imagined primal event that inaugurated reality and determined humanity's situation in the cosmos. Early religious rituals attempted to realize the presence of the divine spirit (*numen*) by returning to a moment when time did not yet exist and experiencing the original act of creation. The most important and enduring representation of the sacred was an *axis mundi* in the form of a centrally located mountain or tree that connected the terrestrial world with supernatural realms located both above and below it. Around this central axis the world was laid out in four directions. Eliade argued that this cosmic plan influenced the location and layout of cities, temples, palaces, and houses, each of which was intended to be a microcosm of the universe. His concepts have been applied to the interpretation of Hindu temple plans and Chinese and Roman urban configurations (Wheatley 1971: 418). While vertical and quadripartite arrangements seem to recur frequently in conceptions of the earth and the universe in early civilizations, the widespread influence of Eliade's theories may have encouraged the interpretation of fragmentary data in ways that exaggerate the extent of cross-cultural uniformity of ideas relating to cosmology. His ideas may have become self-fulfilling.

While the notion of a central vertical axis was strongly marked in the Valley of Mexico and in Maya and Mesopotamian culture and seems to have been present in early China and among the Yoruba, it was not evident among the Inka or in ancient Egypt. Yet the symbolic importance that the Inka assigned to verticality, Egyptian preoccupation with the circumpolar region of the sky, and the ethnocentric belief that every early civilization was located at the centre of the universe can all too easily – and perhaps deceptively – be construed as referring to such a cosmic axis. Although it is often proposed that Chinese and Mesoamerican cosmological concepts were derived from a common set of shamanic beliefs of Siberian origin that were carried to the New World by the earliest Palaeo-Indian settlers, the resemblances between Chinese beliefs and those prevailing among the Indians of the southeastern United States seem to be more detailed than are those between Shang China and highland Mesoamerica. Both the Chinese and the Indians of the eastern United States believed that the underworld was a realm of raw life-forces while the sky world was one of more controlled, intellectual powers. Contrariwise, the people living in the Valley of Mexico viewed the underworld as a place of sterility, death, and disappearance (Allan 1991; B. Smith 1996: 311–16). The theory of Siberian origins also fails to account for the notable differences between Mexican and Peruvian cosmologies, which were presumably based on ideas brought to the New World at the same time. Much more systematic testing of the applicability of Eliade's ideas to hunter-gatherer and other prestate societies around the world is needed before they can be employed to infer the cosmological beliefs of early civilizations. In order to make my data base as independent as possible of Eliade's influence, I have sought to use information collected before as well as since the 1950s. This will help to test the general applicability of Eliade's ideas.

More specific conceptual problems beset the application of Eliade's views. Directionality usually refers to a quadripartite division of the earth's surface. Sometimes, however, it indicates the cardinal directions, as, for example, when the sloping entrance to an Old Kingdom Egyptian pyramid points due north and the pyramid's mortuary temple faces due east. In other instances, it refers to a quartering of the horizon, with the centre of each quarter facing one of the cardinal directions. Among some modern Maya, the words glossed as 'east' and 'west' actually refer to those segments of the horizon where the sun rises and sets in the course of a year, while those glossed 'north' and 'south' refer to the remaining portions of the horizon, where the sun never rises or sets (Watanabe 1983). It is probably more difficult to control for emic variation in the sphere of religious and cosmological beliefs than in any other sector of early civilizations.

The earth, the realm of living human beings, was generally conceptualized in early civilizations as a flat surface (rather than a globe or curving surface), square or circular in outline and only a few thousand kilometres across. It was assumed to be surrounded by the ocean, which at its outer extremity became one with the higher and lower supernatural realms. Above the earth was the realm of the sky, where deities generally associated with life and cosmic order dwelt. The sky realm was often supposed to be supported above the earth by gods, trees, or mountains located at the four corners of the world. Beneath the ground was another realm inhabited by supernatural powers. Sometimes that realm was associated with moisture and life, but more often it was associated with death, albeit a death from which new life might arise. The main points of communication between the upper, middle, and lower worlds were located at their common centre and four corners. Contact occurred at or through hills, sacred trees, caves, tombs, and temples. Within this generic conceptual framework, individual early civilizations elaborated distinctive versions of the cosmos.

The Aztec and their neighbours believed the earth (*cemanahuatl*) to be a disc or square surrounded by four petals or quadrants (*nauhcampa*) set in the midst of sea water that was charged with supernatural power (*teoatl*, *ilhuica-atl*) (D. Carrasco 1999: 104; López Austin 1988, 1: 58–60). The saline waters of Lake Texcoco were believed to be sea water rising up from under the ground (Durán 1971: 168), and their presence made Tenochtitlan, on an island in the middle of that lake, a microcosm of the whole earth. This connection with the sea was emphasized by the sea sand, seashells, and other marine fauna buried in caches in Tenochtitlan's main temple platform (Broda 1987: 99–100).

The terrestrial plane was divided into quadrants. The east was associated with the daily birth and the west with the daily demise of the sun, while the north was associated with the sun's right hand and the south with his left hand as he travelled west across the sky. The north, which was the source of cold, dry winds, tended, like the west, to be associated with death, while the more clement south and east were associated with life. The east was identified with maleness and the west with femaleness. Each of the four quadrants had its own emblematic colour, tree, bird, type of wind, deity, and supernatural powers. The colour symbolism that was associated with the quadrants and the centre was not, however, constant. In one commonly used system, east was associated with red, north with black, west with white, south with blue, and the centre with green (Caso 1958: 10; López Austin 1988, 1: 57). However, east was also associated with yellow, north with red or white, west with blue-green or black, south with white, and the centre with black or red (Aguilera 1989: 132; Berdan 1982: 123; D. Carrasco 1987: 140).

The people of the Valley of Mexico believed that there were thirteen sky levels above the earth, each inhabited by different deities. The lower levels were the realms of the moon, stars, sun, and comets. Above them were skies of various colours, while the top two levels constituted the realm of the creator god Ometeotl (Caso 1958: 64–65). Directly beneath the mountains, fertility deities lived in caves filled with rain-producing clouds, streams, trees, and vegetation. The most important of these paradises, located at the southern edge of the world, was Tlalocan, the home of the rain god Tlaloc. At the northern edge of the world, openings led to the nine levels of Mictlan, the underworld. Mictlan was a cold, dry, dangerous place where the souls of the dead descended from one level to another until those that survived the journey experienced personal extinction in the lowest. The underworld was ruled by Mictlantecuhtli and Mictlancihuatl (the Lord and Lady of the Underworld), who were counterparts of if not the same as Ometeotl (León-Portilla 1963: 109). Each night the dead or jaguar sun passed through the underworld, illuminating it before being reborn as the eagle or daytime sun (Caso 1958: 12–13). The Mexicans believed that at the four corners of the world cosmic energy, which provided rain, sunlight, and plant life, flowed up through caves from the fertile parts of the underworld and down from the skies and then travelled across the surface of the earth before returning to its source at the centre. For the Aztec, the centre was the main temple at Tenochtitlan, the most important and spiritually powerful building in their world (Broda 1987: 122; D. Carrasco 1990: 67; Caso 1958: 56–64; Matos Moctezuma 1988: 123–35).

Many Maya beliefs about the structure of the universe were derived from the same Mesoamerican sources as those in the Valley of Mexico. The Maya pictured a terrestrial world that consisted of a centre surrounded by four quadrants and a primordial sea. East and west were associated with the birth and death of the sun, north with the sky realm, and south with the underworld. There were thirteen sky realms above the terrestrial plane and nine underworlds beneath it. The underworld was a dark, watery (or underwater) locality with its own black water 'sky'. These realms were vertically separated by a cosmic tree located at the centre of the universe with its roots in the underworld and its crown in the sky. The Classic Maya often depicted the sky as a double-headed serpent, their words for 'snake' (*kan*) and 'sky' (*ka'an*) being near-homophones. The earth was pictured as a cayman or turtle resting in water or as a two-headed monster (*kawak*). Both the sky and the earth monster had one living head and one dead one.

The Maya assigned the colour red to the east, white to the north, black to the west, yellow to the south, and blue-green to the centre. Each quadrant had distinctive trees and gods that kept the earth and sky separated. The north, the principal direction from which rains came, was associated with life. Supernatural powers were able to pass from one level of the universe to another through mountains, caves, sinkholes, lakes, and oceans, as well as up and down the world tree and through the bodies of vision serpents that the upper classes conjured up by bleeding themselves and using hallucinogens. Temples were identified with the trees, hills, and caves which facilitated communication between the terrestrial and other realms. The Maya may have regarded the night sky as the underworld, which rotated so that it became visible to the terrestrial world after sunset. The sun rose as a young man from the underworld each day and grew old as he crossed the sky (Freidel and Schele 1988b; Reents-Budet 1998: 78–79; Schele and Miller 1986: 42–47; Sharer 1996: 153–57). The Maya associated the underworld with death and decay, which were a source of fertility and regeneration. The elderly Lords of Death ruled a malodorous realm of rot and disease but one from which major deities and the souls of resourceful rulers were able to escape, at least temporarily, by transforming themselves into the sun, moon, and planets (Schele and Miller 1986: 42, 54).

The Shang and Western Zhou may have conceptualized the terrestrial plane as a square with a square spirit world adjacent to each side. Each spirit world was the home of a different wind and rain, and all of these were surrounded by the ocean (Allan 1991: 75, 173). The Shang viewed the terrestrial plane as constituting a central area (*zhong shang*) surrounded by four lands (*si tu*) named for the cardinal directions. David Keightley (2000) suggests that the east-west axis, associated with the sun, may have been regarded as the paramount one and east as the principal point of the compass. North was the direction of cold and the dead and south the direction of warmth and the living. The Shang viewed themselves as occupying the centre of the earth and surrounded on all four sides by barbarians. In Zhou times these peoples were identified generically as the Rong to the west, the Di to the north, the Yi to the east, and the Man to the south. The Rong and the Di were nomadic peoples (Creel 1970: 197–212). Above the square of the earth was a circular sky world, perhaps composed of nine levels, and below the earth were the Yellow Springs, a moist underworld, perhaps also with nine levels (Allan 1991: 30). This triple-level universe was also conceptualized as a turtle, its upper shell the sky world and its plastron the terrestrial world, swimming in a cosmic sea (104). At the centre of this universe grew the *gianmu*, or fixed mulberry tree, which had nine branches in the sky world and nine roots in the underworld. Shang royal capitals were described as the pole (*ji*), or centre, of the four quarters (76).

The early Chinese appear to have distinguished between celestial spirits, including Shangdi and the royal ancestors, who collectively may have embodied the spirit force (shen) that shaped and ordered the universe, and underworld deities who embodied the primal energies (qi, *feng*), associated with winds and sexual arousal, that animated the cosmos (Lewis 1990: 213–15). It has been suggested that the later culture hero Huangdi (the Yellow Emperor) was originally the ruler of the underworld and hence the underworld counterpart of Shangdi. While the celestial realm was associated with birds, the underworld was associated with dragons (Allan 1991: 65–66, 170). Ten suns were distinguished, each equated with one of the ten sequential days of the Shang ritual calendar. A close association was established between these suns and deceased Shang rulers, each posthumously named after one of the ten days. Every day nine suns, perhaps in the form of birds, stayed in the underworld while the remaining one travelled across the sky. The sun rose from the ocean and ascended into the sky by means of the cosmic mulberry tree before once again plunging into the sea and the underworld (Allan 1991: 50, 172–83; Granet 1958 [1930]: 203; Keightley 2000).

The Mesopotamians imagined the visible universe to consist of two parts, the curved vault of the sky (*an*) and the flat disc of the earth (*ki*), which long ago had been forced apart by the air (*lil*) (Huot 1989: 73). In some early myths these two units had grown through the accumulation of primeval silts; in others they were the body of Tiamat, a primeval cosmic deity that had been torn in two. The surface of the earth had been shaped by the gods, who had dug river channels and raised mountains prior to creating human beings. Southern Mesopotamia was thought to be located at the centre of the terrestrial plane and hence to be the place that had the most effective contact with the gods. It appears to have been assigned to the southern quadrant (*ubda*) of the world, the other quadrants containing Shubur and Hamazi to the east, Martu, the Amorite country, to the west, and Uri to the north (Kramer 1963: 284–85). Above the earth were the air and the sky world, where the major cosmic deities lived. The earth rested on sweet water (*apsu*), which in turn overlay and was surrounded by the heavier salt water of the ocean (*tamtu*).

Beneath the earth was a cavernous underworld (*eretsu*): a dry, dark place containing the city of the dead, which was surrounded by seven walls. Here lived the gods of the underworld, the spirits of disease, and the souls of the dead. The sun travelled through the underworld from west to east each night, briefly bringing light to various parts of it. The moon visited the underworld once a month at new moon to judge the dead. Various deities associated with crops, animal care, and fertility also lived part of each year on earth but had to spend the rest of it in the underworld. Beneath the underworld, a countersky was sometimes envisioned (Bottéro 1992: 273–74; Jacobsen 1976: 168–79). According to some Babylonian cosmologies, there were three sky realms above the earth inhabited by different groups of deities. These combined with the earth, the sweet water, and the realm of the dead to form a six-layered universe (Lambert 1975: 58–60). Beyond the ordered universe was a limitless celestial ocean.

The Inka distinguished an upper or sky world (*hanan pacha*) ruled by the sun and associated with sovereignty, the surface of the terrestrial world (*cay pacha*), which was the abode of living human beings, and a lower realm (*hurin* or *ucu pacha*) composed of the sea and what lay beneath the earth. This lower realm was associated with night and the creator god Wiraqucha. The Inka also thought of the Andean highlands as constituting an upper (*hanan*) moiety, associated with the sky world, and of the coastal plain as constituting a lower (*hurin*) moiety, associated with the sea and fertility (Classen 1993: 31–33; MacCormack 1991: 310).

Cuzco was venerated as the centre of the terrestrial world and the major focus of spiritual power in the Inka kingdom. In the region surrounding it more than three hundred wakas were located along forty-one or forty-two *ceques* (*siqi*), or lines of spiritual force, that radiated from the Qorikancha, the main temple of the sun. Different social groups were responsible for maintaining each of these wakas (Bauer 1998; Cobo 1990: 51–84; I. Farrington 1992; Zuidema 1964). The Cuzco area in turn was surrounded by four divisions (*suyu*) that extended to the frontiers of the Inka kingdom, which was called *tawantinsuyu* (land of the four parts). These quarters not only constituted the largest administrative districts of the Inka state but also were associated with different ecological zones: the northwest (*chinchasuyu*) with the northern highlands, the southwest (*cuntisuyu*) with the Pacific coast, the southeast (*collasuyu*) with the Lake Titicaca area and the Atacama Desert, and the northeast (*antisuyu*) with the Amazonian tropical forest (Kendall 1973: 54). The Inka's two ritual directions were east and west; there were no Quechua words for north or south (Rowe 1944: 300).

The Inka believed the cosmos to be a combination of two sets of reciprocal forces in a creative equilibrium. The first set was characterized by structure, maleness, light, clarity, dryness, rock or earth, fertility, and right-handedness and the second by fluidity, femaleness, darkness, obscurity, moisture, water, fecundity, and left-handedness. Yet water, which was generally conceptualized as female, was also viewed as semen and hence male, while soil, which was impregnated by water, was often regarded as female. The moon, which was always female, was associated with the male sky realm (Classen 1993). Reproduction was a process brought about by water's combining with dry, stable, and enduring earth or rock. High altitudes, including mountain peaks and the sky, were associated with maleness and low-lying regions, including fertile mountain valleys, with femaleness. Life was thought to be sustained by water rising through underground channels from the Pacific Ocean to the highlands, from where it flowed over the earth in the form of rivers back to its source, or, alternatively, transported to the highlands by a celestial llama or the Milky Way and released there as rain. The movement of water into the highlands maintained the equilibrium of the cosmic order by preventing the ocean from rising ever higher and flooding the whole earth. The sun was believed to rise out of Lake Titicaca and sink into the Pacific Ocean, from where it too made its way back into the highlands through underground channels. The Inka viewed death as the separation of the dry and wet aspects of living creatures. While the moist life-force returned to lakes and rivers and finally to the ocean, the dry forces shaping life survived as wakas and mallquis, the dried remains of living things, which were connected with the world inside the earth (Classen 1993: 11–25; Gose 1993: 494–502; Salomon 1991: 15–16; Sherbondy 1992).

The Egyptians viewed the universe as a region of light, life, and ordered activity that had been created and was sustained within Nun (*nw*, *nnw*), a limitless ocean of dark, inert, undifferentiated, and lifeless water that was alien and unknown even to the gods. The earth (t3) was pictured as a flat surface or the upturned, reclining body of the earth god Geb and the sky (pt) as a flat plate made of bronze or meteoric iron held up by four deities or the downward-facing body of the sky goddess, Nut, who was variously pictured as a woman arched over the earth or a cow standing above it. Geb and Nut were separated by their son Shu, who represented air or sunlight. Beneath the earth was the underworld (*dw3t*), which consisted of caverns that extended from the western horizon back to the eastern one. Alternatively, the underworld was identified with the dark sky that extended below the horizon. Below the underworld stretched the feminine portion or counterpart of Nun (*nnwt*) (J. Allen 1988: 3–7).

The Egyptians conceived of the universe as being organized along two main axes: an east-west solar axis and a north-south Nile one. The sun god was believed to grow old as he travelled across the sky each day. In the evening he was swallowed by Nut and rejuvenated as he passed through her body to be reborn the next morning in the east. Alternatively, the sun sank into the underworld and travelled east through it, defeating the forces of disorder and being rejuvenated as he did so, before rising victorious from the eastern horizon the next morning. The Nile River's life-giving waters were believed to well up from the primeval waters in the vicinity of the cataracts and flow north until they reentered the primeval ocean when they reached the Mediterranean Sea. Through endless repetitions of cycles, the sun and the Nile River renewed themselves and provided the necessities of life for the Egyptians.

The east and south were regions that symbolized life and rebirth, while the west and north symbolized both death and the possibility of survival after death. This survival was associated with the Field of Reeds (*sḫt i͗3rw*), a fertile realm of the god Osiris located near the setting place of the sun, and the Field of Offerings (*sḫt ḥtp*), which was associated with the northern circumpolar stars. The Egyptians interpreted the ecliptic (*ḫ*3-channel, 'winding channel') as a river in the sky along which the sun, moon, and planets travelled in their boats. At least in later times, this river was also believed to provide water in the form of rain to foreign lands. Other Egyptologists have associated the Field of Reeds and the Field of Offerings with the portions of the sky located south and north of the ecliptic (Goebs 1998: 10–11).

While the cosmos continued to sustain and renew itself, it constantly had to resist the forces of primeval inertia and disorder (ỉsft) which assailed the gods and threatened the terrestrial realm in the form of deserts, sandstorms, low Niles, rainstorms, night-time, weak rulers, and death. Every night the serpent that personified disorder sought to destroy the weakened sun, every year drought attempted to overwhelm the fertility of the Nile Valley, and over time kings grew older and less competent to rule. The efforts of the solar creator god to renew himself and ensure his eternal youth maintained the delicate balance between the order of the universe and the disorder of the primeval ocean that the creator god had established at the time of creation (*sp tpy*) (Meeks and Favard-Meeks 1996: 197–98).

The Yoruba compared the realm of the gods, or the upper spirit world (*orun*), and the earth to the two halves of a calabash, with the sky set over an earth that was concave downwards. The earth in turn was surrounded by the ocean (Ojo 1966a: 196). The sky was associated with Ifa, the god of certainty and balance, who alone knew the will of the creator god Olorun, and the earth with Esu, the god of uncertainty and disorder (R. Armstrong 1981: 75–76). Yoruba deities climbed up and down between the upper spirit world and the earth along iron chains that hung from the sky or, like the winds, passed between the two realms at the gates of the earth, which were located at the four cardinal directions. The sun, moon, and Venus, the only star that the Yoruba identified individually, all travelled some distance below the dome of the sky. The sun was believed to recross the sky from west to east at midnight (Ojo 1966a: 196–200). The people of Benin drew a similar distinction between the spirit world (*eriui*) and the visible world (*agbo*). The path between these worlds ran through or across the ocean, which surrounded the visible world and was the source of its fertility (Bradbury 1957: 52–54).

Like the Aztec, the Yoruba divided the surface of the earth into four segments, which were identified in relation to the motion of the sun: sunrise, sunset, and the areas to the right and left of the sun as it passed across the sky each day. The east-west axis was regarded as the primary one, the north-south axis as secondary. Noon and midnight, when the sun traversed the zenith, were both regarded as times of special importance and concern. The Yoruba did not venerate the sun, and, while women prayed to the moon for children, they offered no sacrifices to it (Ojo 1966a: 174, 198). Each city ideally had gates that faced the four quarters. In the centre of a town or by each of its gates was a mound dedicated to the four-headed god Olori Merin. Babies were sacrificed to these mounds every three months (Lucas 1948: 166; Ojo 1966a: 200). Yoruba divination correlated specific deities and coloured substances with particular directions. The east was associated with the trickster deity Esu and with sulfur, the north with Ogun, the god of iron, and with redwood, the west with Sango, the god of lightning, and with charcoal, and the south with the creator god Orisala and with chalk. In Ilesa, a special annual cycle of sacrifices was made to Esu in June, Ogun in September, Sango in December, and Orisala in March (Frobenius 1913, 1: 254–59). The Yoruba area was thought to be composed of four parts, each divided into four kingdoms. These were the sixteen kingdoms that had been assigned to the immediate male descendants of Oduduwa, the god who created the world (Ojo 1966a: 200).

The cosmological models propounded by the early civilizations have striking similarities. Those between the Egyptian and the Mesopotamian model may reflect shared beliefs with a single origin somewhere in the Middle East. Those among the various Mesoamerican models have obvious historical connections, although the timing of the development and spread of many religious beliefs remains uncertain. The similarities between Mesoamerican and Chinese cosmologies have tentatively been attributed to shared connections with Siberian shamanism. These particular explanations do not, however, account for the worldwide distribution of many traits. The shared features at least partly reflect the way in which people living in early civilizations would have interpreted the natural world that was familiar to them in the light of their belief that such a world was sustained and animated by supernatural powers. As Alan Sokal and Jean Bricmont (1998: 183 n. 255) observe, 'All beliefs, even mythical ones, are constrained, at least in part, by the phenomena to which they refer'. The best-informed individuals in early civilizations knew about lands many hundreds of kilometres from their own but had no detailed information about regions that were more than a few thousand kilometres away. They tended to think of the terrestrial world as being a relatively flat plane only a few thousand kilometres across. All early civilizations were located close to seas or oceans; therefore it was inferred that salt water encircled the whole earth. Above the terrestrial plane was the sky, which was filled with moving, hence living, celestial bodies. Most cosmographies posited some form of counterpart of the sky located under the earth. Especially in civilizations that interred the dead, this underworld was equated with death and decay and populated with the deities, spirits, and souls of the dead. Because the surface of the earth provided food for humans, it was often concluded that the underworld was a place of regeneration, where death gave rise to new life. The Yoruba's dual division of the cosmos into a purely supernatural sky realm and a terrestrial realm appears to be an exception to this tri-level scheme, but they acknowledged a third cosmically significant level: the sea. Their view of the universe appears to have been more analogous to the Chinese image of the sky and earth as equivalent to the carapace and plastron of a turtle floating on a cosmic sea. The Maya and Aztec viewed the earth as a saurian monster floating on a primordial ocean.

The peopling of the cosmos with deities who animated (or were) the natural world and supplied it with order, light, moisture, fertility, and well-being accords with notions about the fundamental nature of the supernatural shared by the people living in these civilizations. The adverse manner in which natural forces often affected humans also encouraged the belief that the deities who controlled nature were not primarily concerned with human welfare and might under certain circumstances seek to harm human beings.

The belief that spirits and supernatural forces moved from one level of the cosmos to another encouraged symbolic elaboration. The widespread idea that the sun returned from west to east either below the earth or above the sky accorded with a widely shared belief that both earth and sky were opaque bodies that would render such movements invisible. It is also not surprising that an east-west axis, which corresponds to the visible movement of the sun, was generally privileged over a north-south axis. By contrast, the Andean emphasis on the symbolic meaning of verticality in the terrestrial world and the Maya portrayal of the underworld as a place of rank decay, as opposed to the Aztec, Mesopotamian, and Egyptian views of it as a dry, etiolated realm, reflected major differences in the specific ecological settings in which such views were formulated.

It is more difficult to explain the widespread notion of a vertical central axis and quadripartition among the early civilizations. These concepts appear to have been present in many small-scale societies and ultimately may have been grounded in the coordinates that any upright primate would have required to monitor the natural environment. The human body itself would have suggested a vertical axis, while, given the limited range of clear vision, scanning in four directions (front, back, and to each side) would have been necessary to secure the visual coverage required to detect game, as well as animal predators and other dangers. Out of these perceptual foundations may have evolved the tendencies found in early and later preindustrial civilizations to draw complex analogies between the human body and the cosmos (Classen 1993; López Austin 1988).

Without minimizing significant variations in cosmography from one early civilization to another, many similarities can be attributed to parallel analyses of the natural world by people who viewed the universe from generally similar perspectives, including similar views of the supernatural. Such an explanation also helps to account for the greater similarity of views about the terrestrial plane, which were controlled to a greater degree by direct observation, than of ideas concerning the sky world or the underworld. This conclusion accords with the materialist belief that observations of the natural world play a significant role in the development of some religious concepts (J. Furst 1995: 174).

COSMOGONY

All early civilizations sought to understand when and how the universe had come into being and how long it might last. Since it was believed to be animated by supernatural powers, these questions were studied mythologically. Because people in early civilizations saw themselves as following collective patterns of behaviour that the gods had established when they created the world, cosmogonic speculations were intimately concerned with society as well as the natural world.

The people of the Valley of Mexico believed that the whole of creation had evolved from Ometeotl, the bisexual deity living beyond the skies who represented the source of everything that ever was or ever would be in the universe. Ometeotl combined maleness and femaleness, day and night, and all the other complementary and contradictory qualities that made up the universe. At the time of creation, when darkness still prevailed, Ometeotl channelled energy (sometimes specified as fire) to produce four male deities who constructed the temporal and spatial framework of the universe. These were the Red Tezcatlipoca (the agricultural fertility god Xipe Totec) of the east, the Black Tezcatlipoca (Tezcatlipoca, the god of kingship, who could see all) of the north, the White Tezcatlipoca (Quetzalcoatl) of the west, and the Blue Tezcatlipoca of the south, with whom the Aztec identified their patron deity Huitzilopochtli. Huehueteotl, the Old God, or Xiuhtecuhtli, the Old Fire God, identified with Ometeotl, presided over the central axis of the universe. The four Tezcatlipocas created the calendar, the upper sky worlds, the earth, the ocean, the realms of the dead, the other deities, and the heavenly bodies (Heyden 1989: 38–39; León-Portilla 1963: 33–34). In some myths they split in two a female cayman or earth monster floating on the primeval sea in order to create from her body the earth and the sky (Clendinnen 1991: 177).

The sky world and the underworld remained stable, but the terrestrial level was periodically subject to violent transformations (Clendinnen 1991: 222). There had been four successive ages, each lasting from six to thirteen fifty-two-year calendar cycles, during which a different Tezcatlipoca constituted the dominant cosmic force. Each successive age was associated with a different element: earth, wind, fire, and water. Each age was better organized than the one before, but at the end of each the sun of that era failed, a violent cataclysm disrupted the world order, and the human creatures of that period either perished or were turned into animals (León-Portilla 1992: 4). At the beginning of the present era, in A.D. 883, the gods assembled at the ruins of Teotihuacan to raise the sky, which had fallen to earth at the end of the previous era, and renew the earth for a fourth time. Here the god Nanahuatzin immolated himself to become the fifth and apparently final sun, and one by one the other gods hurled themselves into the cosmic fire, where they were consumed, to ensure that the new sun had sufficient life-force to move across the sky. As a consequence of this action the cosmos and the gods were renewed (León-Portilla 1963: 33–48).

The Aztec and neighbouring peoples believed that the new era, identified as that of their patron god, Huitzilopochtli, would come to an end at the termination of one of their fifty-two-year calendar rounds. The world would be destroyed by earthquakes, and supernatural monsters would kill all human beings. It is unclear whether this era was thought likely to be of as short duration as previous ones or whether, because of the superior harmonization of space and time that had been achieved when it was created, it could be expected to last longer. The Aztec believed that by nourishing the sun with human blood the duration of this cosmic order could be extended (Caso 1958: 93–94; León-Portilla 1963: 54–61).

Unlike the Aztec, whose longest year count covered only one fifty-two-year cycle, the Maya had a calendar that used multiples of twenty-year cycles to stretch the counting of days backward and forward over immensely long periods. The Maya equated various cyclical configurations of their calendar with particular controlling deities and believed that the coincidence of the same supernatural forces at different points in time caused human history to repeat itself. In the sixteenth century they believed that their era had begun in 3114 B.C. and would come to an end in A.D. 2012 and that the world had been destroyed, and the sky again raised and the terrestrial realm re-created, at least three times since the beginning of the universe (Schele and Miller 1986: 16).

Both the Classic and the historical Maya thought that the gods brought the universe into being at a cosmic hearth that they identified with the three brightest stars of the constellation Orion. Yet there is growing evidence that the idea of relatively rapid cycles of cosmic creation and destruction may have been introduced to the Maya from central Mexico after the Classic period. While several major Classic-period deities were born or reborn shortly before or after 3114 B.C., there is no indication that that particular year marked the beginning of a new creation for the Classic Maya (Bassie-Sweet 1991: 251). Classic Maya inscriptions referring to anniversaries of royal successions that would occur as late as A.D. 4772 have been interpreted as evidence that the Classic Maya likewise did not believe the present world order would come to an end in A.D. 2012 (Reents-Budet 1998: 78; Schele and Mathews 1998: 106–7, 341).

Such findings call into question significant beliefs that have been attributed to the Classic Maya concerning the creation and history of the world. It has been suggested that they viewed creation as a never-ending pattern of birth, death, and rebirth involving the sowing of cosmic seeds that became celestial bodies, plants, trees, humans, and the dead living in the underworld (D. Carrasco 1990: 100–101). Yet they appear to have believed that the fates of deities and of human individuals and collectivities were predictable from arrays of cosmic forces and planetary motions that could be linked to particular calendrical cycles. They also may have believed that individual gods and other beings had predetermined beginnings and endings that recurred as a result of similar alignments of cosmic forces. Adopting this interpretation creates far greater differences between Aztec and Classic Maya beliefs about cosmological history than were formerly envisaged.

The surviving fragments of Sumerian myths suggest that in the beginning, the wind and storm god, Enlil, separated the sky and the earth, while the god Enki, noted for his cleverness, organized the world much like a large estate. He arranged the land, mountains, marshes, and seas, each with their own deities, put gods in charge of agricultural production, and appointed Utu, the sun god, to look after boundaries. Prior to the creation of human beings, the igigi, a lower order of deities, had to labour to produce food for all the gods. In the course of this labour they dug out the beds of the Euphrates and Tigris Rivers (Bottéro 1992: 222; Jacobsen 1976: 85).

In the later, more detailed, Babylonian creation narrative, *Enuma Elish*, the universe began with a watery waste in which the female salt water, Tiamat, and the male fresh water, Apsu, were commingled. These two engendered silt, which in turn gave rise to time, the horizon, and heaven (an) and earth (ki), the latter probably in the form of two conjoined discs. The god An mated with various goddesses who gave birth to the historical pantheon of deities that controlled the sky, air, earth, sea, and underworld. By impregnating Ki, An gave rise to vegetation. In alternative versions An, the sky, was described as both male (Anum) and female (Antum) and as constituting a married couple who became the ancestors of the gods (Jacobsen 1976: 95, 167–69). The creation of the various generations of gods was followed by a series of conflicts between Apsu and Tiamat, on the one hand, and the younger gods, on the other, in the course of which the older gods were killed in battle and Enki's son, Marduk, was recognized first as the champion of the younger gods and then as their king. Marduk cut Tiamat's body in two and used it to (re-?)create the sky and earth. Next he reorganized the cosmos, created human beings, and assigned administrative tasks to each of the gods. In each of these narratives, creation and cosmic change were accomplished by divine utterances, the same means by which kings and officials commanded things to be done in the human sphere (Jacobsen 1976: 170–88; Kramer 1963: 115).

The cosmic order created by the god An and his descendants was transmitted to the people of Mesopotamia as a model for their society in the form of over one hundred supernatural enabling powers (*mes*) that directed both the operation of the universe and orderly social life among human beings, taking the form of rules, institutions, actions, and symbols (Kramer 1963: 166; Maisels 1990: 281; 1999: 173). The Mesopotamians asserted that royal rule lasted for 241,200 years from the time when it descended from the sky world until the flood, after which the human life-span was shortened to its current length. The first dynasty after the flood, that of the city of Kish, lasted for 24,510 years. After that dynasty, recorded history began (Huot 1989: 231).

It is unclear to what extent the Mesopotamians considered the earth and the universe perishable. Their endurance and the lives of the gods themselves appear to have depended upon the gods' carefully guarding the sources of their power (Oppenheim 1964: 269). The Mesopotamians believed that the gods decreed the fates of individual humans and city-states at an assembly held annually in the temple of Enlil in Nippur, over which the god An presided (Jacobsen 1976: 188). If a tutelary deity abandoned his or her city or his or her support was overruled by the other gods, that city would be destroyed by its enemies. Such a catastrophe could be averted, if at all, only by a pious ruler who was able to divine the wishes of the gods and knew how to placate them. The constant threats that Mesopotamians faced as a result of natural catastrophes, intercity warfare, and foreign invasions were reflected in their pessimistic view of the way in which the gods managed the universe.

The Yoruba believed that in the beginning the earth was a primeval sea or marsh and Olorun and the other deities lived in the sky world. According to accounts that were associated with different city-states, the creation of the terrestrial world was carried out, on Olorun's orders, either by Orisala or by Oduduwa, who descended from the sky world for that purpose. Oduduwa reached the ground at the place where his sacred grove was later located at Ife. He brought with him a supernatural chicken that had been supplied by Olorun, and this chicken created the earth by scratching up soil from the bottom of the swamp. Oduduwa became the first ruler of Ife, and his immediate descendants established the first sixteen Yoruba monarchies (Bascom 1969: 10; Awolalu 1979: 12–13).

There is no indication that the Yoruba believed either the gods or the natural order to be threatened with destruction. While Olorun determined the destinies of individual humans and deities could harm as well as assist people, communities, and the natural world, deities did not periodically determine the fate of city-states, as Mesopotamians believed their gods did. Because they were ruled by descendants of Oduduwa, Yoruba states were expressions of the cosmic order. Through divination and worship, the Yoruba sought to minimize supernatural disruptions in both the natural and the political realm.

The best-documented cosmogonies of a territorial state are the ancient Egyptian ones. The Egyptians referred to the creation of the universe as 'the time of Re' (*rk r*ʿ) or 'the time of the gods' (*rk nṯrw*) (J. Allen 2000: 126). The universe had begun as the result of movement or life stirring within the cosmic sea of non-existence. While each major cult centre had its own creation myth, all of them agreed that a primeval deity or deities had produced the gods and in the course of doing so had ordered the universe and all that inhabited it. In Heliopolis this creator was identified as the sun god Atum (finisher), who shaped the universe after he appeared upon a mound (*st wrt*, 'great seat/place') that had emerged in the primeval sea and slain or repelled the serpent of non-order. A bisexual though physically male-appearing deity, Atum masturbated and then combined his own semen and spittle to create the god Shu (sunlight) and the goddess Tefnut (moisture), who was also identified as the goddess Ma ʿet (cosmic order). They in turn engendered the earth god, Geb, and the sky goddess, Nut, whose four children were Osiris (or Horus the Elder) and Seth and their sister-wives Isis and Nephthys. Osiris represented the fertility of the Nile Valley, Seth the sterility of the desert. The first generations of male gods (Atum, Shu, Geb) successively ruled on earth for a long time, but eventually, as each of them grew older and less able to manage things, disorders broke out which the younger gods had to quell. At that point each older god ascended to the sky world, where he was able to renew his youthful vigour by passing, like the sun, through cosmic cycles of death and rebirth. Osiris's murder by his brother Seth was the first death among the major gods, although not necessarily the first death in the terrestrial sphere. Following a brief revival on earth, Osiris was consigned to the eternal changelessness of the realms of the dead. At the same time he was reborn as his posthumously conceived son, Horus the Younger. Thus the two forms of survival, through endless renewal (nḥḥ) and total changelessness (ḏt), associated with mummification and dryness, were established. With the eventual accession to the throne of Egypt of Osiris's son Horus, modern conditions were achieved. One king after another aged, died, and became identified with the god Osiris while leaving behind a son or incarnation to rule over the whole terrestrial world (J. Allen 2000: 143–45; Meeks and Favard-Meeks 1996: 13–32).

In an alternative Memphite version of creation, that city's creator god, Ptah, who was equated with the primeval mound, brought the other gods, including the sun, into existence and created the universe and social order by formulating concepts in his heart and making them realities by means of his divine utterances (*ḥw*) (J. Allen 2000: 171–73; Lichtheim 1973: 54–55). At Hermopolis the sun was caused to emerge from the primeval waters by four pairs of male and female deities who represented various attributes of nonexistence: inertness, formlessness, darkness, and hiddenness (J. Allen 2000: 126–27).

The Egyptians believed that the universe was constantly threatened by the forces of cosmic disorder, but they were confident that, so long as the proper rituals were performed, it was likely to endure for millions of years. The renewal of the universe was essential to protect not only life on earth but also the gods from the ravages of time. Ultimately, they believed, the universe would come to an end and merge into the creator god, who in turn would be absorbed into the primeval waters (Hornung 1982: 163).

In the ethnically and socially diverse Andean highlands, many different creation myths appear to have coexisted. Branches of the Inka royal family maintained that either one or many Wiraquchas or the lowland deity Pachakamaq had created the universe (MacCormack 1991: 350–51). Wiraqucha, who seems to have been eternal, was associated with the sea, which was viewed as the ultimate source of a major ingredient of life. When Wiraqucha first created the earth and sky, all remained dark. At that time he created stone giants whom he decided not to bring to life. Then he created smaller humans, later to turn some of them back into stones and drown the rest in a great flood. Finally, at Lake Titicaca, he created the sun, moon, and stars. The sun, which was associated with the sky, fire, light, and mountains, was the opposite of Wiraqucha, who represented earth, water, darkness, the coast, and the sea. Both were viewed as essential to support crops and animal life. In some traditions, Wiraqucha was the father and mother of the sun and moon, who produced the morning and evening stars and they in turn Lord Earth (Camac Pacha) or Mother Earth (Pacha Mama) and Lady Ocean (Mama Cocha) (Classen 1993: 19–25). Wiraqucha also reshaped the landscape and provided it with everything that humans would need to survive. When creation was finished, Wiraqucha and two assistants made their way from Lake Titicaca north to Ecuador, where they disappeared into the Pacific Ocean (Demarest 1981; Gose 1993: 490–91; Kendall 1973: 182–89; Rowe 1944: 315–16; 1960; Sullivan 1985).

The Spanish recorded that the Inka believed that the cosmic order periodically disintegrated or was overturned. According to one variant of these myths, five successive worlds had been created, each one lasting between eight hundred and twenty-eight hundred years. Every creation had its own sun, and successive creations were separated by major episodes that were called *pachakuti* (world reversals or earthquakes). According to another version, each sun lasted one thousand years and significant changes occurred every five hundred years, the rulers at such times being called Pachakutiq. The Inka Pachakutiq was said to be the ninth ruler of that name, and his reign was asserted to have marked the beginning of the fifth world (Kendall 1973: 201; Zuidema 1964: 219–34). The upheavals separating different epochs might be cosmologically traumatic. Sometimes the terrestrial world was flooded when water ceased to be drawn from the ocean into the highlands; sometimes the surface of the earth was turned over and the realms of the living and the dead were reversed. The rapid expansion of the Inka state was another kind of upheaval. It has been suggested, however, that all these myths may have resulted from Spanish scholars' inadvertently superimposing European or Mexican concepts on poorly understood Andean myths (Zuidema 1992: 39; Duviols 1989). Thomas Zuidema (1964: 219–20) argues that in Peru the various worlds or cosmic periods existed both simultaneously and consecutively. We must therefore interpret this material with extreme caution. There is no evidence concerning what the Inka believed would be the ultimate fate of creation.

In early civilizations there was much more variation in speculation about the age of the universe, how it was created, and how it might end than there was about the structure of the universe. This is scarcely surprising, since much less empirical evidence was available to constrain thinking about these historical issues. It is often assumed that in most ancient cosmogonies an initial period in which there were no gods or only one was followed by an age in which multiple deities emerged and created the basic structure of the universe and then by the present era, in which human beings live on earth (Meeks and Favard-Meeks 1996; M. Wright 1995). This scheme does not do justice to the complexity of the cosmogonies associated with early civilizations.

While each early civilization evolved its own general narrative about the creation of the universe, there was considerable variation in these accounts within both city-state systems and territorial states. In city-state systems much of this variation was from one city-state to another, each state having its own learned elite and its own traditions. In territorial states regional variation reflected the limited control that central governments exerted over intellectual life in large kingdoms. In all early civilizations, variations were associated with political factions within the upper class.

The Aztec, Yoruba, and Inka appear to have regarded deities such as Ometeotl, Olorun, and Wiraqucha as uncreated. The Egyptians and Mesopotamians believed that the universe had evolved out of some sort of watery, motionless, limitless, and eternal uniformity. The Mesopotamians calculated that this had happened about three hundred thousand years ago, while the Egyptians also believed that the universe had been created many thousands of years in the past. Yet all but a short period of Egyptian cosmological history represented a time when gods had ruled on earth, and most of Mesopotamian history was a mythical time when humans lived far longer than they have done since. The Aztec seem to have believed that the universe had existed in any form for only a few thousand years and that the present creation was only a little over seven hundred years old. In most Yoruba states fifty reigns or fewer separated kings recorded in the nineteenth century from the god Oduduwa, who had created the earth and become the first king (Lloyd 1960: 223). The suggestion that the Inka believed the universe to be about forty-five hundred years old is highly suspect.

There was a general tendency in early civilizations to view creation as a time of superior power and authority, when the gods had established a model cosmic and social order that later human rulers strove to copy as best they could (Maisels 1990: 280). Creation time was often believed to continue alongside historical time. In Egypt and the Valley of Mexico, the daily rising of the sun repeated the act of creation; among the Maya, rulers' souls' escaping from the underworld in stellar forms replicated the Hero Twins' rescuing themselves from the forces of death.

It is unclear how long most early civilizations expected the present cosmic order would endure. The Egyptians believed that, provided their kings performed the proper rituals, their universe would last for a very long time but not forever, while the Aztec feared that the Fifth Sun and perhaps the entire universe might collapse at the completion of any fifty-two-year calendar cycle. The Inka may have believed that the world experienced a destructive upheaval every millennium or less and the Classic Maya that the universe would be destroyed and re-created approximately every five thousand years, but neither of these beliefs can be attributed to them with certainty. The Mesopotamians doubted that individual cities would endure for long periods, given the fickleness of the gods, but surviving myths reveal nothing about the end of the universe; nor do those of the Yoruba. Whatever they believed about cosmic cycles, the Maya appear to have had similar doubts about the long-term survival of cities and other political institutions as a consequence of their belief in cyclicity and the cosmically predetermined fortunes of all things. All early civilizations viewed the cosmos as an ordered system in which everything had a clearly defined function and was interrelated to everything else. Yet no one explicitly believed this orderly arrangement to be eternal.

Some early civilizations associated the creation of the cosmic order with gods that existed prior to and independently of time and space. This was the case with Ometeotl, Olorun, and probably Wiraqucha. The Egyptians viewed creator gods such as Atum or Ptah as a potential for order that existed in the primeval ocean but did not come into being until order had differentiated itself from disorder. The Mesopotamians likewise identified the earliest gods as engendering powers within a cosmic ocean, but the gods to which they gave birth had to slay them before they could order the universe in its present form. Maya cycles suggest a sense of some kind of overarching, impersonal fate, and this sense was also present in the cosmogonies of the Valley of Mexico.

While the deities in early civilizations were always gendered, the gender of creator deities varied. Some of them, such as Olorun, were clearly male. Others, such as Atum and Wiraqucha, appeared to be male but were described as bisexual, indicating that they embodied, at least potentially, the whole of creation. The Aztec conceptualized their deity Ometeotl as a balanced combination of male and female forces. The Mesopotamians believed that a primordial pair of male and female deities engendered the other gods but ascribed a more prominent role to the female. They also may have conceived of an ultimate mother of the gods, while An, the sky god, was sometimes said to take both male and female forms. The younger and more active deities that replaced Tiamat and Apsu were invariably governed by male deities.

Creation myths thus combined a limited set of general ideas about what might have existed before the current cosmos or world order (a creator god? disorder? eternal cycles?) with a belief in the gendered nature of the gods (the creator gods being male, female, both, or bisexual). The aggregate result among the early civilizations was a limited but randomly distributed set of speculations about the origins and history of the cosmos. Similarities between Mesopotamian and Egyptian creation myths that were not shared by any other early civilizations, such as their belief in an ordered universe proceeding out of a watery uniformity, and the Aztec, Maya, and possibly Inka emphasis on periodic transfigurations of the cosmos may result from specific historical links among these societies. There is no obvious connection between the type of creation myth and whether it is associated with city-states or territorial ones. This suggests that the primary aim of cosmogonies was to account for the origins and history of natural phenomena rather than to link the specifics of these phenomena to political issues. This is a conclusion that runs counter to the current emphasis on trying to establish the social role of creation myths in early civilizations (van Zantwijk 1985; Zuidema 1990).

We must, however, consider a possible objection to this conclusion. Thorkild Jacobsen long ago suggested that the instability of the Mesopotamian environment was reflected in its inhabitants' fear of changes in divine favour, while the greater ecological stability of Egypt encouraged the conviction that disorder could be resisted for a long time (Frankfort et al. 1949: 137–40). More recent research confirms that serious problems were indeed encountered in cultivating southern Mesopotamia, but the punishments that the gods regularly meted out to human groups were devastating military defeats, foreign invasions, and epidemics, the major ecological disaster – the great flood – being a unique event. At the same time, both long-term and short-term variations in the height of the Nile flood presented greater ecological challenges than Jacobsen and his colleagues recognized (Butzer 1976). Egyptian cosmology appears to have incorporated a recognition of these ecological problems into its interpretation of the universe as an unstable equilibrium between the forces of order, which among other things ensured agricultural prosperity, and the forces of disorder, which threatened the viability of the universe. This suggests that the cosmic insecurity of the Mespotamians may have reflected to a much greater degree the political instability of their city-state system, while the Egyptians' optimism reflected the stable political order that their territorial state was able to maintain over long periods (Trigger 1979).

If this is so, it might be hypothesized that city-state systems would have attributed greater instability to the cosmic order than territorial states. The city-state systems in the Valley of Mexico had an even greater sense of cosmic insecurity and pessimism than the Mesopotamian ones. As in Mesopotamia, hegemonic relations among city-states were fragile and subject to dramatic reversals. Yet the Valley of Mexico suffered from volcanic eruptions and disastrous crop failures caused by periodic droughts and the region's susceptibility to frosts. While the vast extension of chinampa agriculture and the imposition of extensive tribute in foodstuffs on areas surrounding the Valley of Mexico had considerably alleviated the ecological threat by the late fifteenth century, these solutions were both ecologically and politically fragile. Thus it is impossible to estimate to what extent cosmological pessimism in the Valley of Mexico and Mesopotamia reflected ecological or political problems or a combination of the two.

Not enough is known about Classic Maya beliefs to measure either their sense of ecological instability or the extent to which they interpreted political reversals as deliberate divine interventions as distinguished from cyclical, astrologically predictable realignments of cosmological forces. There is general agreement that, as population density increased in the Late Classic period, Maya agriculture was adversely affected by deforestation and soil erosion on hillsides (Fash 1991: 170–81). Yoruba city-states experienced swift reversals in their political fortunes, but they do not appear to have linked these reversals to cosmic instability. As in Egypt and Mesopotamia, kingship was viewed as the continuation of patterns established when the world was created.

The correlation is no clearer with territorial states. The Egyptians believed that the cosmic order could be maintained over vast periods. This belief also implied that the political order that the gods had established for Egypt and the world at the time of creation would endure despite minor perturbations. But neither the cosmic nor the political order could be taken for granted; both had to be maintained by kings performing the correct rituals. The situation is more uncertain for China and Peru. The Shang appear to have regarded their regime as a symbolic reversal of the previous mythical (or at least mythologized) Xia Dynasty. While they associated themselves with fire, birds, sun, life, and light, they associated their predecessors with the reverse qualities: water, dragons, moon, death, and darkness (Allan 1991: 17–18). This suggests that changes in ruling families or the conquest of one territorial state by another may already have been associated with notions of cosmic reversal. We do not, however, have enough information to determine how stable the Shang believed either their environment or the supernatural order was. The much later Chinese concept of the Mandate of Heaven (*tianming*), which was adumbrated at the beginning of the Zhou Dynasty, reconciled periodic political upheavals with a belief in cosmic and ultimately political stability by blaming political change on the misconduct of rulers. Such misconduct, by angering Heaven, led to ecological disasters, uprisings, and eventually the overthrow of bad governments.

In highland Peru it may have been believed that the cosmos underwent major changes, if not destruction and re-creation, every five hundred or one thousand years. This suggests a sense of cosmic instability approximating that found in the Valley of Mexico. Such a sense of instability would not have been inappropriate in a region subject to severe earthquakes, El Niño episodes, and climatic marginality at high altitudes. Yet it is uncertain whether cosmic cyclicity was an indigenous Andean concept or invented by early Spanish scholars. Even if this view were indigenous, given the brief dominance of the Inka state over much of the Andean region it would be impossible to be certain whether this view was associated with earlier territorial states, such as the Chimu kingdom on the north coast of Peru or Tiwanaku and Wari in the southern highlands, or with the rivalrous chiefdoms that had prevailed until the time of Inka rule in the central highlands.

Thus there is not enough evidence to associate belief in cosmic instability with city-state systems and belief in cosmic stability with territorial states.

Despite varying degrees of optimism and pessimism, all early civilizations entertained doubts about the powers of their deities to control the universe and about the unequivocal willingness of these deities to help human beings. Like the inhabitants of all complex societies, those who lived in early civilizations appear to have been aware of the devastating impacts of both ecological and political calamities and projected these fears into the supernatural realm. Views of cosmic instability may have reflected both political and ecological concerns. In at least some cases, however, they may also have represented the views of earlier and quite different societies persisting under altered circumstances. It is therefore not surprising that, on the whole, these views appear to reflect concerns more about ecological instabilities than about political organization.

COSMOGRAMS

The realm of the gods was the main reference point for maintaining political order in early civilizations. Egyptian kings were believed to continue a rulership that had been established by the creator gods before they retreated to the sky world. Mesopotamian myths asserted that kingship and its paraphernalia descended to earth from the kingdom that the younger gods had established in the sky realm. The Yoruba supreme god Olorun, who lived in the sky world, was king of all the gods, and the world-creating god Oduduwa was the common ancestor and prototype of Yoruba kings. The Inka regarded their ruler as the earthly incarnation of Inti, the chief deity of the sky world, and the Shang kings may have claimed to be descendants of the supreme sky deity Shangdi. Aztec, Maya, and Yoruba kings sought to incorporate into their own persons the powers of one or more major deities.

Wilfred Lambert (1975: 49) has pointed out that in ancient Mesopotamia no clear distinction was drawn between the world of nature and the products of human beings. At the time of creation the gods brought cities into existence, just as they produced rivers and mountains. Mesopotamian temples were viewed as mountains (*kur*) which connected the sky and terrestrial realms (Mander 1999). They bore names such as 'House of the Universe' (*éšárra*) and 'House That Is the Bond of the Sky and the Earth' (*éduranki*) (George 1993: 80, 145). In Egypt the god Ptah created cities in the course of fashioning the natural world (Lichtheim 1973: 55). Such understandings encouraged efforts to strengthen the symbolic alignments between social and political organization, on the one hand, and supernatural powers, on the other, by creating earthly structures and community plans that duplicated those existing in the realm of the gods.

Efforts to relate the terrestrial realm more closely to that of the gods often took the form of aligning public buildings and tombs with solar, lunar, or stellar rising and setting points. The main axes of at least some Egyptian temples were oriented to the rising or setting positions of the sun, moon, or particular stars on certain days of the year (R. Wilkinson 2000: 36–37). The sides of Egyptian pyramids faced the cardinal directions. Features of Maya building complexes were aligned with a series of rising points of the sun or particular planets (Harrison 1999: 53–55). From earliest Shang times, the entrances to major buildings faced away from the malign supernatural influences coming from the north, including the cold north winds of winter. Later Chinese scholars believed that Zhou altars to the soil god were regularly faced with earth of an appropriate directional colour: the east with blue-green, the north with black, the west with white, the south with red, and their summit with yellow. This, however, may have been a late Zhou innovation (Creel 1970: 370; Wheatley 1971: 434).

Beyond this, buildings were created to be cosmograms – miniature replicas of the universe. The Aztec interpreted their Great Temple, which they believed stood at the centre of the cosmos, as such a microcosm. Its three tapered tiers, each with four sides, and top platform represented the thirteen levels of the sky world, its supporting platform the earth, and its foundations the underworld. Its northern half, dedicated to the rain god Tlaloc, was Tonacatepetl, 'the Hill of Sustenance', and its southern half was Coatepec Hill, where Huitzilopochtli had defeated his sister and brothers shortly after he was born. These two sacred hills joined together symbolized the portals of Mictlan, the realm of the dead (Broda, Carrasco, and Matos Moctezuma 1987; Matos Moctezuma 1988: 123–45).

Maya temples represented sacred mountains or the cosmic tree that facilitated human communication with the sky world and the underworld. Classic Maya urban building complexes often had a ritual area to the north, consisting of pyramid temples erected over the burials of former rulers, and a palace complex to the south, with a ball court between. The funerary temples, which reached the highest elevation, symbolized the sky world, the palace complex represented the human realm and the underworld, and the ball court was believed to be a major point of communication with the underworld (Ashmore 1989: 273–74). Shang royal graves, which had four ramps descending to a central wooden chamber, also appear to have been cosmograms (Allan 1991: 88). In Egypt most major urban temples were constructed along east-west axes. From early Shang times or even before, royal palaces contained important ritual structures. Yoruba palaces were of great ritual importance but, while they were divided into outer, semi-public and inner, private sections, they did not exhibit any standard, ritually significant layout.

It is frequently maintained that entire cities were planned as cosmograms. Davíd Carrasco (1989: 9) asserts that all Mesoamerican cities exhibited such plans. Tenochtitlan was laid out, much as nearby Teotihuacan had been over a millennium earlier, with a major ritual and governing complex at the centre that was approached by avenues coming from the four cardinal directions. Tenochtitlan's layout, which is said to have been dictated by the god Huitzilopochtli (Durán 1964: 32), made it a duplicate of Aztalan, the mythical city where the Aztec claimed to have originated, and of Tollan, the city that had been ruled by the god Quetzalcoatl and from which the Aztec nobility and artistic skills were thought to have been derived (Gillespie 1989: 178–79). It is uncertain, however, to what extent other communities, large and small, in the Valley of Mexico physically approximated such an ideal. Texcoco, the second-largest city, does not appear to have implemented such a plan.

The Inka capital, Cuzco, was laid out with four roads extending from Cusipata, its main square, to the four quarters of the kingdom. The adjacent Cusipata and Wakapata squares were covered with a layer of sand brought from the Pacific coast to honour the god Wiraqucha. This sand symbolized the life-giving waters of the ocean which the gods continuously transported to the highlands. Like most highland communities, Cuzco was physically divided into upper and lower moieties. Curiously, the principal temple of the sun god, who was the chief deity of the upper moiety, was located in Lower Cuzco, while the shrine of Wiraqucha, the chief deity associated with the lower moiety, was located in Upper Cuzco. The city as a whole was said to represent a puma, with the fortress and ritual complex of Saqsawaman being its head. The ceque system turned the surrounding Cuzco Valley into a vast ritual area (Classen 1993: 100–106; Hyslop 1990: 29–65; Sherbondy 1992: 61–62; Zuidema 1964).

David O'Connor (1989) has postulated that, at least in the New Kingdom, royal Egyptian cities were laid out along a north-south axis, associated with the king, and an east-west axis, associated with the sun god. Where the two axes met in the centre of the city were located the main temple and, just north of its western entrance, the official palace where the king appeared as the earthly representative of the creator god. Royal residential palaces were located on the outskirts of such cities. From these the king approached the centre of the city as the sun god approached it from the eastern horizon each morning. Such a plan duplicated the solar and Nile axes that structured the terrestrial and sky realms. Barry Kemp and Salvatore Garfi (1993: 78–79) argue, however, that too much symbolism is being read into these urban plans. Recent efforts to assign complex religious meanings to the distribution of cult centres throughout Egypt and Nubia (O'Connor 1998) are even more weakly supported. Efforts to impute celestial patterns to the relative locations of Old

Kingdom pyramids (Bauval and Gilbert 1994) have been received with great scepticism.

There is no evidence for a symbolic layout of early Chinese urban centres, but this may be the result of inadequate data. Mesopotamian and Yoruba cities appear to have been functionally arranged, although G. J. A. Ojo (1966a: 200) argues that, for cosmological reasons, Yoruba cities had central cult places and city gates arranged in fours or multiples of four. Maya city plans are highly diverse and may not have had any generic cosmic significance, although individual buildings and building complexes clearly did.

The desire to create cosmograms does not appear to have been as obvious or widespread in early civilizations as Eliade and his followers have maintained. Tenochtitlan was a city with a central temple that represented the vertical axis uniting heaven, earth, and the underworld and a clear layout of streets and districts representing the four quarters. In other cases, individual temples, palaces, or complexes of such buildings served as cosmic symbols connecting the vertical realms and oriented to the four quarters. Certain general ideas about the nature of the cosmos that Eliade noted may be very old and widely shared, but it has not been established how widespread were the more specific beliefs that he postulated as universals. His general ideas seem to have been applied too dogmatically and in some cases without sufficient local warrant to the physical layout of structures. This does not mean that the broader range of culturally specific meanings that were assigned to topographic features did not play an important role in determining the location and shaping the layout of urban centres or that, as the Inka 'new Cuzcos' illustrate, such meanings were not read into existing topographic or built features (Brady and Ashmore 1999; Richards 1999; van de Guchte 1999).

THE CIVILIZATION IN THE UNIVERSE

All early civilizations visualized the earth and the cosmos as being much smaller than they are now perceived to be and the cosmos as consisting of two or more vertically arranged and intercommunicating levels. Above, and usually below, the terrestrial plane were realms that were occupied exclusively by deities and by the dead. The terrestrial plane, which was the abode of living humans but was also constituted and animated by supernatural power, was flat and round or square in outline and extended to an encircling ocean. Every early civilization believed itself to be located in the centre of the terrestrial plane and to enjoy a privileged location in relation to the gods and the rest of the universe. There was a tendency to view the terrestrial plane as divided into four quarters related to the cardinal directions or the course of the sun across the sky. The main connections between the terrestrial and supernatural realms were found at the extremities and the centre of the world.

It appears likely that many of these similarities resulted from attempts by people living in early civilizations to explain observable natural phenomena in light of their understanding of the supernatural forces that animated (or were) the universe. Widespread vertical and quadripartite divisions of the cosmos may have been derived from still older belief systems influenced by widely shared individual orientations to the environment.

Theories of cosmogony displayed considerably more variation. There was much less agreement about what had preceded the creation of the universe, how stable the terrestrial and cosmic orders were, and what the ultimate fate of the universe might be. This greater variety reflected the lesser degree of constraint by direct observation and hence the greater scope for culturally guided speculation. People in all early civilizations appear to have doubted the ability or willingness of supernatural powers to maintain the cosmos or to treat human beings in a consistently friendly manner. They were aware of the potentially devastating effects of political and ecological breakdown and of ecological disasters and generally attributed these failures to interventions by supernatural beings. Yet beliefs about the stability of the natural environment and the human realm varied considerably, and there is no correspondence between political stability and belief in cosmic stability. The most probable explanation is that, because people living in early civilizations did not distinguish the natural, supernatural, and social realms, all cosmogonies were attempting to understand what we regard as the physical and social realms simultaneously.

21 Cult

In early civilizations' relation with the supernatural, cult or ritual predominated over other forms of devotion (C. Bell 1992). The central feature of these cults was sacrifice, which has been described, along with prayer, as one of the two 'fundamental acts of worship' (Faherty 1974: 128), and prayer and sacrifice were closely linked. The Roman writer Sallust, although living at a time when deities were viewed both more transcendentally and more sceptically than in early civilizations, still described prayer accompanied by sacrifice as animated words – prayer supplying meaning to sacrifice and sacrifice giving power to prayer (Lewis 1990: 3).

Sacrifice has been defined as 'a religious rite in which an object is offered to a divinity in order to establish, maintain, or restore a right relationship of man to the sacred order' (Faherty 1974: 128). The offering transferred the life-force or power of the object from humans to the supernatural, which for early civilizations meant the forces that activated the natural world.

Anthropologists have long discussed the origins and meaning of sacrifice. Edward B. Tylor described it as gifts that fearful humans gave to their deities to win their favour or placate their hostility. William Robertson Smith argued that it constituted a form of communion of a society with its deities that involved eating the gods' totem, or earthly manifestation. James Frazer saw it as a technique for rejuvenating deities and ensuring the continuity of the cosmos, Marcel Mauss as a means to ensure that power continued to flow both ways between human beings and the gods. Gerardus van der Leeuw interpreted sacrifice as a way to open a source of supernatural benefits for humankind. Valerio Valeri (1985) argued that most offerings simultaneously symbolized and were seen as a part of the deity, the donor, and the officiant and thus created, rather than merely reflected or reinforced, a relationship among them. These explanations capture aspects of sacrifice in various societies, but each is specific and partial in its coverage.

Numerous intentions were ascribed to sacrifice by those who practised it. Their goals included to propitiate the gods or avert their anger, to purify wrongdoers or taboo breakers, to establish communication with a deity, to express gratitude for a divine favour already received, to strengthen a request for a favour being requested, to seek protection for worshippers against their human enemies or from evil powers, to cure epidemics, to avoid war or famine, and to replenish the earth (Ajisafe 1924: 92; Faherty 1974: 132–33; Awolalu 1979: 137, 144). The Yoruba and Aztec believed that one of the tasks performed by human sacrifices was to transmit messages, including requests for help, to deities or dead ancestors (Caso 1958: 72; Connah 1987: 145; Soustelle 1961: 99).

The most important function of sacrifice in early civilizations and the one that integrated most of the more specific meanings ascribed to it was to return energy or life to its divine source, thereby rejuvenating the power of that source to animate nature and assist humans. A Roman priest said to the deity to whom he was offering a sacrifice, 'Be thou increased (*macte*) by this offering'. Sacrifice was the impetus that ensured the continuing reciprocal flow of divine life-force between its source and its various manifestations in the terrestrial realm (Faherty 1974: 128). In transcendental religions such as Judaism, Christianity, and Islam, where the omnipotence of a single god renders that god's existence totally independent of his creation, sacrifice becomes merely a token of individual or collective human gratitude for the deity's favours. In early civilizations, individual deities were not viewed as being sufficiently powerful to render them independent of human support. On the contrary, deities and humans were regarded as depending on each other. Because most anthropologists believe that religious concepts are shaped wholly by cultural factors and thus expect them to exhibit considerable cross-cultural variation, the possibility that all early civilizations shared a belief in the dependence of deities and human beings on one another is unexpected and requires verification and explanation.

GODS AS PROVIDERS

In all early civilizations it was believed that deities had created the universe and kept it functioning. As the powers which animated and controlled nature, they supplied (or were) the energy or life that permitted the universe, including human beings, to exist and sustain itself. They were regarded as the source of the light, warmth, activity, nourishment, and fertility that humans required to live and reproduce themselves. Since humans depended on the natural world for their survival, they also depended on the gods. Agriculture was not simply the principal source of nourishment and livelihood but also the primary means by which the gods sustained human life. The gods not only fed humans but in some instances were viewed as the food humans ate.

But why did deities sustain human life and at what cost to themselves? The Egyptian 'Instruction Offered to King Merikare', which dates from the First Intermediate Period, suggests that the creator god fashioned the universe for the sake of human beings, that he shone as the sun in the sky for them, and that he provided them with food and leaders who could maintain order amongst them (Lichtheim 1973: 106). This work, which superficially appears to have anticipated a transcendental, post-axial view of the universe, reflected the 'solar theology' of the Old Kingdom, which celebrated the creative power of the sun god. Yet, while the statement that human beings were the creator god's 'cattle' may be construed as a metaphorical reference to a transcendental deity's loving care for humans, it may instead indicate the sun god's dependence on humans for his nourishment. Elsewhere it is made clear that the Egyptian creator god brought the universe into existence primarily in order to have a realm in which he and the other gods could exist. The sun's daily trip across the sky not only benefited human beings but also allowed the creator god to remain vigorous by passing through ceaseless cycles of death and regeneration (Meeks and Favard-Meeks 1996: 79, 197–98).

In most early civilizations the gods kept the universe functioning primarily to ensure their own survival and well-being. Humans existed in the Mesopotamian universe to provide services – labour and sacrifice – for the gods that significantly improved the quality of their lives (Jacobsen 1976: 117–18). In Mesoamerica, where the concept of religious sacrifice was elaborated to an exceptional degree, it was believed that the gods periodically sacrificed their own or each other's lives to ensure the continuity of the universe and facilitate the survival of humanity. As we have seen, the Aztec claimed that the Fifth Sun had been enabled to move across the sky by the gods' casting themselves into a cosmic fire and that, still earlier, by splitting the female Earth Monster into two parts to form the earth and sky, the gods had made it possible for her to bring forth all the life on earth (Clendinnen 1991: 177). The Aztec believed that plants and animals flourished mainly because the gods sacrificed their own lives to support them (Berdan 1982: 186). Each autumn the sun god died and descended into the underworld to marry the Earth Goddess, who gave birth the following spring to the maize god – the sun reborn in a different aspect. Human sacrifices were interpreted not simply as offerings to the sun but as embodiments of divine power, representing the gods' sacrificing themselves to renew the world (Broda 1987: 70, 75). The Maya likewise believed that their deities sacrificed themselves so that the world might be renewed and human beings live. Humans were made from maize, which was the flesh of the gods and contained divine soul power or life-force that was sacrificed for humans' benefit at harvest time. This power passed from maize into human bodies, where it became particularly concentrated in human blood (Freidel, Schele, and Parker 1993: 195; Miller 1986: 19). Thus humans depended on the gods for their survival.

The Pyramid Texts suggest that the Egyptian sun god nourished and empowered himself each morning by slaughtering and consuming the multitude of stars, thereby appropriating their power. As he crossed the sky, creating and sustaining terrestrial life with his energy, he grew older and weaker, and his remaining power was dispersed again each evening (Goebs 1998). In Egypt and Mesopotamia myths also associated the death and rebirth of the gods with the agricultural cycle. Inanna's essential role in ensuring the agricultural fertility of the earth required that, when she was executed by her sister, the god Enki had to send spirits to the underworld to revive her and secure her release in return for the confinement of various other agricultural deities in the underworld for several months of each year (Jacobsen 1976: 55–61). The Egyptians believed that crops sprouted from the body of Geb or Osiris when it was moistened by the Nile flood, which represented the god's own power of fertility. The murder of Osiris by his brother Seth was represented as part of an ongoing struggle between cosmic order and disorder, while the annual cycle of Nile floods and crop growth constituted the cycle by which Osiris renewed himself (Frankfort 1948: 190–97). Whether the gods were represented as deliberately sacrificing themselves or not, their cycles of life, death, and rebirth sustained the universe upon which, ultimately, all humans depended.

NOURISHING THE GODS

In all the early civilizations human beings offered nourishment to the gods in the form of sacrifices. Sacrifices took the form of killing animals or human beings, offering meat, vegetables, and alcoholic or non-alchoholic beverages, and presenting inedible materials believed to contain special supernatural powers. The Inka offered lumps of gold and silver or images made from these metals to the gods, and the Egyptians offered unworked metals and semiprecious stones, all these substances being considered especially rich in cosmic energy (Daumas 1979; MacCormack 1991: 150; Rowe 1944: 307). The Inka offered thorny oyster (*mullu*) shells from the Pacific Ocean, whole or powdered, to springs and rivers in the highlands (Gose 1993). The Maya believed that burning incense, made from tree resin, provided deities with an especially potent form of divine energy (Freidel, Schele, and Parker 1993: 204).

The Inka burned large amounts of fancy cloth as offerings, thus releasing for the gods the energy that had gone into making it (Murra 1962). Worshippers in Mesopotamia and elsewhere donated goods to temples as thanks offerings to gods (Postgate 1992: 135), but it is not clear whether they were also viewed as sacrifices that would have helped to sustain and empower the gods.

Sacrifices were made to the gods by individuals or groups. Some were made at regular intervals (daily, weekly, or yearly), others on special occasions to expiate sins, thank the gods, or celebrate life-cycle events. In general, the upper classes made more lavish offerings and sometimes sacrificed to more important deities than the lower classes. While Aztec commoners offered quails, tortillas, green maize, and flowers to the gods, nobles and rich merchants offered human captives, cacao beans, exotic bird feathers, and jade (Clendinnen 1991: 243). Sacrifices offered by the king on behalf of the whole nation were the most costly and elaborate of all. While, especially in Mesoamerica, human sacrifice was represented as an honour for the victim, upper-class adults rarely if ever freely volunteered themselves. Human victims were mostly prisoners of war, criminals, strangers, and children.

Erik Hornung (1982: 203) has suggested that the Egyptian gods were transcendental – that they did not need either cult or offerings for their own well-being and therefore offerings were merely tokens of gratitude. New Kingdom texts suggest, however, that, when the gods ceased to receive offerings in the reign of King Akhenaton, they abandoned Egypt, which resulted in military defeats and other disasters (Baines 1995a: 28–29). Other Egyptologists assert that the Egyptians believed that their deities needed human support in order to survive and that the main purpose of temple offerings was to preserve the universe (Daumas 1979: 705; Quirke 1992: 70–103). In particular, the gods required sustenance in the form of food (Silverman 1991: 28–29). Sacrificial offerings returned to Egyptian deities the energy they had expended on the creation and maintenance of the universe. The more offerings a deity received, the more powerful that deity became. Consequently, the most vital concern of the Egyptian gods was the apportioning of their offerings (Meeks and Favard-Meeks 1996: 37, 102, 123). Food offerings were also essential to maintain the life-force of dead humans, who were regarded as gods. Offerings to deceased rulers were a major focus of Old Kingdom religious ritual.

Offerings were essential features of daily Egyptian temple and mortuary cults. Animals were killed in temple abattoirs, and it appears to have been the presentation of their flesh to the gods rather than the act of slaughtering them that constituted the offering. The Egyptians believed that gods entered or were drawn into their cult images three times each day to consume the supernatural energy from their food offerings. In the morning these images were also washed and dressed by their priests. These rituals, performed in the most secluded part of the temple, were essential for maintaining the cosmic order (Robins 1993: 157). Food was regarded as possessing magical power as well as creative energy which made it the essence of life or being (Goebs 1998: 280–81). The term for 'cosmic order' was etymologically closely related to *m3ʿw*, which meant 'offerings', just as *ḥw*, which referred to the divine power of creative utterance, was identical with or similar to a word that meant 'life-sustaining nourishment' (Meeks and Favard-Meeks 1996: 103). Evidence suggests that human sacrifice was performed in cultic settings in Early Dynastic times, but in later periods the only manifestation of it may have been the infrequent slaying of enemy leaders as apparent offerings to the gods (Gardiner 1961: 199–200; R. Wilkinson 2000: 265–67). Statues of bound enemies or written lists of such people appear to have served as substitutes for living individuals in the execration rituals that were performed during the Middle Kingdom to drain the king's enemies of power (Posener 1940).

Mesopotamians believed that all human beings were the servants of the gods. It was their duty to grow food, weave clothes, build earthly residences, cook, and clean for their deities. Gods needed food in order to function effectively, and this was provided by their temple staff in the form of two meals each day (Oppenheim 1964: 188–91; Postgate 1992: 119–20). Without these offerings, the gods would have grown malnourished and ceased to function effectively. The legend of the flood recounted that, after water covered the earth, offerings ceased and the gods grew hungry and began to repent their destruction of humanity. When the water receded and the one surviving family, led by Utnapishtim, emerged from its boat and offered a burnt sacrifice, the deities crowded 'like flies' around the rising smoke, which transmitted to them for the first time in many days the spiritual power of food produced by humans. Because of this, the gods forgave Enki for having surreptitiously rescued a few humans who could continue to serve them (Jacobsen 1976: 120). A later, perhaps facetious Mesopotamian text suggested that, if sacrifices were withheld from a neglectful personal deity, that deity could be forced to beg for food as a hungry dog does from its master (Bottéro 1992: 255–58).

The food and drink that were offered to Mesopotamian gods resembled what was consumed by humans. As in Egypt, animals were slaughtered on temple premises, but there is no indication that the killing of the animal, as opposed to the offering of meat, was regarded as sacrifice. Some animal sacrifices were burned. There is no evidence of human sacrifice, except perhaps the killing of lower-class individuals temporarily substituting for a monarch who feared that the gods might be seeking to destroy him. In serving the gods, priests acted as their household servants, the king as their chief steward, and commoners as their estate workers (Bottéro 1992: 223–25). The Mesopotamians appear to have believed that the gods collectively could survive without human assistance and had done so prior to the creation of humanity. That, however, would have required them to grow and prepare their own food, which meant that their standard of living and position in the cosmos would have been considerably lower than it was after the creation of humanity. The spirits of dead humans received sacrifices, usually together with the deities that were worshipped by individual households (Bottéro 1992: 279–82).

Sacrifice was ubiquitous among the Yoruba. Most personal prayers were accompanied by modest offerings (Awolalu 1979: 108). If devotees depended upon gods for protection and support, gods depended upon devotees to feed them, glorify them, and keep secret the ritual knowledge that was required to serve them. This knowledge could be rendered ineffectual or even harmful if it were divulged to unauthorized humans (Apter 1992: 223; K. Barber 1981: 738). Offerings were normally made to individual deities every four days and at special annual festivals. The more offerings a deity received, the greater became his or her power and willingness to help humans (Armstrong 1981: 71; R. Thompson 1976: P/1). Cults nourished deities in return for past, present, and anticipated favours (Apter 1992: 98, 184). Sacrifice was part of a cycle in which life was exchanged for life, making death essential for prolonging and renewing life. Worshippers did not hesitate to coerce deities by threatening to transfer their devotions and material support to other, more generous gods (Apter 1992: 223; K. Barber 1981: 737–38). The routine goal of cults was, however, to feed and empower deities so that they could renew the cosmos and promote the welfare of the groups and individuals who worshipped them (Apter 1992: 124). Ogun, the god of iron, consumed the flesh of sacrificed dogs and, in return for this nourishment, supplied the iron tools that made agriculture and therefore human life possible (Pemberton and Afolayan 1996: 171).

Yams, kola nuts, palm wine, palm oil, and cowrie-shell money were routine offerings. More elaborate sacrifices included fish, chickens, sheep, goats, and cows. The most prestigious and awe-inspiring offerings were human beings: prisoners of war, slaves, children, and condemned criminals or strangers supplied by the king. Human beings were sacrificed infrequently and usually only a few at a time. The major exceptions occurred during critical phases of wars, when divine assistance became particularly important (Awolalu 1979: 188–89). At Ife choice human victims from Ijesa were thought to be preferred by the gods because of their powerful physiques and phlegmatic natures (S. Johnson 1921: 21). Some human victims were venerated and accorded great honours prior to their deaths and were believed to become gods afterwards. Others were assured that their life-forces would be reborn to a higher social position in a subsequent life (Lucas 1948: 215–17). Victims were often gagged before being sacrificed so they could not curse their executioners (Willett 1967: 49). Because in many Yoruba rituals the victim represented the sacrificer, in offering human lives to the gods the king was symbolically offering a substitute for himself (Apter 1992: 111). The archaeological discovery of forty-one female skeletons thrown into a pit at Benin City indicates that human sacrifices were made there as early as the thirteenth century A.D. (Connah 1975: 49–66). The bodies of human and animal sacrifices were often left to decay before a symbol of the deity for whom they had been killed or disposed of in the forest. It was the life-force and blood of these victims that was offered to the gods.

Individual Yoruba deities had favourite offerings and rejected others. Ogun preferred dogs and palm wine, Sango rams, and Esu fowls. Orisala liked snails, whose juices were associated with calmness and easing pain (Awolalu 1979: 163–64). Libations were offered everywhere to the god of the soil to thank him for the harvest (Ojo 1966a: 168). It was regarded as improper to offer palm wine to Orisala because it was drunkenness that had caused him to ignore Olorun's order to create the world (Awolalu 1979: 164). Particular sacrifices were considered appropriate for specific requests: dogs for longevity, eggs to prevent losses, a ram, sheep, and cock together for victory, and a wild hog to counteract plots (Lucas 1948: 208). The appropriateness of each sacrifice was confirmed by divination prior to its being made, and the sacrifice's efficacy was verified by divination afterward (Awolalu 1979: 162–81).

The Yoruba also made sacrifices to the dead. Prior to human burials, the blood of sacrificed animals was poured or sprinkled on corpses, especially those of notable people, in order to strengthen their souls (Ajisafe 1924: 80–81; K. Barber 1991: 314). Extended families regularly presented food offerings to their dead ancestors. Some spirits of the dead, including those of a few human sacrifices, became gods and received their own offerings.

The Inka regarded sacrifice as the principal focus of religion (Rowe 1944: 305). Its function was to nourish the gods. Smoke rising from burnt offerings sustained the sun god and gave him the strength to stay young and continue moving. Without offerings, wakas grew hungry, disconsolate, and ineffectual (Cobo 1990: 114; MacCormack 1991: 304, 306). Religious sacrifices ensured the continuing circulation of life-giving supernatural energy through the universe (Aveni 1989: 303; Salomon 1991: 16). The term *hucha* designated sacrificial relations between human beings and the sun and upper world generally; *cuyac* designated sacrificial relations with Wiraqucha and the lower world (Dover 1992: 9). The Inka sacrificed male llamas, guinea pigs, birds, and animal fat but not dogs to their deities. They also offered them cooked vegetables, fermented drinks, cocoa, cloth, and metal. The gods preferred food and alcoholic beverages made from maize flour. Libations, sometimes further empowered by being mixed with powdered seashells, were poured into basins, holes in the ground, and springs. Other offerings were burned. White llamas were sacrificed to the sun, brown ones to Wiraqucha, and parti-coloured ones to Illapa, the thunder god. In Cuzco, three or four llamas were offered to the sun each day; their throats were cut in the square in front of the Qorikancha and their bodies burned on an open altar in the square (Rowe 1944: 306–7).

The most valuable offerings were human lives. When new provinces were conquered, the Inka sacrificed some of the best-looking people of that region as a thanks offering to the sun. The rest of the human sacrifices were children selected to become chosen women and yanakuna. These sacrifices had to be without any physical blemish. The children were feasted and made intoxicated and then were strangled, had their throats cut or their hearts removed, or were buried alive. Human sacrifices were offered to the gods during public crises such as famines, pestilence, military defeats, or the illness of the king (Rowe 1944: 306). They were restricted to major temples and government-sponsored rituals (Kendall 1973: 196–97). Some children of subordinate rulers who were chosen for sacrifice became objects of veneration and sources of oracles after their bodies were returned to their birthplaces for burial (Silverblatt 1988b).

The blood of animal sacrifices nourished the gods and was daubed on the faces of worshippers, young men being initiated into adult status, sacred and royal statues, buildings, and mummies in order to strengthen them. Only the mummies and statues of Inka rulers and the images of gods were daubed with human blood (MacCormack 1991: 112–13). Sacrifices were also made to dead ancestors to nourish them so that they could better sustain their living descendants.

The Shang and Western Zhou Chinese offered sacrifices to sustain nature deities and the souls of their dead ancestors. Deities depended on these offerings to maintain their strength, and powerful deities required more sacrifices than minor ones (Allan 1991: 124; Keightley 1978b: 213; Li Boqian 1999). Provisioning lavish sacrifices was one of the main occupations of the upper classes and a primary justification for both warfare and hunting. Hunting and warfare had a shared vocabulary, including the word *huo*, which meant both 'booty' and 'sacrificial victim'. The main reason for hunting was said to be to provide victims for sacrifice (Lewis 1990: 17–21).

The offerings made to Shang royal ancestors and to nature deities consisted of grains, millet-ale libations, animals, and human beings (Keightley 1978b: 213). Animals that were routinely sacrificed included dogs, pigs, wild boars, sheep, and cattle; birds and horses were less common. The humans appear to have been mainly prisoners of war, with the Qiang, a western herding people, being favoured victims. The burial of whole army units, including chariot crews, during foundation rituals for the palaces built at Anyang appears to have involved the sacrifice of royal retainers (Keightley 1969: 374).

Royal sacrifices frequently consisted of combinations of several species of animals together with human victims. A total of one to ten victims was normally sacrificed, but occasionally several hundred were killed at one time. It was divined in advance what sacrifices specific gods or ancestors wished. Libations and blood were poured on the ground, and the bodies of animal and human victims were burned, buried, drowned, or dismembered. Deities were believed to drink the blood of slaughtered victims, and the large-scale killing of animals and humans was a central feature of royal sacrificial rites (Creel 1937: 197–206; Lewis 1990: 20). The heads or ears of human enemies killed in battle were presented at temples to feed ancestral spirits and deities. Shang kings appear to have offered the most elaborate sacrifices to their more remote and more powerful ancestors, even though they relied more heavily on their immediate ancestors to act as intermediaries on their behalf (Keightley 1978b: 218). The royal ancestors depended on food transmitted to them through sacrifices and could punish failure to deliver these sacrifices by harming their descendants or afflicting the Shang kingdom with poor crops, costly wars, military defeats, and plagues (Creel 1937: 175).

The Maya believed that the gods depended on human beings to care for and nurture them and renew their powers (D. Carrasco 1990: 107; Schele and Miller 1986: 176). The Maya's principal cosmic task was to keep the supernatural realm working by nourishing the gods (Hendrickson 1989: 129; Schele and Freidel 1990: 65). This was construed as part of a contractual obligation between human beings and the gods in which each side provided the other with the divine power that they required to survive (Freidel, Schele, and Parker 1993: 195). Throughout Mesoamerica, sacrifice was regarded as a form of debt repayment, with humans returning to the gods the cosmic energy that the gods had expended to provide them with food, make them fertile, and enable humanity to endure (D. Carrasco 1990: 49, 107).

Freidel, Schele, and Parker (1993: 195) point to the central role that meals and offerings played in Maya religious life. The gods were offered incense and a wide selection of foods, but their preferred nourishment was human flesh and blood (Baudez 1994: 275–76). Individual humans were killed, and living humans drew blood from their ear lobes, tongues, and other parts of their bodies and presented it to the gods on strings or pieces of paper (Schele 1984). Maya were expected to offer their own blood to the gods at frequent intervals throughout their lives. The most potent offering was the blood of a king or one of his close relatives, and the most prized human sacrifice was a captured ruler. A royal prisoner was often kept alive for a long period awaiting a special occasion such as the formal designation of a king's heir. Kings and their close female relatives shed copious amounts of blood in painful ways that caused them to enter into trance states during which they communicated with their ancestors and with major deities. These offerings were regarded as an especially effective way to nourish the gods and reinforce the cosmic cycles on which the well-being of all things depended (Schele and Miller 1986: 71).

The Aztec and other peoples in the Valley of Mexico believed that their gods were starved for life-giving forces and required constant sacrifices to revive them and sustain the cosmic order (López Austin 1988, 1: 377). Sacrifice was the means by which human beings could return to the gods the energy that these deities had expended to keep the world and individual humans functioning (Townsend 1992: 136, 154). If this did not occur, the earth would become infertile, the power of the sun would fail, the cosmos would disintegrate, and supernatural forces of disorder, terror, and destruction would be unleashed against humanity. The Aztec made offerings of cooked food and objects made of precious substances, but it was human blood and flesh that best nourished and animated the gods (B. Brown 1984; D. Carrasco 1999; Caso 1958: 12, 96; Clendinnen 1991: 320; Davies 1984; López Austin 1988, 1: 376–77; Soustelle 1961: 97).

While some nourishment for the gods was provided by warriors slain in battle, the most valued and abundant source was human sacrifice. The majority of those killed were captive warriors, and the primary aim of warfare was to obtain such captives. Prisoners offered to Huitzilopochtli were referred to as 'stars', an allusion to the star brothers that the sun had slain and consumed at the time of his birth and at the dawn of every day thereafter (Caso 1958: 93). Male and female slaves of foreign origin and local children born on inauspicious days or possessed of inauspicious physical traits were also slain. Warriors were differentially valued as human sacrifices according to how closely their culture resembled that of the peoples living in the Valley of Mexico. The unconquered Tlaxcalans, living to the east of the Valley of Mexico, were regarded as particularly choice offerings. Victims were despatched in many different ways: heart excision, decapitation, drowning, burning, and combinations of these methods. Different techniques were thought appropriate for particular deities (Durán 1971).

While it is often suggested that the blood of human sacrifices nourished sky deities and their flesh animated earth deities, the Earth Mother was described as crying for human blood and unable to produce crops unless she was drenched with it (Clendinnen 1991: 183, 195). Sacrificed children were believed to become *tepictoton*, spirits who empowered the rain and fertility god,

Tlaloc (Broda 1987: 73). The Aztec sacrificed the largest number of prisoners to their patron solar deity, Huitzilopochtli, in the belief that their blood and hearts would sustain the sun and delay the end of the present creation. This belief provided an ideological justification for the wars that had created and sustained the Aztec tributary system, representing Aztec aggression as altruistic and self-sacrificing (Soustelle 1961: 96–101). In addition to human sacrifices, from earliest childhood the Aztec often collected their own blood on bark cloth or paper which they burned to transmit its life-giving power to the gods (Clendinnen 1991: 74).

Because human flesh and blood were formed from corn, which was a terrestrial manifestation of the gods' life-force, the sacrifice of human life to feed the gods was a potent means of sustaining the cosmic cycle on which everyone depended. As among the Maya, such sacrifice was construed as a form of debt repayment (*nextlaoaliztli*) (D. Carrasco 1990: 49; Clendinnen 1991: 74–75, 208–9). Human sacrificial victims were referred to as 'tortillas for the gods', and their flesh was regarded as equivalent to the maize flour from which tortillas were made. Thus human sacrifices were regarded as equivalent to the deity to whom they were offered (Soustelle 1961: 98) and eating the flesh of a sacrificial victim as the same as eating the flesh of a god (Caso 1958: 75).

As the Aztec state grew more powerful, slaves and prisoners of war were increasingly used as foci for manifestations of the gods. Unlike other human ixiptlas, slaves and prisoners were sacrificed after their representations had run their cycle and were believed to be suffused with the power of the deity to whom, through sacrifice, this power was returned. Sometimes priests wore the flayed skins of such sacrifices, thus turning themselves into ixiptlas. They might also dress as the god to whom they were making a human sacrifice and thus temporarily invest themselves with that god's power; here a terrestrial manifestation of a god was sacrificing another manifestation of that god to the deity itself (Clendinnen 1991: 249). Some of the more prominent ixiptlas enjoyed comfortable and honoured, if circumscribed, lives during the period, sometimes as long as a year, that led up to their being killed. Prisoners or slaves were supposed to look forward with pleasure to dying in this manner and were often made to consume alcoholic beverages or mind-altering hallucinogens just before their deaths to ensure they behaved appropriately.

In all early civilizations sacrifice channelled energy back into the supernatural realm to sustain and animate deities, propitiate them, and make certain they continued to have the power to maintain the natural and social realms. It was believed that, without ensuring the continuing power and goodwill of the gods, crops would cease to grow, women would become barren, and people would sicken and die. G. F. Il'yin and Igor Diakonoff (1991: 378) note that in Vedic India 'because it was believed that the world exists and that people thrive only thanks to the gods, and because the gods live by sacrificial offerings, sacrifices were the main duty of believers'. While individuals and society as a whole depended on the strength and goodwill of the gods, the gods depended no less on the material support of human beings.

In all the early civilizations gods supplied human physical needs, but farmers ultimately provided the food, services, and human lives that were essential for the well-being or even the survival of the gods. Thus they played the same role in relation to the gods as they did in relation to upper-class humans; they supplied food and labour in return for order. The labour of the lower classes ensured the well-being not only of the upper classes but also of individual deities and the universe. This belief differed radically from that of modern transcendental religions, whose deities require no human support. It also differed from the religious beliefs of early small-scale societies, which perceived humans as depending far more on the supernatural forces that animated nature than those forces depended on human beings.

SIGNIFICANCE OF HUMAN SACRIFICE

One of the most important differences among early civilizations in sacrificing to the gods was the extent to which human beings were viewed as the primary or most valuable offerings. In Egypt and Mesopotamia, human sacrifice appears to have been rare even in the earliest periods and soon all but disappeared. In the five other early civilizations, human sacrifices were a regular occurrence, although their number and frequency varied.

In Andean myths humans and llamas were regarded as interchangeable (MacCormack 1991: 171). If animal and human sacrifices had generally been viewed as equivalent, it could be hypothesized that human sacrifices would have been more common in those early civilizations that had the fewest domestic animals, and this might explain the heavy emphasis on human sacrifice in Mesoamerica. It does not, however, explain why there was a strong emphasis on human sacrifice in Shang China and Inka Peru, where large numbers of domestic animals were also sacrificed, or its restrained practice among the Yoruba, who kept fewer domestic animals.

It is frequently suggested that human sacrifice was common in warlike societies where there was little need for extra labour, human sacrifice being a way of disposing of prisoners of war. While this might account for the frequency of human sacrifice in the Valley of Mexico, with its high population density, or among the Shang Chinese, who seem to have resorted to territorial expansion to keep their population density low, it does not explain the situation in Early

Dynastic Mesopotamia, where large numbers of male prisoners appear to have been slaughtered but not sacrificed. Nor does it account for the Inka, who either killed or freed prisoners of war and collected most human sacrifices from among their subject population's children. The evidence also does not suggest that large-scale human sacrifice was widely used to intimidate enslaved captives, although such intimidation might provide a functional explanation for the regular but limited sacrifice of slaves among the Yoruba. The threat of human sacrifice was not employed to intimidate the large numbers of foreign captives that the ancient Egyptians sought to incorporate into their society.

I do not have enough evidence to test the hypothesis that human sacrifice was more commonly employed as an instrument of social control in the formative periods of early civilizations than it was after more effective techniques had been developed (Childe 1945). There is, however, no cyclical correlation in any early civilization between political weakness and frequency of human sacrifice. Once human sacrifice ceased to be practised in an early civilization, it does not appear to have recurred as a normative practice. Human sacrifice died out in China during the Zhou period and was never as common among the Zhou as it had been among the Shang. It also declined rapidly soon after the formation of the Egyptian state and (in the form of retainer sacrifice) after the Early Dynastic period in Mesopotamia. In contrast, it had a long history in West Africa, Mesoamerica, and Peru. In Mesoamerica the incidence of human sacrifice appears to have increased in at least some states that acquired hegemonic status, whose greater power permitted fuller realization of a cultural ideal. It is also highly probable that the Aztec used large-scale prisoner sacrifice to intimidate subject peoples over whom their political control was tenuous. There were cults in the valley, associated with the worship of Quetzalcoatl Topiltzin, the ruler of the ancient city of Tollan, that questioned the value of human sacrifice and promoted alternative ways to nourish the gods. While this movement may have enjoyed some royal patronage at Texcoco, even there it never seriously challenged the ubiquitous belief that large-scale human sacrifice was required to sustain the universe (D. Carrasco 1990: 63).

There is thus no simple functional explanation of human sacrifice. The variations in its occurrence appear to be largely cultural. The Maya and Aztec, who emphasized human sacrifice and blood-letting, were part of a common Mesoamerican tradition, while the Egyptians and Mesopotamians, whose cultures had roots in a Middle Eastern Neolithic tradition, placed special emphasis on animal sacrifice. Nevertheless, all seven early civilizations in this sample shared the belief that living creatures were particularly suitable for nourishing the gods, and five of them (only two of which lacked domestic animals) identified human beings as the most valued offerings.

RITUAL INTERMEDIARIES

In all early civilizations kings and members of the upper classes claimed a special role as mediators between the terrestrial realm and the gods. It was through their intervention that the energy on which the gods, and hence the universe and all human beings, depended for their survival was channelled from the human realm back into the supernatural one. Ordinary people had contact with the supernatural through household and local cults, prayer, divination, visions, dreams, and spirit possession. Many minor deities concerned with various aspects of human well-being were accessible to everyone. Individual families, craft associations, landowning groups, and villages had their protective deities or ancestor spirits. All these groups offered sacrifices to tutelary spirits, and these sacrifices made these groups minor energy-recycling units mediating between the human and the supernatural world. Kings, high-ranking officials, and major institutions tended to monopolize communication with the more powerful supernatural forces because their wealth and power enabled them to make more lavish offerings. The ability to maintain contact with the gods was the most important source of political authority. As a later Chinese tale put it, in former times first shamans and then everyone could communicate with the spirit world, but eventually only rulers could do so (K. Chang 1983: 44–45).

In Egypt kings had established, at least by the Middle Kingdom and possibly much earlier (Seidlmayer 1996), that only they could sponsor the sacrifices that nourished the creator gods and related deities in temples throughout Egypt. This claim was based on the belief that the king was the son or earthly manifestation of each creator deity; the king's offering sacrifices to the gods was equated with sons' making offerings to their deceased fathers. (In reality, the king's role was delegated to numerous priests who presented offerings to the gods each day in his name.) When the king offered food to the gods, he was symbolically offering them both provisions and cosmic order (*m3ʿt* signifying both) (Silverman 1991: 64–67; Shafer 1997b: 23–25). Kings also claimed the ultimate right to provision the souls of the dead, all of whom were classified as gods.

Mesopotamian kings were responsible for ensuring that offerings were regularly made to their city's patron deity and, more generally, to any god or goddess who had a temple in the city-state. Economic prosperity and social harmony constituted evidence that a king enjoyed the favour of his city's principal deities. Some rulers had been priests before they became kings, but in any case they served as religious leaders. They could personally make offerings on behalf of their city-state and its people to any god and were responsible for overseeing the construction and repair of temples and ensuring that temple estates were managed properly. Kings also presented gifts of land, captives, and valuable ornaments to temples and frequently implied that they sought to accumulate riches to adorn temples rather than for their own glorification. Mesopotamian kings played key roles in certain religious rites, such as the New Year festival and the purification of armies before battles. The staff of each temple offered sacrifices to its deity or deities every day. Yet, despite competition between palace and temples, a king's ultimate responsibility for ensuring that a city's gods were well served and his ultimate dependence on their favour set him apart from and above other men (Postgate 1972; 1992: 262–65).

Among the Yoruba, every residential compound had shrines to one or more tutelary deities whose worship was directed by the compound's headman. The patron deities of the patrilineages of quarter and ward leaders were publicly worshipped by these officials and their followers. In addition to revering family and local deities, individuals were free to worship whatever gods they chose.

The Yoruba king had special relations with the patron deity or deities of his royal lineage, whose shrines were located close to or within the outer compound of the royal palace. He also exercised ultimate authority over every cult performed within his kingdom and had the final say in all religious matters. The king authorized community festivals and was represented by an Ifa priest, relative, or palace official at all public sacrificial rites (Apter 1992: 21; K. Barber 1981: 730; Bascom 1969: 34). His sacrifices and the annual festivals he sanctioned assured the stability and good fortune of his kingdom (Apter 1992: 183; Awolalu 1979: 17). Richard Bradbury's (1973: 74) description of the king of Benin as a living vehicle for the mystical forces that ensured the vitality of his kingdom applies equally to Yoruba rulers. Kings personally compounded secret 'medicines' that promoted the collective welfare of their subjects (Bascom 1969: 37). As did the gods, they accepted sacrifices that were offered to them by individuals and groups so that the gift of life might be given to these people in return (Pemberton and Afolayan 1996: 97). In Oyo, the centrally organized cult of Sango expressed and reinforced the authority of Oyo's living ruler. At the royal shrine the senior priests initiated all the king's bodyguards, official messengers, and agents into the Sango cult. The ability to be possessed by Sango provided them with a temporary supply of supernatural power that exceeded that of tributary kings and could be used, when necessary, for dealing with such rulers (Pemberton and Afolayan 1996: 152). Thus, even in this highly decentralized society, kings played the principal role in guiding the rituals that empowered the gods.

In the Valley of Mexico, kings were endowed with divine power which made them the spiritual leaders of their nations. They were expected to watch the earth and sky for supernatural signs, offer appropriate sacrifices, visit shrines, and ensure that priests performed their duties properly (Townsend 1979: 42). In April or May each year, the Aztec king visited the shrine on Mount Tlaloc, located on the eastern flank of the Valley of Mexico, to call forth rain from the mountain. Dressed as the god Tlaloc, he entered the long entrance to the temple carrying food and the blood of a sacrificed child as offerings to its deities. The rituals he performed fertilized the womb of the earth, calling forth its life. In performing these rituals he was not simply a suppliant but, as a manifestation of Tlaloc, was believed to play an active role in changing the seasons (Townsend 1992: 132–36). The king was also regarded as the surrogate of the Old Fire God, Xiuhtecuhtli (Ometeotl), and therefore as the father and mother of his people (Heyden 1989: 38–39). At the same time, rejuvenating the gods and sustaining the cosmic order were activities that upper-class males and ennobled warriors regarded as their collective prerogative (D. Carrasco 1990: 23). Lords wore or sponsored the wearing of the attire of deities at festivals. These costumes drew the deities into closer contact with humans and helped humans to forge more intimate and beneficial relations with them (Townsend 1992: 22).

The Inka ruler and his queen were the supreme mediators between their people and the supernatural forces of the sky and the lower world. The Inka king maintained the cosmic order (Bauer 1996: 333; Classen 1993: 110–11; Silverblatt 1987: 54). He could replace any priest as the chief worshipper or oracle medium of a god. State sacrifices were offered to all deities in the name of the king, except those to the creator god Wiraqucha, which were made on behalf of other deities and possibly paid for by those gods' foundations (Rowe 1944: 305).

The Chinese nobility was, according to Mark Lewis (1990: 28), set apart from the general population by the key role it played in sacrificial rites. The nobles' wealth and privileged access to the rewards of warfare and hunting enabled them to conduct more elaborate rituals than commoners (Allan 1991: 124). Their authority was manifested and reinforced by their ability to nourish and sustain in a spectacular manner the souls of their ancestors and the nature gods who fed them and their followers. Only altars of the soil that were patronized by rulers were nourished by the blood of military captives and condemned criminals (Lewis 1990: 17, 254). The connection between political power and religious ritual was strengthened by the Chinese belief that ancestral souls would accept sacrifices only from their most senior direct living male descendant (21). This meant that higher-ranking nobles had access to more ancient and therefore more powerful souls. Only the king, through the mediation of his royal ancestors, could communicate with the supreme sky god Shangdi (Chao 1972: 143–44). Winning Shangdi's favour and keeping the universe functioning properly required not only sacrifices but ritually correct behaviour (Keightley 1978b: 213–15).

The Maya believed that their kings played a crucial role as both sacrificers and victims in nourishing the gods, thus ensuring that the earth would remain fruitful and the cosmos would survive (Baudez 1994: 280; Houston and Stuart 1996; Schele and Miller 1986: 17, 104, 301). Rulers mediated between the different levels of the cosmos and drew deities and divine power into the human world (Freidel, Schele, and Parker 1993: 224). They communicated by means of elaborate rituals with the gods and the souls of the dead (Schele and Miller 1986: 104). Their blood sacrifices re-enacted the creation of the gods and of the world order and strengthened both (Tate 1992: 101). Through the king's association with 'God K', who appears to have been the ancestor of all royal lineages, life-sustaining essences were able to flow from Maya communities into the supernatural realm. Waging war provided royal and noble victims for sacrificial rituals, and this, combined with the personal blood-letting practised by rulers and nobles, gave the upper classes an especially important role in nourishing the gods and sustaining the cosmic order. Both rulers and gods sacrificed themselves so that life could continue (Miller 1986: 19).

The principal religious role of kings in all early civilizations was to mediate between the human realm and that of the gods, either directly or through royal ancestors who in some instances were also major nature deities. Kings ensured a continuous flow of energy from the human world to the gods and from the gods back to the human realm. For Egyptian, Inka, and Aztec rulers to claim that, without their support, the cosmic order would collapse was not a metaphorical boast or an ideologically driven exaggeration but a statement of profound conviction about how the universe functioned (Silverman 1991: 67). Even in Egypt and Mesopotamia, where it appears to have been believed that the gods might survive the cutting off of a flow of energy back into their realm, it was thought that the universe, and in particular the human realm, would be severely harmed by such a disruption. No such belief appears to have existed in earlier, more egalitarian societies, and there is no reason to believe that it diffused from one early civilization to another, except within Mesoamerica and perhaps between Mesopotamia and Egypt. How could such a belief in the central role played by kings and the upper classes in maintaining the cosmic order have originated independently in at least five and perhaps seven early civilizations?

In all the early civilizations, the gods and kings, assisted by the upper classes, played similar managerial roles in relation to the cosmos and society respectively. Commoners seem to have tacitly acknowledged that, without the domestic peace and order and the defence against foreign attack that the state provided, everyday life would have been far worse for them. Taxes and labour were the material compensation that commoners paid to the upper classes for these benefits. It was therefore easy for people in these civilizations to imagine all human beings performing the same role in relation to the gods that farmers and labourers performed for the upper classes. Sacrifice was the equivalent of paying taxes or tribute to the supernatural. Just as the upper classes could not possess the power they did without the surplus food turned over to them as taxes, so the gods could not survive without sacrifices. It was by the king that offerings were transmitted to provision the major gods so that they could continue to sustain the universe.

Individual rulers were manifestly inferior in power to the major gods. They lived no longer than other humans, even if the office they held was regarded as immortal, yet they were pivotal for maintaining the cosmic order. They alone could discern the will of the gods and ensure that the gods' needs were supplied. Kings thus performed dual functions as guarantors of a hierarchical society and sustainers of the supernatural order on which both nature and society depended. Because kings mediated between the human world and the gods, they and their office partook to varying degrees of the attributes of both worlds. Yet farmers and manual labourers were also recognized as playing a vital role in feeding the gods and therefore in maintaining the universe. Rulers and deities depended for their survival and well-being on the labour of farmers no less than farmers depended for an ordered, habitable, and fruitful universe on the upper classes and the gods. The three groups were linked by a pragmatic interdependence.

RELIGION AS POLITICAL CONSTITUTION

Many anthropologists have treated the religions of early civilizations as theocracies, maintaining that the upper classes used assertions of supernatural support to enhance their authority and frighten the lower classes into obeying them (Conrad and Demarest 1984; Godelier 1986; Steward 1949; L. White 1949). Instead, however, we find a view of cosmic processes in which farmers produced food to sustain themselves, the upper classes, and the gods, the gods sustained an environment in which crops could be grown, and the upper classes maintained order, which permitted populations to produce food, and played a key role in channelling energy back into the supernatural realm through sacrifice.

In recent discussions of changing views of the supernatural as societies grew more complex, some anthropologists have argued that in hunter-gatherer societies nature and the spirits that animate it are believed to provide food unconditionally to humans as a parent does to children (Bird-David 1990). Others have pointed out that in these societies nature embraces malevolent as well as benevolent powers and suggested that addressing nature as parents is more likely to be an appeal for favourable treatment than the expression of a belief that it is inevitably generous and caring (Ingold 1996: 151). The Cree of northern Quebec regard humans as only one among many forms of personhood that make up the cosmos and believe that good relations between hunters and animal spirits, usually expressed in terms of kinship, cause animals to sacrifice their lives to feed humans (Feit 1978; Tanner 1979). Human and animal spirits vary in individual power, and it is this difference which determines the nature of the personal relations they establish with each other. Cultivators living in small-scale societies are said to have viewed the environment and the spirits animating it not as indulgent parents but as demanding ancestors or elders who yielded the necessities of life only in return for favours rendered (Ingold 1996: 123). In early civilizations, in contrast, nature spirits were thought to behave like kings. The cosmos was conceptualized as a kingdom, but it was a kingdom in which the powers of the upper classes were based more on the consent of the governed and less on the exercise of coercion than in many later preindustrial societies. Early civilizations stressed not only the dependence of farmers on kings and gods but also the dependence of gods and kings on farmers.

The religious beliefs of early civilizations have been interpreted as straightforward justifications of an unequal social order. Were religious beliefs simply another means of intimidating ordinary people, as Leslie White (1959: 303–28) used to maintain? The notion that ideological claims made by ruling groups went uncontested by commoners seems highly dubious (Gailey 1987). Many groups living in the Inka kingdom had been conquered only a generation or two earlier, and factional conflicts among the ruling class discouraged any monolithic understanding of the nature of Inka power (Patterson 1991). There is no reason to believe that commoners were inevitably or even habitually duped by the religious claims of their rulers.

Early civilizations were, in theory at least, absolute monarchies. They had no political equivalent of modern constitutions or bills enumerating the rights of the governed. The same 'Instructions Addressed to King Merikare' that defined the role of the Egyptian king as upholding the cosmic order advised the king to suppress troublemakers and curb the common people (Lichtheim 1973: 99). The Aztec king Mochtezuma II's execution of potential opponents of his legislation to restrict government offices to men whose parents were both members of the hereditary nobility was praised as evidence of his power and determination rather than condemned as unjust. In early civilizations there was no way to criticize the behaviour of a superior overtly without also challenging his power.

Segments of Yoruba society could, however, criticize the actions and pretensions of their kings and other leaders in seemingly non-political contexts. During major religious festivals, the king, townspeople, officials, and lineages all asserted their respective rights vis-à-vis one another and questioned claims made by others by means of praise songs and ritual performances. Such behaviour permitted political struggles to be waged without directly challenging the actions or authority of the monarch, thus preserving a precarious balance between centripetal and centrifugal tendencies (Pemberton and Afolayan 1996).

The common features of religious beliefs in early civilizations seem to have been responses to similar political and economic problems faced by all these societies. By recognizing farmers as the producers of most of the goods and services on which not only the upper classes but also the gods depended, these beliefs empowered subordinates. Abuse of power by kings, nobles, or officials could not be protested directly without inviting retribution, but such behavior could be criticized and opposed indirectly on religious grounds. The Greek historian Herodotus reported that Khufu and Khafre, the builders of the two largest Egyptian pyramids at Giza, were remembered as tyrants who had ignored the worship of the gods and oppressed the people, while their successor, Menkaure, who had constructed a much smaller pyramid, was celebrated as a good and generous king. This story appears to have roots in beliefs about these kings that were already current during the Middle Kingdom and may reflect Old Kingdom views. If the first two rulers pushed their persistent demands on the economy to the point where their behaviour began to threaten the unity of Egypt, Menkaure made a timely adjustment after which no ruler except perhaps Akhenaton in the New Kingdom ever again tried to monopolize the wealth of Egypt for his own purposes in this way. Yet opposition to the policies of Khufu and Khafre seems to have been overtly focused not on their treatment of people but on their treatment of the gods. Relations between the king and local groups or their leaders were expressed in religious rather than political terms, the key issue being how carefully kings attended to the needs of the gods on whose well-being the cosmic order depended.

Similarly, no human was permitted to criticize the behaviour or policies of the Inka ruler directly, but objections to his policies could be expressed by his royal ancestors and by wakas throughout the kingdom speaking through their oracle priests. On a number of occasions each year, the king encountered all the mummified bodies of his royal ancestors and publicly conversed with them through their attendant priests. Every year the king had portable wakas brought to Cuzco from all parts of the kingdom so that he might question them. Children of local rulers who had been sacrificed by the king and whose bodies had been returned to their birthplaces for burial established oracular links between the king and regions where such ties had not existed previously. By consulting these oracles, the king in effect sounded the opinions of his subjects to help him decide if proposed policies would work. While oracles dared to criticize the king and to predict bad outcomes for his policies, kings exercised some reciprocal control over wakas by monitoring the accuracy and usefulness of their pronouncements and altering the amount of material support that they received from the central government. Wakas that seriously displeased the king or aligned themselves with rival factions of the royal family might be decommissioned (Gose 1996).

In Mesopotamia, the expansion of temple estates may have been partly a response to the growth of royal authority. Community elders, lineages, and individuals whose power was threatened by increasing centralization appear to have sought closer association with temples, which consequently increased in wealth and power as royal authority grew (Yoffee 1991: 301). By the Early Dynastic period, Egyptian kings were building larger temples and providing more offerings for deities of provinces whose leaders had conspicuously supported the emerging central government while at the same time subverting the authority of all hereditary local leaders (Seidlmayer 1996). Similarly, as Aztec kings became more powerful they honoured calpolli gods with grants of land and shares of foreign tribute but curtailed the political power of calpolli leaders.

Thus in early civilizations the struggle to protect local and individual rights of subjects against increasing exploitation by kings, government officials, and individual members of the upper classes was conducted primarily in a religious idiom. Misbehaviour by the upper classes was believed to infringe first and foremost on the rights of local deities. Undue appropriation of resources by kings and members of the upper classes for their own use endangered the cosmic order by restricting or threatening the food supply of the gods. Religious concepts thus supplied a constitution phrased in terms that were intelligible to people in early civilizations. These concepts did not overtly control or limit the powers of the king or the upper classes but assigned mutual responsibility to workers, the upper classes, and deities for promoting their common welfare and ensuring their joint survival.

Such beliefs exerted moral pressure on farmers to produce food surpluses to feed the upper classes, who regulated the political order and sacrificed to the major deities that sustained the cosmic order. They also stressed the need for rulers and administrators to keep ordinary people moderately prosperous and healthy. The gods had a vested interest in maintaining a cosmos in which enough energy was returned to them to ensure their survival and well-being. Far from being theocracies, the early civilizations were societies in which checks and balances were preserved and ordinary people were understood to have de facto rights. These ideas were expressed in a form that was appropriate for political discourse in societies in which religious concepts had replaced kinship as the principal way of understanding society and the universe. The development of such ideas explains why early civilizations were considerably more stable than the early state societies which had preceded them.

22 Priests, Festivals, and the Politics of the Supernatural

To possess the detailed esoteric knowledge necessary to perform the religious rituals that were patronized by the upper classes in early civilizations required considerable training. In many instances such knowledge, including rituals, prayers, hymns, incantations, and divination formulae, was the prerogative of priests, who were expected to manage the technical details of human relations with the supernatural. In early civilizations or still earlier smaller-scale societies, a shaman or sorcerer might learn how to relate to the supernatural from ecstatic experiences or by seeking personal instruction from a experienced master of these arts. Most individuals became part of a corporate priesthood by receiving formal instruction in a religious school or apprenticing with a religious cult or institution.

One of the fantasies that many religious scholars have propagated concerning early civilizations is that they were characterized by struggles for power between priests and secular authorities. The extensive nineteenth-century historical literature concerning competition for political supremacy between kings and popes in medieval Europe convinced many anthropologists that such conflicts characterized most complex premodern societies (L. White 1949: 233–81). To evaluate such relations objectively, it is necessary to examine the training, lifestyle, organization, and roles of priests in specific early civilizations.

Each city-state in the Valley of Mexico had its own religious institutions, and every major deity possessed its own temple or temples. All the larger temples had their own priests (*tlamacazqui*), who lived in special residences adjacent to the temple while they were on duty. Calpolli temples were tended by part-time priests (*quacilli*) (Soustelle 1961: 41, 51–52).

The king was the spiritual leader of his city-state and the symbolic head of its priesthood, and he presided in person over many major rituals. In Tenochtitlan, the two highest-ranking clergy were the high priests (*quequetzalcoa*) of the main gods, Tlaloc and Huitzilopochtli. Appointed by the king and his council, they appear not only to have been in charge of the cults of these two deities but also to have exercised some kind of supervisory control over all public cults and priests in the city-state.

Under the two high priests was an overseer of all state-sponsored cults (*mexicatl teohuatzin*). Some Spanish writers stated that this individual supervised worship throughout the Aztec tributary system; more likely, among his various duties was tending the cult images of foreign deities that the Aztec kept in a special temple in the central religious complex of Tenochtitlan. These images were hostages for the good behaviour of their worshippers and the proper veneration of the images of the god Huitzilopochtli, which the Aztec required to be installed alongside local deities in the main temples of tributary states. The overseer had two assistants: one responsible for ritual and the other for supervising the education of priests. There was also a treasurer (*tlaquimilolteculitli*), who managed temple property, including the land endowed for the support of state religious cults (Soustelle 1961: 52–53; Townsend 1992: 194).

Each temple had its own chief priest or priests and other clergy, whose number varied according to the importance of the temple and its deities. Eight or nine of the temples that were part of the central religious complex at Tenochtitlan had residences where priests lived while they were on duty. While chief priests seem invariably to have been male, temples dedicated to goddesses as well as to some male gods, such as Mixcoatl, had numerous female priests. Some priests served at temples on a long-term basis, rising from the rank of *tlamacazton* (novitiate) to *tlamacazqui* (regular priest) and sometimes to *tlamamacac* (high-ranking priest). Others worked on a rotational basis, usually for months or weeks, or dedicated themselves to a temple for a brief but fixed period in the hope of being cured of illness or gaining divine favour. More than five thousand people were reported to have served in the central religious complex at Tenochtitlan. In addition to their cult duties, highly trained full-time priests directed Aztec artistic and intellectual life. Priestly specialists also served their communities as diviners, vision interpreters, fortune-tellers, and calendricists (Berdan 1982: 10, 63, 130–33; Caso 1958: 82–84, 89; Durán 1971: 133–34; Soustelle 1961: 50–56; Townsend 1979: 61–62; 1992: 193–94).

Some Aztec children were consecrated by their parents to become priests (Berdan 1982: 130), and others, occasionally commoners who displayed special aptitude for a priestly career, were selected by religious officials. All male priests were trained in the schools normally reserved for the sons of nobles, which were controlled by one of the members of the Council of Four. Priestly training was rigorous. In addition to learning esoteric knowledge, good manners, and self-restraint, students had to fast, bleed themselves, and stay awake all night to keep watch and perform rituals. Their mistakes were punished by beating them, stabbing them with maguey spikes, or throwing them into the lake. Successful students were enrolled as novitiate priests about the age of fifteen (Caso 1958: 86–87).

Priests are described as wearing their hair uncut, unwashed, and often matted with blood, with their ears shredded as a result of frequent blood-letting. While on duty they observed frequent fasts and watches and led an austere life that left them gaunt (Clendinnen 1991: 128–29; Townsend 1992: 192). Both students and priests were executed if they did not refrain from sexual activity. Priests could retire from full-time service of the gods whenever they wished to marry; high-ranking priests were married and even polygamous but had to refrain from sexual activity while they lived and served in the temples. During certain major festivals, all Aztec were forbidden to engage in sexual activity or to wash their heads to strengthen their supernatural powers. The gods were believed to punish with illness anyone who violated these prohibitions (López Austin 1988, 1: 306–7). Priests who became intoxicated were executed (Berdan 1982: 97–98).

It has been claimed that Aztec men were trained to be priests while women were regarded as priests by nature (Clendinnen 1991: 207). Yet some daughters of nobles were trained to be priests, partly in the *cuicacalli*, where all girls and boys were taught ritual songs and dances, but also in temples, where they spent a year around the age of twelve learning to cook and clean for the cult images and the priests. The ecclesiastical training of women was not, however, as long or as rigorous as that of men. Female priests were required to remain celibate so long as they served the gods. Most of them left the priesthood at a relatively young age to marry (Berdan 1982: 88; Caso 1958: 83).

In Mesopotamia the temples in each city-state were controlled by local rulers or hegemons to varying degrees at different times, but for the most part each large temple functioned independently of the rest. Ekur, the temple of Enlil in Nippur, served as a pan-southern-Mesopotamian religious meeting-place, but its priests did not control other temples. Temples possessed estates of varying sizes, and their staff was divided into administrative, cultic, and domestic personnel. The chief administrator of the temple and its estate was called the *sanga*. His position was a full-time one, well remunerated and frequently inherited. A single sanga might be in charge of several temples. Under him were various high-ranking officials who bore titles such as iššakku (farm steward), *paé* (temple overseer), and *idu* (doorkeeper). These officials supervised agricultural labourers, collected rents from tenant farmers, managed commercial transactions, and guarded temple property (R. Harris 1975: 154–88).

While kings could personally sacrifice to any deity, the most prestigious religious official in a major temple, such as one belonging to the patron deity of a city-state, was the en, a title often translated as 'high priest or priestess'. Where the deity was male, the en was usually female, and where the deity was female the en was male. The en lived in the *gipar*, a palace-like structure within the temple enclosure, and appears to have been regarded as a spouse of the deity (Oates 1978: 476). In Ur, the high priest of the moon god, Nannar, was often the daughter of a hegemonic ruler (Lerner 1986: 66–68).

A regular priest, called the *gudu* (Akkadian *pišišu*) of the god he served, offered sacrifices and organized festivals. The highest-ranking priests were called *gudapsu* (hairy priests), perhaps because they did not cut their hair; several of them often served in a large temple at one time. Regular priests' positions were not necessarily full-time jobs; a particular office might be divided into twelve-day allotments (*isqum*), each held in turn by a different person over the course of a year. During Early Dynastic times, libation priests, who directly tended the needs of a temple's resident deity, were depicted as naked or wearing only loincloths, while the offering-bearers who accompanied them were fully clothed. In the Akkadian period priests were distinguished by having their heads shaved (Furlong 1987: 266–76; R. Harris 1975: 168–71; Postgate 1992: 128).

Also attached to temples were diviners (*barum*), dream-interpreters, various types of omen-readers, and ecstatics, who determined the meaning of different forms of divine communications (R. Harris 1975: 176, 188; Postgate 1992: 132). In addition to their regular temple duties, priests and diviners offered sacrifices for ordinary people, interpreted their dreams, made prognostications, administered oaths, participated in legal hearings, and assisted with burial rituals (Postgate 1992: 125). The fees charged for such services belonged either to the priests or to their temple. Other ritualists included professional musicians, praise-singers (*nar/narum*), and lamentation-singers (*gala/kalum*) of various ranks (Crawford 1991: 162; R. Harris 1975: 172–75), who were believed capable of activating divine power and eliciting divine favour (Jacobsen 1976: 15).

Apart from female en priests, the most important women associated with religious activities in Old Babylonian times were the naditum (fallow women). Apparently treated as daughters-in-law of a temple's resident god, they cleaned the interior of the temple and presented special food offerings (*piqittu*) on festival days. They were often daughters of wealthy men, and each lived with her servants in relative luxury in her own house, located within a walled enclosure (*gagum*) attached to a temple. They were not, however, allowed to marry, have children, or alienate family property. Other women, who could marry but not have children, played a role in the cults of female deities (R. Harris 1975: 188–200, 305–12; Jacobsen 1970: 185; Postgate 1992: 97–98, 131–32). Also associated with temples were lower-class women known as *qadistu* (consecrated ones), *istaritu* (devotees of Ishtar), and *harimtu* (ones set apart). They appear to have been, perhaps in addition to having other occupations, prostitutes who modelled their behaviour on that of the goddess Inanna (Ishtar), and their sexual promiscuity was believed to promote the fertility and prosperity of the land. Associations of male prostitutes performed homosexual acts (*asakku*) that were not practised by the gods but entertained the fertility goddess Inanna (Bottéro 1992: 189–92; Lerner 1986: 128–31).

Non-priestly temple staff included snake-charmers, bee-keepers, and acrobats, whose jobs may have been to protect, provision, and entertain deities, cooks who prepared offerings, and sweepers who kept the outer temple buildings clean. At least some of these tasks were performed by different people working in rotation throughout the year (Postgate 1992: 125–27).

Yoruba religious practices were less centralized than were those of the Valley of Mexico or Mesopotamia. Instead of being focused on temples and controlled by hierarchical organizations of priests, they were associated with a large number of cults dedicated to the worship of particular deities or sets of deities. Individuals joined one or more cults as a result of family affiliation, unusual experiences, special physical characteristics, or personal preferences. A deity might torment a person until he or she agreed to worship that deity. Hunchbacks, cripples, dwarfs, albinos, and people born in a caul were believed destined to become worshippers of Orisala, the god who fashioned people in the womb. Each cult had one or more shrines located within or close to a community and its own praise chants, songs, rhythms, dances, musical instruments, insignia, symbols, scar patterns, myths, taboos, and sacrificial foods (Bascom 1969: 81, 97). Initiation into each of these cults could take up to several months and involved seclusion in shrines, the learning of esoteric rituals, the shaving of heads, and sometimes spirit possession by the deity (Bascom 1969: 77–78). Failure to serve a deity once initiated was supernaturally punished. Individual performance and social status played significant roles in determining vertical mobility within such cults.

Some religious cults were important instruments of social control. The Ogboni society, which focused on the worship of the earth god, had as its primary mission to root out and destroy evil and corruption. Its members, who were mostly town and palace officials, collected debts for others, settled blood disputes, acted as judges, and executed criminals. The Oro society, which worshipped a deity associated with the god of medicine, disposed of witches and sorcerers and executed kings who refused to obey orders to commit suicide. The Egungun society, which was concerned with limiting the powers of death, also executed witches. Membership in these three societies remained secret, as did many of their rituals (Ajisafe 1924: 90–93; Bascom 1944; 1969: 31, 92–93; R. Thompson 1976: 6/1–6/4).

The majority of religious cults had as their aim the worship of specific deities, from whom particular benefits were expected. The high god Olorun was exceptional in having no cult; he was believed to benefit from the offerings made to all the other deities. Images of the god Esu received frequent offerings in every household and in public places but he had no priests of his own. One of his duties was to convey the spiritual power of sacrifices to the deities who were their intended beneficiaries.

All other cults had their own local priests, although most of these offices were part-time ones. Priests were believed to be especially endowed with the power of the god they worshipped (Pemberton and Afolayan 1996: 90). Both men and women became priests. Although most priestly offices tended to be hereditary (Lucas 1948: 183), qualifying for them required varying degrees of training, usually in the form of an apprenticeship. Priests and their assistants had to prepare for sacrificing by prayer, fasting, and observing appropriate taboos (Awolalu 1979: 170).

Families, lineages, and quarters each worshipped specific deities or groups of deities, with their political leaders serving as the hereditary priests of their cults. Leading officials often headed cults that played a key role in communitywide religious festivals (Awolalu 1979: 113). In many Yoruba states, former royal lineages that had been dethroned by newcomers or the leaders of kin groups that claimed to have lived in an area before there was any king were acknowledged to have special priestly powers (Pemberton and Afolayan 1996: 38).

Cults whose membership cut across lineage organizations were headed by priests (*aworo*) who had achieved their positions as a result of outstanding service in the cult or divine designation. Such priests officiated at rituals performed every four days and at various annual festivals, offered sacrifices, led devotions, announced their deities' will, and guarded and maintained shrines (*ile orisa*, *ojubo*) and objects of worship. Divination played a major role in determining what sacrifices were required to propitiate specific deities (Awolalu 1979: 111–13). Priests who served Ore, the god of hunting, atoned for acts of incest, those of Orisala buried women who had died while pregnant, and those of Sango purified houses that had been hit by lightning, which was a certain sign that Sango was angry with the people who lived in them (Bascom 1969: 80–84). In Ife, special *otu* priests, attached to the palace, disposed of sacrifices made within the palace grounds and conducted installation ceremonies for the king and the city's leading officials (Bascom 1969: 38).

The most highly trained and revered priests were the diviners (*babalawo*), attached to the cult of Ifa (Orunmile), the god of divination. Ifa transmitted requests for sacrifices and other messages from the gods, including Olorun, to human beings. While Ifa divination was usually performed using sixteen palm nuts, a priest had to have memorized over one thousand verses and learned their meanings to be able to interpret the 256 resulting combinations. This knowledge, which has been described as an encyclopedic compendium of every aspect of Yoruba thought and was kept highly secret, was acquired during an apprenticeship lasting many years (Abimbola 1973; Bascom 1969: 70–71, 80; Lucas 1948: 72). Diviners determined the causes of illnesses and misfortunes and identified possible solutions. Their services were eagerly sought after, making it proverbial that 'a babalawo never starves' (Lucas 1948: 72). The central Ifa shrine was at Ife, where its deity had first descended to earth, but the cult had branches throughout the Yoruba region.

The centre of the cult of Sango was at his shrine in Koso, which was controlled by the king of Oyo. Its operation was supervised by the *otun iwefa*, the Oyo royal eunuch in charge of religious matters. Many important offices in the cult were held by members of high-ranking Oyo lineages. Priests for provincial branches of the Sango cult were trained by the *mogba* (senior priests) at the Koso shrine (Apter 1992: 24–25; Pemberton and Afolayan 1996: 152). At Benin sacrificial rites in honour of dead kings were performed by special priests from Ihoghe who claimed that their ancestors had accompanied the founder of the royal lineage from Ife to Benin (Bradbury 1957: 55).

While the Maya had priests in the sixteenth century A.D., no evidence of priests has been found in either Maya art or surviving texts for the Classic period (Coe 1993: 184). Only kings and members of the royal family are depicted presenting offerings to deities. This may have been, as it was in Egypt, an iconographic convention stressing the crucial role claimed by the king in communicating with the gods and making offerings to them. Many officials, even if they only acted as substitutes for the king, must have been needed to manage the numerous temples and carry out the rituals associated with them. It is unknown whether these duties were performed by priests or by secular deputies for the king and whether such responsibilities occupied individuals full-time or only part-time.

In Egypt all cults for both the gods and the dead were performed in the king's name, but the only Old Kingdom temples that were fully managed by the central government appear to have been royal funerary chapels, the main temples in Memphis and nearby Heliopolis, and some Fifth Dynasty sun temples at Saqqara that were associated with royal funerary cults. Priests, craft workers, and farmers working for funerary temples were granted various exemptions from taxes and corvée labour in the Old Kingdom. Kings supplied cult statues to provincial temples and may have arranged for provincial government officials to finance the daily operations of these temples. Yet, prior to the Middle Kingdom, the construction of most provincial temples appears to have been initiated and carried out locally. Each temple seems to have had its own administrators, workmen, and priests, although in the Old Kingdom some priests may have been responsible for a number of cults in the same district (Goedicke 1979: 129).

The priests who served a particular cult were organized hierarchically. At the top of the hierarchy were the servants of the god (*ḥmw nṯr*), who might be under the control of an overseer of such priests (*ỉmy-r ḥmw nṯr*). They were responsible for the daily rituals of feeding and tending the deity's cult statue (Morenz 1973: 301), assisted by a lector priest (*ẖry ḥbt*), who read aloud the appropriate prayers and incantations, and *stm* priests, who washed, clothed, and applied cosmetics to the cult statue. The general care of the temple was the task of *wʿb* priests (purified ones), who cleaned the buildings, slaughtered animals, cooked for the gods, and guarded and handled sacred objects. All priests had to have their entire bodies shaved, bathe frequently, avoid sex, and wear only linen clothing while they were on duty in the temple. They were supported by large numbers of farmers, craftsmen, and temple labourers (Hawass 1995: 241–45; Sauneron 1960; Shafer 1997b; Strouhal 1992: 223–33).

There is no evidence of full-time priests during the Old and Middle Kingdoms. Instead priests were drawn from other professions to serve in teams (*s3*) for part of each year. The highest-ranking ones were selected from among government administrators and scribes, while lower-ranking ones were recruited among craftsmen and farmers. In the Middle Kingdom, priests were organized in four teams, each of which served in rotation for one lunar month. In the Old Kingdom, there had been five teams, each divided into two sections, which served for one of every ten solar months (A. Roth 1991a: 2–4). Such an arrangement ensured that temples, with their rich endowments, did not become autonomous institutions that were able to challenge the power of the king. It also distributed temple revenues widely among officials and ordinary people (A. Roth 1991b: 120). *Ḥmw k3* were priests who were under contract to perform the mortuary cults of deceased members of the upper class and of well-to-do scribes and other professionals and were paid for their services from perpetual tomb endowments. Offerings frequently came from temples, and many of these priests probably also worked as ordinary priests in these temples.

In the Old Kingdom many upper-class women served as priests (*ḥmwt nṯr*) in the cults of deities throughout Egypt, especially those of the female deities Hathor and Neith. Women also served as funerary priests (*ḥmwt k3*). While a few low-ranking *wꜥbt* priestesses were still attached to the cult of Hathor in the Middle Kingdom, the priests of other cults had become exclusively male. Women continued, however, to serve as musicians and dancers in temple rituals into the New Kingdom (Fischer 1989: 18–20). Their erotic performances were believed to play a vital role in sexually arousing male creator deities and thus ensuring the continued functioning of the universe (Robins 1993: 142–45). It was not until the New Kingdom that full-time priests began to be put in charge of temples. They were appointed and could be dismissed at the king's pleasure.

In the Central Andean highlands, ayllu or village leaders appointed elderly men and women to act as part-time priests. Their responsibilities included offering sacrifices to the ayllu's wakas and the souls of its dead ancestors and being the oracles through whom these supernatural beings spoke to humans (Cobo 1990: 158–59; Kendall 1973: 192; MacCormack 1991: 422–28). Throughout the Inka kingdom, the government appointed priests and chosen women to serve in state temples. The highest-ranking priest in the kingdom was the *willaq umu*, who was the head priest at the main temple of the sun in Cuzco. He was a close relative of the Inka king and seems to have belonged to either Inka Wiraqucha's or Lloque Qhapaq Yupanki's panaqa. He held this post for life or at the king's pleasure and was the chief oracle of Inti, the sun god. The Spanish described the willaq umu as a 'pope' who was in charge of all priests throughout the Inka state. He outranked any other priest and was responsible for organizing the annual visits to Cuzco of portable wakas from the provinces. Yet, whenever the king wished, he could take the willaq umu's place and himself offer sacrifices and transmit oracular messages from the sun god. It is reported that, early in his reign, King Wayna Qhapaq removed the willaq umu from office and personally assumed the role of high priest of the sun (Gose 1996a: 23; Kendall 1973: 191).

The sun temple, the Qorikancha, was reported to have been served by two hundred male priests and five hundred chosen women. Ten priests, called *hatun wilka*, were of higher rank than the rest and belonged to the nobility; ordinary priests were called *yana wilka*. These priests were said to come from the Tarpuntay ayllu, one of the pre-Inka groups in the Cuzco area whose members had been made Inka-by-privilege (Kendall 1973: 191; MacCormack 1991: 112, 158). It was claimed that the solar temple at Vilcas had forty thousand servants and forty gatekeepers, but these figures probably include the farmers who worked the fields assigned to the temple and the total number of gatekeepers who served the temple in rotation each year (MacCormack 1991: 99). Corvée labour may have played as important a role in supplying staff for temples as it did in providing other labourers for the Inka state. Bernabé Cobo (1990: 9) reported that in the Cuzco area more than one thousand men – priests and their apprentices, who had to remember flawlessly all the rituals associated with the wakas they served – were employed solely to conserve religious lore. Cobo also noted that a small group of nobles was specially concerned with religious matters.

The title 'yana wilka' might indicate that ordinary priests were yanakuna, but more likely it simply designated them as servants of the gods (Kendall 1973: 191). The priesthood was to some extent hereditary in certain ayllus or lineages, from which individuals were selected by kinsmen, local rulers, and the Inka government. Individuals were also called to be priests by visions, while children born during thunderstorms were destined in old age to serve the storm god Illapa (Cobo 1990: 158–59; MacCormack 1991: 299, 422). Priests were ranked according to the importance of the wakas they served, by whether and how well their temples were supported by the government, and by their relative positions among the priests serving in a particular temple.

The principal duties of priests were to tend wakas, sacrifice to them, maintain their particular traditions, and transmit this esoteric knowledge to their successors (Cobo 1990: 159). Only nobles and attendant priests were allowed to enter major temples such as the Qorikancha. That required ritual purification and avoidance of foods such as salt, chillies, meat, and corn beer for up to a year (MacCormack 1991: 67). Priests were expected to serve as oracles for their deities, interpret dreams and omens, pray for people, transmit messages from the dead, and diagnose and treat diseases (Kendall 1973: 192). At small shrines one or two priests probably performed all these duties, but at large temples there was some division of labour.

Divination and oracular possession were employed to diagnose diseases, identify hostile sorcerers, locate lost property, determine what was happening to people far away, establish appropriate sacrificial offerings, and settle controversies. Four hundred seventy-five officially sanctioned diviners (*omo*), many of them elderly priests, were reported to have lived in the Cuzco area. Most divination involved sacrifice, and diviners were allowed to keep for themselves the parts of offerings that were not consumed by fire (Cobo 1990: 160–63; Rowe 1944: 302).

Hearing confessions was another important duty of priests. Only deeds and words, not thoughts, were regarded as sinful, but undisclosed sins such as murder, poisoning, theft, seduction, audibly cursing the king or a god, and practising witchcraft were believed to anger the gods and invite supernatural punishment in the form of illness. The gods might punish persons who committed crimes, members of their families, or community leaders. Confession and subsequent purification were the only way to avoid such supernatural retribution. Priests cast lots to determine whether a confession was complete and prescribed penances, which included sacrifices, abstaining from luxury foods, and avoiding sexual relations for a fixed period, all of which were followed by washing in running water (Cobo 1990: 122–25; Rowe 1944: 304–5).

The Inka queen was the principal officiant at Cuzco of the cult of Paksamama, the moon goddess. Women made up most if not all the officiants in the cults of at least some female deities and participated in many other religious rituals performed at cult centres throughout the kingdom. Many of the participants were chosen women, who were ranked and had religious duties assigned to them on the basis of their age and their families' social status. Senior chosen women (mamakuna), who were of royal or noble birth, played important roles in religious rituals, which made them the female counterparts of priests, and also heard all confessions by women (Kendall 1973: 70, 192–93; Silverblatt 1987: 99–106).

There is no clear evidence of a professional priesthood in Shang or Zhou China. Kings, lords, and lineage heads sacrificed to the gods and to their ancestors, assisted by their wives, mothers, sisters, and retainers (Creel 1937: 338). Female attendants (*shifu*) supervised the care of ritual vessels and the preparation of sacrificial foods, attended sacrificial rituals, and organized the ceremonial activities of other women living in the royal palace (C. Chang 1986: 112).

Divination, which involved communicating (*bin*) with royal ancestors, played a major role in determining the detailed content and divine recipients of sacrificial offerings. Such divination has been interpreted as an effort to turn sacrifices into a form of spell-casting that would predispose the royal ancestors to influence nature and intervene in human affairs in a predetermined, favourable manner (Allan 1991: 113–23; Keightley 1978b: 213). At the royal court divination took the form of scapulimancy, with fire being applied to turtle plastrons and the shoulder-blades of butchered oxen. Replies were read from the shapes of cracks that developed as a result of the heat. The dates of divinations, the propositions tested, and sometimes the actual outcomes of events were recorded in writing on the shells or bones used for divination. Divining at the royal court clearly required specialized knowledge, but it is not clear whether royal diviners were regarded primarily as priests or as court officials. Nor is it known whether being a diviner was a full-time occupation (Keightley 1978a).

Royal diviners (*bu*, *zhen*) included princes and nobles as well as individuals of lesser rank. Some diviners appear to have come from settlements or regions whose names they bore to serve the Shang kings. In the earliest oracle texts from Anyang, the names of diviners accompanied the records of their findings. Towards the end of the Shang Dynasty, divination rites were increasingly performed only in the king's name. Yet deputies may have continued to divine and sacrifice for the king (Chou 1968: 60, 137–38; Keightley 1979–80). The strongest evidence of highly skilled ritual specialists working at the Shang court are the two so-called schools for sacrificing to the royal ancestors identified by Tung Tso-pin. Sacrifices were carried out in ten-day cycles, the sacrifice to a particular royal ancestor being performed on the day of the cycle that bore the same 'heavenly stem' designation as appeared in that ancestor's posthumous name. A full set of sacrifices took a whole year to complete (Chao 1972: 132; Creel 1937: 202; Li Chi 1977: 134, 248–54). Tung's Old or Conservative School offered elaborate sacrifices to a large number of ancestors who had preceded the first Shang king, Dayi; the New or Progressive School restricted the number of male ancestors and the categories of queens to whom sacrifices were offered and, instead of divining the contents of individual sacrificial rituals, prescribed standardized offerings. The two schools were also associated with differences in writing styles and calendrical usage. For some reason they alternated every two or three reigns. This suggests that at least two groups of specialists, each with its own distinctive practices, persisted alongside one another in Shang royal circles for over 150 years (Chêng 1960: 178–79, 222; Hsu and Linduff 1988: 110).

Royal sacrifices appear to have been offered regularly only at the royal court. They were also made to some powerful local nature deities when the king was travelling. Princes sacrificed to their own ancestors and to local deities in their provinces and districts (Chêng 1960: 204–6, 223–24). All these rituals must have required numerous officials to ensure that temples were maintained, gather sacrificial offerings, and assist the king or lord in carrying out major sacrifices. Singers and musicians were also employed in these rituals. These people were probably religious specialists only on a part-time basis.

There were also ritualists who were called *xi* if male and *wu* if female, both terms usually being translated as 'shaman'. Such ritualists worked either singly or in groups. It has been suggested that their primary role was to facilitate communication with the supernatural by summoning the souls of the dead back into the terrestrial world or projecting their own souls into supernatural realms (Allan 1991: 85–86; K. Chang 1976: 162). Kwang-chih Chang (1983: 44–54) suggested that Shang kings claimed preeminent shamanistic powers for themselves. In divination, the king's soul ascended into the sky to communicate with the souls of his royal ancestors or their spirits descended from the sky into the body of the king or his diviner. Yet Shang kings were never referred to as shamans (Yates 1997: 82). David Keightley's (1978b: 223–24) proposal that the Shang rulers confronted their ancestors bureaucratically rather than ecstatically seems to accord better with what is known about royal divination in China.

One of the clearly attested duties of shamans was to perform elaborate rain-making rituals (*hun wu*). Occasionally they seem to have allowed themselves to be set on a blazing pyre or exposed to the sun in the hope of inducing rain to end a drought. That these shamans risked being burned to death suggests that they may have been commoners who were sometimes recruited, either by farmers or the government, to perform rituals intended to control the weather. In later times shamans belonged to the lower levels of society and authorities carefully regulated their activities (Allan 1991: 42; Chêng 1960: 224, 226; Yates 1997: 82).

The idea of priests and kings as rivals and of competition between church and state in early civilizations is not supported by the evidence. Concepts that seemed appropriate for understanding the history of medieval Europe have been misapplied to these societies. In all early civilizations individuals were specially trained to conduct rituals and perform other religious tasks. Often such training necessitated acquiring large amounts of esoteric knowledge and maintaining a state of ritual purity. Ritual experts came from different classes and were organized in hierarchies of varying complexity; while some performed their religious duties full-time, others alternated religious tasks with administrative, craft, or agricultural work. The most important role performed by these specialists was to offer, in the name of the king, the sacrifices that played an essential role in providing the gods with what they needed.

The closest approximation to competition between church and state occurred in Mesopotamia, where from time to time in some city-states there was considerable rivalry between kings and the managers of major temple estates. At other times and places, Mesopotamian kings controlled the operation of temples. In all situations, however, Mesopotamian kings were recognized as the chief stewards and agents of their cities' patron deities. In Old and Middle Kingdom Egypt, priests served part-time as deputies for the king, who alone was deemed capable of offering sacrifices to the gods. The same situation may have prevailed among the Classic Maya, assuming that they actually recognized priestly offices as opposed to full-time government officials performing religious rites when required. Shang and Early Zhou sacrifices were offered by lineage heads, the most important of whom were also political leaders. Shang kings and high-ranking nobles were assisted by diviners and others who possessed expert knowledge about how to deal with the supernatural, but these specialists may have simultaneously held other court or administrative appointments. The Aztec and Inka had full-time priests, but kings and other officials could assume their roles during major rituals. The Yoruba had many cults, with different and even rival groups worshipping the same deities. Each of these cults had its own priests and hierarchical organization. Yoruba kings were regarded as supernaturally essential for maintaining the unity of their kingdom and the well-being of the world.

There has also been a tendency to imagine that the cult personnel found in each state constituted a centrally controlled and disciplined hierarchy carrying out a common programme of worship mandated by the government or by religious leaders. In Old Kingdom Egypt, the royal mortuary cults were centrally controlled. The temples in provincial administrative centres appear to have remained partly under local management until the Middle Kingdom, although the central government subsidized their cults to some degree. There was no overall hierarchy of Egyptian priests, and the part-time nature of local priesthoods further limited their ability to exercise political power. The Inka chief priest of the sun in Cuzco, acting in the king's name, normally dealt with wakas throughout the kingdom, distributed royal largess to their cults, curbed potentially dangerous political activities by their oracle priests, and may have coordinated solar rituals in the various provincial administrative centres. Yet he did not impose a centralized control over local cults, most of which remained self-financing and self-managing. Nor is there evidence to sustain the view that Aztec high priests controlled worship throughout the Aztec tributary network.

In none of these societies does there appear to have been an overall religious hierarchy paralleling or overreaching the political order. Even in individual city-states, a single high priest rarely regulated all the temples, and in territorial states it was considered unnecessary to impose a rigidly hierarchical religious organization on local cults. The staff of large temples or cults tended to be complexly and hierarchically arranged. Their priests wore elaborate costumes, observed numerous taboos, and specialized in various branches of knowledge related to communicating with and serving the gods. Yet in every case kings claimed to be the chief intermediaries between their people and the supernatural powers that animated and sustained the universe. This role did not inevitably confer divinity or even great political power on kings, but it made them symbols of the unity of the state and responsible for sustaining the cosmic order. Priests, if they existed at all in particular early civilizations, were subordinates rather than rivals of the king.

PUBLIC RITUAL

Sacrificing to deities was routinely carried out by priests or officials in precincts from which most people were usually excluded. These sanctuaries constituted a ritually safe environment for encountering the supernatural and protected unconsecrated people from the dangers of inadvertent exposure to supernatural power. Such seclusion increased the mystery and importance of these rites in the minds of the people who were not permitted to participate in them.

Large numbers of people were, however, expected or required to participate in other public rituals. These rituals sought to tap the fertility, power, and creativity of supernatural forces for the benefit of the social realm by making that realm more closely resemble its supernatural prototype. They also sought to sustain, renew, and stabilize the cosmos for the benefit of humanity, to draw society into closer harmony with the natural environment, and to reinforce respect for the political hierarchy by stressing its resemblance to the supernatural realm. These goals were pursued by performing rituals that were believed to duplicate what went on among the gods or had happened on earth long ago. In addition to reinforcing cosmological beliefs and promoting social integration, these public rituals sometimes provided a stage for acting out and partially resolving political tensions that were not publicly acknowledged (Bauer 1996; Clendinnen 1991: 235–43).

In the Valley of Mexico, the entire population of city-states joined in numerous acts of collective worship. All the residents of calpollis, quarters, or cities were expected to attend their religious festivals. All teenage boys and girls were taught how to participate in these rituals (Durán 1971: 289–91). Public rituals involving large numbers of celebrants drawn from all classes were performed at various times of the year in plazas adjacent to the central temples of each city, as well as at temples and shrines elsewhere in the city and in the surrounding countryside.

The elaboration of public rituals expressed the relative power of different city-states. As Aztec power grew, the frequency and magnificence of Tenochtitlan's religious rituals increased, along with the number of human sacrifices that accompanied them. The Aztec's main public rituals were keyed to an annual calendar. Nine twenty-day summer 'months' were associated with agricultural rituals that sequentially blessed the seed, encouraged rain, fed hungry commoners before the harvest, celebrated the harvest, and honoured the dead. The nine winter months, stretching between harvest and planting, were devoted to rituals associated with war. Thus the first half of the year was focused on the fertility god Tlaloc, the second half on the solar war god and patron deity, Huitzilopochtli. While most Aztec public rituals involved human sacrifice, the largest numbers of human lives were offered during four brief periods of religious observance each year. The most were killed at *tlacaxipeualiztli* (the flaying of men), the first major festival of the solar year, which occurred at the beginning of the second Aztec month, in late March, and was associated with the fertility god Xipe Totec (Clendinnen 1991: 91, 295–97; Durán 1971: 172, 412–65).

Special public rituals were enacted at four-, eight-, and fifty-two-year intervals, the latter by everyone living in the Valley of Mexico, to renew or re-create the cosmos at the end of a calendar round (Berdan 1982: 134–35). Inga Clendinnen (1992: 76) observes that, while Aztec public rituals united all classes to honour the gods, they also emphasized the hierarchical social order and the need for commoners to defer to the upper classes. This was paralleled by general human submission to a supernatural order that was perceived as being either highly capricious or determined without reference to human interests. The alternative 260-day calendar largely designated feasts related to individual humans and deities and was used for divination.

Yoruba worship tended to occur in public. Shrines were usually small, compelling all but the most esoteric rituals to be carried out around rather than inside them. The king performed special rituals for the welfare of the kingdom in secluded parts of the palace, but even religious societies with secret memberships conducted masked rituals in the streets. Women were excluded from participating in some public rituals and men from participating in others. Religious festivals (*odun*) played a conspicuous role in Yoruba community life. At Ife only twenty-five days each year were without public festivals (Bascom 1969: 34). Elaborate annual ceremonies propitiated deities for the benefit of the community and sought to draw spiritual power from the bush into towns and cities to ensure that women remained fertile, make crops grow, and keep the king strong (Apter 1992: 98). In the course of its major festivals, each Yoruba urban centre sought to re-create the world from its own point of view and to re-establish a precarious balance between the political unity of the state and the diversity of its constituent groups (Apter 1992: 21, 175–76).

In the community of Ila Orangun, the first major public festival of the year, held in March, was Odun Ogungun (the festival of the ancestors). In the course of this festival, the townspeople reasserted their traditional rights and freedoms vis-à-vis the king. Odun Ogun, celebrated in June, dramatized the conflict between an individual's loyalty to the state, as embodied by the king, and his loyalty to his kin group. Odun Oba, in late August and early September, reaffirmed the king's power. These major community festivals were followed by and interpersed with festivals honouring particular deities (Pemberton and Afolayan 1996: 101–96).

At Ife the annual Oduduwa festival celebrated the creation of the world and the genealogical unity of all Yoruba kings and people. The sacrifice of a five-toed chicken and the performances of dancers dressed in chicken costumes commemorated the bird from the sky realm that helped Oduduwa create the earth (Bascom 1969: 10–11). Three New Year yam festivals performed by Ifa priests between late June and August allowed the king of Ife and his retainers, then the worshippers of Ifa and other beneficent deities associated with the colour white, and finally the worshippers of other deities to eat new yams. These festivals also ritually renewed the fertility of the soil (Bascom 1969: 19).

Because of the large number of people living in individual Yoruba extended family compounds, especially in the northern regions, the cults carried out by them had a public character. Every four days, the compound head sacrificed to the various deities that were worshipped by his extended family. A series of major festivals to honour these deities was held during the course of the year. Women worshipped their husbands' deities, but in addition every woman returned to her father's compound to participate in its cults after she had married, and her children sometimes joined her (Bascom 1969: 77).

In Mesopotamia, an important form of public ritual was the journeying of cult statues from one temple to another. Sometimes the images of deities were transported from their temples to the surrounding countryside. This became a major feature of the later *akitum* (New Year) festival at Babylon. Cult statues from different city-states also visited one another. Pre-Sargonic texts record such journeys between Lagash and Girsu and as far away as Uruk, while later records tell of visits by deities from southern Mesopotamia to Nippur and Eridu (Postgate 1992: 123–24). The images of deities were also paraded around cities during their festivals. Standards or symbols of deities were regularly taken from temples to assist in collecting tithes and to be used for swearing oaths in legal cases.

New-moon festivals were celebrated in every Mesopotamian temple, along with feasts specific to each god (Jacobsen 1976: 97–98). The most important annual religious festival was the New Year celebration, which extended over approximately twelve days in March and early April. This elaborate ritual, which followed the annual harvest, sought to renew the cosmos by re-enacting its divine creation and supernatural ordering (Kuhrt 1987: 31–40). It was an occasion for the public to feast on food provided by the king and temples, and in the third millennium B.C. it was also a time when the fertility of the land was renewed by a ritual marriage between the king, temporarily incarnating a god, and his wife or some priestess, incarnating a goddess (Bottéro 1992: 226; Furlong 1987: 33–34; Hooke 1958; Postgate 1992: 123). It has been suggested that this ritual began in Uruk, with a priestess representing the goddess Inanna and the en priest or king representing the god Dumuzi. In the Early Dynastic period, sacred marriages were performed in the temples of many fertility deities (Lerner 1986: 126–27).

Numerous Maya rites were performed in relative seclusion by members of royal families or their deputies inside temples, palace complexes, or small, enclosed plazas surrounded by elite structures. It is not known who was permitted to witness these rites or the religious ball games that were played in courts located within palace complexes, which reenacted the escape of the Hero Twins from the underworld. Maya urban centres did, however, have large, open courtyards adjacent to temples and palaces where huge crowds could have assembled to witness the dedication of royal stelae at the end of twenty-year periods and to celebrate various other rituals.

At Cuzco, the Inka rulers celebrated an elaborate cycle of religious rites that corresponded with the solar year. These rituals were primarily concerned with the planting, harvesting, and storage of crops and with promoting the welfare of the king and the Inka nobility. They celebrated both the king's military prowess and his control over the reproductive resources of society. The festival of Qhapaq Raymi, at the start of the rainy season in December, involved an elaborate set of rituals at Wanakawri (Huanacauri), a major waka associated with the arrival of the Inka royal family in the Cuzco region. In the course of these rituals, the endurance and military skills of young members of the nobility were tested and they were formally initiated into adulthood. In January, rituals were performed for the health of the king. February-March was the time for encouraging crops to grow, and in May the maize harvest was celebrated. In June, the feast of Inti Raymi involved elaborate sacrifices on the hillsides near Cuzco to strengthen and ensure the return southward of the winter sun. In July, irrigation and sod-turning rituals were performed. In August, new crops were ritually sown in sacred fields. In September, Quya Raymi (the queen's festival) was celebrated and diseases were driven from the capital. In October, rituals were performed if drought threatened, while November was associated with preparations for Qhapaq Raymi. Special rituals were performed at times of major threats to the well-being of the state such as wars, earthquakes, or widespread disease (Cobo 1990: 126–51; Kendall 1973: 198–99; Rowe 1944: 308–11).

The king, queen, and high-ranking members of the nobility played prominent roles in these rituals. In July, the king, assisted by Inka nobles, ceremonially inaugurated the agricultural cycle by using a gold-tipped foot plough to begin to turn the sod of a sacred maize field dedicated to the sun at Collcampata, on Saqsawaman Hill, and at Sausero, east of Cuzco. These two fields were associated with the first Inka ruler, Manqu Qhapaq, and his sister-wife Mama Waqu. The ritual initiated the working of other fields belonging to various gods and dead kings and then the rest of the land in the Cuzco region and throughout the Inka kingdom. The following May, the sacred maize fields around Cuzco were harvested by the sons of Inka nobles who were preparing to be initiated into manhood (Bauer 1996: 330; Cobo 1990: 143–44; Kendall 1973: 199; MacCormack 1991: 162; Rowe 1944: 310–11).

Singing and dancing were important features of Inka public worship. Large quantities of beer were consumed by celebrants. Coca leaves were chewed on these occasions by nobles and used for divining and in sacrificial rites (Rowe 1944: 291–92). The religious festivals that involved the greatest mass participation were held in the two adjacent central squares of Cuzco or at major wakas surrounding the city and were attended by the king and the mummies of previous monarchs together with their oracle priests. During some of these rituals, residents of the Cuzco region who were not Inka or Inka-by-privilege were required to vacate the area (Rowe 1944: 310–11). State rituals had set programmes, including special dances and songs, and different social classes were assigned specific roles. The same songs were sung at rituals relating to war as at those relating to agriculture. Official maize-planting rituals were performed by young men wearing military regalia, and warriors played a major role in harvesting ritual crops. The Inka leadership regarded agriculture and military force as equally important for the welfare of the state and therefore ritually equated them (Bauer 1996: 331).

Agricultural and other state rituals were also performed in and around the main temples in provincial administrative centres. There is archaeological evidence that lavish hospitality was offered at these centres to celebrants from the surrounding province (Morris and Thompson 1985). At the community level, ayllu priests offered sacrifices and libations to local wakas and ancestral mummies both before planting and after harvesting the crops (Gose 1993: 486–87). Harvests were also celebrated with community dancing, feasts, and the drinking of corn beer, while shrines containing cobs of corn wrapped in cloth were set up in every house to honour the maize goddess.

In Egypt public and semi-public rituals sustained the monarch, the seasonal cycles, and the gods themselves (Morenz 1973: 89). The ceremony that is best documented prior to the Fourth Dynasty was the Sed festival. For it, cult statues were assembled from every part of Egypt to assist in the ritual death and rebirth of an aging king. This ritual revived his power to sustain the cosmic order. It was usually first performed around the thirtieth year of a king's reign and every few years thereafter (Frankfort 1948: 79–88; T. Wilkinson 1999: 212–15).

Egyptian cult statues participated in religious festivals that required them to leave their temples. They often visited one another, sometimes travelling from one provincial town to another as Hathor of Dendera and Horus of Edfu did each year to celebrate a ritual marriage. Other deities travelled from one temple to another within a single district. At the New Kingdom Opet festival, held during the inundation season, the cult statues of the Theban deity Amon, his wife Mut, and their son Khonsu left their adjacent temples at Karnak to visit the Luxor temple. There Amon and Mut conceived the god Khonsu and by so doing strengthened the powers of the living king, with whom Khonsu was closely identified. Beginning early in the Middle Kingdom, the statue of Amon of Karnak crossed to the west bank of the Nile at harvest time to celebrate the Beautiful Festival of the Valley. This involved visiting royal mortuary temples as well as temples of Hathor and of Amon in the form of a primeval creator god (Finnestad 1997; R. Wilkinson 2000: 95–98). In the Old and Middle Kingdoms, priests carried cult statues in palanquins; in the New Kingdom the palanquins were replaced by small portable boats.

Some celebrations, such as the Festival of the Opening of the Year, were observed annually in every temple. In the Middle Kingdom the festival of Pokar, which commemorated the death and revival of the god Osiris, attracted pilgrims from all over Egypt to Abydos. Temples throughout Egypt held annual festivals to which people came from considerable distances to honour local deities. The most important of these festivals were subsidized by the king and supervised by royal officials acting in his name (Kees 1961: 241–43). The main goal of all these festivals was to promote fertility and rebirth and to renew gods, nature, and human beings (R. Wilkinson 2000: 96–97).

The Shang religious rituals that we know most about were those related to the royal ancestor cult. These rites were performed privately in a restricted palace setting. Among the public rituals was that of Ji (royal tillage). Each February, at the beginning of the farming season, the king and certain high-ranking officials observed a five-day fast and then cultivated a sacred field and offered sacrifices for a good harvest to the god Shangdi. Food and drink were served to the officials and farmers who participated in this ritual. In the autumn, the king offered the food grown on this field as a thanksgiving sacrifice for the harvest. This festival also recognized the farmers' toil, which made the production of food possible (Granet 1958 [1930]: 307; Hsu and Linduff 1988: 370; Keightley 1969: 111–23). Nobles may have performed similar planting and harvest rites in honour of lesser deities at their regional and local centres. The sacrifices that kings and nobles offered at earth altars in connection with war and agriculture also appear to have been public rituals.

In all early civilizations state religious rituals such as enthronements, royal funerals, and offerings to the gods had public as well as esoteric aspects. The esoteric elements stressed the special and restricted nature of the upper classes' relations with the gods. The public rituals displayed the wealth, power, and privileges of the upper classes, who controlled these events, but they required the participation of ordinary people to align human activities with the cosmic and divine orders. Public rituals strengthened the cosmos and drew energy from it for the benefit of humans. They re-enacted the creation of the universe and reinforced the harmony between the annual cycles of human society and those of the natural/supernatural world. The social order was justified by proclaiming it to be modelled on the natural world and the supernatural forces that animated it.

There does not appear to have been any significant distinction between the ways in which religious festivals were controlled and organized in city-states and in territorial states. The vast resources that rulers of individual territorial states had at their disposal were lavished on religious rituals to varying degrees and in different ways. City-states seem to have been characterized by even more diversity. Early Egyptian rulers devoted more of their resources to constructing their burial complexes and maintaining their funerary cults than to any other form of religious activity. Elaborate, state-managed public calendars of festivals developed in both the Valley of Mexico and Inka Peru, while less centralized forms of public ritual, focused on individual temples and cults, played a more important role among the Yoruba, in Mesopotamia, and in ancient Egypt.

In Mesopotamia, kings and temple officials may have contested control of religious rituals, while among the Yoruba individual initiative, combined with even more decentralized political power, made public rituals a focus for political contestation and mediation. Egyptian kings organized ceremonies of extraordinary magnificence and national importance, but public ritual away from the royal court and a few major centres appears to have been left largely to local management. While the Inka imposed considerable uniformity on major cults both in Cuzco and in provincial administrative centres, in Egypt the central government did not try to control religious cults in provincial centres to nearly the same extent, at least during the Old Kingdom. In China, responsibility for ritual performance seems to have been linked to the segmentary allocation of political power. The main role of public religious festivals in all early civilizations was to establish ritual connections between ordinary people and gods whose cults were controlled by the upper classes. By constraining the lower classes to acknowledge this network of unequal relations through their participation, these rituals emphasized the subordination of the lower classes to the powerful and rich.

WITCHCRAFT AND SOCIAL CONTROL

In addition to the practice of religion in communal and family settings there were relations between individuals and the supernatural, some of them socially sanctioned and others entered into for harmful and illicit purposes. Many turned on the assumption that the powers that could be used for good purposes could also be used for bad ones.

In early civilizations people greatly feared spirits that sought to harm humans by causing illness, death, and misfortune to young and old alike. The Mesopotamians believed that swarms of malicious spirits were unleashed upon humanity by the deities who ruled the underworld. Neglected souls of the dead also roamed the world seeking to feed or otherwise prey on relatives and strangers (Bottéro 1992: 282–85). The Aztec believed that the souls of women who had died in childbirth returned to earth to murder children (López Austin 1988, 1: 246). In Egypt, hosts of demons collectively representing the forces of disorder threatened humans, especially during the night (Pinch 1994: 141–42). Among the Inka malevolent spirits (*sopay*) appeared in various forms, such as floating heads and long-breasted women (Rowe 1944: 297–98).

To try to control these dangerous spirits, people had recourse to prayers, amulets, and spells. In Egypt, amulets manufactured in a wide range of materials were purchased and worn by rich and poor alike. Most Egyptian amulets referred to and drew their power from episodes in the many myths that related how the young god Horus was protected from danger by the magical skills of his mother, Isis, and how he finally overcame his uncle Seth. Spells, which often claimed to be ones that the Egyptian gods used to protect themselves, were written on small pieces of papyrus, which were worn by individuals, dipped into water which was then drunk, or recited over someone. Priests known as *ḥry sšt3* (knowers of secrets), sometimes wearing masks and equipped with boxes of amulets and charms, deployed supernatural powers (ḥk3) to assist in childbirth or the curing of disease (Davies and Friedman 1998: 171–76). The Yoruba used charms and incantations to counteract witchcraft, protect property, solicit good luck, shorten the distances they had to travel, avoid dangers, and make their enemies obey them. When building a new house the Yoruba propitiated malevolent local spirits in the hope that they would leave the new residents alone and apologized to good spirits for having disturbed them (Lucas 1948: 279–82; Awolalu 1979: 70, 160). The Inka regarded amulets (*ilya, ayaylya*) as a form of waka (Rowe 1944: 296).

Andean peoples, as we have seen, feared supernatural punishment for personal misconduct. In Mesopotamia, people feared divine punishment if they disobeyed a god's wishes or violated his prohibitions, even inadvertently; in retaliation gods might instruct the demons of illness and misfortune or dissatisfied souls of the dead to pursue and punish wrongdoers (Bottéro 1992: 227–29, 283). By the second millennium B.C. there was a growing emphasis on personal deities, both male and female, who could protect individuals from such dangers by interceding for them with the high gods. Personal deities were often passed down from father to son. Individuals petitioned these deities to identify what wrongdoings they should repent, accept their atonement, supply them with the good luck needed to succeed in life, and protect them from demons. Unusually bad behaviour could cause a personal deity to desert the person being protected (Jacobsen 1976: 150–60). In Egypt there was a gradually increasing tendency to appeal for help to major deities in times of personal trouble. It was assumed that some deity had inflicted misfortune on a person in retribution for misbehaviour and that winning the forgiveness and support of a powerful deity constituted the best hope of redemption (Assmann 1995). The Yoruba feared misfortune as a consequence of perjury, mistreating others, or neglecting a god or ancestor. To punish such behaviour the gods might inflict bad luck or even shorten a person's life. Propitiatory sacrifices were necessary to atone for misdeeds (Awolalu 1979: 156). Aztec, when threatened by personal misfortune, sought the protection of their calpolli's tutelary deity (López Austin 1988, 1: 252).

While conducive to moral behaviour, fear of divine punishment also encouraged a search for charms, incantations, and rituals that would prevent individual misconduct from being noticed and punished by the gods. These were the same means by which the assaults of malicious spirits might be deflected. Individual humans sought to acquire supernatural power that would protect them from the different forms of supernatural attack being directed against them either as a result of malice or in the form of just punishment.

In all early civilizations, people feared witchcraft. It was believed that, consciously or unconsciously, some people sought to harm others by supernatural means, either because of envy or in retaliation for some injury that a person or group was believed to have perpetrated against them. Such people were often well known to their victims, but they could also be complete strangers. There were also sorcerers who were able and willing to help supernaturally inexperienced people practise witchcraft against others. These sorcerers might be clandestine practitioners wholly devoted to the use of supernatural powers for evil purposes or priests, shamans, diviners, or curers who, while they publicly used their skills to protect and cure some people, secretly employed their knowledge to harm others.

In small-scale societies fear of witchcraft, in combination with gossip and ridicule, was a powerful force encouraging generosity and modesty. Individuals who were more skilled, more hard-working, more enterprising, or simply luckier than their neighbours were prepared to share their surplus produce with them rather than risk illness, misfortune, and death for themselves and their families as a result of their neighbours' envy being supernaturally directed against them. People who exercised leadership in these close-knit societies likewise took care not to flaunt their power in a way that would arouse envy or annoy people (Lee 1990; Trigger 1990b).

In early civilizations the fear and practice of witchcraft must have continued to function in this manner among ordinary people, while members of the upper classes also practised witchcraft against each other, often with the help of specialists. Yet the most urgent concern about witchcraft among the rich and powerful in early civilizations was their dread that lower-class people might use it to avenge insults, injustices, or mistreatment that they had suffered at the hands of their superiors. It was especially feared that lower-class people might resort to witchcraft to harm rulers in situations where overt resistance was hopeless. Thus, among the upper classes, witchcraft became intimately associated with concern that the people they controlled and exploited were seeking to harm them.

To some degree such fears may have helped to curb the exploitative behaviour of the rich. Their main effect, however, was probably to make rulers fear their subjects more than they would have done otherwise, and this encouraged a determined effort to uncover and punish witches and sorcerers who might be seeking to harm them. The power of the upper classes to punish witches turned the fear that authorities might accuse ordinary people of being witches into a powerful means for intimidating and controlling the lower classes. Thus accusations of witchcraft, which in smaller-scale societies had served to promote social and economic equality, became in early civilizations a means by which the powerful could intimidate their subordinates.

The Inka state construed all crimes, regardless of the social status of the victims, as acts of sorcery and treason. Every form of misconduct threatened the well-being of the kingdom and the health of the king by angering the gods. Rulers sought to regulate wrongdoers' relations with the supernatural by making the expiation of wrongdoing dependent on confession of the offence to authorized priests or high-ranking chosen women (Kendall 1973: 194). They also sought to control the clandestine manipulation of supernatural power by experts. These included sorcerers (*kawco*), who killed people by means of magical potions and images into which bits of hair, fingernails, or teeth of the intended victim had been inserted. It was believed that some priests, curers (*hampikamayuq*), and authorized diviners (omo) also secretly performed criminal acts of sorcery. The activities of these clandestine manipulators of supernatural power were greatly feared by ordinary people as well as by the state. People carefully destroyed or kept their own hair and nail clippings (Kendall 1973: 66, 76, 94; Rowe 1944: 302, 312, 314). Divination was employed to expose clandestine sorcerers, and any person found to have murdered someone in this manner was slain along with the rest of his family (Rowe 1944: 314). Kings must have dreaded that such intriguers would become involved in factional intrigues among the Inka nobility. At the same time, rulers employed sorcery to enhance their own power. They had priests burn snakes, toads, and jaguars to weaken the power of gods who supported rival rulers and then examined the hearts of sacrificed llamas to see if the ritual had been successful (Kendall 1973: 100–101).

Yoruba of all classes feared witches (*aje*). Many witches were female, and the power to be one tended to be inherited in the female line. Such power could also be purchased from a practising witch and ingested in the form of ritually treated food. The souls of witches were believed to enter the bodies of animals at night, while their own bodies slept. In that form they travelled about spreading disease and sucking blood and vitality from their victims. Witches were assumed to be inherently evil. They killed close relatives, drained life-forces from children, ruined their husbands' businesses, and caused infertility. Divination was frequently employed to determine whether a death was from natural causes. A public form of behaviour that was closely related to witchcraft, *epe* (formal cursing), involved the overt employment of supernatural power to injure a rival or an enemy (Lucas 1948: 272–84; Awolalu 1979: 81–92).

There were in Yoruba society both people actively seeking to inflict supernatural harm on those whom they envied or believed had injured or insulted them and people who believed that they and their families were the victims of such behaviour. The Gelede society, which worshipped Yemoya, goddess of rivers and mother of witchcraft, as well as other deities associated with sorcery, sought to control witchcraft by offering sacrifices to the souls of unidentified witches. These sacrifices were intended to appease witches and deflect them from their intended victims. Individuals who felt threatened by witchcraft attempted to placate unknown witches by offering them animal sacrifices as substitutes for their own lives. The Egungun society had as one of its missions to confront and overcome witches, especially when their power was directed against hunters and small children. Older members of the Egungun and Oro societies hunted down and killed witches who persisted in threatening the well-being of society.

Some Yoruba communities also performed special rituals that were intended to drive witches from their midst (Bascom 1969: 93–95; Awolalu 1979: 154–58; R. Thompson 1976: 14/1–15/2). Diviners were employed to determine who might be secretly performing witchcraft. Those who were accused of witchcraft were tried by ordeal and executed if found guilty. If they confessed, however, they were usually released, since confession was believed to annihilate their power to do evil (Lucas 1948: 277, 284; Awolalu 1979: 83).

In the Valley of Mexico, curers, midwives, and sorcerers were hired to perform various rituals to alter individual destinies and control the weather. These specialists often worked in conjunction with local priests to help people, but sometimes they used their knowledge to inflict harm on those they disliked or the enemies of those who employed them. The Aztec especially feared the activities of sorcerers, who had obtained the power to manipulate the supernatural by having been born on a particular day or having been trained by a practising sorcerer. *Tlacatecolotl* (owl men) cast spells on others which caused them to get ill or die. Nahualli were able to project their souls into animal forms (*nagual*), which roamed about while their human bodies slept. Nahualli intent on harming people penetrated the bodies of their intended victims and consumed the powers that animated them, causing sickness and death. If, however, the nagual was killed, the resident soul could not return to its human body, and this caused the nahualli to perish. Sorcerers also used charms, especially the arm of a woman who had died while delivering her first child, to render themselves invisible and rob houses.

Aztec priests and curers attempted to discern the source of ailments that had been caused by witchcraft by tossing twenty maize kernels onto a cloth and interpreting the pattern they formed. They also counteracted sorcery with various rituals. Efforts were made to search out and punish those practising witchcraft and supernaturally aided robbery. In Texcoco such crimes were tried by the religious rather than the legal council (Berdan 1982: 139–41; Clendinnen 1991: 54–56; López Austin 1988, 1: 364–73; Offner 1983: 149; M. E. Smith 1996: 261). The Aztec believed that individuals lived to an old age by stealing life from other people, who as a consequence died young. As a result, elderly people were credited with possessing great supernatural power, and people treated them with deference in the hope they would steal life from someone else. A normal life span was considered to be one calendar round of fifty-two years (López Austin 1988, 1: 257–58).

In Egypt, people had recourse to charms and spells to assist them to commit criminal acts such as robberies and murders. In the New Kingdom a plot to murder King Ramesses III involved smuggling into the palace wax images of the king that would help to ensure the success of the conspiracy. Priests and sorcerers who were willing to manufacture such equipment (Grimal 1992: 276) must have been regarded as a considerable threat by the king and the upper classes. At the same time, the widespread manipulation of the supernatural not only to keep the cosmos running but to cure illness and help the souls of the dead escape punishment for their crimes in life must have made it difficult to determine who was using the same powers to harm other people. Moreover, the Egyptian state used magic to weaken and subdue its enemies. The Middle Kingdom 'execration texts' employed supernatural techniques to control the foreign enemies of the Egyptian king (Posener 1940).

RITUAL AND HIERARCHY

A vast amount of wealth was expended in early civilizations on temples, sacrifices, religious festivals, and priests. Remains associated with religious beliefs and activities loom large in the archaeological and textual records of early civilizations. Yet early civilizations were not theocracies. Priests did not constitute a social order in any of the early civilizations we are studying; they were drawn from and remained members of various social classes. In ancient Egypt and among the Yoruba the priesthood was only a part-time occupation, and in China and among the Maya priests as a group may not have been distinguished from administrators and support staff. The most important priests were high-ranking officials and the king was ultimately responsible for his society's relations with the supernatural. Local or family cults might express a group's political aspirations to manage their own affairs, but they could not directly challenge royal authority. Because political and religious roles were not clearly distinguished, there was no opportunity for serious political competition between priests and secular rulers.

Much of the routine worship of the gods was conducted in enclosed areas without public participation, but at various times of the year religious festivals required the participation or at least the presence of large numbers of people. These public rituals reinforced the collective identity of society but also reaffirmed the hierarchical organization of early civilizations by stressing the key role that the upper classes played in representing society as a whole in its relations with the supernatural. Finally, fear of witchcraft, now focused on the concerns of the upper classes about malevolent forces that the weaker and less affluent members of society might direct against them, was transformed from what it had been in smaller-scale societies – a way to frighten the more prosperous members of society into being more generous – into yet another means for the upper classes to intimidate and repress the lower classes. Yet witchcraft also provided the lower classes with a way of resisting the demands of the upper classes that was covert and considered effective.

23 The Individual and the Universe

If views about humans' relations to the cosmos – about the creation of human beings, the purpose of human existence, and the fate of individuals after death – reflected the roles that different classes played in society, one might expect the self-image of lower-class people to have been humbler and more pessimistic where the upper classes advanced the most extravagant claims concerning their own superiority. Such assertions tended to be made in territorial states and in city-state systems where nobles were distinguished as a hereditary group from commoners. Combining these two criteria, one might expect the lower classes to have had the most positive self-image among the Yoruba and Mesopotamians (city-states with no formally defined hereditary nobility) and progressively humbler ones among the Aztec and Maya (city-states with hereditary nobles), in Egypt (a territorial state that deemphasized its hereditary nobles), and in Shang China and the Inka kingdom (territorial states with strong hereditary nobilities).

The ethnographic literature on the Yoruba provides no detailed account of the creation of the first human beings. Oduduwa, the god most often credited with creating the earth, was also the ancestor of the first Yoruba kings. The god Orisala was charged by the high god Olorun with the ongoing task of creating individual humans – shaping their bodies (*ara*) from semen and menstrual blood in their mothers' wombs. If Orisala were angry, he might produce deformities in fetuses. Olorun then gave each infant life (Bascom 1969: 10; Awolalu 1979: 12; Pemberton and Afolayan 1996: 97, 218).

The Yoruba believed that the human body was animated by multiple souls or life-forces. One of these was the *emi* (breath), which Olorun breathed into each individual. The emi was associated with the lungs and chest and was believed to be the force that allowed people to live, move about, and work. It required food in order to continue functioning. The emi was able to leave the body when a person was asleep and travel about, its experiences taking the form of dreams. If a wandering soul was captured and prevented from returning to its body, the deprived body would die after four days (Bascom 1969: 74; cf. Lucas 1948: 247–48).

Equally important among the Yoruba was a soul called the *ori* (head), which supplied an individual's intellect, personality, destiny, luck, and supernatural protection. Often called the ancestral guardian soul, it was sometimes described as made up of a person's mind (*iye*) and inner self (*ori inu*), as distinguished from the personality that an individual revealed in public (*ori ode*). It was given by Olorun to someone about to be reborn. The ori was regarded as a minor orisa, living inside a person's head. Its well-being depended on its being fed regularly with sacrifices. Individual emi and ori were associated with particular descent groups, and lineage members fed their heads on the same day. In Benin, warriors and other prominent men also sought to strengthen the supernatural power in their right arms, sacrificing to them both before and after special undertakings. In addition, the Yoruba accorded supernatural status to their shadows (*ojiji*), although shadows performed no special function, received no sacrifices, and remained closely linked to the body. (Apter 1992: 199; Awolalu 1979: 9, 12, 53–54; Bascom 1969: 71–74; Bradbury 1957: 58; Lucas 1948: 246–47).

At the time of a person's death, both souls left the body. If the person had died prematurely, they might continue living in a ghostly form in some other community until their allotted life span was used up. Sooner or later, however, all souls travelled to the spirit world, which was generally believed to be located in the sky (Bascom 1969: 75).

The dead were buried in the ground. Men who lived in towns were interred beneath the rooms or courtyards of their residential compounds. Country dwellers were brought for burial to their patrilineages' urban compounds, while women were interred within their fathers' residences. People without descendants were buried simply, while those who had children were interred with elaborate rites and venerated as long as their children lived. Lepers, albinos, hunchbacks, pregnant women, and people killed by lightning were buried in the sacred groves of various deities by priests who ensured that these individuals were reconciled after death with the deity who was responsible for their misfortune (Bascom 1969: 65–66). Various prohibitions were observed; burying red cloth with the deceased, for example, might cause the person to be reborn a leper.

Elaborate burial rites ensured that the souls of the dead reached the supernatural world and did not become wandering ghosts. Animal sacrifices, the blood of which was sprinkled on the corpse, strengthened the souls of the dead and ensured that they were well disposed towards the living (Bascom 1969:

65–68). After the burial, offerings continued to be made to the body in the form of blood and other libations, which were poured down a hole into the grave. The bodies of the dead were also believed to share in the first-fruits offerings that were made to the earth god (Ojo 1966a: 168). The body apparently ceased to have a personal existence after death (Lucas 1948: 246) but was identified with the life-giving powers of the earth.

The Yoruba believed that after death both the emi and the ori went before Olorun, who punished the souls of evil people, sometimes by forbidding them to be reborn. After death, the emi could visit relatives in dreams (Bascom 1969: 75), while the ori became an *ere* spirit, supernaturally supporting its lineage in the sky world by acting as an intermediary on its behalf with Olorun and the other gods (Awolalu 1979: 60; Pemberton and Afolayan 1996: 25). These ancestral souls were feared as a possible source of supernatural punishment for misbehaviour. The ori was called back by the dead person's living descendants to their family shrine to receive offerings of animals and kola nuts in a ritual performed on the same days that its owner had sacrificed to his head while alive (Bascom 1969: 72). Senior Egungun-society priests caused ori to enter the bodies of cult members during festivals in order to bless their descendants, and the ori spoke through the individuals whose bodies they possessed (K. Barber 1991: 253).

The chief aim of an ancestral soul living in the sky was to be reborn, preferably back into its patrilineal extended family as a grandchild of its previous incarnation. It could be reborn as the same or the opposite sex in successive lifetimes. When the time to be reborn had arrived, the ori appeared before Olorun to receive its body (ara), breath (emi), and destiny (*iwa*). It could bargain with Olorun concerning the day of its next incarnation's death and the specific personality, occupation, and luck this incarnation would have. Actions during a person's subsequent lifetime could alter most of these arrangements, either for better or for worse, to some extent, but they could not change the day of death. Therefore much of an individual's fortune depended on the demands that his or her ori made at this time. These concepts reflected the great importance that the Yoruba placed on bargaining and individual self-reliance in everyday life. The former identity of the ori of a newborn child was revealed to his or her kinsmen by the child's physical appearance and behaviour or through dreams and divination (Bascom 1969: 71–72).

Problems were posed by the belief that ancestral guardian souls were reborn but remained in the sky world acting as intercessors for their families. Sometimes it was claimed that there were two guardian souls, one of which stayed in the sky while the other was continually reborn. If the sky-dwelling version, or ere, were an essence from which individual ori were derived, that would explain the Yoruba belief that a number of living people might share the same soul. Although the ori conserved the basic personality and behavioural traits of a dead person, it is unknown whether it retained personal memories of previous incarnations. Such memories were more likely associated with the ancestral guardian spirits that continued to live in the sky world than with ones that returned to earth. In Benin it was maintained that there were two versions of each soul, which alternated generationally with each other in living in the sky and on earth (Awolalu 1979: 58–61; Bascom 1969: 71–76; Bradbury 1957: 56–58).

Mesopotamian myths concerning the creation of human beings were associated with different city-states and ethnic groups. Sumerian texts recount that, at the request of the other gods, after Enlil had separated the earth and the sky he used his hoe to break the hard crust of the earth in Uzué (The Flesh Grower), a garden located within the temple of Inanna in Nippur, where the first humans sprang up like grass. In another Sumerian myth the god Enki created humans from the 'engendering clay' of the watery underworld. These creations were brought to term by Enki's mother Nammu. In an Akkadian version of this myth, when the gods decided to create humans Enki advised that a rebellious minor god named Weé be slain and that the birth goddess Nintur mix that god's flesh and blood with clay to create humans. Fourteen womb goddesses then gestated this mixture and gave birth to seven human couples. In the *Enuma Elish*, Enki alone fashioned humans, using the blood of the slain rebel deity Kingu (Jacobsen 1970: 112–14, 116, 207; 1974: 1004; 1976: 118; Kramer 1963: 123).

In some of these creation myths, human beings were conceived as clay infused with an element of divinity, often the soul (*etemmu*) of a slain god. Originally less important deities, under Enlil's supervision, had performed the physical labour required to shape the terrestrial world and feed, clothe, and house the gods. When they refused to continue working, Enki created or supervised the creation of human beings to do this work instead. The earth goddess Ninhursaga taught humans the arts that transformed them from simple pastoralists into city dwellers, and the institution of kingship was introduced to Mesopotamia from the sky world. Eventually, there were so many humans that they disturbed Enlil's sleep. With the agreement of the other gods, he sent them plagues, drought, crop failures, and finally a great flood that destroyed all but one family and then, to keep population growth in check, he shortened their lives, afflicted them with barrenness and child death, and introduced virgin priestesses and homosexual behaviour amongst them (Jacobsen 1976: 113–21). The Mesopotamians valued competitiveness, and individuals boasted of their efforts to outdo rivals and to gain fame, wealth, and positions of leadership (Kramer 1981: 11). Yet they dreaded the ability of supernatural powers to harm them and sought the support of personal guardian spirits to avoid illness and misfortune. Individual well-being depended on having supportive supernatural powers present inside one's body. These were called *ilu* (god), if male, and *lamassu* (angel), if female, and they promoted good luck (*ilanu*), vitality and sexual potency (*šedu*), and a favourable destiny (*šimtu*). Without them an individual would quickly fall prey to disease and misfortune (Oppenheim 1964: 199–201).

After death, it was believed, the corpse (*šalamtu*) dissolved back into clay. The bones (*esemtu*) remained forever asleep but were often taken along when families moved from one place to another, and the soul (etemmu) survived as a phantom, ghost, or shadow. If, by mischance, a body remained unburied and no proper funeral rites were performed, its soul wandered the earth as a malevolent spirit. Most souls descended into the underworld (*eretsu*) by way of the grave or various openings (*ablal*) and then had to cross a dangerous river. Once there, they lived a cheerless existence in a dark, arid, dusty realm. This was the home of the gods of death, under the command of Erishkegal and her husband Nergal, and of the demons of disease and misfortune. The sun passed through the underworld each night, briefly lighting portions of it; the moon remained for one day each month. Because nothing could be grown there, the souls of the dead were deemed useless to the gods except for assisting the deities of the underworld to harass the living. Escape was impossible, although on rare occasions the soul of a dead person or god might be released in return for the soul of a living one.

Offerings were made to the souls of dead family members at each new moon. These souls were petitioned to intercede for the welfare of their descendants before the council of the Annunaki, the gods who decided the fate of humans. Yet they could not grow their own food or produce their own clothing in the underworld, nor were these necessities provided for them by the deities of that realm. They depended on food offerings from their living descendants if they were not to starve.

The dead were socially ranked in the underworld as they had been in life. Kings lived in gloomy palaces built of lapis lazuli. They received larger food offerings than commoners, and in Early Dynastic times some were accompanied by the souls of slain household servants. They took riches with them into the underworld so that they might bribe the gods of death into treating them better. Even so, their lives were wretched. Conditions were worse for the souls of ordinary people, especially those who were no longer supplied with offerings by their descendants. The sole exceptions to this fate were Utnapishtim and his family, who had survived the great flood. The gods had permitted them to live without aging in a pleasant but inaccessible enclave on the edge of the world.

Mesopotamians believed that the dead maintained their personal identities, at least as long as their souls were fed. The gods of the underworld were said to 'judge' the souls of the dead, but that seems to have involved confirming their rank rather than rendering a moral evaluation; there was no reward or punishment for what they had done while alive. While the deities of the underworld were supposed to have prayed for the welfare of the souls of the dead, these souls endured an etiolated, marginal existence in a realm that was physically little different from the grave. Many, willingly or unwillingly, helped to harass and injure the living. Living people attributed some of their misfortunes to the souls of the dead, especially ones whose bodies had been left unburied or who did not receive offerings. Such souls might attack (literally 'eat') strangers or their own kin. Yet appropriate exorcisms could return the most malevolent souls to the underworld (Bottéro 1992: 230, 271–85, 288; Kramer 1963: 130–35; Postgate 1992: 92).

A favourite myth of the Aztec and their neighbours described how human beings had been created when the cosmic order was restored at the beginning of the era of the Fifth Sun. The god Quetzalcoatl had descended into the underworld (Mictlan) and, having failed to persuade the god who ruled it to part with some bones of the dead from earlier creations, he stole some from Mictlan's lowest depths. Quetzalcoatl accidentally dropped these bones on his way out, and, as a result of his losing some, the humans of the Fifth Sun were smaller than the intelligent creatures of previous creations. Quetzalcoatl brought the bones to Temoanchan, the place of creation at the centre of the cosmos. There the earth mother Cihuacoatl (Snake Woman) ground the bones into a powder or meal, which the male gods moistened with blood drawn from their genitals. From this mixture men and, four days later, women came into being (Clendinnen 1991: 173; León-Portilla 1963: 107–11; López Austin 1988, 1: 188; M. E. Smith 1996: 206–7).

According to another version of this myth, at the time of the creation of the Fifth Sun sixteen hundred gods descended from the sky world to Teotihuacan in the form of a flint nodule, which shattered into that many pieces when it hit the ground. The mission of these gods was to help animate the new sun, create humans, and become the patron deities of ethnic groups and calpollis. These gods were instructed to retrieve the bones and ashes of the people of former ages from Mictlan. The chief creator of humans was either the god Quetzalcoatl or all four of the primary emanations of Ometeotl. These deities mixed their blood with these bones and ashes to create human beings. The first humans lived in caves or wombs in the earth, from which they emerged to serve their patron deities. A less elaborate myth suggested that the sun had shot an arrow into the ground and a man and woman with no bodies below the waist had emerged from the place where the arrow struck; by kissing they had given birth to the first humans (León-Portilla 1963: 107; López Austin 1988, 1: 240–43).

A more erudite myth claimed that the supreme deity, Ometeotl, had created the first humans. The calendar was born with them and a gender-based division of labour, men being ordered to work the soil and women to spin. This original couple appears, however, to have existed prior to the creation of the sky, earth, and underworld and to have been the ancestors of the gods as well as of humans. It is therefore uncertain whether they were humans or gods. It is also unclear whether a few humans were believed to have survived each of the four successive destructions of the cosmic order or different human-like creatures had to be created at the beginning of each cosmic era. Some versions claimed that the human-like creations of one era survived as animals in succeeding ones (López Austin 1988, 1: 238–40).

Hereditary nobles claimed that they, unlike commoners, were descended from the god Quetzalcoatl. Yet, while this descent distinguished nobles from commoners, it may not have indicated that nobles and commoners had been created differently. The nobility claimed as its ancestor Quetzalcoatl Topiltzin, the ruler of the ancient city of Tollan. Following rebellions, he had abandoned his kingdom and made his way east to the Gulf of Mexico, where he rose into the sky to become the Morning Star. It was ambiguous in Aztec mythology whether Quetzalcoatl Topiltzin was the parthenogenic incarnation of the cosmic deity Quetzalcoatl or an entirely human ruler who was empowered by that god (Gillespie 1989: 123–72).

The people of the Valley of Mexico believed that each child was created by or at the command of Ometeotl, who recycled the life-forces that descended with the dead into the lowest point of the underworld and were drawn from there back to the highest level of the cosmos, where the creator deity lived. In the womb the fetus was nourished by energy that came from Ometeotl rather than from the sun (López Austin 1988, 1: 208–10).

The Aztec and their neighbours believed in a complex set of souls or life-forces. The human body became filled with these supernatural powers at conception, birth, and first exposure to fire and sunlight. *Tonalli*, which was received from Ometeotl at conception, was associated with the head, body heat, and blood. It was an impersonal animating power and the source of individual qualities such as strength, vigour, growth, temperament, appetites, rationality, and destiny. Loss of tonalli resulted in illness and disability. Tonalli could leave the sleeping body in dreams or be dissipated as a result of drunkenness, drug use, and too much sexual activity. It could also be stolen by means of witchcraft or by evil spirits or old people who were anxious to appropriate other people's strength to prolong their own lives. Tonalli was the life-force offered to deities in human sacrifices. Hair, because it grew, was believed to inhibit tonalli from leaving the body; hence the forcible cutting of hair not only constituted a severe public humiliation but also threatened a loss of vitality. *Teyolia*, associated with the heart, was the source of memory and personality and was closely related to personal identity. The teyolias of nobles and outstanding commoners were strengthened by gifts of divine force from specific deities, which returned to these deities after a person died. *Ihiyotl*, associated with the liver and with breath, was the source of strong emotions such as bravery, love, hatred, desire, and exhilaration. A person or animal who could separate his ihiyotl from himself or draw another's ihiyotl inside his body was a nahualli and could use this power to harm others surreptitiously. People sought to maintain a harmonious balance among these three soul forces in order to ensure their personal health and well-being. They were not, however, able to prevent the disaggregation of these forces after death (D. Carrasco 1990: 53, 68–70; Clendinnen 1991: 315; J. Furst 1995; López Austin 1988, 1: 213–36, 318–19, 329–31).

The Aztec believed that human life was characterized by hard work, hunger, illness, worry, pain, and sorrow. Individuals were expected to curb their selfish tendencies and try to exercise stoical self-control, limit their appetites, and work hard to support their families and serve their communities. They expected little in return. Humans always had to be ready to sacrifice their lives to maintain a cosmic order that was ultimately beyond human control. The gods compensated humans for their toil and suffering with routine pleasures such as sleep, laughter, families, and sex, although the latter had to be indulged in with appropriate moderation (Clendinnen 1991: 70–72, 238; León-Portilla 1992: 190; López Austin 1988, 1: 189, 249–51, 342–43).

Each individual received a destiny that was determined by the day on which he or she was born. Some days, especially the five supernumerary days at the end of the solar year, were less lucky than others. An unfavourable birth day could be partially offset by selecting a favourable day for naming a newborn child. It was also believed that human effort could alter an individual's fate. Each child was said to be born without a face (*ixtli*), and one of every individual's chief goals in life was to create a face. Through courage and self-discipline one could gradually acquire a good reputation, and by surrendering to frivolous inclinations and dissipation one could very quickly lose it. Just as people sought to promote equilibrium among their inner forces, so they sought equitable relations with the gods, their communities, and their families. An imbalance could be corrected to some degree by a confession, usually made once in a lifetime by a man to a priest of the deity Tlazolteotli (Eater of Filth) or by a woman to a midwife (Clendinnen 1991: 141; León-Portilla 1963: 104, 115–19; López Austin 1988, 1: 267–69).

After death the animating forces left the body and went their own ways. The tonalli or life-force returned to Ometeotl, perhaps later to be infused into a child born to the family of the deceased. The unaugmented teyolia or sentient soul, which preserved the personality of the dead person, experienced a variety of fates determined not by a person's social status or behaviour in life but by the nature of his or her death. Only the souls of infants, who had never had any direct contact with the dirt and filth of the earth, returned directly to the sky world, from where, after a period spent nursing on a breast tree, Ometeotl sent them back to earth to be reborn.

Beginning four days after their bodies had been cremated and their ashes buried under the floors of their houses, the teyolias of people who had died ordinary deaths journeyed to the underworld. Teyolias of kings and some high-ranking nobles were accompanied by those of slain household slaves, while commoners' dogs were often killed so that their teyolias could accompany those of their masters. The teyolia spent four years making its way ever deeper into a cold, dark, barren, and dangerous underworld. If it did not perish from hardship or the terrible dangers encountered on its journey, it passed into oblivion after it had reached the ninth and lowest level. Offerings were made to the souls of the dead every eighty days for four years to help them during their passage through the underworld. After that, their identities were presumed to be extinguished. The power that constituted teyolias survived in some shadowy, vestigial form until it was anonymously recycled back into the living universe by Ometeotl (Caso 1958: 62–64; Coe 1978: 21; León-Portilla 1963: 90, 109).

In contrast, the teyolias of warriors who had died in battle or been killed as human sacrifices travelled to the east, where after eighty days they joined the sun. Each morning for four years these souls accompanied the sun from the eastern horizon to the zenith. After four years they were turned into hummingbirds or butterflies and lived a carefree and memoryless existence for as long as the Fifth Sun lasted. Women who had died in their first childbirth travelled westward and each afternoon for four years carried the weakening sun in a litter from the zenith to the western horizon. Then they became evil spirits who haunted the earth on the five supernumerary days of each solar year, seeking to kill children by means of paralysis or convulsions. People who died as a result of drowning, being struck by lightning, diseases that caused the body to swell, or being sacrificed to Tlaloc and other fertility deities were transformed into spirits who lived in paradises located inside hills. Some believed that these souls were reborn on earth after four years but without any memory of the past.

For the people in the Valley of Mexico, a human being made sense only in this world. After death, the elements that made up an individual had only a short and uncertain existence separate from one another before they were reabsorbed by the gods and recycled to form new human beings or were transformed into birds, butterflies, spirits, or demons, none of which recalled their human identity. There was no belief in punishment or reward after death for what an individual had done while alive (Caso 1958: 58–62; Clendinnen 1991: 178–79; León-Portilla 1963: 124–26; López Austin 1988, 1: 253, 332–41).

No Classic Maya account of the origin of human beings has survived, but myths recorded in the sixteenth century claimed that two ancestral gods had created human beings after they had fashioned the world. The first imperfect creations were formed from mud, the next from wood, and the third from flesh. Finally present-day humans were made from maize flour mixed with the gods' own blood (Coe 1993: 29; Schele and Miller 1986: 144). Ruling families claimed descent from major deities, usually identified with 'God K' (Houston and Stuart 1996: 297; Tate 1992: 20; Taube 1992: 69–79).

The Maya believed that every human shared souls with one or more animal or spirit companions (*wayob*). (The word *way* was etymologically connected with 'sleep'.) Royal spirit companions were represented as fantastic beasts or combinations of beasts. The White Bone House Centipede was associated with the ruler of Palenque, while the Sun-bellied Jaguar was one of the wayob associated with the kings of Calakmul (Houston 2001; Martin and Grube 2000: 81). Through dancing, massive blood-letting, drug-induced trances, and dreams, people sought, individually and collectively, to transform themselves into their spirit companions as a way of accessing the supernatural (Schele and Mathews 1998: 83–84, 417).

The souls of the dead descended into the underworld (*xibalba*) through caves, down the trunk of the cosmic tree (wakah kan), or by falling through the open jaws of the earth monster. All these openings were designated *ol* (door or hole). The souls of the dead, especially those of powerful rulers, could hope to escape from the underworld by challenging, outwitting, and finally killing its rulers, the Lords of Death. Then, by identifying themselves with gods associated with the sun and the planet Venus, they could rise temporarily out of the underworld into the daytime sky. The life-forces of dead rulers could likewise ascend from their tombs and be reborn as future monarchs of their dynastic lines. Divinized souls of kings were briefly called back into the world by their descendants' vision quests. Ordinary souls appear to have been trapped and doomed to oblivion in the underworld (D. Carrasco 1990: 52;

Freidel, Schele, and Parker 1993: 76–78; A. Miller 1989: 183–86; Schele and Mathews 1998: 414; Schele and Miller 1986: 244–45).

The ancient Chinese appear to have believed that each person had at least two souls: the *po*, which supplied the vital life-forces of a living person, and the *hun*, which provided the intellect, emotions, and consciousness. The po, sometimes referred to as the lower soul, was believed to come from the underworld and the hun or upper soul from the sky realm. A child was born with only a po and acquired its hun when it first cried or laughed. Because the souls of peasants were fed mainly on grain, they were believed to be weaker than those of upper-class persons, who frequently ate meat and other more nourishing foods (Granet 1958 [1930]: 256, 323–24; Lewis 1990: 77). When people died, their po souls, like their bodies, descended into the earth. The po travelled from the grave down to the Yellow Springs (*huang quan*), where it remained as a ghost (*gui*) at least until its life-force was recycled. The hun ascended into the sky, where it lived as a shining spirit (*shen ming*) that was able to communicate with its living descendants and intercede for them with the sky deities that controlled the natural world.

Dying lords sought to eat rich food and drink wine to nourish their hun souls and increase their power to survive. The hun souls of dead members of the nobility regularly received offerings of sacred harvests, domestic animals, and game killed in their honour and could punish living descendants who failed to provide them with satisfactory nourishment. Over time, the individuality of dead ancestors faded from memory, as a result of which their hun came to resemble nature spirits more. As this occurred, their name tablets in temples were removed from view and put into a box with those of more remote ancestors. Berthold Laufer (1913) surmised that these tablets were a replacement for earlier ancestral images. Peasant souls, being weaker, seem not to have endured long after death and soon ceased to be useful intermediaries for their descendants. Commoner lineages did not have special temples where the souls of their ancestors were worshipped, but at specified times each year ordinary families seem to have made offerings to their ancestors at altars located within their homes (Granet 1958 [1930]: 256–57, 323–24; Lewis 1990: 87).

It has been suggested that the po, unlike the hun, originally received no cult (Allan 1991: 66). In later times the po was believed to live near the body in its tomb while the hun could be contacted at its lineage's ancestral shrine and communicated with by means of divination. Sacrifices, including human beings and animals, were offered year after year around Shang royal tombs. These rituals appear to have been focused on small mortuary structures atop low stamped-earth platforms. Thus it appears that in the Shang period the po souls or ghosts of royal ancestors were revered at individual graves, while their hun souls were venerated collectively at ancestral temples inside palace complexes (Wu 1988).

Prominent among the Andean accounts of human origins was the Inka claim that, after Wiraqucha had created the sun at Lake Titicaca, he modelled animals and people from clay at the nearby site of the ancient city of Tiwanaku. He distinguished ethnic groups by painting different clothes and hairstyles on these figures, assigned them their distinctive languages, songs, and customs, and endowed them with the materials and skills they needed to survive. In an alternative creation myth, the sun and moon gave birth to Camac Pacha (Lord Earth) and Mama Cocha (Lady Ocean), from whom in turn men and women were descended (Classen 1993: 19–25; Rowe 1960). Wiraqucha commanded the humans he had created to descend into the earth and travel through underground passages to designated dawning places (*pakarina*), which were distributed throughout the world. The ancestors of each ayllu emerged from a specific pakarina. Some pakarinas were caves, others were mountains, tree roots, or other natural features that facilitated movement back and forth between the surface of the earth and the underworld. The founders of each ayllu claimed ownership of the land and water surrounding their pakarina for themselves and their descendants. At the same time, domestic plants emerged from cave pakarinas and domestic animals from lake ones. Before disappearing into the Pacific, Wiraqucha visited every human community, teaching people how they should live.

At every pakarina, one or more of the new arrivals was turned into a waka, often in the form of a rock. Each waka embodied the life-force that would sustain and be revered by a specific ayllu. From the first arrivals future generations of human beings were born as the life-force, which had been created by Wiraqucha and taken up permanent residence in the waka, combined with local water sources to create living descendants. The most powerful beings that Wiraqucha sent to inhabit the earth were four pairs of brothers and sisters, who were children of the sun god, Inti. They emerged from a cave at Paqariktambo, near Cuzco, at the dawn of the first day to become the ancestors of the Inka royal family (Gose 1993; Kendall 1973: 182–83; Rowe 1944: 315–16; 1960; Sherbondy 1992: 63: Urton 1990).

The Andeans believed that life was created as a result of the combination of dry, enduring substances such as earth and rock and moving water. Each human being was believed to have two kinds of souls, one associated with each of these elements. The personal soul (kamaquen) was derived from the enduring power to fashion and vitalize that was possessed in perpetuity by the founding ancestor of an ayllu, who had been transformed into a waka or preserved as a mummified (dried) body (mallqui). The power which vitalized such a waka provided its descendants with food, clothing, agricultural fertility, reproductive capacity, health, and oracular advice. Living in the heart (*sonqo*) of each of its descendants, this eternal power shaped every individual's bodily form and character. The *upani*, an impersonal life-force, was associated with water. Its main role was to transform the enduring essence of the kamaquen into a living being. The upani was regarded as deaf and mute, a force that animated the individual but did not otherwise shape the personality (Gose 1993; Salomon 1991: 14–16). Death resulted from the separation of the kamaquen and upani souls. The physical manifestation of this separation was desiccation, which occurred as water was withdrawn from the body. When a person died, his or her heart and the personal kamaquen associated with it rejoined the waka from which they were derived. For this reason, local wakas were used as burial sites. The upani soul, attracted to water, drifted away and rejoined the nearest lake, river, or spring, increasing its volume and helping to return water to its ultimate source in the ocean.

The survival of an ayllu was made possible by an ongoing cycle of kamaquen souls emanating from their waka to become human beings and then returning to their source when people died. Mummification, which involved drying corpses while preserving their form, was an essential manifestation of this process. While water drained away, the personal kamaquen soul endured as long as the mummified body it was associated with lasted. That mummies of commoners were preserved, fed, reclothed, and consulted as oracles indicates that, while individual humans were manifestations of the generic kamaquen dwelling within their ancestral waka, their individual souls survived after death (Gose 1993; 1995; Salomon 1991: 19–20).

Dead ancestors issued oracles and punished their living descendants with crop failures, disease, and death for improper conduct or neglect. Groups that relocated took the bodies of their ancestors and all or portions of their wakas with them and continued to venerate them in their new homes. Mummified bodies of dead kings became wakas of great importance, living kings having been shaped by and embodying the power of the sun. Their personal kamaquens survived in association with their mummies and cult statues and spoke through their oracle priests. Their kamaquens also rejoined the kamaquen of the sun, and their hearts were placed in an image of the sun god kept in the main temple in Cuzco. Dead kings continued to live in their palaces and country houses but they were also said to have rejoined or become the sun (Gose 1993; MacCormack 1991: 91–98, 424–32).

The Egyptians' solar creator god was said to have formed human beings (*rmṯ*) from his tears (*rmyt*), as a result of which humans lacked the clear vision of the gods. Egyptian deities, according to some accounts, were formed from the creator's sweat or the blood that he lost while circumcising himself. Some rebellious deities were believed to have been transformed into humans as well as into animals destined for sacrifice (Faulkner 1985: 45; Hornung 1982: 149–50; Meeks and Favard-Meeks 1996: 33; Morenz 1973: 183). The potter god Khnum was portrayed as fashioning the body of each child from clay on his potter's wheel. Female deities known as the Seven Hathors assigned individuals their destiny (*š3w*) when they were born. Their pronouncements greatly influenced a person's quality of life, life-span, and cause of death. However, the gods could adjust individual destinies for better or worse throughout a person's lifetime. Responsibility for altering an individual's fate may have been assigned to a guardian deity (Baines 1991a: 140–41; Morenz 1973: 70–73).

The Egyptians believed that at least six elements were necessary for a human being to exist. The body (*ẖt*, *ḥ*ʿ) or physical shell within which every person existed was animated by its heart (*ỉb*), the source of reason, memory, character, emotions, desire, and pleasure. The name (*rn*) and the shadow (*šwt*) were components of personhood, along with multiple souls, most notably the *k3* and *b3*.

The k3, associated symbolically with the placenta and etymologically with the concept of food or provisioning (*k3w*) and fertility (*k3*, bull; *k3t*, vulva) (L. Bell 1997: 282 n. 2), was moulded by the god Khnum at the same time as he fashioned the mortal body. It was portrayed in Egyptian art as a duplicate of the living person. Described as related to physical nourishment, vitality, and emotions, the k3 appears to have been the creative power passed from parents to children within a family line. Each new k3, created for a specific individual and apparently capable of enduring as long as the cosmos, seems to have been a specific manifestation of a supernatural life-force transferred from one generation to the next since the time of creation. Kings and gods possessed multiple k3s while ordinary humans had only one and unlike ordinary humans were able to communicate with them. Periodic unions of rulers and their k3s in special ritual contexts rejuvenated and re-empowered monarchs. The b3 has been described as a supernatural force that provided perception, specific appetites, and the power to influence other sentient beings. It could leave the body and travel in dreams about the earth as well as visit the sky and underworld and has therefore been described as a travelling soul (J. Allen 2000: 79–81; Baines 1991a: 145; L. Bell 1997: 130–32; Kemp 1989: 208; Lichtheim 1973: 65; Morenz 1973: 158).

Death occurred when the k3 departed from the body. It was a depressing event that stole living beings from their families and transferred them from a fertile, living world into a realm of infertility, thirst, darkness, and unconsciousness, where most of the time one person did not know another. Death disrupted the unity of the life-forces that constituted an individual, although Egyptians sought to do all they could to arrest this process. To prevent the disintegration of the corpse (*ẖ3t*) they mummified and buried it in as elaborate a tomb as an individual could afford. Once the body and its internal organs were embalmed, the mouth of the dead person was symbolically opened prior to interment so that the body might once again speak and eat.

In the tomb the corpse was reunited with its k3, which made the deceased like a god (nṯr). Each night, as the sun passed through the underworld (with which the burial chamber was identified), the corpse was restored to life. Both the corpse and its k3 were sustained by offerings of food, drink, and clothing that were supposed to be provided on a daily basis. Rich tombs were decorated with scenes of offerings being presented to the deceased and food being grown and processed for these offerings to nourish the deceased if real food offerings ceased. Texts promising offerings were erected in the accessible parts of tombs; the reading of these formulae would also provide the corpse and its k3 with food. Substitutes for the mummy in the form of cult statues and relief images of the dead person were placed in the tomb chapel and local temples. Equally important for the survival of the deceased was the preservation of his or her name, which sustained the dead person's identity and ensured that offerings reached their intended recipient.

The corpse, animated by its k3, was able to journey to the kingdom of Osiris, a fertile land where food was grown and corvée labour was performed by *wšbty* (*shawabti*, 'answerers'), human figurines magically programmed to act in place of the dead person. It was only possible to stay in the kingdom of Osiris, however, if the heart – the locus of memory – did not supply evidence that a person had committed any one of forty-two misdeeds (*ḥww*) of a ritual, ethical, or criminal nature during his or her earthly existence. If the deceased was not found innocent and acclaimed worthy (*m3ʿ ḫrw*) by the court which judged the dead, his or her soul would be eaten by *ʿm mwt* (the swallower of the dead). Once again, magical means were employed to ensure a favourable verdict. The dead who reached the kingdom of Osiris became identified with its mummified ruler. Life in the tomb and in the kingdom of Osiris provided the dead with a ḏt eternity.

The b3, represented in hieroglyphs by a jabiru stork or a human-headed bird, maintained its life-force by periodically reuniting with the corpse and k3 of the person to whom it belonged. It also visited the terrestrial world to bring back food and drink for the corpse, communicating with living relatives and friends of the dead person in dreams and visions that either reassured or threatened them and haunting people in the form of a dangerous spirit of the dead (*mwt*). The b3 was also the means by which dead males periodically experienced sexual gratification. (This belief was based on the homophony between the words b3 [soul] and *b3ḥ* [phallus].) B3s also descended into the underworld and travelled to the sky, thus participating in the endless cycles of death and rebirth that took place in the natural world and ensuring their possessors of a nḥḥ eternity for as long as the cosmos lasted. By ascending to the sky the b3 could also become an *3ḫ*, a radiant or transfigured spirit, in the form of a star. As one of the circumpolar stars, the b3 could enjoy the same ḏt immortality in the sky that the k3 did in the tomb. The k3, the b3, and the corpse could hope to continue their association for as long as the universe lasted and the individual sustained an existence and a personal identity provided that some trace of his or her name, image, and provisioning endured. The corpse also continued to be associated with attributes such as its shadow.

The Egyptans believed that the dead could use their supernatural powers (ḥk3) to harm people who had treated them badly during their lifetime or relatives who neglected to provision them after death. They could also use their easier access to the gods to intervene in favour of relatives who pleased them. If the dead were thought to be causing harm, letters addressed to them were left at their tombs, seeking to learn what was troubling them and what had to be done to win their approval. Answers appear to have been received mainly in dreams. The supernatural powers of the dead do not appear to have been markedly greater than those they possessed while alive. Moreover, contact between the living and the dead seems to have lasted only as long as people who had known the dead person remained alive (J. Allen 2000: 94–95; Faulkner 1985; Morenz 1973: 187–212; Reeder 1998).

Egyptologists used to maintain that in the Old Kingdom it was believed that only monarchs and those who were able to construct elaborate tombs and endow them with perpetual funerary offerings were able to enjoy life after death. It has long been evident, however, from the village cemeteries that George Reisner (1932) excavated at Naga ed-Deir, in Upper Egypt, that from Predynastic times ordinary people performed scaled-down versions of the funerary cults of the upper classes. Excavations of the burials of craftsmen and workmen who constructed the Fourth Dynasty Giza pyramid complex have revealed small tombs and evidence of cults that were based on the same general ideas that guided the burial practices of the upper classes (Davies and Friedman 1998: 85–88). Hence it appears that, at least as early as the Old Kingdom, all classes had generally similar aspirations concerning life after death, even if the same marked social distinctions were observed in realizing these aspirations that applied in everyday life. By the Middle Kingdom, all who could afford it sought to identify themselves after death with Osiris, the supreme exemplar of a god who was surviving in a changeless ḏt state. This required embalming and the performance of costly, esoteric rituals that during the Old Kingdom had remained the prerogatives of royalty. In the Old Kingdom, the carving in tombs of magical texts to ensure the well-being of the dead was limited to kings and occasionally queens. At the end of the Old Kingdom, these writings became more widely known and, in the form of the Coffin Texts, were part of the burial equipment of all who could afford them.

BELIEF AND SELF-IMAGE

Myths concerning the creation of humanity indicate that in early civilizations it was believed that the first humans were brought into existence not only by the gods but at least to some extent from the substance of the gods. This view accords with the more general belief that the entire natural world was animated by supernatural power, which seems to have been linked to beliefs that prevailed in still earlier and less complex societies. Yet it was also emphasized in early civilizations that human beings had been created differently from the gods and were inferior to them in their capacities. Moreover, upper-class people often asserted that their origin was different from that of commoners.

In early civilizations the human body was believed to be animated by multiple supernatural forces rather than by a single soul. (The Mesopotamians are generally assumed to have viewed the body as being animated by a single soul, but their beliefs may have been inadvertently misinterpreted to make them more closely resemble modern Western ones; the bones may have constituted a separate life-force that complemented the etemmu-soul, which embodied consciousness.) Often the main distinction was between the life-forces that animated the body and made it function and an intellect power that constituted an individual's mind. One or the other of these souls generally had the power to move beyond the living body in dreams and the imagination. In general, it was believed that these souls constituted a unity focused on the body while the person was alive but separated from one another after death. In Egypt and among the Inka the body was regarded as an important component of the dead person; the Mesopotamians, Yoruba, Chinese, and Maya attached importance to the bones of their ancestors and continued to guard and venerate them.

Various life-forces were thought to survive the deaths of individuals and be recycled to younger generations of the same family or to become part of a pool of cosmic energy that animated future human beings or the universe generally. While personality traits or the appearance of the deceased might be transmitted along with such forces, such energy did not conserve any significant aspects of individual consciousness, personal identity, or memory. In contrast to the conception of reincarnation of some later preindustrial South Asian and

East Asian civilizations, the soul does not appear to have been conscious at any point of previous existences. Nor was moral behaviour in one life believed to influence how that energy was reincarnated as it did according to the Hindu doctrine of karma. What varied considerably in early civilizations was the extent to which a personal identity was believed to survive the dispersal of life-forces following death. Wherever such a personal identity survived, it was believed to depend heavily on offerings made by the living, usually its own descendants, for its power and quality of life. There was only a limited tendency to view the fate of human personalities after death as being linked to an individual's conduct while alive. Morality appears to have been generally viewed as a communal matter rather than as a personal or religious one.

The evidence concerning beliefs about the destiny of the individual after death does not indicate that ordinary people living in city-states imagined a better fate than was anticipated by commoners living in territorial states. All the inhabitants of territorial states, whatever their class, seem to have believed they had a better chance of individual survival and a tolerable existence after death than did the inhabitants of city-states. The well-demarcated class hierarchies and the opulence of upper-class life in territorial states encouraged the upper classes to anticipate a comfortable personal survival after death, and this belief may have spread as a result of status emulation among the lower classes (Cannon 1989). In Egypt, for example, from Predynastic times on, burial customs diffused from the royal court to progressively lower social strata, with each class imitating the practices of the upper classes to the extent that its more limited resources and access to esoteric religious knowledge permitted. The spells contained in the Pyramid Texts, which were collated for royal burials, ceased to be royal prerogatives during the First Intermediate Period, when all aspired to be identified after death with the god Osiris (Davies and Friedman 1998: 85–88; Lehner 1997).

In city-state civilizations the existence of a hereditary upper class might be thought to have encouraged the development of a similar optimism about life after death that would have diffused among commoners. Yet the most pessimistic early civilization in our sample was that of the Valley of Mexico, where, despite having a hereditary nobility, people believed that no individual identity survived for more than four years after death. The Yoruba, who did not have a hereditary nobility but had royal clans that traced their descent from the gods, may or may not have believed in the long-term survival of a personal identity for any dead person. The Maya, who appear to have had a hereditary nobility, believed in a relatively favourable survival after death for resourceful members of the upper class but had lower expectations for commoners. The randomness of these cases suggests that formal class stratification by itself did not make a significant difference. A similar situation prevailed among territorial states, where the Egyptians, who tended to de-emphasize hereditary descent and inherited membership in an upper class, were at least as optimistic about life after death as the Inka and Chinese, for whom hereditary upper-class status was a basis of political order.

While the upper classes in territorial states stressed their similarities to the gods, the upper classes in rivalrous city-states, whether or not these classes were formally defined, viewed the world as a risky place in which they as well as commoners existed to serve the gods. While the optimism that all ancient Egyptians and both Inka rulers and their subjects shared about personal life after death contrasted with the pessimism of the Aztec, Mesopotamians, and, to a lesser extent, the Yoruba, the Chinese may have been less optimistic about the fate of commoners than people in other territorial states, while the Maya appear to have been more optimistic about the fate of the upper classes than people in other city-state civilizations. Even so, the view that all Maya shared concerning the underworld was a gloomy one, while the early Chinese appear to have envisaged everyone as sharing a more promising fate after death than the Mesopotamians or the peoples of the Valley of Mexico.

Beliefs about souls and life-forces in early civilizations appear to have been based on ideas that were widespread if not panhuman prior to the development of these civilizations. Yet the adaptation of these views to the needs of hierarchical societies produced numerous unanticipated parallels among historically unrelated societies. In general, the beliefs evolved by the upper classes played a major role in influencing what the lower classes believed. While status differences in early civilizations are reflected in beliefs about the fate of individuals after death, the greater sense of security and self-importance of the ruling classes and the greater opportunities for status emulation in territorial states were very important in determining how these views were expressed in particular societies.

24 Elite Art and Architecture

Class hierarchies are held together by the 'unproductive uses of economic surplus' (Eyer 1984: 52). In early civilizations conspicuous consumption affirmed the power of the upper classes and served to distinguish strata amongst them. Ordinary people – supporting themselves with simple technologies, able to produce only meagre food surpluses, and allowed by rulers to keep only a small portion of those surpluses – easily appreciated the social significance of the ruling classes' being able to expend large amounts of surplus energy on non-utilitarian projects. Key examples of such undertakings were the creation of costly luxury goods and monumental architecture – cost being measured by the amount of labour required to produce them (Maisels 1999: 344). The ability of the upper classes to sponsor such production reinforced their political power in the imaginations of ordinary people, even though it was lower-class craft workers and corvée labourers who were the producers. Public displays of such production encouraged the loyalty and obedience of the lower classes (Tate 1992: 31).

Yet such a functionalist approach does not account for all the evidence. While temples, palaces, and tombs were often impressive from the outside, much elaborate art and architecture remained hidden from public view. Most palaces, temples, and government buildings were located behind walls that prevented ordinary people from observing what was inside them. Functionalists can argue that what was visible only to the upper classes reinforced their self-image and helped to demarcate and reinforce internal hierarchies. Even so, some of the most costly and elaborate art was hidden away in the darkened, innermost rooms of temples, which only a few officials and priests ever entered, or went straight from the workshop to the tomb. This magnificent art was intended to be viewed only by the gods and by the dead, not by living humans.

In considering the art and architecture of early civilizations, it is impossible to separate functional considerations from symbolic ones. An Egyptian pyramid complex may have been the supreme manifestation of royal authority because of its size and elegance, but it was also built to protect the body of a dead pharaoh, nourish his k3 souls, facilitate the movement of his b3 souls back and forth between the earth and the sky, and maintain the cosmic order. Mesopotamian temples were expressions of community pride and identity and of royal power, but they were also manifestations of the supernatural power or auras of their resident deities (Jacobsen 1976: 16). Maya temples were believed to be animated by supernatural power that accumulated as the result of a divine presence within them and made them ever more effective locations for communicating with the gods (Fox 1996: 485; Schele and Freidel 1990: 72–73). Egyptian tomb art sought to nourish the dead, while Egyptian and Yoruba cult statues were created and used to focus supernatural power (R. Thompson 1976: 20/1). In early civilizations, art and architecture were no less vehicles for managing sacred powers and conducting relations with the supernatural than they were social-regulatory statements. Claims of supernatural power acquired meaning and validity through the expenditure of material resources.

Art and architecture are both commonly viewed as quintessential products of idiosyncratically variable cultural traditions. While buildings perform social functions and their design is subject to various material limitations, stylistic innovation in art and architecture is regarded as relatively free from environmental and social constraints and predominantly influenced by cultural traditions. Even modern neophytes can soon learn to distinguish the formal art and monumental architecture of one early civilization from those of another. This is much harder to do with the less elaborate symbolic creations and house types associated with commoners in the same societies. It is therefore assumed that, stylistically, thematically, and iconographically, art and architecture varied idiosyncratically from one early civilization to another and, of the two, art probably varied more because it was subject to even fewer formal constraints.

While the highly stylized art and architecture that were associated with the upper classes had their origins in the less hierarchical cultures that had developed into early civilizations, both art and architecture were strongly influenced by increasing social complexity. They evolved distinctive forms that reflected the growing class hierarchy. This development constituted the differentiation of what Robert Redfield called a 'Great Tradition', the deliberately cultivated lifestyles of the upper classes, from the 'Little Tradition' of the lower classes. While Little Traditions routinely absorbed elements of elite lifestyles, they were basically continuations of long-established cultural traditions at the community level. Within these local traditions, themes, iconography, and style were not consistently harmonized to the same degree as they were in Great

Traditions (Maisels 1999: 355–56; Marriott 1955; Redfield 1941). It seems appropriate to refer to the art associated with these two traditions as 'elite art' and 'commoner art' respectively. Philip Dark (1973: 61–62) has noted that in Benin there were what he called 'court' and 'plebeian' versions of the cutaway mud sculpture used to decorate the walls of shrines, the court style being limited to Benin City and the work of specialized priests. While ordinary people might carry on traditions inherited from earlier and simpler times, each Great Tradition and its associated elite art and architecture were new creations that involved the radical transformation of old ways of doing things to satisfy new social needs (Haselberger 1961).

ELITE ART

Formal, highly sophisticated art was produced by unusually skilled craft workers for the upper classes. Some were employed full-time by particular patrons. Especially in territorial states, the most skillful artisans worked for the government or for kings, setting standards of excellence for the whole society. In these cases, Redfield's Great Tradition is often called a 'court culture' (Kemp 1989: 64–65; Willett 1967: 162). The quality of what skilled artisans created reflected the extent to which patrons supported their work, greater investment permitting more specialization, the use of more costly and exotic materials, and greater attention to detail.

Highly sophisticated art that is acclaimed for its aesthetic qualities was also produced by part-time specialists working in small-scale societies. The sculpture of the aboriginal peoples of coastal British Columbia, for example, has been compared to that of Classical Greece (Lévi-Strauss 1982). Art of this sort did not, however, employ as wide a range of exotic materials or such elaborate technologies as did the art created in early civilizations. Moreover, even if high-ranking persons commissioned the production of such art as a strategy for self-promotion, this art resulted from the relentless competition for prestige among rival individuals, kin groups, age-grades, and communities rather than the use by established upper classes of distinctive forms of art to represent their superior status in early civilizations. What the two forms of artistic production shared was the investment of wealth to produce highly visible material status symbols.

While modern scholars conventionally refer to the items that were specially produced for the upper classes in early civilizations as works of 'art' and to their producers as 'artists', there is no evidence that concepts genuinely equivalent to these existed in early civilizations (Tate 1992: 30). High-quality work was produced by elite artisans who possessed the specialized skills, raw materials, and resources needed to create the superior work desired by their patrons. Minor officials who had special drawing skills and knowledge of iconography were often involved in designing such items and overseeing their production. These officials would have been the intermediaries between upper-class patrons and the craft workers who physically manufactured luxury goods.

Individual works of high quality were frequently produced by teams of artisans labouring together. Egyptian workshop scenes depict a number of sculptors working simultaneously on large stone statues. Bas-reliefs appear to have been designed and drawn onto limestone or plaster walls by literate scribe-artists who specialized in such work and then chiselled out by stonemasons and coloured by specialized painters (Andreu 1997: 61–65). Designing and drawing also seem to have been separate from stone-carving among the Classic Maya. Two or more Maya designers, as well as two or more stonecutters, sometimes worked on the same monument (Tate 1992: 40–49). Fourteen sculptors are reported to have jointly carved a now destroyed statue of the Aztec ruler Mochtezuma II at Chapultepec (Berdan 1982: 153). Shang bronze-casting required large, well-coordinated teams of highly specialized artisans to produce high-quality vessels (Treistman 1972: 84–93). At least one Egyptian sculptor recorded his name and a small image of himself in a tomb that he decorated for a high-ranking official of the Old Kingdom, presumably with the permission of the tomb's owner (Strouhal 1992: 166–67). Maya individuals associated with the production of stone monuments recorded their names on some carved stone lintels and stelae (Tate 1992: 45–47). However, while skilled artisans appear to have been greatly valued and well-treated by their patrons or clients, most of them remained anonymous.

The teamwork and general anonymity of the people who produced the major art works of early civilizations more closely approximate the modern concept of a skilled artisan or master craft worker than they do the idea of an artist. Like modern artisans, master artisans in early civilizations sought to work within established aesthetic traditions rather than to transcend them by dramatic acts of personal creativity. Especially skilled Yoruba wood-carvers acquired reputations for being able to infuse their creations with unusual amounts of spiritual power, and this ensured that they received important commissions. Yet such reputations were based on their ability to innovate within a traditional framework (R. Thompson 1976: 19/1). Master craft workers were the response to a growing demand for outstanding products by upper-class individuals or institutions. Such patrons provided artisans with the resources that allowed them to devote large amounts of time to developing skills and producing high-quality items.

In early civilizations there was no equivalent of art for art's sake. Artistic creations indicated their owners' or donors' social standing as well as serving religious and practical functions. Upper-class Egyptian jewellery, in addition to signifying the social status of its wearers, incorporated or took the form of amulets that protected such individuals from attacks by evil spirits. The elaborate gold vessels used to serve food and drink to the Inka ruler distinguished him from other people and also symbolically reaffirmed his connection with the sun god. John Baines and Norman Yoffee (1998: 235) have proposed that 'aesthetic items' would be a more appropriate designation than 'works of art' for the special creations of early civilizations. It is tempting to go still farther and designate these items 'elite goods', thereby eliminating any reference to subjective and little understood artistic considerations. Moreover, some highly prized crowns and royal insignia were manufactured from inexpensive, locally available materials using widely practised and not especially elaborate techniques. What distinguished these products was that only certain people were allowed to make and use them. These elite insignia may have been no less valued by the upper classes, but they differed in terms of how they were manufactured from goods produced from rare and valuable materials by highly specialized artisans. The cost of producing the latter items ensured that they could not be copied or usurped by the lower classes. It therefore seems appropriate to retain the designation 'elite art' as an admittedly approximate and ethnocentric gloss for elite goods that required special skills and high economic expenditures to produce.

Each early civilization created elite art that was stylistically unique. Even the Classic Maya and the inhabitants of the Valley of Mexico, whose cultures were expressions of a single Mesoamerican cultural tradition, created highly divergent art. Egyptian relief sculpture, with its serene, hieroglyphic-like human figures arranged in registers against a flat background, shared numerous features with Aztec relief sculpture (Pasztory 1983; Nicholson and Quiñones Keber 1983; Robins 1997; Townsend 1979), but the iconographies of the two sculptures were completely different. The Egyptian symbolic variations in figure size, more open backgrounds, and more elaborate arrangements of registers are not found in the relief styles of the Valley of Mexico. Neither relief style can be confused with that of the Classic Maya, with its flowing lines and dense, convoluted layouts (Baudez 1994; Benson and Griffin 1988). Nor can Maya vase-painting, with its sinuous lines and washed colours, be confused with the mural or codex paintings of the Aztec and their neighbours, which featured heavy outlines filled with bright, uniform colours, expressionless faces, and a strong emphasis on the symbolic details of costumes (Coe 1978; M. E. Smith

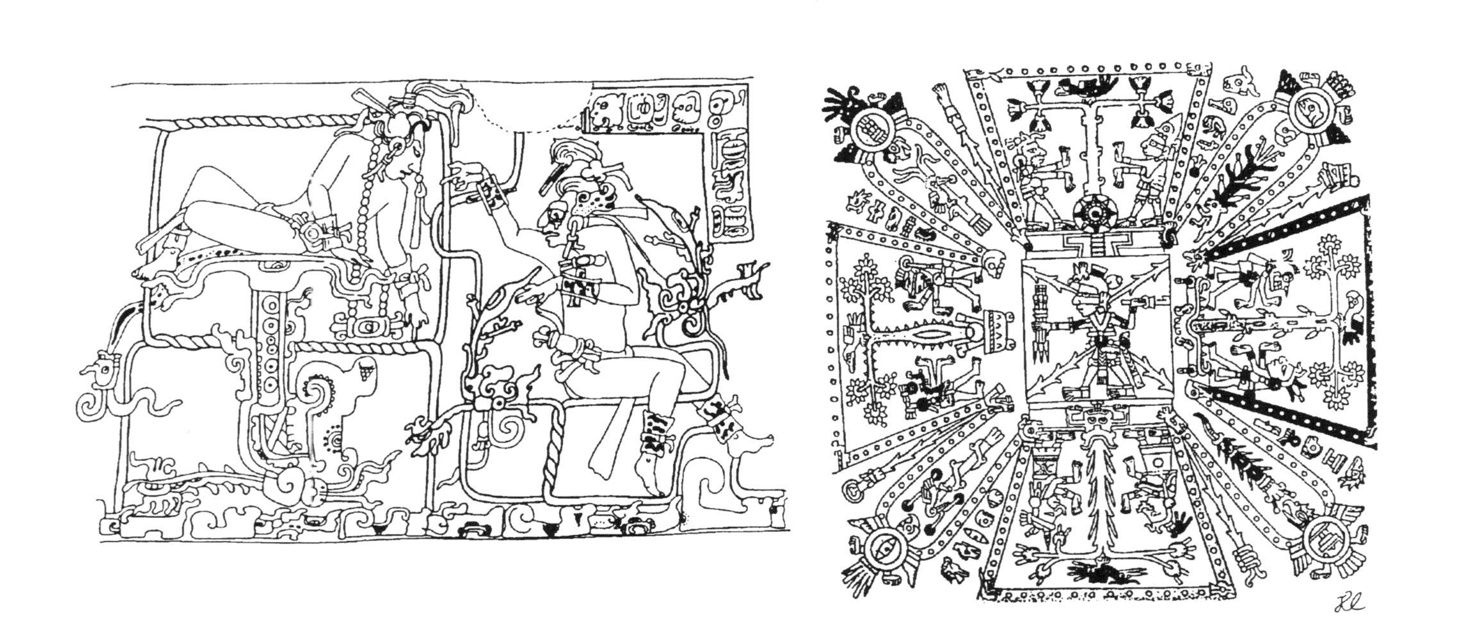

24.1. Classic Maya and Valley of Mexico painting styles: (a) detail from the Quirarte vase, apparently showing gods of the Maya underworld; (b) first page of a ritual almanac, the Codex Fejervary-Mayer. The highland Mexican Fire God Xiuhtecuhtli is shown in the centre, east is at the top. Sources: (a) after Bassie-Sweet 1991: 139; (b) with thanks to the Board of Trustees of the National Museums and Galleries on Merseyside [Liverpool Museum].

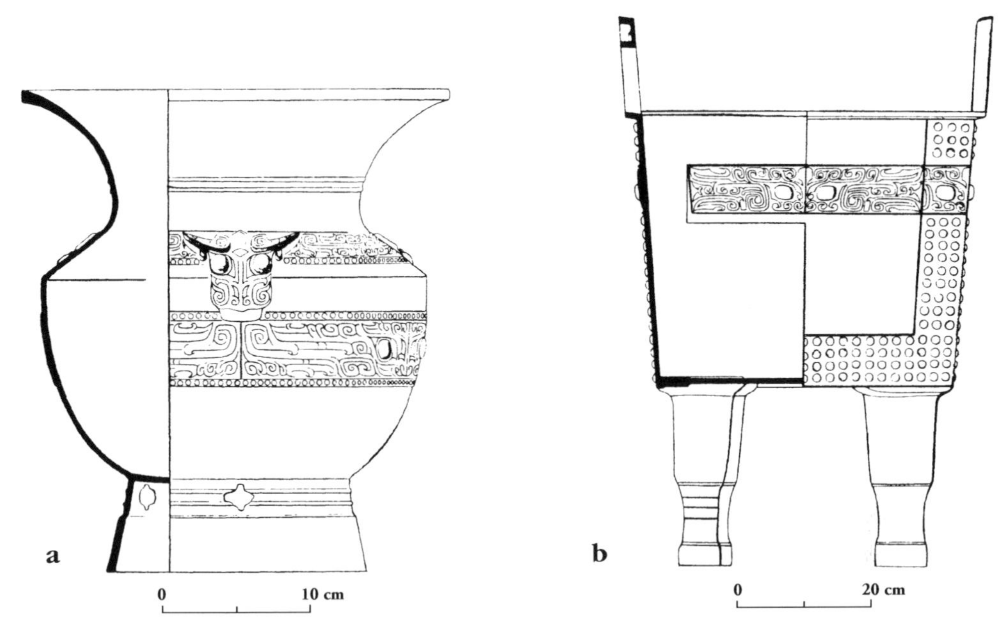

24.2. Early Shang ritual vessels cast in bronze from Zhengzhou. Sources: Wen Wu, no. 3, 1983, pp. 53–57.

1996: 263–64; Smith and Heath-Smith 1980) (Fig. 24.1). Shang metallurgy and wood-carving, with their abstract, balanced, and geometricized figures of animals or parts of animals covering whole surfaces (Fig. 24.2), cannot be mistaken for the more realistic and simply decorated statues of people, anthropomorphic deities, and animals fashioned by Inka craft workers (Chêng 1960: 233–38; Stierlin 1984). Yoruba wood sculpture, with its large heads, simplified extremities, and emphasis on cylindrical shapes, was very different from Egyptian stone or wood sculpture, with its frontality, symmetry, blockiness, and idealized naturalism, and from Mesopotamian stone statues, with their large round eyes, introspective gaze, and elongated forms (Abiodun, Drewal, and Pemberton 1994; R. Armstrong 1981; Ben-Amos 1995; Ben-Amos and Rubin 1983; Dark 1973; Forman, Forman, and Dark 1960; R. Thompson 1976) (Fig. 24.3). Mesopotamian relief sculpture differed from that of Egypt in terms of its more deeply cut figures, greater emphasis on human musculature, and more crowded compositions, as well as its different themes (Caubet and Pouyssegur 1998).

In territorial states centralized control and patronage of the production of sophisticated art tended to promote a polity-wide uniformity of style. In Old and Middle Kingdom Egypt, the production of luxury goods was centred around the royal court, near Memphis, while in the New Kingdom there were

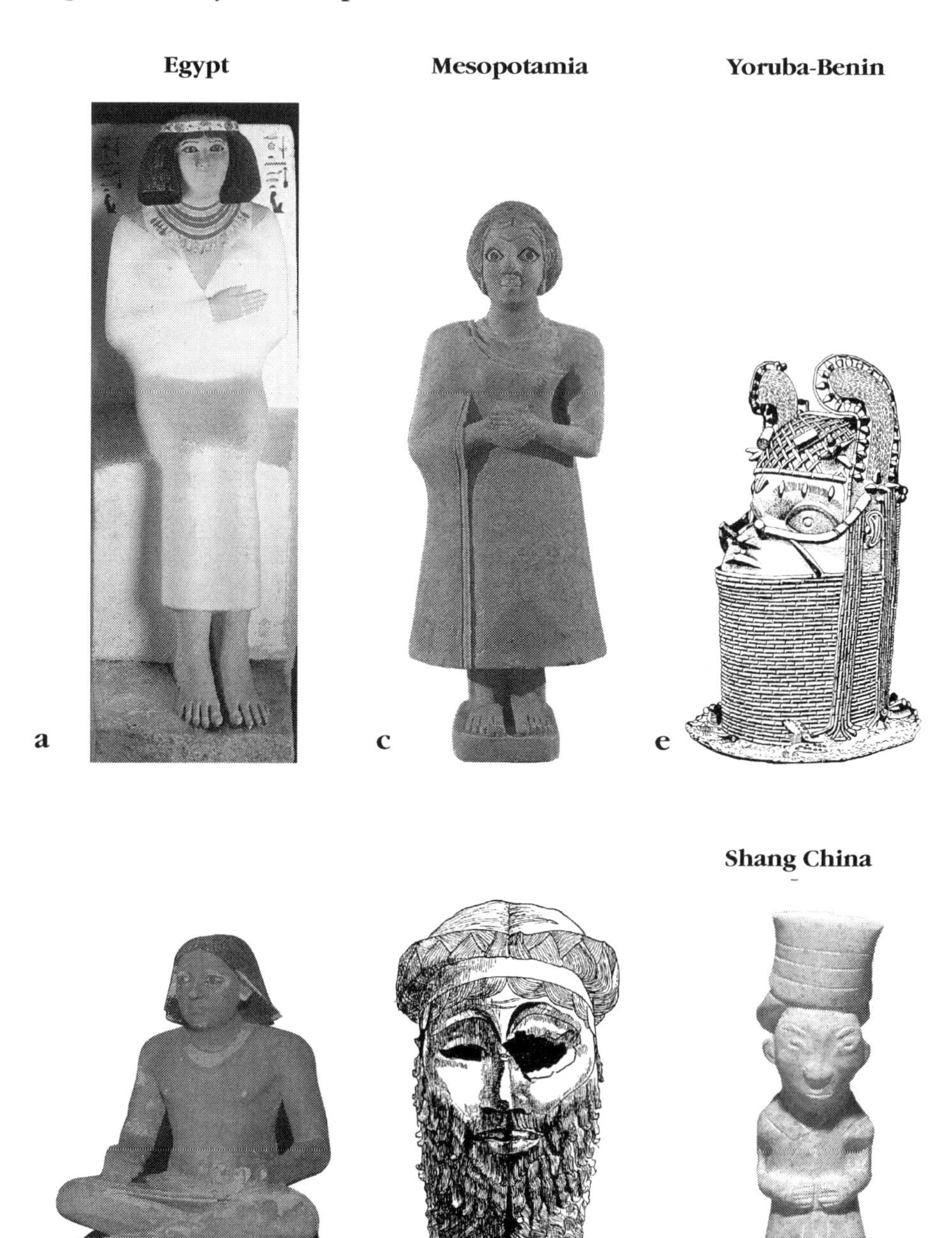

Egypt
Mesopotamia
Yoruba-Benin
a
c
e
Shang China
b
d
f

subtle stylistic differences between goods produced at Memphis and at Thebes (Fuerstein 1999; Martin 1991). The Inka rulers established a uniform style of elite craft production that was evident both in objects made of precious metals, created at a small number of government workshops, and in painted pottery, manufactured at numerous sites throughout the kingdom. The Shang state was characterized by a distinctive art style that would have required standardizing bronze-casting activities at various administrative centres (Thorp 1985).

Each city-state system also had a distinctive, shared art style, presumably disseminated and sustained by interstate contacts among the upper classes of neighbouring city-states, the trading of luxury produce, and sometimes the movement of elite craft workers from one state to another. Shared styles reflected and reinforced a sense of cultural identity among the upper classes of neighbouring city-states and facilitated communication concerning numerous matters of common interest. Yet individual city-states and their upper classes also expressed their identities with local variations in art styles. Western Maya kingdoms such as Palenque and Piedras Negras were the only Classic Maya states to move from single-figure to multiple-figure sculptural compositions. In addition to erecting the free-standing vertical stelae found in most Maya states, the rulers of these kingdoms decorated buildings with elaborately carved stone wall panels and lintels. While upper-class costumes and the use of symbols also varied from one Maya urban centre to another (Tate 1992: xii), changes in the representation of dress and the positioning of figures permit stelae throughout the Maya area to be dated to within less than a century on the basis of stylistic criteria (Proskouriakoff 1950). This suggests that artists in different Maya centres must have communicated extensively with one another.

Yoruba art also varied in style and motifs from one region and one urban centre to another (R. Armstrong 1981: 91). This variation is clear in both woodcarving, which varied regionally, and the ritual bronze heads produced at Ife and the brass ones of Benin. Although the tradition of casting these heads

---

24.3. Statues in early civilizations: (a) Egyptian painted limestone statue of Nofret, wife of Rahotep, a high official and member of the royal family, from Meidum, early Dynasty IV, height 120 cm; (b) painted limestone statue of a scribe from Saqqara, name lost, Dynasty V, height 50 cm; (c) Mesopotamian limestone female worshipper statue, from Khafaja, Early Dynastic period, height 37 cm; (d) bronze head of Akkadian monarch, either Sargon or Naramsin, found at Nineveh, height 37 cm; (e) brass head of the Late Period (nineteenth century) from Benin, probably associated with the cult of a dead ruler, height 52 cm; (f) jade statuette of a standing dignitary, Shang period, height 9 cm. Sources: (a),(b) Egyptian Museum, Cairo (photos courtesy of Scala/Art Resource, NY and Fototeca Internacional Lda/Art Resource, NY); (c) Iraq Museum, Baghdad (photo courtesy of Scala/Art Resource, NY); (d) J. G. Macqueen, *Babylon* (London, 1964), 25; (e) after Willett 1967: 155; (f) courtesy of the Arthur M. Sackler Museum, Harvard University Art Museums, Bequest of Grenville L. Winthrop (photo Michael Nedzweski and Junius Beebe, ©President and Fellows of Harvard College).

is reported to have been introduced to Benin from Ife, the oldest surviving heads at Benin have a different, more stylized form from contemporary Ife ones (Dark 1973: 8–9). Art styles also appear to have varied from one Mesopotamian city-state to another and among different states in the Valley of Mexico. It has not been ascertained, however, to what extent observed differences represented expressions of local identity. Both in the Valley of Mexico and among the Yoruba, towns tended to specialize in the production of different kinds of luxury goods, which were traded over considerable distances.

Elite art traditions could evolve rapidly when social circumstances were propitious. In Egypt such a tradition developed, beginning in Upper Egypt, in the generations that immediately preceded and followed the unification of the country. Rows of animals and antithetical arrangements of humans on stone palettes and ivory knife handles gave way to scenes that were increasingly dominated by the monarch, who came to be represented as acting without any human assistance. At the same time, human beings, animals, and plants were represented in ever more conventionalized forms that were to persist with only minor modifications for over three thousand years. Apart from the appearance of a few short-lived motifs that may have been of Mesopotamian or Elamite origin, this appears to have been a purely internal development (Joffe 2000; Kemp 1989: 19–63).

The Aztec, in contrast, acquired their first elite stone-sculptors following their conquest, early in the fifteenth century, of the neighbouring hegemonic city of Azcapotzalco, to which they had hitherto been tributary. Previously Azcapotzalco and Culhuacan had been the two major centres of stone-carving in the Valley of Mexico. Aztec sculptors drew inspiration from the large stone images visible in the ruins of the ancient city of Tula, seventy kilometres to the north, some of which they brought to Tenochtitlan. They and others in the southern part of the valley also adopted Huaxtec models for producing three-dimensional cult effigies. As Aztec power grew, craft workers evolved a dynamic new style that emphasized bolder compositions and more dynamic and anatomically observant representations of the human body. By the late fifteenth century Tenochtitlan was the pre-eminent centre of stone-carving in central Mexico.

While the Egyptians had to invent their own style of monumental art, the Aztec were able to draw upon various older traditions. Relatively quickly, however, they evolved their own distinctive style of stone-carving, which they employed alongside introduced ones (Townsend 1979). Maya art was influenced by earlier Olmec and Izapan styles, which the Maya transformed to create a new and distinctive style (Coe 1977; Quirarte 1977). Shang elite productions retained the basic shapes of the Neolithic art of northern China while their technical expertise and the flamboyance of their decoration increased dramatically, creating an ever-greater contrast with the goods produced by and for the lower classes (Bagley 1999: 146–53; Keightley 1969: 60).

In some early civilizations elite art acquired a uniform style regardless of the material that was being worked. In Egypt jewellery, furniture, sculpture, and relief carvings that were produced for the upper classes exhibited the same style and ornamentation whether they were manufactured from stone, metal, or wood. Pottery by this time had become purely utilitarian and was largely undecorated. Throughout the course of ancient Egyptian civilization, the elite style slowly changed, but any innovations continued to influence goods produced in all materials. It is known from historical records that different materials were worked by separate groups of craft specialists. The stylistic unity of Egyptian art therefore reflected the taste of patrons and the control that the royal court and bureaucracy were able to exert over various groups of artisans. It also indicated the extent to which the upper classes viewed the goods made for their use as material expressions of their class identity and unity vis-à-vis ordinary people. Although the stylistic unity of elite craft products was disrupted during the First Intermediate Period, a unified style remained the ideal and once again became a reality in the Middle Kingdom (W. Smith 1958).

Shang bronze-casting, the carving of jade, turquoise, marble, ivory, shell, and wood, and the manufacturing of ornate pottery all employed the same highly stylized composite animal motifs and the same complex geometrical patterns (Chêng 1960: 233–38). This uniformity attests to the ability of upper-class patrons to impose their shared tastes on groups of craft specialists living and working in small communities.

Inka production of elite goods appears to have been less stylistically unified. Gold and silver ornaments produced for the state tended to emphasize simplicity and plainness, while pottery and fancy cloth were decorated with extremely complex geometrical patterns (Fig. 24.4). These varied productions tended to share an underlying sense of order, formal clarity, balanced proportions, and clean outlines (Jones 1964: 5; Stierlin 1984). Thus in each territorial state an elite art style which exhibited varying degrees of stylistic homogeneity in relation to different raw materials played a major role in reinforcing a sense of unity within a governing class that was dispersed over a large region.

In city-states elite and commoner art tended to be less sharply differentiated than in territorial states. There was also less stylistic unity in the output of different crafts. The lack of a clear distinction between art created for the upper classes and commoner art resulted in part from skilled artisans' producing for a broader social spectrum than artisans in territorial states.

24.4. Inka art styles: (a) hollow anthropomorphic silver figurine – such figurines, often clothed in miniature textile garments were used as offerings, height 20.3 cm; (b) silver image of a llama made of pieces of hammered sheet silver soldered into place, also used as offering, height 12.7 cm; (c) – (f) Inka decorated ceramics. All these objects would have been manufactured in state production centres. Sources: (a) – (f) after V. W. von Hagen, *Realms of the Incas* (New York, 1957), 78, 90, 168, 172.

Particularly in city-state systems that lacked a hereditary nobility, different crafts tended to have their own styles. Among the Yoruba, the style employed by wood-carvers in any one community differed from the styles associated with ironworking, bronze- or brass-casting, terracotta-figure-making, stone-carving, pottery-making, bead work, leather work, resist-dyeing, and the decoration of calabashes (Bascom 1969: 111; R. Thompson 1976: 1/1). In Mesopotamia the same motifs and styles were used on stone cylinder seals, metal temple and palace decorations, and stone relief-carving but absent on a wide range of mundane objects, including clay statues intended for household use. The representational motifs employed in painting and sculpture were totally absent from elite jewellery. This suggests that temple and palace institutions imposed some degree of uniformity on artisans who worked for them full-time or even part-time but could not (or chose not to) influence the full range of their production. That temples and palaces appear to have patronized similar art styles may reflect either an attempt to impose a common elite identity on the art sponsored by these two types of institutions or, more likely, kings' patronizing the production of major art works for temples

(Caubet and Pouysseggur 1998; Collon 1987; Crawford 1991: 155–67; Frankfort 1954).

Aztec stone-carvers, employed mainly by the state, evolved a distinctive style, although stone cult images continued to be manufactured in the Huaxtec style. Feather workers, who may originally have been of foreign origin, carefully adhered to local iconography. Gold jewellery stylistically resembled what was produced by the Mixtec, but it too incorporated local iconography. Manuscript and mural-painting were executed in a style that appears to have been derived from Puebla and Cholula. While there were some tendencies towards greater stylistic unity in Aztec art, the upper classes appear to have tolerated and even valued foreign styles that enjoyed regional prestige. This same attitude may have encouraged the highest levels of Aztec society to use only painted ceramic vessels imported from Cholula (M. E. Smith 1996: 99–107).

The Classic Maya employed similar styles for carving stone, wood, and jade objects and for painting murals such as the ones that decorated the interior of a small three-room temple at Bonampak. Scenes painted on high-quality ceramic vessels were executed in a more fluid style, and the iconography was different from that used in public art, but the general approach was much the same. Similar forms governed the production of elaborate representational (so-called eccentric) flints (Hanks and Rice 1989). The stylistic uniformity of Classic Maya art may partly reflect the greater geographical isolation of most Maya groups from alternative artistic traditions than was the case with states in the Valley of Mexico. It may also, however, indicate that the Maya upper class, like that of territorial states, exerted stronger controls over the production of various groups of elite specialists, who lived and worked in separate residential groups in Maya urban centres.

The materials used to manufacture high-quality art varied considerably from one culture to another. The ancient Egyptians produced stone statues, relief sculpture, and fancy jars and dishes. In the Old Kingdom, statues varied from small to more than life-size. By the Middle Kingdom, some colossal stone statues were being produced for kings and hereditary nobles. Limestone and sandstone were most frequently worked, but harder rocks, such as granite and diorite, were also carved (DePutter and Karlshausen 1997). In addition, life-size statues were made of wood and sheet copper and small ones cast of precious metals. Gold and semiprecious stones were used to create fancy jewellery, copper and gold to fashion serving vessels, and imported cedar wood and gold leaf to produce ornate furniture and burial equipment. Faience, or blue frit, was a cheap substitute for turquoise.

The Mesopotamians used limestone and alabaster, which they quarried close by, and sometimes imported harder rocks, such as diorite, to carve reliefs, stelae, small statues, doorpost sockets, and cylinder seals. Precious metals were employed to produce jewellery and copper and bronze to manufacture vases and statues.

The Maya carved stelae, lintels, and decorated panels from limestone, tufa, and hardwoods and fashioned painted reliefs of moulded or carved plaster. Painted scenes were also applied to flat plaster surfaces. Jewellery was made of jade and fancy painted vessels and statues of pottery.

The Aztec carved statues, temple furniture, and relief sculpture from stone, painted murals on plaster, and manufactured jewellery and ornaments from jade, obsidian, wood inlaid with turquoise, gold, and copper. Feathers and feather work were highly valued. While high-quality pottery vessels were imported from beyond the valley, large terracotta statues were manufactured locally.

The Shang Chinese lavished their greatest artistic skills on the casting of ritual vessels and elite weapons from bronze. They also carved and lacquered wood, sometimes in the form of large room panels, and manufactured ornaments from jade, shell, and bone. Only a few small human and animal statues were carved from stone. Fancy pottery was decorated with stamped and incised patterns.

The Inka fashioned statues and ornaments from gold, silver, and bronze. They also produced high-quality painted pottery and wove fancy clothing. Although they could work hard stone with great precision, they did not carve statues or bas-reliefs from it. Stone buildings were ornamented with trapezoidal niches but only rarely with simple carved motifs.

The most elaborate and highly prized Yoruba artistic creations were ritual human heads cast from copper or brass and elaborately decorated metal plaques that were used to cover wooden doors and pillars. The most common material for works of art was wood, which was carved and painted to produce statues, masks, and fancy doors for shrines, palaces, and officials' houses. Art works were also made of ivory. At Ife nearly life-size statues were moulded from terracotta (Ojo 1966a: 252). Jewellery and cult equipment were manufactured from brass, iron, and carved ivory. Red coral and glass beads, especially glass beads fom Ife, were highly valued. The stone statues carved in some localities were very crudely executed (Stevens 1978).

There was no cross-cultural uniformity in the materials preferred for artistic expression. Egyptians, Maya, Mesopotamians, and Aztec lavished particular attention on carved stone, but other early civilizations did not. This neglect was especially curious for the Inka, who worked even the hardest types of rock expertly for architectural purposes. Moreover, the ruins of Tiwanaku, which may have inspired Inka stone construction, contained numerous stone reliefs and statues. Metals were important vehicles for artistic expression among the Chinese, Inka, Mesopotamians, Egyptians, and Yoruba but of minor importance in the Valley of Mexico and rare and entirely imported among the Classic Maya. Various forms of jadeite were highly valued by the Chinese and Maya and in the Valley of Mexico. Wood-carving was a significant art form among the Yoruba, in Egypt, in Shang China, and among the Maya. Pottery vessels were a focus of elite art among the Maya, Inka, and Shang Chinese and to a lesser degree in the Valley of Mexico, while high-quality ceramic statues were produced by the Aztec, Yoruba, and Maya. Elsewhere, even where ceramics had formerly been a significant artistic medium, as in Egypt and Mesopotamia, it was reduced to utilitarian status as new, more exotic materials became the preferred means of artistic expression. Murals painted on plaster played an important role in Aztec, Maya, Mesopotamian, and Egyptian culture. Feather work was greatly prized in the Valley of Mexico and among the Maya. Fancy cloth was an especially important medium of artistic expression among the Inka.

It is difficult to correlate these variations with the availability of materials. Egyptians and Andean highlanders had equal access to many types of stone, but the Inka made almost no use of them except for their extensive architectural projects. While both the Yoruba and the Maya had access to a wide variety of hardwoods, the Maya tended to use stone instead. Everywhere there was some preference for durable materials and for scarce and exotic ones, but this emphasis was not overwhelming. The selection of materials for creating elite art seems to have reflected many idiosyncratic cultural preferences.

More cross-cultural regularity can be discerned when art is examined thematically. Elite art in most early civilizations emphasized images of rulers and deities. In general, anthropomorphic beings were portrayed in a more detailed, naturalistic fashion and to a much greater degree in early civilizations than in the small-scale societies from which they had evolved. The Assyriologist V. K. Afanasieva (1991: 128) suggests that art produced prior to the development of early civilizations depicted human beings, if at all, only as integral parts of nature. She maintains that the emphasis on human figures and their more realistic portrayal in early civilizations reflected a new self-confidence and sense of power resulting from greater control over nature and perhaps increased isolation from it. There is, however, no obvious support for this generalization.

The elite art of the ancient Egyptians, Mesopotamians, Classic Maya, and the Valley of Mexico accorded prominence to naturalistic, if often highly stylized, anthropomorphic figures, with a special emphasis on deities, kings, and other persons of high rank. The Yoruba produced naturalistic representations of rulers and their retinues but frequently rendered other anthropomorphic figures in a more abstract style that was also applied to animals. Yoruba anthropomorphic religious figures were usually representations of kings or worshippers rather than of deities (Bascom 1969: 111).

Apart from metal statues of gods and rulers, which were used for cult purposes, the Inka did not produce anthropomorphic representations of any sort; human figures on Inka-style pottery appear to date from the early colonial period. Nor did they create naturalistic representations of anything else, apart from the metal images, sometimes life-size, of plants and animals produced for ritual purposes (Earle 1987: 73). Despite the prominence of anthropomorphic representations in the elite art of earlier civilizations in the southern Andean highlands and the contemporary lowland states that had been absorbed into the Inka kingdom, their overwhelming preference was for elaborate aniconic designs.

Shang art was focused heavily on animal figures, with human or humanoid representations playing only minor and subordinate roles. Kwang-chih Chang (1983) has interpreted the general absence of human figures in Shang and Western Zhou art as resulting from the inspiration of shamanistic themes, with humans being less important than the animals into which shamans transformed themselves. Yet there is much uncertainty about what roles shamans actually played and the beliefs associated with shamanism in early Chinese society. By contrast, Maya artists rendered indubitably shamanistic themes in a format that emphasized the human aspects of the participants (Schele and Miller 1986). One might, following Afanasieva, argue that the minimal importance accorded to human figures in Shang art indicates that Shang society remained at a chiefdom level of development, as Judith Treistman (1972: 130) once claimed. Yet later Chinese elite art, while representing humans to a much greater degree than Shang or Western Zhou art, never accorded as much importance to representations of kings as the art of Egypt, Mesopotamia, the Valley of Mexico, the Maya, or the Yoruba. The art associated with the early civilizations of China and Inka Peru seems to have been based on culturally distinctive choices concerning what was important or appropriate to represent.

In Maya civilization the decoration of temples underwent a major alteration during the Classic period. In Late Preclassic and Early Classic times, temple platforms were faced with elaborate murals executed in moulded and painted plaster. These murals portrayed frontal images of deities or cosmic forces represented in a highly abstract and symbolic form that in some of its general principles resembled Shang art. In the Late Classic period relief sculpture, confined to the shrines atop temple platforms, represented relations between realistically portrayed human kings and anthropomorphized supernatural beings and was accompanied by texts documenting the dynastic claims of the rulers. Arthur Miller (1986: 28–29, 72–80) interpreted this change as reflecting a growing emphasis on the linear inheritance of Maya kingship. Yet more recently deciphered Maya inscriptions indicate that linear inheritance was already well established by the Early Classic period. Stelae displaying the images of kings were first produced in the Tikal region and spread from there to other urban centres in Early Classic times. This makes it unlikely that the switch from cosmic symbolism to royal representations was associated with a major redefinition of kingship. It may, however, have reflected the growing political and ritual power of kings, who became capable at this point of imposing their own identities on major temples until then associated with communities.

A similar increasing emphasis on rulers in monumental art appears to have occurred in Mesopotamia during the Early Dynastic period. Small stone statues that have been conventionally identified as 'priest-kings' and other images that have been speculatively interpreted to be of rulers were produced in Mesopotamia as early as the Uruk period, but figures of kings identified by name do not occur before Early Dynastic times. The appearance of these named images did not, however, correlate with major changes in the programmes of temple decoration as happened among the Maya. Depictions of rulers became common on stone cylinder seals beginning in Ur III times; up to this point such seals had been decorated with banqueting, mythological, and religious scenes (Collon 1987: 123–30). Maya and Mesopotamian evidence casts doubt on the likelihood that the sparseness of surviving anthropomorphic representations in Inka and Shang art necessarily indicates that these civilizations were institutionally less developed than the others. Instead, it suggests that the development of anthropomorphic and royal themes was neither an inevitable nor an automatic concomitant of the rise of early civilizations.

Nevertheless, the early civilizations in which representational art did develop show significant cross-cultural thematic parallels. Statues of gods, rulers, and members of the upper-classes were produced for cult purposes. Life-size statues of rulers and of high-ranking officials and their families were manufactured for funerary purposes in ancient Egypt. These statues were usually carved from stone in an idealized but naturalistic style by sculptors attached to the royal court (Fuerstein 1999). Smaller stone statues of kings and officials were set up in Egyptian temples so that the k3 souls of these individuals could share in the daily food offerings made to the gods. The creation under royal auspices of cult statues of deities was regarded as important enough for years to be named for such events during the First Dynasty. Although no early examples have survived, these statues appear to have been small and made of precious metals (T. Wilkinson 1999: 267–69).

The Mesopotamians manufactured statues of deities, kings, and prosperous citizens for placement in temples. Cult statues may have been made of wood overlaid with metal. Stone statues of men and women were placed in temples to offer perpetual devotion to a deity on behalf of some individual or to remind the deity of that person's devotion. Royal statues were sometimes works of high quality portraying kings in a semi-idealized form. Most worshipper statues exhibit relatively simple workmanship and few, if any, individualizing traits and may have been bought ready-made by well-to-do persons to place in temples. Some of the statues of kings who aspired to divine status may have been intended as objects of worship rather than as images of worshippers (Crawford 1991: 160–64; Postgate 1992: 118).

The Inka made some large sheet-metal statues of major deities and of living and dead rulers. The power of living and dead kings was thought capable of entering into such statues and speaking through their medium priests, thus allowing kings to be present in two or more places at once and facilitating the delegation of royal power (Gose 1996a: 19–20). While no large statues of this sort have survived, small metal images of anthropomorphic beings and llamas have been recovered from the burials of sacrificed children.

In the most powerful Yoruba states, metal heads were cast to serve as cult objects for the veneration of dead rulers. Lesser families were restricted to using ritual heads made of wood or ceramics. Other three-dimensional bronze castings depicted kings or queen-mothers with their retainers. Statues of Yoruba deities or their worshippers were normally carved from wood (Bascom 1969: 111–13; Dark 1973).

The Aztec produced numerous stone statues of deities, while others were fashioned from wood. They also carved stone images of warriors, flag-bearers, and various guardian figures to ornament their temple precincts. Statues of Aztec kings were carved in stone outcrops at Chapultepec, among them one showing King Ahuitzotl wearing the costume of the fertility god Xipe Totec (Townsend 1979: 32–33). These images, which were probably objects of veneration, did not survive the early colonial period. The Maya equivalents of royal statues were deeply carved stelae, each displaying the image of the monarch on its front face. The Maya also carved wooden cult statues of deities, which appear to have been kept wrapped in cloth bundles in temple sanctuaries (Baudez 1994; Houston and Stuart 1996: 303–4).

It therefore appears that in any civilization where anthropomorphic statues were produced, some of them represented gods and others kings. Only in Egypt, Mesopotamia, and among the Yoruba were high-quality statues regularly created representing other prominent individuals: in Egypt as recipients of funerary offerings and in Mesopotamia and among the Yoruba as suppliants or worshippers. The Egyptians also produced small worker statues for interment with the upper classes.

The number of anthropomorphic statues produced varied considerably from one early civilization to another. Scarcely any such statues were fashioned by the Shang, but large numbers were created by the Egyptians. They also varied according to the type of being portrayed. The Aztec produced many statues of gods but relatively few of rulers, while, in the Old and Middle Kingdoms, the Egyptians manufactured many life-size statues of kings, administrators, and their families but fewer and much smaller statues of the gods. Most statues were produced in a style that emphasized a youthful and idealized rather than a literal likeness of an individual.

Relief carvings and painted murals (which are usually not so well preserved) depicted anthropomorphic creatures doing things to a much greater extent than did statues, which in early civilizations tended only to portray prominent individuals standing, sitting, or kneeling. Much of the elite relief art of early civilizations was focused on kings. Scenes portrayed rulers interacting with the gods or with their ancestors, performing rituals, defeating or dominating their foes (Fig. 24.5), and being attended by high-ranking subjects.

Except in the Terminal Classic period, Maya stone relief sculpture appears to have been a monopoly of rulers. It often portrayed kings alone or in the company of supernatural beings, including their ancestors. Occasionally kings were accompanied by a female member of the royal family, and in the western part of the Maya zone they were sometimes attended or assisted by nobles and courtiers. Maya kings were depicted wearing the costumes of gods, performing rituals such as bleeding themselves, militarily defeating enemy rulers, and dominating and humiliating rivals and enemies in various ways, such as standing on their crouching, bound bodies. Sometimes kings were portrayed on a larger scale than commoners or vanquished enemies. Enemies were often shown stripped of their regalia and dishevelled. Stone relief sculpture is found in other than royal or temple settings only from the end of the Classic period, when, at places such as Copan, it began to appear in the residential complexes of some high officials (Baudez 1994; Fash 1991: 162–63; Joyce 1992; 1996; Tate 1992).

In Egypt little official, non-funerary relief art did not portray the king. Public monuments and temple reliefs depicted kings defeating their enemies, receiving blessings from the gods, and performing rituals, which most often involved offerings to deities. Defeated foes were often represented stripped of their insignia and the clothing that was appropriate to their high social status. These themes endured with only minor changes throughout ancient Egyptian history. Kings were represented on a larger scale than any other humans

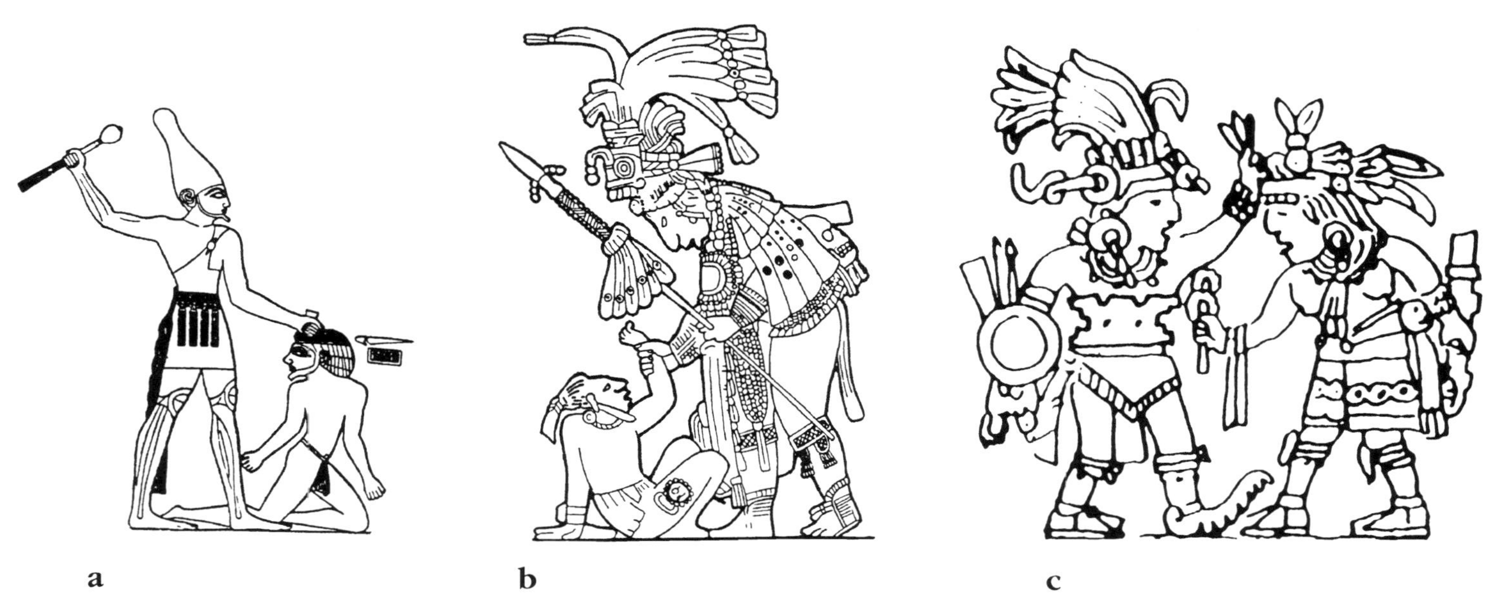

24.5. Kings subduing enemies: (a) Egyptian King Narmer defeats Wʿš, the leader of a northern Egyptian or Libyan people, ca. 3000 B.C.; (b) Bird Jaguar IV, ruler of the Maya city of Yaxchilan, captures Jewelled Skull, A.D. 755; (c) the Aztec ruler Tizoc is represented defeating a warrior from nearby Culhuacan, probably its king – this scene is one of a set of similar images around the circumference of the Tizoc Stone, dated ca. A.D. 1481, symbolizing Aztec hegemony over various city-states. Sources: (a) after Gardiner 1950: 7; (b) adapted from John S. Henderson, *The World of the Ancient Maya*, 2nd ed. (Ithaca, 1981), ©1981 by Cornell University, and used with permission of the publisher, Cornell University Press; (c) adapted from Joyce Marcus, *Mesoamerican Writing Systems* (Princeton, 1993), ©1993 by Princeton University Press, and used with permission of Princeton University Press.

except royal wives and on the same scale as the gods. No one was ever shown helping the king. If anyone else was present, it was simply to witness his achievements.

During the Old and Middle Kingdoms, neither the king nor the gods were represented in the tomb art of the upper classes. Tombs of nobles and officials contained wall reliefs showing food being grown, processed, and presented to the deceased tomb owner. The owner was represented on a larger scale than the commoners who served him. A considerable amount of private tomb art of this sort was produced during the Old and Middle Kingdoms. An unusual religious genre consisting of scenes celebrating the earthly creativity of the sun at different seasons was associated with Fifth Dynasty solar temples (Harpur 1987; Lustig 1997b; Robins 1997).

Early Dynastic Mesopotamian reliefs, often carved on stone stelae, depicted kings leading armies in victorious battles, building temples, and presiding over the feasts that celebrated such accomplishments. Kings were often portrayed on a larger scale than other individuals, but many reliefs emphasized the participation of large numbers of commoners in civic enterprises. Defeated enemy soldiers were depicted naked, being caught in a net by the victorious ruler, clubbed by uniformed and well-armed adversaries, trampled by foot-soldiers and chariots, led away as prisoners, or with their bound and prostrate bodies forming a deity's throne (Caubet and Pouyssegur 1998; Furlong 1987: 16, 21; Parrot 1960; Strommenger and Hirmer 1964).

Aztec relief sculpture depicted mainly deities, anonymous warrior figures, standard-bearers, stacked human skulls, calendrical dates, and miscellaneous religious symbols. Fewer deities were depicted on stone in relief than in the form of three-dimensional sculptures. Royal figures were rare, but the reliefs on the monumental Tizoc stone portrayed that king defeating a series of elaborately dressed human figures, each associated with a tributary city-state. A relief celebrating King Ahuitzotl's enlargement of the main Aztec temple in 1487 records that date and shows him and his predecessor, Tizoc, dressed as priests and engaged in ritual blood-letting (Nicholson 1971a: 112–33; Townsend 1979: 41–42).

Benin brass plaques, which were the equivalent of relief sculpture, were produced not as cult objects but as palace decorations recording historical events and scenes of everyday life. Some showed the king, occasionally on horseback, accompanied by retainers (usually soldiers) and larger than some of them. None showed him in action (Dark 1973: 24–28). Nor did any of these plaques portray recognizable deities. No examples of relief art depicting human or anthropomorphic figures are associated with Shang China or the Inka state.

Where anthropomorphic figures were depicted, their relative size often corresponded with the social importance of the individuals they represented. In Egypt and to a lesser extent in Mesopotamia and among the Maya and Yoruba, kings were shown larger than their subjects. Egyptian officials were likewise portrayed on a larger scale than their subordinates in tomb art.

Conventions for portraying human beings in relief also displayed considerable cross-cultural uniformity. Human faces were usually depicted in profile, eyes and shoulders frontally, and the lower torso, legs, and feet as if viewed from the side. This style of representation, which emphasized each aspect of the body in its most easily drawn or most easily recognized form, exhibited the most intricate conventions in Egypt. In Egyptian relief art, both feet were shown from the side but with their big toes facing the viewer.

In public representational art, the main focus was generally on the king. He was frequently portrayed leading others in Mesopotamian art and as a passive figure accompanied by his followers among the Yoruba. Egyptian rulers and, with some exceptions, Maya ones were shown either alone or as the dominant human figure. In Egypt only the king could be represented as performing a significant action in any scene in which he was portrayed, and therefore in the Old and Middle Kingdoms kings are shown personally defeating enemies but not leading armies. In one panel from Yaxchilan, an eighth-century Maya king is shown fighting alongside one of his subordinate lords, each of them subduing an opponent.

It is not surprising that what many art historians judge to be the finest art of early civilizations was produced in the two territorial states that endured the longest: the stone sculpture and relief carving of Old Kingdom Egypt and the bronze ceremonial vessels of Shang China. The quality of such art was largely determined by how much wealth patrons were able and willing to invest in its production. The best work was produced in small quantities and its distribution controlled by the state and a small upper class. In Old Kingdom Egypt all elite art appears to have been produced by craft workers associated with the royal court and displayed a uniform style. From earliest times, even the smallest and least significant products of royal workshops were coveted by minor officials and village leaders (Aldred 1971: 174–75). While multiple centres of bronze-casting and jade-working appear to have flourished within the Shang kingdom, the unified style of this art suggests that its production was under centralized control. The Inka elite maintained a uniform style for luxury goods that were manufactured from precious metals at a few places and for decorated pottery and fancy cloth fabricated in production centres located throughout the kingdom. In all three territorial states there was a vast gap between the consistently high-quality luxury goods produced by the state and the inferior and uneven quality goods produced in farming villages and market towns.

By contrast, in smaller and less centralized Mesopotamian city-states, the decorations and furnishings of temples and palaces were cruder and less clearly distinguished from what was found in ordinary houses. Temples, palaces, and individuals purchased the work or services of the same full-time artisans. The quality of palace and temple art was much higher in hegemonic cities. The bronze statue head often attributed to Sargon I and the excellent composition and carving of the stela celebrating Naram-Sin's victory over inhabitants of the Zagros Mountains provide examples of the high artistic levels achieved by elite specialists working for the Akkadian Dynasty. The royal statues of the Ur III Dynasty and the stela bearing Hammurabi's law code are examples of the distinguished artistic accomplishments made under the patronage of later rulers (Strommenger and Hirmer 1964).

In the Yoruba ritual centre of Ife bronze-casting reached its highest level of sophistication during the fourteenth century and then declined in quality as that city's political power waned (Willett 1967: 149). The casting of brass heads for the royal court is said to have begun in Benin in the fourteenth century and achieved peaks of excellence in the sixteenth and again in the eighteenth century. These peaks corresponded with exceptional periods of unity and prosperity in Benin's history (Dark 1973: 5–13). The production of Oyo's best art likewise coincided with that city's greatest power and prosperity in the eighteenth century and was disrupted by internal strife and military defeat in the nineteenth. For this reason, Frank Willett (1967: 162), Michèle Coquet (1998), and others identify the highest-quality art in the Yoruba region as court art.

In the Valley of Mexico, high-quality artistic production also tended to be correlated with periods of heightened power and prosperity of various city-states and especially with Tenochtitlan's gradually becoming the dominant regional centre. Richard Townsend (1979: 20) praises the dynamic forms and great plastic force of the key artistic achievements of Aztec sculptors in the late fifteenth century. A similar pattern prevailed among the Classic Maya city-states, with major episodes of artistic creativity generally corresponding with periods of military success and the cessation of production of public monuments with periods of disastrous military defeat and external domination. Yet the leadership of some Maya states continued to produce notable works of art despite political setbacks. In the eighth century, Copan's leaders responded to the capture and sacrificial killing of their thirteenth king by the ruler of the smaller neighbouring state of Quirigua by erecting richly decorated structures that reaffirmed Copan's unity and dynastic history (Fash 1991: 139–46).

More than in any other early city-state system, numerous Maya dynasties succeeded in sustaining distinctive local traditions of elite art over long periods. This accomplishment cannot be attributed simply to major Maya centres' being farther apart than Mesopotamian ones or those in the Valley of Mexico, since the Yoruba states, whose main centres were also relatively far apart, experienced severe cultural fluctuations similar to those of the other city-state systems in our sample.

Elite art differed radically in style from one early civilization to another. Less extreme variations in style also occurred among city-states. The upper classes sponsored the creation of elaborate works of art that symbolized their power and social exclusivity. The degree of elaboration of such art, its stylistic unity, and the extent to which it was differentiated from ordinary artistic productions depended on the wealth and political stability of its patrons. These conditions favoured greater development of elite art in territorial states.

The preferred media of artistic expression and their thematic content also varied significantly from one early civilization to another. Human imagery was highly restricted in Shang and Inka culture. This absence calls into question claims that poorly documented early civilizations that lack obvious representations of kings must have had no kings. In early civilizations where human representation was common, its primary focus tended to be on the king alone (most Classic Maya states), the king and members of the upper class (Egypt), or the king and larger groups of people (Mesopotamia, Yoruba). Only the Aztec, among those early civilizations that portrayed human forms regularly, appear to have paid relatively little attention to kings in their surviving monumental civic art. Kings and members of the upper classes were often depicted worshipping the gods and defeating their enemies in battle. Yet, when civilizations that did not widely portray human forms are taken into account, the art of early civilizations was characterized by almost as much thematic as stylistic diversity.

MONUMENTAL ARCHITECTURE

Among the creations of the upper classes in early civilizations, buildings of unusual size and splendour played a special role. Large buildings were highly visible and attested publicly to the ability of governments, institutions, and individuals to concentrate labour and resources. Royal tombs, palaces, and temples bore witness to polities that were believed to be legitimated by divine power and inseparable from the cosmic order. In most cases the size and elaborateness of such buildings and the costly materials used to embellish them far exceeded what their practical use would have required. This explains, at least in general and functionalist terms, why, as societies grew increasingly inegalitarian, monumental architecture loomed larger in the archaeological record (Abrams 1989; Trigger 1990a). It has been suggested that, in some chiefdoms, phases dominated by monumental construction may have alternated with phases characterized by elite-controlled production of high-status goods (Trubitt 2000). While periods of hypertrophy in the construction of monumental buildings suggest that this process also may have fluctuated in importance in early civilizations, monumental construction and the production of elite goods occurred together at all times.

Despite architecture's symbolic role only a few functional types of buildings were constructed. Temples, royal palaces, and upper-class residences existed in all early civilizations and elaborate upper-class tombs in many of them. Palaces often combined royal residences with administrative centres, meeting places for the upper classes, storehouses, workshops, and barracks. Kings sometimes had private residential and recreational palaces as well as official ones. Temples were the dwelling places of deities or places where contact could take place on a regular basis between the supernatural and designated representatives of human communities rather than places for congregational worship (L. Bell 1997: 135). Temples, palaces, and tombs were not as clearly differentiated in all early civilizations as they are in modern nomenclature. Aztec and Maya temples were often the burial places of rulers. Most Maya temples seem to have been constructed for the cults of dead rulers as well as for the worship of cosmic deities. Yoruba palaces contained important public shrines, and Inka palaces became the tombs of dead kings. Maya 'palaces' were ritual as well as residential and administrative in function. In early China, temples for the veneration of royal ancestors were located inside palaces. Temples, palaces, and royal tombs appear to have been clearly distinguished from one another only in Egypt and Mesopotamia.

Temples, palaces, and tombs were all derived from and generally continued to be identified as the houses of deities, rulers, and the dead. The Sumerian word for temple, *édingir*, signified 'house (or household) of a god', while the Yoruba term *ile orisa* and the Nahuatl *teocalli* meant literally 'house of a god'. The Egyptians called a temple *pr nṯr* (house of a god) or *ḥwt nṯr* (mansion of a god). Maya terms for temple included *yotot* (his house) and *k'ulnah* (holy house). In Sumerian a palace was called *égal* (great house) or *élugal* (house of a king). The Egyptian term was *pr nsw* (house of the king) or *ʿh*. In Egyptian an elaborate non-royal tomb was called a *ḥwt k3* (mansion of the life-force).

Some early civilizations constructed city walls, frontier forts, and border defences. In highland Mexico and the Maya region, ritual ball courts were elaborate stone structures (Fox 1996). The Inka constructed large halls with gabled roofs (*kallanka*) to shelter soldiers or corvée labourers travelling on official business and as places where public festivals could be held indoors in inclement weather. Few other buildings were constructed for public use.

Archaeological studies of temples in precolonial Hawaii demonstrate that, as state power developed, open structures, which had been used for public feasting, were walled off and access to them was restricted to high-ranking officials (Kolb 1994). In early civilizations entry to temples, palaces, and administrative buildings was carefully monitored. Such buildings were often raised on massive platforms or enclosed by walls penetrated by only a few carefully guarded entrances. Rituals were performed by officials high above the commoners who witnessed them or within enclosures to which ordinary people were denied entry. These arrangements heightened the mystery of what was going on in such places and made it easier for the upper classes to emphasize the importance of their activities.

The materials used for monumental construction varied from one early civilization to another. The Yoruba and Shang employed stamped earth to construct monumental buildings and thatch to cover their gabled roofs. Chinese palaces were erected on stamped-earth (*hang-tu*) platforms. Wooden pillars and poles supported gabled roofs, while the curtain walls of houses were also constructed of stamped earth (Chêng 1960: 52–53; Hsu and Linduff 1988: 22–24). Roof tiles were not employed in China until the Zhou period, and even in early Zhou times tiles covered only the crests of roofs (Hsu and Linduff 1988: 297). The Yoruba's buildings were erected directly on the ground and had thick roof-bearing walls constructed of stamped earth. Free-standing enclosure walls and the houses inside them were covered with broad thatched roofs to protect the stamped earth from tropical rains (Bascom 1969: 30; Ojo 1966b: 63–66).

Large Mesopotamian buildings were constructed mainly of mud-brick, although fired bricks and stone slabs were sometimes used for foundation courses. Outer walls were either plastered with mud or lime or encased in fired bricks. Roofs were flat and constructed of logs covered with mats and several layers of clay (Crawford 1991: 53–56).

The Inka built elaborate structures with thick stone bearer walls or constructed the lower walls, which were most exposed to the rain, of stone blocks and used stamped earth above. The most important buildings were constructed of carefully shaped stone blocks, while more utilitarian structures were built of field stones set in mud. The broad, gabled roofs of Inka buildings were thatched, and important state structures had intricate patterns worked into their roofs (Gasparini and Margolies 1980; Hyslop 1990: 6–18; Protzen 1993).

People living in the Valley of Mexico and in the Maya area constructed major buildings of cut-stone facing blocks and rough stone fill. In the Valley of Mexico, roofs of residential structures were either flat and covered with poles and waterproof plaster or gabled and thatched. Major temples had high, sloping wooden roofs. Important Maya buildings either had thatched roofs or were covered by corbelled vaults (Abrams 1994; M. E Smith 1996: 153–61).

The Egyptians constructed elaborate tombs and later temples of cut stone, but palaces, large houses, and administrative buildings continued to be built of plastered mud-brick, although they often had stone doorways and decorative elements. Roofs were flat and constructed of mats and earth supported on horizontal poles. Outer enclosure walls were constructed of mud-brick.

Choices of building materials were influenced at least partly by practical considerations. The Mesopotamians, Shang Chinese, and southern Yoruba lived on plains where stone of any sort was rare. It is therefore not surprising that they used stamped earth or mud-brick to construct even large buildings. Yet, in northern Yoruba territory, where there was abundant Precambrian rock, people did not use it as building material. While this stone is difficult to cut, it is friable and could easily have been used to construct house walls. Nevertheless, stoneworking of any sort was limited among the Yoruba.

The Maya lived in a karst region, where there were vast deposits of limestone and the scarcity of groundwater encouraged the excavation of massive reservoirs to sustain large population centres. The digging of these reservoirs provided building stone and raw material to make plaster, reducing the cost of these materials for construction purposes (Abrams 1994). The Maya also economized on construction costs by subtly incorporating natural features such as hillsides into temple platforms wherever possible in order to create buildings that looked larger and higher than they really were. The Egyptians, the Inka, and the inhabitants of the Valley of Mexico lived in areas where stone was abundant. In the highland Peruvian countryside, constructing buildings and terraces using boulders and rough stone blocks set in mud had long been part of the tradition of vernacular architecture. The Inka government used large blocks of limestone to build forts and lay foundations for other structures, polygonal blocks of diorite to build enclosure walls, and carefully squared blocks of andesite to erect their highest-quality buildings (Rowe 1944: 226). The Egyptians constructed tombs and temples of limestone and sandstone blocks, using granite (which was much harder to work) for special features. Such construction often required transporting blocks of stone by boat for long distances along the Nile.

The amount of energy that had to be expended to utilize these different raw materials varied. Stone was the most difficult material to work, and the extent to which it was employed provides an approximation of the amounts of labour invested in different forms of architecture. Stone was used sparingly in the monumental architecture of Mesopotamia, the Yoruba, and Shang China, in considerable amounts (usually in the form of small blocks) in the Valley of Mexico and by the Classic Maya, and in large amounts (often in the form of massive blocks) by the Inka and the ancient Egyptians (Heizer 1966). Yet the Mesopotamians constructed mud-brick temples, palaces, and city walls of monumental proportions and great architectural beauty; the Shang surrounded some of their administrative compounds with stamped-earth walls of immense size; and the larger Yoruba and Benin palaces were impressive stamped-earth structures. It therefore seems misleading either to overrate the influence of the environment on the choice of materials used for monumental architecture or to equate architectural achievement with a preference for any particular material.

Architectural styles differed greatly from one early civilization to another. Despite their common use of stamped earth, a Shang palace, with its bilaterally symmetrical arrangement of buildings around a linear series of courtyards, could never be mistaken for a Yoruba one, with its cluster of state and private rooms located within a large enclosure wall. Temples were built on solid platforms of varying heights in Mesopotamia and the Valley of Mexico and among the Maya. In all three early civilizations higher, multistage platforms, often referred to as truncated pyramids, were associated with major temples. Yet no one could confuse a Mesopotamian ziggurat with a major temple from the Valley of Mexico. In addition to being constructed of brick rather than stone and rubble, a ziggurat had steeper sides, a single or triple rather than a double stairway on the front face, and one rather than two shrines at the top. Nor would a large platform temple in the Valley of Mexico, with its squarish profile, fail to be distinguished from a Maya temple, with its more slender, steep-sided platform and elaborately decorated roof comb (Fig. 24.6).

Within the Maya region, each major urban centre developed styles of monumental architecture that expressed its own identity or that of its ruling dynasty (Tate 1992: xii). Temples similar to those of Late Classic Tikal, which rose steeply for over forty-six metres, were not constructed in any other Maya city. These temples celebrated the revived political power of Tikal's rulers after a long period of subordination to Calakmul (Harrison 1999). Palenque, to the northeast, was a much smaller centre that lacked a notable Early Classic history. Chan-Bahlum, one of its first major rulers, sought to emphasize the legitimacy of his royal lineage by erecting a series of triple temples that emulated standard types of the much earlier Late Preclassic Maya period. He also had himself portrayed wearing Early Classic–style regalia long abandoned at established centres such as Tikal. Although Palenque's resources were limited, its architecture was distinguished by its elegance (Freidel and Schele 1988b: 64–67).

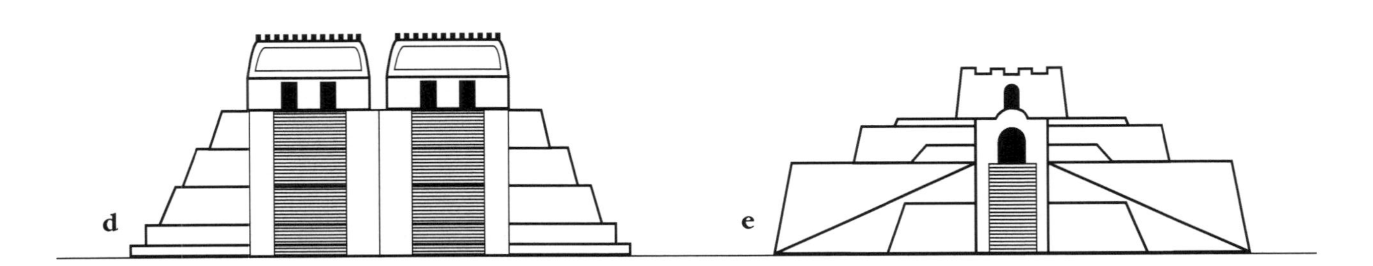

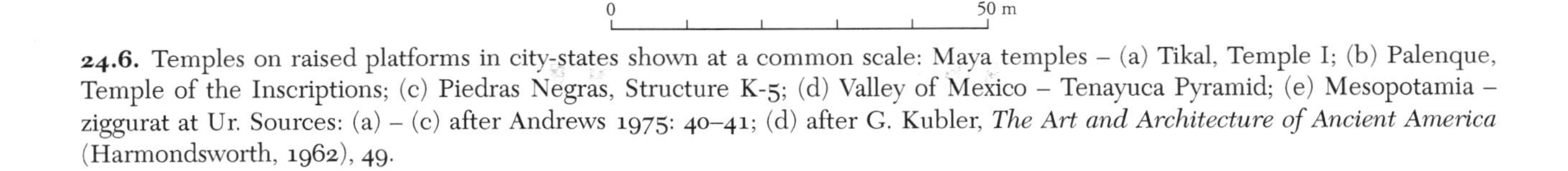

24.6. Temples on raised platforms in city-states shown at a common scale: Maya temples – (a) Tikal, Temple I; (b) Palenque, Temple of the Inscriptions; (c) Piedras Negras, Structure K-5; (d) Valley of Mexico – Tenayuca Pyramid; (e) Mesopotamia – ziggurat at Ur. Sources: (a) – (c) after Andrews 1975: 40–41; (d) after G. Kubler, *The Art and Architecture of Ancient America* (Harmondsworth, 1962), 49.

The architecture of Copan was distinguished from that of other Maya cities by the connected arrangements of its buildings and the impression of massiveness achieved by juxtaposing various structures (Fash 1991). Distinctive architecture and urban plans made every Maya urban centre visually unique.

By contrast, Inka state architecture, with its heavy, unadorned (though sometimes gold-plated) rectangular buildings and distinctive trapezoidal niches, exhibited a uniform style throughout the central Andean highlands. This architecture was visually different from that produced by any earlier or contemporary Andean culture. Egyptian formal architecture, with its distinctive geometrical precision and flat surfaces, likewise evolved as a homogeneous correlate of the Egyptian state.

Constructing large buildings required far more engineering and managerial skills than building ordinary houses. As size and weight increase, even solid structures can collapse from internal stresses if they are not properly built (Mendelssohn 1974). The largest single Egyptian pyramid, at Giza, is estimated to contain over 2.3 million blocks of limestone, each weighing an average of 2.5 tonnes. Even if most of these blocks were quarried nearby, using them to build a massive symmetrical structure 160 metres high in about twenty-five years (the reign of a single king) would have required a vast amount of specialized knowledge (Kemp 1989: 130–36; Lehner 1997: 200–225).

Engineering techniques were limited, although what was understood was applied to good effect. The outside walls of large buildings in most early civilizations were battered, not only giving them an imposing appearance but also helping to steady them. The Egyptians made limited use of corbelled stone ceilings in royal tombs and regularly used barrel vaults to roof mud-brick storerooms, but the roofs of major temples invariably consisted of flat stone slabs supported on short beams running between heavy pillars. The Mesopotamians used bricks to construct true arches in doorways and small domed ceilings. The more elaborate of Maya stone buildings had corbelled roofs. In the other early civilizations, large buildings had walls of stone or stamped earth that supported flat roofs formed of poles covered with earth or plaster in relatively dry climates and gabled, thatched roofs where rainfall was more abundant. Only the Chinese used pole-and-beam structures, a prototype of modern structural steel construction, to support the weight of roofs. The basic architectural techniques that were applied to monumental architecture were generally the same ones that were used to construct ordinary houses, but the increasing size of buildings and sometimes the use of unfamiliar construction materials required the development of new and more specialized engineering skills.

The Egyptians ascribed the construction of the Step Pyramid complex at Saqqara, the oldest collection of stone buildings in Egypt, to Imhotep, a high official of Djoser, the first king of the Third Dynasty, and regarded him as the inventor of stone architecture. However, recent discoveries suggest that large-scale stone construction may have begun at Saqqara at least a generation earlier (Davies and Friedman 1998: 64–69). In the Fourth Dynasty, work on royal funerary complexes was under the control of the Overseer of All the Works of the King (*ỉmy-r k3t nbt nswt*), who at that time was a close relative of the king. Under him a large team of officials and scribes dealt with engineering problems and scheduled, fed, and deployed large numbers of full-time masons and the still more numerous rotating teams of corvée labourers who hauled the stone blocks. Many later Egyptian mathematical texts were concerned with the pragmatic reckonings involved in administering such projects (Strudwick 1985: 217–50).

Archaeologists have observed how, in successive pyramid construction projects, better solutions were found to problems of ensuring the stability of the building blocks and preventing the collapse of inner chambers under the weight of the heavy masses erected above them. Over the course of a few reigns, builders learned that it was more efficient to work with large stone blocks, that horizontal courses were more stable than courses aligned obliquely to the face of a pyramid, and that heavy structures needed to be sited on firm bedrock. Given their unprecedented size, it is surprising how few serious errors were made in constructing these early stone pyramids (Lehner 1997: 218–23).

The largest single Inka building project was Saqsawaman, a fortress and ritual centre located on a hill adjacent to the royal residential precinct at Cuzco. According to Inka tradition, twenty thousand people had worked on this construction at any one time for about seventy-six years prior to the Spanish conquest. Major Inka building projects were supervised by members of the Inka nobility. Sinchi Roka, a half-brother of Wayna Qhapaq, was responsible for major state buildings erected in and near Cuzco during that king's reign. While clay and stone models guided the construction of Inka state buildings, we know little about the lower-level officials who routinely supervised such work. The large size of the buildings that were erected in provincial centres and elsewhere throughout the core of the Inka kingdom and of many of the individual stones that were used to construct them required manipulative techniques that were unfamiliar to ordinary workers (Hyslop 1990: 51–57; Kendall 1973: 122; Niles 1993: 161; Rowe 1944: 224).

The kinds of monumental structures that were accorded greatest prominence varied from one early civilization to another. In most city-states, temples were the earliest monumental buildings. Later one large temple or temple complex in the centre of the city continued to symbolize the unity of the state. Throughout Mesoamerica, temples were repaired periodically and enlarged if resources were available to do so. In the Valley of Mexico, the main temple honouring the two principal gods of each city-state stood in the centre of a complex of smaller temples, priests' residences, elite schools, and ritual plazas enclosed by a wall (Matos Moctezuma 1988: 59–83). Maya temples consisted of a shrine to a single deity built atop a pyramidal platform. Large ones tended to be free-standing, while smaller ones were often incorporated into an architectural agglomeration that included plazas and palaces (Andrews 1975). The earliest Mesopotamian temples were erected on low platforms that grew higher as they were rebuilt. In the Ur III period ziggurats were erected in honour of the patron deity of each major city throughout southern Mesopotamia. At the same time, standardized plans replaced the more variable temple layouts of the Early Dynastic period. The central room of a temple, which was approached from the side, contained the cult statue of the resident deity. Major temples were surrounded by a walled area containing the residence of the high priest or priestess, storerooms, workshops, and sometimes cemeteries (Crawford 1991: 57–81).

Mesopotamian temples were referred to as mountains (*kur*) and believed to be places for communication between the earth and the sky; ziggurats represented an extreme expression of this concept (George 1993). Aztec temples were viewed as microcosms of the universe, mountains of fertility, symbols of mythic events that had happened long ago to deities who were patrons of local ethnic groups, and places where special connections with the sky world and the underworld could be achieved (van Zantwijk 1985: 200). The Maya described their temples as world trees (wakah kan) or mountains (*witz*) through which it was possible to communicate with the higher and lower supernatural realms. The shrines inside temples, where images of the gods were kept, were regarded as caves, which provided direct contact with the gods. These shrines were called *pib nah* (underground house), *kunul* (conjuring place), *kun* (seat), or *waybil* (resting place) (Freidel, Schele, and Parker 1993: 136–55; Schele and Freidel 1990: 72; Schele and Mathews 1998: 29).

At the centre of each Yoruba city was a royal palace (*afin*), which contained complexes of private living quarters for the king, his wives, and his children, official meeting rooms, servants' quarters, storerooms, and shrines of important deities. The royal palace at Benin also had a series of large enclosures each of which contained the shrine of a dead king. Neither the palace nor ordinary houses were more than one storey high, but the royal palace at Benin had a tower rising over twenty metres, ornamented with the wooden image of a python, which provided a visual focus for the whole city (Gallagher 1983: 26). Leading town officials occupied large house compounds located around the perimeter of the palace, and the central market was usually in front of its entrance. Near the market were important temples or shrines, the more elaborate of which had one to three forecourts or rooms. Prior to the disruptive wars of the nineteenth century, Yoruba temples were reported to have been elaborately decorated with carved wooden beams and mud sculpture. Some of them were also larger than any temples of more recent times (Apter 1992: 100; Awolalu 1979: 114–17; Krapf-Askari 1969; Mabogunje 1962; Ojo 1966a: 186; Pemberton and Afolayan 1996: 201).

In other city-state systems, palaces seem to have developed later than temples (Fig. 24.7). Maya 'palaces' were one- or two-storey stone structures built on low platforms. They consisted of large numbers of relatively small, corbel-vaulted rooms arranged around open courts. It has not been resolved whether these structures were inhabited by the royal family or used for administrative and ritual purposes while the royal family lived in lighter and airier wooden buildings nearby (Schele and Miller 1986: 134). David Freidel (1992: 122–25) has suggested that at least parts of 'palaces' served for communication with the supernatural and as dynastic shrines, while 'temples' were the cult places of specific royal ancestors.

In the Valley of Mexico, palaces were built of stone, with rooms opening off a number of inward-facing courtyards. Usually these palaces were located just outside the central temple precinct and close to the main city market. The palace of Mochtezuma II was described as a rectangular structure 220 metres long, with blank outer walls and few entrances. Its rooms were arranged around three courtyards, with the apartments of the king and his family being located on the second storey. The ground floor contained council halls, law courts, guest rooms, meeting rooms for warrior societies, dining halls, servants' quarters, kitchens, a jail, arsenals, accounting rooms, and storerooms. Nearby palaces of former rulers, considered too small or old-fashioned to be lived in, were used as storerooms and perhaps offices (Bray 1968: 104–6).

Mesopotamian palaces were located either near the central temple complex or in a different part of the city where more building space may have been available. They consisted of complexes of rooms, sometimes two storeys high, arranged around one or more internal courtyards. These rooms served as residences for the king and his dependents, audience chambers, barracks, workshops, and storerooms (Crawford 1991: 81–91; Margueron 1982).

In three of the four city-state civilizations there was little emphasis on royal funerary monuments. Aztec kings were cremated along with a few sacrificed retainers and their ashes interred in or near the platform of the main temple (Durán 1964: 178, 210). Yoruba kings were buried in sacred places in the palace grounds or outside the city. Their bodies were often dismembered and parts of them buried in different locations. The heads of at least some of the rulers of

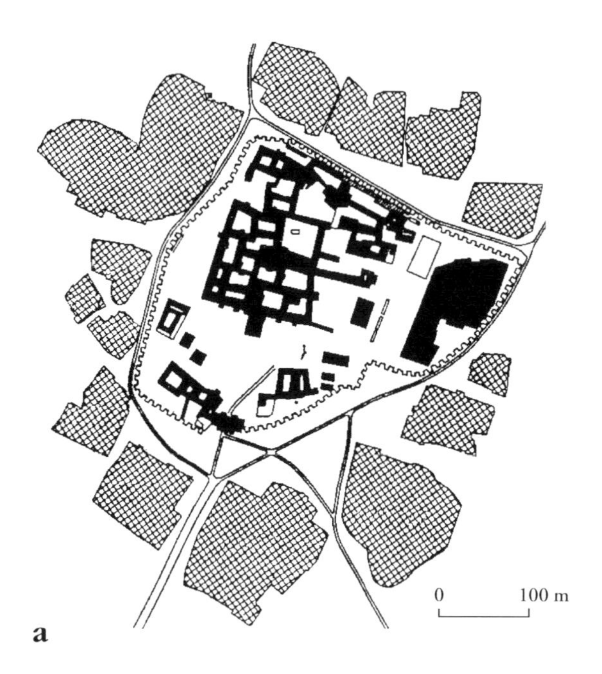

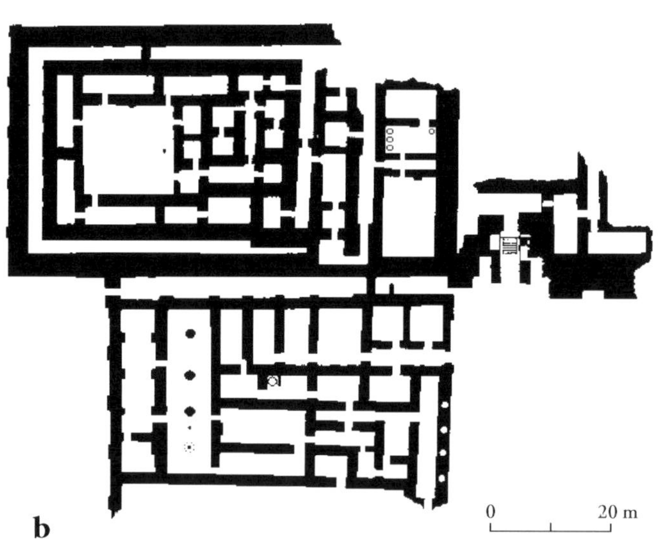

24.7. Royal palaces in city-states: (a) Yoruba – afin of the king of New Oyo surrounded by the compounds of his functionaries and state officials; (b) Mesopotamia – plan of Palace A at Kish, Early Dynastic Period; (c) Maya – palace at Palenque, seventh-eighth centuries A.D.; (d) Valley of Mexico – a courtyard of the palace of King Nezahualcoyotl at Texcoco, from Mapa Quinatzin, officials sit in council (illustrations not to common scale). Sources: (a) after Mabogunje 1962: fig. 12; (b) after Strommenger & Hirmer 1964: 391, fig. 17; (c) adapted from Tracy Wellman, *Chronicle of the Maya Kings and Queens* by Simon Martin and Nikolai Grube (London, 2000), with permission of the publisher Thames & Hudson Ltd.; (d) after G. Kubler, *The Art and Architecture of Ancient America* (Harmondsworth, 1962), 54.

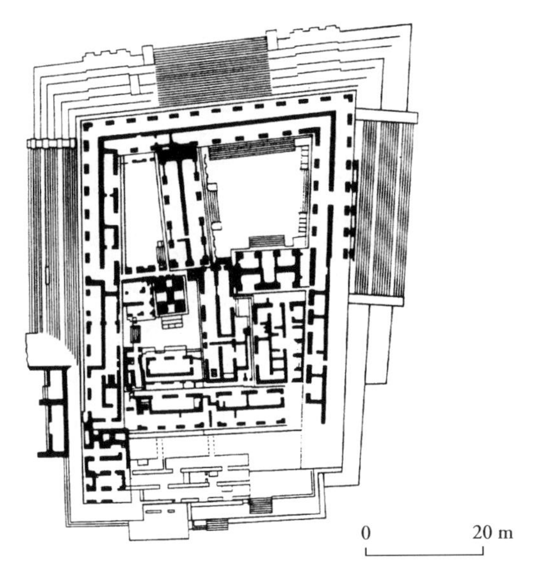

c

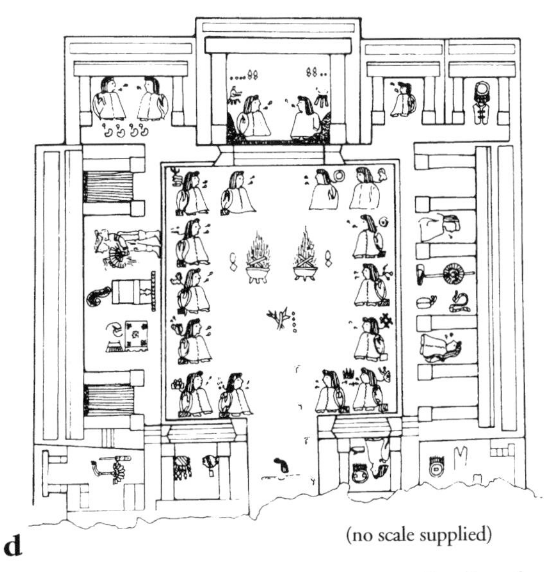

d

24.7. *Continued.*

Benin were interred at Ife in a special burial ground called Orun Oba Ado (The Spirit World of the Benin Kings) (Bradbury 1958: 22; Pemberton and Afolayan 1996: 27). At Oyo and elsewhere, the underground wooden burial chamber for the body of the king and some of his sacrificed retainers was covered by a small mound and became a place where his remains were venerated (S. Johnson

1921: 55). Some Mesopotamian kings and high-ranking women were buried underground in domed or vaulted brick or fieldstone chambers. The Early Dynastic royal burials at Ur were accompanied by richly dressed court women and male servants. Ur III rulers had large brick funerary chapels erected over their graves. (Crawford 1991: 104–12; Huot 1989: 209–18).

Maya provisions for dead rulers were considerably more elaborate (Coe 1988). Kings were buried with a few retainers in underground tombs dug out of bedrock or constructed of masonry. The most elaborate was that of King Hanab-Pakal at Palenque, which contained a magnificently carved sarcophagus. On top of or near these tombs rulers built large funerary temples dedicated to the gods with whom they were identified (Houston and Stuart 1996: 296–97). Michael Coe (1957; 1961) has drawn a close parallel between these temples and the royal funerary temples in which deceased Cambodian rulers were once identified with Hindu deities.

Considerable energy was expended on large-scale defensive architecture in some city-state civilizations. Yoruba cities were surrounded by moats and earth ramparts pierced by fortified gateways (Connah 1975: 244). Some Yoruba city-wall systems expanded or contracted over time, creating multiple fortifications, and in certain urban centres internal walls separated one section of the community from another. Defensive walls, often planted with thorn bushes, were also constructed along the borders of some Yoruba states. The small kingdom of Ijebu-Ode had a rampart 130 kilometres long enclosing 1,036 square kilometres of farm land (Bascom 1969: 4). The mud-brick walls that surrounded Mesopotamian cities in Early Dynastic times were celebrated as physical testimonials to the relative power and affluence of different city-states, becoming a major component of their identity as well as their defence (Jacobsen 1976: 196). Vanquished states were required to breach or demolish their walls.

Mesoamerican cities were rarely walled. Tikal, with its north and south earth ramparts, was a partial exception. Tenochtitlan was connected to the mainland by four causeways and by aqueducts that carried fresh water into the city centre. In addition to serving a defensive function, the causeways were major architectural works that added to the splendour and impressiveness of the Aztec capital.

The symbolic role of monumental architecture in city-states was to glorify and express the power and unity of the community and the effectiveness of its leaders. Yet different kinds of buildings occupied city centres in the various early civilizations. Yoruba palaces were the residences and property of successive kings, but they were also identified with the multifocal government of a state and played a major role in the religious life of the community. In the Valley of Mexico and Mesopotamia, temples marked the city centre. Palaces were located either adjacent to the central temple complex or elsewhere in the city. They tended to increase in size as royal power grew and were largest in relation to temples in hegemonic city-states. At the same time, victorious rulers also manifested their power and wealth by building larger and more splendid temples. In small city-states, both palaces and central temples were small. Among the Maya, the major 'temples' were higher and more prominent than the 'palace' complexes, but these temples were associated with the funerary cults of dead kings as well as with the worship of the gods with whom kings were identified.

In territorial states, monumental architecture celebrated the power of the king and of the central government. The Inka rulers constructed imposing temples, palaces, residences for chosen women, and public halls in Cuzco and other highland administrative centres from Ecuador to Lake Titicaca. The uniform style of Inka state buildings made them symbols of royal power in a kingdom that was characterized by great ethnic diversity and numerous pockets of settlement separated by rough mountainous terrain. Artisans were sent to Tumipampa, in Ecuador, to teach local masons how to construct Inka-style buildings after the area was incorporated into the Inka state (von Hagen 1959: 77). While Inka official buildings were constructed of cut stone, their basic pattern was that of the traditional commoner farmstead, a rectangular walled enclosure with a number of rectangular one-room, one-storey dwellings, constructed of field stones set in mud plaster, located around the inside of the wall.

Inka palaces consisted of a series of intercommunicating courtyards surrounded by a blank stone wall. A main entrance, which was well guarded, led into the outer courts, which contained large and small reception halls and offices and accommodations for palace officials. The inner, more private, courts were reserved for the king and his family. This section also contained gardens and bathing facilities, as well as apartments and work areas for retainers and domestic servants (Kendall 1973: 128–29). Kings and other members of the royal family built rural palaces in the vicinity of Cuzco as places for relaxation (Niles 1987; 1993; von Hagen and Morris 1998: 161–98).

The main temple in Cuzco was constructed of especially fine masonry and partly covered with gold plaques. Cuzco also contained a large residential complex for chosen women and large halls for state rituals. At least in the highlands, every provincial capital was a little Cuzco, with its own state temple, government residences, offices, residence for chosen women, rest-houses for people travelling on state business, and, on the edge of the settlement, well-built government storehouses. The residences of provincial governors were smaller versions of royal palaces that the king probably occupied when he visited. Provincial nobles lived in local-style residences in ethnic communities rather than at the provincial administrative centres (D'Altroy 1992; Hyslop 1990; LeVine 1992; Morris and Thompson 1985; Malpass 1993b).

The greatest architectural creations of Old and Middle Kingdom Egypt were the tombs of kings built near Memphis, which remained the capital of a united Egypt except during the Eleventh Dynasty, when the capital was located at Thebes. The most complete royal funerary complex of the Third Dynasty, that of King Djoser, had a rectangular stone enclosure wall 1,645 metres long and 10.5 metres high, containing a 60-metre-high step pyramid, as well as stone chapels and other facilities for celebrating the Sed festivals that would permit the king to continue renewing himself after death. Beginning with the Fourth Dynasty, royal burial complexes consisted of large pyramid-shaped tombs, with adjacent cult temples reached by covered ramps from valley temples located alongside canals. This change represented a growing emphasis on the king's relation to the sun god. In the Old Kingdom, other members of the royal family and high-ranking officials constructed smaller, rectangular stone tombs above burial chambers cut into the rock (Edwards 1985; Hawass 1995; Lehner 1997).

Egyptian palaces were surrounded by rectangular mud-brick enclosure walls and contained staterooms, the king's private apartments, separate residences for the royal women and children, and gardens, as well as food storage facilities and administrative offices. One such palace, The Lotus Blossom of King Isesi, built for a Fifth Dynasty king, appears to have measured 640 by 231 metres (Lehner 1997: 231). The original *Ỉnb ḥḏ* (White Wall), which came to symbolize the unity of Egypt, was undoubtedly a combined palace and national administrative centre that King Menes was reputed to have built near the border between Upper and Lower Egypt. The city of Memphis, which grew up around this palace, was relocated as the course of the Nile shifted eastward, but successive versions of the palace and the adjacent temple of Ptah remained the nucleus of Memphis for the rest of that city's history (Baines and Malek 1980: 136; Davies and Friedman 1998: 38–44; O'Connor 1989). In addition to using this administrative palace, Old Kingdom rulers appear to have built important residential palaces near the construction sites of their pyramids. During the Fourth Dynasty, one or more such palaces appear to have been located adjacent to the Giza plateau. Residential palaces no longer used by the king might have continued for a time to be employed as administrative offices.

Egyptian temples were considerably smaller and simpler during the Old and Middle Kingdoms than they became later. They appear to have developed from shrines or royal funerary chapels, surrounded by rectangular mud-brick enclosures, that were constructed in the Early Dynastic period (R. Wilkinson 2000: 16–19). Most temples were built, like palaces and ordinary houses, of mud-brick, although during the Middle Kingdom it became increasingly common for the inner parts of temples to be made of stone. The best-preserved temples of the Old Kingdom are two solar temples at Abu Sir, near Memphis. Used for royal funerary cults, they were first constructed of mud-brick and then rebuilt in stone. Each contained an open court in the centre of which stood a large obelisk that was a symbol of the sun god. Most Old and Middle Kingdom temples were roofed, houselike structures whose architecture and decoration turned them into models of the cosmos. The shrine containing the cult statue of the principal deity, which was lodged in the innermost, most elevated, and most secluded portion of the temple, symbolized the creator deity standing on the mound of creation.

Although the central government appears to have played a major role in building and maintaining the main temples at Memphis and nearby Heliopolis, there seems to have been no standardized temple architecture in provincial capitals prior to the Middle Kingdom (Kemp 1989: 65–83; O'Connor 1992; Seidlmayer 1996). Whereas the Inka emphasized their authority by imposing a uniform architectural style on administrative centres throughout the kingdom, the Egyptian rulers stressed theirs by enhancing the distinctiveness of their capital. One reason for this difference may have been the much smaller size of the Egyptian kingdom. Because it was likely that, in the course of corvée labour or military service, most male Egyptians would visit the capital region from time to time, focusing attention on its architecture was a symbolically effective way to express the unity of the state.

The Shang kings and nobility erected large building complexes on stamped-earth platforms, sometimes within rectangular enclosures surrounded by massive stamped-earth walls. These buildings had doors and windows facing south, away from the cold winter winds. The main palace structure excavated at Anyang was entered through a south gate flanked by two large towers. This gate opened onto a courtyard containing a great hall at the far end and two side halls. Beyond, along the main axis of the building, was another large hall and still farther north another courtyard with an ancestral temple at the north end. Nearby were servants' houses. The general layout of palaces appears to have been established no later than early Shang times (G. Barnes 1993: 126–28; Thorp 1991). The residences of regional officials were probably of similar design but built on a smaller scale and with greater emphasis on fortifications in districts that were exposed to uprisings or attack. Ancestral shrines were an integral part of all upper-class residential complexes, while earth altars were associated with administrative centres.

Shang royal tombs were dug deep into the earth and had burial chambers constructed of carved and lacquered wooden panels. Many people were killed and buried alongside kings in these graves, together with horses, chariots, bronze vessels, and other luxury goods. Only royal graves appear to have had stepped entrance passages approaching them from four sides, a design that had cosmological significance. Burial complexes of other members of the royal family and of nobles were smaller, of simpler design, and contained fewer grave goods. Although no superstructures survive, a stamped-earth platform and shrine appear to have been built over each royal grave (Li Boqian 1999; Wu 1988; Yang 1986).

The largest buildings erected in Old Kingdom Egypt were royal tombs, some of which were the largest single structures created by any preindustrial society. In Shang China the largest buildings seem to have been palaces, which contained temples for ancestor worship. The Inka assigned equal importance to royal palaces and temples for state deities, and the two types of buildings were similar in design. Inka palaces became tombs and centres of mortuary cults for dead kings. The largest single Inka building complex was Saqsawaman, which was both a fortress and a royal ritual centre. Enclosure walls were constructed around royal residences (Egypt, Inka, China), regional administrative centres (Egypt, China), temples (Egypt), and royal tombs (Egypt). The chief aim of monumental architecture in territorial states was to facilitate and glorify royal authority.

William Sanders (1974: 109) has argued that in states corvée labour was employed mainly to erect palaces, which served as administrative centres, while in chiefdoms it was used to build temples and tombs, which served communal (including religious) functions. Yet, while it is true that the largest temple platform in the Valley of Mexico in the Late Aztec period was smaller than the much earlier Pyramid of the Sun at Teotihuacan (Willey and Phillips 1958: 184, 193–94), and that the largest pyramid-temple complexes at Tikal were smaller than the two largest Preclassic complexes at El Mirador, Danta and El Tigre, broader evidence does not support this conclusion. Egypt was not a chiefdom when the Great Pyramid was built and, while palaces constituted the largest Yoruba architectural complexes, there is no evidence that Yoruba polities were more statelike than Mesopotamian or Valley of Mexico ones, where temples rather than palaces dominated city centres and symbolized urban corporate identity. Yoruba data also call into question the notion that palaces as secular entities can be distinguished from temples as religious ones. Likewise, Classic Maya 'palaces' may have served various ritual functions, while temples were associated with cosmic deities that were not only related to the city as a whole but also identified with individual deceased rulers. In the Valley of Mexico during the Late Aztec period, as well as in Mesopotamia and among the Classic Maya, increasing palace size and opulence appear to have been the consequences of expanding royal power, which was accompanied in hegemonic states by the increasing size of temples. In the Valley of Mexico and Mesopotamia this situation reflected either a balance of power between rulers and other powerful institutions or, more likely, growing royal patronage of religious institutions that continued to symbolize the community. Among the Maya, the increasing size of both 'temples' and 'palaces' may have reflected greater royal control over the economy. This evidence further calls into question the suggestion that general stages of development can be differentiated among early civilizations. In territorial states, temples, tombs, and palaces served in various ways and combinations as symbols of royal power.

The energy expended on monumental architecture was considerable in all early civilizations but appears to have varied significantly from one to another. While it is impossible, given the limited data that have survived, to calculate precise energy expenditures on monumental architecture, rough approximations based on current population estimates and the largest surviving structures are possible. Among territorial states constructing the stone pyramids and upper-class tombs of Old Kingdom Egypt appears to have required a greater expenditure of energy in relation to total population than the impressive monumental stone architecture of the Inka. The Egyptian pyramids of the Fourth Dynasty were the most ambitious short-term building projects undertaken by any early civilization. While the construction of massive stamped-earth walls and platforms in Shang China necessitated considerable expenditures of energy, the work time estimated to have built the main enclosure at Zhengzhou (ten thousand persons working for four years [Hsu and Linduff 1988: 20]) falls far short of the labour required to build the largest Egyptian pyramid.

Among city-state civilizations, the Maya's ubiquitous construction of stone temples, palaces, and elite residences probably represented the highest per capita expenditure of energy on monumental architecture. The various city-states in the Valley of Mexico and Mesopotamia, with their stone and brick temples and palaces, seem to have occupied a middle position. While the stone, rubble, and mortar construction of the Valley of Mexico was probably more labour-intensive than the brick construction of Mesopotamia, the total per capita labour input required to build its temples and palaces was probably less than that required to construct Mesopotamia's many temples, palaces, and city walls. The Yoruba's stamped-earth buildings and less elaborate earth walls seem to have been the least labour-intensive of all the early civilizations we have examined.

Energy expenditures on monumental architecture in territorial states appear to have exceeded those in city-states, and this suggests that the major factors promoting the construction of monumental architecture were the power and resources of different governments. Among city-states, the elaboration of architecture varied directly with the hegemonic status and prosperity of individual rulers. While, in Mesopotamia, kings and temple corporations may have begun erecting larger and more splendid buildings as symbols of their conflicting political claims within city-states, the increasing power of kings eventually enabled rulers to sponsor all forms of monumental construction.

CULTURAL TRADITIONS

The elite art and architecture of each early civilization were stylistically distinct from those of every other, and within city-state systems urban centres exhibited varying degrees of stylistic diversity. Art and architectural styles changed slowly, usually as the result of innovations within ongoing local traditions. Some Early Classic Maya copied aspects of the building styles and motifs of Teotihuacan in emulation of that far-off but powerful foreign state, but in general their art and architecture remained distinctively Maya (Culbert 1991c; Henderson 1981: 137–38). Inka state architecture grew out of local forms of rural construction, although Inka stoneworking techniques may have been inspired by monuments created much earlier by states in the Lake Titicaca region. Palaces and major public buildings dating from the reigns of successive Inka kings can be distinguished stylistically, and these differences may have served to identify the accomplishments of individual rulers in a non-literate society (Niles 1993: 155–64; 1999). Egyptologists can likewise differentiate the art styles of successive reigns, although the monarchs who sponsored these works also identified themselves by having their names engraved on them. This suggests that artists and architects, as well as their patrons, in early civilizations approved of and may have encouraged limited innovation within well-established artistic canons.

In Egypt, the collapse of the central government at the end of the Old Kingdom massively disrupted the work of skilled artisans and temporarily ended high-quality artistic production. Yet basic styles survived, and, as political unity was restored, the artistic achievements of the past were successfully emulated. In China the expansion of the Zhou kingdom was accompanied by an effort to emulate the artistic and architectural achievements of the Shang rulers. At the same time, however, the Zhou developed their own distinctive styles (Hsu and Linduff 1988: 311–18). The introduction of many forms of highland Mexican art and architecture into the Maya lowlands during the Postclassic period is believed to have been associated with significant ethnic movements (Henderson 1981: 206–16). In general, however, the art and architecture of early civilizations appear to have been characterized by continuities in culturally specific styles.

More cross-cultural uniformity is evident in functional aspects of art and architecture. The materials that were locally available played a significant though not determining role in the choice of building materials. At the same time, exotic materials were often favoured for manufacturing elite luxury goods. A limited range of engineering options restricted the structure and hence the shape of buildings. No large domed buildings were erected in any early civilization, and tall buildings consisted mainly of solid platforms. In the Valley of Mexico and Mesopotamia and among the Maya imposing truncated pyramid-temples evolved from simple house platforms originally intended to raise ordinary dwellings above flood waters or damp soil. Shang ancestral temples were built on the same low stamped-earth platforms as upper-class residences, and all Egyptian, Inka, and Yoruba houses and temples were built at ground level. In Egypt, grave mounds provided the inspiration for pyramids and mastabas, which were largely of solid construction.

Monumental buildings belonged to a limited range of types: palaces, temples, tombs, fortifications, and various combinations thereof. The first three were thought of as different kinds of houses. Large buildings were not designed to be public amenities – the closest approximation to such a structure being the Inka kallanka. This limited range of functional types reflected the evolutionary proximity of early civilizations to small-scale societies, in most of which houses were the only significant structures.

Most of the two-dimensional state-sponsored art in early civilizations, when it was representational, portrayed the activities of rulers. Kings were shown worshipping the gods and, often single-handedly, conquering enemy peoples. The requirements of Egyptian upper-class tombs encouraged the development of elaborate art portraying the production of food and other goods and the presentation of these goods to dead tomb owners and their families. Not all early civilizations were, however, committed to the production of representational art. Shang two-dimensional art concentrated on abstract and highly symbolic portrayals of animals and comparable Inka art on elaborate geometrical patterns. One cannot predict either the style or content of the art that will be found in any particular early civilization. Yet, while stylistically art and architecture vary entirely idiosyncratically from one early civilization to another, structurally and thematically they display not idiosyncrasy but weak-to-moderate degrees of cross-cultural regularity.

25 Literacy and Specialized Knowledge

Lifestyle and culture sharply distinguished the upper classes from commoners in early civilizations. The upper classes lived in larger, more imposing, and often cleaner houses, were waited on by servants who attended to their comforts, ate more nutritious food, wore costlier and showier clothing and jewellery, were more fastidious about their personal appearance and hygiene, and cultivated more refined manners. Behavioural stereotypes were dramatically displayed in the upper-class tomb art of Old Kingdom Egypt, where the calm, dignity, and physical perfection of the upper classes were contrasted with the quarrelsomeness, rustic manners, dishevelled appearance, and occasionally malnutrition and physical deformities of the lower classes.

The upper classes often spoke either a more refined version of the national language or a completely different language from most of their subjects. The Aztecs contrasted *macehuallatolli*, the form of Nahuatl spoken by commoners, with *tecpillatolli*, the form spoken by the nobility and at the royal palace (Davies 1980: 216; León-Portilla 1963: 140; Marcus 1992a: 528). While the Classic Maya spoke Cholan Mayan in the southern lowlands and Yucatec Mayan farther north, their writing recorded a prestige version of Cholan that developed in the Peten and appears to have been adopted by the upper classes throughout the Maya region (Henderson 1981: 50–52; Houston, Robertson, and Stuart 2000). It is now agreed that *emesal* was a refined, not a women's, dialect of Sumerian (Oppenheim 1964: 371). Egyptians studying to be scribes had to learn the written version of their language, which was based on Old Kingdom and later Middle Kingdom forms that over time diverged increasingly from everyday speech. Written Egyptian was also presumably based on a refined version of the language spoken at the royal court and intended to transcend regional dialects among officials and administrators. Knowing written Egyptian presumably influenced the language that was spoken by the educated classes in much the same way that knowing modern literary Arabic modifies colloquial speech (J. Allen 2000: 1–2). The royal version of Quechua spoken by the Inka upper class differed from the Quechua that served throughout their kingdom as a language of administration. Quechua had spread as a lingua franca from the central coast of Peru and been used for trading and interethnic communication in the central highlands long before the Inka adopted it as their official language of administration. The Inka elite appear originally to have spoken a language of their own. The royal version of Quechua that replaced this language coexisted with the Quechua used throughout the Andean area and the parent Quechua languages that were spoken in central coastal Peru (Gose 1993: 505; Rostworowski and Morris 1999: 807–9; Salomon 1986: 189).

A major source of the identity, self-esteem, and power of the upper classes was possession of specialized knowledge, some of which increased their ability to organize themselves and administer society. One of the most interesting technological innovations of early civilizations was the development of complex systems for storing information. The structural properties of writing provide detailed insights into the factors that produced cross-cultural similarities and differences in a particular aspect of culture. More esoteric forms of knowledge were believed to enhance the ability of upper-class people to manipulate supernatural forces for their own benefit as well as to promote the general well-being of society. Especially elaborate knowledge of this sort included calendrics, medicine, divination, and magic. Both administrative and esoteric knowledge increased not only the self-confidence of the upper classes but also the respect and awe with which ordinary people regarded them.

RECORDING SYSTEMS

In the eighteenth century, writing was identified as the key feature defining civilization (Childe 1950; Gelb 1963: 221; Morgan 1907 [1877]: 12; Sjoberg 1960: 32–34, 38). Jack Goody (1986; Goody and Watt 1963) has argued, in conformity with that view, that writing has made literate societies totally different from non-literate ones, facilitating elaborate record-keeping and making possible the systematic development of scientific knowledge, philosophy, and literature. Goody maintains that writing encouraged forms of thinking that are increasingly decontextualized, more universal, and more concerned with logical coherence. He also argues that writing promoted discovery, invention, and technological progress and facilitated the growing independence of institutions from state control as well as the development of private property. Yet the extent to which recording systems were developed or used varied considerably from one early civilization to another. Writing as Goody defines it occurred in only four of the early civilizations in our sample. The recording systems used in other early civilizations varied in nature and in what they were intended to accomplish.

The oldest and most generally accepted definition of 'writing' is that it is a system which records sequences of words in durable signs. Thus a competent reader who has never before encountered a particular text can read from it the same sequence of words that its author wrote down. No writing system records every feature of actual speech (the loudness and speed of utterances are rarely indicated), and many early forms of writing failed to supply grammatical and phonetic elements that could easily and unambiguously be inferred by the native speakers of a language. Whether or not every morpheme (minimal meaningful semantic unit) is represented, writing, as defined above, is distinguished from protowriting or, more properly (since not all 'protowriting' evolved into writing systems), semasiography. Semasiography uses pictograms and ideograms to represent ideas. A pictogram is a sign that has a specific meaning but one that may be expressed verbally in different ways. Thus a pictogram in a list of North American Plains Indian year names that represents the year 1876 by depicting the death of a long-haired United States cavalry officer could have been 'read' in any Plains Indian language as 'the year Long-Hair was killed by the Sioux', 'the year we defeated General Custer', or 'the year we won the Battle of the Little Bighorn' (Nabokov 1996: 39–41). In such a recording system pictograms represent specific objects or events metonymically, by depicting some well-known aspect of them. Ideograms are signs that arbitrarily represent specific concepts which, like pictograms, can be read in any language. Examples are the Arabic numerals 1, 2, and 3.

In semasiography more abstract concepts are sometimes represented by rebuses, or phonetic extensions, which display an object that represents a word that sounds similar to what is intended. Unlike pictograms and ideograms, rebuses can normally be read only in a specific language. Examples in English are representing the pronoun 'I' by drawing an eye or the prefix 'be-' by drawing a bee. The most rudimentary applications of rebuses are to record personal or place names that have literal meanings, such as 'Red Cloud' and 'Big Bear'. Semasiography can be used to record limited and isolated sets of concepts such as personal names, toponyms, types of goods, or calendar dates and to suggest sequences of events in mnemonic form. It cannot, however, record consecutive speech, only certain general concepts and words belonging to certain specific semantic categories. As such limited recording systems evolve in the direction of representing speech, they typically first indicate sequences of nouns and verbs, then begin to specify adjectives, adverbs, conjunctions, and prepositions, and finally note tense markers and other strictly grammatical morphemes (Hanks 1989: 18; Sampson 1985: 49–50).

In recent years some Mesoamericanists have sought to have complex highland Mexican forms of semasiography, including those found in the Valley of Mexico, accepted as writing systems. They argue that the term 'writing' should be extended to cover any form of recording that represents some specific words as well as ideas (Boone and Mignolo 1994; Marcus 1992a; M. Smith 1973). In two early civilizations, Egypt and Mesopotamia, it is now possible to trace the transformation of semasiography into writing. Yet, while acknowledging that there can be a continuum between complex semasiography and writing which makes the boundary separating them arbitrary, conflating the two practices fails to recognize their fundamental and irreducible differences. Writing and semasiography can more profitably be treated as two different types of recording systems rather than as different types of writing.

Early recording systems served at least three different functions. One function was commemorating kings and their deeds. This sort of recording flourished in Egypt in the late Predynastic period, most notably on elaborate stone maces and palettes. These objects, produced for the royal court and decorated with scenes of royal activity, bore signs that specified the names of rulers, toponyms, and the names and titles of officials. They marked the beginning of a long tradition of labelled representations of Egyptian monarchs and officials (Davis 1992). Labelled representations of kings also provide a large part of the surviving corpus of Maya inscriptions.

The second major function was administrative. This is attested in Mesopotamian temple complexes beginning as early as the second half of the fourth millennium. Over time such records developed into an elaborate corpus of temple, palace, and eventually personal records associated with the receipt and ownership of goods, the sale of land, houses, slaves, and other property, loans and other commercial agreements, royal decrees and regulations relating to commerce, and legal proceedings concerning economic matters. At a very early period sign lists were compiled for training Mesopotamian recorders that helped to standardize and ensure mutual comprehensibility of the records produced by different scribes (Nissen, Damerow, and Englund 1993; Postgate 1992: 66–68). Early Egyptian records on papyrus have been lost, but surviving wood, bone, and ivory labels from the Predynastic and Early Dynastic periods identify the owners, contents, and places of origin of jars, boxes, and bolts of cloth (T. Wilkinson 1999: 41–42).

Finally, early recording systems were used for religious purposes. In China the oldest surviving texts are the oracle-bone inscriptions, which were related to divination. The Shang also appear to have regarded burning messages written on strips of bamboo as an effective way to communicate with their ancestors and the gods (Creel 1937: 161–62; 1938: 38). In Mesopotamia, to ensure that no mistakes were made in rituals, prayers were recorded in written form already by the Early Dynastic period, while in Egypt written petitions for ensuring the provisioning of the dead appeared early in the Old Kingdom. The enduring role played by lector priests in Egypt suggests that literacy was as important for ensuring the correct performance of rituals in that country as it was in Mesopotamia (Postgate, Wang, and Wilkinson 1995).

Papyrus scrolls, which existed in Egypt as early as the First Dynasty, and bamboo strips, which are known to have been used in Shang China, endured less well than Mesopotamian clay tablets. Mesoamerican inscriptions on stone and pottery have survived better than have Mesoamerican parchment and bark-cloth books. Yet, despite the problems posed by the unequal survival of evidence, what has endured appears to reflect real differences in the uses that were made of recording systems by the various early civilizations. No one function, such as administration, seems to have been everywhere more important than any other in spurring the initial development of recording systems. Writing developed in different institutional milieus, such as temples and palaces, and for the most part continued to be employed for different purposes in such milieus. Only in Mesopotamia, Egypt, and China does writing appear gradually to have come to be used for private purposes by literate individuals or those who could afford to employ professional scribes to read and write for them.

Use of semasiography began in Mesopotamia about 3400 B.C., during the Uruk IV period. The oldest known clay tablets have been found in temple contexts at Uruk (Fig. 25.1). These early recording devices may have replaced or developed out of a still earlier recording system that used clay tokens (Schmandt-Besserat 1992), although the relationship between these two systems is problematical (Yoffee 1995: 285–86). Much later, Mesopotamian scribes claimed that writing had been invented (presumably in a fully developed state) by Enmerkar, a priest-king of early Uruk, so that messages could be transmitted more accurately (Kramer 1981: 22–23; Postgate 1992: 56). Yet early texts made no attempt to record speech. They itemized different types of goods, noting quantities and possibly owners' marks in no standardized order.

It was not until around 2900 B.C. that homophony began to play a significant role in expanding the range of concepts that could be recorded (Bottéro 1992: 80). Only later, in the Early Dynastic period, were efforts made to record speech. Yet, while the signs in these earliest examples of true writing were ordered in accordance with Sumerian grammar, their main purpose seems to have remained mnemonic. Grammatical elements that were deemed

a b

25.1. Early recording in Mesopotamia and Egypt: (a) a clay ledger tablet from Uruk, Uruk IV period – the obverse uses signs to record names and numbers, the reverse records a total of 54 cattle; (b) small labels from Tomb U-j at Abydos, Egypt, dated 3250 B.C. – the round holes were bored for attachment to goods; these labels record place names as well as quantities and appear to employ signs as phonograms as well as logograms. Sources: (a) after Gelb 1963: 64; (b) after K. A. Bard (ed.), *Encyclopedia of the Archaeology of Ancient Egypt* (London, 1999), 111.

unnecessary or that native speakers of Sumerian could have supplied unambiguously from context were omitted. These included many prefixes and suffixes that indicated tense, person, case, number, and mood. A fully developed writing of the Sumerian language, which was not provided until the Ur III period, was probably devised to satisfy the needs of Akkadian-speakers at a time when Sumerian was ceasing to be a spoken language (Bottéro 1992: 83–85; Huot 1989: 52–55; Nissen, Damerow, and Englund 1993; Postgate 1992: 54–66). From the beginning, Mesopotamian writing was done primarily on clay tablets, which only occasionally were baked to harden them for long-term

Word	Meaning	Original Form	Rotated 90° ca 3000 B.C.	Early Dynastic 2500 B.C.	First Millennium B.C.
SAG	head				
KA	mouth				
KU(A)	fish				
GUD	ox				
ŠE	grain				
ŠAR	orchard				
APIN	plough				
DU	foot, leg				

25.2. Development of Mesopotamian signs from the Uruk IV period to the first millennium B.C., showing how signs were altered to improve them for writing on clay tablets and enhance their clarity. Sources: after Gelb 1963: 70, and Cooper 1996: 39.

preservation. At first, signs were drawn on clay; later they were composed entirely of wedge-shaped marks impressed with a stylus. The directions and lengths of these marks were increasingly standardized, making the signs ever more abstract (Fig. 25.2).

The semasiographic recording of goods, place-names, and personal names is first evidenced in southern Egypt in connection with the growing royal power that accompanied the gradual unification of Egypt. Small tags from Tomb U-j at Abydos, which is dated about 3250 B.C., appear to be inscribed with phonetic signs as well as word signs (Davies and Friedman 1998: 35–38). Thus, when it is first attested, Egyptian semasiography was probably more advanced in its techniques for representing spoken words than was its Mesopotamian counterpart. Semasiography continued to be used by royal officials during Early Dynastic times to record personal names, toponyms, dates, the contents of containers, and, in an increasingly complex mnemonic fashion, the events of particular years. Continuous speech began to be recorded only in the late

Second or early Third Dynasties (Baines 1983). Around that time the signs being used were also standardized and their number greatly reduced. Even then, because Egyptian writing did not specify vowels, precise grammatical forms and the pronunciation of words had to be inferred by the reader. This arrangement persisted throughout Egyptian history.

Beginning in the Old Kingdom the Egyptians used a pictorial, or hieroglyphic, form of writing for religious texts and monumental display. Texts in this script were carved on stone and wood or drawn with a brush on papyrus. Hieratic, a cursive version of hieroglyphic, was used for administrative purposes and normally written on papyrus (Fig. 25.3). Although, because it is not pictorial, modern scholars find it more difficult to master, hieratic was used by many scribes who never learned to write hieroglyphs. While royal and religious texts appear to have been more frequent in relation to administrative texts in Egypt than in Mesopotamia, the bulk of the texts produced in both civilizations was probably administrative. The administrative records produced by state-controlled institutions were already highly developed in Egypt during the Old Kingdom. Writing appears to have been restricted to the ruling and administrative classes during the Old and Middle Kingdoms (Baines 1983; Gardiner 1950: 6–10).

Despite a tendency to ascribe great antiquity and sometimes divine origin to specific texts in order to enhance their importance, literary, religious, and professional writings appeared later than administrative, royal, and cultic texts. In Egypt, a corpus of didactic wisdom, which itemized the sorts of behaviour required to be a successful official, and the Pyramid Texts and some other ritual compositions are all the 'literary' works that survive from as late as the Fifth Dynasty. Some short narrative passages occur in royal and funerary inscriptions from the Fourth Dynasty, but even terse autobiographies only start to appear in funerary contexts in the late Old Kingdom (Lichtheim 1973). Literary works, political manifestos of rulers, and medical papyri were first composed in Egypt during the First Intermediate Period and the Middle Kingdom. Many of these writings were used for centuries as school texts and for this reason survive in multiple copies. No Egyptian composition was longer than a modern short story (Lichtheim 1973; 1976; Williams 1964).

Mesopotamian scribes recorded numerous stories, epic poems, myths, hymns, proverbs, disputations, and laments in late Sumerian times, but the stories and epic poems were not worked into larger literary compositions such as the *Enuma Elish* until the second millennium B.C. Beginning in Early Dynastic times, Mesopotamian royal inscriptions, including proclamations and records of military and administrative actions, were recorded on stone stelae. In both Egypt and Mesopotamia administrative accounts, because of their

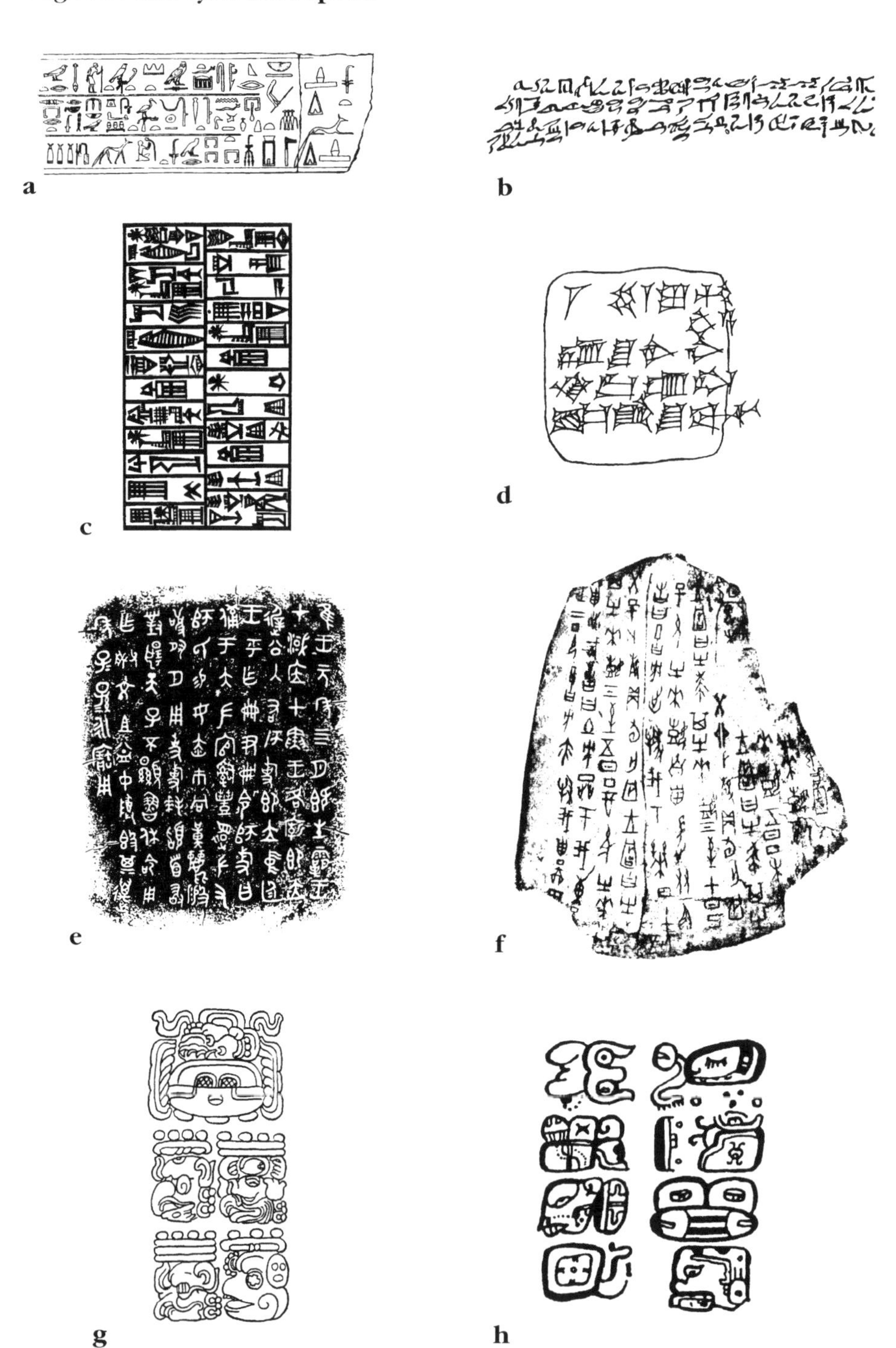
a
b
c
d
e
f
g
h

ledger-like organization, retained many of the characteristics of semasiography long after the spoken word was routinely being recorded in other genres (Kramer 1963: 168–226).

In China inscribed oracle bones from Shang and Zhou royal sites provide the only significant corpus of texts surviving from prior to 1100 B.C. Inscriptions are attested only after 1200 B.C., when Anyang became a Shang royal centre. There is no archaeological record of the early development of Chinese writing or of semasiography in the immediately preceding Erligang and Erlitou periods (Boltz 1999). Graphs etched on pottery of the Dawenkou culture of Shandong, which dates approximately 2500 to 2000 B.C., may mark an early stage in the development of the Chinese recording system. While limited evidence of writing for divinatory purposes has been found at other sites (Chêng 1960: 180), it is not known to what extent writing was limited to royal court circles during the Shang period. The Chinese later claimed that, before the development of writing, they had kept records on knotted cords (Creel 1938: 33), as did the Inka and some African societies (Lagercrantz 1968). The late Shang also made 'books' (*che*) of bamboo strips bound together with strings, but none of these have survived. The Zhou writing system, which is first attested in the late Shang period, is obviously of Shang origin. Oracle texts found at the two courts differ mainly in the size of characters and their dating systems (Hsu and Linduff 1988: 46–47).

In the earliest known examples of the Chinese script, sentences were already being written in the same subject-verb-object order used in modern spoken Chinese. Pronouns and prepositions were also being indicated. The longest known Shang oracle-bone inscriptions contain about 160 characters, but texts on bronze vessels, which identify individuals and clans, rarely consist of more than a few characters (Boltz 1986; 1994). Songs, speeches, and

---

25.3. Formal characteristics of writing systems in early civilizations: (a) portion of offering formula carved in hieroglyphs on limestone block from an Old Kingdom tomb; (b) Egyptian literary hieratic of Dynasty XII; (c) Akkadian inscription carved on stone; (d) hand copy of Ur III bookkeeping entries on a small clay tablet; (e) Western Zhou inscription cast on a bronze vessel; (f) Shang oracle-bone inscription carved on the shoulder blade of an ox; (g) Maya hieroglyphs carved on Stela A from Copan; (h) painted Maya glyphs from the Dresden Codex. Sources: (a) from H. Junker, *Giza* (Vienna, 1922–1955); (b) from A. Gardiner 1950, pl. 2; (c) from J. Friedrich, *Extinct Languages* (New York, 1957), 36; (d) from C. E. Keiser, *Neo-Sumerian Account Texts from Drehem: Babylonian Inscriptions in the Collection of James B. Nies* (New Haven, 1971), document 448; (e) after K. Chang, *The Archaeology of Ancient China*, 2nd ed. (New Haven, 1968), 188; (f) from Lo Chen-yu, *Yin-hsu, Shu-ch'i Ching-hua* (Peking, 1914); (g) from S. G. Morley, *An Introduction to the Study of Maya Hieroglyphs* (Washington, D.C., 1915), p. 166; (h) from E. W. Förstemann, *Die Maya-Handschrift der Königlichen Bibliothek zu Dresden* (Berlin, 1962), p. 58.

historical records preserved in the traditional Chinese literary canon that are ascribed to the Shang period have been demonstrated on linguistic grounds to have been composed during the Western Zhou period. They were either written by Zhou propagandists or created by the Song principality, which was ruled by descendants of the Shang kings (Creel 1938: 50).

It is not clear what non-oracular uses were made of writing in Shang times. Oracle-bone inscriptions incorporate detailed calendars for sacrifices and annal-like accounts of military expeditions and other events, but there is no direct evidence for the use of writing except by royal officials for divinatory and display purposes. Early Western Zhou bronze vessels were inscribed with much longer texts that were often of a historical or ritual nature. Yet even these texts do not appear to have precisely represented the spoken language of that period. Inscriptions are extremely terse and lack the connectives expected in spoken Chinese (Creel 1938: 24).

Chinese writing was done with brush and ink on bamboo slips, bone, and cloth, but on oracle bones texts were also engraved. Characters retained their pictographic quality, and many can easily be recognized as representations of the objects with which they were associated either semantically or phonetically. Most characters became less representational and the brush strokes which composed them more standardized over time. Characters cast on Shang bronzes tended to be less schematized and simplified than were those engraved on oracle bones (Chêng 1960: 177–94; Creel 1938: 24–47; Hsu and Linduff 1988: 46–49).

The Classic Maya were also able to record speech. Few texts survive except ones carved on stone monuments, which are mainly records of kings and dynastic histories, together with short labels painted on fancy pottery. The Classic Maya also produced books, written on bark cloth or parchment. No book survives, however, from the Classic period in legible condition, and the few later ones that have been preserved deal exclusively with divination. It is unknown whether the Classic Maya used writing to record administrative data, historical chronicles, or religious texts.

The Maya script, which is abundantly attested only after A.D. 250, appears to have evolved from the same Olmecoid recording system (1100–400 B.C.) that gave rise to complex semasiography in highland Mexico (Justeson 1986). Maya inscriptions consisting of block glyphs with minimal syntactical transparency and syllabic content appear in the archaeological record between A.D. 1 and A.D. 150. Shortly after, the addition of pronouns makes it clear that the Mayan language was being represented. Syllabograms were used by the beginning of the Early Classic period, around A.D. 250. Phoneticism, the representation of grammatical particles, and the optional substitution of syllabograms for logograms increased after that time. After A.D. 650 witnessed the creation of more syllabic signs that produced still greater phonetic clarity (Hanks 1989: 18; Houston 2001; Justeson 1989: 29; Justeson, Norman, and Hammond 1988). Maya glyphs were highly calligraphic, suggesting a painterly origin. Individual signs were elaborate. They were arranged in square blocks consisting of principal glyphs accompanied by phonetic complements and associated grammatical particles. The same forms of signs were carved on stone as were drawn with a brush on pottery and books. There is no evidence that the forms of signs were simplified over time (Coe 1992; Coe and Kerr 1998; Houston 2001).

The other early civilizations did not develop writing, and their recording systems were highly idiosyncratic. The Yoruba had no indigenous recording systems. In neighbouring Dahomey, however, numerical records were kept by storing pebbles in boxes and bags (Dalton 1975: 100). These served as simple mnemonic devices, with those in charge having to remember to what the various quantities referred. The Inka kept accounts on sets of knotted cords (*khipu*). Different colours and thicknesses of strings denoted different goods, while various-sized knots represented different quantities in decimal order. Accountants (*khipukamayuq*) kept detailed records of goods entering and leaving government storehouses and could report precisely what these storehouses contained at any time. Sometimes two or more accountants were responsible for keeping track of the same information so that higher officials could compare their accounts. It is unclear to what extent particular colours and types of cords were used to record specific types of information or each record-keeper had to remember individually what the various strings on his khipus represented. Experts therefore disagree whether khipus were purely mnemonic devices or to some extent ideographic. It has been suggested that information relevant to the long-term management of storehouses could have been recorded on khipus, but it has not been demonstrated that this was done. Such recording would have required ways of indicating to what periods various information applied. No one suggests that memory did not play an important role in providing semantic interpretations of khipus. Calculations relating to the numerical information stored on khipus were done by manipulating sets of stones (Ascher and Ascher 1981; Quilter and Urton 2001; Urton 1998). King Pachakutiq is said to have had painted boards representing his official version of Inka history placed in the Qorikancha (Kendall 1973: 45). These were presumably mnemonic devices of a pictographic or even purely pictorial nature. There is no evidence that the Inka used rebuses as phonetic indicators to suggest personal names and toponyms.

In the Valley of Mexico a complex form of semasiography was employed. Books (*amatl*) were made of deerskin parchment or, more often, of paper manufactured from the native wild fig tree or from maguey fibre, sized with a thin coating of white lime. The pages of these books were folded accordion-wise. In these books or on single sheets of paper were recorded ritual, divinatory, calendrical, astronomical, historical, and genealogical information, maps showing state boundaries, records of landholding, laws, tribute lists, and itineraries for travellers. Such writings were stored in *amoxcalli* (book houses) in palaces and temple complexes. The art of recording such information was said to have been introduced into the Valley of Mexico by Mixtec scribes (León-Portilla 1992: 58; Marcus 1992a: 53).

Accounts and tribute lists consisted mainly of drawings of different sorts of goods, characterized by both shape and colour, accompanied by conventional numbers. The rebus principle was used to suggest the names of people and places. On the Tizoc Stone, dating from the 1480s, the town of Tochpan was represented by a rabbit (*tochtli*) and Matlatzinco by a mat (*matatl*). There were, however, almost no secondary signs indicating locatives or diminutives. It has been suggested that after 1480 more use was made of phonetics to record proper names, but there is no evidence that phonetic signs were used to record abstract concepts or speech prior to the arrival of the Spanish. Historical information was recorded in the form of standardized representations of various kinds of events, such as migrations of peoples and families and the births, marriages, military exploits, and deaths of important people. These representations were accompanied by standardized date signs, while the names of people and places were suggested by rebuses. History was referred to both as *ihtoloca* (what is said about something) and *xiuhamatl* (written records) (León-Portilla 1992: 39).

In Egypt and Mesopotamia, where the development of writing is now reasonably well documented, it took between six hundred and eight hundred years for complex semasiography to evolve into a script that was well equipped to record language. In early civilizations that had writing systems, only a tiny fraction of the population was literate, and most of these were rulers and administrators. Shulgi, an Ur III king, boasted that he could write, which suggests that in Mesopotamia not all rulers were literate (Postgate 1992: 69). While literacy was overwhelmingly a male prerogative, there were female scribes in Old Kingdom Egypt. In Mesopotamia a few women belonging to the upper classes could write, including Enheduana, a daughter of Sargon I, whose temple hymns became part of the literary canon (Postgate 1992: 26).

In Mesopotamia, a basic literacy seems to have been more widespread than in any other early civilization. There, at least by the Old Babylonian period, many merchants were literate, and writing facilitated more elaborate forms of economic transactions than elsewhere (Postgate 1992: 69). Literate Egyptians used their ability to read and write to transact personal business, but literacy appears to have been more closely tied to government and temple administration than it was in Mesopotamia. Those who could not read or write depended on scribes to record and transmit information for them. In Shang China and among the Classic Maya there is no evidence that writing extended beyond royal courts and state administration, although this may reflect the limitations of current sources of information. In Egypt, China, and among the Maya, because of the pictorial aspects of scripts, some non-literate people may have recognized the symbols representing the names of their city, major gods, or the reigning king. Such knowledge, however, did not constitute or even approximate literacy.

Historical records began as brief accounts of events incorporated into royal annals, monumental royal inscriptions, and funerary texts. Such records often contained important elements of political propaganda (Marcus 1992a). The systematic destruction and self-serving revision of historical records were carried out by the Aztec king Ahuitzotl as part of his political centralization of the Aztec kingdom (León-Portilla 1992: 100). Early Zhou rulers may have destroyed the official records of their Shang predecessors (Creel 1938: 1–50). Yet, while the accumulation of historical records eventually permitted a more systematic understanding of the past in some early civilizations, no literature developed in early civilizations that resembled the detailed studies of human history, the works of abstract philosophy, or the systematic analyses of the natural world that characterized scholarship in the Classical civilizations of Greece and Italy and in China beginning in the late Zhou period. Writing in the early civilizations did not produce the intellectual transformation that Goody (1986) associates with it.

There is also no evidence that the political integration of the Inka kingdom, which lacked writing, was any less effective than that of ancient Egypt or Shang China, despite the importance that these two kingdoms attached to writing as an instrument of bureaucratic control. The political systems of the Yoruba city-states, which lacked any form of writing or semasiography, were in no way inferior to those of Late Aztec city-states, which had a complex form of semasiography, or those of Mesopotamia, which had a fully developed script. A well-developed script appears to have provided a significant advantage only for financial transactions in Mesopotamia and perhaps for calendrical and astronomical studies among the Maya. Writing continued to play significantly different roles in different early civilizations and was not a precondition for early civilizations to evolve and function. It is no longer warranted to claim that, because the Inka and the Yoruba were unable to record speech, their cultures were less developed than was that of the Old Kingdom Egyptians.

Nor can it be claimed that the Classic Maya, who had a fully developed script, were more advanced than the Aztec, who did not.

The writing systems of early civilizations display extraordinary similarities in their developmental patterns and basic structure. All of them were constructed on the same general principles, although no two were structurally identical. All the scripts associated with early civilizations were of a logophonic variety and used from several hundred to several thousand signs.

No fully developed writing system can employ a different sign (logogram) to represent each word or morpheme without some kind of ciphering, which takes the form of supplying phonetic elements that help to link the script to the spoken language. Therefore all the scripts associated with early civilizations were a mixture of logograms (word or morpheme signs), sound signs, and sometimes taxograms (determinatives). Taxograms do not represent speech but clarify the reading of logograms by assigning them to particular semantic classes. Such scripts evolved by semantically extending the logograms for items that were easy to depict to represent more abstract concepts. Thus the Egyptians used a circle, which represented *rʿ* (sun), to write *hrw* (day), while the Shang used the sign for *kou* (mouth) to write *ming* (to call). In addition, logograms were extended phonetically to represent homonyms or near homonyms. Thus the Egyptian sign for 'basket' (*nbt*) was also used to represent *nb* (lord) and *nb* (all), while the Shang used a single sign to write *wang* (king) and *wang* (to go to town). Resulting ambiguities could be resolved by adding a phonetic complement to indicate the pronunciation of a logogram or a taxogram to indicate the semantic class to which a word sign belonged (Boltz 1994: 12–13).

The writing systems of early civilizations varied, however, in the manner by which sounds were indicated. The Sumerian script was logosyllabic. Logograms, many of which were derived from earlier pictograms, were used to write the predominantly monosyllabic roots, or unbound morphemes, of the language. Unbound morphemes included nouns, verbs, and adjectives. Syllabic signs, which were easily derived from monosyllabic root words, were used to write prefixes and suffixes and to provide phonetic complements that clarified the readings of logograms. Syllabic signs took the forms CV (consonant + vowel), V, VC, and CVC (or CV + VC). By 2500 B.C., Sumerian was written using several hundred logograms, one hundred to one hundred and fifty syllabograms, and a few taxograms. As a result of increasing systematization, the total number of signs being used declined from more than one thousand in 3000 B.C. to approximately three hundred around 2400 B.C.

Old Akkadian began to be written at the time when Mesopotamian semasiography was being perfected to record the Sumerian language. Akkadian was a Semitic language, which meant that roots composed of one to three consonants expressed semantic meanings while grammatical relations were indicated by changes in interconsonantal vowels and by prefixes and suffixes. The numerous sound changes that this produced within words favoured the development of syllabic writing (Postgate 1992: 65). While Sumerian cuneiform remained heavily logographic, in Akkadian almost any word could be written phonographically or logographically according to the preferences of individual scribes. In discursive texts, logography rarely exceeded 15 percent. Because Sumerian signs were used to write Akkadian words, relations between sounds and signs grew increasingly complex as Akkadian-derived sound values were added to but did not systematically replace existing Sumerian readings of phonograms. This made taxograms more important for specifying correct readings. Yet, at most periods, scribes used only two hundred to three hundred signs to write Akkadian, although a scholar had to be familiar with both the syllabic and logographic values of approximately six hundred signs in order to read a wider corpus of texts (Cooper 1996: 45–57; Nissen, Damerow, and Englund 1993: 117–18; Sampson 1985: 47–56).

The Maya script, like the Mesopotamian ones, was logosyllabic. It had approximately 800 signs, but only about 200 to 300 were actively employed at any one time. The Maya used a large number of logograms to write nouns, verbs, and other unbound morphemes and a relatively compact syllabary of CV combinations to write affixes, clarify the meaning of multivocalic logograms, and sometimes replace logograms. The word *pakal* (shield), which was the name (or part of the name) of a seventh-century king of Palenque, could be written with a single logogram (a shield), a logogram with phonetic complements, or a set of three syllabograms. The Maya script does not appear to have employed any taxograms. About 150 of its signs had syllabic functions (Coe 1992: 262–63; Justeson 1989).

Ancient Egyptian was an Afroasiatic language and therefore historically related to Akkadian. It too had roots, usually made up of two or three consonants, which supplied semantic meanings, while grammatical relations were indicated by prefixes, suffixes, and intervocalic vowels, as well as by syntax. Unlike the Akkadian script, however, Egyptian writing was based on the principle that, whenever it was possible for a native speaker to infer the correct vowels and other grammatical elements, only the basic consonants were written. Hence ancient Egyptian writing developed not as a logosyllabary but as a logoconsonantary composed of logograms, consonant signs, and taxograms. There were twenty-five uniliteral signs representing single consonants, about eighty biliteral signs representing two successive consonants, and some seventy triliteral signs representing three successive consonants, all without the intervening vowels. Many of these phonograms were derived from logograms for words containing one to three consonants. Egyptian scribes made extensive use of consonant signs to supply, where necessary, phonetic complements that designated the precise word to which a logogram referred. Taxograms were employed to distinguish the meaning of homonyms or to identify categories of words, including personal names (distinguished by gender). Taxograms were also used to separate words. Throughout most of Egyptian history about seven hundred signs were used at any one time (J. Allen 2000: 1–31; Ritner 1996).

The Chinese script is often described as purely logographic because it provides a separate sign or character for each word (morpheme). In the Late Shang period, when the script is first attested, the vast majority of known signs, which total about one thousand, were unit characters representing single morphemes, often in pictorial form. Because most words in Early Chinese were monosyllabic, there were no characters without semantic meaning. Even then, however, as characters underwent either phonetic or semantic extension in an effort to write words that had more abstract meanings, it became necessary to supply clues to either their pronunciation or their meaning in order to maintain intelligibility. This was done by combining two unit signs to create compound characters, one segment of which provided a clue to the pronunciation while the other suggested the meaning.

Later, in the Han Dynasty, a tendency to use alternative homophonic signs (ignoring tone) to write the same word – a movement in the direction of syllabic writing – was arrested by imposing semantic classifiers on all characters to ensure that they remained logographic. Gradually the semantic classifying element (or radical) came to be written on the left side of the character and the phonetic indicator on the right. This procedure ensured that every homonym was represented by a different sign. Despite this triumph of logography, 66 percent of the characters used to write modern Mandarin are described as 'functionally syllabograms' and 99 percent offer some phonetic specification for their readings. Thus from Shang times on, Chinese writing has been a logosyllabic script disguised as a logographic one. Although ninety-five hundred characters were included in a Chinese language lexicon by A.D. 100 and fifty thousand characters are listed in modern dictionaries, twenty-four hundred characters suffice to write 99 percent of the words used (Boltz 1986; 1994; 1999; Sampson 1985: 145–81; Unger and DeFrancis 1995: 52).

There is general agreement, based on their idiosyncratic formal and structural properties, that the writing systems of Mesopotamia, China, and the Maya originated independently of one another. Although it has been argued that the development of complex semasiography in Upper Egypt was stimulated by knowledge of the recording system used in Mesopotamia (Diringer 1962: 47;

A. Spencer 1993: 61–62), not only the signs but also the general principles developed for representing sounds in the two scripts were completely different. Moreover, when it is first attested, Egyptian semasiography appears to have been more advanced in its techniques for representing sounds than its Mesopotamian counterpart (Davies and Friedman 1998: 35–38). Each of the four writing systems, then, appears to have developed independently of the other three. These are the only 'pristine' writing systems associated with early civilizations that are well documented and reasonably well understood.

That all four scripts were logographic in nature suggests that in the development of early writing systems the representation of words everywhere had cognitive priority over the representation of sounds. Yet it also appears that a script based on the representation of words alone would have been too cumbersome to be workable; users would not have been able to remember so many different signs. Hence all these developing scripts had to combine word signs (logograms) and sound signs (phonograms) to represent sequences of spoken words (DeFrancis 1989: 58; Hill 1967; Unger and DeFrancis 1995: 53). Yet early scripts created sound signs in different ways. The Mesopotamian and Maya scripts both utilized syllabograms, although the Maya had a much more regular syllabary than the Mesopotamians (Trigger 1998b). Ancient Egyptian was consonantal, and Chinese was logographic in the sense that each sign retained its own semantic value, although indications of sound values were built into many characters. All four writing systems had a large number of signs by comparison with later writing systems based solely on the representation of syllables (both syllabaries and South Asian–style alphasyllabaries [*abugidas*]) or phonemes (both alphabets and Semitic consonantaries [*abjads*]) (Daniels 1996a: 4; Trigger 1998b). The Sumerian and Maya scripts actively used three hundred to eight hundred signs, ancient Egyptian about seven hundred, and Shang Chinese over one thousand. While the number of signs diminished as the Sumerian and Egyptian scripts became more standardized, the number of Chinese characters continued to increase.

The signs that composed the Mesopotamian and Chinese writing systems acquired increasingly abstract forms over time. In Mesopotamia this was related to signs' ceasing to be drawn on clay and instead being impressed with a stylus, a change that increased the speed of writing. Abstraction was also increased when sign columns on clay tablets were rotated ninety degrees so they could be written horizontally from left to right rather than vertically. This shift, which made writing physically easier, occurred about the middle of the third millennium, although on stone stelae vertical columns continued to be carved until much later (Postgate 1992: 63–64). Chinese signs were conventionalized to accord with an increasingly standardized set of brush strokes.

The Mesopotamian and the Maya scripts each had a single form. The Chinese employed a single script, which had two or more calligraphic versions of varying degrees of formality. The Egyptians quickly developed a highly abstract, hieratic version of their script for everyday use but maintained the elaborate pictorial or hieroglyphic version for display and religious purposes. In all early civilizations aesthetic considerations played a significant role in the development of scripts.

Once established, logophonic scripts persisted over long periods (Gelb 1963: 165). There is no example of such a script's ever evolving directly into a predominantly phonographic one. On the contrary, the number of signs used for Egyptian hieroglyphic writing increased from about seven hundred to more than five thousand in the Greco-Roman period (332 B.C.–A.D. 400), prior to the script's being replaced by a slightly modified version of the Greek alphabet (Ritner 1996: 74). This elaboration reflected the increasingly esoteric nature of traditional Egyptian religion. Reversing early trends toward phonography, the use of logographs also increased in Babylonian cuneiform during the late second and first millennia B.C. until logograms were being used to write over 85 percent of words in divinatory, astrological, and other technical records (Cooper 1996: 53). In the seventh and sixth centuries B.C., the Babylonian language, with its cuneiform script, was superseded as the lingua franca of the Middle East by the Aramaic language, with its twenty-two-letter consonantary, although a few conservative priests and scholars continued to use Babylonian cuneiform into the first century A.D.

The major shifts towards more phonographic writing occurred when scripts were adopted by foreign peoples, who were not constrained by firmly established cultural traditions of literacy and by pedagogical and professional interests that were tied to an existing script (Gelb 1963: 165). Increased phoneticization occurred when the early Sumerian writing system was adapted to write Akkadian. In this case, however, the cultural milieu remained the same, and the benefits of increased phoneticism were largely offset by the increasing multivalency of syllabograms as Akkadian sound values were added to signs that already expressed Sumerian sound values. While the Semitic consonantaries from which all alphabets and South Asian alphasyllabaries are derived may have been inspired by Egyptian uniliteral signs, these scripts were not invented in Egypt, nor is there any evidence that Egyptians played a role in their creation (Millard 1986). It is generally agreed that the principles that guided the writing of ancient Egyptian would have made it difficult for Egyptian scribes to realize that they could have written their language using only uniliterals. Even if any Egyptian scribes had realized that this was technically possible, they almost certainly would have resisted abandoning their more complex writing system, into which many cultural values had been pictorially encoded (Kroeber 1948: 517).

It is often assumed that, because logophonic scripts were complex and difficult to learn, they were inherently inferior to phonographic and especially alphabetic scripts. Yet in modern China and Japan heavily logographic scripts have not impeded the development of mass literacy, the high consumption of published material, and the functioning of modern industrial economies. These developments suggest that the practical advantages of phonemic scripts are less than is usually believed (Unger and DeFrancis 1995: 54–55). They also call into question the widespread assumption that in early civilizations scripts were deliberately kept complex to ensure that they stayed the exclusive possession of a small administrative or upper class. Literacy remained restricted for numerous economic, social, and cultural reasons. In Egypt hieroglyphs were called *mdw nt̲r* (the words of the god), and their invention was attributed to Thoth, the god of wisdom; learning to write in this fashion or to write at all was viewed as a sacred art not meant to be widely shared. In East Asia, simplified, more phonemic versions of scripts have been regarded as appropriate for use only by women, children, and the lower classes (Daniels 1996b; King 1996: 218, 226; J. Smith 1996: 212). It appears that, once a logophonic script developed, the prestige that was associated with using it reduced its chances of being replaced by a structurally simpler script so long as there was no serious disruption of elite cultural patterns (Trigger 1998b).

ORAL LITERATURE

Along with the uses that were made of writing in early civilizations, strong emphasis continued to be placed on the oral transmission of knowledge. In non-literate early civilizations and among the non-literate lower classes in early civilizations that had writing, oral transmission was the only means of preserving knowledge. Even the upper classes in civilizations that had writing systems accorded high status to the oral communication and presentation of knowledge. Eloquence was greatly valued, and material that was intended to be remembered was often composed in metrical or poetic form.

The Yoruba preserved the histories of individual patrilineages in the form of *itan*, oral prose narratives recited by male elders. Itan recounted the migrations and extolled the achievements of a patrilineage and its most renowned members, traditions that were often at odds with the official histories of towns and their dynastic rulers. Elders, both male and female, also preserved their lineages' distinctive lullabies, folktales, and riddles. Those responsible for sacrificing to the gods had to remember their families' special prayers, incantations, and blessings (Pemberton and Afolayan 1996: 8). *Oriki* (praise songs), poetical compositions performed in honour of deities, communities, households, individual persons, both living and dead, and even special trees and animals, played a significant role in struggles among individuals and groups to enhance their social and political status. While they were recited by many people, the most elaborate ones were composed and performed at public festivals by professional praise-singers, most of whom were women (K. Barber 1991; Pemberton and Afolayan 1996: 7–10). The official historians of the state of Oyo (*arokin*), the ruler's bards, drummers, and cymbalists, were responsible for remembering and reciting the official myths, histories, and praise songs of the royal lineage. These works affirmed the priority of the king of Oyo in relation to other Yoruba rulers. Royal reciters, it was claimed, could be executed if they made a single error in their performances (Apter 1992: 14; Mercier 1962: 46).

In the Andean highlands, local political leaders had their predecessors' deeds remembered in poems that had rigid phonetic structures but rarely rhymed. Local religious officials also had to remember and transmit to their successors the prayers and hymns that related to the cults for which they were responsible. The Inka royal court and the various Inka royal descent groups cultivated their own origin myths and historical traditions. Each set of traditions sought to promote the political interests of a particular branch of the royal family. Pachakutiq's revised version of Inka history, which was composed following his usurpation of royal power in the fifteenth century, appears to have been sustained by subsequent Inka rulers. Royal promotion of stories supernaturally associating the origins of the Inka royal family with the Lake Titicaca region may have been intended to facilitate the integration of that important region into the Inka state. Learned men (*amautakuna*) at the Inka royal court composed narratives, songs, and dramas about the royal ancestors that were performed on feast days, as well as prayers, hymns, and love songs. These compositions were memorized, and the most esteemed were transmitted from one generation to the next (Kendall 1973: 46–49).

In the Valley of Mexico, elderly commoners addressed elaborate, formulaic speeches (*huehuetlatolli*) to newborn infants, young people, and newly married couples, exhorting them to work hard, behave soberly, and diligently discharge their responsibilities to their families and society. Composing and reciting more elaborate and original works were pastimes of the nobility and ways in which talented commoners could win royal favour and lasting fame. Rhythmic songs, ceremonial addresses, and accompanying music were called *toltecayotl*. Sung poetry was referred to as *xochicuicatl* (flower songs), and beautiful speech was compared to precious jade and quetzal feathers. Song was believed to have existed before the universe, and it was said to bring humans into closer contact with the forces of creation as represented by Ometeotl and fill their hearts with the creative power that had brought the universe into existence. Songs celebrated the deeds of great warriors and explored such themes as friendship and death. They also expressed hopes, fears, and doubts that ran counter to the martial beliefs that were being accentuated by the Aztec state. Palaces employed salaried professional singers to compose and perform works that praised the achievements, wealth, and greatness of reigning kings and their predecessors, celebrated their victories and conquests, and traced royal genealogies. These works were sung at palace celebrations and public religious ceremonies. Temples also employed professional singers to compose chants and hymns that celebrated the deeds and greatness of their gods. Both sorts of singers were called *cuicapicque* (Berdan 1982: 155–58; Clendinnen 1991: 219–22; Durán 1971: 299; León-Portilla 1963: 180–81; 1992: 71).

Samuel Kramer (1963: 170) has maintained that the *nar* (poet-singer or minstrel) is the key to understanding Mesopotamian literature. Some poet-singers were employed by temples to train singers and conduct liturgies. Others worked for kings, for whom they trained court singers and composed and recited myths and epic poems. Prior to the extensive use of writing, poet-singers must have played an essential role in preserving and promoting knowledge of the past as did the 'bards' at the Inka and Aztec royal courts. These poet-singers probably began to compose elements of the Gilgamesh epic around 2100 B.C., presumably for the Ur III rulers, who claimed Gilgamesh as their ancestor. The epic was not drawn together, however, before 1600 B.C., and its final version was edited six hundred years later. The known corpus of Mesopotamian literary works, including myths, epics, hymns, laments, disputes, and proverbs, has been estimated to amount to about twenty-eight thousand lines. Most of these works are characterized by systematic repetition, parallelism, epithets, similes, and other characteristics of poetry. Hence much Mesopotamian recorded literature appears to have been grounded in or stimulated by an oral literary tradition (Jacobsen 1976: 195; Kramer 1981: 289–90).

There is no significant record of or about purely oral literature in ancient Egypt, but Egyptian written texts appear to reflect the pervasive influence of orality. Many hymns, spells, and religious petitions that were carved on the walls of tombs and temples and on amulets were intended to be read aloud. Didactic literature was presented as a written record of verbal advice that an elderly official had given to his son or pupil. While surviving 'Songs of the Harper', a genre that expressed scepticism about traditional beliefs concerning life after death, were engraved on the walls of tombs, they were represented as songs that were sung by male professional musicians. Short stories, such as

'The Story of Sinuhe', 'The Tale of the Eloquent Peasant', 'King Khufu and the Magician', and 'The Shipwrecked Sailor', seem modelled on the sort of tale that a public storyteller might have presented. They were all relatively short and had simple, dramatic story lines. Some were largely naturalistic stories set in earlier times; others were filled with supernatural elements. The style of writing indicates that these stories were composed in written form, and it has been suggested that some of them were intended as propaganda to support the kings who were re-establishing centralized royal power in the early Middle Kingdom (Williams 1964). It is unclear, however, whether these politically engaged stories were composed as models for public storytellers, who might have worked as agents for the central government, or were intended only for the administrative classes, whom they reached in written form. Most of these stories have survived because they were used as school texts (Lichtheim 1973: 169–84, 211–35).

Among the Egyptian writings more obviously intended only for a literary audience were compositions extolling the benefits of being a scribe and the political testaments ascribed to rulers of the First Intermediate Period and the early Middle Kingdom. In general, the composition of works of political propaganda that sought to justify the new political order ceased as the Twelfth Dynasty became more securely established. These compositions were replaced by hymns or songs celebrating the power of reigning kings (Lichtheim 1973: 134–63, 198–201). Yet, while the milieu of literate Egyptian bureaucrats was socially and culturally remote from that of farming villages, their literary compositions were not very different from storytelling among the rural population.

The important role assigned to oral literature in shaping and transmitting the values of the upper classes in early civilizations, whether or not these civilizations had fully developed writing systems, helps to explain why writing was less crucial for them than was once thought. Writing was used to record various types of information, but the qualitative difference between what was written and what was spoken was not great, if a gap existed at all (Halverson 1992; Havelock 1986). Nothing appears to have been created in early civilizations that resembled the systematic philosophical treatises or studies of nature produced by later Greek and Roman writers. Scholarship of that sort, while strongly influenced by literacy, may have owed more to the desacralization of the natural world than to a widespread ability to read. Writing invariably facilitated a more detailed conservation of knowledge and its transmission without the necessity of person-to-person contact. Even this advantage does not appear, however, to have been widely recognized and systematically exploited until later. While the knowledge possessed by the upper classes of early civilizations differed in content and elaboration from that of the lower classes, the two sorts did not yet differ radically in their degree of generalization or abstraction.

ELITE EDUCATION

The ways in which specialized knowledge and skills were transmitted among the upper and administrative classes varied considerably from one early civilization to another.

Inka rulers paid careful attention to the education of male members of the nobility and of chosen women. Chosen women were trained to weave fine clothing and cook and brew for the state; those of higher social rank were also instructed in religious matters. About the age of ten, the sons of Inka nobles, Inka-by-privilege, and some high-ranking provincial nobles were required to attend *yachawasi*, special schools run by learned men (amautakuna) who were members of the nobility. While at school, sons of provincial nobles and Inka governors constituted de facto hostages for their fathers' loyalty. Students are reported to have remained at these schools for four years, studying the court version of the Quechua language, Inka rituals and calendrics, khipu record-keeping, and Inka history and learning about the law, how to govern, how to lead armies, and how to behave in a manner appropriate to their social class. Living in the Inka capital and often serving as pages at the royal court helped to prepare such young men to become government officials (Kendall 1973: 65, 77–78; Rowe 1944: 282–83).

In Egypt the only official school for training scribes and administrators during the Old Kingdom appears to have been attached to the royal court. There the sons of major officials were educated together with the king's sons. Boys also appear to have been educated to be scribes and administrators by their fathers or by being sent to live with important officials. In the Middle Kingdom the main school continued to be located at the royal residence and may have been divided into separate sections for princes and the sons of lesser officials. There were also, however, smaller schools in communities such as Kahun, where the individuals who took turns tending the funerary cult of Senwosret II lived. These schools probably were sustained on a fee-paying basis. Children attended such schools between the ages of five and ten. They then continued for a decade or longer to learn how to be bureaucrats by working in a subordinate capacity in a government office or on the staff of a government official. At school students first learned to write words in the hieratic script and went on to memorize and learn to record simple stories, formulae, and sentences from an elementary textbook and then study classical Middle Kingdom texts. Learning to read and write was accompanied by the acquisition of elementary arithmetical and bookkeeping skills and a growing understanding of the behaviour and values of the ruling and administrative classes. In the New Kingdom still more schools were established in temples to supply a growing need for administrators (David 1986: 120; Janssen and Janssen 1990: 69–83; Williams 1972). The main centres where knowledge accumulated and could be consulted in Egypt were the 'Houses of Life' (*pr ʿnḫ*), or scriptoria, attached to major temples. The writings preserved in these institutions concerned not only theology, temple ritual, and architecture but also astronomy, medicine, history, and all other forms of knowledge related to the gods and their creation (R. Wilkinson 2000: 74).

In Shang China there appears to have been a palace school where the king's sons, children of collateral royal lineages, and sons of non-royal administrators were educated (Chao 1972: 25–26). These boys were instructed in martial arts as well as administrative skills, which in some cases may have included learning how to write. Alternatively, writing may have been the prerogative of a small group of specialists who learned it from their patrilineal kinsmen as a form of highly respected craft knowledge.

Among the Yoruba all transmission of knowledge seems to have been accomplished by apprenticeship. Sons of officials and members of palace and town associations acquired their administrative skills and knowledge of specialized rituals by assisting office-holders. Often knowledge was acquired through initiation into ritual societies and organizations and rising slowly through their ranks. The most demanding apprenticeship was that required to become a diviner (babalawo). Divination was required to gain the approval of the god Ifa to be instructed in the secret knowledge of his cult. Three years of intensive study were needed to qualify for the lowest rank of the Ifa priesthood. Such experts generally divined for their extended families. Many more years of instruction were required to rise to the second and third ranks, the third being that of a high priest (Abimbola 1973; Bascom 1969: 70–71; Eades 1980: 125–26).

The Aztec required all boys to attend one of two sorts of schools. Sons of nobles and a few commoners attended schools attached to major temples where they were trained to become priests, high-level administrators, and scribes. This required intensive instruction in astrology, calendrics, dream interpretation, record-keeping, oratory, and the martial arts, as well as in the cultivated speech and manners of the nobility (Berdan 1982: 88–90, 143; León-Portilla 1963: 134–39). Probably associated with these schools were the *tlamatinime* (learned men), who are described as composers and teachers of songs that encoded scientific and historical knowledge and advisers to rulers. The Texcocan kings were renowned for promoting such scholarship (Berdan 1982: 143; León-Portilla 1963: 16, 69–74).

In Mesopotamia record-keeping was first associated with temples. Standardized word lists suggest that record-keepers were being formally trained already in the Uruk period. At least as early as 2500 B.C., schools called *édubba* (tablet houses) were located next to temples and palaces, where scribes (*dubšar*) were trained to manage the affairs of these institutions. These schools were the major centres in which Mesopotamian culture was conserved and elaborated. By the Ur III period there were also private schools for children from families that could afford tuition. Every school was under the authority of an *adda édubba* (school father), who was assisted by one or more senior students or assistant teachers, called 'big [or older] brothers' (*šešgal*). The students were *dumu édubba* (school's sons). Boys (only very rarely girls) began attending these schools when they were between five and seven years old. They were taught writing, elementary mathematics, and the forms of legal and administrative documents. They first learned to write syllabograms and logograms, then multisign words, and then short and long texts, which they copied or memorized. Semitic-speaking children also had to learn Sumerian, which, although it continued to be of literary and sometimes administrative importance, was ceasing to be a spoken language. Bilingual lists of words, accompanied by phonetic renderings of the Sumerian ones, were compiled to facilitate this study. The establishment of private schools was associated with the spread of literacy beyond the confines of temple and palace administrations, in particular among merchants and some craft workers, but hymns were included in the libraries of private schools that had no direct connection with temples. Schools as an institution aspired to be centres of learning where old texts were copied and preserved and new ones composed (Kramer 1963: 229–45; 1981: 3–16; Nissen, Damerow, and Englund 1993: 104–10; Postgate 1972: 814; 1992: 67–70, 153).

Thus, in the two best-documented territorial states, Inka Peru and ancient Egypt, the royal court was the main centre of formal education and the place where sons of the most important administrators were trained. A similar arrangement probably existed in Shang China. In Egypt the growing need for scribes to handle administrative matters led to the creation of schools that were community-based and privately supported. Specialized education was more variable in city-states. Among the heterarchical Yoruba, all education was by apprenticing or initiation into a society or cult. In Mesopotamia, where class membership was not formally hereditary, the increasing use of writing encouraged the development of private schools in addition to temple and palace ones. In the Valley of Mexico, where class divisions were hereditary, upper-class education was controlled by the state and managed through temples and priests. Formal schools seem to have been the most developed and varied in states where writing or complex semasiography became essential for bureaucratic management and private business.

SPECIALIZED KNOWLEDGE

Societies that did not distinguish the natural and supernatural realms could not differentiate as we do between natural science and religion. Miguel León-Portilla (1963: xxi) maintains that the Aztec did not distinguish philosophy, religion, and science. The sixteenth-century Yucatec Mayan term *miats* covered what the Spanish differentiated as philosophy, science, art, culture, and wisdom (Tate 1992: 30). Modern distinctions do not accord with the cosmological understandings of early civilizations.

Notably absent in the surviving records of literate early civilizations are documents relating to their extraordinary architectural and other technological achievements. While Egyptian school texts contain formulae for calculating the approximate volumes of pyramids, no manuals describe how a real pyramid was planned and built. Nor are there early Chinese texts dealing with bronze-casting. Either these operations were carried out by non-literate craftsmen or such records and instruction guides as existed were insufficiently numerous or appreciated to have survived. There is therefore no way to know whether Chinese bronze-casting was treated as a straightforward technological process or whether magic and ritual played an integral role in casting ceremonial vessels, as it did in at least some metal-casting in Benin. Much more documentation is available concerning calendrics, medicine, divination, and magic, which routinely combined what we would interpret as rational practices with magical and religious ones.

Anthony Aveni (1989), in his comparative study of calendar systems, concludes that all governments of early civilizations bureaucratically organized time. Calendars took account of the periodicities of astronomical bodies and of seasonal and biological cycles and related them to human activities. Day and night, monthly lunar cycles (which affected how much light was available for activities after sunset), and annual rounds of changing weather were important features of the natural world to which government activities and planning had to adapt. Yet arbitrary choices were necessarily involved in determining the relative importance accorded to specific factors and how different cycles were integrated with one another. There was still greater variation in the extent to which, and how, different early civilizations recorded time over long durations. This paralleled the greater variation among cosmogonies than among more observation-based cosmologies.

The Egyptian diurnal cycle began at dawn. Egyptian officials divided each daylight period (*hrw*) and each night (*grḥ*) into twelve equal hours (*wnwt*), which altered in length as the duration of day and night varied throughout the year. The Egyptians also recognized an ecological year that began with the rising of the Nile flood, as presaged by the first observed rising (*prt*) of the star Sirius (*spdt*) just before dawn in mid-July. Egyptian officials utilized a civil year (*rnpt*) of 365 full days (*sw*). This year was divided into three seasons (*tr*): inundation (*3ḫt*), the growing season (*prt*), and summer (*šmw*). Each season consisted of four months (*3bd*) of 30 days each, followed by 5 additional days (*ḥryw rnpt*). Each month was divided into three 10-day weeks, called 'first', 'middle', and 'last'. Although it was originally timed to begin with the heliacal rising of the star Sirius, the civil year fell one day behind the solar year every four years, with the result that the calendrical 'inundation' season eventually occurred during the actual growing season and then during the dry season. It took approximately 1,460 years for the civil calendar to correspond once more with the solar year. This suggests that the civil year may have been created about 2773 B.C., probably in the Third Dynasty.

A twelve-month lunar calendar was used to organize everyday life. To keep this calendar in accord with the solar year, an extra lunar month was added whenever the first day of the lunar year preceded the heliacal rising of Sirius in mid-July. This month had to be added approximately once every three years. The Egyptians also used this lunisolar calendar to determine the dates for religious festivals. Priests divided the ecliptic, or path of the sun through the sky, into thirty-six decans, each marked by a star constellation. At night the rising of each new decan in the east indicated that two-thirds of an hour had passed. The rising of different decans at a particular time of night also divided the solar year into thirty-six units of approximately ten days (one Egyptian week) each.

Initially, each year was named after one or more distinctive events, either in anticipation of these events or after they had occurred. During the Fifth and Sixth Dynasties, years were numbered according to the biennial cattle counts of each monarch's reign. Finally, beginning in the Middle Kingdom, they were numbered consecutively according to the years of a king's reign. In the Middle Kingdom, the second year of a king's reign began on the first day of the 'inundation' season following his accession. In the New Kingdom, each regnal year began on the actual day of the king's accession; thus each civil year consisted of parts of two regnal years (J. Allen 2000: 104–6; L. Bell 1997: 157–59; Gardiner 1950: 203–6).

In Mesopotamia each daily cycle commenced at sunset. The Sumerians divided each night and each day into three watches, while the Babylonians divided the time from one sunset to the next into twelve equal parts. The year was divided into two seasons, with summer (*emeš*) beginning in February or March and winter (*enten*) in September or October. The Mesopotamian calendar was a lunisolar one, based on real lunar months of twenty-nine and thirty days. These months were named differently in different cities. The financial year began two months after the spring grain harvest, but for other purposes the year began with the harvest. An extra lunar month was inserted into the calendar approximately every three years to keep it in line with the seasons. This was done at different times in different cities. By 2400 B.C., a schematic year composed of twelve thirty-day months was introduced for accounting purposes. Years were named after auspicious events such as military victories or the building of a temple. In the Old Babylonian period, they began to be numbered, as in Egypt, according to regnal years (Kramer 1963: 91, 140).

The Shang daily cycle began during the night or at dawn. Daytime (*ri*) was divided into at least eight periods defined by the position of the sun and by daily human activities; the night (*xi*) was not subdivided. The Shang observed a ten-day week (*xun*) and had a lunisolar calendar in which 'big moons' (*da yue*) thirty days long usually alternated with 'little moons' (*xiao yue*) of twenty-nine days. A normal year began with the first new moon after the winter solstice and lasted twelve lunar months. The lunar calendar was kept in time with the seasons by intercalating seven extra thirty-day months every nineteen years. The conservative ritualists added these months at the end of years, the progressive ritualists whenever the need for an adjustment was perceived. Each day was assigned what at least since Han times has been called a *ganzhi* name. Ten so-called celestial stem (*tiangan*) names and twelve terrestrial branch (*dizhi*) names were permuted to produce a series of sixty day-names that were used in divination and sacrifice. Towards the end of the Shang dynasty, six successive ganzhi cycles made up an ancestral cult cycle (*si*) that nearly corresponded with a solar year but was not synchronized with it. These cult cycles were numbered according to how many had occurred during a king's reign. Only much later in Chinese history were the ganzhi combinations also utilized to label successive years. King's names were sometimes mentioned in connection with dates, but this, together with a combination of ganzhi and lunar dates that formed a thirty-one-year cycle, was inadequate to order years sequentially over long periods. Later king lists and other chronological information that have been confirmed by Shang oracle-bone texts suggest that the Shang must have preserved information about the length of each king's reign as the basis for constructing a long-term chronology (Chêng 1960: 228–33; Keightley 1999b: 249–51; 2000).

The Aztec and their neighbours, in accordance with their ideas about the construction of the universe, divided days into thirteen hours (equivalent to the number of sky worlds) and nights into nine hours (equivalent to the number of underworlds). The *tonalpohualli* (counting of days) permuted thirteen numerals and twenty day-names to identify 260 consecutive days and was used for divination and guiding personal affairs. The *xihuitl* or solar calendar consisted of 18 *meztli*, each with its own name and made up of 20 numbered days plus 5 and perhaps in some years 6 extra days (*nemontemi*) to produce a 365-day year. Despite its short duration, the term *meztli* literally meant 'moon'. The two calendars ran concurrently to produce a recurring fifty-two-year calendar round known as a *xiuhmolpilli* (bundling of years). Although two such calendar rounds were recognized as corresponding with thirteen 584-day cycles of the planet Venus, the 52-year round was the longest calendrical unit explicitly differentiated by the Aztecs. Thus there is often uncertainty about the precise calendar round in which a specifically dated event occurred. Different city-states also used different day-names and appear to have begun their years with different months. Historical records kept track of events that occurred over consecutive calendar rounds (Berdan 1982: 143–48; Bray 1968: 163–71; Caso 1971; León-Portilla 1992: 47; M. E. Smith 1996: 253–58; van Zantwijk 1985: 226).

The basic structure of the Maya calendar was also a ritual year of 260 days and a solar year of 365 days that ran concurrently to form a fifty-two-year calendar round. In addition, however, the Maya used a long count of consecutively numbered days. In this system, 20 days (*kin*) constituted one *winal*, 18 winals one *tun* (roughly a year), 20 tuns one *katun*, and 20 katuns one *baktun*. Thus the date 9.18.5.0.0 fell 9 baktuns, 18 katuns, and 5 tuns, or 1,427,400 days, after the start of the current baktun on August 13, 3114 B.C. This date corresponds to September 15, A.D. 795 of the modern calendar. By embedding baktuns in progressively longer cycles, the Maya, alone among the early civilizations, could extend their long count forward or backward indefinitely. Inscriptions dealing with the supernatural record dates that are up to nineteen positions above the baktun and hence extend over many billions of years. The greatest span of time known to be indicated is 142 nonillion (142 followed by 36 zeros) years. According to Maya calculations, all the cycles above the baktun currently stood at the thirteenth position (Aveni 1989: 190–254; A. Miller 1986: 17–29; Schele and Miller 1986: 316–22; Tate 1992: 13–15).

The long count did not conceptualize time as linear. Instead, it viewed time as composed of short cycles of days embedded in successively longer rounds. The Maya used their long count to correlate calendar-round dates over long periods. Dates were cited in terms of the long count followed by the day in the 260-day cycle, the phase of the moon in a 29- or 30-day cycle, which of nine ruling lords of the night was presiding, and finally the solar date. Long-count dates were first recorded in the late third century A.D. This suggests that the long count was introduced at a time when dynastic kingship was becoming more important. Yet, if the principal goal of the long count was to record dynastic continuity, the Maya calendar dramatically overshot its mark. It became a vehicle for speculating about continuities and transformations in the cosmic order on a temporal scale unmatched in any other early civilization. The importance that the Maya accorded to astrology as a means of divination appears linked to the extraordinary development of their calendar.

The Inka used a calendar of twelve lunar months named for qualities, activities, and rituals associated with particular seasons. The solstices and the time for planting were ascertained by establishing the positions of the rising and setting sun in relation to stone towers (*sukanka*) constructed on the skyline to the east and west of Cuzco. An extra lunar month was probably added approximately every three years to adjust the lunar calendar to the solar cycle. It is unclear whether the year began with the month of Qhapaq Raymi, which corresponded with the southern summer solstice, or the month of Inti Raymi, which occurred at the time of the winter solstice. The solar year was also divided into twelve months, each made up of three ten-day weeks. It is not understood how the solar and lunar months were correlated, and there is no evidence on the way in which successive years were identified. These difficulties, combined with a lack of written records prior to European contact, greatly complicate understanding Inka dynastic history (Bauer and Dearborn 1995; Julien 2000; MacCormack 1991: 166; Rowe 1944: 308; Sadowski 1989: 212; Ziolkowski and Sadowski 1989b: 167–69).

The Yoruba observed a lunar year made up of thirteen 'months', each composed of seven four-day 'weeks'. These 'weeks' were associated with the holding of markets as well as with ritual observances. Each day of the week was named for a local market held on that day. It is not clear how or whether the lunar calendar of 364 days was correlated with the solar year. Years were identified according to the regnal years of a particular king, memorable events, or the cultivation of particular plots of land (Bascom 1969: 25; Ojo 1966a: 296–307).

The common use of a lunisolar calendar, which sought to correlate a set of lunar months and a solar year, and the eventual adoption of a schematic year for administrative purposes might have resulted from the various historical links between Egypt and Mesopotamia. The employment of calendar rounds for ritual purposes in early China and Mesoamerica also might be interpreted as evidence of some sort of historical connection between these two regions. Yet the development of lunisolar calendars in Peru as well as China and of a schematic administrative calendar in Peru as well as in Egypt and Mesopotamia indicates that these sorts of reckonings may have been invented independently in Egypt and Mesopotamia. The Chinese and Mesoamerican divinatory cycles are also very different, suggesting that any historical connections were very remote and general. The Maya long count was unique. To explain the similarities and differences in the calendrical systems of early civilizations, more than historical connections must be considered.

All early civilizations recognized units of time approximating a solar year divided into 'months' approximating a lunar cycle and 'weeks' of four to ten days. It has been suggested that days, months, and solar years may reflect human circadian rhythms that developed as long-term, selective adaptations to cycles in the natural environment (Aveni 1989: 28). Yet, while some 'months' measured actual lunar cycles, others were arbitrarily fixed at twenty-eight, twenty-nine, or thirty days. The Aztec and their neighbours even more arbitrarily divided the solar year into eighteen 'months' of twenty days each. The calendars of early civilizations appear to have been divided into 'months' in order to take account of the changing seasons as these related to agricultural activities, state projects such as waging war, and the rituals associated with these projects. Four-to-ten-day 'weeks' facilitated the scheduling of repetitive, short-term labour tasks in agricultural societies, and in early civilizations they were used to regulate short-term administrative and ritual activities. As elaborated by the governments of early civilizations, calendars also became complex devices for correlating the terrestrial and cosmic realms and managing relations with the supernatural. Annual calendars have numerous generic similarities that reflect the similar purposes they served in all early civilizations, but their idiosyncratic differences indicate the culturally specific ways in which these goals were realized.

The Yoruba, Mesopotamian, Valley of Mexico, Shang, Egyptian, and Inka upper classes carefully recorded the names of successive rulers, but their calendars were not equipped to order events chronologically over long periods. The fifty-two-year calendar round used in the Valley of Mexico was the most extensive of these systems. In Egypt and Mesopotamia, careful records were kept for administrative purposes first of the names used to identify successive years and later of counts of each king's regnal years in order to track the passage of time over long periods. Yet episodes of political disruption and associated breaks in record-keeping created problems for maintaining such chronologies, particularly when it was no longer remembered which rulers had reigned sequentially and which concurrently. Only the Classic Maya long count, by embedding short cycles in exponentially longer ones, created a device for recording all possible events in a comprehensive chronological order. While, in general, early civilizations that possessed writing or complex semasiographies were better equipped to order events chronologically over long periods than were ones that did not, the vast qualitative difference between the general principles governing the Maya long count and all other systems for recording time over long periods provides striking evidence of the culturally specific factors shaping such phenomena.

Medicine in early civilizations was a combination of what we would regard as natural methods, such as applying herbal remedies that were known empirically to have specific beneficial effects, and supernatural methods. This combination did not distinguish medicine from other forms of technological practice.

That people in early civilizations distinguished between illnesses that could be cured by natural means and other diseases that required supernatural intervention is often interpreted as signifying that they believed that at least some illnesses had natural causes. It does not follow, however, that diseases that could be cured by natural methods were believed to be naturally caused. In cultures in which the natural and supernatural were not clearly separated no such distinction was possible. A wound that could be treated naturally might have been caused by a god's failure to protect someone in battle, and supernatural help would be sought for any infection that did not respond quickly to regular herbal treatment. Ultimately, therefore, all medical problems were caused and could be cured supernaturally.

The Yoruba attributed diseases to deities who used them to punish social misconduct and offences committed against the supernatural. Oya, Sango's favourite wife and the goddess of the Niger River, afflicted worshippers who displeased her with sometimes fatal throat diseases; Yemoja, Sango's mother and the goddess of the Ogun River, caused stomach-aches and drowned her enemies; Sopona, Sango's brother, spread smallpox far and wide. Numerous illnesses were also attributed to witches and sorcerers. The Yoruba sought to cure illnesses by atoning for their sins and wrongdoings and by having specialists or ritual societies perform ceremonies that would counteract or placate the malevolent beings who were seeking to harm them. While there is no evidence among the Yoruba for herbalists or ritual specialists who cured only the upper classes, wealthy and powerful individuals could afford treatments that ordinary people could not (Bascom 1969: 87–95).

In the Valley of Mexico it was believed that illness was inflicted by the gods as punishment for human wrongdoing or as a result of divine malevolence, as well as by sorcerers who manipulated supernatural forces to harm others. The god Tlaloc released cold winds that caused gout, palsy, swellings, the withering or stiffening of limbs, ulcers, leprosy, and dropsy. The spirits of women who had died in childbirth paralysed young people, while Xipe Totec caused skin and eye diseases. Excessive sexual activity, which displeased the gods, produced melancholy and tuberculosis in families, and failure to obey ritual prohibitions was punished by venereal diseases, haemorrhoids, and skin ailments. Sorcerers produced illnesses by injecting powerful charms into people's bodies.

The Aztec and their neighbours sought to avoid the gods' anger and to elicit their help to overcome diseases by means of rituals and amulets. There were two types of doctors. The more specialized were the *ticitl*, who were considered tlamatinime (wise men) and had been trained in the calmecacs. Ticitl were also priests. Of lower status were female curers and midwives. Doctors sought, by means of divination, to discover what god or sorcerer had caused an illness. This involved casting lots, staring into a bowl of water, or ingesting hallucinogenic substances and, on the basis of what was revealed, prescribing cures. Treatments for illnesses that were determined to be curable using natural remedies included purgatives, teeth-cleaning, bone-setting, lancing of boils, suturing, bleeding, and steam baths. Over twelve hundred herbal remedies were also used. If an illness was determined to have been caused by witchcraft, efforts were made to locate the charms – worms, pieces of paper, pebbles, or stone chips – that were responsible for it and extract them from the sick person's body. Special offerings were made to deities who were reputed to be able to cure particular illnesses. (These deities were not always the same ones that caused the disease.) Midwives and curing women prescribed food taboos for nursing mothers.

The standing of doctors in Aztec society appears to have been related not to the kinds of diagnosis and curing they attempted but to the wealth and status of their clients. Both ticitl and curing women sought to heal diseases that were believed to require supernatural as well as natural treatment, and both supernaturally diagnosed the causes of illnesses. Ticitl were more thoroughly trained and therefore considered better able to diagnose and cure illnesses; they were also feared because they were thought to have the power to cause as well as cure illnesses (Berdan 1982: 148–50; Bray 1968: 182–85; Ortiz de Montellano 1990; Ruiz de Alarcón 1984: 156–208; M. E. Smith 1996: 260–63; Soustelle 1961: 191–200).

Mesopotamian society also supported two kinds of specialists in curing diseases. The *asû* (doctor) was trained in the medical lore associated with the city of Isin. He did not examine the body but noted symptoms and prescribed medicines. The medicines (*šammu*) consisted of herbs, animal products (fat, blood, milk, bone), and certain minerals. These substances, none of which was rare or expensive, were mixed with beer, vinegar, honey, or tallow to be swallowed or administered as enemas, suppositories, lotions, and salves. Other remedies included laxatives, diuretics, and cough syrups. Asûs consulted clay tablets that listed symptoms, cures, and sometimes a sick person's chances of recovery.

The second type of healer, the *ašipu* (diviner physician), was said to have been trained in the lore of the city of Eridu. He carefully observed the sick person's body, treating its temperature, colour, and pulse as omens that would reveal the cause of the disease and allow him to propose a cure. Cures consisted of a combination of the traditional pharmacopoeia and conjuration. An ašipu sought to persuade the gods to reverse their sentence by employing exorcistic rituals (*namburbū*) that transferred the illness to someone else or to an image (*salmu*). Animal sacrifices might be offered to Erishkegal, the ruler of the underworld, as a substitute (*pūhu*) for the sick person. Doctors and diviner physicians shared the view that disease was mainly caused by supernatural powers, including divine intervention and witchcraft (Bottéro 1992: 142–43; Oppenheim 1964: 288–305).

Doctors had the same social status as innkeepers and bakers, and they and the midwives plied their trade on a freelance basis. Diviner physicians were superior to them but also generally self-employed. The most successful were appointed as palace staff. Surgical interventions were rare and discouraged by laws that inflicted draconian punishments on medical practitioners if an operation caused the death of a patient (Pritchard 1955: 175–76, laws 215–23). Leo Oppenheim (1964: 298–301) noted that very little development occurred in Mesopotamian medical practice after the Old Babylonian period. He attributed this to the stultifying effect of reducing any practice to writing (a view contrary to Goody's) and to Mesopotamian fatalism.

According to John Rowe (1944: 312), the highland Peruvians believed that all diseases (*oñqoy*) had supernatural causes: the actions of evil spirits, the annoyance of deities over sinful behaviour (including neglect of their cults), sorcery, or loss of the soul as a consequence of fright. Most people were treated by *soñqoyoq* or *kamasqa*, old men and women who had acquired knowledge of the medicinal properties of plants or had themselves recovered from severe illness. The nobility were treated by *hampikamayuq* (medical specialists). Both sorts of curers sought to divine the causes of ailments and apply appropriate natural or supernatural treatments. Collawayna people, who were reputed to possess great knowledge of the curative powers of plants, were obliged to serve the king as doctors. Doctors also recommended purges and bleeding and set broken bones. They sought to counteract witchcraft by removing magical charms that had secretly been injected into people's bodies. Hampikamayuq put some high-ranking sick persons to sleep, presumably using drugs, and claimed to open their bodies and cleanse them of the toads and other charms that sorcerers had injected into them. Ordinary people regarded washing in flowing rivers as a way to cleanse their bodies of diseases. It is unclear if the trepanning – cutting holes in skulls of living people – that was practised in the

Cuzco area was intended to treat injuries to the brain or to remove supernatural charms.

Sacrifices played an important role in Inka healing. The treatment of broken bones involved not only setting them but also sacrificing to appease the spirit who had caused the injury. A high-ranking noble who contracted a very serious illness might sacrifice one of his own children in the hope that the supernatural powers who were attacking him would accept the child's life in place of his own. Midwives got their power from bearing twins and besides delivering babies turned foetuses and induced abortions (Cobo 1990: 164–67; Kendall 1973: 91–94; Rowe 1944: 312–15).

In Egypt the upper classes and perhaps corvée labourers were treated by professional physicans who belonged to the scribal class. Physicians employed by the state were enmeshed in a bureaucratic hierarchy of at least five levels: ordinary (*swnw*), chief (*wr swnw*), inspector (*sḥḏ swnw*), overseer (*ỉmy-r swnw*), and controller (*ḫrp swnw*). The higher ranks may have been medical administrators. Some doctors worked for the king and others for the palace, various members of the royal family, officials, and apparently commoners (*swnw mrt*). In the Old Kingdom female physicians, who were other than midwives, attended high-ranking female members of the royal family. In the service of the upper classes were specialists who treated the eyes, stomach, rectum, teeth, and other parts of the body. Dentists (*swnw ỉbḥ*) were distinguished from tooth-makers (*ỉry ỉbḥ*), who were craft workers. Physicians who served the king often played prominent roles at the royal court. Other royal doctors, who also served as wʿb priests, attested the suitability of sacrificed animals, and doctors may have certified the fitness for human consumption of animals slaughtered for the royal kitchens. The goddess Sakhmet, who was associated with the awesome power of the eye of Re, was the patron deity of doctors.

Despite the great religious significance of embalming, the practical work of mummification was performed by low-ranking craft workers. Doctors do not appear to have taken advantage of the opportunities that embalming offered to study human anatomy. Their medical manuals suggest that their anatomical knowledge was based largely on the examination of animals' entrails. The heart was thought to be the location of an individual's life-force, reason, character, and emotions. It was also the source of all significant bodily functions; blood, tears, saliva, semen, urine, faeces, gases, and bodily poisons came from the heart and were distributed to other parts of the body through veins and other channels (*mtw*). It was believed that female reproductive organs opened into the interior of the body and that the eye was connected to the ear. The Egyptians did not know that blood returned to the heart. The brain's only function was thought to be as a source of mucous.

The Egyptians viewed illnesses as punishments by the gods, demonic afflictions, and results of witchcraft. Disease was believed to be brought about by the blockage of channels, which resulted in the accumulation within the body of bad substances of both internal and external origin. Egyptian medical books identified over two hundred different types of illnesses, none of which related to the lungs, liver, gall-bladder, spleen, pancreas, or kidneys, and prescribed treatments. Specialized works dealt with subjects such as gynaecology and the treatment of physical injuries. Herbs were often used as medicines, but other frequent ingredients included blood, animal faeces, and fingernail dirt. The use of these substances reflected the belief that the best way to purge noxious substances was to accumulate more of them in the body. The frequent use of enemas, vaginal douches, and emetics reflected a similar concern to purge the body of disease-causing impurities. Doctors tended to treat illnesses by natural means unless they proved resistant; then they resorted to supernatural cures. While some medical treatises claimed great antiquity, their writing style indicates otherwise; most major surviving texts appear to have been compiled in the Middle Kingdom. Thereafter, the same medical treatises continued to be copied and consulted for many hundreds of years without any serious attempt to expand, rethink, or replace them (Andreu 1997: 56–57; David 1986: 123–30; Ebeid 1999; Ghalioungui and el Dawakhly 1983; Jonckheere 1958; Nunn 1996; Strouhal 1992: 243–49).

Both of the territorial states for which we have information, Egypt and Inka Peru, had specialists to treat the upper classes. In city-states, the same types of medical practitioners seem to have been available to all classes on a fee-paying basis. The Aztec distinguished medical specialists from folk doctors, but the methods they used were based on the same general principles. In Mesopotamia diviner physicians worked for kings, but the difference between them and ordinary curers was not simply a class one; their basic approaches to healing were quite different.

All early civilizations believed that some or all diseases were caused by witchcraft or the anger and malevolence of the gods. It is not clear that people thought of any illnesses or misfortunes as being purely natural or fortuitous. When it was known how to treat diseases effectively by natural means, this was done. Illnesses that were known not to respond to natural treatment or failed to respond to such treatment were handled supernaturally. Such behaviour accords with a general view in which the world was understood to exhibit cause-and-effect relations in much of its daily working but was also believed to be animated and therefore ultimately controlled by supernatural powers.

None of the early civilizations gave rise to anything resembling the highly distinctive, more elaborate, and far more systematized bodies of medical theory that characterized the later preindustrial civilizations of China, India, Greece, and Rome (Bates 1995). Physicians in early civilizations nevertheless entertained many ideas that were similar to those of these later systems.

A concern with the supernatural dominated other major intellectual creations of the early civilizations. While the production of new medical knowledge appears to have reached a virtual standstill in late Middle Kingdom Egypt, the collection and editing of spells intended to ensure the well-being of individuals after death remained a vital focus of that civilization's intellectual activity. In the Old Kingdom the Pyramid Texts, which were inscribed in royal tombs, performed this function first for kings alone and then for a few queens as well (Faulkner 1969). In the First Intermediate Period the Pyramid Texts evolved into the Coffin Texts, which were available to all who could afford to have them inscribed on their coffins. In the New Kingdom spells, some based on Coffin Texts, were inscribed on papyrus scrolls which were sold to individuals to be buried with them. Almost two hundred chapters of spells were assigned to 'The Spells of Coming Forth by Day' (*rw nw prt m hrw*), better known in English as 'The Book of the Dead'. Some of these chapters, such as 'The Declaration of Innocence' and 'The Judgement of the Dead', were deemed essential elements of this work, but no surviving copy contains every chapter. At the same time, special funerary texts were being inscribed in royal tombs. The composing of new texts to assist the souls of the dead ceased only at the end of the New Kingdom (Sørensen 1989). All these works were based on the belief that magic (ḥk3) played a major role in maintaining the cosmic order. Another form of organized supernatural knowledge was lists of lucky and unlucky days (or parts of days) accompanied by advice for coping with the unlucky ones (D'Auria 1988; Englund 1989b: 24; Faulkner 1985).

In Mesopotamia the main focus of upper-class study was divination. Omen texts appear late in the Old Babylonian period, but allusions to divination abound in historical and religious texts in Early Dynastic times. In later periods neighbouring peoples regarded divination as the Mesopotamians' major intellectual achievement. Mesopotamians believed that the gods communicated their wishes and warnings to humans through dreams, bird flights, the movement of smoke, patterns formed by oil floating on water, earthquakes, thunder, rain, hail, and the births of multiple or malformed children and animals. The most common form of divination was based on the size, shape, and colouring of the livers and other entrails of sacrificed animals. Astronomical observations did not become the major focus of divination until after 1500 B.C. The interpretation of each class of natural phenomena required its own diviner priests. Their goal was to extract the correct messages from omens, so that rituals could be performed to ensure that bad prognostications did not come to pass. While diviners worked for private individuals as well as kings, anxiety for both their own welfare and that of the state made kings the chief patrons of the art of divination.

To try to improve the accuracy of their predictions, diviners kept records of specific divinations and their outcomes. They also amassed detailed information concerning events in the natural world. They sought to transform these observations into generalized statements about what natural occurrences revealed concerning the will of the gods and what might happen in the future if ritual actions were not taken to alter the situation. While these activities have been interpreted as leading to the development of the scientific method, their goal was to assist relations with a universe that was believed to be controlled by powerful and quixotic supernatural forces (Bottéro 1992: 105–42; Crawford 1991: 24; Oppenheim 1964: 206–24).

The Aztec also devoted much attention to divination. Divinatory methods were taught in the religious schools, recorded in almanacs and other manuals, and cultivated by specialist priests. Deities and humans alike were believed to be subject to shifting cosmic forces that vitally affected their personal destinies. Mexicans sought to divine the future so that they could take action to avoid personal and collective misfortune. Aztec diviners determined the fate of a newborn child by casting lots to ascertain how the gods associated with the day of its birth might influence its destiny. Likewise, a merchant setting out on a trading expedition would have his chances of success or failure divined. If the prognostications were not good, sacrifices would be offered to try to improve the situation. There were pictographic guides for interpreting dreams, which were viewed as messages from the supernatural realm. Ball games constituted a form of divination used by rulers. Divinations for the king and members of the nobility were usually performed by expert priests, who were better trained and more highly regarded than those who divined for commoners (León-Portilla 1963: 116–20; Ruiz de Alarcón 1984: 141–55; M. E. Smith 1996: 240–41, 256).

The Maya were deeply interested in the future. The divinations for their upper class appear to have been based largely on astronomical observations. Maya rulers supported detailed studies of the movements of the sun, moon, and planets over long periods in the hope of being able to foretell the future of individuals, kingdoms, and the cosmos. The Maya believed that events of the past repeated themselves in accordance with the motions of heavenly bodies. Cycles of planetary movements were correlated with each other and linked to cycles of the Maya long count, and these observations used to forecast supernatural and historical events. Because of the detailed astronomical data base which their calendar allowed them to create, expert Maya diviners were able to extend their calculations of planetary and stellar conjunctions far beyond anything commoners could attempt (Aveni 1992).

The Inka elite also elaborated special forms of divination. Fire divination, practised by specialists called *yakarka* who came from Waro, near Cuzco, was used to uncover treason. A special form of lung divination (*kalpa*), which involved inflating the lungs of sacrificed llamas, was employed to determine issues of major importance to the king, such as the outcome of military campaigns or the choice of an heir to the throne. More routine issues were divined using the lungs of birds or guinea pigs. Other forms of divination included observing the forms taken by smoke rising from sacrifices, casting pebbles, beans, or maize kernels, and observing the movements of spiders or snakes. These simpler forms were used for deciding whether to plant crops, travel, or marry and how to cure common illnesses. Guidance was also sought from the dead speaking through spirit mediums, through spirit possession involving the thunder god Illapa and other nature deities, and by having mediums prophesy while they were intoxicated or influenced by drugs. Both divination and oracular communication were practised by commoners as well as by the upper classes, but the forms employed by the latter were more elaborate and more carefully controlled by the state (MacCormack 1991: 303–6; Rowe 1944: 302–4).

At the Shang court, divination received lavish royal attention and patronage. Scapulimantic diviners kept records of the successes and failures of their divinations, apparently in an effort to improve their methods. They also kept records of solar and lunar eclipses, including ones that were observed only in remote provinces, and information about the weather and the movements of the planets, which were believed to affect the fortunes of the kingdom and its rulers (Chêng 1960: 226–27; Keightley 1978a; 1999b; 1999c).

A Yoruba diviner had to memorize and learn the various meanings of more than one thousand verses that facilitated the interpretation of divinatory procedures and guided him in prescribing sacrifices that were appropriate for gaining a desired blessing or averting misfortune.

The most important upper-class intellectual activities in early civilizations were concerned with improving relations with the supernatural powers that animated the cosmos. These activities were focused on divining the will of the gods, deflecting their anger, maintaining the cosmic order, averting illness, helping individuals after death, and averting social calamities. Analogous concerns were shared by the lower classes, but the upper classes were able to sponsor specialists to develop divinatory techniques that they hoped would benefit themselves and their kingdoms. Such efforts often encouraged the detailed observation of natural phenomena, but their primary goal was to regulate relations with the supernatural and natural orders.

KNOWLEDGE AND ITS USES

Scholars such as Gordon Childe (1965 [1936]) and Benjamin Farrington (1936) maintained that theoretical as opposed to practical knowledge was first produced by the scribes of early civilizations, but they believed that the initial objective of systematic observation of the natural world was not the enhancement of technical knowledge but the cultivation of techniques for sociopolitical control and the manipulation of the supernatural. Technological knowledge, when its development was not actively discouraged, was regarded as the preserve of craft workers and farmers. Thus the distinction between a managerial class that was exempt from manual labour and lower-class artisans and farmers was reflected in a dichotomy between thinking about nature and acting on it. This distinction, Childe and Farrington claimed, in some early civilizations eventually created hitherto unknown dichotomies between mind and matter, subject and object, and society and nature. They argued that the rulers of early civilizations rejected the pursuit of scientific knowledge in favour of magic and superstition because they regarded the latter as powerful techniques for social control and therefore supportive of their own despotic power. Childe, as a Marxist, identified technological change as a threat to the established social order that early ruling classes instinctively feared. As a result of upper-class patronage of magic and superstition, he suggested, far more magical lore than craft knowledge was preserved in written form, and craft knowledge itself was probably riddled with ritual and magic designed to restrict highly developed crafts to small groups of practitioners.

This sort of functional explanation may be misleading. Early civilizations had inherited a general view of the cosmos in which no significant distinction was drawn between the natural and supernatural realms and these realms differed from society only in degree. Perception of the social order as a terrestrial copy of the cosmic order precluded the concept of cultural progress that Childe and Farrington saw the rulers of early civilizations resisting. However much early civilizations changed, the most powerful models for human behaviour and social order were believed to have been revealed to humans by supernatural forces when the world was created. Cause and effect were understood to be operative in everyday life but regarded as contingent aspects of a cosmic order that reflected the potentially changeable will of the divine powers that animated the natural world. In some early civilizations the ultimate causality was an unalterable fate built into the structure of the universe, but more often and more proximally it was a personal process by which individual deities created and managed the cosmos by issuing orders. The aim of rulers was to sustain the divine model of social organization that had long ago been established or revealed to humans by the gods. Within this framework, no one was likely to have regarded a lack of significant development in medicine or technology as abnormal or technological change as something that had to be resisted. The long-term attention paid to the elaboration of divination and magic in Egypt and Mesopotamia is evidence of the importance that the rulers of early civilizations accorded to understanding the supernatural and finding ways to placate or control it.

While supernatural concerns sometimes encouraged careful observations of the natural world that in later, neighbouring civilizations would play a role in the development of scientific knowledge, these observations were made within a framework in which science and magic were not distinguished from one another because nature and the supernatural were not differentiated. Rulers sought supernatural power to control the natural forces on which the welfare of society and ultimately their own political and personal power depended. The same view of the cosmos encouraged farmers and craft workers to combine their detailed knowledge of cause and effect and of ritual to produce food and goods. Rulers seeking to control relations with the supernatural with respect to matters about which there were no routine understandings of cause and effect were forced to rely on divination and magic.

A concern with manipulating and gaining the support of supernatural powers was ubiquitous in early civilizations. Amulets, incantations, and divination were employed to ward off evil and win the protection of benevolent deities, and scribes and priests were encouraged to develop ever more effective techniques. The worldview of early civilizations encouraged the conviction that the natural world could be most effectively controlled by supernatural means. The main aim of research was to obtain a better understanding not of the nature of things but of how to shape more favourable relations with the supernatural. In this endeavour, general similarities among the beliefs of early civilizations appear to have been grounded in ideas that were already present in the various societies that gave rise to them. This does not rule out the possibility that common psychological tendencies were important in shaping human behaviour in these societies. It does suggest, however, that these psychological factors must be understood in a broader historical context.

26 Values and Personal Aspirations

Beliefs varied greatly from one early civilization to another concerning the nature of an ideal human life and what characterized a successful individual. Despite many similarities in social and economic institutions, life as experienced by an Aztec must have differed greatly from life as it was experienced by a Mesopotamian or a Yoruba. Inspired by the views of the eighteenth-century German philosopher Johann Herder, cultural relativists have interpreted these experiential variations as vindicating the humanist claim that every culture is a unique expression of the human spirit that is worthy of study for its own sake (Vernant 1995).

The source materials available for studying these variations largely concern the understandings and aspirations of high-ranking males, but these ideals were probably shared or at least admired to some extent by most people in the society. Consensus could have been either a product of status emulation or a reflection of long-established, culturally specific views that were retained and adapted to new situations as societies developed more complex class hierarchies. The lack of comparable data concerning the values and aspirations of women in early civilizations invites the suggestion that greater cross-cultural similarities in their roles as wives, mothers, and homemakers made their views about themselves more similar than those of men, but this conclusion may simply impose androcentric prejudices on early civilizations. Opportunities for women to participate in the political and economic activities of their societies varied greatly from one early civilization to another. Women must have used the varied social ideologies of their societies to construct culturally distinctive roles for themselves within their families and communities. It would seem that, along with male commoners, they participated to varying degrees in a set of social values and aspirations that were realized most fully in the lifestyles of upper-class males and are documented most fully in relation to such individuals. Women must often have exploited these ideals in pursuit of their own objectives. At the same time, they would have had reasons to view male ideals and aspirations ambivalently and even critically.

IDEAL LIFESTYLES

Ideal behaviour for the ancient Egyptian male was expounded in great detail in Egyptian books of wisdom or instruction (*sb3yt*) – in fact, career manuals – which began to be composed in the late Old Kingdom. The model was the successful government official. The ideal official sought always to appear calm, polite, self-effacing, and cautious as well as transparently honest and efficient. He was described as a 'silent' or 'reserved' man (*gr*) and as a 'knowing' man (*rḫ*), which meant that, unlike a 'fool' (*wḫ3*), he was able to control his anger and conceal both his resentments and his ambitions. He knew how to behave so as not to offend his superiors or annoy equals with whom he had to cooperate as well as compete. He treated those under his command politely and with consideration but made sure that they respected and obeyed him. He was generous as a way of cultivating friends and recruiting supporters.

The ideal official was expected to remain composed even when subjected to severe provocation. Every aspect of his conduct was guided by rules of dignified behaviour that he had learned in the course of his education. Self-control, combined with administrative talent, was viewed as the best way to avoid being disgraced by enemies and rivals and to attract the notice, support, and preferment of senior officials. Responsible behaviour was viewed as according with the cosmic order upon which the survival and satisfactory functioning of both Egypt and the universe depended. In the terrestrial realm, the chief force sustaining that order was the Egyptian monarch, and being a good team worker was a manifestation of loyalty to the king.

Moderation under all circumstances was advocated. To be successful a man had to avoid boasting, drinking too much wine, losing his temper, getting into brawls, or associating with men who had a reputation for behaving badly or who might be suspected of subversive behaviour. Adulterous affairs and relations with prostitutes were to be avoided not for moral reasons but so as not to be drawn into dangerous disputes and entanglements with their male kinsmen. Early marriage with a suitable woman was advocated as the best means to ensure a man's respectability. A prudent bureaucrat would never eat too much, especially when invited to dine with his superiors, since gluttony suggested a general lack of self-control. He had to avoid engaging in idle gossip or saying things that might embarrass or annoy his superiors. A superior's mistakes were to be drawn to his attention privately and very discreetly, if at all. The wisest course was often to let a superior get himself into trouble rather than oppose his policies and risk angering him. Functionaries who carefully followed these instructions could take comfort in the thought that superiors or rivals who were boastful, greedy, dishonest, or quarrelsome would eventually be demoted or barred from holding office.

The ultimate ambition of an Egyptian official was to be sufficently successful that he could live a quiet family life free from the cares and conflicts of public office. The favourite setting for such a life was a rural estate, where an official could relax, fish, and perhaps hunt for his amusement, enjoy the visits of his friends, and oversee farming operations. These ideals, which were explicitly formulated and expounded by administrators and scribes and inculcated in members of the upper and administrative classes in the schools, provided a model of male conduct for the whole of society. While the lower classes were caricatured as quarrelsome and violent, status emulation encouraged them to copy the manners and attitudes exemplified by their social superiors (J. Allen 2000: 258–59; Morenz 1973: 117–23).

Men and women living in the Valley of Mexico were urged to cultivate moderation, responsibility, and restraint in their communal life. Politeness was a key virtue and boasting a manifestation of extreme bad taste. The more high-ranking people were, the more selflessly they were expected to behave. Individuals were expected to be serious and calm – to speak, eat, and walk slowly, avoid interrupting others, obey superiors and elders, and help the needy. Honesty, hard work, and service to family and city were extolled as virtues, and competitiveness and aggressiveness were supposed to be curbed by a deep concern for the welfare of fellow citizens. Humour was not valued. Individuals were encouraged to feel that they were constantly being observed and evaluated by those around them. Although violence in the form of war and human sacrifice was common, its occurrence was carefully controlled by the state. Yet, despite these ideals, Aztec men were competitive, and eager to enhance their positions in society. Commoners were described by the upper classes as being quarrelsome and litigious. Gambling, ritual ball games, and especially warfare were sources of considerable prestige for men who were successful in these endeavours, but soldiers could lose their lives and gamblers end up as debt slaves. These activities were viewed as ones in which individual prowess, skill, bravery, and supernatural favour counted for more than effective teamwork.

The supreme male ideal was to be a successful warrior. All men were expected to be prepared to sacrifice their lives defending their city-state or trying to enhance its power. The public oration that accompanied the birth of every Aztec boy asserted that his main purpose in life was to be a soldier. Schools for commoners concentrated principally on military training, while young men of the upper class received military instruction as part of a more extensive education. Women's reproductive functions were militarized by equating child-bearing with a man's risking his life in battle. Young noblemen were required to validate their hereditary privileges by distinguishing themselves in military operations and risking debilitating wounds and capture or death in battle. For commoners the only legitimate way to advance was by capturing enemy warriors in battle. Valour was rewarded by kings' publicly conferring on individual warriors the right to wear elaborate, minutely graded costumes and insignia, memberships in military orders, and extensive social and economic privileges according to the number of enemy warriors they had captured. Men who never captured an enemy in battle were subjected for the rest of their lives to various public humiliations. The sacrifices it required of men made waging war the key activity defining their worth. Long-distance traders were despised because they did not fight for their city-states, but even they carried arms and were prepared to defend themselves valiantly if attacked (Bray 1968: 35–38; Clendinnen 1991: 46, 141–45; Soustelle 1961: 217–24).

Early Dynastic Mesopotamian elite art and literature glorified male political competition and heroic struggle (Pollock 1991: 383). Rulers sought to increase their power and wealth by dominating one another and extending their control over adjacent city-states, while individual scribes and craft workers competed to be recognized as outstanding in their professions (Kramer 1981: 11). The hero-rulers of ancient times dared to taunt and oppose deities, although they never succeeded in overcoming them (R. McC. Adams 1966: 151). Yet, in their everyday lives, Mesopotamians were enmeshed in activities related to farming and commerce. For men the most important source of prestige was owning enough farm land and urban property to live comfortably on the income derived from their investments rather than having to engage personally in manual labour or long-distance trade. Such a life was modelled on that of the gods, the divine landowners for whom all human beings worked as paid labourers or tenant farmers. Men who owned much property had the leisure to participate in the business of city councils and law courts, and these activities enhanced their prestige and political power. Successful merchants invested their profits in land and property in the hope that eventually they could abandon long-distance trading and shift from the traders' area into the city proper to participate in its esteemed lifestyle (Oppenheim 1969; Van De Mieroop 1999: 212–13).

Western Zhou society, according to Mark Lewis (1990: 7), was dominated by a militaristic upper class set apart from the rest of the population by its devotion to elaborate ancestral cults. These cults involved blood sacrifices that the nobility supplied in part through warfare and hunting. The ritually encoded acts of violence that characterized the lives of the Zhou ruling class were therefore linked to their most venerable religious practices. Such relations appear to have characterized the value system of the Shang upper class to an even greater degree. David Keightley (1978b: 222–23) has argued that the rituals which governed relations between the Shang upper class and its ancestors were characterized by a love of order that effectively bureaucratized these relations. He maintains that office-holding was regarded as superior to any other occupation and that in due course gaining administrative office became a man's chief goal in life. Holding high administrative office was, however, intimately associated with warfare, violence, and human sacrifice. Keightley (1987) also argues that a marked concern for modularity and the imposition of unusual forms and uses on material objects in late prehistoric times anticipated a later preoccupation with ritual and decorum among the Chinese upper class. These differences may have been linked to the segmentary, rather than bureaucratic, nature of the regional political administration in northern China, looser political organization having encouraged more use of ritual and symbolism to promote political unity.

The Yoruba emphasized competition as the quintessential affirmation of the individual, but, they also valued a combination of forcefulness (*ase*), composure (*itutu*), and character (*iwa*) – which resulted in the use of power to benefit rather than harm other people (R. Thompson 1976: P/1). Competition not only occurred overtly in the economic and political arenas but was symbolically encoded in community and religious rituals. Political contests occurred between leaders on the same level of government or different ones and often involved efforts by untitled but ambitious men to increase their reputations and followings.

Andean males from earliest childhood cultivated the ability to ignore pain (Classen 1993: 75). Coming-of-age rituals involved personal endurance tests and military contests. These rituals were especially elaborate in the case of the Inka male nobility, whose collective coming-of-age ceremony was held under the auspices of the royal court in and around Cuzco each December as part of the summer solstice feast of Inti Raymi. In the course of this ceremony, which involved beatings and armed combat to test their bravery, young nobles were transformed into adult warriors and instructed that their principal duty was to risk their lives to defend and enlarge the Inka state. Bernabé Cobo (1990: 126–33, 215) reports that military activities were considered the most important and noble ones in which an Inka man could engage.

COUNTER-IDEALS

There were also counter-ideals. In New Kingdom school texts Egyptian scribes scolded young men who thought of abandoning their formal education to join the army (Lichtheim 1976: 171–72), contrasting the superficial attractions of a military career with the brutal realities of army life and the long-term benefits of becoming scribes. The existence of this literature suggests that the adventure associated with military life appealed strongly to many young men. Throughout Egyptian history, military officers were never portrayed wearing military uniforms; instead they were represented as scribes and government officials (Martin 1991: 47–88). It was impossible for a man to become a high-ranking military officer without first becoming literate and a member of the administrative class. This demonstrates both the strength of the idea of the official as the model to which all men should conform and the extent to which bureaucratic ideals intruded into even the least pacific spheres of Egyptian society.

In the Valley of Mexico, long-distance traders celebrated their adherence to their own ideals of commercial rivalry with competitive feasting, which established relative social status among them. They also sacrificed prisoners, whom they had purchased rather than captured, in an attempt to win public esteem. This was especially important for aspirants to leadership roles in the merchant community that involved interaction with the king and royal officials. Yet to offer human sacrifices merchants had to secure the support of leading warriors, and therefore these sacrifices also symbolized the subordination of merchants and their distinctive values to the hegemonic values that were associated with the larger society and especially with its military leaders (Clendinnen 1991: 136–38).

A more radical counter-ideal was embodied in the religious movement in the Valley of Mexico that opposed the idea of blood sacrifices to sustain the cosmic order. This movement, promoted by certain learned men, appears to have received some support from Nezahualcoyotl, the king of Texcoco. He was angered by the Aztec upper class's manipulation of Mesoamerican religious-military beliefs to justify not only their control of a vast tributary network but also their increasing political domination of their allies within the Triple Alliance. These alternative concepts claimed historical and religious roots in the Quetzalcoatl who had ruled the ancient city of Tollan, but they do not appear to have been sufficiently influential to produce any fundamental questioning of the aspirations and understandings that shaped individual values throughout the region (León-Portilla 1992: 163–67, 190; Townsend 1979: 35–36).

The Yoruba subscribed to two antithetical lifestyles: that of the successful warrior-politician, who mobilized supporters and acquired wealth and power within a community, and that of the contemplative sage or wise man, who was expected to use his divinatory skills to promote harmony and well-being and hold families and communities together. The warrior-politician and the sage exemplified the complementary qualities of compulsion and harmony that the Yoruba regarded as fundamental components of the supernatural realm. These qualities were linked to an equally fundamental dichotomy between disorder and order that was associated with the trickster god Esu and Ifa, the god of wisdom, and with the cities of Oyo and Ife (Apter 1992: 29). Yet, among both violent and contemplative individuals, struggles for personal preeminence were consistent with the competitiveness that constituted the universally shared value of Yoruba culture. What distinguished the Yoruba from the Egyptians, Aztec, and Mesopotamians, with their single-minded focus on bureaucratic skill, warfare, or landowning as a cultural ideal, was the Yorubas' acceptance that two radically different goals could be equally important. Nevertheless, many more Yoruba men sought to excel as warriors and politicians than as sages.

THE IMPACT OF CULTURAL TRADITIONS

Early civilizations exhibited a broad range of behavioural ideals. Some of this variation may have been influenced by social and ecological factors. For one thing, there appears to have been greater emphasis on individual competitiveness in city-state systems and on personal subordination to bureaucratic routines or state goals in territorial states. Again, the strong emphasis on militarism in the Valley of Mexico may have been encouraged by the exceptionally dense population of that region in late pre-Hispanic times, increasing competition over land and other resources. The high value placed on land ownership in southern Mesopotamia could have been related to the importance of controlling crop surpluses in that alluvial region as a basis for procuring essential raw materials by means of long-distance trade. The Egyptians' idealization of the quiet, self-controlled official could perhaps only have developed in a society that had no significant external enemies. The similar values of the Chinese mandarinate did not acquire ascendancy until after the Chinese state came to control so much of East Asia that it no longer had any serious rivals; in Shang and Zhou times military prowess was valued much more highly than it was later. It has also, however, been suggested that privileging learning instead of violence evolved within the framework of formalist values that already had a long history in Chinese culture (Keightley 1978b).

Yet short-term functional explanations of this sort do not explain the development of enduring cultural traditions. While the Yoruba appear to have been as warlike as the Aztec or the Inka, instead of glorifying military prowess as the supreme male ideal they embraced a life of action and a life of contemplation as equally acceptable alternatives. Moreover, while Chinese history demonstrates that concepts of the self can change significantly with political and economic conditions, ancient Egyptian and Mesopotamian ideals endured for millennia despite significant political and ecological transformations. Aztec values, which were grounded in a belief that war and bloodshed were required to sustain the cosmic order, appear to have been of great antiquity in Mesoamerica. The values that influenced personal aspirations in early civilizations often seem to have taken the form of long-enduring cultural traditions. While particular social or ecological factors may at some early period have significantly influenced these traditions, the values themselves acquired sufficient autonomy to survive considerable alteration in material circumstances.

The impact of these idiosyncratic values on life in the various early civilizations was far from trivial. Men who were temperamentally predisposed to feel comfortable in Egyptian society probably would have felt psychologically stressed and ill at ease had they found themselves living among the Aztec, while individuals temperamentally suited to pursue Aztec goals would have found life dull and repressed had they lived in ancient Egypt. Yoruba civilization offered a choice of ideal lifestyles within a general framework that stressed individual competitiveness. While the plasticity of human nature probably led most people to accept as normal the goals set by the society into which they were born, it is clear that the core values of different early civilizations made life in each early civilization unique.

In an examination of later preindustrial civilizations, John Hall (1986: 33–83) has argued that, from the Han Dynasty to the beginning of the twentieth century, the Confucian mandarinate succeeded in inhibiting the development of dynamic, semi-autonomous economic and military sectors in Chinese society. They did this in part to protect the interests of their own governing class but also to safeguard the large but fragile Chinese state from changes that might have encouraged institutional or regional autonomy. Hall also attributed the weakness of the political order in India to the withdrawal of the Brahmins from the political sphere, although they continued to play an important role in regulating Hindu daily life, and asserted that the way in which these two preindustrial civilizations were organized precluded developments analogous to the industrial revolution.

Christopher Hallpike (1986: 288–371) suggests that inflexible 'core principles' – patterns of behaviour and belief that are not directly related to modes of subsistence – supply sets of general propositions that guide the elaboration of the knowledge and values of historically related societies. He maintains that these sets of values originate as a result of historical accidents analogous to the operation of random variation or the founder's effect in biological evolution but, once formulated, influence cultural development for long periods. Their role is therefore a constraining one. Hallpike identifies the core principles that have shaped Chinese society since at least the late first millennium B.C. as including rejection of a series of activities that were highly valued in some other cultures: war, militarism, interpersonal conflict, public debate, litigation, and the public humiliation of high-ranking individuals. All these activities were believed to violate a cosmic order in which forces that were antithetical and unequal to one another but essential for the operation of the cosmos constituted a harmonious, self-regulating, organic unity. Thus the use of military force or the resort to legal action to regulate relations between individuals was viewed as threatening to undermine the cosmic and therefore the social order (312–29).

The core principles shared by the Indo-European-speaking peoples, according to Hallpike, included approval of competitive individualism as manifested in athletic competitions and verbal exchanges, admiration of warfare combined with personal loyalty to military leaders, uninhibited use of civil law to regulate interpersonal disputes, the individual pursuit of wealth, and the idea of representative government as embodied in an assembly. Both legal systems and assemblies were viewed as terrestrial versions of arrangements that operated on the cosmic level. While the Chinese regarded large patrilineal descent groups as constituting the basis of social order, the Indo-Europeans, although also favouring patrilineal forms of social organization, avoided large descent groups. Free Indo-Europeans were divided into three orders – priests, warriors, and farmers – which provided the basis for a later dichotomy between church and state (1986: 329–49). By contrast, the Chinese, from the late Zhou period on, divided society into a descending hierarchy of officials, farmers, artisans, and traders, attaching little importance to priests and equating religion (*zhao*) with moral teaching (315).

That the cultural traditions defined by core principles can persist over long periods despite major changes in technology, environmental settings, and demography is evident, Hallpike claims, in the many features shared by Indo-European societies, despite these societies' being dispersed over a region stretching from Western Europe to India. This, he says, means that it is possible to predict more about a culture by knowing the linguistic family to which it belongs than by knowing its environmental setting. He also argues that capitalism is not a universal stage of human development but a specific manifestation of Indo-European values (370–71), a position that generally agrees with Hall's. If Hallpike is right, enduring cultural traditions that were at least semi-autonomous with respect to ecological adaptation helped to shape the value systems and functioning of early civilizations.

The fact that early civilizations that had broadly similar class structures, analogous arrangements that permitted the upper classes to appropriate most surplus production, a limited range of political organization, and formally similar religious beliefs should have developed such distinctive and persistent beliefs concerning what constituted a good life indicates the power of culturally constructed understandings to shape some aspects of human behaviour independently of materially adaptive factors. Unlike art styles, which displayed idiosyncratic variation but had no practical impact on everyday life, these values exerted enormous influence on how people behaved in early civilizations, how they thought about themselves, and how their civilizations functioned.

The religiously based military ethos of highland Mesoamerica encouraged armed conflict and socially and politically devalued long-distance trade. The importance accorded to military prowess made it impossible for merchants to compete for political power. The Egyptian idealization of bureaucratic values may explain why, despite their large population, they were never as formidable militarily as their numbers might suggest. The extension of civilian administrative values to the military sphere seems to have inhibited the development of a distinctive military ethos even in the New Kingdom, when the army had become institutionally more differentiated from the rest of society than ever before. Personal value systems played a key role in shaping behaviour in every early civilization. Contrary to what materialist anthropologists have claimed, these value systems were neither epiphenomenal nor socially irrelevant.

Yet cross-cultural regularities indicate that the power of such ideals to shape behaviour was subject to important limitations. This is particularly so with respect to material self-interest. Whether the highest ideal posited by a society was for a man to be an outstanding warrior, a rich landowner, or a successful bureaucrat, those who were successful all believed that it was essential for them to sustain their power, privileges, and luxurious lifestyles at the expense of farmers and other manual workers. The Egyptian bureaucrat who strove to embody the ideals of the 'quiet man' was no less prepared to use coercion and violence to suppress opposition among the lower classes than the Aztec warrior-official. Doing this involved exercising similar kinds of social controls, including military and police repression, upper-class manipulation of legal systems, continued recruitment of corvée labour, protection of institutional and private forms of land ownership, and maintenance of ideologies that sought to justify the upper classes' domination over the labouring classes. Those controls, rather than some innate obsession with cruelty and violence (D. Carrasco 1990; Sagan 1985), encouraged the development of similar attitudes towards power and upper-class rights in all early civilizations. While most Aztec, as well as the Imperial Chinese ruling class, may have despised and socially penalized the commercial acquisition of wealth (Hallpike 1986: 325), all members of the upper classes appreciated the need to control wealth in order to retain power and continue to enjoy an enhanced standard of living. Economic and political interests thus tended to be viewed similarly, and these uniformities imposed significant cross-cultural limitations on the operations of idiosyncratic cultural traditions. Thus the role of such traditions in shaping behaviour, while important, may have been more restricted than some extreme cultural determinists have maintained.

VALUES AND SELF-INTEREST

Idiosyncratic cultural traditions which assigned specific values to particular sorts of individual behaviour had the power to privilege certain kinds of actions at the expense of others. Such traditions not only established differing social agendas that distinguished one early civilization from another but, more important, constrained their development in idiosyncratically specific ways over long periods. Scholars who study differing perceptions and values have no difficulty in demonstrating that each early civilization was a unique expression of human creativity. Yet, while all human behaviour is culturally mediated, culturally idiosyncratic solutions guided human behaviour only in those spheres where similar ecological constraints or universal considerations of self-interest did not directly constrain such behaviour. In these underdetermined spheres, cultural choices provided the cognitive and psychological structuring that was required for a society to function properly. Without adequate agreement about what constituted appropriate behaviour, disruptions, conflict, and personal disorientation would render a society dysfunctional. As Ernest Gellner (1982) argued, what is purely cultural must impose some kind of order or structure on itself in order to be comprehensible. This does not mean that cultural prescriptions had to be inflexible or that everyone had to accept and follow them precisely, but an individual cannot rebel against rules unless rules exist.

Despite these great variations in lifestyle, in matters that relate to economic and political self-interest we find that the ruling classes of early civilizations conceptualized their power and privileges and the way in which they should deal with the lower classes in much the same manner. Their behaviour was therefore grounded in something other than idiosyncratic or free cultural choice. Evolutionary ecologists, who focus on the clearly adaptive aspects of human behaviour, have tended to interpret all such cross-cultural uniformities as a justification for an ecologically based, unilinear view of cultural evolution, but this approach ignores vast differences in the environmental settings, demography, and productive arrangements of early civilizations. Many of the important cross-cultural similarities that relate to political power and the control of wealth in early civilizations appear by default to be grounded in little-understood species-specific tendencies to handle these issues in similar ways. This again raises important psychological questions.

27 Cultural Constants and Variables

The collective identity of each early civilization was expressed by a distinctive and highly elaborated upper-class culture that formally symbolized that civilization's unity and differentiated it from neighbouring societies. The patronage of these elite traditions helped to distinguish the upper from the lower classes while identifying the upper classes with the civilization as a whole. Each early civilization possessed its own religious beliefs, myths, and festivals and its own distinctive style(s) of art, architecture, music, and dance. The most ambitious forms of conspicuous consumption in early civilizations were the sponsorship by rulers and the upper classes of the production of monumental architecture and high-quality works of art. The deployment of large amounts of lower-class labour to erect buildings that became symbols of upper-class dominance constituted further evidence of the power of the upper classes.

In territorial states, the culture of rural dwellers was regionally variable, while that of the upper classes was statewide and unitary. In city-state systems, local variants of the elite culture frequently distinguished one polity and its leaders from another, while pancivilizational similarities signalled the shared membership of the upper classes in a broader upper-class interaction network. There were, however, differences in the extent to which upper-class traditions were distinguished from those of commoners. In city-state systems, especially those that lacked a hereditary nobility, high-quality art tended to be a technically superior and aesthetically more sophisticated version of commoner art, while in territorial states it developed radically different canons and was produced by artists working full-time for the state rather than simultaneously for upper-class patrons and the marketplace. In territorial states, stringent upper-class controls and guidelines tended to unify production stylistically, while in city-states different groups of craft workers developed and perpetuated their own styles. There was also considerable variation among early civilizations in the materials that were preferred for making works of art. Imported raw materials were often used to produce luxury goods for upper-class clients. Although elite art works were created, as material expressions of secular and supernatural power, for the ruling classes in all early civilizations, the styles of these works varied idiosyncratically from one early civilization to another. There was iconographic as well as stylistic cross-cultural variation, although iconographic differences were not totally idiosyncratic. The particular styles and iconography of upper-class art and architecture tended to be established at an early stage in the development of a civilization. While such art changed slowly thereafter, innovations occurred within the context of an established cultural tradition.

In all early civilizations, monumental architecture was consistently distinguished from ordinary structures. In addition to having a distinctive and unified style, monumental architecture was used symbolically in various other ways to integrate societies. In city-states, large buildings – temples or palaces or both – invariably marked the centres of cities. While monumental architecture manifested the political power and wealth of those who sponsored it, the basic functional types remained strictly limited: tombs, temples, palaces, and fortifications. All forms of monumental architecture developed from earlier fortifications and from houses, which in early civilizations were differentiated for the use of kings and other members of the upper classes, gods, and dead members of the upper classes. In city-states, temples and palaces tended to express community identity as well as royal and divine authority, while in territorial states palaces, temples, walled administrative compounds, forts, and rulers' tombs signalled royal authority.

Each early civilization cultivated distinctive social values and personal aspirations. These were most explicitly defined for high-status males and, once formulated, endured for long periods. There may have been a tendency to value individual competitiveness more highly in city-states and conformity to bureaucratic and state goals more highly in territorial ones. Yet specific value complexes, such as Aztec militarism, Egyptian self-control, and Yoruba competitiveness, while too enduring to be explainable in narrowly functional terms, influenced individual behaviour and thus each society's capacity to pursue specific goals. These values also made each early civilization unique. They did not, however, impact the ability of the upper classes to control resources and manpower and to protect their privileges using very similar techniques.

RELIGION

In addition to a vast array of idiosyncratic concepts, religious beliefs displayed significant cross-cultural uniformity. The presence of religious beliefs in all human societies seems associated with panhuman cognitive abilities that must have been produced by natural selection in the course of biological evolution. These abilities include heightened individual self-awareness, the pervasive role of metaphor in thinking, and habitual anthropomorphization (Boyer 1994; 1996; Mithen 1996; Tilley 1999). As individual humans grew more conscious of the perils that confronted them in the natural and social realms, they sought to alleviate psychic stress by postulating a universe controlled by supernatural forces that were not indifferent to humans and might be persuaded to protect them. Religious beliefs sought to account for the origin and nature of the cosmos and the forces that animated it, the origin and nature of human beings, the fate of individual humans after death, and the way in which humans might regulate relations with the supernatural to their advantage. The beliefs that were associated with specific early civilizations seem to have represented attempts by people of particular cultures to answer essential questions about the nature of the universe and their relations to it.

The rulers of all early civilizations expended vast amounts of wealth and energy on religious buildings, cult equipment, celebrations, and sacrifices. Each early civilization venerated its own deities, conceptualized them in terms of distinctive beliefs, myths, and legends, and devised rituals to worship them. The totality of religious beliefs and practices associated with each early civilization was an original and unique creation.

At the same time, the people in every early civilization assumed that the supernatural was immanent in the natural world as the power animating the physical landscape, plants, animals, and human beings. While this power consisted of primal energy, it was invariably personified and manifested itself not as one but as many individual deities. Individual deities often took more than one form, and their degree of physical anthropomorphization varied from one early civilization to another. Deities were capable to varying degrees of merging with one another or separating to form distinctive entities. They represented powers of the natural world that were believed to possess human faculties and personalities, including gender identity. Because they had these attributes, it was possible for human beings to communicate and bargain with them. Yet, because they also represented the forces of nature, they were far more powerful and long-lived than individual human beings. They were also unequal in power among themselves and often in conflict with one another. While deities formed hierarchies that corresponded with their respective degrees of power, these were often loose hierarchies resembling the arrangement of forces found in the natural world. Apart from a few creator gods, hierarchies among deities were not immutable.

The concept of nature's being animated by supernatural forces that possessed human-like personalities meant that no clear distinction could be drawn between what today we see as the natural, supernatural, and social realms. Because of this, the natural world was not viewed as something that could be manipulated solely or even principally by means of systematic observation, understanding, and practical action. People living in early civilizations understood causal relations and regularly used such knowledge to exploit the natural world, but their belief that the cosmos was animated by supernatural powers inspired the conviction that ultimately humans could most effectively manipulate the natural world for their own purposes by establishing friendly relations with the deities that controlled it or gaining power over these deities. This conviction precluded the recognition of any need to develop a scientific view of the cosmos.

People in all early civilizations believed that a supernaturally animated nature sustained human life and that the gods depended on human offerings to replenish their powers. This mutual dependence generated a cosmic cycle in which energy was circulated from the supernatural realm into the human world and back again. The degree of self-sufficiency attributed to the gods varied from the Mesopotamians' belief that without humans the lesser gods would have to cultivate fields and build temples to the Aztecs' conviction that, without an endless supply of human blood, the supernatural forces that sustained the universe would quickly cease to operate. Offerings were intended to nourish the gods literally rather than metaphorically and normally consisted of food and drink or the lives of animals and human beings. Because of their dependence on offerings, deities in the early civilizations were not transcendental as they were in most later preindustrial civilizations. It was only once the gods were no longer believed to depend on human support that offering them sacrifices became a purely metaphorical or symbolic act.

Within this system of belief, farmers created the resources that sustained themselves, the upper classes, the gods, and the cosmic order. Every family made offerings to deities, who often included their dead ancestors, but the upper classes and in particular the king were especially important intermediaries in conveying energy from the human to the supernatural realm. Their ability to accumulate surplus resources on a larger scale than anyone else made it possible for them to sustain the gods more lavishly than commoners. They also possessed specialized ritual knowledge about how to relate to the gods. The ritual activities of the king were viewed as crucial for maintaining the universe. Kings, not priests, were responsible for offering major sacrifices. When priests sacrificed on behalf of the king, they did so as his substitutes or agents. Major sacrifices were usually made in ritually exclusive settings, such as the interiors of temples and on elevated temple platforms – places accessible only to rulers, priests, and members of the upper classes. Public participation in state-sponsored rituals involved mass dancing, singing, and participation in religious dramas that celebrated the natural changes and human activities associated with the annual seasonal cycle. These rituals sought to renew the world and reinforce the social order by strengthening relations with the gods and revitalizing the universe.

While beliefs concerning what was appropriate for sacrifice and how sacrificial rituals should be performed varied from one early civilization to another, the basic concepts concerning sacrifice were the same. Since these ideas differed significantly from concepts of sacrifice in less complex societies and could not have diffused from a single point of origin among all the early civilizations, they must have been formulated separately in individual early civilizations. There appears, however, to have been a high degree of cross-cultural uniformity in the general patterns of religious beliefs among the societies out of which early civilizations had developed. Not clearly distinguishing the natural, supernatural, and social realms seems to have been typical of all societies prior to the desacralization of nature that took place in most Eurasian civilizations in the middle of the first millennium B.C. In simpler societies, where all social relations tended to be modelled on kinship ties, relations between the human and the natural/supernatural spheres were formulated in terms of requests for parental benevolence from the supernatural or the need for humans to sustain and obey the spirits of deceased ancestors who controlled the fertility of the land. In early civilizations, views of the supernatural as real or metaphorical kin gave way to a belief that the gods constituted a superior social stratum. The understanding of the supernatural that developed in early civilizations therefore seems to have resulted from the reworking of a relatively uniform set of beliefs about the supernatural in earlier societies to reflect the more hierarchical structure of societies that were no longer being held together at the highest levels by kinship relations.

The conceptualization of sacrifice in the early civilizations must have developed from earlier beliefs concerning reciprocity and exchange between human beings and the supernatural. These beliefs were, however, radically reformulated as a consequence of the evolution of complex systems of taxation and tribute. Sacrifice in early civilizations represented a projection into the supernatural realm of the observation that farmers materially supported the upper classes, who in turn maintained the larger political and social order that was essential for a complex agricultural economy to function and for farmers to prosper. Such projections made sense to both farmers and rulers, who viewed each other as components of inegalitarian societies for which no viable alternative could be imagined. Rulers were accepted as necessary to maintain political stability; hence, by extrapolation, the role of the gods was to maintain the cosmic order, and to do this deities required material support. If rulers became too exploitative or permitted the upper classes to appropriate too many resources from farmers for their own use, they endangered not only the production of food but also the continuation of the cosmic order. Thus religious beliefs helped to curb exploitation by the upper classes on the grounds that restraint was necessary to nourish deities and keep both the political and the cosmic systems working.

Cross-cultural uniformities in the religious beliefs of early civilizations resulted from analogous reflections on the taxation systems that were generically common to all these societies. Sacrifice projected the taxation system into the cosmic realm. Essential roles were assigned to farmers as producers of food for the upper classes and the gods, to the human upper classes for maintaining the social and political order that made a productive economy possible, and to the gods for maintaining the cosmic order on which all life depended. The upper classes played a vital role in sustaining the gods but depended on farm labour to produce the food that was needed to do this. Therefore they were answerable to the gods for their treatment of farmers, just as farmers were answerable to the gods if they did not regularly produce food surpluses. Sahlins (1976: 211–12) has maintained that religious beliefs were the dominant focus of symbolic production in the early civilizations. They provided powerful concepts that helped to regulate political relations among classes in societies that had grown too large and too complex to be managed by notions of real or metaphorical kinship.

The concept of sacrifice thus supplied the equivalent of political constitutions for early civilizations. While farmers and other lower-class people were explicitly excluded from decisions about how society was to be governed and denied the right to criticize the actions of the upper classes overtly, their duty to ensure the continuity of the political and cosmic orders by feeding the upper classes and the gods was balanced by the need for the upper classes to make sure that farmers had the social peace and resources they needed to produce enough food to sustain the cosmic order. The failure of either farmers or the upper classes to respect and sustain the other threatened the functioning of the universe.

The common features of beliefs about sacrifice in the various early civilizations therefore appear to have been more than passive, epiphenomenal reflections of an effective ecological adaptation. They represented a shared understanding of the nature of social relations in early civilizations and of the limits to which one class could exploit another without endangering the whole system. Ideas about sacrifice and cosmic order in early civilizations constituted an implicit discourse on political power that mediated class relations and limited dangerous behaviour in the form of either lower-class rebelliousness or the overexploitation of farmers by the upper classes.

Whatever beliefs about the cosmos or the gods may have been shared by the societies that developed into early civilizations, major features of the religious beliefs of early civilizations were shaped by thinking about economic and political institutions that did not exist prior to the development of these societies. This process illustrates the capacity of widely separated groups of human beings at a particular level of development to transform common experiences into similar understandings of the supernatural. The development of these concepts also provides an astonishing demonstration of the ability of the human mind to construct analogous religious concepts under similar economic and political conditions and to use these ideas to stabilize convergent forms of social organization. This suggests that practical reason played a more extensive and important role in formulating general patterns of religious beliefs than cultural particularists allow.

THE UNIVERSE AND HUMANS

Individual early civilizations produced numerous accounts, often differing in detail, concerning the structure and creation of the universe, the origin of humans, the nature of human souls, and the fate of humans after death. Some of these versions were associated with various cults or with different kinship or ethnic groups that had been drawn together in larger political structures as early civilizations developed. Others were deliberately synthesized for political reasons. Yet these accounts displayed numerous cross-culturally recurrent patterns.

Cosmologies exhibited many similarities. The universe was conceptualized as a series of superimposed levels: a single terrestrial plane, one or more sky realms above, and one or more underworlds beneath. The sky and underworld planes were the exclusive realms of the gods and the dead, while the earth was shared by living people and the supernatural. These levels were interconnected, most often at the centre and around the edges of the terrestrial realm, through hills, trees, caves, and temples. The gods and supernatural energy were able to move through these gateways, conveying life-giving powers from the purely supernatural realms to the human one and back again.

The earth was generally believed to be a flat plane, round or square in outline, at most a few thousand kilometres across, and surrounded by a salt-water ocean. Each early civilization and usually each city-state believed itself to be located at the centre of the terrestrial plane, which had been created especially for its benefit. The terrestrial plane was often thought to be divided into quarters either according to the cardinal directions or at the points that marked the rising and setting points of the sun at the summer and winter solstices. This model took account of the geographical knowledge of the world that was possessed by well-informed people who lived in early civilizations. Such information declined exponentially beyond the borders of each early civilization. Knowledge of particular seas or oceans was extrapolated as signifying that the world was surrounded by salt water.

Lacking the contribution of practical knowledge, beliefs about the celestial and underworld levels showed much less cross-cultural uniformity. While the Mesoamerican civilizations postulated thirteen sky realms and nine underworlds associated with specific deities and the Chinese likewise imagined multiple levels, the Egyptians and the Mesopotamians postulated only one major supernatural realm in the sky and another beneath the earth.

The understanding of the earth and the cosmos may also have been influenced by views held in earlier, less complex societies. Mircea Eliade (1954) maintains that all early cultures believed in a multitiered universe, a vertical *axis mundi* both separating and joining the different levels, accessibility between the natural and supernatural levels, and the importance of shamans for communicating between them. Unfortunately, we would need more detailed and systematic information about small-scale societies to evaluate these claims. If Eliade is even partially correct, however, cross-culturally uniform beliefs that had existed prior to the development of early civilizations would help to account for many otherwise inexplicable cross-cultural uniformities in the cosmologies of early civilizations.

Myths concerning the creation and transformations of the universe were cross-culturally more varied than cosmologies. A crucial factor shaping these myths was measurement of time. Early civilizations tended to group days into short periods of from four to ten days, longer periods of twenty to thirty days, and various approximations of the sidereal year. These units facilitated adaptations to seasonal changes, as well as the organization of labour, markets, and tax collection. While the improved record-keeping of early civilizations encouraged greater awareness of longer time-scales, there was much variability in conceptualizing longer periods of time. The Aztec, Maya, and Inka thought of time as moving in cycles of days, years, and longer units associated with disintegrations and renewals of the cosmic order. Other early civilizations, such as Egypt, Mesopotamia, and that of the Yoruba, appear to have believed that a stable or self-renewing cosmos had been created at some point in the past and would last indefinitely. It is clear that ideas concerning the origin and functioning of the universe were far more speculative and less subject to empirical constraints than formulations dealing with the layout of the earth's surface. The overt importance accorded to cyclical processes in all three New World civilizations probably arose from shared cultural traditions, which in the case of the Maya and the Aztec are well documented.

It has been suggested that the Egyptians believed the cosmic order to be more stable than the Mesopotamians did, because Egypt was ecologically more stable than Mesopotamia (Frankfort et al. 1949: 137–39). Recent research on the ecology of these civilizations has cast doubt on this interpretation, showing significant instability in Egypt as well; and the fact remains that the supernatural punishments envisioned in Mesopotamia were rarely ecological disasters. Alternatively, it has been proposed that, because of their greater political stability, territorial states encouraged belief in an ordered cosmos more than city-states, which were frequently battling one another for hegemony (Trigger 1979: 40). The Maya, the inhabitants of the Valley of Mexico, and the Mesopotamians viewed the rise and fall of individual city-states as events decreed by the gods or inherent in the structure of the universe. Yet the Inka seem to have viewed the universe as similarly unstable, although this may be because they and their subjects in the central Andean highlands had only briefly constituted a territorial state. Moreover, the Maya, who thought that the fortunes of city-states were unstable because of ever-shifting relations among cosmic powers, believed that the natural order was stable for periods lasting at least five thousand years, and the Mesopotamians and the Yoruba, no less than the ancient Egyptians, appear to have believed that the cosmic order would endure far longer. These observations preclude any simple correlation between beliefs about cosmic instability and city-state or territorial-state forms of political organization. Such beliefs appear to have been shaped by various combinations of ecological and political factors. Instability was attributed to supernatural punishment of specific human acts as well as to forces inherent in the supernatural order.

Accounts of human origins tended to be highly variable even within the same early civilizations, but it was widely believed that all humans contained some divine element. It was also claimed in many early civilizations that the upper classes differed in origin from commoners. People in all early civilizations believed that human beings had two broad types of souls – impersonal life-forces that animated bodies and souls associated with intelligence and personality. These souls were assembled at or near birth and tended to separate at death, but one or both continued to exist. As did the gods, they required sustenance from the human world to function properly both before and after death. Yet the fortunes of the dead varied from one early civilization to another. In Mesopotamia food offerings merely sustained the intellect soul of the dead person, which was fated to live in misery in the underworld, whereas elsewhere they empowered souls. In most early civilizations, the dead served as intermediaries between their living descendants and the gods, the souls of kings doing so on behalf of the entire society. Families feared that the souls of dead members would punish them for misbehaviour or neglect.

It is tempting to interpret what happened to the souls of commoners after death, as understood in different early civilizations, as a reflection of their social status during life. This would suggest that commoners in city-states, especially those that lacked a hereditary nobility, ought to have enjoyed a more favourable existence after death than awaited commoners in territorial states. Yet, among the Egyptians and Inka, the souls of commoners were believed to fare better than the souls of commoners in city-states. As a result of status emulation, the beliefs of the upper classes appear to have raised rather than lowered commoners' self-evaluation and expectations. In city-states, both upper- and lower-class Yoruba, Mesopotamians, and Aztec expected less for themselves after death. The fates of dead Maya rulers, although seemingly dependent on the results of their individual efforts to outwit the gods of the underworld, appear to have more resembled those of their counterparts in territorial states.

SPECIALIZED KNOWLEDGE

There was considerable cross-cultural uniformity in the sorts of specialized knowledge that the upper classes chose to patronize in early civilizations. The elaborate technological understanding developed by skilled craft workers generally went unrecorded, except indirectly in connection with supplying artisans with raw materials and paying them for their work. The same is true for architects; a few ceremonial plans and models of buildings have survived but no detailed information about how major construction projects were planned and carried out. Presumably, even in literate early civilizations, many of the highly specialized skills required to perform this work were transmitted orally. Genealogies and the deeds of former kings and great men were celebrated in writing, oral traditions, or a combination of both. Bards and scribes helped to preserve an understanding of the past.

In general, the knowledge that was of greatest practical concern to the upper classes and regarded as most worthy of elaboration had as its goal improving relations with the supernatural. Ascertaining the will of the gods through reading omens and practising divination was highly elaborated in all the early civilizations. Concerns about health made medicine a subject of special interest to the rich and powerful. Although some diseases were known to be curable using natural remedies, no disease was believed to have only a natural cause, and all diseases were considered susceptible to supernatural treatment. There was also widespread fear of witchcraft or sorcery. Whereas in egalitarian societies fear of becoming a victim of witchcraft or of being accused of having practised it had encouraged generosity and redistribution, in early civilizations the ability of the upper classes to accuse commoners of witchcraft transformed such accusations into a powerful means of intimidation. Witchcraft also continued, however, to frighten the upper classes, who feared it as a covert form of resistance to their authority. This encouraged the development of more effective techniques for detecting witches and for counteracting witchcraft, demonic powers, and even the ill will of the gods using magical spells, amulets, and esoteric rituals.

Thus the forms of knowledge that were most assiduously cultivated under upper-class sponsorship in early civilizations were linked to trying to find ways to deal with aspects of the natural/supernatural realm that could not be controlled by natural means. This kind of specialized knowledge remained the prerogative of the upper classes, highly trained priests, and administrative specialists. The cultivation and preservation of specialized knowledge appears to have been primarily associated with temples or religious groups in city-state systems and with royal courts in territorial states. In some early civilizations the upper classes were taught such knowledge, along with record-keeping and other administrative skills, at special schools.

More complex understandings of cosmology, human origins, divination, and medicine grew out of earlier beliefs that were elaborated by specialists employed in the higher echelons of early civilizations. Creating new and more effective ways to control relations with the supernatural required understanding the specific wishes of the gods. The purpose of such knowledge was to enlist their political support and their assistance in counteracting human illness, misfortune, and witchcraft and to use divine power to reinforce upper-class control over the lower classes. These common concerns encouraged analogous elaborations of ideas in all the early civilizations. Such elaborations manifested the greatest degree of cross-cultural regularity in those domains of culture that exhibited the greatest continuity from earlier periods and were most strongly influenced by direct observation.

Early civilizations were the first societies in which, for functional reasons, speech, as opposed to ideas about specific topics, was recorded. Writing did not, however, develop in all early civilizations, and the uses that were made of it remained everywhere more restricted than in later preindustrial civilizations and modern industrial societies. Systems that were able to record speech developed in only four of the early civilizations we are examining. Despite evidence of an independent origin for at least three and possibly all four of these scripts, they were all logophonic. The representation of sounds was achieved differently, however, by each writing system. There was no precedent for the principles of writing as it developed in these four early civilizations. Even where it had been present, semasiography operated very differently. Yet these earliest scripts indicate that, when people first sought to record speech, they habitually began with logography rather than by trying to represent phonemes or syllables. Once a functioning logophonic writing system had been created, there was no indication of any further evolution within individual early civilizations towards more phonetic scripts. The creation of phonetic scripts happened (and then not always) only when logophonic scripts were used to write new languages in hitherto non-literate societies. The development of writing systems provides dramatic evidence that precedents were not required for the occurrence of striking parallel or convergent developments in particular domains of culture.

RELIGIOUS BELIEFS AND PRACTICAL REASON

Much of the knowledge that characterized the elite cultures of early civilizations was derived from religious, cosmological, and therapeutic concepts of earlier times, altered and elaborated to serve the needs of larger and more complex class societies. Changes included the recognition of a larger terrestrial world and longer periods of time, although, except with the Maya concept of time, both space and time remained limited by comparison with modern understandings. Cross-culturally similar beliefs in early civilizations often appear to have resulted from the adaptation of already similar earlier beliefs to analogous new conditions. Class societies created elaborate art and architecture that symbolized the unity of society at the same time as they reaffirmed the dominance of the upper classes over commoners. Early civilizations also exhibited idiosyncratic differences in aspirations and values which, because they influenced human behaviour, affected the functioning of these societies in significant ways.

The most dramatic and far-reaching intellectual innovations that these class societies produced were those related to religious beliefs. While the gods were credited with supplying the cosmic energy that supported human life, humans nourished the gods, and earthly rulers became the supreme intermediaries in the process by which the cosmic cycle was maintained. This analysis projected into the supernatural realm the simultaneously complementary and antagonistic relations that bound together the upper and lower classes in early civilizations. By assigning farmers, rulers, and gods significant roles in maintaining the cosmic order, this view imposed moral limitations on the exploitative behaviour of the upper classes that enhanced the viability of society. Since there had been no need for religious beliefs of this sort prior to the development of larger, class-based societies, their cross-cultural uniformity in early civilizations suggests that they were products of practical reason as it related to some universal forms of self-interest. The same explanation can be offered for the cross-cultural regularity of the measures that the upper classes employed to protect their wealth and power. The logographic preference in the writing systems of early civilizations seems to reflect as yet little understood cognitive biases that all human beings share.

While scholars have long been fascinated with the cultural diversity of early civilizations, there was much similarity in the basic religious concepts, cosmologies, beliefs concerning souls, and forms of knowledge that were thought worth elaborating. Ironically, scholars seem less intrigued by truly unique forms of knowledge, such as the Classic Maya view of time, than by diverse expressions of similar themes. While we have encountered much specific diversity in subsistence economies in early civilizations and at least two radically different approaches to political organization, there appears to have been only one major view of the operation of the supernatural. Far from being an epiphenomenal reflection of culture as an adaptive system, this view appears to have been the convergent outcome of profound reflections on how class societies served the practical needs of their members. In early civilizations, religion was not only the main locus of symbolic production but also the principal medium for vital discussions and debates on political issues.

Discussion

28 Culture and Reason

Anthropologists agree that all human perception is culturally and therefore symbolically mediated. Even the most extreme positivists acknowledge that an understanding of the world is mediated by the categories and associated meanings that individuals learn as members of societies and that, human behaviour therefore represents an adaptation not to the world as it really is but to the world as individuals imagine it to be. Yet anthropologists disagree violently about the significance of symbolic mediation and especially about the degree to which culturally constructed images of the world approximate reality. They also hold many different views concerning the forces that shape culture (Trigger 1998c).

At one extreme are the ecological determinists, who seek to understand human behaviour in terms of the same factors that govern the behaviour of all other animal species. Culture for them is one component of an adaptive system that modifies human behaviour in response to changing demographic and natural conditions – a mechanism that helps a species to achieve adaptive fitness. While acknowledging the unusually prominent role of symbolic manipulation in guiding human behaviour, they see culture as shaped by practical activity and utilitarian interests. The human mind, in their view, is a device for formulating rational adaptive stategies, and culture is a mnemonic for encoding and facilitating the implementation of these strategies. For most practical purposes, they consider behaviour rather than culture the primary object of scientific study.

Supporters of this view argue that, even if the world that humans adapt to is one of ideas, it has to bear a very close resemblance to the real world if human groups are to survive. This discounting of the explanatory value of cognition and an accompanying tendency to treat culture as a black box encourage ecological determinists to emphasize the generically animal aspects of human behaviour and to treat the specifically human aspects as epiphenomenal. Such an approach tends to minimize the significance of cultural traditions in favour of short-term, functionalist explanations of human behaviour and beliefs. There is also a strong preference for Locke's view of the mind as a *tabula rasa* on which sensory impressions are inscribed for rational analysis (R. N. Adams 1988).

At the opposite extreme are those who attach supreme importance to cultural meanings in the shaping of human perception and behaviour. For them cultures are texts that are modified by endless individual decodings and encodings and no two individuals ever understand the same utterance or event in precisely the same way. Advocates of this approach insist that principles of classification and understanding are culturally specific and historically derived and therefore cannot be inferred from any objective qualities of the real world (Sahlins 1976: 47). They also maintain that a vast array of alternative cultures could be associated with any particular set of material conditions. They see no clear order or direction to change, which they consider mainly a result of the random variations (memory tricks) produced by ceaseless recodings of messages. George P. Murdock (1956) called this process 'miscopying' and likened it to genetic mutation, and it is also the hallmark of a historical-particularist approach. Cultural relativists emphasize cross-cultural differences and treat culturally mediated understandings as the most important factors shaping human behaviour. Many of them also attribute the persistence of cultural traditions to the inability of the people who are guided by a culture to formulate significant alternatives – a conclusion that is incompatible with the ethnographic observation that cultures characteristically provide multiple ready-made options for dealing with ecological and social challenges (Salzman 2000). Carried to the extreme of cultural determinism, a relativist approach becomes the idealist counterpart of ecological determinism.

Between these two extremes lies a broad range of options. Structuralists treat culture as a text but see it as controlled by hypothetical underlying structures that limit variation and change. Within structuralism there are harder and softer options. Some theorists believe that the underlying structure inhibits change to the extent that French culture will remain identifiably French regardless of how much economic or social change occurs. Others, in keeping with the approach's Saussurean origins, view structure as more analogous to grammar, which does not preclude any particular thought from being expressed but determines how difficult it may be to communicate a specific idea in any particular language. Late Boasian anthropology believed that an innate human need for psychological consistency required cultures to acquire patterns that were reassuring to individuals. The need for such patterning was claimed to be far more important than the specific nature of any pattern (Benedict 1934).

On the materialist side, classical Marxism identified economic competition rather than ecological adaptation as the primary source of social and cultural change, at least in class societies. This approach, by assigning primary importance to individual and group strategies as they relate to political power and the control of resources, conceptualized human beings as active agents shaping their collective destiny rather than as passive entities subject to ecological or cultural forces. Still more permissive was the older Boasian belief that, provided that a culture satisfied a basic set of functional prerequisites, such as food and protection, cultural variation could be random (Aberle et al. 1950; R. E. Adams 2000: 2–6; Murdock 1945). This approach, which had much in common with Bronislaw Malinowski's belief that social institutions were grounded in the biological needs of individuals, posited that functional prerequisites could be satisfied in many different ways and that culture was shaped by the idiosyncratic operation of diffusion as well as by the aggregate outcomes of individual preferences.

Each of these theories has its supporters, and all of them have fluctuated in popularity over time. The cyclical rather than unilinear nature of these fluctuations suggests that these theories are deeply embedded in the competing values of Western society, especially those associated with rationalism and romanticism. For social scientists to proclaim that they are Marxists, cultural ecologists, or cultural relativists is to assert that they are prepared to act as if one of these explanations of how societies function and change constituted the best approximation of the truth. Such a commitment is largely an act of faith.

The evidence that has been examined concerning early civilizations does not support the once widely accepted ecological-evolutionary position that, because sociocultural phenomena are shaped most powerfully by ecological or economic constraints, societies at the same level of development will show the most cross-cultural regularity in their economic institutions, less in their social and political organization, and still less in the cultural sphere. The assumption here is that the features of most adaptive significance will be selected for most powerfully by material constraints, while less significant ones will display opportunistically determined random patterning (Friedman and Rowlands 1978b). In every aspect of early civilizations we have encountered idiosyncratic practices and beliefs. In general, cross-cultural parallels have tended to be of a generic sort, while idiosyncratic features have been more specific. The evidence does not, however, support the view that cross-cultural regularities existed mainly at the level of economic and social behaviour as opposed to that of belief. This unexpected distribution of cross-cultural patterning suggests the need for a more careful analysis of the factors that produced both idiosyncrasies and uniformities among early civilizations.

CULTURALLY IDIOSYNCRATIC PATTERNS

Art styles, not surprisingly, varied idiosyncratically from one early civilization to another, even among the neighbouring Maya and Aztec. Similar idiosyncratic variation differentiated the monumental architecture produced for upper-class patrons in each of the early civilizations. The elite styles of art and architecture that characterized specific early civilizations evolved from local prototypes but acquired their distinctive features at an early stage in the development of each civilization. Because of their greater formality and elaboration, such styles often bore little resemblance to their antecedents. Yet, despite stylistic differences, important features were shared. Lavish support by the upper classes favoured the creation of more sophisticated and coherent styles. Conspicuous consumption is evident in the large size of buildings, the vast amount of labour required to erect them, and the specialized skills that were invested in producing high-quality products. Luxury goods were frequently manufactured from exotic and expensive raw materials. These forms of behaviour exhibited in material form the wealth and power of the upper classes.

Distinctive art styles symbolized the political unity of particular territorial states, the broader cultural affiliations of member polities of city-state systems, and the separate identities of individual city-states. Yet the extent to which the art styles of the various elite crafts in individual early civilizations were integrated varied. While innovations took place and to some extent were valued in the art and architecture of all early civilizations, they occurred within the constraints of well-defined cultural traditions. Individual craft specialists sought to produce works of art that were of exceptional quality, but their aim was excellence within existing canons. The aesthetic principles underlying the art of individual early civilizations changed over time and varied among individual artists. Yet, the principles that defined a single cultural tradition constituted no less impressive a manifestation of patterning in human behaviour than the strongest cross-cultural regularity. The materials used and the available technology imposed few functional limitations on stylistic variation. The continuing pressure for stylistic unity came mainly from the sociocultural sphere, with the upper class encouraging internal coherence and the maintenance of distinctive cultural traditions. Yet the stylistic features of an early civilization's elite art and architecture constituted a self-contained manifestation of culture that exerted no specific functional constraints on everyday life.

Propositions about goals for individual humans were also cross-culturally variable. These propositions were not purely stylistic, however; they established norms to which individuals had to conform in order to win public approval. Dominant cultural ideals represented values of the upper classes as those of the entire society and thus encouraged society to function in accordance with those classes' interests. To some limited degree these values may have accorded functionally with different forms of sociopolitical organization. A heightened emphasis on competitiveness seems to have been associated with city-state systems and obedience to authority with territorial states. Such correlations were not, however, very specific. As did art styles, attitudes relating to ideal individual behaviour tended to persist for long periods. The ancient Mesopotamian belief that kings were not inherently different from their subjects stubbornly survived strenuous efforts by some hegemons and later rulers of Mesopotamian regional states to persuade their subjects to regard them as gods.

Cultural ideals also focused the performance capabilities of whole societies. The Aztec, like the early Indo-Europeans, glorified individual males as warriors; the Egyptians and increasingly the Chinese idealized the ordered and harmonious conduct of public affairs; and the Mesopotamians and Yoruba, each in their own way, positively valued interpersonal competition. The same set of values tended to be shared by people living in all the states making up a city-state system. The often very different values that prevailed in nearby less complex societies exerted little influence on early civilizations and were frequently dismissed as barbarous. Even when long-established civilizations came to be coerced by societies whose ideals differed from their own, a set of values that had become less than optimally adaptive could persist indefinitely.

It is frequently asserted that aspects of culture that vary idiosyncratically among historically unrelated cultures are 'stylistic' rather than 'functional' and therefore selectively neutral (Dunnell 1978; Wenke 1997a). This argument is problematical for several reasons. First, some features of human behaviour that are idiosyncratically variable are highly adaptive. Because there was great variation in the types of environments that the different early civilizations exploited and in the performance characteristics of their domestic plants and animals, there was also great variation in the ways these resources were managed. Diverse agricultural regimes made food production effective in different environmental settings. Most of these practices were continuations of adaptive patterns that had evolved separately in each region long before the rise of civilization. There was also considerable variation in agricultural technology, which ranged from simple digging sticks in some early civilizations to a broad range of metal hand tools in others. While some of this technology developed in early civilizations, most of it has been shown to have been a heritage from earlier times. Thus there was great idiosyncratic variation among early civilizations in quintessentially adaptive features. Neoevolutionists such as Julian Steward (1949), who maintained that early civilizations had similar subsistence economies, wrongly assumed that all these civilizations had developed in similar environmental settings. They failed to recognize the variability in the subsistence patterns of early civilizations as a prime example of ecological adaptation. Unlike stylistic variation in art and architecture, idiosyncratic variation in agricultural practices was adaptive to varied ecological settings.

Style has long been recognized as a symbolic way to assert ethnic, class, and gender identity. Sahlins (1976: 203) noted that an unconscious dress code can create a cohesive society out of perfect strangers. In early civilizations, elite art and monumental architecture both expressed and reinforced the power of the upper classes and the corporate identities of early civilizations and individual states. Values and lifestyles defined generally acceptable behavioural patterns and thus provided individuals with needed guidance and reassurance. Patterns for living were powerfully sanctified by tradition and religion as well as by familiarity. In addition to privileging certain general types of behaviour, each society provided specific guidelines applicable to relations between parents and children, men and women, old and young, and people of higher and lower rank. While these values played mainly a neutral facilitating role in relation to society as a whole when early civilizations existed in relative isolation from one another, they acquired strong, if unpredictable, selective values when competition developed between societies with different values. The sort of warfare practised in the Valley of Mexico, which was focused on gaining individual prestige and maintaining the universe through prisoner sacrifice, fared badly when the Aztec had to confront Spanish forces that fought for different reasons and by different rules. Yoruba personal competitiveness, by contrast, proved highly adaptive for coping with British colonial administration. It therefore seems unlikely that an operational distinction can be drawn between style and function.

The ubiquity of patterns of elite art, monumental architecture, and refined, upper-class lifestyles suggests that they fulfilled significant functions that were necessary for the operation of early civilizations, providing symbols that structured identity, promoted psychological stability, and gave meaning to life. From a vast range of possibilities, they created coherent cultural patterns, goals, and aspirations for people to follow. It is unclear whether the specific choices made reflected some deep structure underlying cultural patterns, the operation of a conscious set of core principles, or mere chance. Whatever their source, the resulting configurations provided meaning to what people did in what would otherwise have been a chaotic situation.

Idealists maintain that idiosyncratic cultural patterns represent the quintessence of creativity of the human spirit, free from ecological constraints, and celebrate each cultural pattern as a unique creation of the human spirit. Yet at the same time they see cultural change as the result of a random succession of unique understandings that each human mind brings to culturally transmitted experience, every decoding being another encoding. This theory implies that cultures ought to change in a random fashion and exhibit random cross-cultural patterning, and many historical particularists and postprocessual archaeologists in fact assert that such randomness characterizes all of human behaviour.

Postmodernist claims about cultural idiosyncrasy revive long-standing anthropological debates about the relation between cultural traditions and functionality. Nineteenth-century anthropologists treated cultural traditions as a dead weight constraining human behaviour and the means by which obsolete and often irrational ideas from the past survived into the present. Edward B. Tylor (1871) defined the main goal of evolutionary anthropology as exposing the useless and even dangerous survivals of more primitive stages of human development in modern society. This approach encouraged anthropologists to view culture as an uncritically accepted and change-resistant set of customs inherited from the past.

Later many social anthropologists argued in opposition to this idea that there was no such thing as a 'survival'; any concept that persisted from the past either continued to perform its original function or had acquired a significant new one. They also argued that there was no reason that new functions needed to resemble previous ones. Cultures had to be understood in terms of the relations that their various parts bore to the whole at any given time. Social anthropologists who followed A. R. Radcliffe-Brown (1958) stressed the primary importance of social relations and viewed culture as acquiring its functional significance from the relations that individual beliefs, habits, and bodies of knowledge bore to social behaviour.

Classical Marxism posited a more complex and reflexive relation between tradition and function. According to Karl Marx, 'human beings make their own history ... not under conditions chosen by themselves, but ones directly encountered, given, and transmitted from the past' (Marx and Engels 1962, 1: 247). In other words, each generation starts with a heritage of past beliefs and practices that individuals and groups reshape to accord with their changing needs and aspirations. Culture simultaneously guides human behaviour, provides ideas that can be used to bring about change, and encourages resistance to change. Old institutions can be either rejected or altered to serve new purposes. Gordon Childe (1965 [1936]: 98) argued that no one could infer the details of British parliamentary government in the nineteenth century from a purely theoretical understanding of the capitalist mode of production. Although there was a close connection between the economic dominance of the entrepreneurial bourgeoisie in nineteenth-century Britain and the form of power that was exercised in that country, the specific nature of the British constitution had to be understood in relation to an evolving set of English political institutions and practices that had originated during the medieval period.

A powerful tendency, derived from functionalism, nevertheless persists to dismiss cultural traditions as non-explanations of human behaviour (Binford 1989: 14–16). Culture continues to be regarded as a passive residue of ideas inherited from the past that is destined to be either discarded or reshaped to serve present needs. This view has been seriously challenged by the ecologists Robert Boyd and Peter Richerson (1985), who point out that the great selective advantage of the symbolic capacity of human beings is the ability it confers to benefit from the experiences of others without having to share or even witness them. The vast majority of the ideas that guide behaviour are learned symbolically from others either in infancy or later in life. Individuals therefore do not have to reinvent the wheel, nor do they have to alter established ways of doing things unless they conclude that there is a compelling reason for doing so.

Boyd and Richerson (1985: 95–116, 276) maintain that ideas inherited from the past are generally superior to innovations, in part because repeated use and modification have enhanced their effectiveness as guides for individual behaviour. While innovations are initially devised to serve personal ends, as they are applied by large numbers of people over long periods they become better adapted to serving the needs of society as a whole. Innovations may become necessary as a result of ecological or economic changes, but because they are untested they generally have higher initial social costs than traditional solutions. If this is the case in modern industrial societies, it must have been even more so in earlier societies, where, because of the slower rate of change, the necessity to alter existing rules of human behaviour would usually have been less pressing.

This argument calls into question the notion that it is practical reason that accounts for cross-cultural uniformities and cultural reason that explains cross-cultural particularities. Ecological patterns are adaptive precisely because they are variable from one natural setting to another. Other idiosyncratic cultural patterns persist not because stylistic traits are selectively neutral but because they are selected for internal consistency in situations that relate to identity, cooperation, and psychological well-being rather than to serve a cross-cultural goal.

CROSS-CULTURAL REGULARITIES

Early civilizations had many similarities. Marshall Sahlins and Elman Service (1960) identified cross-cultural regularities as products of general evolution, arguing that these were features that, for functional reasons, all societies that reached a particular level of complexity had to develop. Neoevolutionists assumed that the explanation for these similarities was primarily ecological.

In all the early civilizations, farmers produced modest agricultural surpluses, of which a disproportionate amount was appropriated by the upper classes. All of them had generally similar class hierarchies, one of two basic types of political organization (city-states and territorial states), and three types of administration (heterarchical, delegational, and bureaucratic). Their religious beliefs did not distinguish the natural, the supernatural, and the social any more than those of smaller-scale societies. Early civilizations had convergently created a single model of how the cosmos functioned and of the relations linking humans and the supernatural, and in each early civilization the upper classes patronized the study of a natural world that was believed to be animated by supernatural forces.

The rulers of each early civilization used various economic, political, and religious incentives to induce farmers to produce agricultural surpluses and surrender a large portion of them to the state and the upper classes. While these 'tributary' relations had features in common with the support of elders and big men in some small-scale agricultural societies, the bureaucratic and coercive measures that were used to ensure the regular production and delivery of surpluses were different. The size of surpluses continued to be restricted by simple technologies, which made human labour a relatively inflexible variable, and by the limited extent to which farmers could be persuaded or coerced to produce beyond their families' immediate needs. Farmers paid moderate rates of taxes with little protest in return for the state's organizing defence against foreign enemies, maintaining internal peace, and sometimes coordinating projects that promoted economic development. Increasing taxation beyond these modest limits would have required increasing use of force and hence greater managerial organization and expense. Unlike some later preindustrial civilizations, early civilizations opted for a low-force/low-yield solution. Probably only about 10 percent of total food production was surrendered to the state.

Higher population densities were associated with more intensive forms of food production. While more intensive agriculture yielded more food per unit of arable land, it often required more human labour to produce the same amount of food and under these circumstances was not undertaken without a good reason. While all early civilizations appear to have been able to intensify food production, this was accomplished in locally specific ways. Intensification was mainly based on knowledge that ordinary farmers already possessed. Where population densities or opportunities to sell food were increasing, initiatives for more intensive food production usually came spontaneously from farmers.

Early civilizations required extensive areas of fertile, easily worked soils and moderately dense, sedentary human populations. Population density by itself was not, however, necessarily the key variable, and neither was the circumscription of a region with great agricultural potential by a much poorer one. More important was a growing need to protect agricultural land and other forms of immovable property as increasing amounts of labour were invested in them. As possession of such property was increasingly threatened by rival polities, pastoral marauders, and poorer or landless elements within society, farmers became willing to submit to authority and pay taxes in order to ensure that their property was adequately protected (Linton 1933). The development of larger states often produced conditions propitious for agricultural intensification and population expansion. Such expansion made landowners even more dependent on government protection, but where denser populations necessitated more labour to produce sufficient food, overall surplus production may occasionally have declined. In situations where denser populations could have been supported without adopting more labour-intensive forms of agriculture, rulers sometimes sought to increase food production and their own revenues by attracting foreign immigrants or settling prisoners of war. Despite the close correlation between population density and the intensity of agricultural production, there appear to have been many different strategies for managing both population growth and agricultural intensification. Population density cannot be treated as an independent variable in the development of early civilizations.

There were three main types of land ownership in early civilizations: collective, institutional, and private. While it is unclear to what extent collectively owned land was a primordial form in all early civilizations, institutional land was independently created in several and private land in at least two (Mesopotamia and Egypt). We are prevented from positing an evolutionary sequence of landholding from collective through institutional to private by the considerable variation in combinations of these types of ownership from one early civilization to another and the varying capacity of collective and institutional forms to resist erosion.

All early civilizations required corvée labour from commoners, although the amount and importance of this form of tax varied. While the Inka collected taxes only in the form of labour, other civilizations required in addition the regular payment of taxes either on land or on harvests and herds. In most early civilizations they were collected in kind, but in Mesopotamia they were eventually paid in silver. Aztec and Yoruba leaders extracted considerable revenues by means of a sales tax, while Yoruba authorities also imposed duties on the local and regional transport of goods. In many early civilizations, governments, temples, and officials derived income from institutionally or privately owned land by requiring landless farmers to work it in return for being allowed to keep enough produce to feed themselves and their families or by hiring wage labourers, renting land, or sharecropping it. While the means varied, the result was the same: a large portion of the crops produced on such lands was appropriated by the government and the upper classes.

The development of systems of taxation and appropriation involved the repeated invention of a limited number of techniques for extracting resources from commoners and the use of different combinations of these techniques. An increasing variety of techniques appears to have been employed in individual early civilizations over time. By disguising the total amount of wealth that was being appropriated from individuals by the state and the upper classes, this elaboration probably facilitated the increasing economic exploitation of the lower classes. Tribute from conquered states further increased the revenues of kings and the upper classes.

Although early civilizations displayed a wide range of kinship organization, these forms exhibited a stronger masculine bias than that associated with less complex societies. The position of women varied considerably in early civilizations, perhaps partly because of the differing status of women in the societies that gave rise to them, but in no early civilization were women equal to men. Moreover, where the position of women can be monitored over time it deteriorated rather than improved.

Early civilizations were characterized by a degree of division of labour and craft specialization unprecedented prior to their origin. These developments resulted mainly from growing demands for luxury goods, more effective weapons, and higher-quality domestic goods. While some households continued to manufacture goods for their own use and part-time craft workers supplied local markets, there was a great increase in the number of full-time artisans. Through a combination of market sales and commissioned production, the self-employed full-time craft workers that were characteristic of city-state systems made goods of varying quality available to all levels of society. The elite craft workers of territorial states produced luxury goods exclusively for the government and the upper classes while part-time rural craft specialists manufactured goods for the lower classes. In Mesopotamia and the Valley of Mexico and among the Yoruba, long-distance traders, operating independently of government control, imported exotic raw materials and circulated high-quality produce among neighbouring, and often warring, city-states. In territorial states, the government controlled both the local procurement of valuable raw materials and the conduct of foreign trade.

Early civilizations possessed many analogous political institutions. The most important of these was kingship. Monarchs were conceptualized differently in the various early civilizations. In some the king was proclaimed to be a universal ruler; in others he was simply one head of state among many. Some kings effectively governed their kingdoms; others tended to be figureheads. Although in most early civilizations kings led their armies into battle, the Yoruba regarded such behaviour as incompatible with a ruler's holiness. Egyptian, Inka, Aztec, Maya, and Yoruba kings were believed to be infused with the powers of one or more major cosmic deities; Mesopotamian rulers were regarded as ordinary humans who had to depend on the goodwill of the gods for their success. Despite the varied ways in which they were conceptualized, kings invariably represented the unity of a state. They were also regarded as at least symbolically responsible for the welfare of their kingdoms: for their agricultural prosperity, social harmony, defence, legal systems, and dealings with the supernatural. It appears that in early civilizations it was impossible to conceive of political unity except as it was embodied in a single person.

All the early civilizations had essentially similar class hierarchies based on a dichotomy between rulers and workers. At the top, a king and a tiny upper class monopolized most of the resources of a society and made all the important policy decisions. The upper class was hierarchized, with a royal family at the apex. In many early civilizations, membership in the upper class was formally ascribed and hereditary. In others, upper-class status was attributed to individuals or families either on the basis of relative power and wealth or position in a government hierarchy. Male members of the upper class governed and were military leaders; they did not engage in manual labour.

Below the upper class were full-time specialists – administrators and minor civil servants, full-time soldiers, and craft workers. The bulk of the population were farmers, landowning or landless, and at the bottom of society, except in the Andes and perhaps in China, were slaves – debtors, criminals, military captives, purchased foreigners, and their descendants. In all the early civilizations, the social hierarchy was also one of power and wealth. The number of people belonging to each free class increased exponentially from the top to the bottom of the class hierarchy. Vertical mobility, where it was allowed, was controlled from above, and classes tended to be endogamous. Perhaps the most important distinction in the organization of social hierarchies was between early civilizations that had hereditary nobilities and those that lacked them.

Early civilizations exhibited two types of political organization: city-states and territorial states. These types differed not only in size but in political, economic, and social organization. In city-states, large numbers of farmers lived in urban centres and full-time craft workers produced for an extensive clientele, including farmers, who bought their goods at urban markets and shops. In territorial states, urban centres were inhabited only by rulers, administrators, retainers, and skilled craft workers who produced goods for the state and the upper classes. Farmers lived in rural settings, where they manufactured the goods they needed on a part-time basis. This created a two-tiered economy integrated only by a system of taxation that funnelled surplus resources from the bottom to the top.

Charles Maisels (1999: 342–59) attributes the origin of territorial states to the greater extent to which differences in strategies of ecological adaptation permitted ruling classes to exploit commoners. He argues that the solidarity of rural communities in Egypt and of clan organization in China facilitated their more effective exploitation. Much idiosyncratic argument is required to make the four Old World civilizations that Maisels studies conform to this generalization, and even more difficulties are involved in extending it to cover the early civilizations of the Western Hemisphere. Moreover, the valid correlations that he establishes between city-states and reciprocal exchange and between territorial states and exploitative economies may have been the result rather than the cause of these differences in political organization.

It is clear, however, that early civilizations had either territorial states or city-states but both sorts did not occur together in a single early civilization. While many unilinear evolutionists believe that city-states were consolidated to form territorial states and Joyce Marcus (1998) has argued that early territorial states broke apart to form city-states, there is no evidence that one of these types of state ever evolved into the other. Both, however, in some instances evolved into preindustrial regional states, a type of polity that combined some features of both earlier forms with other, completely new features.

Early civilizations displayed limited variation in their forms of administration. In a city-state, power was vested in the government located in the main urban centre, which was often heterarchical in structure. Territorial states required more formal, hierarchical administration, either delegational or bureaucratic. The information theorists of the late 1960s and 1970s viewed these forms as having developed through the necessary delegation of authority to make various administrative decisions to lower-level officials and the organization of hierarchies to process information and monitor whether higher-level orders were being carried out (see, e.g., D. Clarke 1968: 88–101). Problems first developed, they argued, when societies expanded beyond the point where all adults could know each other individually. Above the threshold of about four hundred people there was increasing need for brokers or intermediaries to shape public opinion and produce consensus. As groups became still larger, the ever-greater amounts of time required to reach agreement about public policy rendered consensual decision-making increasingly ineffective. Once communities expanded much beyond fifteen hundred people, leaders had to be authorized to make crucial decisions that were accepted as binding on their followers (G. Foster 1960: 178; Heidenreich 1971: 129–34). People agreed to obey officials in order to avoid chaos. The alternatives for political management in early complex societies were, according to these theorists, extremely limited. They proposed that the number of levels in an administrative hierarchy had to increase as the state expanded and, more specifically, that whenever approximately seven additional units required coordination a new level of control had to be established (G. Johnson 1973; 1978; G. Miller 1956; van der Leeuw 1981). William Rathje (1975) argued that, as the range and intensity of control increased, controls became more standardized and eventually lower-level units were encouraged to become largely self-regulating to reduce their cost to the central government. Information theorists did not attempt to explain why societies grew more complex or why in particular societies a bureaucratic or delegational form of administration was preferred (Flannery 1972), but they did show how a limited variety of workable solutions may have limited the types of administration that were possible.

The military forces in early civilizations depended on peasant corvées to supply most of the soldiers needed to defend frontiers and fight in foreign campaigns. A corps of full-time soldiers and police was employed to guard members of the upper class, protect government installations, arrest criminals, and intimidate dissidents. As states grew more powerful they relied increasingly on full-time soldiers. Armed forces, whether made up of conscripts or professional soldiers, were organized in a modular, hierarchical fashion, no doubt for the same reasons that the political administration was. Some physical coercion was required to punish rebels and ensure the payment of taxes. In general, such punishment seems to have been easier to impose in territorial states than in city-states. The boundaries of territorial states were fortified or patrolled, making it difficult for dissidents to escape. Armed rebellions were generally local and easily crushed. In city-state systems, in contrast, malcontents and rebels could flee to neighbouring states, where they had a good chance of being welcomed by kings who were rivals or enemies of their own ruler. Central governments also generally sought to curb blood feuds, especially ones that might be directed against the sovereign.

The basic elements of legal procedures – socially recognized rules with universal applicability, authorities who rendered judgements, and some means of enforcement – were already widespread and probably universal among small-scale societies (Pospisil 1958). What early civilizations added was a hierarchical dimension that paralleled the political hierarchy. The king was ascribed ultimate authority in legal matters, especially with respect to life-and-death decisions. Law courts were established at various administrative levels. Because of the greater ability of the state to deploy force, decisions by higher courts tended to be rapid, definitive, and often arbitrary. Yet administrative economy was achieved by allowing lower-level tribunals to regulate legal problems within extended families and local groups as much as possible. At this level decisions were generally enforced by public opinion. Higher-level courts were controlled by members of the upper classes, and their judgements reflected the self-interest of that social stratum. They normally imposed much harsher penalties on lower-class individuals than on upper-class ones. Only the Aztec and their neighbours inflicted more severe penalties on the upper classes, in this case for a series of personal misdemeanours that called into question their self-control and hence the supernatural power they were supposed to possess. Witchcraft accusations, which in small-scale societies had been used to enforce redistribution and protect economic equality, were redirected to coerce the less powerful and affluent.

Whether the upper classes in specific early civilizations viewed themselves as self-disciplined bureaucrats, audacious warriors, or comfortable landowners, they agreed about the need to protect their privileges and possessions by keeping the lower classes subservient. They also agreed about the means, including both physical and legal coercion, by which this could be accomplished. It is, however, also clear that those who controlled early civilizations relied heavily on at least the passive consent if not the active support of a substantial majority of the governed. Rulers could never have deployed enough force to suppress even a significant minority of their subjects. It is also evident that governments of early civilizations did not interfere unduly in the affairs of the lower classes. Kin groups and communities were allowed to regulate their internal affairs so long as their doing so did not interfere with the privileges of the powerful. The frequent delegation of political and legal power demonstrated a preference for less expensive government, even if it increased the risk of disintegration. The state focused its administrative skills and resources on key concerns of the upper classes, such as collecting taxes. Because the wealth that was available to the upper classes was limited, leaders preferred to expend as much of it as possible on their own lifestyles and on creating symbols of power and therefore sought to spend only what was necessary on coercion.

The most potent source of power for the upper classes was probably the pervasiveness and hence the seeming normality of inequality. Hierarchical relations pervaded almost every aspect of life. Relations between a ruler and his subjects provided a model for relations between male heads and other members of extended or nuclear families, as well as between adults and children, teachers and pupils, employers and employees, and masters and slaves. All such relations tended to be construed as father-son relations. As the result of a growing emphasis on male public leadership, the position of women declined. Thus, from birth, children lived in families and communities that were characterized by institutionalized inequality and the dominance of male authority figures.

The training of children regularly involved physical punishment, which was used to deal not only with disobedience but also with failure to perform up to the level expected of them. Pupils, apprentices, and employees were required to respect and obey those in authority. Thus the experiences of everyday life in early civilizations encouraged obedience to authority figures. These relations contrasted dramatically with what was found in small-scale societies, where social control was enforced by public opinion and children were rarely, if ever, physically coerced or punished (Trigger 1985b). Smaller-scale societies often lacked even the concept of obedience, in the sense of one person's being thought to have the moral right to tell another person what to do. This distinction is understandable in terms of the information-theoretical notion that the development of control hierarchies resulted from the need to regulate increasingly large-scale societies. Information theory also explains why decision making came to be associated with people who did not perform manual labour and manual labour was associated with the carrying out of orders. The cultural encoding of concepts of status and power into family life, gender relations, and relations between young and old might appear to be a hierarchizing of social relations at an intimate level where hierarchy was not operationally required. Yet, only by making hierarchical relations pervasive in everyday life could unequal relations be made to appear sufficiently natural that they operated effectively at the societal and hence the political level. Unequal relations probably diffused through complex societies as a result of status emulation.

The need to develop a command hierarchy to manage complex societies does not, however, explain why decision-makers and their families invariably acquired such exalted social status and appropriated such large amounts of surplus wealth for their personal use. Few social scientists have recognized this as an issue worth investigating. Instead they have assumed that power, wealth, and social status are naturally correlated. Opposed to such a correlation is the religious ideal of service without personal or material benefit, as embodied in the Christian belief that a true leader should serve his followers. Occasionally ascetic religious figures appear to be satisfied with moral influence alone, but even in religious hierarchies leaders normally control wealth and live more luxuriously than their followers. In general, power over others is correlated with control of wealth as well as with enhanced social status.

Several explanations have been proposed for this correlation. Leaders need to possess wealth to reward their supporters and sustain subordinate officials. Unless those in command control sufficient material resources, a hierarchical system cannot be created or maintained. Public displays of wealth may also have been necessary to signal the importance of leaders and elicit respect for them. To survive, people had always had to extract more calories in the form of food from the environment than they expended in doing so, and this had made them implicitly aware of the practical importance of Zipf's (1949) law of least effort. The ability to flout this law by indulging in conspicuous and often wasteful consumption was therefore a statement of power that would have been immediately comprehensible (Trigger 1990a; Veblen 1899).

In small-scale societies leadership is not correlated with the possession of wealth. Hunter-gatherer societies are mobile, and those who live in them have little opportunity to accumulate possessions. The sharing of food results in balanced reciprocity, which promotes the well-being of everyone and is therefore highly adaptive. The most successful hunters share their catches with less successful hunters and their families and in return are accorded implicit positions of leadership. Any lack of generosity or of appropriately modest behaviour is punished by gossip and ridicule and believed to incite assaults of witchcraft (Lee 1990). In small-scale sedentary societies, leaders and their kin and supporters labour hard to produce surplus wealth that can be given away to incur moral indebtedness and thus sustain political support, often working harder than their followers and sometimes being poorer (Sahlins 1972; Trigger 1990b).

Eighteenth-century reports of such behaviour were interpreted by Jean-Jacques Rousseau and other Enlightenment philosophers as evidence that civilization had corrupted instinctive human generosity – an idea taken up in turn by Marxist thinkers, who attributed oppression to the development of hierarchy rather than to human nature. David Erdal and Andrew Whiten (1996) have argued that there must be some innate human predisposition that favours egalitarian behaviour in small-scale societies that is not present among other higher primate species. Yet it is clear that the social and economic egalitarianism of small-scale societies is everywhere a product of social engineering that requires the vigorous support of public opinion for its enforcement. When leaders acquire the power to control public communication and silence criticism of their behaviour, they invariably begin to accumulate wealth, which they use not only to perform public duties but also to confer disproportionate social and material benefits on themselves and their families.

That social and economic inequality becomes universal under these circumstances suggests that the tendency to equate power and wealth relates to a general acquisitiveness that is deeply embedded in human behaviour. In small-scale societies, such acquisitiveness is effectively suppressed by public opinion, which enforces the redistribution of such wealth as exists. Public opinion also imposes modesty on individuals who possess talents that are important for the well-being of their societies and make them de facto leaders. Yet, while in preindustrial civilizations public criticism and discontent were directed against the arbitrary appropriation of wealth and the abuse of power, economic inequality was accepted as a normal condition (Weber 1976 [1896]: 258). Revolutionary activity, when it occurred, sought to curb excesses rather than to eliminate the class system. Small-scale societies recognize acquisitiveness and domination as tendencies in human behaviour and seek ways to curb them through the exercise of public opinion. These mechanisms fail to control leaders as societies grow more complex, and power begins to be expressed through the conspicuous consumption of wealth. Neither cultural ecology nor information theory can readily explain why this happens.

Religions in early civilizations were based on the belief that supernatural forces animated (or were) the natural world; hence they did not distinguish the natural and the supernatural. Supernatural forces were ascribed minds, wills, and senses resembling those of human beings. These capacities facilitated communication between the human and the natural/supernatural realms. Human beings believed themselves to be animated by supernatural power, which further reduced the distinction between the social and the natural/supernatural. Because humans depended on the natural environment, they sought to guarantee their well-being by maintaining good relations with the supernatural beings that controlled nature. These relations constituted the central focus of religion in early civilizations. Morality remained primarily a social rather than a religious concern.

Not distinguishing the natural, supernatural, and social realms appears, on the basis of comparative ethnographic data, to have been an inheritance from the past. Yet much older ideas of supernatural power as animal spirits that had kinship relations with humans or as supportive but demanding ancestors were increasingly displaced by the perception of major deities as powerful natural or cosmic forces on whose support the welfare of all human beings depended. This broader vision of the supernatural was stimulated by a growing appreciation of the importance of political articulation and control for the survival and well-being of societies (Swanson 1960: 191–93). As forces of nature, deities were born, died, competed with one another, changed, and revealed both good and bad qualities. They were not all equally powerful, and weaker deities were subordinated in various ways to stronger ones. Thus widely shared beliefs that antedated the development of early civilizations were transformed in significant ways in the context of more complex and hierarchical social structures.

Out of this process emerged a set of distinctive beliefs that were common to all early civilizations. Humans saw themselves as dependent on the supernatural energy that sustained the universe and provided for their material needs. The gods, as the forces of nature, were the source of all life and sustenance, but they depended on the energy that human beings returned to them in the form of sacrifices. This complex of beliefs distributed complementary roles that were believed essential for sustaining the cosmos among commoners, the upper classes, and the gods. Deities provided the energy and order that animated the universe and all that was in it, including human beings. Farmers supplied the food and labour that supported the upper classes and the gods, while the upper classes provided the political order that allowed farmers to produce food surpluses and ritually cycled into the supernatural realm the energy that permitted the gods to maintain the cosmic order.

By assigning responsibility for nourishing the gods to the king and the upper classes, religious beliefs in early civilizations imposed strict limitations on the upper classes' exploitation of farmers. If food production faltered as the result of mistreatment of commoners by the upper classes, not only the stability of human society but the cosmic order was threatened – a situation for which human rulers were answerable to the gods. The maintenance of balanced and reciprocal relations between the upper and lower classes may explain why class conflict was not a major feature of early civilizations.

Nothing resembling this conceptualization of relations between human beings and the cosmic order could have existed before. Its tenets represented a projection into the supernatural realm of the general relations of production and government that linked farmers and the upper classes in early civilizations. Yet these religious beliefs cannot be dismissed as epiphenomenal. Nor, although based in part on views inherited from earlier times, can they be described as a simple or predictable reworking of these beliefs to fit new circumstances. They were instead products of profound reflections concerning the nature of society that took account of the general practices and accommodations that best governed relations among classes and extended these relations to the supernatural forces that were thought to maintain (or be) the universe. Relations between social classes were used analogically to conceptualize relations between human beings and the natural/supernatural forces on which humans had to rely. Through a conceptual inversion, the organization of the supernatural came to be perceived as a model and justification for human political and religious conduct. In a social realm that had become too large to be conceptualized in terms of kinship metaphors, religious concepts provided the basis for thinking about political issues and creating the equivalent of a constitution. It is highly significant that, in all the early civilizations, religion offered the context for such formulations and that, despite many specific differences in social organization and in beliefs concerning both the cosmic order and the gods, the same view of a sociocosmic order was created.

These conclusions are very different from those I would have reached had I discovered, for instance, that the people in every early civilization in my sample had believed in a powerful male deity named Ra, who was identified with the sun. Such evidence would have supported an Egyptocentric, or perhaps an Atlantean, explanation of the origins of religious beliefs in early civilizations. The fact that detailed similarities of this sort were not shared by early civilizations, combined with the lack of evidence of major historical links (except those of Mesoamerica) among the early civilizations being examined, strongly supports the view that we are dealing with a series of independent intellectual constructions.

The early civilizations also shared many general beliefs concerning the structure of the universe. Ideas about a multilevel cosmos with exclusively supernatural levels above and beneath the earth, a terrestrial world divided into quarters and surrounded by an ocean, and communication between levels occurring mainly at the centre and the outer edges of the earth may have been derived from beliefs that were already widespread prior to the development of the various early civilizations. These beliefs were supplemented by the more extensive empirical knowledge of the world that people in early civilizations were able to assemble as a result of contacts with increasingly distant societies and their recording of observations of natural phenomena over lengthy periods. The constraints of empirical knowledge account for the greater cross-cultural uniformity associated with beliefs concerning the terrestrial plane than with beliefs about the celestial and underworld levels and those relating to cosmology by comparison with more speculative topics such as creation, cosmic history, and the ultimate fate of the universe.

The idea that human beings possessed multiple souls, which disaggregated after they died, also appears to have been a continuation of earlier widespread beliefs. So too was the notion that an individual's identity survived, though not necessarily permanently, after death. Belief in the ability of souls to enjoy an enhanced existence after death appears to have been stronger in territorial states than in city-state systems. These optimistic beliefs seem to have developed among the upper classes and to have spread through status emulation to the lower classes.

The most important forms of learning that were patronized by the upper classes included divination and medicine. Doctors not only had to be familiar with natural remedies but had to know how to practise divination, interpret oracles, and discern the will of the gods in relation to health and sickness. Divination, oracles, and magic were also thought to enable leaders to learn the will of the gods concerning political and personal matters, avoid divine anger, control deities, ward off evil, and uncover witches. Much of this specialized knowledge was focused on regulating relations between human beings and the supernatural. This focus was not an obfuscation of practical knowledge that the upper classes hoped would halt technological and social progress and hence protect their special privileges, as Marxist historians of science once argued (Childe 1965 [1936]; B. Farrington 1936). While the people of early civilizations coped with most everyday problems in a practical and straightforward manner (Hallpike 1979), their view of the cosmos encouraged them to rely on the supernatural to try to resolve any problems that did not have an obvious pragmatic solution. To the upper classes, discovering techniques for managing relations with the supernatural was a supremely practical activity.

The development of writing systems provides detailed insights into the mixture of conceptual uniformity and idiosyncratic variation underlying a major intellectual achievement of some early civilizations. Writing systems were invented in at least four early civilizations, and all four scripts adopted similar logophonic approaches. Logograms, or word signs, were of primary importance, but sounds also had to be represented to resolve ambiguities resulting from their semantic extensions. Three different methods were employed for representing sounds: the Sumerians and Maya used syllabograms, the Egyptians noted only consonants, and the Chinese increasingly combined two signs, one of which functioned as a logogram while the other suggested its pronunciation. Purely syllabic or alphabetic scripts were produced only in societies that lacked writing systems but were aware of existing logophonic scripts. This pattern suggests a natural tendency for humans to privilege logography when developing systems to record speech.

THEORETICAL IMPLICATIONS

Comparative study reveals abundant idiosyncratic variation from one early civilization to another. Some of this variation was ecologically adaptive. Other variation helped to define the identity and status of different ethnic or political groups. Idiosyncratic variation characterized the content of the myths, art styles, and knowledge of early civilizations. Because all understanding is symbolically mediated, it is not surprising that idiosyncratic cultural traditions shaped human behaviour in highly significant and often unpredictable ways. Yet there is also abundant evidence of cross-cultural regularities that cannot be explained by historical relations. These regularities structured important aspects of the economies, social and political organization, and belief systems of early civilizations. There is no sector of early civilizations that did not display a significant combination of cultural idiosyncrasies and cross-cultural regularities. Such findings do not correspond with the expectations of either neoevolutionists or cultural determinists.

Neoevolutionary anthropologists have long been preoccupied with explaining cross-cultural similarities that appear to have arisen independently in societies at the same level of development. Most anthropologists assume that in the course of hominid evolution natural selection favoured the development of the biological capacity to manipulate symbols as a more flexible means of adaptation to the environment (Mithen 1996). This assumption has encouraged many archaeologists and anthropologists to interpret cultural transformations as rational responses to changing ecological conditions. Demographic and environmental changes and shifting patterns of competition with other societies require alterations in the ways in which human groups adapt to their environments. Most neoevolutionists have assumed that sociocultural change occurs only when ecological shifts require it. These ideas accord with the views articulated by Boasian cultural anthropologists and Durkheimian social anthropologists late in the nineteenth century and differ from those of a minority of materialists (mainly Marxists), who believe that systemic changes occur as a result of competition over resources. Both approaches view convergent change as a product of what Sahlins (1976) called 'practical reason' (Sanderson 1990).

Cultural ecologists regard human intelligence as individuals' ability to regulate, rationally and often on the basis of near-perfect knowledge, their relations with the natural world and with other human beings. Considerations of least effort and risk avoidance allow human groups to implement optimally adaptive solutions. People who must cope with similar problems in analogous environments are expected to devise similar solutions. For these theorists, necessity is truly the mother of invention. They disagree, however, on the level at which ecological influences are manifested. Leslie White (1949: 390–91) suggested that technological subsystems shaped social subsystems, while both together influenced philosophies and the arts, but he maintained (1945: 346) that these influences shaped cultural patterns only in a general fashion. Marvin Harris (1974; 1977; 1979), in contrast, has gone to great lengths to demonstrate that adaptive strategies shape very specific aspects of human behaviour and beliefs. He assumes that all aspects of cultures are functionally interrelated and that adaptive changes produce alterations throughout cultural systems. He further regards values and beliefs as epiphenomenal and determined by adaptation to the environment. Culture is treated as a facilitator – a way to encode adaptive behaviour and make it automatic.

Others, whose views are closer to White's, regard change as limited to an adaptive 'core' of society, while allowing that established aspects of behaviour and belief, which promote adaptation or are neutral with respect to it, persist. Julian Steward (1949) argued that the adaptive core revealed itself through cross-cultural regularities, while less adaptive features of culture survived as particularities. Thus kingship would have been identified as a core feature of early civilizations, while the symbolic association of monarchs in specific cultures with crowns, stools, or parasols would have constituted historical particularities. Steward (1955: 209) equated the study of cross-cultural regularities with science and that of particularities with history, arguing that there was no place for the study of particularities in a science of anthropology. He also stressed, however, that it was necessary to determine empirically which features were cross-culturally recurrent and which were not – an idea that underlies the present study. Robert Dunnell (1978) made a similar point when he argued that functional traits, which are affected by selection and therefore nonrandom, have to be distinguished from stylistic ones, which are functionally neutral and therefore have random or stochastic distributions. The problems inherent in distinguishing between style and function have already been noted. Roy Rappaport (1968) and Kent Flannery and Joyce Marcus (1976) have assigned a more proactive role to traditional beliefs, which they believe may play a significant role in regulating adaptive behaviour. The epiphenomenal role of culture was further called into question by Ian Hodder's (1982a) demonstration that material culture was not limited to reflecting social relations (also Cannon 1989).

Drawing on ideas derived from Enlightenment philosophy, neoevolutionists emphasized similarities in all human behaviour and the unilinear nature of cultural development throughout the world. Their approach encouraged belief in the similarities of responses of societies that were at the same level of development. Marshall Sahlins and Elman Service (1960) formulated their distinction between specific and general evolution in a similar vein. They argued that, while cultures necessarily adapted in diverse ways to various types of environments, the resulting specific differences were eventually overwhelmed by similarities in the successively more complex general adaptations that made more advanced societies dominant over less advanced ones. Steward, with his concept of multilinear evolution, appears to have advocated specific evolution, but in adopting Wittfogel's idea that all early civilizations had evolved in areas where irrigation was necessary he subjected cultural evolution to a unilinear straitjacket (Steward 1949; 1955: 178–209). It is now evident that early civilizations did not develop in a single type of environment or as the result of a particular agricultural practice such as extensive reliance on irrigation. Because subsistence adaptation always occurred in relation to particular local conditions, it had to be specific and was therefore highly variable.

Nor does much support remain for the suggestion that population pressure was the main factor promoting the development of early civilizations. Despite claims to the contrary by Ester Boserup (1965) and Mark Cohen (1977), population growth is not an independent variable but is influenced by numerous economic, social, and cultural factors. Much remains to be learned about relations between forms of government and population density. In New Guinea, communities have traditionally tended to split when their population rises above three hundred rather than grow larger and develop more elaborate forms of government. This process continues in areas that have overall population densities that are as high as 135 persons per square kilometre (Forge 1972). There was great variation in population density in relation to the amount of arable land in early civilizations.

The most important factor relating to agriculture that encouraged the development of early civilizations appears to have been the investment of labour in the long-term improvement of land, which created a need for protection against predation. State support ensured the owners of the best agricultural land that others could have access to it only on terms that they set (Linton 1933; 1939). Alternatively, where land was abundant but labour scarce, the state was looked to as a power that could guarantee the contractual rights of the affluent to the labour of the poor. Kent Flannery (1972) has noted that trade and many other factors promoted the development of early civilizations. The emergence of states created conditions that encouraged population growth and agricultural intensification. These developments increased the dependence of affluent groups on the government's capacity to maintain law and order.

The factors promoting the development of early civilizations thus appear to have been less ecological than economic or political. Land and labour were of less consequence in their own right than because they were regarded as forms of property, and ownership of land became less important than appropriation of the surpluses produced on that land.

As societies expanded, they required more complex hierarchical administrative structures. Kent Flannery (1972) has suggested that determining how these structures worked is more important for the functional understanding of early civilizations than discovering the varied and often idiosyncratic factors that encouraged the formation of specific large-scale political entities. In addition, authorities had to be able to deploy force to protect the society as a whole, uphold the rights of its more privileged members, and ensure that officials' orders were carried out. Achieving these goals required the development of armies, police forces, and law courts that served the interests of the upper classes. City-state systems and territorial states constituted alternative political structures for achieving those ends. These two varieties of political organization exemplify the complex roles played by functional constraints in shaping social organization.

More specific attention must be paid, however, to the correlation between the development of decision-making hierarchies and increasing social and economic inequality. It is generally assumed that, to be effective, authoritative decision-making roles in early civilizations had to be associated with wealth and high status. The accumulation of wealth for the personal benefit of the upper class cannot, however, be explained from a purely functional or rational perspective. Instead, it appears to be rooted in higher-primate behaviour and in a universal human tendency to interpret conspicuous consumption as evidence of political power.

Chimpanzees combine a strong predisposition for sociability and membership in groups with intense rivalries for positions of dominance and influence within those groups. Alliance making, deceit, and betrayal characterize these rivalries (Conroy 1990). The development of complex human societies undermined the highly effective social mechanisms that had been developed for combating self-assertiveness and acquisitiveness in hunter-gatherer societies, where generalized reciprocity had been important for survival. In complex societies, leaders who controlled the public dissemination of information were able to curb any public gossip and ridicule directed against them and suppress and punish their critics. The unprecedented isolation of rulers in their houses and then their palaces made them still more immune to public criticism (P. Wilson 1988). In these ways, individuals in positions of authority could protect and reinforce their power. Public deference was demanded from the vast majority of people, and overt criticism of the upper classes was not tolerated. Under these conditions, the lower classes lost any active role in governing society as a whole. Yet, while the upper classes were at least passively accepted and economically supported in return for the regulatory benefits they conferred on society, they remained subject to covert public opinion, which could become openly hostile if their control became ineffectual or their behaviour grew too oppressive.

Steven Mithen (1996) has argued that human social behaviour is biologically grounded not in general intelligence but in specific forms of cerebration that were already highly developed in humanity's ancestors prior to their separation from the great apes. His modular view of human intelligence lacks anatomical substantiation, and many neuroscientists emphasize the flexibility and adaptability of the modern human brain (Dubrovsky 1999). Yet some aspects of human behaviour do appear to be controlled by biological factors. The human cortex, which is associated with the capacity to reason, is anatomically linked to the limbic system, the seat of the emotions. Close connections between reason, will, and emotions are essential if reason is to promote effective goal-oriented and social behaviour (E. Armstrong 1991). Tendencies towards sociability and competitiveness seem likely to be genetically encoded in all the higher primates. If this is so, a biologically based tendency toward individual competitiveness, the overt expression of which had been held in check by public opinion among hunter-gatherers, came to be expressed more openly as societies grew more complex. As the state replaced public opinion as the principal instrument for maintaining social order, mechanisms for reinforcing social cooperation and solidarity of great antiquity were suppressed.

Egalitarian societies and states sought to promote different basic human behavioural tendencies. Thus there is no basis for claiming that, because they had temporal priority, egalitarian societies present human nature more accurately than do hierarchical ones. Yet societies appear to have been shaped not only by the adaptive requirements of their environments but also by aspects of human nature that are a product of long-term biological evolution. Practical reason cannot be equated solely with ecological adaptation. The human brain is not simply a rational calculating machine but a biological organ with its own needs and its own biologically determined modes of operation (E. White 1993). Phylogenetic and evolutionary psychological approaches point to the error of assuming that the inegalitarian behaviour that has emerged relatively recently in the course of human history is entirely culturally determined, just as information theory and functional analyses generally reveal that not everything that characterizes societies at a particular stage of cultural development is necessarily biologically determined.

Equally challenging to explain is why the upper classes everywhere lived luxuriously. Wealth is essential to maintain supporters and officials, and the conspicuous display and consumption of resources is universally interpreted as a sign of power. Yet this does not account for the enthusiasm with which the upper class lavished wealth on itself. Although better nutrition, superior housing, and less physical labour had selective advantages for an upper-class family, the luxury of upper-class lifestyles vastly transcended what was biologically required. Indeed, it may even have been counterproductive in terms of personal health. While hierarchically organized decision-makers were essential to ensure the functioning of complex societies, if these leaders and their families had lived frugal personal lives they would still, as administrative specialists, have been able to make the decisions necessary to regulate their societies.

Luxurious lifestyles are unique to humans living in class societies, but they are also universal in these societies. At most, other primates quarrel over the possession of food. In the early stages of hominid evolution, prior to the development of generalized reciprocity, competitive behaviour with respect to food probably had a significant selective advantage in periods of life-threatening scarcity. In the course of human evolution, this behavior may have expanded to include striving for all sorts of possessions whenever public opinion was insufficient to enforce generosity.

As societies came to be marked by increasing political inequality, the accumulation of wealth invariably paralleled the acquisition of political power, and conspicuous consumption was interpreted as evidence of power. Thus wealth and status became mutually reinforcing. In early civilizations, political power was both an important means of obtaining wealth and essential for protecting it. Conversely, controlling wealth was necessary to maintain political power. Yet there was little opportunity for economic and political interests to compete (Eisenstadt 1963). Wealth alone could not confer high social status on long-distance traders. Sociopolitical forces were clearly more important determinants of early class societies than economic ones. Yet humans appear to opt for wealth as well as political power whenever the opportunity arises. Under these circumstances, culturally specific explanations of inequalities in wealth appear to be epiphenomenal rationalizations of a universal human tendency. This universality calls into question the relativist claim that the object of wants is always particular and historically determined (Sahlins 1976: 152). Despite the group-enforced equality of hunter-gatherer societies, the correlation between power, status, and wealth appears to be deeply rooted in the human psyche.

Western individualism has encouraged an understanding of self-interest as the pursuit of strictly personal goals. In many other societies, in contrast, personal rewards, prestige, and well-being are believed to be derived from working with and for others. Yet the checks on material accumulation that existed in small-scale societies were subverted in every early civilization, and human beings displayed increasing personal acquisitiveness as well as a desire for publicly acknowledged status and power. This suggests that there may be significant genetic limits to humans' ability to sacrifice personal interest for the common good and that whenever personal acquisitiveness is not effectively controlled by public opinion it prevails over cultural conventions (Alexander 1987).

The development of analogous forms of behaviour as societies grew increasingly complex was paralleled by the development of analogous beliefs. The similar views held in early civilizations about relations between human beings and the natural/supernatural partly represented a continuation of ideas that were already shared by less complex societies. The same appears to hold, with varying degrees of regularity, for ideas about the structure of the universe, its functioning, the nature of souls, and healing. Yet all these understandings were significantly transformed in the hierarchical context of early civilizations. Novel but similar beliefs about mutually supportive relations between human societies and the supernatural arose through the development of analogous concepts in each early civilization. Similar parallelisms characterized other developments, including the upper classes' cultivation of esoteric knowledge related to the intentions of the gods, symbolizing the unity of the state through a single person who was believed to be responsible for the functioning of all aspects of society as well as the principal intermediary with the supernatural, and the belief that deities required human support to function properly. Enlightenment philosophers and nineteenth-century evolutionary anthropologists attributed such similarities to 'psychic unity'. Unfortunately, they treated psychic unity as if it were an explanation rather than a phenomenon or a set of phenomena to be explained.

Anthropologists still do not know enough about the reasons for widespread uniformities in human understandings. This is at least partly because they have too long accepted Emile Durkheim's (1964 [1895]) dogmatic separation of the social and the psychological and therefore paid insufficient attention to the role of psychological and biological factors in shaping human behaviour. Many cultural anthropologists perfunctorily acknowledge that human needs, drives, motives, desires, feelings, and sentiments are innate and universal. They also accept that biological factors not only influence ecologically adaptive behaviour but also account for the presence of art, music, and religious beliefs in all human societies. Boas and Malinowski both included psychological factors among culture's functional prerequisites, but because they believed that there were many possible cultural solutions for the problems that each functional prerequisite posed, they did not regard these prerequisites as significantly inhibiting cultural diversity. Neoevolutionary archaeologists accepted psychological predispositions as universals but discounted their importance in shaping human behaviour by comparison with ecological considerations. Classical Marxists accepted the reality of psychological drives but, so as not to compromise their millenarian ambitions to transform the human condition, denied that these drives constituted a fixed human nature (Geras 1983). Relativists regarded psychological predispositions as subordinate to and controlled by cultural conventions which alone guided human behaviour.

The idea that human behaviour must be explained without reference to psychology encouraged belief in an intelligence that rationally adapted individuals and groups to their natural and social environments. Today, however, it is increasingly acknowledged that certain abilities are neurologically and hormonally grounded (Butterworth 1999; Gazzaniga 1992; 1998; Low 2000; Mithen 1996). These claims are not to be confused with those of sociobiology, which maintains that, as a result of natural selection, predispositions for very specific forms of human behaviour become biologically embedded in the human brain over periods as short as a few thousand years (E. Wilson 1978). Given the accelerating rate of cultural change during the course of hominid development, such a process would have had few adaptive advantages and many disadvantages; hence it is difficult to understand how it might have evolved or persisted (Boyd and Richerson 1985: 199). Short-term biological encoding, which is highly susceptible to regional evolutionary trends, also does not account for what appear to be the overwhelming universal similarities in human nature.

The difficulties posed by sociobiology do not, however, rule out the possibility that the biological basis of the human mind has been shaped by natural selection acting over very long periods. The most important long-term challenge to which natural selection has adapted human beings does not appear to have been the natural environment, which became increasingly varied as human beings expanded around the globe. Instead, it was living in small groups within which individuals related to one another in both cooperative and competitive ways. The human mind remains best equipped to make informed decisions that relate to the activities of small groups rather than large ones and to the immediate future rather than the long term. This suggests that individuals are better adapted for pursuing immediate goals for themselves and their families than for pursuing the long-term welfare of larger collectivities (Boyd and Richerson 1985; Carrithers 1992).

Mithen (1996) has argued, on the basis of archaeological data and comparative primate ethology, that hominids' capacities to manipulate technology and analyse biological and physical phenomena developed far more recently than their capacity to manage social relations (Byrne and Whiten 1988). The cognitive linking together of these specialized forms of thought, which may have occurred between one hundred thousand and forty thousand years ago, appears to have made human comprehension more flexible and abstract. The development of language, at least some aspects of which have a complex genetic basis (Gopnik 1997), vastly increased the ability of humans to transmit knowledge by inculcation. This form of learning is adaptively much more efficient than learning by demonstration or by trial and error. The development of language not only accelerated the rate of cultural change but vastly altered and expanded human awareness and self-awareness and enhanced human analytical abilities. This made it possible for humans to adapt ever more quickly to varying ecological conditions and eventually, for better or worse, to dominate the planetary ecosystem (Deacon 1997; Mellars and Gibson 1996; Noble and Davidson 1996). Mithen claims that the interrelating of what were originally specialized forms of cerebration also made possible the obsessive anthropomorphization that still characterizes human thought.

Recent cognitive research suggests that the human mind understands the world through a complex web of metaphors that structures perception, action, and social relations (Lakoff 1987; Lakoff and Johnson 1980; Tilley 1999). Thus it appears that cognitive evolution has endowed the human mind with various general and specific analytical capacities that predispose humans to attribute analogous symbolic meanings to their perceptions of the natural and social realms. The sun, because of its extreme brilliance, has often been used as a symbol of supreme power, the snake, because it sheds its skin, as a symbol of renewal, and a physically elevated position as an indication of superior social rank (Hallpike 1979: 149–67; von Gernet 1992; 1993). The widespread myths that identify kings or elites with strangers (Feeley-Harnik 1985; Gillespie 1989) equate varying social status with ethnic differences, and Mary Helms (1998) claims that this equation derives its legitimacy and authority from cosmological beliefs. Concepts that in the past have been cited as examples of psychic unity need to be studied in far greater detail not only from an anthropological perspective but from the perspectives of evolutionary psychology and neuroscience. Only then will anthropologists be in a position to understand why many aspects of culture display varying degrees of cross-cultural uniformity. Such an approach may eventually provide a reliable methodology for distinguishing between cross-cultural uniformities resulting from the operation of similar psychological factors and similarities resulting from historical connections.

It is misleading to deny emergent properties in society and culture in order to support the erroneous positivist concept of a unified science. Yet the psychological and biological bases of human cognition must be considered in explaining human behaviour. This will require a determined effort to overcome the extreme antireductionist biases of Durkheimian sociology and cultural anthropology. One benefit of closer ties between the social sciences, on the one hand, and psychology and biology, on the other, would be a better understanding of those aspects of human behaviour that are influenced by long-term human biological evolution. The present study suggests that such factors may contribute in significant ways to the shaping of human understanding and behaviour. This sort of interdisciplinary research might also advance the social sciences' still rudimentary understanding of the mechanisms that structuralists claim pattern human thought.

29 Conclusion

The comparative study of early civilizations documents the capacity of the human mind to generate an almost infinite variety of beliefs and ideas. Art styles, myths, and ecological knowledge differed radically from one early civilization to another, and people's lives were shaped and provided with meaning by values and aspirations that were unique to each. These observations accord with the relativist view that every human group lives in its own culturally constructed environment. While it is impossible to test Marshall Sahlins's (1976: 19) assertion that human beings live in meaningful cultural schemes of their own devising that are never the only ones possible, there is much evidence that makes this proposition appear plausible.

Cultural change does not, however, occur merely as the result of accidental miscopying or alteration in the course of individual decodings of messages. Culture resists random changes by striving to maintain cognitive structures and psychological consistency. The relation between form and meaning is highly complex. In some cases, while texts or icons remain the same, interpretations of them alter significantly over time. Conversely a series of highly varied or rapidly changing texts or symbols may continue to express a single message (Goodenough 1953–68; Marx and Engels 1964: 97–118; 287–347; Panofsky 1939). In these ways, cultural traditions can persist over long periods and adapt to changing conditions.

Yet early civilizations also displayed a vast amount of cross-cultural uniformity, especially in the sociopolitical and religious spheres. Subsistence patterns were concerned with adaptation to local conditions and necessarily displayed much variation. By contrast, early civilizations possessed one general form of class structure, only two main forms of sociopolitical organization, and one set of key religious beliefs. These findings are inconsistent with both the view that early civilizations were shaped wholly by idiosyncratic factors and the view that their similarities resulted only from ecological constraints.

Another type of functional constraint that was cross-culturally uniform was the need for more formal and hierarchical systems of decision-making as societies increased in scale. It appears, furthermore, that only a limited number of sociopolitical arrangements had enough functional coherence to exist as viable systems – an observation that George P. Murdock (1949) first made with respect to kinship systems. Christopher Hallpike (1986) suggests than an ever more limited range of institutions and value systems is able to survive as societies grow larger and more likely to compete with one another. Isolated early civilizations, which displayed two major political variants, fall midway between highly variable small-scale societies and structurally even less variable industrial civilizations. It has been suggested that the collapse of the Soviet Union after fewer than seventy years of competition with capitalist societies indicates that only a single general type of industrial economy has proved competitively viable (Harris 1992). Only one sort of early civilization was viable in any one region. Territorial states and city-states were not superseded by each other but replaced by new and more complex forms of preindustrial civilization.

Societies are altered in various ways by the need to adjust effectively to changing ecological conditions. They are also reshaped by rational calculations in the economic sphere, where competitive advantages are achieved by making more efficient use of available energy and resources. Contrary to the claims of extreme relativists, human beings devise rational strategies to outmanoeuvre competitors and seek to alter the rules of society in their own interest. While relativists argue that self-interest is always culturally defined such interests in all early civilizations appear to have been based on competitive advantages in controlling material resources and human labour.

Finally, the independent development of similar understandings not only about practical matters but also with respect to religious beliefs and symbolism is abundantly documented for early civilizations. Some of the parallels appear to result from the operation of practical reason, while others reflect little-understood tendencies of the human mind to produce particular types of analogies.

Traditional rationalists, including the neoevolutionists of the 1960s, sought to understand how human beings used a general capacity for rational calculation to adapt to their environments. Yet, in addition to being capable of rational calculation, the human brain provides the organic basis for human drives, personality, and affective capacities. These drives and affects not only motivate human behaviour but also constitute biological realities to which culture must accommodate. Specialized analytical capacities that have developed in the course of human evolution may channel thought in particular directions. Consequently, anthropologists are discussing not so much Sahlins's 'practical reason' as a more complex form of 'human reason' that provides for the cognitive and psychological as well as the physical needs of human beings. This view transcends the traditional dichotomies that Western thought draws between body and intellect, matter and mind. For such an approach to have any scientific value, however, anthropologists must shun subjective and ethnocentric speculations, especially those of the Hegelian tradition which seek to understand a timeless human spirit (Karlsson 1998: 188).

The background for understanding the biological component of human behaviour is changing rapidly as a Lockean belief in general, calculative reason gives way to the possibility of specific as well as general forms of intelligence such as those associated with metaphorical thought or with particular aspects of numeracy and language. What is needed is a better understanding, derived from psychology and neuroscience, of how the human brain shapes understanding and influences behaviour. Nothing about such an approach undermines or calls into question a materialist and evolutionary (as opposed to a narrowly ecological or environmental) approach to the understanding of human behaviour. On the contrary, given what we know about biological evolution, only a materialist and evolutionary approach is sustainable. Nor is any challenge posed to viewing cultures as adaptive systems. The problem is to understand how humans, as biological and behaviourally predisposed products of long-term natural selection possessing both unique capacities for culture and distinct cultural heritages, adapt to each other and to their environment. Social scientists must cease analysing human behaviour without reference to humans as biological entities. Evolution, both biological and cultural, is a process that adapts humans with specific but as yet poorly understood biological, social, and psychological predispositions and needs to the natural and social environment in which they live.

The preoccupation of processual archaeology with rationalist ecological adaptation represents an unacceptably simplistic understanding of the evolutionary process. Humans adapt to their surroundings as beings with specific cognitive capacities, psychological predispositions, and hormonally based drives, not just as entities equipped with the ability to calculate optimal energetic relations with the environment. All these needs and capacities must be considered as relevant for understanding human adaptation. Cognition is not just instrumental or epiphenomenal but active in identifying human goals and shaping human adaptation. Cultural traditions provide the understandings with which specific groups cope with life and attempt to solve new problems. Knowledge concerning technology and economic matters is no less a cultural heritage from the past than are ideas about social organization or religious beliefs.

Nevertheless, instrumental reasoning, biologically defined human needs, and innate predispositions are more important in shaping or resisting changes in human behaviour than postprocessual archaeologists or postmodernist anthropologists acknowledge.

Cross-cultural regularities are not restricted to aspects of human behaviour in which ecological concerns about the efficient use of energy predominate. A materialist approach must also explain cross-culturally similar patterns of historically unrelated religious thought. Species-specific biological behaviour, including specific analytical capacities of the human mind, may be necessary to account for cross-cultural parallels of a symbolic nature. All the early civilizations shared a considerable number of features that were the convergent products of human needs and natural constraints transforming existing knowledge and behaviour to specific ends. Yet this uniform cultural core (to borrow Steward's terminology) was accompanied by idiosyncratic features derived from historical traditions that did not evolve convergently, among them art styles, highly specific religious beliefs, and, most surprisingly, values and personal aspirations.

The present study suggests that a broader spectrum of factors must be taken into account to explain similarities and differences among early civilizations than is fashionable in most current theorizing. There are no grounds for accepting sociobiology's claim that human behaviour becomes biologically grounded in the short term, but it appears that human behaviour cannot be explained purely in cultural and social terms. Human beings are products of biological evolution operating over a very long period. Natural selection has shaped the human capacity to think and communicate symbolically. Increasing evidence indicates that these operations are grounded not only in a general intelligence but also in various specific cognitive capacities that developed separately over time. In addition, human beings have a broad set of needs, desires, and emotions that is biologically grounded. Relativists argue that these tendencies can be culturally managed in a vast number of ways, but this claim does not appear to accord with the full range of cross-cultural uniformities that characterize human behaviour. To explain such uniformities, it is necessary to take account of biological and psychological, as well as social and cultural, factors.

Social and cultural phenomena have their own emergent properties and cannot wholly be explained in psychological or biological terms. Yet neither can human behaviour or the nature of society and culture be understood without judiciously taking account of the findings of evolutionary psychology and neuroscience. It would appear to be in these sciences that anthropologists must seek explanations of certain cross-cultural uniformities in human behaviour, such as tendencies towards inequality in status and wealth. The failure of social scientists to address these issues in the past has contributed to some of the major disasters in utopian social engineering attempted during the twentieth century, most notably in Stalinist Russia and Maoist China. Evolutionary psychology and neuroscience remain underdeveloped, and the findings of evolutionary psychology are strongly influenced by various social stereotypes and activist agendas. Therefore they are not panaceas. Many cross-cultural regularities can be explained functionally in terms of ecological or information theory. Yet the rift created by Durkheimian and, more recently, anthropological relativist preoccupations with purely social or cultural explanations needs to be bridged to produce more holistic and convincing explanations of cross-cultural similarities and differences in human behaviour.

References

Aberle, D. F., A. K. Cohen, A. K. Davis, M.-J. Levy, Jr., and F. X. Sutton. 1950. The Functional Prerequisites of a Society. *Ethics* 60: 100–111.

Abimbola, Wande. 1973. 'The Literature of the Ifa Cult', in S. O. Biobaku, pp. 41–62.

Abiodun, Rowland, H. J. Drewal, and John Pemberton III. 1994. *The Yoruba Artist: New Theoretical Perspectives on African Arts.* Washington, DC: Smithsonian Institution Press.

Abrams, E. M. 1989. Architecture and Energy: An Evolutionary Perspective. *Archaeological Method and Theory* 1: 47–87.

1994. *How the Maya Built Their World: Energetics and Ancient Architecture.* Austin: University of Texas Press.

Abu-Lughod, J. 1969. 'Varieties of Urban Experience: Contrast, Coexistence, and Coalescence in Cairo', in I. M. Lapidus, pp. 159–87.

Adams, Richard E. W., ed. 1977. *The Origins of Maya Civilization.* Albuquerque: University of New Mexico Press.

1986. Río Azul. *National Geographic* 169: 420–51.

2000. 'Introduction to a Survey of the Native Prehistoric Cultures of Mesoamerica', in R. E. W. Adams and M. J. MacLeod, pt. 1, 1–44.

Adams, R. E. W., and M. J. MacLeod, eds. 2000. *The Cambridge History of the Native Peoples of the Americas.* Vol. 2. *Mesoamerica.* 2 parts. New York: Cambridge University Press.

Adams, R. E. W., and W. D. Smith. 1981. 'Feudal Models for Classic Maya Civilization', in W. Ashmore, pp. 335–49.

Adams, Richard N. 1988. *The Eighth Day: Social Evolution as the Self-Organization of Energy.* Austin: University of Texas Press.

Adams, Robert McC. 1960. 'Early Civilizations, Subsistence, and Environment', in C. H. Kraeling and R. McC. Adams, pp. 269–95.

1965. *Land behind Baghdad: A History of Settlement on the Diyala Plains.* Chicago: University of Chicago Press.

1966. *The Evolution of Urban Society: Early Mesopotamia and Prehispanic Mexico.* Chicago: Aldine.

1974a. Anthropological Perspectives on Ancient Trade. *Current Anthropology* 15: 239–58.

1974b. 'Historic Patterns of Mesopotamian Irrigation Agriculture', in T. E. Downing and M. Gibson, pp. 1–6.

1981. *Heartland of Cities: Surveys of Ancient Settlement and Land Use on the Central Floodplain of the Euphrates.* Chicago: University of Chicago Press.

1992. 'Ideologies: Unity and Diversity', in A. A. Demarest and G. W. Conrad, pp. 205–21.

Adams, R. McC., and H. J. Nissen. 1972. *The Uruk Countryside.* Chicago: University of Chicago Press.

Adetugbo, Obiodun. 1973. 'The Yoruba Language in Yoruba History', in S. O. Biobaku, pp. 176–204.

Afanasieva, V. K. 1991. 'Sumerian Culture', in I. M. Diakonoff, pp. 124–36.

Aguilera, Carmen. 1989. 'Templo Mayor: Dual Symbol of the Passing of Time', in D. Carrasco, pp. 129–35.

Ajayi, J. F. A., and Robert Smith. 1971. *Yoruba Warfare in the Nineteenth Century.* 2d ed. Cambridge: Cambridge University Press.

Ajisafe, A. K. 1924. *The Laws and Customs of the Yoruba People.* London: Routledge.

Akintoye, S. A. 1971. *Revolution and Power Politics in Yorubaland, 1840–1893.* London: Longman.

Aldenderfer, M. S., L. R. Kimball, and April Sievert. 1989. Microwear Analysis in the Maya Lowlands: The Use of Functional Data in a Complex-Society Setting. *Journal of Field Archaeology* 16: 47–60.

Aldred, Cyril. 1971. *Jewels of the Pharaohs: Egyptian Jewellery of the Dynastic Period.* London: Thames and Hudson.

Alexander, Richard. 1987. *The Biology of Moral Systems.* Hawthorne, NY: Aldine de Gruyter.

Allam, Schafik. 1981. Quelques aspects du mariage dans l'Egypte ancienne. *Journal of Egyptian Archaeology* 67: 116–35.

1989. 'Women as Owners of Immovables in Pharaonic Egypt', in B. S. Lesko, pp. 123–35.

1991. Egyptian Law Courts in Pharaonic and Hellenistic Times. *Journal of Egyptian Archaeology* 77: 109–27.

Allan, Sarah. 1991. *The Shape of the Turtle: Myth, Art, and Cosmos in Early China.* Albany: State University of New York Press.

Allchin, F. R. 1995. *The Archaeology of Early Historic South Asia: The Emergence of Cities and States.* Cambridge: Cambridge University Press.

Allen, J. P. 1988. *Genesis in Egypt: The Philosophy of Ancient Egyptian Creation Accounts.* Yale Egyptological Studies 2.

2000. *Middle Egyptian: An Introduction to the Language and Culture of Hieroglyphs.* Cambridge: Cambridge University Press.

Allen, R. C. 1997. Agriculture and the Origins of the State in Ancient Egypt. *Explorations in Economic History* 34: 135–54.

Amin, Samir. 1976. *Unequal Development: An Essay on the Social Formations of Peripheral Capitalism.* New York: Monthly Review Press.

An Chin-huai. 1986. 'The Shang City at Cheng-chou and Related Problems', in K.-C. Chang, 1986b, pp. 15–48.

Andreu, Guillemette. 1997. *Egypt in the Age of the Pyramids.* Ithaca: Cornell University Press.

Andrews, G. F. 1975. *Maya Cities: Placemaking and Urbanization.* Norman: University of Oklahoma Press.

Apter, Andrew. 1992. *Black Critics and Kings: The Hermeneutics of Power in Yoruba Society.* Chicago: University of Chicago Press.

Armstrong, E. 1991. The Limbic System and Culture. *Human Nature* 2: 117–36.

Armstrong, R. P. 1981. *The Powers of Presence: Consciousness, Myth, and Affecting Presence.* Philadelphia: University of Pennsylvania Press.

Ascher, Maria, and Robert Ascher. 1981. *Code of the Quipu: A Study in Media, Mathematics, and Culture.* Ann Arbor: University of Michigan Press.

Ashmore, Wendy, ed. 1981. *Lowland Maya Settlement Patterns.* Albuquerque: University of New Mexico Press.
1989. 'Construction and Cosmology: Politics and Ideology in Lowland Maya Settlement Patterns', in W. F. Hanks and D. S. Rice, pp. 272–86.
Ashmore, Wendy, and A. B. Knapp, eds. 1999. *Archaeologies of Landscape: Contemporary Perspectives.* Oxford: Blackwell.
Assmann, Jan. 1995. *Egyptian Solar Religion in the New Kingdom: Re, Amun, and the Crisis of Polytheism.* London: Kegan Paul International.
Atran, Scott. 1993. Itza Maya Tropical Agro-Forestry. *Current Anthropology* 34: 633–700.
Aveni, A. F. 1989. *Empires of Time: Calendars, Clocks, and Cultures.* New York: Basic Books.
ed. 1992. *The Sky in Mayan Literature.* Oxford: Oxford University Press.
Awolalu, J. O. 1979. *Yoruba Beliefs and Sacrificial Rites.* London: Longman.
Bacus, E. A., and L. J. Lucero, eds. 1999. *Complex Polities in the Ancient Tropical World.* Archeological Papers of the American Anthropological Association 9.
Baer, Klaus. 1960. *Rank and Title in the Old Kingdom: The Structure of the Egyptian Administration in the Fifth and Sixth Dynasties.* Chicago: University of Chicago Press.
Bagley, R. W. 1980. 'The Zhengzhou Phase (The Erligong Period)', in W. Fong, pp. 95–108.
1999. 'Shang Archaeology', in M. Loewe and E. L. Shaughnessy, pp. 124–231.
Bailey, A. M., and J. R. Llobera, eds. 1981. *The Asiatic Mode of Production: Science and Politics.* London: Routledge and Kegan Paul.
Baines, John. 1983. Literacy and Ancient Egyptian Society. *Man* 18: 572–99.
1991a. 'Society, Morality, and Religious Practice', in B. E. Shafer, pp. 123–200.
1991b. Egyptian Myth and Discourse: Myth, Gods, and the Early Written and Iconographic Record. *Journal of Near Eastern Studies* 50: 81–105.
1995a. 'Kingship, Definition of Culture, and Legitimation', in D. O'Connor and D. P. Silverman, pp. 3–47.
1995b. 'Origins of Egyptian Kingship', in D. O'Connor and D. P. Silverman, pp. 95–156.
Baines, John, and Jaromir Malek. 1980. *Atlas of Ancient Egypt.* Oxford: Phaidon.
Baines, John, and Norman Yoffee. 1998. 'Order, Legitimacy, and Wealth in Ancient Egypt and Mesopotamia', in G. M. Feinman and J. Marcus, pp. 199–260.
Bairoch, Paul. 1988. *Cities and Economic Development: From the Dawn of History to the Present.* Chicago: University of Chicago Press.
Ball, J. W. 1993. 'Pottery, Potters, Palaces, and Polities: Some Socioeconomic and Political Implications of Late Classic Maya Ceramic Industries', in J. A. Sabloff and J. S. Henderson, pp. 243–72.
Barber, E. W. 1994. *Women's Work – The First 20,000 Years: Women, Cloth, and Society in Early Times.* New York: Norton.
Barber, Karin. 1981. How Man Makes God in West Africa: Yoruba Attitudes towards the *Orisa. Africa* 51: 724–45.
1991. *I Could Speak Until Tomorrow:* Oriki, *Women, and the Past in a Yoruba Town.* Washington, DC: Smithsonian Institution Press.
Barlow, R. H. 1949. *The Extent of the Empire of the Culhua Mexica.* Ibero-Americana 28. Berkeley: University of California Press.
Barnes, Barry. 1974. *Scientific Knowledge and Sociological Theory.* London: Routledge and Kegan Paul.
Barnes, G. L. 1993. *China, Korea, and Japan: The Rise of Civilization in East Asia.* London: Thames and Hudson.
Barnes, S. T., ed. 1989. *Africa's Ogun: Old World and New.* Bloomington: Indiana University Press.
Barnes, S. T., and P. G. Ben-Amos. 1989. 'Ogun, the Empire Builder', in S. T. Barnes, pp. 39–64.

Barraclough, Geoffrey, ed. 1984. *The Times Atlas of World History*. Rev. ed. London: Times Books.

Bascom, William. 1944. *The Sociological Role of the Yoruba Cult-Group*. American Anthropological Association Memoir 63.

1955. Urbanization among the Yoruba. *American Journal of Sociology* 60: 446–54.

1969. *The Yoruba of Southwestern Nigeria*. New York: Holt, Rinehart and Winston.

Bassie-Sweet, Karen. 1991. *From the Mouth of the Dark Cave: Commemorative Sculpture of the Late Classic Maya*. Norman: University of Oklahoma Press.

Bates, D. G., ed. 1995. *Knowledge and the Scholarly Medical Traditions*. Cambridge: Cambridge University Press.

Baudez, Claude-François. 1994. *Maya Sculpture of Copán: The Iconography*. Norman: University of Oklahoma Press.

Bauer, B. S. 1996. Legitimization of the State in Inca Myth and Ritual. *American Anthropologist* 98: 327–37.

1998. *The Sacred Landscape of the Inca: The Cusco Ceque System*. Austin: University of Texas Press.

Bauer, B. S., and D. S. P. Dearborn. 1995. *Astronomy and Empire in the Ancient Andes*. Austin: University of Texas Press.

Bauval, Robert, and Adrian Gilbert. 1994. *The Orion Mystery: Unlocking the Secrets of the Pyramids*. London: Heinemann.

Becker, M. J. 1973. Archaeological Evidence for Occupational Specialization among the Classic Period Maya at Tikal, Guatemala. *American Antiquity* 38: 396–406.

Bell, Barbara. 1971. The Dark Ages in Ancient History. 1. The First Dark Age in Egypt. *American Journal of Archaeology* 75: 1–26.

Bell, Catherine. 1992. *Ritual Theory, Ritual Practice*. Oxford: Oxford University Press.

Bell, Lanny. 1997. 'The New Kingdom "Divine" Temple: The Example of Luxor', in B. E. Shafer, pp. 127–84.

Ben-Amos, Paula. 1983. 'In Honor of Queen Mothers', in P. Ben-Amos and A. Rubin, pp. 79–83.

1995. *The Art of Benin*. 2d ed. London: British Museum Press.

Ben-Amos, Paula, and Arnold Rubin, eds. 1983. *The Art of Power, the Power of Art: Studies in Benin Iconography*. UCLA Museum of Cultural History Monograph Series 19.

Benedict, Ruth. 1934. *Patterns of Culture*. Boston: Houghton Mifflin.

Benson, E. P., and G. G. Griffin, eds. 1988. *Maya Iconography*. Princeton: Princeton University Press.

Berdan, F. F. 1982. *The Aztecs of Central Mexico: An Imperial Society*. New York: Holt, Rinehart and Winston.

Berdan, F. F., R. E. Blanton, E. H. Boone, M. G. Hodge, M. E. Smith, and Emily Umberger. 1996. *Aztec Imperial Strategies*. Washington, DC: Dumbarton Oaks.

Betanzos, Juan de. 1996. *Narratives of the Incas*. Trans. and ed. Roland Hamilton and Dana Buchanan from the Palma de Mallorca Manuscript. Austin: University of Texas Press.

Bethell, Leslie, ed. 1984. *The Cambridge History of Latin America*. Vol. 1. *Colonial Latin America*. New York: Cambridge University Press.

Betzig, L. L. 1986. *Despotism and Differential Reproduction: A Darwinian View of History*. New York: Aldine.

Bierbrier, Morris. 1982. *The Tomb-Builders of the Pharaohs*. London: British Museum Publications.

Bierhorst, John. 1985. *Cantares Mexicanos: Songs of the Aztecs*. Stanford: Stanford University Press.

Binford, L. R. 1962. Archaeology as Anthropology. *American Antiquity* 28: 217–25.
1971. 'Mortuary Practices: Their Study and Their Potential', in *Approaches to the Social Dimensions of Mortuary Practices*, J. A. Brown, ed., pp. 6–29. Memoirs of the Society for American Archaeology 25.
1972. *An Archaeological Perspective.* New York: Seminar Press.
1978. *Nunamiut Ethnoarchaeology.* New York: Academic Press.
1980. 'Willow Smoke and Dogs' Tails': Hunter-Gatherer Settlement Systems and Archaeological Site Formation. *American Antiquity* 45: 4–20.
1983. *In Pursuit of the Past: Decoding the Archaeological Record.* London: Thames and Hudson.
1989. *Debating Archaeology.* San Diego: Academic Press.
2001. *Constructing Frames of Reference: An Analytical Method for Archaeological Theory Building Using Ethnographic and Environmental Data Sets.* Berkeley: University of California Press.
Biobaku, S. O., ed. 1973. *Sources of Yoruba History.* Oxford: Oxford University Press.
Bird-David, Nurit. 1990. The Giving Environment: Another Perspective on the Economic System of Gatherer-Hunters. *Current Anthropology* 31: 189–96.
Blacker, Carmen, and Michael Loewe, eds. 1975. *Ancient Cosmologies.* London: Allen and Unwin.
Blanton, R. E., G. M. Feinman, S. A. Kowalewski, and P. N. Peregrine. 1996. A Dual-Processual Theory for the Evolution of Mesoamerican Civilization. *Current Anthropology* 37: 1–14.
Blanton, R. E., S. A. Kowalewski, G. Feinman, and J. Appel. 1981. *Ancient Mesoamerica: A Comparison of Change in Three Regions.* Cambridge: Cambridge University Press.
Bloch, Maurice, ed. 1975. *Marxist Analyses and Social Anthropology.* London: Malaby Press.
1985. *Marxism and Anthropology: The History of a Relationship.* Oxford: Oxford University Press.
Boas, Franz. 1963 (1911). *The Mind of Primitive Man.* New York: Crowell-Collier.
Boltz, W. G. 1986. Early Chinese Writing. *World Archaeology* 17: 420–36.
1994. *The Origin and Early Development of the Chinese Writing System.* New Haven, CT: American Oriental Society.
1999. 'Language and Writing', in M. Loewe and E. L. Shaughnessy, pp. 74–123.
Bonnet, Hans. 1999 (1939). On Understanding Syncretism. *Orientalia* 68: 181–98.
Bontty, Monica. 1997. Concerning *hp*. *Journal of the Society for the Study of Egyptian Antiquities* 27: 1–8.
Boone, E. H., ed. 1984. *Ritual Human Sacrifice in Mesoamerica.* Washington, DC: Dumbarton Oaks.
Boone, E. H., and W. D. Mignolo, eds. 1994. *Writing Without Words: Alternative Literacies in Mesoamerica and the Andes.* Durham, NC: Duke University Press.
Boserup, Ester. 1965. *The Conditions of Agricultural Growth: The Economics of Agrarian Change under Population Pressure.* Chicago: Aldine.
Bottéro, Jean. 1992. *Mesopotamia: Writing, Reasoning, and the Gods.* Chicago: University of Chicago Press.
Bottomore, T. B. 1974. 'Social Differentiation and Stratification', in *The New Encyclopaedia Britannica*, 15th ed., *Macropaedia*, Vol. 16: 953–59.
Boyd, Robert, and P. J. Richerson. 1985. *Culture and the Evolutionary Process.* Chicago: University of Chicago Press.
Boyer, Pascal. 1994. *The Naturalness of Religious Ideas: A Cognitive Theory of Religion.* Berkeley: University of California Press.
1996. What Makes Anthropomorphism Natural: Intuitive Ontology and Cultural Representations. *Journal of the Royal Anthropological Institute* 2: 83–97.

Bradbury, R. E. 1957. *The Benin Kingdom and the Edo-Speaking Peoples of South-Western Nigeria.* London: International African Institute.
1973. *Benin Studies.* Edited by Peter Morton-Williams. London: Oxford University Press.
Brady, J. E., and Wendy Ashmore. 1999. 'Mountains, Caves, Water: Ideational Landscapes of the Ancient Maya', in W. Ashmore and A. B. Knapp, pp. 124–45.
Bram, Joseph. 1941. *An Analysis of Inca Militarism.* American Ethnological Society Monographs 4.
Braudel, Fernand. 1982. *Civilization and Capitalism 15th–18th Century*. Vol. 2: *The Wheels of Commerce.* New York: Harper and Row.
Bray, Warwick. 1968. *Everyday Life of the Aztecs.* New York: Dorsey.
Broda, Johanna. 1987. 'Templo Mayor as Ritual Space', in J. Broda, D. Carrasco, and E. Matos Moctezuma, pp. 61–123.
Broda, Johanna, Davíd Carrasco, and Eduardo Matos Moctezuma. 1987. *The Great Temple of Tenochtitlan: Center and Periphery in the Aztec World.* Berkeley: University of California Press.
Bronson, Bennet. 1966. Roots and the Subsistence of the Ancient Maya. *Southwestern Journal of Anthropology* 22: 251–79.
Brook, Timothy, ed. 1989. *The Asiatic Mode of Production in China.* Armonk, NY: M. E. Sharpe.
Brown, B. A. 1984. 'Ochpaniztli in Historical Perspective', in E. H. Boone, pp. 195–210.
Brown, D. E. 1991. *Human Universals.* Philadelphia: Temple University Press.
Brumfiel, E. M. 1980. Specialization, Market Exchange, and the Aztec State: A View from Huexotla. *Current Anthropology* 21: 459–78.
1983. Aztec State Making: Ecology, Structure, and the Origin of the State. *American Anthropologist* 85: 261–84.
1987. 'Elite and Utilitarian Crafts in the Aztec State', in E. M. Brumfiel and T. K. Earle, pp. 102–18.
1991. 'Weaving and Cooking: Women's Production in Aztec Mexico', in J. M. Gero and M. W. Conkey, pp. 224–51.
1994. 'Ethnic Groups and Political Development in Ancient Mexico', in E. M. Brumfiel and J. W. Fox, pp. 89–102.
1996. 'Figurines and the Aztec State: Testing the Effectiveness of Ideological Domination', in R. P. Wright, 1996a, pp. 143–66.
1998. 'The Multiple Identities of Aztec Craft Specialists', in C. L. Costin and R. P. Wright, pp. 145–52.
Brumfiel, E. M., and T. K. Earle, eds. 1987. *Specialization, Exchange, and Complex Societies.* Cambridge: Cambridge University Press.
Brumfiel, E. M., and J. W. Fox, eds. 1994. *Factional Competition and Political Development in the New World.* Cambridge. Cambridge University Press.
Burger, R. L. 1995. *Chavin and the Origins of Andean Civilization.* London: Thames and Hudson.
Burgess, E. W. 1926. *The Urban Community.* Chicago: University of Chicago Press.
Butterworth, Brian. 1999. *What Counts: How Every Brain Is Hardwired for Math.* New York: Free Press.
Butzer, K. W. 1976. *Early Hydraulic Civilization in Egypt: A Study in Cultural Ecology.* Chicago: University of Chicago Press.
Byrne, R. W., and Andrew Whiten, eds. 1988. *Machiavellian Intelligence: Social Expertise and the Evolution of Intellect in Monkeys, Apes, and Humans.* Oxford: Oxford University Press.

Calnek, E. E. 1972. Settlement Pattern and Chinampa Agriculture at Tenochtitlan. *American Antiquity* 37: 104–15.
1973. The Localization of the Sixteenth-Century Map Called the Maguey Plan. *American Antiquity* 38: 190–95.
1976. 'The Internal Structure of Tenochtitlan', in E. R. Wolf, pp. 287–302.
Cannadine, David, and Simon Price, eds. 1987. *Rituals of Royalty: Power and Ceremonial in Traditional Societies.* Cambridge: Cambridge University Press.
Cannon, Aubrey. 1989. The Historical Dimension in Mortuary Expressions of Status and Sentiment. *Current Anthropology* 30: 437–58.
Carmack, Robert. 1973. *Quichean Civilization: The Ethnohistoric, Ethnographic, and Archaeological Sources.* Berkeley: University of California Press.
1981. *The Quiche Mayas of Utatlan: The Evolution of a Highland Guatemala Kingdom.* Norman: University of Oklahoma Press.
Carneiro, R. L. 1970a. 'Scale Analysis, Evolutionary Sequences, and the Rating of Cultures', in *A Handbook of Method in Cultural Anthropology*, R. Naroll and R. Cohen, eds., pp. 834–71. New York: Columbia University Press.
1970b. A Theory of the Origin of the State. *Science* 169: 733–38.
Carpenter, L. K. 1992. 'Inside/Outside, Which Side Counts? Duality-of-Self and Bipartization in Quechua', in R. V. H. Dover, K. E. Seibold, and J. H. McDowell, pp. 115–36.
Carrasco, Davíd. 1987. 'Myth, Cosmic Terror, and the Templo Mayor', in J. Broda, D. Carrasco, and E. Matos Moctezuma, pp. 124–62.
ed. 1989. *The Imagination of Matter: Religion and Ecology in Mesoamerican Traditions.* British Archaeological Reports International Series 515.
1990. *Religions of Mesoamerica: Cosmovision and Ceremonial Centers.* San Francisco: Harper and Row.
1999. *City of Sacrifice: The Aztec Empire and the Role of Violence in Civilization.* Boston: Beacon Press.
Carrasco, Pedro. 1981. Comment on Offner. *American Antiquity* 46: 62–68.
Carrithers, Michael. 1992. *Why Humans Have Cultures: Explaining Anthropology and Social Diversity*. Oxford: Oxford University Press.
Caso, Alfonso. 1958. *The Aztecs: People of the Sun.* Norman: University of Oklahoma Press.
1971. 'Calendrical Systems of Central Mexico', in *Handbook of Middle American Indians*, Vol. 10, *Archaeology of Northern Mesoamerica*, pt. 1, pp. 333–48. Austin: University of Texas Press.
Caubet, Annie, and Patrick Pouyssegur. 1998. *The Ancient Near East.* Paris: Editions Pierre Terrail.
Celenko, Theodore, ed. 1996. *Egypt in Africa.* Indianapolis: Indianapolis Museum of Art.
Chakrabarti, D. K. 1997. *Colonial Indology: Sociopolitics of the Ancient Indian Past.* New Delhi: Munshiram Manoharlal Publishers.
Chang Cheng-lang. 1986. 'A Brief Discussion of Fu Tzu', in K.-C. Chang, 1986b, pp. 103–19.
Chang Kwang-chih. 1962. 'China', in *Courses toward Urban Life: Archaeological Considerations of Some Cultural Alternatives*, R. J. Braidwood and G. R. Willey, eds., pp. 177–92. Chicago: Aldine.
1976. *Early Chinese Civilization: Anthropological Perspectives.* Cambridge, MA: Harvard University Press.
1977. 'Ancient China', in *Food in Chinese Culture: Anthropological and Historical Perspectives*, K.-C. Chang, ed., pp. 23–52. New Haven: Yale University Press.
1978. '*T'ien Kan*: A Key to the History of the Shang', in *Ancient China: Studies in Early Civilization*, D. T. Roy and T.-H. Tsien, eds., pp. 13–42. Hong Kong: Chinese University Press.

1980. *Shang Civilization.* New Haven: Yale University Press.
1983. *Art, Myth, and Ritual: The Path to Political Authority in Ancient China.* Cambridge: Harvard University Press.
1984. Ancient China and its Anthropological Significance. *Symbols*, Spring/Fall, pp. 2–4, 20–22.
1986a. *The Archaeology of Ancient China.* 4th ed. New Haven: Yale University Press.
ed. 1986b. *Studies of Shang Archaeology.* New Haven: Yale University Press.
1999. 'China on the Eve of the Historical Period', in M. Loewe and E. L. Shaughnessy, pp. 37–73.
Chang Ping-ch'üan. 1986. 'A Brief Description of the Fu Hao Oracle Bone Inscriptions', in K.-C. Chang, 1986b, pp. 121–40.
Chao, Lin. 1972. Shang Government. Ph.D. diss., University of Chicago.
Charlton, T. H., and D. L. Nichols. 1997a. 'The City-State Concept: Development and Applications', in D. L. Nichols and T. H. Charlton, pp. 1–14.
1997b. 'Diachronic Studies of City-States: Permutations on a Theme, Central Mexico from 1700 B.C. to A.D. 1600', in D. L. Nichols and T. H. Charlton, pp. 169–207.
Chase, A. F., and D. Z. Chase. 1996. More Than Kin and King: Centralized Political Organization among the Late Classic Maya. *Current Anthropology* 37: 803–10.
Chase, D. Z., and A. F. Chase, eds. 1992a. *Mesoamerican Elites: An Archaeological Assessment.* Norman: University of Oklahoma Press.
1992b. 'An Archaeological Assessment of Mesoamerican Elites', in D. Z. Chase and A. F. Chase, pp. 303–17.
Chase, D. Z., A. F. Chase, and W. A. Haviland. 1990. The Classic Maya City: Reconsidering the 'Mesoamerican Urban Tradition'. *American Anthropologist* 92: 499–506.
Chêng, Tê-k'un. 1960. *Archaeology in China.* Vol. 2. *Shang China.* Cambridge: Heffer.
1963. *Archaeology in China.* Vol. 3. *Chou China.* Cambridge: Heffer.
Childe, V. G. 1928. *The Most Ancient East: The Oriental Prelude to European Prehistory.* London: Kegan Paul.
1930. *The Bronze Age.* Cambridge: Cambridge University Press.
1934. *New Light on the Most Ancient East: The Oriental Prelude to European Prehistory.* London: Kegan Paul.
1945. Directional Changes in Funerary Practices during 50,000 Years. *Man* 45: 13–19.
1950. The Urban Revolution. *Town Planning Review* 21: 3–17.
1951. *Social Evolution.* New York: Schuman.
1956a. *Society and Knowledge: The Growth of Human Traditions.* New York: Harper.
1956b. *Piecing Together the Past: The Interpretation of Archaeological Data.* London: Routledge and Kegan Paul.
1958. *The Prehistory of European Society.* Harmondsworth: Penguin.
1965 (1936). *Man Makes Himself.* London: Watts.
Chisholm, Michael. 1962. *Rural Settlement and Land Use: An Essay in Location.* London: Hutchinson.
Chou Hung-hsiang. 1968. Some Aspects of Shang Administration: A Survey Based Solely on Texts Available in the Oracle Bone Texts. Ph.D. diss., Australian National University.
Claessen, H. J. M., and Peter Skalník, eds. 1978. *The Early State.* The Hague: Mouton.
Clancy, F. S., and P. D. Harrison, eds. 1990. *Vision and Revision in Maya Studies.* Albuquerque: University of New Mexico Press.
Clarke, D. L. 1968. *Analytical Archaeology.* London: Methuen.
Clarke, W. H. 1972. *Travels and Explorations in Yorubaland 1854–1858*, J. A. Atanda, ed. Ibadan: Ibadan University Press.

Classen, Constance. 1993. *Inca Cosmology and the Human Body.* Salt Lake City: University of Utah Press.

Clendinnen, Inga. 1991. *The Aztecs: An Interpretation.* Cambridge: Cambridge University Press.

Clifford, James. 1988. *The Predicament of Culture: Twentieth-Century Ethnography, Literature, and Art.* Cambridge, MA: Harvard University Press.

Cobo, Bernabé. 1979. *History of the Inca Empire.* Austin: University of Texas Press.

1990. *Inca Religion and Customs.* Austin: University of Texas Press.

Coe, M. D. 1957. The Khmer Settlement Pattern: A Possible Analogy with that of the Maya. *American Antiquity* 22: 409–10.

1961. Social Typology and the Tropical Forest Civilizations. *Comparative Studies in Society and History* 4: 65–85.

1977. 'Olmec and Maya: A Study in Relationships', in R. E. W. Adams, pp. 183–95.

1978. *Lords of the Underworld: Masterpieces of Classic Maya Ceramics.* Princeton: Art Museum, Princeton University.

1988. 'Ideology of the Maya Tomb', in E. P. Benson and G. G. Griffin, pp. 222–35.

1992. *Breaking the Maya Code.* London: Thames and Hudson.

1993. *The Maya.* 5th ed. London: Thames and Hudson.

Coe, M. D., and Justin Kerr. 1998. *The Art of the Maya Scribe.* New York: Harry N. Abrams.

Cohen, Abner. 1972. *Arab Border-Villages in Israel: A Study of Continuity and Change in Social Organization.* Manchester: Manchester University Press.

Cohen, M. N. 1977. *The Food Crisis in Prehistory: Overpopulation and the Origins of Agriculture.* New Haven: Yale University Press.

1989. *Health and the Rise of Civilization.* New Haven: Yale University Press.

Cohen, Ronald, and Elman Service, eds. 1978. *Origins of the State: The Anthropology of Political Evolution.* Philadelphia: Institute for the Study of Human Issues.

Collier, G. A., R. I. Rosaldo, and J. D. Wirth, eds. 1982. *The Inca and Aztec States 1400–1800: Anthropology and History.* New York: Academic Press.

Collon, Dominique. 1987. *First Impressions: Cylinder Seals in the Ancient Near East.* Chicago: University of Chicago Press.

Connah, Graham. 1975. *The Archaeology of Benin: Excavations and Other Researches in and around Benin City, Nigeria.* Oxford: Oxford University Press.

1987. 'African Civilizations: Precolonial Cities and States', in *Tropical Africa: An Archaeological Perspective.* Cambridge: Cambridge University Press.

Conrad, G. W., and A. A. Demarest. 1984. *Religion and Empire: The Dynamics of Aztec and Inca Expansionism.* Cambridge: Cambridge University Press.

Conroy, G. C. 1990. *Primate Evolution.* New York: Norton.

Cooper, J. S. 1996. 'Sumerian and Akkadian', in P. T. Daniels and W. Bright, pp. 37–57.

Coquet, Michèle. 1998. *African Royal Court Art.* Chicago: University of Chicago Press.

Costin, C. L. 1991. Craft Specialization: Issues in Defining, Documenting, and Explaining the Organization of Production. *Archaeological Method and Theory* 3: 1–56.

1996. 'Exploring the Relationship between Gender and Craft in Complex Societies: Methodological and Theoretical Issues of Gender Attribution', in R. P. Wright, 1996a, pp. 111–40.

1998a. 'Introduction: Craft and Social Identity', in C. L. Costin and R. P. Wright, pp. 3–16.

1998b. 'Housewives, Chosen Women, Skilled Men: Cloth Production and Social Identity in the Late Prehispanic Andes', in C. L. Costin and R. P. Wright, pp. 123–41.

Costin, C. L., and M. B. Hagstrum. 1995. Standardization, Labor Investment, Skill, and the Organization of Ceramic Production in Late Prehispanic Highland Peru. *American Antiquity* 60: 619–39.

Costin, C. L., and R. P. Wright, eds. 1998. *Craft and Social Identity*. Archeological Papers of the American Anthropological Association 8.
Coult, A. D., and R. W. Habenstein. 1965. *Cross Tabulations of Murdock's World Ethnographic Sample*. Columbia: University of Missouri.
Cowgill, G. L. 1997. State and Society at Teotihuacan, Mexico. *Annual Review of Anthropology* 26: 129–61.
Crawford, Harriet. 1991. *Sumer and the Sumerians*. Cambridge: Cambridge University Press.
Creel, H. G. 1937. *The Birth of China: A Study of the Formative Period of Chinese Civilization*. New York: Raynal and Hitchcock.
1938. *Studies in Early Chinese Culture: First Series*. American Council of Learned Societies. Studies in Chinese and Related Civilizations 3. London: Routledge.
1970. *The Origins of Statecraft in China*. Vol. 1. *The Western Chou Empire*. Chicago: University of Chicago Press.
Cressey, George. 1955. *Land of the 500 Million: A Geography of China*. New York: McGraw-Hill.
Crone, Patricia. 1989. *Pre-Industrial Societies*. Oxford: Blackwell.
Crumley, C. L. 1987. 'A Dialectical Critique of Hierarchy', in T. C. Patterson and C. W. Gailey, pp. 155–69.
Culbert, T. P., ed. 1973. *The Classic Maya Collapse*. Albuquerque: University of New Mexico Press.
ed. 1991a. *Classic Maya Political History: Hieroglyphic and Archaeological Evidence*. Cambridge: Cambridge University Press.
1991b. 'Maya Political History and Elite Interaction: A Summary View', in T. P. Culbert, 1991a, pp. 311–46.
1991c. 'Polities in the Northeast Peten, Guatemala', in P. T. Culbert, 1991a, pp. 128–46.
Culbert, T. P., Laura Kosakowsky, R. E. Fry, and W. A. Haviland. 1990. 'The Population of Tikal, Guatemala', in T. P. Culbert and D. S. Rice, pp. 103–21.
Culbert, T. P., L. J. Levi, and Luís Cruz. 1990. 'Lowland Maya Wetland Agriculture: The Rio Azul Agronomy Progam', in F. S. Clancy and P. D. Harrison, pp. 115–24.
Culbert, T. P., and D. S. Rice, eds. 1990. *Precolumbian Population History in the Maya Lowlands*. Albuquerque: University of New Mexico Press.
Curtin, P. D. 1984. *Cross-Cultural Trade in World History*. Cambridge: Cambridge University Press.
Dallos, Csilla. 1997. Identity and Opportunity: The Gender and Politics of Decision-Making among the Lanoh, Peninsular Malaysia. MS, McGill University.
Dalton, George. 1975. 'Karl Polanyi's Analysis of Long-Distance Trade and His Wider Paradigm', in J. A. Sabloff and C. C. Lamberg-Karlovsky, pp. 63–132.
D'Altroy, T. N. 1987a. Introduction: Inka Ethnohistory. *Ethnohistory* 34: 1–13.
1987b. Transitions in Power: Centralization of Wanka Political Organization under Inka Rule. *Ethnohistory* 34: 78–101.
1992. *Provincial Power in the Inka Empire*. Washington, DC: Smithsonian Institution Press.
D'Altroy, T. N., and T. K. Earle. 1985. Staple Finance, Wealth Finance, and Storage in the Inka Political Economy. *Current Anthropology* 26: 187–206.
Daniels, P. T. 1996a. 'The Study of Writing Systems', in P. T. Daniels and W. Bright, pp. 3–17.
1996b. 'The Invention of Writing', in P. T. Daniels and W. Bright, pp. 579–86.
Daniels, P. T., and William Bright, eds. 1996. *The World's Writing Systems*. Oxford: Oxford University Press.
Dark, P. J. C. 1973. *An Introduction to Benin Art and Technology*. Oxford: Oxford University Press.

Daumas, François. 1979. 'Les textes géographiques du trésoir D du temple de Dendara', in Edward Lipinski, pp. 689–705.
D'Auria, Sue. 1988. *Mummies and Magic: The Funerary Arts of Ancient Egypt.* Boston: Boston Museum of Fine Arts.
David, A. R. 1986. *The Pyramid Builders of Ancient Egypt: A Modern Investigation of Pharaoh's Workforce.* London: Routledge and Kegan Paul.
Davies, Nigel. 1980. *The Aztecs: A History.* Norman: University of Oklahoma Press.
1984. 'Human Sacrifice in the Old World and the New: Some Similarities and Differences', in E. H. Boone, pp. 211–26.
Davies, Vivian, and Renée Friedman. 1998. *Egypt Uncovered.* New York: Stewart, Tabori and Chang.
Davis, Whitney. 1992. *Masking the Blow: The Scene of Representation in Late Prehistoric Egyptian Art.* Berkeley: University of California Press.
Deacon, T. W. 1997. *The Symbolic Species: The Co-Evolution of Language and the Brain.* New York: Norton.
DeFrancis, John. 1989. *Visible Speech: The Diverse Oneness of Writing Systems.* Honolulu: University of Hawaii Press.
Demarée, R. J. 1983. *The 3ḫ ỉkr n Rˁ-Stelae on Ancestor Worship in Ancient Egypt.* Egyptologische Uitgaven 3. Leiden: Nederlands Instituut voor het Nabije Oosten.
Demarest, A. A. 1978. 'Interregional Conflict and "Situational Ethics" in Classic Maya Warfare', in M. Giardino, B. Edmonson, and W. Creamer, eds., *Codex Wauchope: A Tribute Role*, pp. 101–11. New Orleans: Human Mosaic.
1981. *Viracocha: The Nature and Antiquity of the Andean High God.* Peabody Museum Monographs 6.
1992. 'Ideology in Ancient Maya Cultural Evolution: The Dynamics of Galactic Polities', in A. A. Demarest and G. W. Conrad, pp. 135–57.
Demarest, A. A., and G. W. Conrad, eds. 1992. *Ideology and Pre-Columbian Civilizations.* Santa Fe: School of American Research Press.
Denzer, LaRay. 1994. Yoruba Women: A Historiographical Study. *International Journal of African Historical Studies* 27: 1–39.
DePutter, T. J. M., and Christina Karlshausen. 1997. In Search of the Lost Quarries of the Pharaohs. *KMT* 8(3): 54–59.
Desroches-Noblecourt, Christiane. 1986. *La femme au temps des pharaons.* Paris: Stock.
DeVore, Irven, and K. R. L. Hall. 1965. 'Baboon Ecology', in *Primate Behavior: Field Studies of Monkeys and Apes*, I. DeVore, ed., pp. 20–52. New York: Holt, Rinehart and Winston.
Diakonoff, I. M., ed. 1969a. *Ancient Mesopotamia: Socio-Economic History.* Moscow: Nauka.
1969b. 'The Rise of the Despotic State in Ancient Mesopotamia', in I. M. Diakonoff, 1969a, pp. 173–203.
1974. *Structure of Society and State in Early Dynastic Sumer.* Malibu: Undena.
1987. 'Slave-Labor vs. Non-Slave Labor: The Problem of Definition', in M. A. Powell, pp. 1–3.
ed. 1991. *Early Antiquity.* Chicago: University of Chicago Press.
Diamond, Stanley, ed. 1960. *Culture in History: Essays in Honor of Paul Radin.* New York: Columbia University Press.
1974. *In Search of the Primitive: A Critique of Civilization.* New Brunswick, NJ: Transaction Books.
Diop, Cheikh Anta. 1974. *The African Origin of Civilization: Myth or Reality.* Westport, CT: Lawrence Hill.
Diringer, D. 1962. *Writing.* New York: Praeger.
Donadoni, Sergio, ed. 1997. *The Egyptians.* Chicago: University of Chicago Press.

Donald, Leland. 1997. *Aboriginal Slavery on the Northwest Coast of North America.* Berkeley: University of California Press.
Donkin, R. A. 1979. *Agricultural Terracing in the Aboriginal New World.* Viking Fund Publications in Anthropology 56.
Doolittle, W. E. 1990. *Canal Irrigation in Prehistoric Mexico: The Sequence of Technological Change.* Austin: University of Texas Press.
Dover, R. V. H. 1992. 'Introduction', in R. V. H. Dover, K. E. Seibold, and J. H. McDowell, pp. 1–16.
Dover, R. V. H., K. E. Seibold, and J. H. McDowell, eds. 1992. *Andean Cosmologies through Time: Persistence and Emergence.* Bloomington: Indiana University Press.
Downing, T. E., and McGuire Gibson, eds. 1974. *Irrigation's Impact on Society.* Anthropological Papers of the University of Arizona 25.
Drew, David. 1999. *The Lost Chronicles of the Maya Kings.* London: Weidenfeld and Nicolson.
Drewal, H. J. 1989. 'Art or Accident: Yoruba Body Artists and Their Deity Ogun', in S. T. Barnes, pp. 235–60.
Drewal, M. T. 1989. 'Dancing for Ogun in Yorubaland and in Brazil', in S. T. Barnes, pp. 199–234.
Driver, H. E. 1966. Geographical-Historical versus Psycho-Functional Explanations of Kin Avoidances. *Current Anthropology* 7: 131–82.
Dubrovsky, Bernardo. 1999. 'Evolutionary Psychiatry and Psychology: Conflicts with Evolutionary Science', Plenary Lecture, Fifth International Congress of Psychiatry.
Dunn, S. P. 1982. *The Fall and Rise of the Asiatic Mode of Production.* London: Routledge and Kegan Paul.
Dunnell, R. C. 1978. Style and Function: A Fundamental Dichotomy. *American Antiquity* 43: 192–202.
Dunning, N. P. 1996. 'A Reexamination of Regional Variability in the Pre-Hispanic Agricultural Landscape', in S. L. Fedick, 1996a, pp. 53–68.
Durán, Diego. 1964. *The Aztecs: The History of the Indies of New Spain.* New York: Orion.
1971. *The Book of the Gods and Rites and the Ancient Calendar.* Norman: University of Oklahoma Press.
Durkheim, Emile. 1964 (1895). *The Rules of Sociological Method.* New York: Free Press.
Duviols, Pierre. 1989. 'Las cinco edades primitivas del Perú según Guaman Poma de Ayala: ¿Un método de computo original?' in M. S. Ziolkowski and R. M. Sadowski, pp. 7–16.
Eades, J. S. 1980. *The Yoruba Today.* Cambridge: Cambridge University Press.
Earle, T. K. 1985. 'Commodity Exchange and Markets in the Inca State: Recent Archaeological Evidence', in *Markets and Marketing*, Stuart Plattner, ed., pp. 369–97. Lanham, MD: University Press of America.
1987. 'Specialization and the Production of Wealth: Hawaiian Chiefdoms and the Inka Empire', in E. M. Brumfiel and T. K. Earle, pp. 64–75.
ed. 1991. *Chiefdoms: Power, Economy, and Ideology.* Cambridge: Cambridge University Press.
1994. Wealth Finance in the Inka Empire: Evidence from the Calchaqui Valley, Argentina. *American Antiquity* 59: 443–60.
Earle, T. K., and T. N. D'Altroy. 1989. 'The Political Economy of the Inka Empire: The Archaeology of Power and Finance', in *Archaeological Thought in America*, C. C. Lamberg-Karlovsky, ed., pp. 183–204. Cambridge: Cambridge University Press.
Ebeid, Nabil. 1999. *Egyptian Medicine in the Days of the Pharaohs.* Cairo: General Egyptian Book Organization.
Edens, Christopher. 1992. Dynamics of Trade in the Ancient Mesopotamian 'World System'. *American Anthropologist* 94: 118–39.
Edwards, I. E. S. 1985. *The Pyramids of Egypt.* Rev. ed. Harmondsworth: Penguin.

Eggan, Fred. 1966. *The American Indian: Perspectives for the Study of Social Change.* Chicago: Aldine.
Egharevba, Jacob. 1960. *A Short History of Benin.* Ibadan: Ibadan University Press.
Ehrenreich, R. M., C. L. Crumley, and J. E. Levy, eds. 1995. *Heterarchy and the Analysis of Complex Societies.* American Anthropological Association Archeological Papers 6.
Eisenstadt, S. N. 1963. *The Political Systems of Empires.* Glencoe: Free Press.
ed. 1986. *The Origins and Diversity of Axial Age Civilizations.* Albany: State University of New York Press.
Eisenstadt, S. N., Michel Abitbol, and Naomi Chazan. 1988. *The Early State in African Perspective: Culture, Power, and Division of Labour.* Leiden: E. J. Brill.
Eliade, Mircea. 1954. *The Myth of the Eternal Return.* New York: Pantheon Books.
Elias, Norbert. 1978. *The Civilizing Process.* Vol. 1. *The Development of Manners: Changes in the Code of Conduct and Feeling in Early Modern Times.* New York: Urizen Books.
1982. *The Civilizing Process.* Vol. 2. *State Formation and Civilization.* Oxford: Blackwell.
Ellis, M. deJ. 1976. *Agriculture and the State in Ancient Mesopotamia: An Introduction to Problems of Land Tenure.* University of Pennsylvania, University Museum, Babylonian Fund, 1.
Ember, Melvin, and C. R. Ember. 1983. *Marriage, Family, and Kinship: Comparative Studies of Social Organization.* New Haven: HRAF Press.
Englund, Gertie, ed. 1989a. *The Religion of the Ancient Egyptians: Cognitive Structures and Popular Expressions.* Uppsala Studies in Ancient Mediterranean and Near Eastern Cultures 20. Stockholm: Tryckeri Balder.
1989b. 'Gods as a Frame of Reference: On Thinking and Concepts of Thought in Ancient Egypt', in G. Englund, 1989a, pp. 7–28.
Engnell, Ivan. 1967. *Studies in Divine Kingship in the Ancient Near East.* Oxford: Blackwell.
Eno, Robert. 1990. Was There a High God *Ti* in Shang Religion? *Early China* 15: 1–26.
Erdal, David, and Andrew Whiten. 1996. 'Egalitarianism and Machiavellian Intelligence in Human Evolution', in P. Mellars and K. Gibson, pp. 139–50.
Erdosy, George. 1988. *Urbanisation in Early Historic India.* British Archaeological Reports International Series 430.
Evans-Pritchard, E. E. 1962. 'Anthropology and History', in *Essays in Social Anthropology*, pp. 46–65. London: Faber.
Eyer, Joe. 1984. 'Capitalism, Health, and Illness', in *Issues in the Political Economy of Health Care*, J. B. McKinlay, ed., pp. 23–59. London: Tavistock Publications.
Eyre, C. J. 1984. Crime and Adultery in Ancient Egypt. *Journal of Egyptian Archaeology* 70: 92–105.
1987a. 'Work and the Organisation of Work in the Old Kingdom', in M. Powell, pp. 5–47.
1987b. 'Work and the Organisation of Work in the New Kingdom', in M. Powell, pp. 167–221.
1994. The Water Regime for Orchards and Plantations in Pharaonic Egypt. *Journal of Egyptian Archaeology* 80: 57–80.
1999. 'The Village Economy in Pharaonic Egypt', in *Agriculture in Egypt: From Pharaonic to Modern Times*, A. K. Bowman and Eugene Rogan, eds., pp. 33–60. Proceedings of the British Academy 96.
Faherty, R. L. 1974. 'Sacrifice', in *The New Encyclopaedia Britannica*, 15th ed., *Macropaedia*, Vol. 16, pp. 128–35.
Falkenstein, Adam. 1974 (1954). *The Sumerian Temple City.* Malibu: Undena.
Falola, Toyin. 1991. The Yoruba Caravan System of the Nineteenth Century. *International Journal of African Historical Studies* 24: 111–32.
Farrington, Benjamin. 1936. *Science in Antiquity.* London: Butterworth.

Farrington, I. S. 1992. Ritual Geography, Settlement Patterns, and the Characterization of the Provinces of the Inka Heartland. *World Archaeology* 23: 368–85.

Fash, W. L. 1991. *Scribes, Warriors and Kings: The City of Copán and the Ancient Maya.* London: Thames and Hudson.

Faulkner, R. O. 1969. *The Ancient Egyptian Pyramid Texts, Translated into English.* Oxford: Oxford University Press.

1985. *The Ancient Egyptian Book of the Dead.* London: British Museums Publications.

Fedick, S. L., ed. 1996a. *The Managed Mosaic: Ancient Maya Agriculture and Resource Use.* Salt Lake City: University of Utah Press.

1996b. 'Conclusion: Landscape Approaches to the Study of Ancient Maya Agriculture and Resource Use', in Fedick 1996a, pp. 335–47.

Fedick, S. L., and Anabel Ford. 1990. The Prehistoric Agricultural Landscape of the Central Maya Lowlands: An Examination of Local Variability in a Regional Context. *World Archaeology* 22: 18–33.

Feeley-Harnik, Gillian. 1985. Issues in Divine Kingship. *Annual Review of Anthropology* 14: 273–313.

Feinman, G. M. 1998. 'Scale and Social Organization: Perspectives on the Archaic State', in G. M. Feinman and J. Marcus, pp. 95–133.

Feinman, G. M., and Joyce Marcus, eds. 1998. *Archaic States.* Santa Fe: School of American Research Press.

Feit, Harvey. 1978. Waswanipi Realities and Adaptations: Resource Management and Cognitive Structure. Ph.D. diss., McGill University.

Fernea, Robert. 1970. *Shaykh and Effendi: Changing Patterns of Authority among the El-Shabana of Southern Iraq.* Cambridge, MA: Harvard University Press.

Feucht, Erika. 1997. 'Women', in S. Donadoni, pp. 315–46.

Finnestad, R.B. 1997. 'Temples of the Ptolemaic and Roman Periods: Ancient Traditions in New Contexts', in B. E. Shafer, pp. 185–237.

Fischer, H. G. 1968. *Dendera in the Third Millennium B.C. down to the Theban Domination of Upper Egypt.* Locust Valley: Augustin.

1989. 'Women in the Old Kingdom and the Heracleopolitan Period', in B. S. Lesko, pp. 5–24.

Flannery, K. V. 1972. The Cultural Evolution of Civilizations. *Annual Review of Ecology and Systematics* 3: 399–426.

ed. 1982. *Maya Subsistence: Studies in Memory of Dennis E. Puleston.* New York: Academic Press.

1998. 'The Ground Plans of Archaic States', in G. M. Feinman and J. Marcus, pp. 15–57.

1999. Process and Agency in Early State Formation. *Cambridge Archaeological Journal* 9: 3–21.

Flannery, K. V., and Joyce Marcus. 1976. Formative Oaxaca and the Zapotec Cosmos. *American Scientist* 64: 374–83.

2000. Formative Mexican Chiefdoms and the Myth of the 'Mother Culture'. *Journal of Anthropological Archaeology* 19: 1–37.

Folan, W. J., E. R. Kintz, and L. A. Fletcher. 1983. *Coba: A Classic Maya Metropolis.* New York: Academic Press.

Folan, W. J., J. Marcus, S. Pincemin, M. del Rosario Dominguez Carrasco, L. Fletcher, and A. Morales López. 1995. Calakmul: New Data from an Ancient Maya Capital in Campeche, Mexico. *Latin American Antiquity* 6: 310–34.

Fong Wen, ed. 1980. *The Great Bronze Age of China: An Exhibition from the People's Republic of China.* New York: Alfred A. Knopf.

Ford, C. S., ed. 1967. *Cross-Cultural Approaches: Readings in Comparative Research.* New Haven: HRAF Press.

Forde, C. D. 1934. *Habitat, Economy, and Society: A Geographical Introduction to Ethnology.* London: Methuen.
Forge, Anthony. 1972. 'Normative Factors in the Settlement Size of Neolithic Cultivators (New Guinea)', in P. J. Ucko, R. Tringham, and G. W. Dimbleby, pp. 363–76.
Forman, Werner, Bedrich Forman, and Philip Dark. 1960. *Benin Art.* London: Hamlyn.
Foster, B. R. 1981. A New Look at the Sumerian Temple State. *Journal of the Economic and Social History of the Orient* 24: 225–41.
1982. *Administration and Use of Institutional Land in Sargonic Sumer.* Mesopotamia: Copenhagen Studies in Assyriology 9. Copenhagen: Akademisk Forlag.
Foster, G. M. 1960–61. Interpersonal Relations in Peasant Society. *Human Organization* 19: 174–78.
Fox, J. G. 1996. Playing with Power: Ballcourts and Political Ritual in Southern Mesoamerica. *Current Anthropology* 37: 483–509.
Fox, J. W., G. W. Cook, A. F. Chase, and D. Z. Chase. 1996. Questions of Political and Economic Integration: Segmentary versus Centralized States among the Ancient Maya. *Current Anthropology* 37: 795–801.
Fox, R. G. 1977. *Urban Anthropology: Cities in Their Cultural Settings.* Englewood Cliffs: Prentice-Hall.
Frankfort, Henri. 1948. *Kingship and the Gods: A Study of Ancient Near Eastern Religion as the Integration of Society and Nature.* Chicago: University of Chicago Press.
1954. *The Art and Architecture of the Ancient Orient.* Harmondsworth: Penguin.
1956. *The Birth of Civilization in the Near East.* New York: Doubleday.
Frankfort, Henri, H. A. Frankfort, J. A. Wilson, and Thorkild Jacobsen. 1949. *Before Philosophy: The Intellectual Adventure of Ancient Man.* Harmondsworth: Penguin.
Franklin, U. M. 1983. 'The Beginnings of Metallurgy in China: A Comparative Approach', in G. Kuwayama, pp. 94–99.
1990. *The Real World of Technology.* Toronto: CBC Enterprises.
Franklin, U. M., J. Berthong, and A. Chan. 1985. Metallurgy, Cosmology, Knowledge: The Chinese Experience. *Journal of Chinese Philosophy* 12: 333–69.
Freidel, D. A. 1986. 'Maya Warfare: An Example of Peer Polity Interaction', in C. Renfrew and J. Cherry, pp. 93–108.
1992. 'The Trees of Life: *Ahau* as Idea and Artifact in Classic Lowland Maya Civilization', in A. A. Demarest and G. W. Conrad, pp. 115–33.
Freidel, D. A., and Linda Schele. 1988a. Kingship in the Late Preclassic Maya Lowlands: The Instruments and Places of Ritual Power. *American Anthropologist* 90: 547–67.
1988b. 'Symbol and Power: A History of the Lowland Maya Cosmogram', in E. P. Benson and G. G. Griffin, pp. 44–93.
Freidel, D. A., Linda Schele, and Joy Parker. 1993. *Maya Cosmos: Three Thousand Years on the Shaman's Path.* New York: William Morrow.
Fried, M. H. 1967. *The Evolution of Political Society: An Essay in Political Anthropology.* New York: Random House.
Friedman, Jonathan, and M. J. Rowlands, eds. 1978a. *The Evolution of Social Systems.* Pittsburgh: University of Pittsburgh Press.
1978b. 'Notes towards an Epigenetic Model of the Evolution of "Civilisation"', in J. Friedman and M. J. Rowlands, 1978a, pp. 201–76.
Friedman, Renée, and Barbara Adams, eds. 1992. *The Followers of Horus: Studies Dedicated to Michael Allen Hoffman.* Egyptian Studies Association Publication 2, Oxbow Monograph 20. Oxford: Oxbow Books.
Frobenius, Leo. 1913. *The Voice of Africa.* 2 vols. Translated by Rudolf Blind. London: Hutchinson.

Fuerstein, Carol, ed. 1999. *Egyptian Art in the Age of the Pyramids*. New York: Metropolitan Museum of Art.

Fuller, Peter. 1980. *Beyond the Crisis in Art*. London: Writers and Readers.

Furlong, Iris. 1987. *Divine Headdresses of Mesopotamia in the Early Dynastic Period.* British Archaeological Reports International Series 334.

Furst, J. L. M. 1995. *The Natural History of the Soul in Ancient Mexico.* New Haven: Yale University Press.

Furst, P. T. 1977. 'The Roots and Continuities of Shamanism', in *Stones, Bones, and Skin: Ritual and Shamanic Art*, A. T. Brodzky, R. Danesewich, and N. Johnson, eds., pp. 1–28. Toronto: Society for Art Publications.

Fussell, G. E. 1966. *Farming Technique from Prehistoric to Modern Times.* Oxford: Pergamon Press.

Gailey, C. W. 1987. 'Culture Wars: Resistance to State Formation', in T. C. Patterson and C. W. Gailey, pp. 35–56.

Galarza, Joaquin. 1997. 'Deciphering the Aztec Script', in *Virtual Archaeology: Re-creating Ancient Worlds*, Maurizio Forte and Alberto Siliotti, eds., pp. 264–71. New York: Harry N. Abrams.

Gallagher, Jacki. 1983. 'Between Realms: The Iconography of Kingship in Benin', in P. Ben-Amos and A. Rubin, pp. 21–26.

Gardiner, Alan. 1950. *Egyptian Grammar: Being an Introduction to the Study of Hieroglyphs.* 2d ed. Oxford: Oxford University Press.

1961. *Egypt of the Pharaohs: An Introduction.* Oxford: Oxford University Press.

Garner, B. J. 1967. 'Models of Urban Geography and Settlement Location', in *Models in Geography*, R. J. Chorley and Peter Haggett, eds., pp. 303–60. London: Methuen.

Garrard, T. F. 1983. 'Benin Metal-casting Technology', in P. Ben-Amos and A. Rubin, pp. 17–20.

Gasparini, Graziano, and Luise Margolies. 1980. *Inca Architecture.* Bloomington: Indiana University Press.

Gazzaniga, M. S. 1992. *Nature's Mind: The Biological Roots of Thinking, Emotions, Sexuality, Language, and Intelligence.* New York: Basic Books.

1998. *The Mind's Past.* Berkeley: University of California Press.

Geertz, Clifford. 1965. 'The Impact of the Concept of Culture on the Concept of Man', in *New Views of the Nature of Man*, J. R. Platt, ed., pp. 93–118. Chicago: University of Chicago Press.

1973. *The Interpretation of Cultures: Selected Essays.* New York: Basic Books.

1979. 'From the Native's Point of View: On the Nature of Anthropological Understanding', in *Interpretive Social Science: A Reader*, Paul Rabinow and W. M. Sullivan, eds, pp. 225–41. Berkeley: University of California Press.

1984. Anti Anti-relativism. *American Anthropologist* 86: 263–78.

Gelb, I. J. 1963. *A Study of Writing.* 2d ed. Chicago. University of Chicago Press.

1973. Prisoners of War in Early Mesopotamia. *Journal of Near Eastern Studies* 32: 70–98.

1979. 'Household and Family in Early Mesopotamia', in E. Lipinski, pp. 1–97.

Gellner, Ernest. 1982. 'What Is Structuralisme?' in *Theory and Explanation in Archaeology: The Southampton Conference*, Colin Renfrew, M. J. Rowlands, and B. A. Segraves, eds., pp. 97–123. New York: Academic Press.

1983. *Nations and Nationalism.* Oxford: Blackwell.

1988. *Plough, Sword and Book: The Structure of Human History.* London: Collins Harvill.

George, A. R. 1993. *House Most High: The Temples of Ancient Mesopotamia.* Winona Lake, IN: Eisenbrauns.

Geras, Norman. 1983. *Marx and Human Nature: Refutation of a Legend.* London: Verso.

Gero, J. M., and M. W. Conkey, eds. 1991. *Engendering Archaeology: Women and Prehistory.* Oxford: Blackwell.
Ghalioungui, Paul, and Zeinab el Dawakhly. 1965. *Health and Healing in Ancient Egypt.* Cairo: Dar Al-Maaref.
Gibson, McGuire. 1974. 'Violation of Fallow and Engineered Disaster in Mesopotamian Civilization', in T. E. Downing and M. Gibson, pp. 7–19.
1977. Nippur: New Perspectives. *Archaeology* 30: 26–37.
Gibson, McGuire, and R. D. Biggs, eds. 1991. *The Organization of Power: Aspects of Bureaucracy in the Ancient Near East.* 2d ed. Studies in Ancient Oriental Civilization 46. Chicago: Oriental Institute of the University of Chicago.
Giddens, Anthony. 1979. *Central Problems in Social Theory: Action, Structure, and Contradiction in Social Analysis.* Berkeley: University of California Press.
1981. *A Contemporary Critique of Historical Materialism.* Vol. 1. *Power, Property, and the State.* London: Macmillan.
1984. *The Constitution of Society: Outline of the Theory of Structuration.* Berkeley: University of California Press.
1985. *A Contemporary Critique of Historical Materialism.* Vol. 2. *The Nation-State and Violence.* Cambridge: Polity Press.
Gillespie, S. D. 1989. *The Aztec Kings: The Construction of Rulership in Mexica History.* Tucson: University of Arizona Press.
2000. Rethinking Ancient Maya Social Organization: Replacing 'Lineage' with 'House'. *American Anthropologist* 102: 467–84.
Glassner, J.-J. 1989. 'Women, Hospitality, and the Honor of the Family', in B. S. Lesko, pp. 71–90.
Gledhill, John. 1984. 'The Transformation of Asiatic Formations: The Case of Late Prehispanic Mesoamerica', in M. Spriggs, pp. 135–48.
Godelier, Maurice. 1978. 'Economy and Religion: An Evolutionary Optical Illusion', in J. Friedman and M. J. Rowlands, pp. 3–11.
1986. *The Mental and the Material: Thought, Economy, and Society.* London: Verso.
Goebs, Katja. 1998. Symbolic Functions of Royal Crowns in Early Egyptian Funerary Literature. Ph.D. diss., Oxford University.
Goedicke, Hans. 1979. 'Cult-Temple and "State" during the Old Kingdom in Egypt', in E. Lipinski, pp. 113–31.
Goelet, Ogden, Jr. 1994. 'A Commentary on the Corpus of Literature and Tradition Which Constitutes *The Book of Going Forth by Day*', in E. von Dassow, pp. 137–70.
Gohary, Jocelyn. 1992. *Akhenaten's Sed-Festival at Karnak.* London: Kegan Paul International.
Goodenough, E. R. 1953–68. *Jewish Symbols in the Greco-Roman Period.* 13 vols. New York: Pantheon Books.
Goody, Jack. 1980. 'Slavery in Time and Space', in J. L. Watson, 1980a, pp. 16–42.
1986. *The Logic of Writing and the Organization of Society.* Cambridge: Cambridge University Press.
Goody, Jack, and Ian Watt. 1963. The Consequences of Literacy. *Comparative Studies in Society and History* 5: 304–45.
Gopnik, Myrna, ed. 1997. *The Inheritance and Innateness of Grammars.* Oxford: Oxford University Press.
Gose, Peter. 1993. Segmentary State Formation and the Ritual Control of Water under the Incas. *Comparative Studies in Society and History* 35: 480–514.
1995. Les momies, les saints et les politiques d'inhumation au Pérou, au xviie siècle. *Recherches Amérindiennes au Québec* 25 (2): 35–51.

1996a. Oracles, Divine Kingship, and Political Representation in the Inka State. *Ethnohistory* 43: 1–32.
1996b. The Past Is a Lower Moiety: Diarchy, History, and Divine Kingship in the Inka Empire. *History and Anthropology* 9: 383–414.
2000. The State as a Chosen Woman: Brideservice and the Feeding of Tributaries in the Inka Empire. *American Anthropologist* 102: 84–97.
Gossen, G. H., and R. M. Leventhal. 1993. 'The Topography of Ancient Maya Religious Pluralism: A Dialogue with the Present', in J. A. Sabloff and J. S. Henderson, pp. 185–217.
Graham, Elizabeth. 1991. 'Women and Gender in Maya Prehistory', in *The Archaeology of Gender: Proceedings of the 22nd Annual Chacmool Conference*, D. Walde and N. D. Willows, eds., pp. 470–78. Calgary: Archaeological Association of the University of Calgary.
1999. 'Stone Cities, Green Cities', in E. A. Bacus and L. J. Lucero, pp. 185–94.
Granet, Marcel. 1958 (1930). *Chinese Civilization.* New York: Meridian Books.
Grant, Michael. 1973. *Roman Myths.* Rev. ed. Harmondsworth: Penguin.
Griffeth, Robert, and C. G. Thomas, eds. 1981. *The City-State in Five Cultures.* Santa Barbara: ABC-Clio.
Grimal, Nicolas. 1992. *A History of Ancient Egypt.* Oxford: Blackwell.
Grou, Gilbert. 1989. La rôle des spécialistes dans l'armée inca: Un subjet à reconsidérer. *Culture* 9(2): 49–60.
Guthrie, Stewart. 1993. *Faces in the Clouds: A New Theory of Religion.* New York: Oxford University Press.
Haas, Jonathan. 1982. *The Evolution of the Prehistoric State.* New York: Columbia University Press.
Hall, John. 1986. *Powers and Liberties: The Causes and Consequences of the Rise of the West.* Harmondsworth: Penguin.
Hallo, W. W. 1957. *Early Mesopotamian Royal Titles: A Philologic and Historical Analysis.* American Oriental Society, American Oriental Series 43.
Hallpike, C. R. 1979. *The Foundations of Primitive Thought.* Oxford: Oxford University Press.
1986. *The Principles of Social Evolution.* Oxford: Oxford University Press.
Halverson, John. 1992. Goody and the Implosion of the Literacy Thesis. *Man* 27: 301–17.
Hammond, Norman. 1991. 'Inside the Black Box: Defining Maya Polity', in T. P. Culbert, 1991a, pp. 253–84.
2000. 'The Maya Lowlands: Pioneer Farmers to Merchant Princes', in R. E. W. Adams and M. J. MacLeod, pt. 1, pp. 197–249.
Hancock, Graham, and Santha Faiia. 1998. *Heaven's Mirror: Quest for the Lost Civilization.* London: Michael Joseph.
Hanks, W. F. 1989. 'Word and Image in a Semiotic Perspective', in W. F. Hanks and D. S. Rice, pp. 8–21.
Hanks, W. F., and D. S. Rice, eds. 1989. *Word and Image in Maya Culture: Explorations in Language, Writing, and Representation.* Salt Lake City: University of Utah Press.
Hansen, M. H., ed. 2000. *A Comparative Study of Thirty City-State Cultures: An Investigation.* Historisk-filosofiske Skrifter 21. Copenhagen: Royal Danish Academy of Sciences and Letters.
Hardin, G. J. 1968. The Tragedy of the Commons. *Science* 162: 1243–48.
Harner, Michael. 1977. The Ecological Basis for Aztec Sacrifice. *American Ethnologist* 4: 117–35.
Harpur, Yvonne. 1987. *Decoration in Egyptian Tombs of the Old Kingdom: Studies in Orientation and Scene Content.* London: KPI.

Harris, Marvin. 1968. *The Rise of Anthropological Theory: A History of Theories of Culture.* New York: Crowell.

1974. *Cows, Pigs, Wars, and Witches.* New York: Random House.

1977. *Cannibals and Kings: The Origins of Cultures.* New York: Random House.

1979. *Cultural Materialism: The Struggle for a Science of Culture.* New York: Random House.

1992. Anthropology and the Theoretical and Paradigmatic Significance of the Collapse of Soviet and East European Communism. *American Anthropologist* 94: 295–305.

Harris, Rivkah. 1975. *Ancient Sippar: A Demographic Study of an Old-Babylonian City (1894–1595 B.C.).* Uitgaven van het Nederlands Historisch-Archaeologisch Instituut te Istanbul 36.

1989. 'Independent Women in Ancient Mesopotamia?' in B. S. Lesko, pp. 145–56.

Harrison, P. D. 1990. 'The Revolution in Ancient Maya Subsistence', in F. S. Clancy and P. D. Harrison, pp. 99–113.

1999. *The Lords of Tikal: Rulers of an Ancient Maya City.* London: Thames and Hudson.

Harrison, P. D., and B. L. Turner, II, eds. 1978. *Pre-Hispanic Maya Agriculture.* Albuquerque: University of New Mexico Press.

Haselberger, Herta. 1961. Method of Studying Ethnological Art. *Current Anthropology* 2: 341–84.

Hassan, F. A. 1993. 'Town and Village in Ancient Egypt: Ecology, Society, and Urbanization', in *The Archaeology of Africa: Food, Metals, and Towns.* Thurstan Shaw, Paul Sinclair, Bassey Andah, and Alex Okpoko, eds., pp. 551–69. London: Routledge.

1997. The Dynamics of a Riverine Civilization: A Geoarchaeological Perspective on the Nile Valley, Egypt. *World Archaeology* 29: 51–74.

Hassig, Ross. 1985. *Trade, Tribute, and Transportation: The Sixteenth-Century Political Economy of the Valley of Mexico.* Norman: University of Oklahoma Press.

1988. *Aztec Warfare: Imperial Expansion and Political Control.* Norman: University of Oklahoma Press.

Hastorf, C. A. 1990. The Effect of the Inka State on Sausa Agricultural Production and Crop Consumption. *American Antiquity* 55: 262–90.

Havelock, E. A. 1986. *The Muse Learns to Write: Reflections on Orality and Literacy from Antiquity to the Present.* New Haven: Yale University Press.

Haviland, W. A. 1968. 'Ancient Lowland Maya Social Organization', in *Archaeological Studies in Middle America*, M. A. Harrison and Robert Wauchope, eds., pp. 93–117. Middle American Research Institute, Tulane University, Publication 26.

1974. Occupational Specialization at Tikal, Guatemala: Stoneworking-Monument Carving. *American Antiquity* 39: 494–96.

1988. 'Musical Hammocks at Tikal: Problems with Reconstructing Household Composition', in R. R. Wilk and W. Ashmore, pp. 121–34.

1992. Status and Power in Classic Maya Society: The View from Tikal. *American Anthropologist* 94: 937–40.

Hawass, Zahi. 1995. 'The Programs of the Royal Funerary Complexes of the Fourth Dynasty', in D. O'Connor and D. P. Silverman, pp. 221–62.

Hayes, W. C. 1955. *A Papyrus of the Late Middle Kingdom in the Brooklyn Museum (Papyrus Brooklyn 35.1446).* Wilbour Monographs 5. New York: Brooklyn Museum.

Heichelheim, F. M. 1958. *An Ancient Economic History.* Vol. 1. *From the Palaeolithic Age to the Migrations of the Germanic, Slavic, and Arabic Nations.* Leiden: Sijthoff's.

Heidenreich, C. E. 1971. *Huronia: A History and Geography of the Huron Indians, 1600–1650.* Toronto: McClelland and Stewart.

Heizer, R. F. 1966. Ancient Heavy Transport, Methods and Achievements. *Science* 153 (3738): 821–30.

Helms, M. W. 1998. *Access to Origins: Affines, Ancestors, and Aristocrats.* Austin: University of Texas Press.

Henderson, J. S. 1981. *The World of the Ancient Maya.* Ithaca: Cornell University Press.

Henderson, J. S., and P. J. Netherly, eds. 1993. *Configurations of Power: Holistic Anthropology in Theory and Practice.* Ithaca: Cornell University Press.

Hendrickson, Carol. 1989. 'Twin Gods and Quiché Rulers: The Relation between Divine Power and Lordly Rule in the Popol Vuh', in W. F. Hanks and D. S. Rice, pp. 127–39.

Hester, T. R., and H. J. Shafer. 1994. 'The Ancient Maya Craft Community at Colha, Belize, and Its External Relationships', in G. M. Schwartz and S. E. Falconer, pp. 48–63.

Heyden, Doris. 1989. *The Eagle, the Cactus, the Rock: The Roots of Mexico-Tenochtitlan's Foundation Myth and Symbol.* British Archaeological Reports International Series 484.

Hicks, Frederic. 1982. Tetzcoco in the Early 16th Century: The State, the City, and the Calpolli. *American Ethnologist* 9: 230–49.

1994. 'Alliance and Intervention in Aztec Imperial Expansion', in E. M. Brumfiel and J. W. Fox, pp. 111–16.

Hill, A. A. 1967. 'The Typology of Writing Systems', in *Papers in Linguistics in Honor of Léon Dostert*, W. M. Austin, ed., pp. 92–99. The Hague: Mouton.

Ho Ping-ti. 1975. *The Cradle of the East: An Inquiry into the Indigenous Origins of Techniques and Ideas of Neolithic and Early Historic China, 5000–1000 B.C.* Chicago: University of Chicago Press.

Hobhouse, L. T., G. C. Wheeler, and Morris Ginsberg. 1915. *The Material Culture and Social Institutions of the Simpler Peoples: An Essay in Correlation.* London: Chapman and Hill.

Hodder, B. W., and U. I. Ukwu. 1969. *Markets in West Africa: Studies of Markets and Trade among the Yoruba and Ibo.* Ibadan: Ibadan University Press.

Hodder, Ian. 1982a. *Symbols in Action: Ethnoarchaeological Studies of Material Culture.* Cambridge: Cambridge University Press.

1982b. *The Present Past: An Introduction to Anthropology for Archaeologists.* London: Batsford.

1986. *Reading the Past: Current Approaches to Interpretation in Archaeology.* Cambridge: Cambridge University Press.

ed. 1987. *The Archaeology of Contextual Meanings.* Cambridge: Cambridge University Press.

Hodge, M. G. 1984. *Aztec City-States.* Memoirs of the Museum of Anthropology, University of Michigan, 18.

1997. 'When Is a City-State? Archaeological Measures of Aztec City-States and Aztec City-State Systems', in D. L. Nichols and T. H. Charlton, pp. 209–27.

1998. Archaeological Views of Aztec Culture. *Journal of Archaeological Research* 6: 197–238.

Hodge, M. G., and M. E. Smith, eds. 1994. *Economies and Polities in the Aztec Realm.* Albany: Institute for Mesoamerican Studies.

Hoffman, M. A. 1979. *Egypt before the Pharaohs: The Prehistoric Foundations of Egyptian Civilization.* New York: Knopf.

Holl, A. F. C. 2000. 'Metals and Precolonial Society', in *Ancient African Metallurgy: The Sociocultural Context*, M. S. Bisson, S. T. Childs, Philip de Barros, and A. F. C. Holl, pp. 1–81. Walnut Creek, CA: AltaMira Press.

Hooke, S. H., ed. 1958. *Myth, Ritual, and Kingship: Essays on the Theory and Practice of Kingship in the Ancient Near East and in Israel.* Oxford: Oxford University Press.

Hornung, Erik. 1982. *Conceptions of God in Ancient Egypt: The One and the Many.* Ithaca: Cornell University Press.

1997. 'The Pharaoh', in S. Donadoni, pp. 283–314.

Hosler, Dorothy. 1988. Ancient West Mexican Metallurgy: South and Central American Origins and West Mexican Transformations. *American Anthropologist* 90: 832–55.
Houston, S. D. 1993. *Hieroglyphs and History at Dos Pilas: Dynastic Politics of the Classic Maya*. Austin: University of Texas Press.
2001. Into the Minds of Ancients: Advances in Maya Glyph Studies. *Journal of World Prehistory*. In press.
Houston, S. D., John Robertson, and David Stuart. 2000. The Language of Classic Maya Inscriptions. *Current Anthropology* 41: 321–56.
Houston, S. D., and David Stuart. 1996. Of Gods, Glyphs, and Kings: Divinity and Rulership among the Classic Maya. *Antiquity* 70: 289–312.
Howell, Nancy. 1979. *Demography of the Dobe !Kung*. New York: Academic Press.
Hsu, C.-Y., and K. M. Linduff. 1988. *Western Chou Civilization*. New Haven: Yale University Press.
Huber, L. G. F. 1988. The Bo Capital and Questions Concerning Xia and Early Shang. *Early China* 13: 46–77.
Hudson, Michael. 1996. 'The Dynamics of Privatization, from the Bronze Age to the Present', in Michael Hudson and B. A. Levine, pp. 33–72.
Hudson, Michael, and B.A. Levine, eds. 1996. *Privatization in the Ancient Near East and Classical World*. Peabody Museum of Archaeology and Ethnology Bulletin 5.
Hunt, Eva. 1972. 'Irrigation and the Socio-Political Organization of Cuicatec Cacicazgos', in *The Prehistory of the Tehuacan Valley*, Vol. 4, F. Johnson, ed., pp. 162–259. Austin: University of Texas Press.
Hunt, R. C. 1987. Agricultural Ecology: The Impact of the Aswan High Dam Reconsidered. *Culture and Agriculture* 31: 1–6.
1991. 'The Role of Bureaucracy in the Provisioning of Cities: A Framework for Analysis of the Ancient Near East', in M. Gibson and R. D. Biggs, pp. 141–68.
Huntington, Ellsworth. 1956. *Principles of Human Geography*. 6th ed. New York: J. Wiley.
Huot, J.-L. 1989. *Les Sumériens: Entre le Tigre et l'Euphrate*. Paris: Errance.
Hyslop, John. 1984. *The Inka Road System*. Orlando: Academic Press.
1990. *Inka Settlement Planning*. Austin: University of Texas Press.
Il'yin, G. F., and I. M. Diakonoff. 1991. 'India, Central Asia, and Iran in the First Half of the First Millennium B.C.', in I. M. Diakonoff, pp. 366–86.
Ingold, Tim. 1996. 'Hunting and Gathering as Ways of Perceiving the Environment', in *Redefining Nature: Ecology, Culture, and Domestication*, Roy Ellen and Katsuyoshi Fukui, eds., pp. 117–55. Oxford: Berg.
Inomata, Takeshi. 2001. The Power and Ideology of Artistic Creation: Elite Craft Specialists in Classic Maya Society. *Current Anthropology* 42: 321–49.
Isaac, B. L. 1993. 'AMP, HH & OD: Some Comments', in V. L. Scarborough and B. L. Isaac, pp. 429–71.
Isbell, W. H. 1997. *Mummies and Mortuary Monuments: A Postprocessual Prehistory of Central Andean Social Organization*. Austin: University of Texas Press.
Jacobsen, Thorkild. 1943. Primitive Democracy in Ancient Mesopotamia. *Journal of Near Eastern Studies* 2: 159–72.
1970. *Toward the Image of Tammuz and Other Essays on Mesopotamian History and Culture*. Cambridge, MA: Harvard University Press.
1974. 'Mesopotamian Religions', in *The New Encyclopaedia Britannica*, 15th ed., *Macropaedia*, Vol. 11, pp. 1001–1106.
1976. *The Treasures of Darkness: A History of Mesopotamian Religion*. New Haven: Yale University Press.

1982. *Salinity and Irrigation Agriculture in Antiquity: Diyala Basin Archaeological Projects, Report on Essential Results, 1956–58.* Malibu: Undena.
James, T. G. H. 1962. *The Ḥeḳanakhte Papers and Other Early Middle Kingdom Documents.* Publications of the Metropolitan Museum of Art Egyptian Expedition 19.
Janssen, J. J. 1978. 'The Early State in Ancient Egypt', in H. Claessen and P. Skalník, pp. 213–34.
Janssen, R. M., and J. J. Janssen. 1990. *Growing Up in Ancient Egypt.* London: Rubicon Press.
1996. *Getting Old in Ancient Egypt.* London: Rubicon Press.
Jaspers, Karl. 1953. *The Origin and Goal of History.* New Haven: Yale University Press.
Jing, Zhichun, George Rapp, Jr., and Tianlin Gao. 1997. Geoarchaeological Aids in the Investigation of Early Shang Civilization on the Floodplain of the Lower Yellow River, China. *World Archaeology* 29: 36–50.
Joffe, A. H. 2000. Egypt and Syro-Mesopotamia in the 4th Millennium: Implications of the New Chronology. *Current Anthropology* 41: 113–23.
Johnson, G. A. 1973. *Local Exchange and Early State Development in Southwestern Iran.* University of Michigan Museum of Anthropology Anthropological Papers 51.
1978. 'Information Sources and the Development of Decision-Making Organizations', in *Social Archeology: Beyond Subsistence and Dating*, C. L. Redman et al., eds., pp. 87–112. New York: Academic Press.
Johnson, Samuel. 1921. *The History of the Yorubas from the Earliest Times to the Beginning of the British Protectorate*, O. Johnson, ed. London: Routledge.
Jonckheere, Frans. 1958. *Les médecins de l'Egypte pharaonique: Essai de prosopographie.* Bruxelles: Fondation Egyptologique Reine Elisabeth.
Jones, Julie. 1964. *The Art of Empire: The Inca of Peru.* New York: Museum of Primitive Art.
Jorgensen, J. G. 1966. Addendum: Geographical Clusterings and Functional Explanations of In-Law Avoidances: An Analysis of Comparative Method. *Current Anthropology* 7: 161–82.
ed. 1974. *Comparative Studies by Harold E. Driver and Essays in His Honor.* New Haven: HRAF Press.
Joyce, R. A. 1992. 'Images of Gender and Labor Organization in Classic Maya Society', in *Exploring Gender through Archaeology: Selected Papers from the 1991 Boone Conference*, Cheryl Claassen, ed., pp. 63–70. Monographs in World Archaeology 11. Madison: Prehistory Press.
1996. 'The Construction of Gender in Classic Maya Monuments', in R. P. Wright, 1996a, pp. 167–95.
2000. *Gender and Power in Prehispanic America.* Austin: University of Texas Press.
Julien, C. J. 1988. How Inca Decimal Administration Worked. *Ethnohistory* 35: 257–79.
2000. *Reading Inca History.* Iowa City: University of Iowa Press.
Justeson, J. S. 1986. The Origin of Writing Systems: Preclassic Mesoamerica. *World Archaeology* 17: 437–58.
1989. 'The Representational Conventions of Mayan Hieroglyphic Writing', in W. F. Hanks and D. S. Rice, pp. 25–38.
Justeson, J. S., W. M. Norman, and Norman Hammond. 1988. 'The Pomona Flare: A Preclassic Maya Hieroglyphic Text', in E. P. Benson and G. G. Griffin, pp. 94–151.
Kamenka, Eugene. 1989. *Bureaucracy.* Oxford: Blackwell.
Kanawati, Naguib. 1977. *The Egyptian Administration in the Old Kingdom: Evidence on Its Economic Decline.* Warminster: Aris and Phillips.
1980. *Governmental Reforms in Old Kingdom Egypt.* Warminster: Aris and Phillips.
Kane, V. C. 1974–75. The Independent Bronze Industries in the South of China Contemporary with the Shang and Western Chou Dynasties. *Archives of Asian Art* 28: 77–107.
Karlsson, Håkan. 1998. *Re-thinking Archaeology.* Göteborg: Novum Grafiska.

Ke Changji. 1989. 'Ancient Chinese Society and the Asiatic Mode of Production', in T. Brook, pp. 47–64.
Keatinge, R. W. 1988. *Peruvian Prehistory: An Overview of Pre-Inca and Inca Society*. Cambridge: Cambridge University Press.
Kees, Hermann. 1961. *Ancient Egypt: A Cultural Topography*. Chicago: University of Chicago Press.
Keightley, D. N. 1969. Public Work in Ancient China: A Study of Forced Labor in the Shang and Western Chou. Ph.D. diss., Columbia University.
1978a. *Sources of Shang History: The Oracle-Bone Inscriptions of Bronze Age China*. Berkeley: University of California Press.
1978b. The Religious Commitment: Shang Theology and the Genesis of Chinese Political Culture. *History of Religions* 17: 211–25.
1979–80. The Shang State as Seen in the Oracle-Bone Inscriptions. *Early China* 5: 25–34.
ed. 1983a. *The Origins of Chinese Civilization*. Berkeley: University of California Press.
1983b. 'The Late Shang State: When, Where, and What?' In D. N. Keightley, 1983a, pp. 523–64.
1987. Archaeology and Mentality: The Making of China. *Representations* 18: 91–128.
1999a. 'The Environment of Ancient China', in M. Loewe and E. L. Shaughnessy, pp. 30–36.
1999b. 'The Shang: China's First Historical Dynasty', in M. Loewe and E. L. Shaughnessy, pp. 232–91.
1999c. Theology and the Writing of History: Truth and the Ancestors in the Wu Ding Divination Records. *Journal of East Asian Archaeology* 1: 207–30.
2000. *The Ancestral Landscape: Time, Space, and Community in Late Shang China, ca. 1200–1045 B.C.* University of California Center for Chinese Studies, China Research Monograph 53.
Kelley, D. H. 1971. 'Diffusion: Evidence and Process', in C. L. Riley et al., pp. 60–65.
Kellogg, Susan. 1995. The Woman's Room: Some Aspects of Gender Relations in Tenochtitlan in the Late Pre-Hispanic Period. *Ethnohistory* 42: 563–76.
Kemp, B. J. 1977. The Early Development of Towns in Egypt. *Antiquity* 51: 185–200.
1983. 'Old Kingdom, Middle Kingdom, and Second Intermediate Period c. 2686–1552 BC', in B. G. Trigger et al., pp. 71–182.
1989. *Ancient Egypt: Anatomy of a Civilization*. London: Routledge.
Kemp, B. J., and Salvatore Garfi. 1993. *A Survey of the Ancient City of El-'Amarna*. Egypt Exploration Society Occasional Publications 9.
Kendall, Ann. 1973. *Everyday Life of the Incas*. London: Batsford.
Kennedy, J. S. 1992. *The New Anthropomorphism*. Cambridge: Cambridge University Press.
Kenoyer, J. M. 1997. 'Early City-States in South Asia: Comparing the Harappan Phase and Early Historic Period', in D. L. Nichols and T. H. Charlton, pp. 51–70.
King, Eleanor, and Daniel Potter. 1994. 'Small Sites in Prehistoric Maya Socioeconomic Organization: A Perspective from Colha, Belize', in G. M. Schwartz and S. E. Falconer, pp. 64–90.
King, Ross. 1996. 'Korean Writing', in P. T. Daniels and W. Bright, pp. 218–27.
Klor de Alva, J. J. 1982. 'Spiritual Conflict and Accommodation in New Spain: Toward a Typology of Aztec Responses to Christianity', in G. A. Collier, R. I. Rosaldo, and J. D. Wirth, pp. 345–66.
Köbben, A. J. F. 1952. New Ways of Presenting an Old Idea: The Statistical Method in Social Anthropology. *Journal of the Royal Anthropological Institute* 82: 129–46.
1973. 'Comparativists and Non-Comparativists in Anthropology', in *A Handbook of Method in Cultural Anthropology*, Raoul Naroll and Ronald Cohen, eds., pp. 581–96. New York: Columbia University Press.

Kolb, M. J. 1994. Monumentality and the Rise of Religious Authority in Precontact Hawai'i. *Current Anthropology* 35: 521–47.

Krader, Lawrence. 1975. *The Asiatic Mode of Production: Sources, Development, and Critique in the Writings of Karl Marx*. Assen: Van Gorcum.

Kraeling, C. H. and R. McC. Adams, eds. 1960. *City Invincible: A Symposium on Urbanization and Cultural Development in the Ancient Near East*. Chicago: University of Chicago Press.

Kramer, S. N. 1963. *The Sumerians: Their History, Culture, and Character.* Chicago: University of Chicago Press.

1981. *History Begins at Sumer: Thirty-nine Firsts in Man's Recorded History*. 3d rev. ed. Philadelphia: University of Pennsylvania Press.

Krapf-Askari, Eva. 1969. *Yoruba Towns and Cities: An Enquiry into the Nature of Urban Social Phenomena*. Oxford: Oxford University Press.

Kroeber, A. L. 1948. *Anthropology*. 2d ed. New York: Harcourt, Brace.

Kuhrt, Amélie. 1987. 'Usurpation, Conquest, and Ceremonial: From Babylon to Persia', in D. Cannadine and S. Price, pp. 20–55.

Kuwayama, George, ed. 1983. *The Great Bronze Age of China: A Symposium*. Los Angeles: Los Angeles County Museum of Art.

La Barre, Weston. 1984. *Muelos: A Stone Age Superstition about Sexuality*. New York: Columbia University Press.

Lacovara, Peter. 1997. *The New Kingdom Royal City*. London: Kegan Paul International.

Lagercrantz, Sture. 1968. African Tally-Strings. *Anthropos* 63/64: 115–28.

Lakoff, George. 1987. *Women, Fire, and Dangerous Things: What Categories Reveal about the Mind*. Chicago: University of Chicago Press.

Lakoff, George, and Mark Johnson. 1980. *Metaphors We Live By*. Chicago: University of Chicago Press.

La Lone, D. E. 1982. 'The Inca as a Nonmarket Economy: Supply on Command versus Supply and Demand', in *Contexts for Prehistoric Exchange*, J. E. Ericson and T. K. Earle, eds., pp. 291–316. New York: Academic Press.

La Lone, M. B., and D. E. La Lone. 1987. The Inka State in the Southern Highlands: State Administrative and Production Enclaves. *Ethnohistory* 34: 47–62.

Lamberg-Karlovsky, C. C. 1996. *Beyond the Tigris and Euphrates: Bronze Age Civilizations*. Beer-Sheva: Ben-Gurion University of the Negev Press.

Lambert, W. G. 1975. 'The Cosmology of Sumer and Babylon', in C. Blacker and M. Loewe, pp. 42–65.

Landsberger, Benno. 1976. *The Conceptual Autonomy of the Babylonian World*. Malibu: Undena.

Lapidus, I. M., ed. 1969. *Middle Eastern Cities: A Symposium on Ancient, Islamic, and Contemporary Middle Eastern Urbanism*. Berkeley: University of California Press.

Larsen, M. T. 1976. *The Old Assyrian City-State and Its Colonies*. Copenhagen: Akademisk Forlag.

Laufer, Berthold. 1913. The Development of Ancestral Images in China. *Journal of Religious Psychology* 6: 111–23.

Law, Robin. 1977. *The Oyo Empire, c. 1600–c. 1836: A West African Imperialism in the Era of the Atlantic Slave Trade*. Oxford: Oxford University Press.

Lechtman, Heather. 1993. 'Technologies of Power: The Andean Case', in J. S. Henderson and P. J. Netherly, pp. 244–80.

Lee, R. B. 1972. 'Population Growth and the Beginnings of Sedentary Life among the !Kung Bushmen', in *Population Growth: Anthropological Implications*, Brian Spooner, ed., pp. 329–42. Cambridge, MA: MIT Press.

1990. 'Primitive Communism and the Origin of Social Inequality', in S. Upham, pp. 225–46.

Leemans, W. F. 1950. *The Old-Babylonian Merchant: His Business and His Social Position.* Leiden: E. J. Brill.
1954. *Legal and Economic Records from the Kingdom of Larsa.* Leiden: E. J. Brill.
1960a. *Legal and Administrative Documents of the Time of Hammurabi and Samsuiluna (mainly from Lagaba).* Leiden: E. J. Brill.
1960b. *Foreign Trade in the Old Babylonian Period.* Leiden: E. J. Brill.
Lehner, Mark. 1997. *The Complete Pyramids.* London: Thames and Hudson.
León-Portilla, Miguel. 1963. *Aztec Thought and Culture: A Study of the Ancient Nahuatl Mind.* Norman: University of Oklahoma Press.
1984. 'Mesoamerica before 1519', in L. Bethell, pp. 3–36.
1992. *The Aztec Image of Self and Society: An Introduction to Nahua Culture.* Salt Lake City: University of Utah Press.
Leprohon, R. J. 1999. The Concept of Family in Ancient Egyptian Literature. *KMT* 10(2): 50–85.
Lerner, Gerda. 1986. *The Creation of Patriarchy.* New York: Oxford University Press.
Lesko, B. S. 1989. *Women's Earliest Records: From Ancient Egypt and Western Asia.* Brown Judaic Studies 166. Atlanta: Scholars Press.
Levi, L. J. 1996. 'Sustainable Production and Residential Variation: A Historical Perspective on Pre-Hispanic Domestic Economies in the Maya Lowlands', in S. L. Fedick, 1996a, pp. 92–106.
LeVine, T. Y. 1987. Inka Labor Service at the Regional Level: The Functional Reality. *Ethnohistory* 34: 14–46.
ed. 1992. *Inka Storage Systems.* Norman: University of Oklahoma Press.
Lévi-Strauss, Claude. 1962. *La pensée sauvage.* Paris: Plon.
1982. *The Way of the Masks.* Seattle: University of Washington Press.
Lewis, M. E. 1990. *Sanctioned Violence in Early China.* Albany: State University of New York Press.
Li Boqian. 1999. The Sumptuary System Governing Western Zhou Rulers' Cemeteries, Viewed from a Jin Rulers' Cemetery. *Journal of East Asian Archaeology* 1: 251–76.
Li Chi. 1977. *Anyang.* Seattle: University of Washington Press.
Lichtheim, Miriam. 1973. *Ancient Egyptian Literature: A Book of Readings.* Vol. 1. *The Old and Middle Kingdoms.* Berkeley: University of California Press.
1976. *Ancient Egyptian Literature: A Book of Readings.* Vol. 2. *The New Kingdom.* Berkeley: University of California Press.
Linton, Ralph. 1933. *The Tanala: A Hill Tribe of Madagascar.* Field Museum of Natural History Anthropological Series 22.
1939. 'The Tanala of Madagascar', in *The Individual and His Society: The Psychodynamics of Primitive Social Organization*, Abram Kardiner, ed., pp. 251–90. New York: Columbia University Press.
Lipinski, Edward, ed. 1979. *State and Temple Economy in the Ancient Near East.* Leuven: Departement Oriëntalistiek, Katholieke Universiteit Leuven.
Liverani, Mario. 1996. Reconstructing the Rural Landscape of the Ancient Near East. *Journal of the Economic and Social History of the Orient* 39: 1–41.
Lloyd, P. C. 1955. The Yoruba Lineage. *Africa* 25: 235–51.
1960. Sacred Kingship and Government among the Yoruba. *Africa* 30: 221–37.
1962. *Yoruba Land Law.* London: Oxford University Press.
1974. *Power and Independence: Urban Africans' Perception of Social Inequality.* London: Routledge and Kegan Paul.
Loewe, Michael, and E. L. Shaughnessy, eds. 1999. *The Cambridge History of Ancient China: From the Origins of Civilization to 221 B.C.* Cambridge: Cambridge University Press.

López Austin, Alfredo. 1988. *The Human Body and Ideology: Concepts of the Ancient Nahuas*. 2 vols. Salt Lake City: University of Utah Press.
Loprieno, Antonio. 1997. 'Slaves', in S. Donadoni, pp. 185–219.
Lounsbury, F. G. 1986. 'Some Aspects of the Inka Kinship System', in J. V. Murra, N. Wachtel, and J. Revel, pp. 121–36.
Low, B. S. 2000. *Why Sex Matters: A Darwinian Look at Human Behavior.* Princeton: Princeton University Press.
Lu Liancheng. 1993. Chariot and Horse Burials in Ancient China. *Antiquity* 67: 824–38.
Lucas, J. Olumide. 1948. *The Religion of the Yorubas*. Lagos: C. M. S. Bookshop.
Lucero, L. J. 1999. 'Water Control and Maya Politics in the Southern Maya Lowlands', in E. A. Bacus and L. J. Lucero, pp. 35–49.
Lumbreras, L. G. 1974. *The Peoples and Cultures of Ancient Peru*. Washington, DC: Smithsonian Institution Press.
Lustig, Judith, ed. 1997a. *Anthropology and Egyptology: A Developing Dialogue*. Sheffield: Sheffield University Press.
1997b. 'Kinship, Gender and Age in Middle Kingdom Tomb Scenes and Texts', in J. Lustig, 1997a, pp. 43–65.
Mabogunje, A. L. 1962. *Yoruba Towns*. Ibadan: Ibadan University Press.
McAnany, P. A. 1993. 'The Economics of Social Power and Wealth among Eighth-Century Maya Households', in J. A. Sabloff and J. S. Henderson, pp. 65–89.
1995. *Living with the Ancestors: Kinship and Kingship in Ancient Maya Society*. Austin: University of Texas Press.
MacCormack, Sabine. 1991. *Religion in the Andes: Vision and Imagination in Early Colonial Peru*. Princeton: Princeton University Press.
McDowell, A. G. 1999. *Village Life in Ancient Egypt: Laundry Lists and Love Songs*. Oxford: Oxford University Press.
McNeill, W. H. 1976. *Plagues and Peoples*. Garden City: Anchor.
Mace, Ruth, and Mark Pagel. 1994. The Comparative Method in Anthropology. *Current Anthropology* 35: 549–64.
Maekawa, Kazuya. 1984. Cereal Cultivation in the Ur III Period. *Bulletin on Sumerian Agriculture* 1: 73–96.
Maisels, C. K. 1990. *The Emergence of Civilization: From Hunting and Gathering to Agriculture, Cities, and the State in the Near East*. London: Routledge.
1993. *The Near East: Archaeology in the 'Cradle of Civilization'*. London: Routledge.
1999. *Early Civilizations of the Old World: The Formative Histories of Egypt, the Levant, Mesopotamia, India, and China*. London: Routledge.
Malek, Jaromir. 1997. Review of *Ancient Egyptian Kingship*, D. O'Connor and D. P. Silverman, eds. *Journal of Egyptian Archaeology* 83: 227–28.
Malek, Jaromir, and Werner Forman. 1986. *In the Shadow of the Pyramids: Egypt during the Old Kingdom*. Norman: University of Oklahoma Press.
Malinowski, Bronislaw. 1939. The Group and the Individual in Functional Analysis. *American Journal of Sociology* 44: 938–64.
Malpass, M. A., ed. 1993a. *Provincial Inca: Archaeological and Ethnohistorical Assessment of the Impact of the Inca State*. Iowa City: University of Iowa Press.
1993b. 'Variability in the Inka State: Embracing a Wider Perspective', in M. A. Malpass, 1993a, pp. 234–44.
Mander, Pietro. 1999. Space-Time Connections in Aspects of Kingship in Ancient Mesopotamia. *Anthropology and Philosophy* 3: 5–13.
Mann, Michael. 1986. *The Sources of Social Power*. Vol. 1. *A History of Power from the Beginning to A.D. 1760*. Cambridge: Cambridge University Press.

Marcus, Joyce. 1976. *Emblem and State in the Classic Maya Lowlands.* Washington, DC: Dumbarton Oaks.

1992a. *Mesoamerican Writing Systems: Propaganda, Myth, and History in Four Ancient Civilizations.* Princeton: Princeton University Press.

1992b. Political Fluctuations in Mesoamerica. *National Geographic Research and Exploration* 8: 392–411.

1993. 'Ancient Maya Political Organization', in J. A. Sabloff and J. S. Henderson, pp. 111–83.

1998. 'The Peaks and Valleys of Ancient States: An Extension of the Dynamic Model', in G. M. Feinman and J. Marcus, pp. 59–94.

Marcus, Joyce, and G. M. Feinman. 1998. 'Introduction', in G. M. Feinman and J. Marcus, pp. 3–13.

Margueron, J.-C. 1982. *Recherches sur les palais mésopotamiens de l'âge du Bronze.* Paris: Paul Geuthner.

Mark, Samuel. 1998. *From Egypt to Mesopotamia: A Study of Predynastic Trade Routes.* College Station, TX: Texas A&M University Press.

Marriott, McKim, ed. 1955. *Village India: Studies in the Little Community*. Chicago: Chicago University Press.

Martin, G. T. 1991. *The Hidden Tombs of Memphis: New Discoveries from the Time of Tutankhamum and Ramesses the Great.* London: Thames and Hudson.

Martin, Simon, and Nikolai Grube. 2000. *Chronicle of the Maya Kings and Queens: Deciphering the Dynasties of the Ancient Maya.* London: Thames and Hudson.

Marx, Karl. 1964. *Pre-Capitalist Economic Formations*, E. J. Hobsbawm, ed. London: Lawrence and Wishart.

Marx, Karl, and Frederick Engels. 1962. *Selected Works in Two Volumes.* Moscow: Foreign Languages Publishing House.

1964. *On Religion.* New York: Schocken Books.

Masuda, Shozo, Izumi Shimada, and Craig Morris, eds. 1985. *Andean Ecology and Civilization: An Interdisciplinary Perspective on Andean Ecological Complementarity.* Tokyo: University of Tokyo Press.

Mathews, Peter. 1991. 'Classic Maya Emblem Glyphs', in T. P. Culbert, 1991a, pp. 19–29.

Matos Moctezuma, Eduardo. 1988. *The Great Temple of the Aztecs: Treasures of Tenochtitlan.* London: Thames and Hudson.

Meeks, Dimitri, and Christine Favard-Meeks. 1996. *Daily Life of the Egyptian Gods.* Ithaca: Cornell University Press.

Mellars, Paul, and Kathleen Gibson, eds. 1996. *Modelling the Early Human Mind.* Cambridge: McDonald Institute for Archaeological Research.

Mendelssohn, Kurt. 1974. *The Riddle of the Pyramids.* London: Thames and Hudson.

Mercier, Paul. 1962. *Civilisations du Benin.* Paris: Société Continentale d'Editions Modernes Illustrées.

Meskell, Lynn. 1998a. An Archaeology of Social Relations in an Egyptian Village. *Journal of Archaeological Method and Theory* 5: 209–43.

1998b. Intimate Archaeologies: The Case of Kha and Merit. *World Archaeology* 29: 363–79.

Mikhaeli, Moshe. 1969. War and Society in Ancient Sumer. M.A. thesis, Department of History, McGill University.

Millard, A. R. 1986. The Infancy of the Alphabet. *World Archaeology* 17: 390–98.

Miller, A. G. 1986. *Maya Rulers of Time: A Study of Architectural Sculpture at Tikal, Guatemala.* Philadelphia: University Museum.

1989. 'Comparing Maya Image and Text', in W. F. Hanks and D. S. Rice, pp. 176–88.

Miller, Daniel, M. J. Rowlands, and Christopher Tilley, eds. 1989. *Domination and Resistance.* London: Unwin Hyman.

Miller, G. A. 1956. The Magical Number Seven, Plus or Minus Two: Some Limits on Our Capacity for Processing Information. *Psychological Review* 63: 81–97.

Mithen, S. J. 1996. *The Prehistory of the Mind: A Search for the Origins of Art, Religion, and Science.* London: Thames and Hudson.

Moholy-Nagy, Hattula. 1997. Middens, Construction Fill, and Offerings: Evidence for the Organization of Classic Period Craft Production at Tikal, Guatemala. *Journal of Field Archaeology* 24: 293–313.

Montmollin, Olivier de. 1989. *The Archaeology of Political Structure: Settlement Analysis in a Classic Maya Polity.* Cambridge: Cambridge University Press.

Moore, F. W., ed. 1961. *Readings in Cross-Cultural Methodology.* New Haven: HRAF Press.

Moore, J. D. 1996. The Archaeology of Plazas and the Proxemics of Ritual. *American Anthropologist* 98: 789–802.

Moore, S. F. 1958. *Power and Property in Inca Peru.* New York: Columbia University Press.

Moorey, P. R. S., ed. 1979. *The Origins of Civilization.* Oxford: Oxford University Press.

1985. *Materials and Manufacture in Ancient Mesopotamia: The Evidence of Archaeology and Art.* British Archaeological Reports International Series 237.

1994. *Ancient Mesopotamian Materials and Industries: The Archaeological Evidence.* Oxford: Oxford University Press.

Moreno García, J. C. 1998. La population *mrt*: Une approche du problème de la servitude dans l'Egypte du IIIe millénaire (1). *Journal of Egyptian Archaeology* 84: 71–83.

Morenz, Siegfried. 1973. *Egyptian Religion.* Ithaca: Cornell University Press.

Morgan, L. H. 1907 (1877). *Ancient Society, or Researches in the Lines of Human Progress from Savagery through Barbarism to Civilization.* Chicago: Kerr.

Morris, Craig. 1998. 'Inka Strategies of Incorporation and Governance', in G. M. Feinman and J. Marcus, pp. 293–309.

Morris, Craig, and D. E. Thompson. 1985. *Huánuco Pampa: An Inca City and Its Hinterland.* London: Thames and Hudson.

Morris, Ian. 1997. 'An Archaeology of Equalities? The Greek City-States', in D. L. Nichols and T. H. Charlton, pp. 91–105.

Murdock, G. P. 1945. 'The Common Denominator of Cultures', in *The Science of Man in the World Crisis*, Ralph Linton, ed., pp. 132–42. New York: Columbia University Press.

1949. *Social Structure.* New York: Macmillan.

1956. 'How Culture Changes', in *Man, Culture, and Society*, H. L. Shapiro, ed., pp. 247–60. New York: Oxford University Press.

1959a. *Africa: Its Peoples and Their Culture History.* New York: McGraw-Hill.

1959b. 'Evolution in Social Organization', in *Evolution and Anthropology: A Centennial Appraisal*, B. J. Meggers, ed., pp. 126–43. Washington, DC: Anthropological Society of Washington.

1981. *Atlas of World Cultures.* Pittsburgh: University of Pittsburgh Press.

Murdock, G. P., and Caterina Provost. 1973. Factors in the Division of Labor by Sex: A Cross-Cultural Analysis. *Ethnology* 12: 203–25.

Murra, J. V. 1960. 'Rite and Crop in the Inca State', in S. Diamond, ed., pp. 393–407.

1962. Cloth and Its Functions in the Inca State. *American Anthropologist* 64: 710–28.

1980. *The Economic Organization of the Inka State.* Greenwich, CT: JAI Press.

1986. 'The Expansion of the Inka State: Armies, War, and Rebellions', in J. V. Murra, N. Wachtel, and J. Revel, pp. 49–58.

Murra, J. V., Nathan Wachtel, and Jacques Revel, eds. 1986. *Anthropological History of Andean Polities.* Cambridge: Cambridge University Press.

Nabokov, Peter. 1996. 'Native Views of History', in B. G. Trigger and W. E. Washburn, pt. 1, pp. 1–59.

Naroll, Raoul. 1961. Two Solutions to Galton's Problem. *Philosophy of Science* 28: 15–39.
Nash, June. 1978. The Aztecs and the Ideology of Male Dominance. *Signs* 4: 349–62.
Nelson, S. M. 1991. The Statuses of Women in Ko-Shilla: Evidence from Archaeology and Historic Documents. *Korea Journal* 31(2): 101–7.
Netting, R. M. 1969. 'Ecosystems in Process: A Comparative Study of Change in Two West African Societies', in *Contributions to Anthropology: Ecological Essays*, David Damas, ed., pp. 102–12. National Museums of Canada Bulletin 230.
Nichols, D. L., and T. H. Charlton, eds. 1997. *The Archaeology of City-States: Cross-Cultural Approaches.* Washington, DC: Smithsonian Institution Press.
Nicholson, H. B. 1971a. 'Major Sculpture in Pre-Hispanic Central Mexico', in *Handbook of Middle American Indians*, Vol. 10, pp. 92–134. Austin: University of Texas Press.
1971b. 'Religion in Pre-Hispanic Central Mexico', in *Handbook of Middle American Indians*, Vol. 10, pp. 395–446. Austin: University of Texas Press.
Nicholson, H. B., and Eloise Quiñones Keber. 1983. *Art of Aztec Mexico: Treasures of Tenochtitlan.* Washington, DC: National Gallery of Art.
Nieboer, H. J. 1900. *Slavery as an Industrial System: Ethnological Researches.* The Hague: M. Nijhoff.
Niles, S. A. 1987. *Callachaca: Style and Status in an Inca Community.* Iowa City: University of Iowa Press.
1993. 'The Provinces in the Heartland: Stylistic Variation and Architectural Innovation near Inca Cuzco', in M. A. Malpass, pp. 145–76.
1999. *The Shape of Inca History: Narrative and Architecture in an Andean Empire.* Iowa City: University of Iowa Press.
Nissen, H. J. 1988. *The Early History of the Ancient Near East, 9000–2000 B.C.* Chicago: University of Chicago Press.
Nissen, H. J., Peter Damerow, and R. K. Englund. 1993. *Archaic Bookkeeping: Early Writing and Techniques of Economic Administration in the Ancient Near East.* Chicago: University of Chicago Press.
Noble, William, and Iain Davidson. 1996. *Human Evolution, Language, and Mind: A Psychological and Archaeological Inquiry.* Cambridge: Cambridge University Press.
Nunn, John. 1996. *Ancient Egyptian Medicine.* Norman: University of Oklahoma Press.
Oates, Joan. 1978. 'Mesopotamian Social Organisation: Archaeological and Philological Evidence', in J. Friedman and M. J. Rowlands, pp. 457–85.
1996. 'Irrigation Agriculture in Mesopotamia', in *Water in Archaeology*, Geraldine Barber and Tertia Barnett, eds., pp. 54–67. Bristol: Wessex Water.
O'Connor, David. 1989. City and Palace in New Kingdom Egypt. *Cahiers de Recherches de l'Institut de Papyrologie et d'Egyptologie de Lille* 11: 73–87.
1990. *Ancient Egyptian Society.* Pittsburgh: Carnegie Museum of Natural History.
1992. 'The Status of Early Egyptian Temples: An Alternative Theory', in R. Friedman and B. Adams, pp. 83–98.
1995. 'Beloved of Maat, The Horizon of Re: The Royal Palace in New Kingdom Egypt', in D. O'Connor and D. P. Silverman, pp. 263–300.
1998. 'The City and the World: Worldview and Built Forms in the Reign of Amenhotep III', in D. O'Connor and E. H. Cline, pp. 125–72.
O'Connor, David, and E. H. Cline, eds. 1998. *Amenhotep III: Perspectives on His Reign.* Ann Arbor: University of Michigan Press.
O'Connor, David, and D. P. Silverman, eds. 1995. *Ancient Egyptian Kingship.* Leiden: E. J. Brill.
Offner, J. A. 1981. On the Inapplicability of 'Oriental Despotism' and the 'Asiatic Mode of Production' to the Aztecs of Texcoco. *American Antiquity* 46: 43–61.
1983. *Law and Politics in Aztec Texcoco.* Cambridge: Cambridge University Press.

Ojo, G. J. A. 1966a. *Yoruba Culture: A Geographical Analysis.* London: University of London Press.

1966b. *Yoruba Palaces: A Study of Afins of Yorubaland.* London: University of London Press.

Olivier, Laurent. 1999. The Origins of French Archaeology. *Antiquity* 73: 176–83.

Oppenheim, A. L. 1964. *Ancient Mesopotamia: Portrait of a Dead Civilization.* Chicago: University of Chicago Press.

1969. 'Mesopotamia: Land of Many Cities', in I. M. Lapidus, pp. 3–18.

Ortiz de Montellano, Bernard. 1990. *Aztec Medicine, Health, and Nutrition.* New Brunswick, NJ: Rutgers University Press.

Otterbein, Keith. 1989. *The Evolution of War: A Cross-Cultural Study.* 3d ed. New Haven: HRAF Press.

Panofsky, Erwin. 1939. *Studies in Iconology: Humanistic Themes in the Art of the Renaissance.* Oxford: Oxford University Press.

Park, T. K. 1992. Early Trends Toward Class Stratification: Chaos, Common Property, and Flood Recession Agriculture. *American Anthropologist* 94: 90–117.

Parkinson, R. B. 1995. 'Homosexual' Desire and Middle Kingdom Literature. *Journal of Egyptian Archaeology* 81: 57–76.

Parrot, André. 1960. *Sumer.* Paris: Gallimard.

Parsons, J. R. 1976. 'The Role of Chinampa Agriculture in the Food Supply of Aztec Tenochtitlan', in *Cultural Change and Continuity: Essays in Honor of James Bennett Griffin*, C. E. Cleland, ed., pp. 233–57. New York: Academic Press.

Pasztory, Esther. 1983. *Aztec Art.* New York: Abrams.

Patterson, T. C. 1987. 'Tribes, Chiefdoms, and Kingdoms in the Inca Empire', in T. C. Patterson and C. W. Gailey, pp. 117–27.

1991. *The Inca Empire: The Formation and Disintegration of a Pre-Capitalist State.* New York: St. Martin's Press.

1997. *Inventing Western Civilization.* New York: Monthly Review Press.

Patterson, T. C., and C. W. Gailey, eds. 1987. *Power Relations and State Formation.* Washington, DC: Publication of the Archeology Section, American Anthropological Association.

Peel, J. D. Y. 1983. *Ijeshas and Nigerians: The Incorporation of a Yoruba Kingdom, 1890s–1970s.* Cambridge: Cambridge University Press.

Pemberton, John, III, and F. S. Afolayan. 1996. *Yoruba Sacred Kingship: 'A Power Like That of the Gods'.* Washington, DC: Smithsonian Institution Press.

Pinch, Geraldine. 1994. *Magic in Ancient Egypt.* London: British Museum Press.

Pohl, Mary, ed. 1985. *Prehistoric Lowland Maya Environment and Subsistence Economy.* Papers of the Peabody Museum of Archaeology and Ethnology, Harvard University, 77.

Pokora, Timoteus. 1978. 'China', in H. J. M. Claessen and P. Skalník, pp. 191–212.

Polanyi, Karl. 1944. *The Great Transformation.* New York: Farrar and Rinehart.

1957. 'Marketless Trading in Hammurabi's Time', in K. Polanyi, C. M. Arensberg, and H. W. Pearson, pp. 12–26.

1968. *Primitive, Archaic, and Modern Economies: Essays of Karl Polanyi*, George Dalton, ed. Garden City, NY: Anchor Books.

Polanyi, Karl, C. M. Arensberg, and H. W. Pearson. 1957. *Trade and Market in the Early Empires.* Glencoe: Free Press.

Pollock, Susan. 1991. 'Women in a Men's World: Images of Sumerian Women', in J. M. Gero and M. W. Conkey, pp. 366–87.

1999. *Ancient Mesopotamia: The Eden That Never Was.* Cambridge: Cambridge University Press.

Posener, Georges. 1940. *Princes et pays d'Asie et de Nubie: Textes hiératiques sur des figurines d'envoûtement du Moyen Empire.* Bruxelles: Fondation Egyptologique Reine Elisabeth.

Pospisil, L. J. 1958. *Kapauku Papuans and Their Law.* Yale University Publications in Anthropology 54.

1971. *Anthropology of Law: A Comparative Theory.* New York: Harper and Row.

Possehl, G. L. 1998. 'Sociocultural Complexity without the State: The Indus Civilization', in G. M. Feinman and J. Marcus, pp. 261–91.

Postgate, J. N. 1972. 'The Role of the Temple in the Mesopotamian Secular Community', in P. J. Ucko, R. Tringham, and G. W. Dimbleby, pp. 811–25.

1992. *Early Mesopotamia: Society and Economy at the Dawn of History.* London: Routledge.

Postgate, J. N., Tao Wang, and Toby Wilkinson. 1995. The Evidence for Early Writing: Utilitarian or Ceremonial? *Antiquity* 69: 459–80.

Potter, D. R., and E. M. King. 1995. 'A Heterarchical Approach to Lowland Maya Socioeconomies', in R. M. Ehrenreich, C. L. Crumley, and J. E. Levy, pp. 17–32.

Powell, M. A. 1985. Salt, Seed, and Yields in Sumerian Agriculture: A Critique of the Theory of Progressive Salinization. *Zeitschrift für Assyriologie* 75: 7–38.

ed. 1987. *Labor in the Ancient Near East.* American Oriental Society, American Oriental Series 68.

Price, T. D., and G. M. Feinman, eds. 1995. *Foundations of Social Inequality.* New York: Plenum.

Priese, K.-H. 1974. 'rm und '3m, das Land Irame: Ein Beitrag zur Topographie des Sudan im Altertum. *Altorientalische Forschungen* 1: 7–41.

Pritchard, J. B., ed. 1955. *Ancient Near Eastern Texts Relating to the Old Testament.* 2d ed. Princeton: Princeton University Press.

Proskouriakoff, Tatiana. 1950. *A Study of Classic Maya Sculpture.* Carnegie Institution of Washington Publication 593.

Protzen, J.-P. 1993. *Inca Architecture and Construction at Ollantaytambo.* Oxford: Oxford University Press.

Pyburn, K. A. 1997. 'The Archaeological Signature of Complexity in the Maya Lowlands', in D. L. Nichols and T. H. Charlton, pp. 155–68.

Quilter, Jeffrey, and Gary Urton, eds. 2001. *Narrative Threads: Explorations of Narrativity in Andean Khipus.* Austin: University of Texas Press.

Quirarte, Jacinto. 1977. 'Early Art Styles of Mesoamerica and Early Classic Maya Art', in R. E. W. Adams, pp. 249–83.

Quirke, Stephen. 1992. *Ancient Egyptian Religion.* London: British Museum Press.

Radcliffe-Brown, A. R. 1952. *Structure and Function in Primitive Society: Essays and Addresses.* New York: Free Press.

1958. *Method in Social Anthropology: Selected Essays.* Chicago: University of Chicago Press.

Rapoport, Amos. 1993. 'On the Nature of Capitals and their Physical Expression', in *Capital Cities: International Perspectives*, John Taylor, J. G. Lengellé, and Caroline Andrew, eds., pp. 31–67. Ottawa: Carleton University Press.

Rappaport, R. A. 1968. *Pigs for the Ancestors: Ritual in the Ecology of a New Guinea People.* New Haven: Yale University Press.

Rathje, W. L. 1975. 'The Last Tango in Mayapan: A Tentative Trajectory of Production-Distribution Systems', in J. A. Sabloff and C. C. Lamberg-Karlovsky, pp. 409–48.

Rawson, Jessica. 1993. Ancient Chinese Ritual Bronzes: The Evidence from Tombs and Hoards of the Shang (c. 1500–1050 BC) and Western Zhou (c. 1050–771 BC) Periods. *Antiquity* 67: 805–23.

1999. 'Western Zhou Archaeology', in M. Loewe and E. L. Shaughnessy, pp. 352–449.

Ray, J. D. 1993. 'The Pharaohs and Their Court', in *Egypt: Ancient Culture, Modern Land*, Jaromir Malek, ed., pp. 68–77. Norman: University of Oklahoma Press.

Read, Kay. 1994. Sacred Commoners: The Notion of Cosmic Powers in Mexica Rulership. *History of Religions* 34: 39–69.

Redfield, Robert. 1941. *The Folk Culture of Yucatan.* Chicago: University of Chicago Press.
Redman, C. L. 1978. *The Rise of Civilization from Early Farmers to Urban Society in the Ancient Near East.* San Francisco: Freeman.
Reeder, Greg. 1998. Musings on the Sexual Nature of the Human-Headed Ba Bird. *KMT* 9(3): 72–78.
Reents-Budet, Dorie. 1998. 'Elite Maya Pottery and Artisans as Social Indicators', in C. L. Costin and R. P. Wright, pp. 71–89.
Reisner, G. A. 1932. *A Provincial Cemetery of the Pyramid Age, Naga-ed-Dêr.* Berkeley: University of California Press.
Renfrew, Colin. 1972. *The Emergence of Civilisation: The Cyclades and the Aegean in the Third Millennium* B.C. London: Methuen.
1975. 'Trade as Action at a Distance: Questions of Integration and Communication', in J. A. Sabloff and C. C. Lamberg-Karlovsky, pp. 3–59.
1997. Review of *Early Civilizations*, by B. G. Trigger. *American Journal of Archaeology* 101: 164.
Renfrew, Colin, and J. F. Cherry, eds. 1986. *Peer Polity Interaction and Socio-Political Change.* Cambridge: Cambridge University Press.
Rice, D. S., and T. P. Culbert. 1990. 'Historical Contexts for Population Reconstruction in the Maya Lowlands', in T. P. Culbert and D. S. Rice, pp. 1–36.
Richards, J. E. 1999. 'Conceptual Landscapes in the Egyptian Nile Valley', in W. Ashmore and A. B. Knapp, pp. 83–100.
Richards, Janet, and Mary Van Buren, eds. 2000. *Order, Legitimacy, and Wealth in Ancient States.* Cambridge: Cambridge University Press.
Riley, C. L., J. C. Kelley, C. W. Pennington, and R. L Rands, eds. 1971. *Man Across the Sea: Problems of Pre-Columbian Contacts.* Austin: University of Texas Press.
Ritner, R. K. 1996. 'Egyptian Writing', in P. T. Daniels and W. Bright, pp. 73–87.
Roberts, Clayton. 1996. *The Logic of Historical Explanation.* University Park: Pennsylvania State University Press.
Robins, Gay. 1993. *Women in Ancient Egypt.* London: British Museum Press.
1997. *The Art of Ancient Egypt.* Cambridge, MA: Harvard University Press.
Rohrlich, Ruby. 1980. State Formation in Sumer and the Subjugation of Women. *Feminist Studies* 6: 76–102.
Ronhaar, J. H. 1931. *Women in Primitive Motherright Societies.* The Hague: J. B. Wolters.
Rostworowski de Diez Canseco, Maria. 1960. Succession, Coöption to Kingship, and Royal Incest among the Inca. *Southwestern Journal of Anthropology* 16: 417–27.
1999. *History of the Inka Realm.* Cambridge: Cambridge University Press.
Rostworowski, Maria, and Craig Morris. 1999. 'The Fourfold Domain: Inka Power and Its Social Foundations', in *The Cambridge History of the Native Peoples of the Americas*, Vol. 3, *South America*, Frank Salomon and S. B. Schwartz, eds., pt. 1, pp. 769–863. Cambridge: Cambridge University Press.
Roth, A. M. 1991a. *Egyptian Phyles in the Old Kingdom: The Evolution of a System of Social Organization.* Studies in Ancient Oriental Civilization 48. Chicago: Oriental Institute of the University of Chicago.
1991b. 'The Organization and Functioning of the Royal Mortuary Cults of the Old Kingdom in Egypt', in M. Gibson and R. D. Biggs, pp. 115–21.
Roth, H. L. 1903. *Great Benin: Its Customs, Art, and Horrors.* Halifax, UK: F. King.
Rounds, J. 1982. 'Dynastic Succession and the Centralization of Power in Tenochtitlan', in G. A. Collier, R. I. Rosaldo, and J. D. Wirth, pp. 63–89.

Rousseau, Jérôme. 1990. *Central Borneo: Ethnic Identity and Social Life in a Stratified Society*. Oxford: Oxford University Press.
2001. Hereditary Stratification in Middle-Range Societies. *Journal of the Royal Anthropological Institute* 7: 117–31.
Rowe, J. H. 1944. 'Inca Culture at the Time of the Spanish Conquest', in *Handbook of South American Indians*, Vol. 2. *The Andean Civilizations*, J. H. Steward, ed., pp. 183–330. Smithsonian Institution Bureau of American Ethnology Bulletin 143.
1960. 'The Origins of Creator Worship among the Incas', in S. Diamond, pp. 408–29.
Rowlands, M. J. 1989. 'A Question of Complexity', in D. Miller, M. J. Rowlands, and C. Tilley, pp. 29–40.
Ruhlen, Merritt. 1994. *The Origin of Language: Tracing the Evolution of the Mother Tongue*. New York: Wiley.
Ruiz de Alarcón, Hernando. 1984. *Treatise on the Heathen Superstitions That Today Live Among the Indians Native to This New Spain, 1629*. Trans. and ed. J. R. Andrews and Ross Hassig. Norman: University of Oklahoma Press.
Ryder, A. F. C. 1969. *Benin and the Europeans, 1485–1897*. London: Longmans.
1984. 'From the Volta to Cameroon', in *General History of Africa*, Vol. 4, *Africa from the Twelfth to the Sixteenth Century*, D. T. Niane, ed., pp. 339–70. Berkeley: University of California Press.
Sabloff, J. A., and J. S. Henderson, eds. 1993. *Lowland Maya Civilization in the Eighth Century A.D.* Washington, DC: Dumbarton Oaks.
Sabloff, J. A., and C. C. Lamberg-Karlovsky, eds. 1975. *Ancient Civilization and Trade*. Albuquerque: University of New Mexico Press.
Sadowski, R. M. 1989. 'A Few Remarks on the Astronomy of R. T. Zuidema's "Quipu-Calendar"', in M. S. Ziolkowski and R. M. Sadowski, pp. 209–13.
Sagan, Eli. 1985. *At the Dawn of Tyranny: The Origins of Individualism, Political Oppression, and the State*. New York: Knopf.
Sahagún, Bernardino de. 1950–82 (1575–77). *Florentine Codex: General History of the Things of New Spain*. 13 vols. A. J. O. Anderson and C. E. Dibble, eds. Santa Fe: School of American Research/Salt Lake City: University of Utah Press.
Sahlins, M. D. 1958. *Social Stratification in Polynesia*. Seattle: University of Washington Press.
1968. *Tribesmen*. Englewood Cliffs: Prentice-Hall.
1972. *Stone Age Economics*. Chicago: Aldine.
1976. *Culture and Practical Reason*. Chicago: University of Chicago Press.
1985. *Islands of History*. Chicago: University of Chicago Press.
Sahlins, M. D., and E. R. Service, eds. 1960. *Evolution and Culture*. Ann Arbor: University of Michigan Press.
Salomon, Frank. 1986. *Native Lords of Quito in the Age of the Incas: The Political Economy of North-Andean Chiefdoms*. Cambridge: Cambridge University Press.
1987. A North Andean Status Trader Complex under Inka Rule. *Ethnohistory* 34: 63–77.
ed. 1991. *The Huarochirí Manuscript: A Testament of Ancient and Colonial Andean Religion*. Austin: University of Texas Press.
Salzman, P. C. 2000. *Black Tents of Baluchistan*. Washington, DC: Smithsonian Institution Press.
Sampson, Geoffrey. 1985. *Writing Systems: A Linguistic Introduction*. Stanford: Stanford University Press.
Sanders, W. T. 1973. 'The Cultural Ecology of the Lowland Maya: A Reevaluation', in T. P. Culbert, pp. 325–65.
1974. 'Chiefdom to State: Political Evolution at Kaminaljuyú, Guatemala', in *Reconstructing Complex Societies: An Archaeological Colloquium*, C. B. Moore, ed., pp. 97–121. Bulletin of the American Schools of Oriental Research suppl. 20.

1976. 'The Agricultural History of the Basin of Mexico', in E. R. Wolf, pp. 101–59.
Sanders, W. T., J. R. Parsons, and R. S. Santley. 1979. *The Basin of Mexico: Ecological Processes in the Evolution of a Civilization.* New York: Academic Press.
Sanders, W. T., and B. J. Price. 1968. *Mesoamerica: The Evolution of a Civilization.* New York: Random House.
Sanders, W. T., and David Webster. 1988. The Mesoamerican Urban Tradition. *American Anthropologist* 90: 521–46.
Sanderson, S. K. 1990. *Social Evolutionism: A Critical History.* Oxford: Basil Blackwell.
Santley, R. S. 1990. 'Demographic Archaeology in the Maya Lowlands', in T. P. Culbert and D. S. Rice, pp. 325–43.
1991. 'The Structure of the Aztec Transport Network', in C. D. Trombold, pp. 198–210.
Sapir, Edward. 1921. *Language: An Introduction to the Study of Speech.* New York: Harcourt, Brace.
Sauneron, Serge. 1960. *The Priests of Ancient Egypt.* New York: Grove.
Scarborough, V. L. 1993. 'Water Management in the Southern Maya Lowlands: An Accretive Model for the Engineered Landscape', in V. L. Scarborough and B. L. Isaac, pp. 17–69.
Scarborough, V. L., and B. L. Isaac, eds. 1993. *Economic Aspects of Water Management in the Prehispanic New World.* Research in Economic Anthropology suppl. 7.
Schaedel, R. P. 1978. 'Early State of the Incas', in H. J. M. Claessen and P. Skalník, pp. 289–320.
Schele, Linda. 1984. 'Human Sacrifice among the Classic Maya', in E. H. Boone, pp. 6–48.
Schele, Linda, and David Freidel. 1990. *A Forest of Kings: The Untold Story of the Ancient Maya.* New York: Morrow.
Schele, Linda, and Peter Mathews. 1991. 'Royal Visits and Other Intersite Relationships among the Classic Maya', in T. P. Culbert, 1991a, pp. 226–52.
1998. *The Code of Kings: The Language of Seven Sacred Maya Temples and Tombs.* New York: Scribner.
Schele, Linda, and M. E. Miller. 1986. *The Blood of Kings: Dynasty and Ritual in Maya Art.* New York: Braziller.
Schmandt-Besserat, Denise. 1992. *Before Writing.* 2 vols. Austin: University of Texas Press.
Schrire, Carmel, ed. 1984. *Past and Present in Hunter-Gatherer Studies.* Orlando: Academic Press.
Schulman, A. R. 1964. *Military Rank, Title, and Organization in the Egyptian New Kingdom.* Münchner Ägyptologische Studien 6. Berlin: Hessling.
Schwartz, G. M., and S. E. Falconer, eds. 1994. *Archaeological Views from the Countryside: Village Communities in Early Complex Societies.* Washington, DC: Smithsonian Institution Press.
Seaman, Gary, and J. S. Day, eds. 1994. *Ancient Traditions: Shamanism in Central Asia and the Americas.* Niwot, CO: University Press of Colorado.
Seidlmayer, S. J. 1987. 'Wirtschaftliche und Gesellschaftliche Entwicklung im Ubergang vom Alten zum Mittleren Reich: Ein Beitrag zur Archäologie der Gräberfelder der Region Qua-Matmar in der Ersten Zwischenzeit', in *Problems and Priorities in Egyptian Archaeology*, Jan Assmann, Günter Burkard, and Vivian Davies, eds., pp. 175–217. London: KPI.
1996. 'Town and State in the Early Old Kingdom: A View from Elephantine', in *Aspects of Early Egypt*, Jeffrey Spencer, ed., pp. 108–27. London: British Museum Press.
Service, E. R. 1971. *Primitive Social Organization: An Evolutionary Perspective.* 2d ed. New York: Random House.
1975. *Origins of the State and Civilization: The Process of Cultural Evolution.* New York: Norton.

Shafer, B. E., ed. 1991. *Religion in Ancient Egypt: Gods, Myths, and Personal Practice*. Ithaca: Cornell University Press.
ed. 1997a. *Temples of Ancient Egypt*. Ithaca: Cornell University Press.
1997b. 'Temples, Priests, and Rituals: An Overview', in B. E. Shafer, 1997a, pp. 1–30.
Sharer, R. J. 1996. *Daily Life in Maya Civilization*. Westport, CT: Greenwood Press.
Shaughnessy, E. L. 1999. 'Western Zhou History', in M. Loewe and E. L. Shaughnessy, pp. 292–351.
Shaw, Thurstan. 1978. *Nigeria: Its Archaeology and Early History*. London: Thames and Hudson.
Shen Chen. 1994. Early Urbanization in the Eastern Zhou in China (770–221 B.C.): An Archaeological View. *Antiquity* 68: 724–44.
Sherbondy, J. E. 1992. 'Water Ideology in Inca Ethnogenesis', in R. V. H. Dover, K. E. Seibold, and J. H. McDowell, pp. 46–66.
Sidrys, Raymond. 1979. Supply and Demand among the Classic Maya. *Current Anthropology* 20: 594–97.
Siegel, B. J. 1947. *Slavery during the Third Dynasty of Ur.* American Anthropological Association Memoir 66.
Silver, Morris. 1986. *Economic Structures of the Ancient Near East*. Totowa, NJ: Barnes and Noble.
Silverblatt, Irene. 1987. *Moon, Sun, and Witches: Gender Ideologies and Class in Inca and Colonial Peru*. Princeton: Princeton University Press.
1988a. Women in States. *Annual Review of Anthropology* 17: 427–60.
1988b. Imperial Dilemmas, the Politics of Kinship, and Inca Reconstructions of History. *Comparative Studies in Society and History* 30: 83–102.
1991. 'Interpreting Women in States: New Feminist Ethnohistories', in *Gender at the Crossroads of Knowledge: Feminist Anthropology in the Postmodern Era*, Micaela di Leonardo, ed., pp. 140–71. Berkeley: University of California Press.
Silverman, D. P. 1991. 'Divinities and Deities in Ancient Egypt', in B. E. Shafer, pp. 7–87.
1995. 'The Nature of Egyptian Kingship', in D. O'Connor and D. P. Silverman, pp. 49–92.
Simpson, W. K. 1974. Polygamy in Egypt in the Middle Kingdom. *Journal of Egyptian Archaeology* 60: 100–105.
Sjoberg, Gideon. 1955. The Preindustrial City. *American Journal of Sociology* 60: 438–45.
1960. *The Preindustrial City: Past and Present*. Glencoe: Free Press.
Smith, B. D. 1996. 'Agricultural Chiefdoms of the Eastern Woodlands', in B. G. Trigger and W. E. Washburn, pt. 1, pp. 267–323.
Smith, J. S. 1996. 'Japanese Writing', in P. T. Daniels and W. Bright, pp. 209–17.
Smith, Mary. 1973. *Picture Writing from Ancient Southern Mexico: Mixtec Place Signs and Maps*. Norman: University of Oklahoma Press.
Smith, M. E. 1986. The Role of Social Stratification in the Aztec Empire: A View from the Provinces. *American Anthropologist* 88: 70–91.
1996. *The Aztecs*. Oxford: Blackwell.
Smith, M. E., and Cynthia Heath-Smith. 1980. Waves of Influence in Postclassic Mesoamerica? A Critique of the Mixteca-Puebla Concept. *Anthropology* 4: 15–20.
Smith, P. E. L. 1976. *Food Production and Its Consequences*. Menlo Park, CA: Cummings.
Smith, Robert. 1969. *Kingdoms of the Yoruba*. London: Methuen.
1973. 'Yoruba Warfare and Weapons', in S. O. Biobaku, pp. 224–49.
Smith, S. T. 1995. *Askut in Nubia: The Economics and Ideology of Egyptian Imperialism in the Second Millennium B.C.* London: Kegan Paul International.
Smith, W. S. 1958. *The Art and Architecture of Ancient Egypt*. Harmondsworth: Penguin.

Snell, Daniel. 1982. *Ledgers and Prices: Early Mesopotamian Merchant Accounts*. New Haven: Yale University Press.
Sokal, Alan, and Jean Bricmont. 1998. *Intellectual Impostures: Postmodern Philosophers' Abuse of Science*. London: Profile Books.
Somerville, Siobhan. 1997. 'Scientific Racism and the Invention of the Homosexual Body', in *The Gender/Sexuality Reader: Culture, History, Political Economy*, R. N. Lancaster and Micaela di Leonardo, eds., pp. 37–52. New York: Routledge.
Sørenson, J. P. 1989. 'Divine Access: The So-called Democratization of Egyptian Funerary Literature as a Socio-cultural Process', in G. Englund, pp. 109–25.
Soustelle, Jacques. 1961. *The Daily Life of the Aztecs on the Eve of the Spanish Conquest*. New York: Macmillan.
Southall, A. W. 1956. *Alur Society: A Study in Processes and Types of Domination*. Cambridge: Heffer.
1988. The Segmentary State in Africa and Asia. *Comparative Studies in Society and History* 30: 52–82.
Spalding, Karen. 1984. *Huarochirí: An Andean Society under Inca and Spanish Rule*. Stanford: Stanford University Press.
Spath, C. D. 1973. The Problem of the Calpulli in Classic Nahuatlaca Social Structure. *Journal of the Steward Anthropological Society* 5 (1): 25–44.
Spencer, A. J. 1993. *Early Egypt: The Rise of Civilisation in the Nile Valley*. London: British Museum Press.
Spencer, Herbert. 1873–1932. *Descriptive Sociology, or, Groups of Sociological Facts, Classified and Arranged by Herbert Spencer.* London: Williams and Norgate.
1876–96. *The Principles of Sociology*. 3 vols. London: Williams and Norgate.
Sperber, Dan. 1985. *On Anthropological Knowledge: Three Essays*. Cambridge: Cambridge University Press.
Spriggs, Matthew, ed. 1984. *Marxist Perspectives in Archaeology*. Cambridge: Cambridge University Press.
Stein, Burton. 1980. *Peasant, State, and Society in Medieval South India*. Oxford: Oxford University Press.
Stein, G. J. 1998. Heterogeneity, Power, and Political Economy: Some Current Research Issues in the Archaeology of Old World Complex Societies. *Journal of Archaeological Research* 6: 1–44.
Steinkeller, Piotr. 1981. The Renting of Fields in Early Mesopotamia and the Development of the Concept of 'Interest' in Sumerian. *Journal of the Economic and Social History of the Orient* 24: 113–45.
1993. 'Early Political Development in Mesopotamia and the Origins of the Sargonic Empire', in *Akkad, The First World Empire: Structure, Ideology, Traditions*, M. Liverani, ed., pp. 107–29. History of the Ancient Near East Studies 5.
Steinmetz, S. R. 1930 (1900). 'Classification des types sociaux et catalogue des peuples', in *Gesammelte kleinere Schriften zur Ethnologie und Soziologie von S. R. Steinmetz*, Vol. 2, pp. 96–210. Groningen: P. Noordhoff.
Stepugina, T. V. 1991. 'The First States in China', in I. M. Diakonoff, pp. 387–419.
Stevens, Phillips, Jr. 1978. *The Stone Images of Esie, Nigeria*. Ibadan: Ibadan University Press.
Steward, J. H. 1949. Cultural Causality and Law: A Trial Formulation of the Development of Early Civilizations. *American Anthropologist* 51: 1–27.
1955. *Theory of Culture Change*. Urbana: University of Illinois Press.
Stierlin, Henri. 1984. *Art of the Incas and Its Origins*. New York: Rizzoli.

Stone, E. C. 1987. *Nippur Neighborhoods*. Studies in Ancient Oriental Civilization 44. Chicago: Oriental Institute of the University of Chicago.
1990. The Tell Abu Duwari Project, Iraq, 1987. *Journal of Field Archaeology* 17: 141–62.
1997. 'City-States and Their Centers: The Mesopotamian Example', in D. L. Nichols and T. H. Charlton, pp. 15–26.
Stone, E. C., and Paul Zimansky. 1995. The Tapestry of Power in a Mesopotamian City. *Scientific American* 272 (4): 92–97.
Storey, Rebecca. 1985. An Estimate of Mortality in a Pre-Columbian Urban Population. *American Anthropologist* 87: 519–35.
Strommenger, Eva, and Max Hirmer. 1964. *5,000 Years of the Art of Mesopotamia*. New York: Abrams.
Strouhal, Eugen. 1992. *Life of the Ancient Egyptians*. Norman: University of Oklahoma Press.
Strudwick, Nigel. 1985. *The Administration of Egypt in the Old Kingdom: The Highest Titles and Their Holders*. London: KPI.
Sullivan, L. E. 1985. 'Above, Below, or Far Away: Andean Cosmology and Ethical Order', in *Cosmogony and Ethical Order: New Studies in Comparative Ethics*, R. W. Lovin and F. E. Reynolds, eds., pp. 98–129. Chicago: University of Chicago Press.
Sumner, W. G. 1906. *Folkways*. Boston: Ginn.
Swanson, G. E. 1960. *The Birth of the Gods: The Origin of Primitive Beliefs*. Ann Arbor: University of Michigan Press.
Tainter, J. A. 1988. *The Collapse of Complex Societies*. Cambridge: Cambridge University Press.
Tang, Jigen, Zhichun Jing, and George Rapp. 2000. The Largest Walled Shang City Located in Anyang, China. *Antiquity* 74: 479–80.
Tanner, Adrian. 1979. *Bringing Home Animals: Religious Ideology and Mode of Production of the Mistassini Cree Hunters*. Memorial University of Newfoundland, Institute of Social and Economic Research, Social and Economic Studies 23.
Tate, C. E. 1992. *Yaxchilan: The Design of a Maya Ceremonial City*. Austin: University of Texas Press.
Taube, K. A. 1992. *The Major Gods of Ancient Yucatan*. Studies in Pre-Columbian Art and Archaeology 32. Washington, DC: Dumbarton Oaks.
Terray, Emmanuel. 1975. 'Classes and Class Consciousness in the Abron Kingdom of Gyaman', in M. Bloch, pp. 85–135.
Textor, R. B., ed. 1967. *A Cross-Cultural Summary*. New Haven: HRAF Press.
Thompson, J. E. S. 1954. *The Rise and Fall of Maya Civilization*. Norman: University of Oklahoma Press.
1970. *Maya History and Religion*. Norman: University of Oklahoma Press.
Thompson, R. F. 1976. *Black Gods and Kings: Yoruba Art at UCLA*. Bloomington: Indiana University Press.
Thorp, R. L. 1985. The Growth of Early Shang Civilization: New Data from Ritual Vessels. *Harvard Journal of Asiatic Studies* 45: 5–75.
1991. Erlitou and the Search for the Xia. *Early China* 16: 1–38.
Tijm, Jan. 1933. *Die Stellung der Frau bei den Indianern der Vereinigten Staaten und Canada's*. Zutphen: W. J. Thieme.
Tilley, Christopher. 1999. *Metaphor and Material Culture*. Oxford: Blackwell.
Tolstoy, Paul. 1963. Cultural Parallels between Southeast Asia and Mesoamerica in the Manufacture of Bark Cloth. *Transactions of the New York Academy of Science*, Series 2, 25: 646–62.
1966. Method in Long-Range Comparison. *Acts of the 36th International Congress of Americanists* 1: 69–89.

Tourtellot, Gair. 1988. 'Developmental Cycles of Households and Houses at Seibal', in R. R. Wilk and W. Ashmore, pp. 97–120.

Townsend, R. F. 1979. *State and Cosmos in the Art of Tenochtitlan*. Studies in Pre-Columbian Art and Archaeology 20. Washington, DC: Dumbarton Oaks.

1989. 'Coronation at Tenochtitlan', in D. Carrasco, pp. 155–88.

1992. *The Aztecs*. London: Thames and Hudson.

Treistman, J. M. 1972. *The Prehistory of China: An Archaeological Exploration*. Garden City, NY: Doubleday.

Trigger, B. G. 1968. *Beyond History: The Methods of Prehistory*. New York: Holt, Rinehart and Winston.

1972. 'Determinants of Urban Growth in Pre-Industrial Societies', in P. J. Ucko, R. Tringham, and G. W. Dimbleby, pp. 575–99.

1976a. *Nubia under the Pharaohs*. London: Thames and Hudson.

1976b. Inequality and Communication in Early Civilizations. *Anthropologica* 18: 27–52.

1978. 'The Inter-Societal Transfer of Institutions', in *Time and Traditions: Essays in Archaeological Interpretation*, pp. 216–28. Edinburgh: Edinburgh University Press.

1979. 'Egypt and the Comparative Study of Early Civilizations', in *Egyptology and the Social Sciences: Five Studies*, K. R. Weeks, ed., pp. 23–56. Cairo: American University in Cairo Press.

1985a. 'The Evolution of Pre-Industrial Cities: A Multilinear Perspective', in *Mélanges offerts à Jean Vercoutter*, Francis Geus and Florence Thill, eds., pp. 343–53. Paris: Editions Recherche sur les Civilisations.

1985b. 'Generalized Coercion and Inequality: The Basis of State Power in the Early Civilizations', in *Development and Decline: The Evolution of Sociopolitical Organization*, H. J. Claessen, Pieter van de Velde, and M. E. Smith, eds., pp. 46–61. South Hadley, MA: Bergin and Garvey.

1989. *A History of Archaeological Thought*. Cambridge: Cambridge University Press.

1990a. Monumental Architecture: A Thermodynamic Explanation of Symbolic Behaviour. *World Archaeology* 22: 119–32.

1990b. 'Maintaining Economic Equality in Opposition to Complexity: An Iroquoian Case Study', in S. Upham, pp. 119–45.

1990c. *The Huron: Farmers of the North*. 2d ed. Fort Worth, TX: Holt, Rinehart and Winston.

1993. *Early Civilizations: Ancient Egypt in Context*. Cairo: American University in Cairo Press.

1998a. *Sociocultural Evolution: Calculation and Contingency*. Oxford: Blackwell.

1998b. Writing Systems: A Case Study in Cultural Evolution. *Norwegian Archaeological Review* 31: 39–62.

1998c. Archaeology and Epistemology: Dialoguing across the Darwinian Chasm. *American Journal of Archaeology* 102: 1–34.

Trigger, B. G., B. J. Kemp, D. O'Connor, and A. B. Lloyd. 1983. *Ancient Egypt: A Social History*. Cambridge: Cambridge University Press.

Trigger B. G., and W. E. Washburn, eds. 1996. *The Cambridge History of the Native Peoples of the Americas*. Vol. 1. *North America*. 2 parts. Cambridge: Cambridge University Press.

Trombold, C. D., ed. 1991. *Ancient Road Networks and Settlement Hierarchies in the New World*. Cambridge: Cambridge University Press.

Troy, Lana. 1986. *Patterns of Queenship in Ancient Egyptian Myth and History*. Uppsala Studies in Ancient Mediterranean and Near Eastern Civilizations 14.

1989. 'Have a Nice Day! Some Reflections on the Calendars of Good and Bad Days', in G. Englund, 1989a, pp. 127–47.

Trubitt, M. B. D. 2000. Mound Building and Prestige Goods Exchange: Changing Strategies in the Cahokia Chiefdom. *American Antiquity* 65: 669–90.

Turner, B. L., II. 1990. 'Population Reconstruction of the Central Maya Lowlands: 1000 B.C. to A.D. 1500', in T. P. Culbert and D. S. Rice, pp. 301–24.

Turner, Victor. 1967. *The Forest of Symbols: Aspects of Ndembu Ritual*. Ithaca: Cornell University Press.

1975. *Revelation and Divination in Ndembu Ritual*. Ithaca: Cornell University Press.

Tylor, E. B. 1871. *Primitive Culture*. London: John Murray.

1889. On a Method of Investigating the Development of Institutions; Applied to Laws of Marriage and Descent. *Journal of the Anthropological Institute of Great Britain and Ireland* 18: 245–72.

Tyumenev, A. I. 1969. 'The Working Personnel on the Estate of the Temple of ^{d}BA-Ú in Lagaš during the Period of Lugalanda and Urukagina (25th–24th cent. B.C.)', in I. M. Diakonoff, 1969a, pp. 88–126.

Ucko, P. J., Ruth Tringham, and G. W. Dimbleby, eds. 1972. *Man, Settlement, and Urbanism*. London: Duckworth.

Unger, J. M., and John DeFrancis. 1995. 'Logographic and Semasiographic Writing Systems: A Critique of Sampson's Classification', in *Scripts and Literacy: Reading and Learning to Read Alphabets, Syllabaries, and Characters*, I. Taylor and D. R. Olsen, eds., pp. 45–58. Dordrecht: Kluwer.

Upham, Steadman, ed. 1990. *The Evolution of Political Systems: Sociopolitics in Small-Scale Sedentary Societies*. Cambridge: Cambridge University Press.

Uphill, E. P. 1988. *Egyptian Towns and Cities*. Aylesbury: Shire Publications.

Urton, Gary. 1981. *At the Crossroads of the Earth and the Sky: An Andean Cosmology*. Austin: University of Texas Press.

1990. *The History of a Myth: Pacariqtambo and the Origin of the Inkas*. Austin: University of Texas Press.

1998. From Knots to Narratives: Reconstructing the Art of Historical Record Keeping in the Andes from Spanish Transcriptions of Inka *Khipus*. *Ethnohistory* 45: 409–38.

Valeri, Valerio. 1985. *Kingship and Sacrifice: Ritual and Society in Ancient Hawaii*. Chicago: University of Chicago Press.

van Buren, Mary. 1996. Rethinking the Vertical Archipelago: Ethnicity, Exchange, and History in the South Central Andes. *American Anthropologist* 98: 338–51.

van de Guchte, Maarten. 1999. 'The Inca Cognition of Landscape: Archaeology, Ethnohistory, and the Aesthetic of Alterity', in W. Ashmore and A. B. Knapp, pp. 149–68.

Van De Mieroop, Marc. 1989. 'Women in the Economy of Sumer', in B. S. Lesko, pp. 53–66.

1999. *The Ancient Mesopotamian City*. 2d ed. Oxford: Oxford University Press.

van der Bij, T. S. 1929. *Ontstaan en Eerste Ontwikkeling van de Oorlog*. Groningen: Wolters.

van der Leeuw, S. E. 1981. 'Information Flows, Flow Structures, and the Explanation of Change in Human Institutions', in *Archaeological Approaches to the Study of Complexity*, S. E. van der Leeuw, ed., pp. 229–329. Cingula 6. Amsterdam: Albert Egges van Giffen Instituut voor Prae- und Protohistorie.

Vandermeersch, Léon. 1977. *Wangdao, ou La voie royale: Recherches sur l'esprit des institutions de la Chine archaïque*. Vol. 1. *Structures cultuelles et structures familiales*. Publications de l'Ecole française d'Extrême-Orient 113.

1980. *Wangdao, ou La voie royale: Recherches sur l'esprit des institutions de la Chine archaïque*. Vol. 2. *Structures politiques, les rites*. Publications de l'Ecole française d'Extrême-Orient 113 (2).

van Zantwijk, Rudolph. 1985. *The Aztec Arrangement: The Social History of Pre-Spanish Mexico*. Norman: University of Oklahoma Press.

1994. 'Factional Divisions within the Aztec (Colhua) Royal Family', in E. M. Brumfiel and J. W. Fox, pp. 103–10.

Veblen, Thorstein. 1899. *The Theory of the Leisure Class: An Economic Study in the Evolution of Institutions*. New York: Macmillan.

Vernant, Jean-Pierre. 1995. 'Introduction', in *The Greeks*, J.-P. Vernant, ed., pp. 1–21. Chicago: University of Chicago Press.

Vila, André. 1970. L'armement de la forteresse de Mirgissa-Iken. *Revue d'Egyptologie* 22: 171–99.

Vining, Rutledge. 1955. A Description of Certain Spatial Aspects of an Economic System. *Economic Development and Cultural Change* 3: 147–95.

von Dassow, Eva. 1994. *The Egyptian Book of the Dead: The Book of Going Forth by Day*. San Francisco: Chronicle Books.

von Gernet, A. D. 1992. 'New Directions in the Construction of Prehistoric Amerindian Belief Systems', in *Ancient Images, Ancient Thought: The Archaeology of Ideology*, A. S. Goldsmith, Sandra Garvie, David Selin, and Jeannette Smith, eds., pp. 133–40. Calgary: University of Calgary Archaeological Association.

1993. The Construction of Prehistoric Ideation: Exploring the Universality-Idiosyncrasy Continuum. *Cambridge Archaeological Journal* 3: 67–81.

von Hagen, Adriana, and Craig Morris. 1998. *The Cities of the Ancient Andes*. London: Thames and Hudson.

von Hagen, V. W., ed. 1959. *The Incas of Pedro de Cieza de León*. Norman: University of Oklahoma Press.

Wachtel, Nathan. 1982. 'The *Mitimas* of the Cochabamba Valley: The Colonization Policy of Huayna Capac', in G. A. Collier, R. I. Rosaldo, and J. D. Wirth, pp. 199–235.

Wallerstein, Immanuel. 1974. *The Modern World-System*. Vol. 1. *Capitalist Agriculture and the Origins of the European World-Economy in the Sixteenth Century*. New York: Academic Press.

Walters, S. D. 1970. *Water for Larsa: An Old Babylonian Archive Dealing with Irrigation*. New Haven: Yale University Press.

Wang Ming-Ke. 1999. Western Zhou Remembering and Forgetting. *Journal of East Asian Archaeology* 1: 231–50.

Ward, W. A. 1989. 'Non-Royal Women and Their Occupations in the Middle Kingdom', in B. S. Lesko, pp. 33–43.

Warrick, G. A. 1990. A Population History of the Huron-Petun, A.D. 900–1650. Ph.D. diss., McGill University.

Watanabe, J. M. 1983. In the World of the Sun: A Cognitive Model of Mayan Cosmology. *Man* 18: 710–28.

Watson, J. L., ed. 1980a. *Asian and African Systems of Slavery*. Oxford: Blackwell.

1980b. 'Slavery as an Institution: Open and Closed Systems', in J. L. Watson, 1980a, pp. 2–15.

Watson, William. 1979. 'The City in Ancient China', in P. R. S. Moorey, pp. 54–77.

Watterson, Barbara. 1991. *Women in Ancient Egypt*. New York: St. Martin's Press.

Weber, Max. 1949. *Max Weber on the Methodology of the Social Sciences*. Trans. E. A. Shils and H. A. Finch. Glencoe: Free Press.

1968. *Economy and Society: An Outline of Interpretive Sociology*, Guenther Roth and Claus Wittich, eds. New York: Bedminster Press.

1976 (1896). *The Agrarian Sociology of Ancient Civilizations*. London: NLB.

Webster, David. 1993. 'The Study of Maya Warfare: What It Tells Us about the Maya and What It Tells Us about Maya Archaeology', in J. A. Sabloff and J. S. Henderson, pp. 415–44.

1997. 'City-States of the Maya', in D. L. Nichols and T. H. Charlton, pp. 135–54.

1998. 'Warfare and Status Rivalry: Lowland Maya and Polynesian Comparisons', in G. M. Feinman and J. Marcus, pp. 311–51.

Wegner, Josef. 2000. A Middle Kingdom Town at South Abydos. *Egyptian Archaeology* 17: 8–10.

Wenig, Steffen. 1969. *The Women in Egyptian Art*. New York: McGraw-Hill.

Wenke, R. J. 1997. 'City-States, Nation-States, and Territorial States: The Problem of Egypt', in D. L. Nichols and T. H. Charlton, pp. 27–49.

Westermann, W. L. 1955. *The Slave Systems of Greek and Roman Antiquity*. Memoirs of the American Philosophical Society 40.

Wheatley, Paul. 1971. *The Pivot of the Four Quarters: A Preliminary Enquiry into the Origins and Character of the Ancient Chinese City*. Edinburgh: Edinburgh University Press.

Whitaker, Ian. 1976. Regal Succession among the Dálriata. *Ethnohistory* 23: 343–63.

White, Elliott. 1993. *Genes, Brains, and Politics: Self-Selection and Social Life*. Westport, CT: Praeger.

White, L. A. 1945. 'Diffusion vs. Evolution': An Anti-Evolutionist Fallacy. *American Anthropologist* 47: 339–56.

1949. *The Science of Culture: A Study of Man and Civilization*. New York: Grove.

1959. *The Evolution of Culture: The Development of Civilization to the Fall of Rome*. New York: McGraw-Hill.

Whorf, B. L. 1956. *Language, Thought, and Reality: Selected Writings of Benjamin Lee Whorf*, J. B. Carroll, ed. Cambridge, MA: MIT Press.

Wilk, R. R. 1988. 'Maya Household Organization: Evidence and Analogies', in R. R. Wilk and W. Ashmore, pp. 135–51.

Wilk, R. R., and Wendy Ashmore, eds. 1988. *Household and Community in the Mesoamerican Past*. Albuquerque: University of New Mexico Press.

Wilkinson, R. H. 2000. *The Complete Temples of Ancient Egypt*. London: Thames and Hudson.

Wilkinson, T. A. H. 1996. *State Formation in Egypt: Chronology and Society*. British Archaeological Reports International Series 651.

1999. *Early Dynastic Egypt*. London: Routledge.

Wilks, Ivor. 1975. *Asante in the Nineteenth Century: The Structure and Evolution of a Political Order*. Cambridge: Cambridge University Press.

Willett, Frank. 1967. *Ife in the History of West African Sculpture*. London: Thames and Hudson.

1973. 'Archaeology', in S. O. Biobaku, pp. 111–39.

Willey, G. R. 1955. 'The Interrelated Rise of the Native Cultures of Middle and South America', in *New Interpretations of Aboriginal American Culture History*, B. J. Meggers and Clifford Evans, eds., pp. 28–45. Washington, DC: Anthropological Society of Washington.

1985. Ancient Chinese-New World and Near Eastern Ideological Traditions: Some Observations. *Symbols*, Spring, pp. 14–17, 22–23.

Willey, G. R., and Philip Phillips. 1958. *Method and Theory in American Archaeology*. Chicago: University of Chicago Press.

Williams, R. J. 1964. 'Literature as a Medium of Political Propaganda in Ancient Egypt', in *The Seed of Wisdom: Essays in Honour of T. J. Meek*, W. S. McCullough, ed., pp. 14–30. Toronto: University of Toronto Press.

1972. Scribal Training in Ancient Egypt. *Journal of the American Oriental Society* 92: 214–21.

Wilson, D. J. 1997. 'Early State Formation on the North Coast of Peru: A Critique of the City-State Model', in D. L. Nichols and T. H. Charlton, pp. 229–44.

Wilson, E. O. 1978. *On Human Nature*. Cambridge, MA: Harvard University Press.

Wilson, J. A. 1960. 'Egypt through the New Kingdom: Civilization without Cities', in C. H. Kraeling and R. McC. Adams, pp. 124–64.

Wilson, P. J. 1988. *The Domestication of the Human Species*. New Haven: Yale University Press.

Wittfogel, K. A. 1938. Die Theorie der orientalischen Gesellschaft. *Zeitschrift für Sozialforschung* 7: 90–122.

1957. *Oriental Despotism: A Comparative Study in Total Power*. New Haven: Yale University Press.

Wolf, E. R., ed. 1976. *The Valley of Mexico: Studies in Pre-Hispanic Ecology and Society*. Albuquerque: University of New Mexico Press.

Wright, H. T. 1998. 'Uruk States in Southwestern Iran', in G. M. Feinman and J. Marcus, pp. 173–97.

Wright, M. R. 1995. *Cosmology in Antiquity*. London: Routledge.

Wright, R. P., ed. 1996a. *Gender and Archaeology*. Philadelphia: University of Pennsylvania Press.

1996b. 'Technology, Gender, and Class: Worlds of Difference in Ur III Mesopotamia', in R. P. Wright, 1996a, pp. 79–110.

1998. 'Crafting Social Identity in Ur III Southern Mesopotamia', in C. L. Costin and R. P. Wright, pp. 57–69.

Wu Hung. 1988. From Temple to Tomb: Ancient Chinese Art and Religion in Transition. *Early China* 13: 78–115.

Yan Wenming. 1999. Neolithic Settlements in China: Latest Finds and Research. *Journal of East Asian Archaeology* 1: 131–47.

Yang Hsi-chang. 1986. 'The Shang Dynasty Cemetery System', in K.-C. Chang, 1986b, pp. 49–63.

Yates, R. D. S. 1997. 'The City-State in Ancient China', in D. L. Nichols and T. H. Charlton, pp. 71–90.

Yoffee, Norman. 1977. *The Economic Role of the Crown in the Old Babylonian Period*. Malibu: Undena.

1988. Aspects of Mesopotamian Land Sales. *American Anthropologist* 90: 119–30.

1991. 'Maya Elite Interaction: Through a Glass Sideways', in T. P. Culbert, 1991a, pp. 285–310.

1993. 'Too Many Chiefs? (or, Safe Texts for the '90s)', in *Archaeological Theory: Who Sets the Agenda?* Norman Yoffee and Andrew Sherratt, eds., pp. 60–78. Cambridge: Cambridge University Press.

1995. Political Economy in Early Mesopotamian States. *Annual Review of Anthropology* 24: 281–311.

1997. 'The Obvious and the Chimerical: City-States in Archaeological Perspective', in D. L. Nichols and T. H. Charlton, pp. 255–63.

Zagarell, Allen. 1986. Trade, Women, Class, and Society in Ancient Western Asia. *Current Anthropology* 27: 415–30.

Zeder, M. A. 1991. *Feeding Cities: Specialized Animal Economy in the Ancient Near East*. Washington, DC: Smithsonian Institution Press.

Zimmerer, K. S. 1993. Agricultural Biodiversity and Peasant Rights to Subsistence in the Central Andes during Inca Rule. *Journal of Historical Geography* 19: 15–32.

Ziolkowski, M. S., and R. M. Sadowski, eds. 1989a. *Time and Calendars in the Inca Empire*. British Archaeological Reports International Series 479.

1989b. 'The Reconstruction of the Metropolitan Calendar of the Incas in the Period 1500–1572 AD', in M. S. Ziolkowski and R. M. Sadowski, 1989a, pp. 167–96.

Zipf, G. K. 1949. *Human Behavior and the Principle of Least Effort*. Cambridge, MA: Addison-Wesley.

Zou Heng. 1999. The Yanshi Shang City: A Secondary Capital of the Early Shang. *Journal of East Asian Archaeology* 1: 195–205.

Zuidema, R. T. 1964. *The* Ceque *System of Cuzco: The Social Organization of the Capital of the Inca*. Leiden: Brill.

1977. 'The Inka Kinship System: A New Theoretical View', in *Andean Kinship and Marriage*, Ralph Bolton and Enrique Mayer, eds., pp. 240–81. American Anthropological Association Special Publication 7.

1990. *Inca Civilization in Cuzco*. Austin: University of Texas Press.

1992. 'Inca Cosmos in Andean Context: From the Perspective of the Capac Raymi Camay Quilla Feast Celebrating the December Solstice in Cuzco', in R. V. H. Dover, K. E. Seibold, and J. H. McDowell, pp. 17–45.

Index

Made in the USA
San Bernardino, CA
30 November 2019

60611156R00430